MW00466570

# CHALLENGES ON THE EMMAUS ROAD

# CHALLENGES ON THE EMMAUS ROAD

*Episcopal Bishops Confront*
   *Slavery, Civil War,*
   *and Emancipation*

T. FELDER DORN

*For Kathleen, a wonderful Caring Deacon and a good friend.*

THE UNIVERSITY OF SOUTH CAROLINA PRESS

© 2013 University of South Carolina

Published by the University of South Carolina Press
Columbia, South Carolina 29208

www.sc.edu/uscpress

Manufactured in the United States of America

22  21  20  19  18  17  16  15  14  13    10  9  8  7  6  5  4  3  2  1

*Library of Congress Cataloging-in-Publication Data*
Dorn, T. Felder.
  Challenges on the Emmaus Road : Episcopal bishops con front slavery, civil war, and emancipation / T. Felder Dorn.
    pages cm
  Includes bibliographical references and index.
  ISBN 978-1-61117-249-2 (alk. paper)
1. Episcopal Church—History—19th century. 2. Church and social problems—United States—History—19th century. 3. Christianity and politics—United States—History—19th century. 4. Church and state—United States—History—19th century. 5. United States—Church history—19th century. I. Title.
  BX5882.D67 2013
  283'.7309034—dc23

                                2013007826

The book was printed on recycled paper with 30 percent postconsumer waste content.

*Dedicated with love and affection to Sara Ruth, Ruth and Gene,*
*Julia, Thomas and Eleanor, Kristine, Allison, and Adam*

# Contents

PART 7  **Aftermath from the Diocesan Perspective and
Concluding Observations**

# Illustrations

## Maps

## Photographs

All maps were drawn by Martin Holloway, professor of graphic design, Kean University, Union, N.J. All photographs were originally published in William Stevens Perry, *The Episcopate in America* (New York: Christian Literature Company, 1895).

This work examines the responses to the issues of their time by a cadre of Episcopal bishops whose episcopates began before or during the Civil War and continued through the war and its immediate aftermath. The issues and events of these years were the most significant of any that have occurred on American soil. The era began with slavery steadily growing toward its peak of four million human beings in bondage, continued with the secession of eleven Southern states from the American Union, encompassed a devastating civil war, and ended with emancipation and reunion.

Part 1 comprises background material, namely the history of slavery in the United States and the structure of the American Episcopal Church. Part 2 first examines the antebellum actions and official words, spoken from the pulpit or at diocesan convention, of the bishops in the states in which slavery was permitted by law in 1860. The stance of the Northern bishops on slavery, as revealed during a church convention at the end of the presecession period, then is explored.

In Part 3, secession, a consequence of slavery and the next great issue confronted by the prelate cadre, is studied from the viewpoint of both the Northern and the Southern bishops. A major response to secession initiated by Southern bishops was division of the church. That issue, including the reaction of the Union bishops also is examined in part 3.

Secession led to war, and the responses of bishops, South and North, to that great conflict are explored in parts 4 and 5. These responses were largely in the form of exhortations through sermons and addresses at diocesan and national conventions, but several bishops in both sections became deeply involved in matters pertaining to the war, and the special activities of these bishops are described. In part 4 the impact of the Civil War on the work of the Southern bishops within their dioceses also is examined.

Parts 6 and 7 explore the major problems and opportunities created for the church by the Union victory and by emancipation. Civil reunion afforded the opportunity for church reunification, but the reunification process was fraught with issues, the most significant of which reached the floor of the October 1865 convention of the Protestant Episcopal Church. That convention and the rump November 1865 convention of the former Confederate Church are examined in part 6. Discussion of the establishment of a churchwide framework to respond to the challenge to provide secular and religious instruction to the freed people concludes part 6. How the bishops in the former slave states led that response at the diocesan level and how those bishops guided their dioceses to confront and act on other postwar issues are the topics of part 7.

# ACKNOWLEDGMENTS

The research on which the manuscript for *Challenges on the Emmaus Road* is based was conducted over a period of ten years. I wish first to express my appreciation for the assistance that I was given by librarians. It truly was the competent, willing, and kind help of library staff members that made it possible for me to write this book. Library staff members at all the institutions below contributed to this work.

Alexander Library at Rutgers, the State University of New Jersey.

Bailey/Howe Library at the University of Vermont, with thanks to Prudence Doherty for securing materials during and after my visit.

Central Library of the Philadelphia Library System, Pennsylvania.

Delia Biddle-Pugh Library, Burlington County Historical Society, New Jersey.

Duke Divinity School Library, North Carolina, with appreciation to Roger Lloyd for his assistance.

Keller Library at General Theological Seminary, where help was received from Emily Knox, Laura Moore, Mary Robison, and the Reverend Andrew Kadel

Kenyon College Library and Information Services, Special Collections and Archives, New Jersey, with many thanks to Carol Marshal for her help before, during, and after my visit.

The Library of Virginia.

Millburn Public Library (where in the early years of this work Barry Devlin was helpful in securing books through OCLC), New Jersey.

Nancy Thompson Library at Kean University, New Jersey.

New York Public Library (Schwartzman Building on Fifth Avenue), where I was privileged to use the Wertheim Study and was assisted first by David Smith and then by Jay Barksdale.

Newark Public Library (at which Dale Colson and Kendell Willis secured many books for me through interlibrary loans), New Jersey.

Perkins Library at Duke University, North Carolina, with thanks to Elizabeth Dunn.

Petersburg, Virginia, Public Library, with thanks to Nancy J. Woodall.

Richmond, Virginia, Public Library, at which Liz Triplett rendered valuable assistance during my visit and by correspondence before and after my time there.

South Carolina Historical Society

South Caroliniana Library at the University of South Carolina.

University Library and Methodist Library at Drew University, New Jersey.

Wilmington Public Library, Downtown, Delaware.
Wilson Library at the University of North Carolina at Chapel Hill.

My appreciation goes as well to the archivists and other members of the staff in diocesan offices with whom I have communicated during the course of this work, especially Elizabeth Allison, historiographer and registrar, Diocese of Vermont; Mary Klein, archivist, Diocese of Maryland; Susan Rehkopf, archivist and registrar, Diocese of Missouri; and Margaret Smith, archivist, Diocese of Connecticut.

Among the many people who answered my requests for information or documents, special thanks must go to Renae Ronayne at Shattuck–St. Mary's School in Faribault, Minnesota, who supplied extensive materials about Bishop Whipple; to Beverly Tetterton at the New Hanover County, North Carolina, Public Library, for documentation concerning African American congregations in North Carolina; and to the parish staff at Emmanuel Church in Brook Hill, Virginia, for information on the early ministry of Bishop Wilmer.

Linda Boyce, parish administrator at the Church of St. Luke and the Epiphany in Philadelphia, gave my wife and me a tour of the church building and provided documents on its history. This was St. Luke's Church in 1865 and was the host church for the General Convention of the Protestant Episcopal Church in America in October of that year. We also were privileged to visit St. Paul's Church in Richmond, site of the 1859 General Convention, and many other churches that have origins during the period in which this book is set.

Assistance also was received by telephone, mail, and e-mail from librarians, archivists, newspaper staff, and others from Florida to Maine and from Minnesota to the Gulf Coast. I am grateful to all.

I appreciate the contribution made by Martin Holloway, professor of graphic design at Kean University, in executing the maps that appear in three of the essays.

Three colleagues, Bonnie Kind, Daniel O'Day, and the Reverend Cornelius Tarplee, read the penultimate draft of the manuscript, which totaled 1,471 pages. I am grateful for their extensive and thoughtful comments, which were invaluable in strengthening this work and sharpening its focus.

Bill Adams, managing editor, directed the process required to convert the manuscript into a book with a consistent style and pleasing appearance. Alexander Moore, acquisitions editor at the University of South Carolina Press, also endured reading the long draft, and his encouragement, suggestions, and calm insistence on a length that would not frighten readers made it possible to get the manuscript in publishable form.

My wife, Sara Ruth, read and offered suggestions on every draft over the past dozen years. For that work and her encouragement and boundless patience I am deeply thankful.

PART 1

# Historical Background

# The Protestant Episcopal Church in the United States

## ✦═══ A Sketch of the Years before 1860

The parent of the Protestant Episcopal Church in the United States was the Anglican Church or Church of England, members of which were among the English immigrants who had come to America during the colonial period. On the eve of the Revolution, there were about two hundred fifty Anglican clergy in the thirteen colonies. These ministers served an approximate combined total of three hundred organized congregations and missionary stations. More than half of the clergymen were in Maryland and Virginia. The ministers in charge of Anglican churches were men who had been ordained in England. Many clergy in the North were missionaries of the Society for the Propagation of the Gospel.[1] All Anglican clergy in the American colonies had subscribed to a solemn vow of loyalty to the English king, the head of the Church of England. Most of these clergy, in fact, remained loyalists, which resulted in tension between the rector and patriot members within congregations and in difficulty between the rector and community members who favored independence.[2] Some clergy were persecuted, others were driven out of the community, and many Anglican clergymen simply departed, seeking refuge in Canada, England, or, in some cases, New York, which British forces held for most of the war.

An issue in the Southern colonies, especially in Maryland and Virginia, was that the Anglican Church was "established," receiving financial support derived from special taxes levied by the colonial legislatures; some of these funds were used for clergy salaries.[3] During the war, colonial legislatures were pressured by those favoring the Revolution to "disestablish" the Church of England. In 1779 in Virginia the legislature did, in fact, abolish the taxes that formerly had been remitted to the church vestries. Other legislatures took similar action as the Revolution wound down. A related issue was that the Anglican Church had been given public lands in states in which it was established; ownership of church property therefore became a matter of controversy when independence was achieved.[4]

When the war ended, what had been the Anglican Church in the colonies was in disarray and dissension and faced a dearth of both fiscal resources and clergy.[5] Besides the problems arising from the war and its aftermath, a pre-Revolution difficulty had become critical, namely the absence of resident bishops to ordain, guide, and support the clergy. Prior to 1776 some nominal supervision had been supplied by the bishop of London. With independence, the need for real oversight and assistance had intensified. Most pressing was the fact that new clergymen to replace the depleted prerevolutionary corps were needed. The only feasible way to build the required indigenous group of clergy was to have resident bishops by whom ordinations could be administered and who could approve assignments for clergy who wished to become part of the new American church.

Church leaders emerged in New England, the middle colonies, and in the South to try to solve these problems and to organize a new Protestant Episcopal Church based on Anglican beliefs and doctrines that could continue in the United States. Among the leaders were clergymen Samuel Seabury of Connecticut, Samuel Provost of New York, William Smith of Maryland, William White of Pennsylvania, and Robert Smith of South Carolina, four of whom later became American bishops.[6]

The church in Connecticut elected Samuel Seabury as bishop in 1783 and sent him to England to be consecrated. A requirement for consecration, however, was subscribing to an oath of allegiance to the king. This, Seabury, of course, could not do. He traveled to Scotland, where bishops in the nonjuror line were willing to consecrate him.[7] He returned to Connecticut in 1785 as the first American bishop. In 1787 William White and Samuel Provost were consecrated in England as bishop of Pennsylvania and bishop of New York, respectively, the English Parliament having passed an act that permitted American bishops to be consecrated.[8] Now that there were three bishops on American soil, the requisite number to hold a consecration rite, all that was needed for an American church to function independently, therefore, was creation of an organizational structure and governance rubrics. The inability of the three bishops to work in unison, however, retarded that initial step.

Both White and Provost were low churchmen and both had favored the American cause in the Revolution. White, in fact, had served as chaplain to the Continental Congress. During the war Provost was the lone Anglican minister in New York City who supported the Revolution.[9] Seabury was a high churchman and was openly a loyalist during the war, at one point having written some Tory propaganda. He also had served as a chaplain to a British regiment.[10] Provost was strongly opposed to Seabury and his consecration by nonjurors; Provost appeared unwilling to cooperate with Seabury in establishing a unified American church or in consecrating new bishops.

The church in New England and the church in the Middle and Southern states both were planning governing rubrics for a national church, but the two branches did not meet together. A barrier in addition to Provost's antipathy toward Seabury was that Seabury was concerned that Middle and Southern states' organizational plans for the new church included the laity and did not afford bishops a strong enough role. William White recognized that unity was essential if an American church were to be formed, and it was his diplomatic skills and maneuvers that brought the two factions together.

In 1789 there were two sessions of a general convention involving Episcopal dioceses in the United States. The first session was held from 28 July through 8 August 1789 and was attended only by representatives from Southern and Middle states, to wit: New York, New Jersey, Pennsylvania, Delaware, Maryland, South Carolina, and Virginia. Bishop White was there, but Samuel Provost was prevented by illness from attending.[11]

During the meeting Bishop White succeeded in getting the convention to acknowledge explicitly the validity of Seabury's bishopric and in winning approval for other measures to placate the Connecticut bishop, namely making provision for a House of Bishops and making lay representation at General Convention an option for each diocese.[12] Another important action that occurred at the first session concerned the "*Act of the Clergy of Massachusetts and New Hampshire* in the election of the Reverend Edward Bass to the episcopate." This act was transmitted to the convention by the Reverend Dr. Samuel Parker of Boston with the request that the three bishops, Seabury, Provost, and White, join in the consecration of Dr. Bass. The convention followed its affirmation of the validity of Seabury's consecration with a request by formal resolution that Bishops White and Provost unite with Bishop Seabury to consecrate the Reverend Dr. Bass.[13]

These actions all were communicated to Bishop Seabury, with the result that he and clergy representatives from Connecticut, as well as Dr. Samuel Parker, who represented the clergy of Massachusetts and New Hampshire, attended the second convention session from 30 September through 16 October. The Connecticut bishop came prepared to work for a unified church.[14]

Bishop Provost's reaction to the actions of the first session was antithetical to that of Bishop Seabury. The New York bishop was invited to preach the opening sermon at the second session; he declined, and, though recovered from his illness, refused even to attend when the convention reconvened in September. He rejected the convention's appeal to unite in a service with White and Seabury to consecrate Dr. Bass and was displeased with the New York delegation for giving its sanction to such an arrangement.[15] Episcopal Church historian James Thayer Addison summed up the New York bishop's behavior, saying that Provost "sulked in his New York tent" while the business of a vital convention transpired.[16]

When the 1789 convention ended, there was in place a constitution, a set of canons, and a prayer book. The Protestant Episcopal Church in the United States of America (PECUSA), with nine charter dioceses, scilicet Connecticut, Massachusetts, New York, New Jersey, Delaware, Maryland, Pennsylvania, Virginia, and South Carolina, was established.[17]

Although Bishop White had no doubts about the validity of Seabury's consecration and very much wanted to see the two lines (Scottish and English) unite to consecrate a bishop on American soil, he was concerned about offending the archbishop of Canterbury and the other English bishops who had consecrated both Samuel Provost and himself in 1787. That consecration had been intended to provide three American bishops in the English line, but one bishop-elect, Dr. Griffith of Virginia, had withdrawn before the consecration could take place. White felt that there was a tacit understanding that three "English Line" bishops would be resident in America before there was a consecration performed by bishops in the American church.[18] Provost's intransigence probably eased White's discomfort over the deferral of action on the request of Dr. Parker.

Then, in 1790, James Madison was consecrated in England as bishop of Virginia, and there were three English line bishops in the United States. In 1792, again as a result of the mediation efforts of William White, the four American bishops, Seabury, White, Provost, and Madison, joined in a consecration to elevate Thomas Claggett to the episcopate of Maryland.[19] An American line of succession with roots to both the English church and the Scottish nonjurors was in place.

Dr. Bass withdrew his name as a bishop-elect after the 1789 convention. He was later re-elected, however, and in 1797 was consecrated by Bishops White, Provost, and Clagget. Bass served as the second bishop of Massachusetts and the first bishop of Rhode Island until his death in 1803.[20]

The 1792 convention opened in New York on 11 September, in accord with the constitutions and canons adopted in 1789. In 1789 Bishop White was the presiding bishop from 28 July until the constitution was adopted in October, at which point Seabury, as senior bishop, presided in the House of Bishops. In the interest of unity, however, the seniority rule was rescinded in 1792, and a rotation system adopted, thereby putting Provost in the presiding bishop's chair for that convention.[21] Bishop White took the chair at the 1795 convention. Seabury died in 1796, and Provost resigned his episcopate in 1800.[22] Although Provost's resignation was not accepted by the House of Bishops, an assistant bishop was consecrated, and Provost never again functioned as bishop. In 1804 the seniority rule was restored and remained in place until presiding bishops began to be elected in the 1920s.[23] William White served as presiding bishop until 1836.

The new Episcopal Church went through some hard times in the next few decades after its founding, and the General Conventions in the early 1800s do not reflect a robust church.[24] Structure and governance rubrics were in place for the new institution, however, and a leadership cadre developed. Bishops such as William Hobart in New York, Alexander Griswold in New England, Philander Chase and Charles McIlvaine in Ohio, John Ravenscroft in North Carolina, James Otey in Tennessee, Jackson Kemper for the Northwest, Leonidas Polk for the Southwest, Stephen Elliott in Georgia, and Alonzo Potter in Pennsylvania came to the episcopate to pursue aggressively the expansion of the church. The road to a watershed convention at Richmond was paved with their achievements.

At the time of its General Convention in Richmond in October 1859, the Protestant Episcopal Church in the United States of America could claim more than 139,000 communicants, 2,065 clergy, more than 1,400 church edifices, and 2,120 parishes (organized congregations). These parishes were administratively housed in 34 domestic dioceses, each one presided over by a bishop.[25] Within many dioceses, especially the ones located in frontier states, there were mission stations served either by missionary clergy or parish rectors who were willing to undertake additional responsibilities. The church also supported domestic missionary bishops for United States' territories (in what are now the lower forty-eight states) not yet organized as dioceses. Foreign missions in China and Africa were headed by missionary bishops.

From the beginning the American Episcopal Church boasted many members influential in government, a characteristic that was still true in 1859.[26] It was also a church with a significant number of members from the upper class. Episcopalian wealth was perhaps most obvious in the South, where many plantation owners (and hence large slaveholders) were churchmen.

An important area in which the Episcopal Church was not a leader was membership, in which it lagged well behind other major Protestant denominations. The small membership was particularly significant in states permitting slavery in that, as will be described in subsequent essays, taking the gospel to slaves was considered part of the church's mission. Of the 139,411 communicants for the United States in 1859, 25,563 were in dioceses in states that would join the Confederacy.[27] By contrast, *The American Ecclesiastical Handbook* reported 994,620 "Regular Baptists" for the United States, 486,826 of whom were in states that would secede, and about 1,700,000 Methodists for the United States, approximately 500,000 of whom were in states that would secede. There were 66,864 "Old School" Presbyterians in the states that would secede, and approximately 700,000 Presbyterians of all types in the United States.[28]

In the years covered by this study, the U.S. Census did not survey for numbers of members or communicants, but it did gather data on the number of church buildings. In 1850, for example, the U.S. Census recorded a total of 29,007 church edifices for the Methodists, Baptists, Presbyterians, and Episcopalians; of these buildings, 1,493 or just under 5.2 percent belonged to the Episcopal Church. This "edifice index" for the Episcopal Church was highest in the Northern free states, being 6.2 percent slightly lower (5.9 percent) in the four slave states that did not secede, and only 3.3 percent in the eleven states that eventually formed the Confederacy. In the latter group of states, the 1850 census reported a total of only 395 Episcopal structures, a number that had risen to 524 by 1860.[29]

## Notes

1. Samuel Wilberforce, *A History of the Protestant Episcopal Church in America* (London: James Burns, 1844), 173. The Society for the Propagation of the Gospel in Foreign Parts was founded by royal charter at the beginning of the eighteenth century. Its original focus was on possessions of Great Britain, and it served both colonists and the people native to the area. See Henry Offley Wakeman, *An Introduction to the History of the Church of England: From the Earliest Times to the Present Day,* 10th ed. (London: Rivingtons, 1923), 410.

2. In his *History of the Protestant Episcopal Church* Wilberforce states that no Anglican minister north of Pennsylvania supported the Revolution, but he estimates that about one-third of the Anglican clergy in the South were on the side of the patriots. According to William Wilson Manross in *A History of the American Episcopal Church* (New York: Morehouse-Gorham, 1950), 175–201, loyalty to the Crown varied by colony. He agrees with Wilberforce that in Maryland and Virginia only about one-third of the Anglican clergy supported the Revolution but claims that in South Carolina the patriot cause was favored by a three-to-one margin among Anglican ministers. James Thayer Addison, in *The Episcopal Church in the United States, 1789–1931* (New York: Charles Scribner's Sons, 1951), 52, concurs, except that he reports that in Virginia two-thirds of the Anglican clergy supported the patriot cause.

3. Wilberforce, *History of the Protestant Episcopal Church,* 173, and Robert W. Prichard, *A History of the Episcopal Church* (Harrisburg: Morehouse Publishing, 1991), 80.

4. G. MacLaren Brydon, "Memorial on Proposed Disestablishment of the Church in Virginia, 1776," *Historical Magazine of the Protestant Episcopal Church* 2 (March 1933): 48.

5. The surrender of Cornwallis at Yorktown in 1781 effectively ended the fighting, but the formal end of the war came in 1783 with the signing of the Treaty of Paris. Writing in 1906, George Hodges, *Three Hundred Years of the Episcopal Church in America* (Philadelphia: Jacobs, 1906), 78, made a pithy summary statement in reference to the impact of the Revolution on the former Anglican Church in the United States: "The Church was almost destroyed."

6. See *Journals of the General Convention of the Protestant Episcopal Church in the United States, 1785–1835,* ed. William Stevens Perry, vol. 1, *1785–1821* (Claremont, N.H.: Claremont Manufacturing, 1874), for accounts of various meetings that occurred from 1784 to 1786 and that in 1789 culminated in the establishment of the Protestant Episcopal Church in the United States.

7. The line of "nonjuror" bishops began in 1688 when James II was forced to abandon the throne and William III of Orange and his wife Mary (the daughter of James II) became king and queen of Britain. The clergy in Scotland, including the bishops, refused to swear allegiance to William and Mary on the grounds that they had previously taken an

oath of allegiance to James II, which was binding until James II died. The label *nonjurors* (non-swearing) was applied to these bishops. The new monarchs decreed that the Anglican Church was no longer the state church in Scotland and replaced it with the Presbyterian Church. The Scottish bishops, however, were in the line of apostolic succession, and perpetuated the nonjuror line. Swearing loyalty to the occupant of the British throne was not a requirement for consecration, and hence Seabury sought and was granted consecration by the nonjuror bishops. See John Moorman, *A History of the Church in England* (London: Adam and Charles Beck, 1953), and Prichard, *History of the Episcopal Church.*

8. Prichard, *History of the Episcopal Church*, 86.

9. Addison, *Episcopal Church in the United States*, 52.

10. Prichard, *History of the Episcopal Church*, 88.

11. "Journal of a Convention of the Protestant Episcopal Church in the States of New York, New Jersey, Pennsylvania, Delaware, Maryland, Virginia, and South Carolina, Held in Christ Church in the City of Philadelphia, 28 July to 8 August 1789," in *Journals of the General Convention*, ed. Perry, 63–90.

12. Ibid., 71. The convention passed unanimously the resolution stating that "it is the opinion of this convention, that the consecration of the Right Reverend Dr. Seabury to the Episcopal office is valid."

13. Charles Comfort Tiffany, *A History of the Protestant Episcopal Church in the United States of America* (New York: Christian Literature Company, 1895), 370–73.

14. Tiffany, *History of the Protestant Episcopal Church*, 375–76.

15. Ibid., 373, 376.

16. Addison, *Episcopal Church in the United States*, 68.

17. New Hampshire was at first part of the Diocese of Massachusetts and did not have its own bishop until 1844. See "Journal of the Proceedings of the Protestant Episcopal Church in a Convention held in Philadelphia, 29 September to 16 October 1789," in *Journals of the General Convention*, ed. Perry. The canons are printed on pages 125–30.

18. Tiffany, *History of the Protestant Episcopal Church*, 373.

19. "Journal of the Proceedings of the Protestant Episcopal Church in a Convention held in City of New York, 11–19 September 1792," in *Journals of the General Convention*, ed. Perry, 164–65.

20. "List of the Bishops of the Episcopal Church in the United States of America," http://en.wikipedia.org/wiki/List_of_Episcopal_bishops_(U.S.). (Accessed 7 January 2013).

21. "Journal of the Proceedings of the Protestant Episcopal Church in a Convention held in City of New York, 11–19 September 1792," 145–79.

22. "Journal of the Proceedings of the Protestant Episcopal Church in a Convention, 1801," in *Journals of the General Convention*, ed. Perry, 257–88.

23. "Journal of the Proceedings of the Protestant Episcopal Church in a Convention, 1804," in *Journals of the General Convention*, ed. Perry, 289–322.

24. The state of the early church in Virginia is noted briefly in the essay "William Meade and John Johns of Virginia," below.

25. *Journal of the General Convention, 1859* (Philadelphia: King and Baird, 1860), 317. A glossary of terms pertaining to the Episcopal Church is provided in Donald S.

Armentrout and Robert Boak Slocum, *An Episcopal Dictionary of the Church: A User-Friendly Reference for Episcopalians* (New York: Church Publishing, 1999).

26. George Washington was an Episcopalian. In the first U.S. Congress (1789–1791), thirteen of the twenty-nine senators and twenty-four of the sixty-six house members were churchmen, representing a much higher membership percentage than any other denomination. *Religious Affiliation of the Senators and Representatives in the First United States Congress,* http://www.adherents.com/gov/congress_001.html (accessed 1 July 2007). There also were Episcopalians within the Confederate government and military, including President Jefferson Davis and General Robert E. Lee.

27. *Journal of the General Convention, 1859,* 318. Four states in which slavery was legal did not secede. The *Journal of the General Convention, 1859,* reported 14,905 communicants in those states.

28. Alexander Schem, *The American Ecclesiastical Year Book: The Religious History and Statistics of the Year 1859* (New York: H. Dayton, 1860), 34, 41, 47. The estimate of "Presbyterians of all types" is taken from *The World Almanac 1868,* Commemorative Edition (New York: Pharos Books [Scripps Howard], 1992), 61. All statistics, except for Episcopal communicant data, are estimates, presented here only to show that the Protestant Episcopal Church had a small fraction of the Protestant church membership both in the United States as a whole and in the South.

The U.S. Census in 1890 did survey for membership data. These were compiled and the collection methods explained in the following work: Department of the Interior, *Report on Statistics of Churches at the Eleventh Census 1890* (Washington, D.C.: Government Printing Office, 1894). The data in this publication show clearly that in 1890 the Episcopal Church was a distant fourth in membership, behind the Methodists, Baptists, and Presbyterians.

29. Historical Census Browser, Geostat Center, University of Virginia Library, http://fisher.lib.virginia.edu/collections/stats/histcensus/ (accessed 1 November 2006). The "edifice index" was constructed as a rough index of membership share.

# Slavery in the United States

## ⊹≒ A Brief History

The international slave trade existed long before the thirteen colonies were founded in North America. By the middle of the fifteenth century, Portuguese ships were removing Africans from their native continent to sell as slaves in Europe.[1] In the sixteenth century the economies of the Spanish empire in the New World and the Portuguese colony in Brazil began to create large demands for slaves. Slave labor was used extensively in agriculture, especially on sugar cane plantations, and later in other pursuits, such as gold mining in Brazil.[2] Portuguese sea captains dominated the slave trade at first, but later the Dutch, and then the English, became the major participants. Other European countries such as France participated to a lesser extent.[3]

The establishment of colonies by countries other than Spain on the east coast of North America in the 1600s opened a new opportunity for slave traders. Slavery began in these colonies when a Dutch man-of-war sold twenty Africans to the English colonists at Jamestown in 1619.[4] In 1636 the *Desire,* the first slave ship, or "slaver," built in the colonies, was launched in Marblehead, Massachusetts.[5] The locus of the trade from colonial ports, however, shifted to Rhode Island, from which 934 voyages were made in the period from 1700 to 1807. These ships brought from Africa a total of more than 106,000 slaves, but only a fraction of these were landed in colonial ports, the others being taken to ports in the West Indies, including Cuba.[6] European slavers continued to dominate the trade. Of the eleven to twelve million people enslaved and removed from Africa during the three to four centuries of the slave-trading era, about 800,000 or 850,000 were brought to what is now the United States.[7]

Those enslaved in Africa were sometimes seized directly by slave-ship forays up coastal rivers, but far more often they were purchased from other Africans, usually from a local king or chieftain who had secured slaves through tribal warfare or kidnapping raids on villages not in his jurisdiction. Slaves were purchased with rum, cloth, gunpowder, and other goods. The unfortunate captives bought by a ship captain were held in slave-holding pens or forts called barracoons near the coast until the slaver had sufficient human cargo to set sail. Once the ship had reached its destination, the slaves were sold, becoming the property of their masters and forced to labor at assigned tasks. In British North America there was a much higher concentration of slaves in the Southern colonies than in the Northern ones. Although a number of slaves were taught to manage household tasks and some were trained in other pursuits, the majority worked in agriculture, especially in the rice, indigo, and tobacco fields of the South. Some slaves in the North worked on farms, but as the 1700s progressed it became clear that Northern agriculture and the Northern economy generally were not well suited for the profitable use of slaves. The disparity between regions with regard to the need for slaves was greatly magnified when Eli Whitney invented the cotton gin just after the Revolution. Indigo production shifted to India after the war, but the market for cotton appeared limitless. The nation became one with two economic systems, one dependent on slave labor and the other not.

After the Revolution, for which the Declaration of Independence was the document of justification, the discussion of slavery as a moral issue intensified. The debate would go on for many decades, but from the outset, at least to some, the spectacle of a nation founded on principles of liberty and equality sanctioning by law the enslavement of a race of people was a grotesque contradiction. Starting with Massachusetts, Northern states began taking action to abolish slavery.

The first year that a census was taken in the United States was 1790, by which time only the thirteen original colonies had become states. The table below provides a comparison of the magnitude and locations of slavery in the United States in 1790 and 1860. Massachusetts in 1790 no longer had slaves within its borders, but there were 681,777 slaves in the other twelve states. Of the states in which slaveholding was permitted, four were states that would later join the Confederacy, and eight would remain Union states. Slavery was abolished by state action in six of those eight states long before the Civil War. By the time of the 1860 census there were 3,950,311 slaves in the fifteen states that still permitted slavery, eleven of which seceded to form the Confederate States. The New Jersey entry of eighteen slaves for 1860, while technically correct, was an aberration that resulted from the wording of that state's earlier emancipation action. There were large numbers of slaves in Kentucky, Maryland, and Missouri, and although the citizens of these states were sharply divided over secession, all three states remained in the Union. Delaware, with only a small number of slaves (1,798) followed the same course.

In March 1807 both Houses of the Congress voted to outlaw the Atlantic Slave Trade, effective 1 January 1808, an action already taken by Great Britain. The opening section of the act set forth its key stipulation:

Be it enacted by the Senate and House of Representatives of the United States of America in Congress assembled, That from and after the first day of January, one thousand eight hundred and eight, it shall not be lawful to import or bring into the United States or the territories thereof from any foreign kingdom, place, or country, any negro, mulatto, or person of color, with intent to hold, sell, or dispose of such negro, mulatto, or person of color, as a slave or to be held to service or labor.[8]

## Number of slaves by state, 1790 census and 1860 census

| | 1790 | 1860 |
|---|---|---|
| *States that seceded to join the Confederacy* | | |
| Alabama | | 435,080 |
| Arkansas | | 111,115 |
| Florida | | 61,645 |
| Georgia | 29,264 | 462,198 |
| Louisiana | | 331,726 |
| Mississippi | | 436,531 |
| North Carolina | 100,783 | 331,059 |
| South Carolina | 107,094 | 402,406 |
| Tennessee | | 275,719 |
| Texas | | 182,566 |
| Virginia | 292,627 | 490,865 |
| **Subtotal** | **529,768** | **3,520,910** |
| *Slave states that remained in the Union* | | |
| Delaware | 8,887 | 1,798 |
| Kentucky | * | 225,483 |
| Maryland | 103,036 | 87,189 |
| Missouri | | 114,931 |
| **Subtotal** | **111,923** | **429,401** |
| *Non-slave Union states in 1860* | | |
| California | | 0 |
| Connecticut | 2,648 | 0 |
| Illinois | | 0 |
| Indiana | | 0 |
| Iowa | | 0 |
| Maine | | 0 |
| Massachusetts | 0 | 0 |

*Non-slave Union states in 1860 (continued)*

|  | 1790 | 1860 |
|---|---|---|
| Michigan |  | 0 |
| Minnesota |  | 0 |
| New Hampshire | 157 | 0 |
| New Jersey | 11,423 | 18 |
| New York | 21,193 | 0 |
| Ohio |  | 0 |
| Oregon |  | 0 |
| Pennsylvania | 3,707 | 0 |
| Rhode Island | 958 | 0 |
| Vermont |  | 0 |
| Wisconsin |  | 0 |
| **Subtotal** | **40,086** | **18** |
| **Grand Total** | **681,777** | **3,950,329** |

*There were 12,430 slaves in the territory of Kentucky in 1790.

*Source:* Data extracted from tables provided by Historical Census Browser, Geostat Center, University of Virginia Library, http://fisher.lib.virginia.edu/collections/stats/histcensus/ (accessed 1 July 2007). As noted on the website, all data provided by the Geostat Center are drawn from the U.S. Census of Population and Housing.

Lack of enforcement made the law banning U.S. participation in the external slave trade at first mostly symbolic. Enforcement was gradually strengthened, however, and the United States began in the 1840s to cooperate with Great Britain worldwide to suppress the slave trade. For a time both U.S. and British naval squadrons patrolled the west African coast to interdict slave ships.[9]

While importation of slaves into the United States was declared illegal, the internal or domestic trading of slaves flourished openly for most of the fifty-three years immediately preceding the Civil War.[10] By 1860 the eight hundred thousand or more slaves that had been imported into the United States during the Atlantic slave trade had grown to nearly four million. Most of the slaves in the United States in 1860, therefore, had been born there. The domestic trade was a mechanism to move slaves from areas where there was a surplus of slave labor into areas of high need. The other mechanism was for a slaveholding family to move with the family slaves from one state to another. During the decade of the 1850s, there were seven states into which more slaves entered than departed and eight states from which more slaves departed than entered. The complete breakdown is shown in the following table.

## Impact of the domestic slave trade in the South

*Net entry (+) and exit (-) of slaves by state for the decade 1850–1859*

(States arranged in descending order of estimated net entry or exit)

*States with an estimated net entry*

| | |
|---|---|
| Texas | +99,190 |
| Mississippi | +48,560 |
| Arkansas | +47,443 |
| Louisiana | +26,528 |
| Florida | +11,850 |
| Alabama | +10,752 |
| Missouri | + 6,314 |

*States with an estimated net exit*

| | |
|---|---|
| Virginia | -82,573 |
| South Carolina | -65,053 |
| Kentucky | -31,215 |
| North Carolina | -22,390 |
| Maryland | -21,777 |
| Tennessee | -17,702 |
| Georgia | - 7,876 |
| Delaware | -920 |

*Source:* These figures (adapted from Michael Tadman, *Speculators and Slaves: Masters, Traders, and Slaves in the Old South*, 12) represent estimates of the number of slaves who moved into or out of each of the slaveholding states during the decade prior to the Civil War, either through the domestic slave trade or by accompanying their owners to another state. Tadman's table, which includes estimates for all decades from 1790–1799 through 1850–1859, was constructed by using the U.S. Census data and the decennial rate of natural increase (DRNI), or the excess of births over deaths for the slave population. Using the slave population at the start of the decade and the DRNI, the expected population at the end of the decade based on the DRNI alone was computed. This number and the actual population from census data were then used to calculate the net influx or outflow of slaves. For the actual calculation formulas and calculation refinements, consult Tadman, *Speculators and Slaves*, appendices 1 and 2, and Frederic Bancroft, *Slave Trading in the Old South*, 384–95.

The top state in the first (net entry) category is Texas, a state that had entered the Union only in December 1845 and which had experienced a huge jump in slave population since 1850. Texas is followed by Mississippi, Arkansas, and Louisiana, all of which had a net-entry estimate in excess of twenty-five thousand for the decade. The large demand for increased slave labor in those four states was fueled by the great expansion of the cotton crop into the Deep South and the Southwest.

All seven states had maintained a positive net-entry figure since achieving statehood, but this figure had peaked in a prior decade for all except Texas, Arkansas, and Florida.

In those states in which more slaves left the state than entered, Virginia's estimate for 1850–1859 had exceeded eighty thousand. Virginia, Maryland, and Delaware had shown decade deficits since 1790; the latter two states, as shown in the first table above ("Number of slaves by state, 1790 census and 1860 census"), had experienced an actual drop in the slave population. North Carolina had been a source of slaves for other states since the decade beginning in 1800, as had South Carolina and Kentucky since 1820. Georgia and Tennessee, in contrast, had shown a positive net-entry figure through the decade 1840–1849.

Slaves were bought and sold in private transactions and also at public auctions, both in Upper South city markets and in markets in cities farther to the south and southwest. Slave traders, men who purchased and then resold slaves for profit, bought slaves in the former locations and sold them in the latter. Slaves were moved from one place to another in groups or "coffles," which usually traveled on foot. Slaves generally were tied together to prevent escape. Very young slaves and mothers sometimes rode in wagons.

Associated with the domestic trade were two particularly shameful features of the institution of slavery. One was the separation of slave families, husbands from wives, children from parents, and siblings from siblings. Some owners did make an effort to buy or sell family units together, but the profit motive trumped other considerations. Owners having to sell slaves to satisfy creditors or to keep from losing their homes were not in a position to enforce a "no separation" policy.

Another shocking feature of the domestic trade was rearing slaves from babyhood to be sold for profit when they reached saleable age. Toward this end, slave owners in some states, particularly in the Upper South and especially in Virginia, fostered "breeding" by slave women. When these newborns had grown into young slaves, six to eight years in age,[11] many were among the slaves from "slave-exporting" states sold to meet the increasing demand for field hands and other workers in states to the South and West.[12] The "home-grown" labor pool comprised slaves who were already acclimated to the system and generally were healthy, factors which made them valuable and more desirable than slaves imported from Africa through the illegal Atlantic slave trade.

Two quotations from Frederic Bancroft's work on slave trading give a perspective on rearing slaves for market. The first quotation is one of a series derived from Bancroft's study of the words of descendants of slave owners.

Moncure D. Conway, whose father was a slaveholder near Fredericksburg, Virginia, wrote: "As a general thing, the chief pecuniary resource in the border states is the breeding of slaves; and I grieve to say that there is much ground for the charges that general licentiousness among the slaves, for the purpose of a large increase, is compelled by some masters and encouraged by many. The period of maternity is hastened, the average youth of negro mothers being nearly three years earlier than that of any free race, and an old maid is utterly unknown among the women."

The stock farmer indifferent to enlarging his herd would be no more of an anomaly than was the planter that did not keep close count of his pickaninnies and rejoice in the profit that grew with them.[13]

Bancroft also includes and discusses an excerpt from an 1832 speech to the Virginia House of Delegates by Thomas Jefferson Randolph: "The exportation of slaves from Virginia to other Southern States has averaged 8,500 [annually] for the last twenty years. . . . It is a practice, and an increasing practice in parts of Virginia, to rear slaves for market. How can an honorable mind, a patriot, a lover of his Country, bear to see this ancient Dominion. . . . converted into one grand menagerie where men are to be reared for market like oxen for the shambles?"[14] Although slavery had once prevailed in all thirteen original colonies, and the American participation in the Atlantic slave trade was centered in Rhode Island, conflict over slavery within Northern states and between Northern and Southern states was present from the start of the new republic.

The South vigorously advocated that the Union maintain a balance of slave states and free states, so that national legislation unfavorable to slave states could not be passed. The first of many congressional struggles over this issue began with the quest of the citizens of the territory of Missouri for statehood. Missouri was expected to enter as a slave state. After extensive debating and maneuvering, an agreement that became known as the Missouri Compromise was effected. Maine was admitted to the Union as a free state in 1820, and Missouri was admitted as a slave state in 1821. In addition, the southern border of Missouri, latitude 360° 30' west, extended westward would be the line north of which slavery was prohibited.[15]

In 1846 a Democratic congressman from Pennsylvania named David Wilmot attached an amendment to an appropriations bill associated with negotiations for a territorial settlement with Mexico following the Mexican-American War. This Wilmot Proviso would have excluded slavery from any territory acquired from Mexico. The bill passed the House of Representatives in two successive sessions but failed twice to pass the Senate. The debate was acrimonious and spilled over into the 1848 presidential election campaign. The determination and bitter feelings on both sides were intensified by the struggle over this proviso.[16]

In 1850 the issue of the extension of slavery into new states was confronted again, and this time it appeared to be a real possibility that the states in the South would leave the Union if an acceptable compromise could not be achieved. An agreement known as the *Compromise of 1850* averted immediate crisis, but its terms included provisions that would lead to future discord. This compromise was actually a series of separate legislative acts. The key provisions insofar as the status of slavery was concerned were as follows:

1.  The territories of New Mexico, Nevada, Arizona, and Utah were free to organize. The decision as to slave state or free state would be made by the territorial inhabitants at the time of application for statehood.
2.  The slave trade was abolished in Washington, D.C. (Slavery was allowed to continue, but the spectacle of a large slave market in the nation's capital was removed.)
3.  California was admitted to the Union as a free state.
4.  The Fugitive Slave Act of 1850 was passed.[17]

Actions 2 and 3 were wanted by the North. Action 1 put the responsibility for slavery's status in a state from the western territories on the prospective state's inhabitants, a "popular sovereignty" model; this was seen as a gain for the South. Action 4 favored the South and in fact was put in the compromise to offset the admission of California to the Union.

The fugitive slave law of 1793 had weak enforcement provisions and often was simply ignored in the North. The 1850 act, however, was a strong law which stipulated that fugitive slaves must be returned to their owners and directed that the federal government assume responsibility for enforcement. The act provided for punishment of individuals who hindered the carrying out of the provisions of the law. Many escaped slaves living in the North fled to Canada for fear that federal marshals, under the provisions of the new law, might seize them. Committed abolitionists were outraged, and many others in the North felt that they were now complicit in protecting an institution in which they did not believe, and which, in fact, was prohibited in their states.[18]

Four years later the time had come to organize the Kansas-Nebraska territory. Prior attempts had met with Southern opposition, in that states created from that territory would be bound by the Missouri Compromise. Senator Stephen Douglas offered a bill that created two territories and that provided for popular sovereignty in the choice of "free" or "slave" when statehood was conferred. This proposal rescinded the Missouri Compromise and led to a prolonged, bitter debate in Congress, with antislavery forces vehemently opposed. With the support of President Pierce and continued activity on the part of Douglas, however, the Kansas-Nebraska Act became law in May 1854.[19]

Both proslavery and antislavery settlers rushed into Kansas, each attempting to organize a government that could apply for statehood.[20] The result was "bleeding Kansas," an extended period of violence between proslavery and free-soil factions that exacerbated the distrust and bitterness that already existed between North and South. Kansas eventually became a free state in January 1861, but by that time the Union had been severed and civil war was only months away. The action in Kansas furnished a man named John Brown and his sons with guerilla experience that he would draw upon later at Harper's Ferry.

Before even the first of the legislative debates over the extension or containment of slavery had begun, there was movement at the grassroots to call for the end of slavery in the United States. Antislavery or abolitionist societies sprang up all over the country, although by the mid-1830s these had ceased to function in the South.[21] Abolitionist leaders included Frederick O. Douglass, a former slave, who had become a powerful orator and uncompromising critic of those in the North who were willing to tolerate the existence of slavery in their country. Another prominent leader was William Lloyd Garrison, a Nova Scotia native who devoted his entire working life to abolitionism until slavery no longer existed in the United States. His weekly paper, the *Liberator,* was the chief vehicle by which his views were disseminated. Garrison was a longtime president of the American Anti-Slavery Society, founded in 1833 to promote the demise of slavery in the United States. By 1838 this society had 1,350 chapters and 250,000 members.[22] Among those active in the movement were woman-suffrage advocate Elizabeth Cady Stanton and her husband Henry. Women's groups were responsible for many petitions delivered to Congress calling for an end to slavery. By far the most famous and effective antislavery publication was Harriet Beecher Stowe's 1852 novel *Uncle Tom's Cabin or, Life among the Lowly.*

Abolitionist voices grew in number, intensity, and influence. Although they had not moved Congress to action, Southerners heard the increasing calls for abolition and observed the increasing militancy of its supporters. Abolitionist speeches, pamphlets, newspapers, and Stowe's novel had, by the mid-1850s, certainly inspired anger and resentment in the South. More tangibly, slaveholders saw the effects of the assistance given by Northern citizens to the Underground Railroad and the growing resistance of Northerners to enforcement of the fugitive slave law.

Just over a month after Lincoln's election in November 1860, South Carolina seceded. A last-minute effort in Congress to save the Union, a compromise proposed by Senator John J. Crittenden of Kentucky, repackaged elements of former compromises. His proposal comprised six proposed constitutional amendments and four proposed congressional resolutions. Although the vote was close in the Senate, the measure failed to pass in both houses in January 1861.[23] By the time the new president was inaugurated on 4 March 1861, seven Southern states had passed ordinances of secession and Jefferson Davis had been sworn in as provisional president of the Confederate States of America.

## Notes

1. Dorothy Schneider and Carl Schneider, *Slavery in America: From Colonial Times to the Civil War* (New York: Facts on File, 2000), 3.

2. See Kathleen J. Higgins, *"Licentious Liberty" in a Brazilian Gold-Mining Region: Slavery, Gender, and Social Control in Eighteenth Century Sabara, Minas Gerais* (University Park: Penn State University Press, 1999).

3. Schneider and Schneider, *Slavery in America*, 16.

4. Clayton E. Jewett and John O. Allen, *Slavery in the South: A State-by-State History* (Westport, Conn.: Greenwood Press, 2004), 259.

5. Schneider and Schneider, *Slavery in America*, 15.

6. Jay Coughtry, *The Notorious Triangle: Rhode Island and the African Slave Trade, 1700–1807* (Philadelphia: Temple University Press, 1981).

7. Estimates of the Africans removed and the number transported to North America during and after the colonial period vary; the figure reported here is derived from Schneider and Schneider, *Slavery in America*, 13.

8. "Statutes of the United States Concerning Slavery," The Avalon Project, Yale Law School Library. http://www.yale.edu/lawweb/avalon/statutes/slavery/sl004.htm. (Accessed 22 January 2013). This website has a copy of the entire act.

9. W. E. B. Du Bois, in *The Suppression of the African Slave Trade to the United States of America, 1638–1870* (New York: Russell and Russell, 1965), devotes an entire chapter to the enforcement problems in the first several decades after the United States outlawed importation of slaves. He also includes in appendix C, "Typical Cases of Vessels Engaged in the American Slave Trade," a list of slavers and their locations documented during this period, some of which were taken into custody, some of which were not. According to Michael Tadman, in *Speculators and Slaves: Masters, Traders, and Slaves in the Old South* (Madison: University of Wisconsin Press, 1996), 11, and other authors, there were not large numbers of importations from Africa after the Atlantic trade became illegal. Certainly the major growth in the slave population did arise from slaves born in the United States, but it also seems clear that the United States was "lax," in the opinion of Du Bois, in enforcing the proscription against importations.

10. Some states did for a time ban or restrict interstate slave trading. These restrictions were removed by most states, however, in the 1840s and early 1850s. See Schneider and Schneider, *Slavery in America*, 68–70.

11. By the time slave children were six to eight years old, they could be "hired out" (with the slave owner paid for the young slave's labor) or sold. See Frederic Bancroft, *Slave Trading in the Old South* (Baltimore: J.H. Furst, 1931. Reprinted. New York: Ungar, 1959), 77.

12. John C. Reed, in *The Brothers' War* (Boston: Little, Brown, 1905), 432, made the blunt statement that "many of these older sections turned from being agricultural communities, into nurseries, rearing slaves for the younger states where virgin soil was abundant."

13. Bancroft, *Slave Trading*, 76–77. Bancroft quoted Conway from Moncure D. Conway, *Testimonies Concerning Slavery* (London: Chapman and Hall, 1865), 20.

14. Bancroft, *Slave Trading*, 60–70.

15. Jewett and Allen, *Slavery in the South*, 175.

16. Don E. Fehrenbacher, *Sectional Crisis and Southern Constitutionalism* (Baton Rouge: Louisiana State University Press, 1995), 34–36.

17. "The Compromise of 1850 and the Fugitive Slave Act," *Judgment Day* (PBS Online website), Part 4, *1831–1865*, http://www.pbs.org/wgbh/aia/part4/4p2951.html (accessed 17 July 2007).

18. Louis Filler, *Crusade against Slavery: Friends, Foes, and Reforms, 1820–1860* (Algonac, Mich.: Reference Publications, 1986), 242–45.

19. See Fehrenbacher, *Sectional Crisis and Southern Constitutionalism*, 45–65, for a discussion of the Kansas-Nebraska Act and its consequences.

20. See also "Bishops in the Slave States," below, the section on Cicero Stephens Hawks's episcopate in Missouri in the "bleeding Kansas" years.

21. Schneider and Schneider, *Slavery in America*, 272.

22. Filler, *Crusade against Slavery*, 87.

23. The Crittenden Compromise is discussed in Don E. Fehrenbacher, *The Dred Scott Case, its significance in American law and politics*, (New York: Oxford University Press, 1978), 545–50. A text of the compromise is provided at http://sunsite.utk.edu/civil-war/critten.html (accessed 6 August 2007).

PART 2

# Episcopal Bishops
# in the Antebellum Era

# Preamble

When secession began in December 1860, there were sixteen bishops of the Protestant Episcopal Church with jurisdictions in the fifteen states in which slavery was legal. The Episcopal Church in each of the eleven Southern states that eventually seceded was led by a bishop, and the Diocese of Virginia also had an assistant bishop. One of these eleven states, Arkansas, did not constitute a diocese, but the Right Reverend Henry C. Lay's purview as missionary bishop for the Southwest encompassed that state. A bishop also led the church within each of the four slave states that were to remain within the Union.

In ten of the fifteen states the bishop serving in 1860 was the first Episcopal bishop for the diocese that was coterminous with that state. In those cases the bishop of necessity had to have as a primary concern the increase of communicants within his diocese. These bishops were heavily engaged in evangelism, in parish organizing, and helping to support church construction. Although the Atlantic states of Maryland, Virginia, North Carolina, and South Carolina had longer Episcopal traditions, the bishops in these states still had to devote much time to diocese building in 1860. Arkansas, as noted above, was part of Bishop Lay's missionary district, and his charge was to provide Episcopal services while he encouraged formation of dioceses within the district.

The bishops in these fifteen states had to confront slavery not as an abstract question, but as a state-sanctioned institution right on their doorsteps that posed questions concerning the role their church should play with respect to the slaves in their midst. Bishops in states that did not permit slavery, as will be described, did not openly come to grips with slavery in the antebellum era.

# Stephen Elliott of Georgia and
# Thomas Frederick Davis of South Carolina

## Stephen Elliott

The Diocese of Georgia was established in February 1823, but many years passed before the new diocese could afford a bishop.[1] Stephen Elliott, its first bishop, was consecrated in Christ Church, Savannah, on 28 February 1841.[2] The new bishop simultaneously began his episcopate and assumed the rectorship of St. John's Church in Savannah. Stephen Elliott set to work to develop his vast diocese, which encompassed a total population of 691,392, including 280,344 slaves.[3] From the beginning Elliott saw his mission as bringing both white and black residents into Christ's fold, and he felt that, in saving souls, race or status was of no importance. Given the social structure, however, including the fact that most slaves were on large plantations, there had to be tactical differences in the approaches used for the two races.

In building white congregations, Bishop Elliott started with 323 communicants and 6 parishes; 9 clergymen attended his first diocesan convention.[4] His evangelical work, which included starting new churches, strengthening struggling ones, and visiting all congregations, continued until the Civil War. His efforts were augmented and reinforced as the diocese gained both fiscal and personnel resources. By 1850 there were 19 churches, 24 clergy, and 862 communicants.[5] In 1860 there were 27 churches, 28 clergymen, and more than 2,000 communicants.[6] When he died, an editorial in the *Macon Telegraph* praised the impact of Elliott's missionary zeal during the first twenty years of his episcopate: "when he entered upon the office of Bishop, Episcopalianism was scarcely known in Georgia beyond the walls of churches in Savannah and Augusta; he closed his labors with congregations in nearly every town of the State, with communicants numbered by thousands, and with thousands more pressing into the fold."[7]

In terms of the geographical spread of the Episcopal Church in Georgia, this editorial painted a true picture, but the reckoning of the number of communicants in the state was overstated. At the May 1861 diocesan meeting, the communicant total was reported by the Committee on the State of the Church as 2,184.[8] This meeting marked the end point for Elliott's diocese building effort, from which his attention was diverted by secession, church division, and war and its consequences.

### Missions to Slaves and the Free Black Population

The 1861 communicant total included more than 500 black persons, most of whom were slaves, and one large mission on the Ogeechee River accounted for 357 of the latter.[9] This major thrust of Elliott's ministry had begun immediately after his consecration. At his first convention in May 1841 Bishop Elliott described visitations held earlier that spring. He reported on having "preached several times to slaves" during his very first episcopal visit, which was to Christ Church on St. Simons Island. He then made his first plea for slaves to be instructed in the Episcopal faith. "There is no arrangement of worship so well qualified as ours, to meet exactly the wants of our colored population. What they need is sound religious instruction. . . . There are very few colored persons of the State of Georgia who have not within their reach, some kind of religious exercise, but it is, for the most part, a religion of excitement, occupied entirely with the feelings, while they need to be instructed in the first principles of the doctrine of CHRIST."[10] He urged parish rectors to count and make a roll of slave children in their parishes and to arrange to instruct them in the faith.

At the 1843 convention Elliott directed a message both to slave owners and to clergy. He appealed first to the slave owners' sense of duty: "One-half, at least, of the large slave holders on the Savannah, the Ogeechee, the Altamaha, the Satilla, and the sea islands which skirt the coast of Georgia are Episcopalian, and it is time they wake up to their responsibilities in this matter."[11] For the clergy and potential deacons, he presented both an opportunity and a challenge: "But it is useless to arouse the Planters to their duty so long as the Ministers of the Church and her candidates for orders shut their eyes to the vast work which is here spread out before them. From this city [Savannah], we can look out upon, at least, ten thousand slaves whose masters are, for the most part, willing that they should be religiously instructed—willing to pay that they might be instructed. . . . and yet among all that vast multitude there is not heard the voice of a single pastor."[12]

The bishop then noted that the problem's scope was even wider but went on to commend the effort being made near the Altamaha River by St. David's, a tiny church in Glynn County: "From the bluff at Darien, there are to be seen plantations containing 5000 slaves, and St. David's is the first Episcopal Church that has offered the glad tidings of great joy to their greedy ears."[13] The officiating minister at St. David's, the Reverend Dr. John Vaughan, reported that he was attempting to serve some 1,000 to 1,200 slaves and that "the coloured people evince a growing attachment" to the services of the Episcopal Church.[14] Elliott praised Vaughan's work and the support given by the five planters who had built the church. This effort adumbrated a model that Elliott soon implemented.

*Missions on the Ogeechee and Savannah Rivers*

In 1845 Bishop Elliott provided a missionary for the slaves who were working the land on several plantations by the Ogeechee River. Charles Lwanga Hoskins, historian of black Episcopalians in Georgia, points out that this was a significant departure from precedent, because "for the first time the church was setting up a work entirely for the slaves and not simply as an adjunct of a white parish."[15] Elliott appointed to the new Ogeechee Mission his student and protégé, the Reverend William C. Williams. Williams, a young deacon, twenty-four years old, faced alone a truly staggering task. His initial reception by the slaves, many of whom viewed him as an agent for the owners, was not cordial, and his first priority was to establish credibility with those whom he wished to proselyte.[16] By the time of the 1846 diocesan meeting, however, Williams had made progress: "I entered upon my duties . . . on the First Sunday in Advent [1845]. I am engaged by several planters to labour among their Negroes. There are not a dozen whites within the limits of the parish, so that my whole time is devoted to the Blacks. I have had service twice on Sunday, besides a weekly lecture, alternating between the different plantations . . . ; on each of the plantations, schools have been established for the oral instruction of the children."[17]

Williams reported that there were a total of eighty children attending the schools. He was pleased with the pace at which they were learning and added that "for permanent success among an ignorant people my chief hope must be in the young, and if they are neglected or only partially instructed, no lasting good can be experienced. The Liturgy has been introduced as fast as possible. The Negroes seem much interested in the responsive part of the service, and I am convinced the constant use of the Liturgy among them will be of the greatest benefit."[18] Williams reported to the diocese in 1852 that he was serving seven plantations. "These plantations lie contiguous, and cover an area of six miles long by three miles wide. Within this space there are between 1,000 and 1,500 souls."[19]

In January 1852 the Reverend R. W. Kennerly began the Savannah River Mission with a model similar to that of the Ogeechee Mission. It got off to a good start. This mission comprised seven plantations, four of which were on the South Carolina side of the river. The total slave population served was between 1,100 and 1,200.[20] The model continued to spread; in December 1860 the Reverend J. M. Meredith, a newly ordained deacon, became the missionary for four plantations by the Altamaha River, serving nearly 800 slaves. The bishop noted that the plantation owners had "made him up a salary of one thousand dollars."[21] In his 1855 report to the diocesan convention, Ogeechee Missionary Williams was able to report that there were 151 communicants and that 330 pupils were in the mission schools. He had baptized 63, including 45 adults, since his last report and the bishop had confirmed 39.[22]

In his 1856 diocesan address Bishop Elliott reported that he had consecrated St. James's Church on the Great Ogeechee. Following the consecration, the largest confirmation service ever held in the diocese was celebrated, when Missionary Williams presented 148 candidates to the bishop. Elliott then expressed his hopes for the continued replication of the work being done by Reverend Williams. "The longer I observe the workings of this [Ogeechee] mission, the better I am satisfied that we could get under our control, and bless with our instructions almost the whole slave population of the Sea-Coast, if the [slave] masters would only do their duty, and if ministers could be found to devote themselves to the work. . . . A very large proportion, fully two thirds of the owners of slaves along the sea-coast of Georgia, is nominally Episcopal . . . ; most of these are in sufficient proximity to each other to form missions, which would demand but a very modest expenditure on the part of each planter."[23]

Elliott expressed frustration that, in spite of the success of the Ogeechee Mission, some planters still believed that the slaves would not accept Episcopal services. It was clear, however, that the bishop was going to continue to assign a high priority to expanding river missions and to the provision of services and religious instruction for slaves throughout the diocese. Even during the early years of the war, the Ogeechee Mission communicant total continued to rise, being reported as 423 at the 1863 diocesan convention.[24]

### *The Institute at Montpelier: A Venture Undergirded by Slavery*

A major initiative begun by Elliott soon after coming to the Georgia bishopric was the establishment of an Episcopal institute at Montpelier that would provide education for the white youth of the diocese. The first step was a school for girls, the purpose of which was "the instruction of young women of this diocese, in that learning and those accomplishments which, according to his [Elliott's] conception of her character and duties, a Christian woman, whose station in life permitted it, ought to know and acquire."[25] A school for boys, in addition to a sound academic curriculum, provided training in "the best mode of performing their duties as owners of slaves and the masters of human beings for whose souls they must give an account."[26]

The unique feature of the Georgia Episcopal institute was that slave labor was the keystone of its funding pattern. Elliott described that pattern in 1842: "Our plan . . . is to make a stock farm cultivated by a slave force owned by the Institute, pay all the expenses of the Schools except for the salaries of the instructors. By throwing only this burden upon the tuition money, we are enabled, should the plan continue to work as it has hitherto done, to furnish the best education, together with all such accomplishments as Christian parents should desire for their children, at a cost far below the usual charges, at the same time that we improve the property and enlarge the schools."[27] Charles Lwanga Hoskins, in his work about black Episcopalians in Georgia, reported the original number of slaves at three hundred and the acreage at eight hundred.[28] St. Luke's Church in Montpelier ministered to slaves as well as to the institute students and staff. For a time it appeared that the venture might succeed, and diocesan reports reflected growth and an expectation of solvency.

Ultimately, though, the substantial capital investment and operational funding required to match Elliott's enthusiasm and desire for excellence outpaced the funds from the institute's income and other sources available to the bishop. Elliott was called to take over the institute administration in 1845, and he moved to Montpelier to do so, but the institution could not survive.[29] The boys' school closed in 1849, and the next year the girls' school closed and then immediately reopened; but the girls' school closed for good at the end of 1855.[30] Elliott used his entire personal fortune to cover the obligations that were unpaid when closure came.[31] His wife also contributed her fortune to meet those obligations, and afterwards, no longer having independent wealth, the Elliotts were solely dependent upon his salary.[32] After this heartbreaking experience, he returned to Savannah to become rector of Christ Church.

### St. Stephen's Church in Savannah

Although the Savannah River Mission was successful, the missionary, the Reverend Sherod Kennerly, found the care of the vast area, two-thirds of which was across the Savannah River in South Carolina, to be beyond his ability to manage. Accordingly, in January 1856 he relinquished to the Diocese of South Carolina the part of the mission that lay in that diocese.[33] He retained the Georgia plantations under his purview, and, under Elliott's guidance, Kennerly began in Savannah another new activity: a mission to free urban black residents; both Christ Church and St. John's Church supported this new outreach. The free black population in Savannah was small, but it was a population that included among the men tailors, carpenters, coopers, and shopkeepers—and pastry cooks and nurses among the women—as well as domestic service for those of both genders.[34] William Cleghorn, a successful black baker, offered the hall above his bakery as a meeting place, and services began there in January 1856. Bishop Elliott celebrated the first Holy Communion in the building, at which seven persons received the sacrament.[35]

The bishop placed the "temporal affairs" of the church entirely in the hands of the all-black vestry, but services were conducted by Kennerly, and, after he departed in 1859, by other white priests or deacons. Elliott made regular episcopal visits to St. Stephen's and reported the resulting number of confirmations in his diocesan addresses.[36] The establishment of St. Stephen's for free blacks certainly was a recognition on Elliott's part that this was a population that was there to stay, and grow, in his diocese—and a recognition that some among Savannah's free blacks wanted a role in the conduct of their local-church affairs.

## Thomas Frederick Davis

### Diocesan Setting and Davis's Initial View of Challenges

When Thomas Frederick Davis, a native of North Carolina, became bishop of South Carolina in October 1853, he was serving Grace Church in Camden, South Carolina, where he had been the rector for seven years. Prior to coming to Camden, he had served churches in Salisbury and Wilmington in his home state.[37]

In 1853 there were in the Diocese of South Carolina sixty-nine clergymen and fifty-six organized congregations, fifty-three of which were parish churches entitled representation at diocesan convention, and three of which were mission congregations. There were 5,456 communicants at the end of 1853, just over half of whom were slaves. The diocese was more than fifty years old and firmly established.[38] When Davis began as bishop, in fact, his diocese was much more developed than was any other slave-state diocese at the point when the bishop who was to lead that diocese during the Civil War came to the episcopate.

Nevertheless, Davis still saw his episcopal jurisdiction as a missionary challenge. The population data for the state of South Carolina for the year 1850 from the U.S. Census were as follows:[39]

| Total | White | Slaves | Free persons of color |
|---|---|---|---|
| 668,507 | 274,563 | 384,984 | 8,960 |

These population figures and the low density of churches, especially in the up-country, suggested that there was much room for growth. The new bishop had a particular concern about the ministry of the church to slaves, a ministry that had been nurtured by his predecessors, Bishops Bowen and Gadsden.

### Earlier Responses by Church to Slavery

In 1835 South Carolina bishop Nathaniel Bowen wrote a pastoral letter on the religious instruction of slaves. Although the letter was over his signature (and he concurred in its message), he made plain that he was communicating the will of the diocesan convention of the Episcopal Church in South Carolina. He then wrote:

> The religious instruction of our slave population is one of deep and vital interest. Forming as we do, a large majority of the slave holders in the low country, we . . . are bound to inquire into the duty and means of affording such instruction to our slaves, as shall make them wise unto salvation. Among us must begin the good work, which, if entered upon with an humble reliance upon Divine Grace, must result in a harvest of abundant blessing to the church and her members, both now and at that day, when we shall be called upon to give an account of our stewardship.[40]

The letter included a message for the slave-owning planters. Part of the message was pragmatic. Religious instruction of slaves resulted in better behavior, stronger relations between master and slave, and better relationships among the slaves. The facts, Bowen noted, "shew happy, practical efficacy of the religious instruction of our slaves."[41] Slave owners were also told that slaves, as human beings, must die and one day give account for their earthly actions. Religious instruction was essential if they were to give a good account—and owners bore responsibility: "Slaves are placed where responsibility is imposed, subject to law and your authority. Will you deprive them of knowledge of higher and more solemn sanction to restrain them from evil?"[42] Bowen provided service outlines and scriptural references as guides. He also included the convention's recommendations for staffing this missionary effort. Clergy were urged to establish Sunday schools for slaves, to secure lay catechists, and to use slave masters, their overseers, and members of the slave owner's family as volunteer staff.

Bishop Bowen recognized that the clergy of the diocese, who already were ministering to white congregations, had limited time. More missionary clergy were needed, and Bowen noted that a full-blown missionary effort, especially on the large plantations, was not possible at that time. His letter, however, committed himself and the diocese to making the strongest effort possible. At one point in his letter Bowen noted that the instruction provided was "of course to be altogether oral." This implicitly acknowledged a state proscription against teaching slaves to read and write.

Twelve years later, at the 1847 diocesan convention, Bowen's successor, Bishop Gadsden, gave his thoughts on the consecration of a chapel built for the use of slaves. In particular, he insisted that chapel be open to all in the parish, because he did not wish to depart "from that interesting feature of true religion, in all its dispensations, namely that 'the rich and the poor in the house of God meet together,' for he is the Maker and Redeemer of them all, and the sanctifier of the true believer, without respect of color, or station, or condition. . . . In our Diocese the master and the servant, the descendants whether of Shem, or Ham, or

Japheth, have been encouraged to unite in public worship and receiving Christian instruction."[43] Gadsden's position was clear; all churches in his diocese should be open to all people.

Under the leadership of Bishops Bowen and Gadsden, the Diocese of South Carolina had accepted formally religious instruction of slaves as a diocesan obligation. Thus, when Davis became bishop he found in place a diocesan commitment and ongoing efforts to take the gospel to slaves.

*An Episcopate for White People and Black People*

Davis did begin work to establish new white churches, and in the years just before secession his efforts bore fruit. He consecrated five churches in 1858, three in 1859, and six in 1860, bringing the total of parish churches in the diocese to sixty-seven. The passion of the early Davis episcopate, however, was expanding and strengthening the outreach of the gospel to slaves.

Davis delivered his first sermon at Grace Church in Camden, where he had served as rector before his election as bishop. He departed Camden on 10 November 1853 and preached on both 12 and 15 November at Trinity Church in Edgefield, where he confirmed three people on 12 November. By late November he was in the lowcountry, preaching and holding confirmation services for both races in and around Charleston. He recorded these visits in his diary.

> *Sunday, Nov. 27th* In St. John's Church, John's Island, I preached and confirmed 14 white persons. After the white congregation were dismissed, a very large assembly of colored persons were gathered together, to whom the Rev. Mr. Prentiss preached; after which I confirmed 121 colored persons. I was forcibly struck with the regard and reverence which these servants paid to their spiritual instructors, and the cordiality and gratefulness with which they received all that we spoke unto them. They shewed that much attention had been paid to them by their pastor, the Rev. Mr. Hall. . . .
>
> *Sunday Jan. 1st*, in morning at St. Matthew's Parish, confirmed 4 white persons. In afternoon at Hampton Chapel, about five miles distant, confirmed 92 colored persons.
>
> *Saturday, Jan. 22nd*, . . . At night, at Hyde Park Plantation, preached and confirmed 13 colored persons.[44]

Davis's first visitation tour therefore focused on strengthening and expanding ministry to the slaves. Although Davis continued to encourage, wherever practicable, what Bishop Gadsden had called "that interesting feature of true religion, in all its dispensations," namely that "the rich and the poor in the house of God meet together," there was little, if any, mingling during worship, and the communion rail was approached separately by the two races. Davis's work to see that the gospel was brought to slaves did include efforts to bring slaves and whites together in worship under the same roof, but "slave chapels" became more and more common on plantations.

In his maiden diocesan address in 1854, Bishop Davis put an emphasis on missionary ministry to the slaves.

> There does seem to be a wider field of usefulness opening to the Church, especially among the colored population. Here is a great field of missionary labor, and one that bears equally upon the consciences of laymen and clergymen. We owe this people religious instruction, and unless we pay it, I do not see how we can be justified in the sight of God and man. . . . The great difficulty lies in the inquiry, how shall it be accomplished? And this leads me to refer to another point, the want of active, earnest devoted missionaries. This is the great want of the church.[45]

Davis thus made clear his commitment to the religious instruction of slaves, but at the same time noted the lack of missionary clergy to carry out the work. A year later, he was still seeking missionaries but in reporting progress he appeared optimistic, praising his clergy, and encouraging the laity. He concluded, though, with a pointed suggestion to slave owners:

> Some of our brethren [in the clergy] are giving themselves to this work. . . and their labors have been much blessed. Let me say to our lay brethren of the church, that when their brethren in the ministry are thus laboring for the good of those souls . . . it is but right. . . that they should meet them, and help them and work with them; that they should. . . see that all obstacles are moved out of their way. This is generally so, but there are cases in which there might be improvement; and especially, *let the whole Sabbath Day be devoted only to religion.*[46] (Emphasis added)

Although not as many as Davis felt were needed, there were missionaries, some of whom served several plantations, conducting services, preaching, and catechizing. Davis visited these plantations to hold confirmations, including a tour after the 1854 convention, during which he preached on successive days on several plantations, each time to a "large congregation of colored persons." One service was in the chapel on the Reverend Stephen Elliott's plantation, where he "confirmed 53 colored persons."[47] In February 1856 he reported: "Confirmed 26 colored persons on the plantation of Thomas Porcher, where there was a new, neat, and commodious chapel erected for the use of its slaves. . . . Confirmed 23 Colored Persons on the plantation of Joshua LaBruce. 10 of these 23 were from other plantations."[48]

At the 1857 convention Davis reported on the facilities available within the diocese for worship by slaves and for their religious instruction. These facilities were largely plantation-based. His findings were as follows: "45 chapels and places of worship for slaves; 150 lay persons, male and female, engaged in giving them catechetical instruction." He concluded that "there must be 150 congregations and catechumens in proportion to the number of teachers above mentioned."[49] Among the 150 laypersons were the wives and daughters of the slave owners on whose property the slave chapels were constructed. Until the Civil War broke out, the diocese continued to grow in communicants; the total confirmations reported by Davis in diocesan journals from 1854 through 1861 were 1,591 white communicants and 2,917 who were black.

### A Difficult Issue

Performing the rite of marriage for slave couples and the implications of doing so were discussed at diocesan conventions in 1856 and 1857. Then, in the convention of 1859, Davis presided over consideration of a report that addressed the issue of slave marriages and in particular the separation of husband and wife when slaves were sold. The report stated that masters were bound, in relation to their treatment of slave marriages, by the same scriptural provisions that applied to their own marriages. Slaves married by the church were bound by the same provisions. The report did offer an exception for circumstances beyond the control of the master (and slave) and permitted second marriages in these cases. The report, though, was clear that its authors disapproved of sales that separated husband and wife. The report was debated thoroughly both in 1859 and 1860, but it was tabled in both years. The debate reflected strong support for a diocesan position that the teachings of the Bible applied to both races, but neither the original motion nor the series of substitute motions or proposed amendments resulted in wording that the convention would accept.[50] The issue remained on the table during the war years.

### Health and Work Style

Davis's health began to deteriorate noticeably in 1858 as a result of his intense work habits, and in 1860 he had an unsuccessful operation to save his eyesight.[51] His vision worsened, and he did suffer permanent blindness in 1862. Neither his health problems nor his failing eyesight nor secession and the concomitant war clouds, however, deterred Davis from his episcopal duties. In 1861, just before hostilities erupted, Davis visited several plantations:

> *April 4th Thursday.* On the plantation of Mr. Plowden Weston, attended at the catechizing of the children. All things here, bear the evidence of great attention to the religious culture of the colored people. The answers of the children when catechized, the number of hymns which they repeated and sang,

and their whole appearance, indicated that they had been very carefully instructed. . . . May there be increased efforts every where for the salvation of these persons committed to our trust.

*April 5th, Friday.* At the plantation of Col. Belin on Sandy Island, preached and confirmed eighteen colored persons.

*April 7th, Sunday—Forenoon.* In the lower Church preached and confirmed eight colored persons. Afternoon—At the plantation of Chancellor Dunkin, Divine service was held, and Rev. A. Glennie and myself addressed the negroes.[52]

In the early morning of 12 April, the bombardment of Fort Sumter began.

### Notes

1. *Diocese of Georgia, 1823,* 3. The formal title of the journal of proceedings for this first meeting was *Convention of the Protestant Episcopal Church in the State of Georgia, 1823* (Augusta: *Chronicle and Advertiser* Office, 1823).

2. *Diocese of Georgia, 1840* (Columbus: *Enquirer* Printing Office, 1840), 23, and William Stevens Perry, *The Episcopate in America* (New York: Christian Literature Company, 1895), 83.

3. Historical Census Browser, Geostat Center, University of Virginia Library, http://fisher.lib.virginia.edu/collections/stats/histcensus/ (accessed 15 September 2008).

4. *Diocese of Georgia, 1840,* 23, and *Diocese of Georgia, 1841* (Columbus: *Enquirer* Printing Office, 1841), 1, 19.

5. *Diocese of Georgia, 1850* (Marietta: Hunt and Campbell, 1850), 3, 39. See also Hubert B. Owens, *Georgia's Planting Prelate* (Athens: University of Georgia Press, 1945), 9.

6. *Diocese of Georgia, 1860* (Savannah: George N. Nichols, 1860), 5, 57.

7. *Augusta Daily Chronicle and Sentinel,* 29 December 1866; reprinted from editorial in the *Macon Telegraph.*

8. *Diocese of Georgia, 1861* (Savannah: John M. Cooper, 1861), 35.

9. Ibid. Data collected from 1861 parochial reports.

10. *Diocese of Georgia, 1841,* 7.

11. *Diocese of Georgia, 1843* (Savannah: W. T. Williams, 1843), 12.

12. Ibid.

13. Ibid., 12–13.

14. Ibid., 26–27.

15. Charles Lwanga Hoskins, *Black Episcopalians in Georgia: Strife, Struggle, and Salvation* (Savannah: Hoskins, 1980), 35.

16. Ibid.

17. *Diocese of Georgia, 1846* (Marietta: *Advocate* Office, 1846), 22. Teaching slaves to read and write was proscribed by state laws in the antebellum South.

18. Ibid.

19. *Diocese of Georgia, 1852* (Macon: Benjamin Griffin, 1852), 48.

20. Ibid., 49.

21. *Diocese of Georgia, 1861,* 25.

22. *Diocese of Georgia, 1855* (Macon: D. F. Griffin, 1855), 45.

23. *Diocese of Georgia, 1856* (Savannah: G. Nichols, 1856), 14–15.

24. *Diocese of Georgia, 1863* (Savannah: E. J. Purse, 1863), 57.

25. Thomas Hanckel, ed., *Sermons by the Right Reverend Stephen Elliott, D.D., Late Bishop of Georgia, with a Memoir* (New York: Pott and Amery, 1867), page x of *Memoir*.

26. *Diocese of Georgia, 1842* (Savannah: W. T. Williams, 1842), 14.

27. Ibid., 12.

28. Hoskins, *Black Episcopalians in Georgia,* 28.

29. Bishop Elliott's daughter, Ellen Elliott Shoup, believed that her father was misled by the prior institute head regarding the financial status of the school when the bishop took over. (Ellen Elliott Shoup, "Sketch of Charlotte Bull Barnwell Elliott," in *Mothers of Some Famous Georgians of the Last Half Century,* ed. Sarah Harriet Butts (New York: J. J. Little, 1902), 19.

30. *Diocese of Georgia, 1856,* 36. The land and buildings were used until 1876 for a private school. Although it was no longer an Episcopal institution, Elliott maintained an association with the new school, as was noted in a newspaper article following Elliott's death. (*Augusta Daily Chronicle and Sentinel,* 29 December 1866; reprinted from the *Macon Telegraph.*)

31. Hanckel, *Sermons and Memoir,* page x of *Memoir.*

32. Shoup, "Sketch of Charlotte Bull Barnwell Elliott," 19.

33. *Diocese of Georgia 1856,* parochial reports, 45.

34. The number of free black persons in Chatham County, Georgia, of which Savannah is the county seat, was 731 in 1850. Historical Census Browser, Geostat Center, University of Virginia Library, http://fisher.lib.virginia.edu/collections/stats/histcensus/ (accessed 1 July 2007).

35. Hoskins, *Black Episcopalians in Georgia,* 50.

36. *Diocese of Georgia, 1866* (Savannah: Purse and Sons, 1866), 22.

37. Perry, *Episcopate in America,* 123.

38. *Diocese of South Carolina, 1854* (Charleston: A. E. Miller, 1854), parish listings and page 56.

39. Historical Census Browser, Geostat Center, University of Virginia Library, http://fisher.lib.virginia.edu/collections/stats/histcensus/ (accessed 9 November 2006).

40. Nathaniel Bowen, *A Pastoral Letter on the Religious Instruction of the Slaves of Members of the Protestant Episcopal Church in the State of South Carolina Prepared at the Request of the Convention of the Churches of the Diocese* (Charleston, A. E. Miller, 1835), 4.

41. Ibid., 7.

42. Ibid.

43. *Diocese of South Carolina, 1847* (Charleston: Miller and Browne, 1847), 25.

44. *Diocese of South Carolina, 1854,* 20–22.

45. Ibid., 22.

46. *Diocese of South Carolina, 1855* (Charleston: A. E. Miller, 1855), 29.

47. Ibid., 22.

48. *Diocese of South Carolina, 1857* (Charleston: A. E. Miller, 1857), 18, 26.

49. Ibid., 30.

50. *Diocese of South Carolina, 1859* (Charleston: A. E. Miller, 1859), 30–35, and *Diocese of South Carolina*, 1860 (Charleston: A. E. Miller, 1860), 39–40.

51. *Diocese of South Carolina, 1858* (Charleston: A. E. Miller, 1858), 34; *Diocese of South Carolina*, 1860, 24; *Diocese of South Carolina*, 1861 (Charleston: A. E. Miller, 1861), 13.

52. *Diocese of South Carolina 1861*, 16.

# William Meade and
# John Johns of Virginia

### Prelude: An Interest in Colonization

On 21 December 1816 a group met in a Washington, D.C., hotel to discuss establishment of a society that would help free black people to emigrate from the United States to a colony set aside for them in Africa or at some other location overseas. The meeting had been called by the Reverend Robert Finley, a Presbyterian minister deeply concerned about the plight of the increasing number of free blacks in America and by his brother-in-law, Elias B. Caldwell, clerk of the U. S. Supreme Court. Francis Scott Key, a prominent attorney in Washington and author of the "Star-Spangled Banner," assisted Finley and Caldwell. The meeting was attended by about twenty people, including a mayor, a general, members of both houses of Congress, clergymen, and others of considerable influence. Henry Clay chaired the meeting. Among the clergymen present was William Meade from the Diocese of Virginia.[1]

As a result of this meeting a society was established with the formal title American Society for Colonizing the Free People of Color in the United States. Known as the American Colonization Society (ACS), this organization was to "collect information" and to assist the United States government in setting up a colony in Africa (or in "such other place as Congress shall deem most expedient") to receive the free persons of color. Emigration was to be voluntary. The society's leadership set about the tasks of (1) urging governmental action, in particular the acquiring the land on which a colony could be established, and (2) winning public support, both endorsements and monetary subscriptions, for the purposes of the society.[2]

The Reverend Mr. Meade became an immediate supporter of the ACS and an active agent on its behalf. In so doing, Meade had the full support of the Virginia diocesan convention, which passed a strong resolution endorsing the goals of the ACS at its meeting in May 1819.[3] Support for the new ACS also was expressed by resolutions of the state legislatures of Virginia, Tennessee, and Maryland.[4] Meade undertook tours, north and south on behalf of the ACS, seeking to explain its mission and to secure donations and pledges. He was an excellent spokesperson for the society, securing favorable publicity and pledges from Savannah to New Haven. Meade remained a supporter of the ACS, but in 1820 his active role as fundraiser and speaker for the society ceased, and Meade returned to Millwood, Virginia, to devote his energies to his church there.[5]

Colonization under ACS auspices began in 1820, and after a rocky start the ACS, with U.S. government help, traveled a long and tortuous path that led to emigration of some twelve thousand free blacks to a colony named Liberia, which became a free and independent republic in 1847.[6] The purpose of the ACS, establishment of a colony to which free black persons who chose to become colonists there would receive assistance in relocating and resettlement, was clearly stated in its founding document, but the motives of its supporters varied. Some, for example, felt that free black persons were a corrupting influence on American society in general and should be encouraged to leave; others felt that white people would never accept black individuals as citizens with equal rights and therefore free blacks should leave for their own protection; still others saw free blacks as a threat to the institution of slavery that needed to be removed; and some saw emigration of free blacks as a way that slave owners who wished to could emancipate slaves without creating a free black population that would generate resentment among neighboring slave owners. Taking the last view, some even saw the ACS plan as the ultimate solution to the problem of slavery—gradual emancipation accompanied by relocation to an African colony. This position, according to his colleague John Johns, was the motivation for Meade's active role in the early days of the ACS.[7]

### Overview of the Meade Episcopate

On 18 May 1814 the Reverend Richard Channing Moore, rector of St. Stephen's Church in New York City, who had just accepted the position of rector at the new Monumental Church in Richmond, was elected bishop of the Diocese of Virginia.[8] Bishop Moore quickly began a vigorous effort to revive the Episcopal Church in Virginia, which had languished since the Revolution. The General Convention of 1811 took note of the sad state of the church in Virginia: "the Church in Virginia is from various causes so depressed, that there is danger of her total ruin, unless great exertions, favoured by the blessing of Providence, are employed to raise her."[9]

One of the new bishop's strong supporters was the Reverend William Meade, an energetic young clergyman who had been ordained in 1811. During the next eighteen years Meade served parishes in Millwood, Winchester, and Alexandria and helped to establish parishes in the several counties surrounding Winchester.[10]

In 1829, when the diocese resolved to proceed with election of an assistant bishop, Meade was chosen.[11] He was consecrated in August of the same year.[12]

The months just after he was consecrated were indicative of the drive that he would bring to his role as a bishop. At the 1830 convention Assistant Bishop Meade reported that his first official act occurred on 30 October 1829, that of consecrating the new building for Christ Church in Winchester. He then embarked on a schedule of visits that took him from Millwood to Martinsburg (in what is now West Virginia), Woodstock (in Shenandoah County), Harrisonburg, and Staunton. He preached in a church at each stop, except for one destination, where he delivered his sermon to "a large assembly in a private house." On Christmas Eve, Meade arrived at Halifax Courthouse and, Christmas Day, preached to a "full house" in the courthouse. He then confirmed ten persons. From Halifax, Bishop Meade went back north to visit in Campbell, where he paid a call on John Henry, son of Patrick Henry. Meade also preached to a "large collection" of neighbors at the home of Spotswood Henry and continued north to conduct visitations in Alexandria.

Strengthening and increasing the membership of the Virginia church was his first priority throughout his episcopate. From late 1829 until early 1862, his health permitting, Meade crisscrossed the Diocese of Virginia on episcopal visits to established churches; on these visits he usually preached, and, if candidates were ready, administered confirmation and assisted with the Holy Eucharist. He also made missionary visits to congregations that had no church or minister, addressed groups in private homes, and preached to slaves on plantations.

Bishop Moore died on 11 November 1841, and William Meade became bishop of Virginia.[13] By October of the following year Virginia had a vigorous new assistant bishop, John Johns, with whom Meade could share the work of the diocese. Johns was a native of Delaware who was serving as a parish priest in Maryland at the time of his election.[14]

The overall growth during the Meade years in certain key indices can be seen in the table below; the data are taken from clergy lists and parochial reports in the diocesan journals for the years concerned.

## Overall diocesan statistics for the Diocese of Virginia, 1829–1860

| Year | Number of clergy | Number of parishes | Number of communicants |
|------|------------------|--------------------|------------------------|
| 1829 | 44  | 40  | 1,462 |
| 1841 | 87  | 99  | 3,702 |
| 1850 | 110 | 109 | 5,347 |
| 1860 | 116 | 123 | 7,876 |

## Ministry to Slaves

When he became assistant bishop, Meade saw his flock as inclusive of bond and free and white and black. Throughout his early ministry and his episcopate, Meade felt that his primary obligation to the slaves and other black people within his diocese was to bring them the message of the gospel of Jesus Christ. His visitation schedules and diocesan addresses document that he sought to bring Christ to all classes, including the servants. Although he supported colonization, and colonization as a concomitant, gradual emancipation, he did not believe that his charge was to call for change in the social order.

Prior to the 1834 convention, Meade wrote a pastoral letter dealing with the "very important duty of giving religious instruction to our servants." His remarks at the convention suggested that he felt that some of his constituents—lay and clerical—were not giving this matter serious attention. "I know the difficulties of the task, but I know that both ministers and people are far too ready to magnify those difficulties, and satisfy themselves with very insufficient excuses for its neglect. If the love of immortal souls, which is the true spirit of Christ, did but reign in our hearts as it ought to do, we should be more apt to teach these, our poor ignorant fellow creatures, and less apt at finding excuses for our neglect of them. I commit the feeble effort in their behalf to God and your consciences, hoping that it may not be altogether in vain."[15]

In 1837 Meade described a visitation in Prince George County with a George Harrison, plantation owner.

> I was much pleased on the evening of that day, to be invited into a warm and comfortable house adjoining his establishment, and to be accompanied to the same by himself and other members of his household, where I found a large collection of his servants ready to receive such religious instruction as I should feel disposed to give. I was much gratified in spending an hour with them in exercises which seemed to interest them and to awaken the gratitude of their hearts. It is the custom of Mr. Harrison and his brother who lives near to him, to assemble their servants at a small church, built by themselves, between their plantations, on every other Sabbath, and to procure the services of a faithful preacher of the gospel for their sole benefit.[16]

At the 1840 diocesan convention a committee of five was appointed to "consider the best means of promoting the religious instruction of servants." Two of the members were Bishops Moore and Meade. Meade reported for the committee at the 1841 meeting. The report stated at the outset that the committee assumed that no reader of the report would question the duty of providing religious education to servants and that the report would focus only on possible means for offering that education. The committee then devoted over one-third of its report to making clear on whom the burden of such religious instruction had to fall. It would be highly desirable to have a class of clergy whose only responsibility was the souls of the slaves, but the likelihood of that happening in Virginia, at least in the immediate future, was small. The work had to move forward immediately, led by the extant diocesan clergy and supported in every way possible by the slave owners and their families.

In those cases in which it was feasible for the slaves to attend Sunday services with everyone else, the clergymen were urged to aim at least some part of the sermon at the slaves each Sunday. If it were not feasible for the slaves to attend regular Sunday morning services, then ministers should make it their practice to hold Sunday-afternoon or week-night services in plantation homes or slave quarters. The committee then argued that catechizing was necessary if the slaves were to participate meaningfully in worship. This work could be shared by the minister with parishioners, and through it the slaves could learn many of the responsive parts of the worship service. This could be accomplished even though all instruction had to be oral. It was also suggested in the report that Sunday schools should be established for black children and that catechizing be done during the Sunday-school hour. The report went so far as to propose that, if there were insufficient staff for both a white and a black Sunday school, the white children might learn at home, with the church program reserved for the slave children.

Finally, the committee urged that family worship be a part of the life of every household and that servants be invited and expected to attend. Families were asked to consider carefully the time chosen for such services. Services should be held at a time when servants would expect to be on duty, not during times which they would expect to have free. One suggestion offered was to take a half hour after the morning meal before everyone started work for the day. The report, coming just months before the death of Bishop Moore and Meade's becoming diocesan, served as a set of expectations regarding the religious instruction of slaves during the twenty years that Meade was bishop of Virginia.[17]

In 1845 the theme of the 1841 document was reinforced by the Committee on the State of the Church. "Is it not then in our interest, as well as our duty, and for the benefit of the community as well as of masters and families, that in all families, plantations, and churches, our colored classes should, as far as possible, be gathered into schools for religious instruction,—just as our children are in Sunday Schools? Is it not a fact that Almighty God holds us just as much bound to train up our servants, as to train up our children, 'in the nurture and admonition of the Lord?'"[18] At intervals throughout the 1840s and 1850s, Meade's addresses and the parochial reports echoed the theme that religious instruction of slaves was a charge from God. In 1852 Meade commended special materials to his clergy for use in this ministry; these included a book of sermons and a booklet for use in catechizing exercises.[19]

## Colonization Redux

In 1837 the Reverend John Payne, an 1836 graduate of the Virginia Seminary, became a missionary to Africa, joining a recently established Episcopal mission at Cape Palmas. Payne became one of the leaders of a missionary movement that grew in scope from the tiny settlement at Cape Palmas to encompass the Colony of Liberia and finally the Liberian Republic. The work of Payne and other missionaries focused on black American colonists, but the church schools established were open to native Africans as well. At the end of January 1838 Payne set up a school at Mt. Vaughan, a mission near Cape Palmas, that enrolled four children of colonists and thirty-seven native children.[20] John Payne was consecrated as bishop of Cape Palmas and Parts Adjacent on 11 July 1851. In 1853 Liberia and Cape Palmas became one missionary district. Bishop Payne made trips to America to secure support for his work in Africa, and Meade, James Hervey Otey of Tennessee, and other Southern bishops were strongly supportive, even though some dioceses were unable to make large contributions.

Although the objectives were not mutually exclusive, the emphasis with regard to Liberia for Meade and many other supporters of Payne gradually shifted from promoting colonization to supporting missionary work. After his consecration Payne still hoped that colonization would ultimately be a major factor in slavery's demise,[21] but the vision of a massive emancipation-emigration movement held by some ACS founders had faded long before the Civil War. Some organized emigration occurred through the late 1800s, but the Episcopal Church focused on missions and not on promotion of colonization.[22]

## An Unpleasant Incident

Although most Virginians, including slave owners, approved of Meade's plans to bring slaves into the Christian fold, his efforts were not without controversy. In May 1856 he confirmed a group of slaves at Lawrenceville and made some remarks to the confirmands. A subsequent letter to the editor of the *Petersburg Daily Democrat* was extremely critical of the bishop, charging that he had made remarks that "elevated" black people socially and politically. This letter began a series of editorials and other letters to the editor, including responses from the bishop's defenders as well as a response from Meade.[23]

The first letter, appearing in the *Daily Democrat* on 20 May 1856, was from an anonymous correspondent from the County of New Brunswick calling himself A. Z. who was not present at the confirmation ceremony. Nevertheless, he labeled Meade an "unsound head of the Church" and unleashed an invective barrage. "Bishop Meade was at Lawrenceville on last Wednesday, and I understand made very objectionable remarks to the congregation on slavery, in the presence of ten or twelve Negroes, who were candidates for confirmation. Public sentiment is very much against him here. The object of this communication is to ask persons who were present to make known what he said, in order that the people of Virginia may know what to expect from him, and deal with him as he deserves."[24]

A. Z. went on to argue that "it ought not to be tolerated" for Bishop Meade or others in "high authority to use expressions to our Negroes calculated to make them believe that they are better than their masters, and thereby render them dissatisfied with their own situations."[25]
In fact, A. Z. argued,

> If Bishop Meade cannot act in a manner becoming a citizen of Virginia, in the present aspect of affairs, and never feels himself more highly honored than when allowed to confirm a slave, he ought to move to that part of the country where it is considered by some more honorable and praiseworthy to rob a slaveholder of his property than to confirm a Negro. . . . His course has certainly deprived him of the ability to do good in any way here; . . . it is a source of regret with several that they did not leave the church. A movement on the part of any person was only necessary, I understand, to have caused him to have only empty benches to lecture to.[26]

Meade's words that he "never felt himself more highly honored than when allowed to confirm a slave" appeared to have been the detonator for the A. Z. diatribe. A. Z., in fact, felt that clergymen should not concern themselves with black individuals and certainly should not minister "particularly to their spiritual wants."[27]

An editorial in the *Petersburg Daily Express* questioned the charges against Meade and expressed the belief that his remarks had been misconstrued. The editor argued that Meade, born and educated in Virginia, was "too closely identified with the South in feelings and interest" to have said anything against the "peculiar institution."[28] A letter to the editor took a bolder and more direct stance in defending Meade. "Bishop Meade has grown gray in his Master's service and in ministering to the spiritual wants of *blacks* as well as *whites*. He and all other ministers should feel highly honored in being the instruments of saving the souls of every class and color. . . So far as the political and moral institution [slavery] is concerned we have a right to expect that Southern ministers should sustain it, but in his ministerial character no minister of any denomination has any right to discriminate between the soul salvation of whites and blacks."[29]

Bishop Meade also responded, noting that "In my address at Lawrenceville, I adverted to the fact that a number of servants were about to be confirmed—and that my saying something suitable to them was proper from me—that GOD, who, of one blood, had made all nations upon earth, had given us a religion suitable to all, and that the Bible had many things addressed to all—rich and poor, bond and free—that the larger portions of the human race had always been in some form of bondage to the other, being poor and dependent."[30]

Meade's address to the newly confirmed slaves went on to encompass several themes. One was that slaves should be grateful that they were born in America and not in some heathen land where the gospel would not have reached them. The freedom conferred on them by God's word was of much greater importance than any earthly liberty. He exhorted them to accept their station that God had mandated and to "rejoice in the many spiritual blessings connected with it." The bishop also asserted that God had allowed them to be brought to America to be Christianized and that ultimately Africa would benefit by having the gospel brought there by former slaves.

He noted that he had been confirming slaves for twenty-seven years and that his sermons and instructions regarding the religious training of servants had been generally circulated and approved. In his view the earthly status, slave or master, of each person was determined by Providence and should be accepted, but all races were of the same origin and deserved equal access to God's love and grace.

Although this incident did generate considerable discussion, in general Meade encountered very little open resistance to religious instruction of slaves. Most of the time, apathy and lack of resources, not hostility, were the chief barriers. There were those, however, who, although silent, shared some of the concerns of the writer of the letter to the editor and were apprehensive of any activity that could potentially lead slaves to aspire to improve their status. In that regard, it should be noted that all religious instruction of slaves that Meade sanctioned was presented orally and was aimed solely at enriching the worship experience for them and deepening their understanding of God. The intention was not to teach slaves to read or to promote their social elevation; a decision to change the earthly status of slaves, Meade felt, could be made only by God alone (and presumably would be communicated to his people when the time came).[31] This incident, though isolated, gives a glimpse of the complexity, conflicted feelings, and convoluted rationales that were intertwined with slavery.

### Status of Meade's Work in 1860 and Future Plans

The efforts made to reach slaves during Meade's episcopate, especially in the light of the clerical resources available, were significant, and appreciable numbers of slaves were reached by preaching and religious instruction. The number actually brought into the Episcopal fold as communicants, however, was only a tiny fraction of the slave population, as can be seen in the table below. The slave population in Virginia in 1850 was in excess of 472,000, and in 1860 it was nearly 491,000.[32]

Diocesan statistics for the Diocese of Virginia with
racial breakdowns, 1850–1861

| | Baptisms | | | Communicants | | | Confirmations | | |
|------|-------|-------|-------|-------|-------|-------|-------|-------|-------|
| Year | White | Black | Total | White | Black | Total | White | Black | Total |
| 1850 | 683 | 166 | 849 | | | 5,347 | | | 287 |
| 1851 | 828 | 117 | 945 | | | 5,412 | | | |
| 1852 | 709 | 149 | 858 | 5,666 | 176 | 5,842 | 408 | 32 | 440 |
| 1853 | 777 | 167 | 944 | | | 5,292 | | | 348 |
| 1855 | 739 | 108 | 847 | 5,793 | 224 | 6,017 | 412 | 17 | 429 |
| 1856 | 727 | 267 | 994 | 6,292 | 235 | 6,527 | 405 | 47 | 452 |
| 1857 | 951 | 164 | 1,115 | 6,281 | | 6,314 | 528 | 86 | 614 |
| 1858 | | | | | | 6,939 | | | |
| 1859 | 1,032 | 301 | 1,333 | 6,740 | 444 | 7,184 | 671 | 64 | 735 |
| 1860 | 1,038 | 178 | 1,216 | 7,762 | 114 | 7,876 | 666 | 22 | 688 |
| 1861 | 940 | 250 | 1,190 | | | 6,398 | 421 | 46 | 467 |

Source: Journals of the Diocese of Virginia for the years 1850 through 1860. Data are taken
from summary sheets for the parochial reports, reports of the Committee on the State of
the Church, and in a few cases by counts from the individual parochial reports.

Note: The sharp drop from baptisms to confirmations, especially for black individuals,
was a problem that the church urgently needed to address. The most reliable statistic was
the number of baptisms; the least reliable was the number of slave communicants, which
parish clergy often found difficult to estimate.

The number of pupils in Sunday school reached 5,000 by the end of the 1850s; in
1861, 695 of those listed as enrolled were black.

In 1858 another special committee was created to review the status of the diocesan ministry to blacks. The authorizing resolution read as follows:

> That a special committee be appointed to ascertain from the parishes, and re-
> port to the next convention, whether any, and, if any, what provision is made
> for the instruction of the colored population of their limits.
>
> And also, to inquire as to the best means of securing the permanent attach-
> ment of that people to our church.[33]

Although this committee did not report in 1859, its membership was increased at
that year's diocesan convention. One of the added members was Bishop Johns,
who assumed the committee chair. Two resolutions were referred to the augmented committee for consideration, one asking that the convention consider
establishing missionary duty for its clergy for the benefit of slaves, the other

requesting that collections be taken up in each parish to provide "suitable places of public worship" for slaves.

The 1858 resolution creating the committee and the resolutions referred to it the next year reflected a feeling that not nearly enough was being accomplished through the ministry to slaves. Implicit in the words of the creating resolution regarding "permanent attachment of that people to our church" was concern over the small fraction of baptisms that translated into confirmations and over the slow growth in number of slave communicants.

### The Johns Report

The committee's 1860 report was delivered by the chair, Assistant Bishop Johns. Johns's report reflected a two-year study and included not only a status report on the religious instruction of slaves but also recommendations to strengthen the missionary work among them. Its first major conclusion was that, although nearly all parishes were making an effort to bring teaching and worship to blacks, the effort across the diocese was not succeeding. Some eight to nine thousand black individuals were being reached by preaching or some form of religious instruction, the committee estimated (out of a population of some 473,000 slaves and 54,000 free persons),[34] but, as is evident in the table above, only a tiny fraction of those being reached committed to the Episcopal Church. The committee reviewed a number of possible reasons for failure.[35]

Committee members rejected lack of accommodations as a cause. Churches appeared to have enough seats, and the committee felt that congregations were willing to increase the size of their churches, if needed, to accommodate more black persons. Also rejected as a significant factor was the preference that black persons appeared to have for baptism by immersion. The liturgy, preaching, and doctrinal views were also dismissed as root causes. The committee identified the cause of failure by the Episcopal Church in Virginia to gather black persons into Christ's fold as a deficiency in the worship environment, namely: the lack of "the blessed privilege of Christian Fellowship." The report included the following explanation:

> Little is done presently to satisfy that need. The Lord's Supper is celebrated for black and white in the same place, but separately. There is no identification with the Church. Any service, communion included, must gratify their intuitive craving for Christian fellowship.
>
> When white and colored persons worship in the same house and partake at the same administration, no more judicious course could be pursued than that which is now uniform practice; and the colored people themselves, under present circumstances, would not have it otherwise. . . .

If this evil [lack of fellowship] is to be remedied, it can only be done by providing for them those privileges within our own pale. And as religion does not require, and this is not the region, nor ours the people, to favor anything approximating amalgamation, such provision they must be led to find among themselves under our supervision, and in accordance with the statutes of the Commonwealth. And this is practicable and unexceptionable. Other denominations have successfully adopted this policy, and we need not fail.[36]

This report, in effect, recognized the need for fellowship but rejected structuring worship in a way that would facilitate Christian fellowship between the races. In the conclusion the committee recommended that the following structure be adopted for providing worship services and religious instruction of the "colored people."

1. The formation of the people of color into a separate and distinct congregation.
2. The provision of a suitable place for their worship.
3. A certain number to be taken from the communicants to assist the minister in the affairs of the congregation, with special reference to admissions, supervision, and discipline of church members.
4. Minister must always be a clergyman of the Diocese of Virginia—either a Rector already—or one appointed by the Diocesan Missionary Society.[37]

This plan would have required a change of approach in most parishes, accompanied by an increase and/or redistribution of resources. Nevertheless, under ordinary circumstances an implementation plan for the committee's carefully crafted proposals probably would have been developed in a timely fashion. Circumstances were far from ordinary, however; concerns about secession and possible war precluded any immediate action, and within a year both secession and war had come. The war's outcome then made the social order to which the committee recommendation applied a thing of the past. A new diocesan report on this matter was produced after the war, when emancipation had altered the relationship between the races. The concept of a "separate and distinct" congregation for black people, however, carried over.

Although there were large numbers of plantation slaves in Virginia, some of whom were served by slave chapels, the focus on missionaries appointed directly by the bishop to minister to plantation slaves was not nearly as pronounced as it was in Georgia and South Carolina. The services thus were more "white-parish" oriented in Virginia, and the resultant sharing of worship facilities by black congregants with their white counterparts no doubt contributed to the feeling of lack of connection to the place of worship that the Johns committee perceived among black communicants.

## Johns's Summary of Meade's Views on Slavery and Colonization

John Johns, who served as William Meade's assistant bishop for twenty years, offered a commentary on Meade's views on slavery. This commentary, reproduced below, serves both as a statement of the philosophy that motivated Meade's actions with regard to slavery and as an insight into the complex issues and conflicting emotions that confronted Meade as a slave-state bishop.

> Slavery, as a civil institution, was never to his taste. He had, however, no conscientious scruples as to its lawfulness, because he believed it to have been distinctly recognized, and formally legislated about, by divine authority in the Sacred Scriptures.
>
> As an institution existing in the United States, he did not hold with those who professed it to be a blessing to the country, but with the distinguished statesmen of Virginia who considered it politically disadvantageous, and hoped it would, in the process of time, be happily terminated. How such termination was to be effected, he did not as yet perceive. In early life he had manumitted and conveyed to non-slaveholding States, such of his servants as he thought capable of taking care of themselves. The results of this, and other similar experiments, which he had watched with much interest, satisfied him that manumission was generally a failure, if the persons freed were to remain in this country, and he decidedly advised against it.
>
> His zeal in the cause of the Colonization Society was kindled by the hope that though it was, in its principles and action, distinctly limited to free people of color, it might ultimately lead to some arrangement for the removal of the entire colored population, without violence or wrong.

Meanwhile, with the Apostle, he taught masters and servants to conform to the relations in which they were providentially placed. Servants by "obeying their masters according to the flesh, not with eye-service as men-pleasers, but with singleness of heart, fearing God," and masters by giving unto their servants that which is just and equal, "knowing that they also have a master which is in heaven."[38]

### Notes

1. P. J. Staudenraus, *The African Colonization Movement, 1816–1865.* (New York: Columbia University Press, 1961), 27–28.

2. Ibid.

3. *Diocese of Virginia, 1819* (Richmond: John Warrock, 1819), 21.

4. John Johns, *A Memoir of the Life of the Right Reverend William Meade, D.D., Bishop of the Protestant Episcopal Church in the Diocese of Virginia, with a Memorial Sermon by the Reverend William Sparrow, D.D.* (Baltimore: Innes, 1867), 119.

5. Staudenraus, *African Colonization*, 70–74.

6. See Staudenraus, *African Colonization*, and Patricia Levy, *Liberia* (New York: Cavendish, 1998), for accounts of Liberian colonization.

7. Staudenraus, *African Colonization*, 28–29, provides insight into the diversity of views at the founding meeting, and an address given some years later by Henry Clay gives a detailed picture of the thinking of a prominent founder of the society. See *An Address delivered to the Colonization Society of Kentucky at Frankfort, Ky, February 17, 1829, by the Honorable Henry Clay* (Lexington: Thomas Smith, 1829).

8. *Diocese of Virginia, 1814* (Richmond: Ritchie and Truehart, 1814), 6.

9. "Journal of the Proceedings of the Protestant Episcopal Church in a Convention, 1811," in *Journals of the General Convention of the Protestant Episcopal Church in the United States, 1785—1835,* ed. William Stevens Perry, vol. 1, *1785–1821* (Claremont, N.H.: Claremont Manufacturing, 1874), 381.

10. *Diocese of Virginia* [journals], *1818–1821* and *1823–1826.*

11. *Diocese of Virginia, 1829* (Richmond: John Warrock, 1829), 14–16.

12. William Stevens Perry, *The Episcopate in America* (New York: Christian Literature Company, 1895), 51.

13. Prior to the election in 1829, when Meade was chosen assistant bishop, a motion had been adopted by the convention that the new assistant bishop would not have right of succession. The House of Bishops did not approve of this proviso but proceeded with Meade's consecration. The diocese subsequently removed the restriction, and Meade's succession in 1841 was without objection at the diocesan convention.

14. Perry, *Episcopate in America*, 87.

15. *Diocese of Virginia, 1834* (Richmond: John Warrock, 1834), 15.

16. *Diocese of Virginia, 1837* (Richmond: B. R. Wren, 1837), 10.

17. The next comprehensive study by a special diocesan committee was presented by Assistant Bishop Johns at the 1860 convention. This report is discussed below.

18. *Diocese of Virginia, 1845* (Richmond: Wm MacFarlane, Messenger Office, 1845), 35–36.

19. *Diocese of Virginia*, 1852 (Washington, D.C.: Jno. T. Towers, 1852), 17.

20. Paul Due, "The Work of the Seminary in Liberia," Section 9, Chapter I, Part 3. In William A. R. Goodwin, *History of the Theological Seminary in Virginia and Its Historical Background*, 2 vols. (New York: Edwin Gorham, 1924), 2: 300–303.

21. See the letter of Bishop Payne to Bishop Otey, reproduced in *Diocese of Tennessee, 1853* (Nashville: J. Roberts, 1853), 38–41.

22. In the 1880s and 1890s there was in the South a revival of interest in emigration to Liberia. Although the ACS participated, this time the movement was initiated and led by African Americans. Kenneth Barnes, in his book *Journey of Hope: The Back to Africa Movement in Arkansas in the Late 1800s* (Chapel Hill: University of North Carolina Press, 2004), examines this movement and gives a thorough and poignant description of the emigration of six hundred black Americans from Arkansas to Liberia.

23. Johns, *Memoir of the Life of Meade*, 473–75, and *Petersburg Daily Democrat*, 20 May 1856, 2.

24. *Petersburg Daily Democrat*, 20 May 1856, 2.

25. Ibid.

26. Ibid.

27. *Petersburg Daily Express,* 22 May 1856, 2.

28. Ibid., 21 May 1856, 2.

29. Ibid., 22 May 1856, 2.

30. *Petersburg Daily Democrat,* 28 May 1856, 1.

31. *Diocese of Virginia, 1845.* The "Report of the Committee on the State of the Church," found on page 35 in this journal, explicitly states that religious instruction of black individuals, bond or free, was to be done orally and was not to involve teaching the pupils to read.

32. Historical Census Browser, Geostat Center, University of Virginia Library, http://fisher.lib.virginia.edu/collections/stats/histcensus/php/state.php (accessed 14 May 2007).

33. *Diocese of Virginia, 1858* (Richmond: Whig Book and Job, 1858), 48.

34. Historical Census Browser, Geostat Center, University of Virginia Library, http://fisher.lib.virginia.edu/collections/stats/histcensus/php/state.php (accessed 14 May 2007).

35. *Diocese of Virginia, 1860* (Richmond: Charles H. Wynne, 1860), appendix C, 63–69.

36. Ibid., 67–68.

37. Ibid., 69.

38. Johns, *Memoir of the Life of Meade,* 476–77.

# Thomas Atkinson of North Carolina and William Rollinson Whittingham of Maryland

## Thomas Atkinson

Thomas Atkinson was consecrated as bishop of North Carolina on 17 October 1853 at St. John's Chapel in New York. Atkinson was assuming charge of a diocese in turmoil; his predecessor, Levi Silliman Ives, had abandoned the diocese when he converted to Roman Catholicism, leaving an acephalous diocese and much disappointment and anger in the wake of his departure, a departure without precedent in the American church. Atkinson had been elected at a North Carolina diocesan convention at which the clerical order had taken more than thirty ballots to nominate a new bishop.[1] Atkinson's election occurred while he was rector of Grace Church in Baltimore; he had served churches in that city since 1843.[2]

### Early Attitude toward Slavery

Atkinson's attitude toward slavery had played a significant role on two earlier occasions when he was considered for a bishopric. His views were neither strongly proslavery nor abolitionist. Joseph Blount Cheshire, who served as a presbyter in North Carolina while Atkinson was bishop, wrote the following description of Atkinson's position: "Bishop Atkinson . . . had a strong sense of the disadvantages and evils of slavery, though he was also sensible of the difficulties of finding any just and practicable means of abolishing it in the South. He had freed all his own slaves who wished to be freed and go to the free states, and kept only those who voluntarily chose to remain in the South."[3]

During his service in Baltimore, he was twice elected bishop of Indiana, declining the first time in 1843 because he did not feel ready to become a bishop. In 1846, however, his decision to decline came after receipt of a letter from a friend resident in Indiana who informed him that the public feeling there against slavery and those who owned slaves was "inflamed and bitter." Atkinson did not believe that he could function effectively in such an atmosphere. In 1853, when under consideration as bishop of South Carolina, he was asked for his thoughts on the institution, he responded that slavery was a "disadvantage," but he saw no way to abolish it. He added that, given a choice between retaining slavery and retaining the Union, he would choose the Union. Cheshire quotes Atkinson as remarking: "So, I was not Bishop of Indiana, because I was not sufficiently opposed to slavery, and I was not Bishop of South Carolina, because I was not sufficiently in favor of it."[4] Later, in 1853, the nomination from North Carolina came, and Atkinson and Thomas Frederick Davis, the nominee for bishop of South Carolina, were consecrated at the same ceremony.

## Primary Charge to Diocesan Clergy

Atkinson's main thesis in delivering his first charge to the clergy at the 1855 diocesan convention was that the church was obligated to bring the gospel to all elements of society. Thus far, he argued, the Episcopal Church was wanting in that regard.

> Surely no candid man can well deny, that on the whole our Church has not reached and leavened the mass of society anywhere in this country. In cities, villages or rural districts, if you enter an Episcopal Church, you will find the congregation composed of nearly the same materials. There are professional men, merchants in the more extensive lines of business, the larger landholders, the retired men of fortune, official persons: these and their families, well-dressed, well-mannered . . . , these attend the services of the Episcopal Church. But where are the mechanics, where are the petty shopkeepers, where are the small farmers, where, at the South, are the overseers, where at the North, are the manufacturing operatives and the farm laborers, where among us, alas! too frequently, are our own slaves? Others are taking care of their souls, or they go uncared for. Surely this ought not to be; this must not continue. We cannot justify it to God or man, if our Gospel reach only ears polite, if our glad tidings never find their way to those who especially need instruction, strengthening and comfort,—the ignorant, the poor, the weary, the heavy-laden.[5]

The new bishop then proceeded to propose that flexibility was needed in the liturgy to reach different classes of people, especially slaves:

> That a congregation of slaves, coming jaded from labor, to worship their Maker and to hear His word, require the same kind and the same length of service as would be appropriate to a body of intellectual people, . . . so unjust

is this, that the most rigid churchmen are wont to shorten and transpose the Service when they use it for the benefit of slaves or among congregations perfectly new to our worship.

... Some relaxation of the Rubrics for the conduct of public worship, seems then to me indispensable for the full efficiency of the Church in its aggressive efforts.[6]

This was a broad charge with a clear theme: the temporal blessings of the church as well as the eternal message of the gospel were meant for all classes of people, from the very wealthy and educated to the indigent and ignorant. Although a master plan or overall strategy for reaching the slave population was not delineated, the fact that slaves were to be assigned a priority in the diocesan mission was clear.

*The Years 1856–1860*

In the period after Atkinson came to North Carolina but before the outbreak of the Civil War, he helped the diocese grow by some nine hundred communicants overall. In choosing a primary focus Atkinson took his own charge seriously, and he devoted much of his energy to promoting the spread of the gospel among the slaves, nearly 289,000 of whom had been recorded by the 1850 census.[7] He personally performed a number of marriages of slave couples and on his visits encouraged his clergy to reach out to slaves and especially to urge them to seek confirmation and to have their children baptized.

In 1857 the Committee on the State of the Church reported the following figures for the number of baptisms during the conventional year just closed: among white congregants, 327 infants and 62 adults; among slaves, 228 infants and 25 adults. Also reported were data for the number of catechumens (persons being instructed in the faith, in preparation for confirmation): white individuals, 1,105; black persons, 345.[8] The committee, probably mindful of their bishop's charge regarding slaves, expressed disappointment in the number of black catechumens reported and urged an increase in "instruction of the colored class."[9]

Atkinson's 1857 report showed that since the 1856 diocesan meeting he had preached 170 times, administered communion 42 times, consecrated two churches, and laid the cornerstone for two churches. His visits to large farms or plantations also were noted. On 26 March 1857 at the Lake Chapel, which served the plantations of Josiah Collins and Charles Pettigrew, the Reverend Mr. Watson preached and afterwards Bishop Atkinson confirmed twenty-six slaves. The next day, in the same chapel, Atkinson preached and celebrated the Holy Eucharist. He commented on the service: "Those who partook of it, probably exceeding a hundred in number, were the families of those gentlemen and mainly their slaves. And I think it right to say here that the more I have seen of the effects of the system pursued in that congregation, the better I am pleased with it."[10] One year later, Atkinson returned to confirm twenty-eight slaves and one white person, as well as to administer communion to a "very large congregation of slaves."[11]

One measure of success of diocesan missionary efforts after Atkinson's 1855 charge was the annual number of confirmations; these data are provided in the table below.

**Confirmations reported for the Diocese of North Carolina, 1856–1860**

| Convention year | White | Black | Total |
|---|---|---|---|
| 1856 | 207 | 64 | 271 |
| 1857 | 255 | 63 | 318 |
| 1858 | 271 | 65 | 336 |
| 1859 | 245 | 106 | 351 |
| 1860 | 198 | 49 | 247 |
| 1861 | 237 | 48 | 285 |

*Source:* Journals of the Diocese of North Carolina for the years 1856 through 1861. Data are taken from the bishop's addresses, except for the year 1857, for which data is from the report of the Committee on the State of the Church.

In 1858 Bishop Atkinson made the following observation about the confirmation of slaves.

> I have indicated more distinctly than heretofore the number of colored persons confirmed. In order that we may better estimate the progress we make in evangelizing that interesting part of our population, who are, among us, in a peculiar sense, Christ's Poor, and to whom therefore His Church is bound especially to minister. In that aspect of things, we have not much cause for self congratulation; while at the same time the great success of efforts earnestly and perseveringly made for the religious welfare of this part of our charge is a sufficient ground for hope, and encouragement to increased diligence for the future.[12]

In this observation, Atkinson recognized that compared to the total slave population the number being confirmed was very small, but that those efforts that were being made were bearing fruit. He expected the number to rise, but the long-term answer, the bishop noted, was in having more clergy and other personnel supervised by clergy available for this missionary effort.[13] In 1860, the Bishop was concerned about the drop in confirmations for both whites and slaves and wondered if the "increased prosperity" of the times had diverted some of the mission focus among his flock to a focus on wealth accumulation.[14]

In October 1859 Atkinson attended the General Convention in Richmond, Virginia, and was greatly encouraged by what transpired, including the consecrations of both diocesan and missionary bishops. He relayed his feelings to the 1860 diocesan convention: "The proceedings of that body [the General Convention] and of the Board of Missions, which was in session at the same time, were of great interest, and of most favorable augury to the extension and prosperity of the Church. The discussions were animated, but harmonious and fraternal. The conclusions reached by a majority were heartily acquiesced in by all. There was but little legislation, yet a good deal was practically accomplished in the way of giving increased efficiency to the Church in her glorious mission."[15]

These words were spoken in May 1860, however, and Bishop Atkinson's hopes for the harmony, extension, and prosperity of the national church, as well as his determined efforts to bring the light of Christ to the slaves in his diocese, were soon to be frustrated by secession and civil war.

## William Rollinson Whittingham

William Rollinson Whittingham was born in New York on 4 January 1805. He was home-schooled by his mother Mary Rollinson, who even tutored him during his preparation for the entrance examinations at General Theological Seminary. After his graduation and ordination to the diaconate, he held positions as church rector first in New Jersey and then in New York City, where he was made priest. He served four years as professor and librarian at General Seminary before being called to be bishop of Maryland.[16]

### Attention to Diocesan Growth

Whittingham was the fourth diocesan of Maryland, which had been served by a bishop since 1792. Whittingham's efforts toward building his diocese began immediately after his consecration in September 1840. From that time until the diocesan convention in 1841, the new bishop traversed the length and breadth of his see—Eastern Shore and Western Shore, north to south—in spite of poor roads and heavy snow storms. He performed his episcopal functions in parishes large and small. He was on the road the entire year, visiting 70 percent of his parishes. He traveled more than 2,900 miles on diocesan duty, consecrating four churches, ordaining one deacon and four priests, instituting one rector, officiating at 49 confirmations at which 446 persons were confirmed, preaching 149 sermons, and administering the Lord's Supper 55 times.[17] During his early years in office Bishop Whittingham seems to have felt at ease with his flock as he visited across the diocese. "There is no fuss," he said, "no parade, no apologies, no departure from the common course of things on the arrival of guests. A larger table, more food, and another log on the fire in the best room is all the change made, and in half an hour I defy anyone to feel strange among them."[18]

Thomas Atkinson, who became bishop of North Carolina after serving as a priest under Whittingham in Maryland for ten years in the 1840s and early 1850s, wrote later that Bishop Whittingham "preached with vigor, enthusiasm, freshness of language, and magnetism" and ran diocesan conventions efficiently. "As Bishop, his gavel at conventions was like the hammer of Thor."[19] Atkinson also reported that during Whittingham's episcopate the number of clergy rose from 58 to 159 and that in Baltimore the number of churches increased from 5 to 23. Much of this growth occurred during the decades between 1840 and 1860, during which his leadership was energetic and inspirational.[20]

*Views on Slavery and Ministry to Slaves*

The first tenet of Bishop Whittingham's position on slavery was that slaves were brothers and sisters to be won to Christ. This was an imperative, and from his first year, when traveling in the diocese he visited with slaves whenever possible. At church services slaves often sat in the gallery or in assigned pews, and Whittingham at times would preach to the slaves after the white congregants had been dismissed. Communion was administered to both groups, although separately.

Whittingham also set before their masters the obligation to provide religious nurture for slaves. William Francis Brand described the bishop's approach: "He never failed, where the opportunity was possible, in church to address some words of instruction to the blacks, and in private homes, at time of family prayers, if the domestics were not present, he would ask that they be called in, and frequently, in public and private, he urged upon masters their duty as Christians to see to the Christian instruction of their 'servants.'"[21]

In his first address to a diocesan convention in 1841, Whittingham's remarks on that subject were not subtle.

> Surely this blood [of our slaves] will be upon the heads of those who suffer them to go down to the pit in brute ignorance or blind fanaticism unwarned, untaught, unfed with the bread of life! . . . I have been happy to find . . . a disposition to hear patiently and approve admonitions to masters to discharge their duty to those whom God has made subject to their will; but it is lamentable to see how little *operative* and *practical* this feeling is, in the majority of cases. A heavy burden lies upon us, my brethren, both of the clergy and the laity, until we do more, much more, than is now done for the servile portion of our church.[22]

The bishop lamented that other churches had become more attractive to the slave population than the Episcopal Church and regretted that the Episcopal Church had not "taken the pains" to adapt the service to meet the needs of this "untutored" population. He noted, however, that slaves almost invariably sought baptism in an Episcopal house of worship and that once that sacrament was administered, the bishop, clergy, and laity were responsible to God for the soul of the baptized.

The second component of Whittingham's position on slavery was that he was categorically opposed to it, and he certainly did not support the Southern clamor for extension of the institution to other states. His third, seemingly contradictory tenet was that abolitionism was a great evil. His thoughts about abolition were articulated in a letter written in December 1842.

> The calumny of abolitionism must be carefully guarded against. This can best be done by the most scrupulous adherence to religious instruction and intercourse with the negroes, and by bringing out fully in such instruction and intercourse the bearing of faith on practice, the Gospel rule on subordination in society, and the compatibility of spiritual privilege with temporal privation, and even oppression. . . . I loathe and abhor the spirit of abolitionism as it has developed itself at the North, firmly believing it to have proceeded from the first great rebel and fosterer of all insubordination. The evils attendant on slavery are aggravated, not cured, by its intervention. These evils, it is my full persuasion, are only to be cured by the operation of the Gospel on the system as it is, introducing into it a new element like one of those powerful solvents in chemistry which change the nature without altering the outward form or texture. [23]

On 1 October 1843, in St. James' First African Church of Baltimore, Bishop Whittingham ordained to the diaconate a free black man, Eli Worthington Stokes. In describing this event in his book *Men of Maryland,* George Freeman Bragg, chronicler of black participation in the Episcopal Church, refers to the "celebrated and learned Bishop Whittingham" and seems to regard him as a friend of black ministers.[24] Whittingham's record of the ordination follows: "On the 16th Sunday after Trinity, October 1, at a special ordination held in St. James' First African Church, in Baltimore, I admitted to the Holy Order of Deacons, Elie Worthington Stokes, a colored man presented by the Rev. J. N. McJilton. His case involving some peculiarities, I consulted on it both the Standing Committee and a council of Presbyters especially convened; and acted finally under the advice of both."[25]

Eli Stokes soon departed Maryland and organized a black Episcopal church in Connecticut, where he was ordained priest. After his time there, he served a church in Rhode Island and then became a missionary in Africa. He worked with fellow missionary Alexander Crummell on the organization of a Liberian church. He died in Africa in 1867.[26] Whittingham must have seen no inconsistency between his views on abolition and his ordination and launching of the career of this pioneer black churchman.[27]

In 1859 Whittingham received an unsolicited copy of a pamphlet that apparently contained proslavery views. The bishop replied through an open letter that was submitted to newspapers. Whittingham's opposition both to abolitionism and to the institution of slavery appear in juxtaposition throughout the letter:

> I have no doubt of the lawfulness of holding slaves. . . .
>
> But a twenty-years' use of unusually good opportunities for examining the results of slavery has satisfied me that the results of slavery are highly deleterious to the interests of the community, civil, moral, and religious. . . .
>
> The white population is most injured, and most of all the entire slaveholding portion. . . .
>
> I am satisfied that no community can permanently thrive, that is, for a course of generations, in which slaveholding prevails. . . .
>
> No doubt, the conditions of free negroes in our country is worse than that of the slaves. But that gives no man the right to make them slaves. . . .
>
> No doubt, the abolition of slavery in the Southern States is impossible, and its attempt, in any way, by the North, an enormous crime. But that is no reason for encouraging the extension of slavery beyond its present limits. With no prejudice against slavery, and with very strong prejudice against amalgamation of races and colors, and in favor of distinctions in society, I have been slowly brought by my own conscientious study of slavery, as I have lived and moved in it, in all its forms and aspects, for almost a quarter of a century, to acquiesce in its condemnation as a great social evil. And I know that it is so regarded by the best and wisest portion of those who have inherited it . . . and have no hope of its being removed.[28]

Whittingham concluded this letter by saying that he knew that he and others who felt that slavery was (1) an evil but that it could not be abolished, and (2) that abolishment should not be attempted, were "right in claiming to be let alone in that position." He added that those holding that position were "at ease about answering to God for it." Bishop Whittingham thus did not believe that it was his responsibility as a Christian leader to promote, or even to support, the overthrow of this "great social evil." In his judgment, his responsibility to God was to do his best to see that the teachings of Christ were brought to everyone, slaves included.

## A Statistical Snapshot

In the two decades of his episcopate before the Civil War, Bishop Whittingham and his clergy had, in fact, made some progress in fulfilling that responsibility. In 1860 the convention journal reported 129 churches with 10,928 communicants for the Diocese of Maryland. During the prior conventional year there had been 2,932 baptisms and 909 confirmations. These statistics were reported in the "Summary of Parochial Reports," within which no breakdown by race was provided.[29] Many individual churches, however, did give statistics by race in their parochial reports. A tally of those revealed that for black people there were 855 baptisms spread among 85 churches, a total of 472 communicants among 57 churches, and 55 confirmations total from the 15 churches that reported at least one confirmation of a black person.[30] The ratio of baptisms of black individuals to the total black population was actually slightly higher than the ratio of baptisms of white individuals to the white population, but comparable ratios for communicants and confirmations were much higher for white persons.[31] St. James' First African Church in Baltimore accounted for 61 black communicants; the others were associated with white churches in which special seating or special services were held for black people.[32]

*End of an Era*

The diocese showed appreciation for its dedicated bishop in 1859 by approving a salary increase.[33] The coming of secession and civil war, and Whittingham's views on those events, however, terminated what had been a period of diocesan growth. Discord soon replaced harmony in the relationship between bishop and flock. Whittingham's biographer, William Francis Brand called 1859 a "watershed" year, adding that "the good fortunes of Bishop Whittingham, as men look upon prosperity, culminated when he had half finished his course as Bishop. God had in store for him some better things than the continuation of human favor."[34]

## Notes

1. Hugh T. Lefler, "Thomas Atkinson, Third Bishop of North Carolina," *Historical Magazine of the Protestant Episcopal Church* 17 (December 1948): 425.

2. William Stevens Perry, *The Episcopate in America* (New York: Christian Literature Company, 1895), 125.

3. Joseph Blount Cheshire, *The Church in the Confederate States: A History of the Protestant Episcopal Church in the Confederate States* (New York: Longmans, Green, 1912), 262.

4. Ibid., 263–64.

5. Thomas Atkinson, "Primary Charge to the Clergy delivered at the Convention at Warrenton in May 1855," 6–7; document attached to *Diocese of North Carolina, 1855* (Fayetteville: Edward J. Hale, 1855).

6. Ibid., 8.

7. Historical Census Browser, Geostat Center, University of Virginia Library, http://fisher.lib.virginia.edu/collections/stats/histcensus/ (accessed 12 January 2009).

8. *Diocese of North Carolina, 1857* (Fayetteville: Edward J. Hale, 1857), 69.

9. Ibid., 69–70.

10. Ibid., 24.

11. *Diocese of North Carolina, 1858* (Fayetteville: Edward J. Hale, 1858), 24.

12. Ibid., 25.

13. Ibid.

14. *Diocese of North Carolina, 1860* (Fayetteville: Edward J. Hale, 1860), 25.

15. Ibid., 19.

16. Perry, *Episcopate in America*, 81.

17. *Diocese of Maryland, 1841* (Baltimore: Joseph Robinson, 1841), 10.

18. Arthur Kinsolving, "The One Hundred and Fiftieth Anniversary of the Organization of the Diocese of Maryland," *Historical Magazine of the Protestant Episcopal Church* 3 (March 1934): 11.

19. Thomas Atkinson, *A Sermon Commemorative of the Rt. Rev. William Rollinson Whittingham, D.D., LL.D., Late Bishop of the Diocese of Maryland* (Baltimore: William Boyle, 1879), 8.

20. Ibid., 11. Bishop Atkinson noted that the Diocese of Maryland divided when the Diocese of Easton was formed in 1868. The growth figures reported refer to the part of the state that remained in the Diocese of Maryland.

21. William Francis Brand, *Life of William Rollinson Whittingham, Fourth Bishop of Maryland*, 2 vols. (New York: E. and J. B. Young, 1883), 1:263.

22. *Diocese of Maryland, 1841*, 21.

23. Whittingham to Dr. John Scott, "catechist to a congregation of Negroes on the Eastern Shore," December 1842; quoted in Brand, *Life of Whittingham*, 1:264.

24. George Freeman Bragg, *Men of Maryland* (Baltimore: Church Advocate Press, 1914), 100.

25. Ibid., 101.

26. Ibid., 102.

27. In Whittingham's judgment abolition was still wrong, even though many persons of abilities comparable to those of Stokes were still bound in slavery.

28. Nelson Waite Rightmeyer, "The Church in a Border State—Maryland," *Historical Magazine of the Protestant Episcopal Church* 17 (December 1948): 412–13. Rightmeyer notes that the bishop received the pamphlet in 1859. Whittingham's response came soon thereafter, but the exact date of the bishop's letter is not provided.

29. *Diocese of Maryland, 1860* (Baltimore: Published by the Convention, 1860), 108–9.

30. Ibid., 38–82.

31. There were 87,189 slaves and 83,342 free black individuals in 1860, for a total black population of 171,131. The white population was derived by subtracting the total black population from the total population of the state, 687,049. Source: Historical Census Browser, Geostat Center, University of Virginia Library, http://fisher.lib.virginia.edu/collections/stats/histcensus/ (accessed 1 November 2008).

32. *Diocese of Maryland, 1860*, 38–82.

33. *Diocese of Maryland, 1859* (Baltimore: Published by the Convention, 1859), 15. The bishop's salary was set at $3,500 per year, plus "use of the Episcopal residence, rent free."

34. Brand, *Life of Whittingham*, 1:46.

# A Tale of Two Bishops

+≈ *An Intersectional Friendship*

## Charles Pettit McIlvaine of Ohio and Leonidas Polk of Louisiana

During the years between establishment of the Episcopal Church in the United States and the Civil War, American bishops formed many friendships with colleagues, some of which were across sectional lines, such as those between John Henry Hopkins of Vermont and Stephen Elliott of Georgia, William Mercer Green of Mississippi and Horatio Potter of New York, Charles McIlvaine of Ohio and William Meade of Virginia, and McIlvaine with both James Otey of Tennessee and Leonidas Polk of Louisiana. These relationships were facilitated by the triennial national conventions, which most bishops attended faithfully. The formation and long duration of one of these friendships will be explored in this essay, and a subsequent essay will describe its rupture during the war.

## United States Military Academy, 1826: An Unusual Baptism

It was the first service of adult baptism ever performed in the chapel at West Point. Two cadets received the sacrament, which was administered by the academy's chaplain, an Episcopal priest and professor of ethics. Some weeks earlier one of the cadets had come to the chaplain—only the second cadet to call, even though Chaplain Charles Pettit McIlvaine had been at West Point for almost a year. Cadet Leonidas Polk had seen a tract given to McIlvaine's first visitor and had been deeply affected. The day after calling on the chaplain, Polk had knelt in chapel during the confession, an action that had not occurred in the chapel previously. Forty days later the corps of cadets and a number of faculty and staff witnessed the profession of faith by Cadets Polk and William B. Magruder.[1]

To conclude the service Chaplain McIlvaine addressed the two men: "Pray your master and saviour to take you out of the world rather than allow you to bring reproach on the cause you have now professed."[2] Cadet Polk's deep, emotional *Amen* echoed through the chapel. Polk thus acknowledged his baptismal commitment. He and Charles McIlvaine had begun a friendship that was strengthened when Polk decided to change his profession from soldier to minister. Although separated in place, they were to walk similar spiritual paths for more than three decades as they went about their Christian duty.

## Leonidas Polk

*Early Life*

Leonidas Polk was a native of North Carolina whose grandfather had served during the Revolution and whose father was a colonel in the United States Army. While Leonidas Polk was in his second year at the University of North Carolina, Colonel Polk secured for his son an appointment to West Point. The young Polk finished the U.S. Military Academy in July 1827, but he resigned his commission in order to enter Virginia Theological Seminary.[3]

While in seminary, Polk was attracted to the American Colonization Society (ACS) and, in fact, entertained briefly the thought that this society might point the way to the gradual abolition of slavery in the United States. After attending an ACS meeting at which Henry Clay and others had spoken, he wrote his father about the society, which was beginning to implement a plan to provide support for the emigration of free blacks to Africa: "The number of applicants for transportation greatly exceeds the means of the Society. There are now about six hundred. The plan seems to be feasible. . . . All that is wanting to remove not only the blacks that are free, but those that are enslaved also is the consent of their owners and the funds to transport them. . . . Now I believe in the course of not many years one State after another will be willing to abolish slavery."[4]

This belief that an emancipation and emigration program could be implemented to rid the South of slavery, however, dissipated rapidly. Polk soon understood that slavery was entrenched as a civil institution in the South. He also came to understand that even if slavery were abolished, it would be impossible to move all black people back to Africa. According to his son and biographer, William Mecklenburg Polk, he continued to regard slavery as a civil and political burden but saw no solution. What he did see clearly was his obligation as a minister to meet the spiritual needs not only of the masters and other white Christians but also of the slaves. He strove to meet this obligation throughout his ministry.[5]

After Polk was ordained to the diaconate in April 1930, his mentor from West Point days, Charles McIlvaine, wanted Polk to take charge of his parish in Brooklyn while McIlvaine traveled overseas, but Polk already had agreed to be the assistant to Bishop Moore of Virginia at the Monumental Church in Richmond. On 6 May 1830 Polk married Frances Ann Devereux of Raleigh, and the following January their first child, a son named Hamilton, was born. Polk was ordained to the priesthood in May 1931. The young Polk family moved to Tennessee in 1833, and early in the next year he took possession of a farm given to him by his father.

His lands and those of his three brothers were in Maury County, Tennessee. His father-in-law provided him with slaves to work the farm.

*Priest in Tennessee*

At the request of Bishop Otey in January 1834, the Reverend Mr. Polk became rector of St. Peter's Church in Columbia, for which he reported seventeen communicants at the diocesan meeting in April of that year.[6] Bouts of poor health plagued the young priest over the next several years, causing him at one point to suspend his clerical duties for several months.[7] Nevertheless, by 1838 the number of communicants at St. Peter's had more than doubled, and Polk had helped Bishop Otey establish a school for girls in Columbia.[8] A major priority for Polk during these years was taking the gospel to slaves, and, in addition to his duties at St. Peter's, Polk held services in his home for his slaves and those of his brothers. Polk's wife recalled her husband's attention to the slaves' religious training: "In the summer of 1837 our house was completed. As soon as we were in it, my husband began holding services for the Negroes every Sunday, and devoted himself to them. The sick were special objects of his affection."[9]

Polk resigned his parish duties at St. Peter's in July 1838, apparently content to devote his attention to his farming interests, his family, and to the spiritual needs of slaves.[10]

## Charles Pettit McIlvaine

*Early Life*

Charles Pettit McIlvaine was a New Jersey native, born in Burlington on 18 January 1799. He was graduated from Princeton University, studied at Princeton Theological Seminary, and was ordained deacon in June 1820. His ordination to the priesthood took place in Baltimore in March 1821, and he began his ministry at Christ Church in Georgetown in the District of Columbia.[11] While at Christ Church, he was appointed chaplain to the United States Senate and befriended John C. Calhoun, who was serving as secretary of war. With Calhoun's support, McIlvaine secured appointment as chaplain and professor of ethics at the United States Military Academy at West Point in 1825, where he remained for two years during which he helped to bring about the conversion of Cadet Leonidas Polk.[12] Polk's influence was strong among his classmates, and his example, together with McIlvaine's sermons, started a wave of interest in religion at West Point. Many cadets came to see the chaplain, often brought by Polk to McIlvaine's office. Some cadets who came under McIlvaine's influence at West Point went on to become military officers in the Civil War. McIlvaine moved from West Point to become rector of St. Ann's Church in Brooklyn and soon thereafter became professor of "Revealed Religion and Sacred Antiquities" in the University of the City of New York.[13]

## Bishop of Ohio

In 1832 McIlvaine was elected bishop of Ohio, a position vacated by Bishop Philander Chase as a result of tension between Chase and the diocesan leadership. The service of consecration for McIlvaine and three other new bishops was held soon thereafter, on 31 October, at St. Paul's Chapel in New York.[14]

Bishop McIlvaine's first priority was to build new congregations and strengthen existing ones, and he dedicated himself to this task in spite of travel hardships and a personal constitution unused to the primitive conditions in many parts of Ohio. The cities were small; according to the 1830 census, Cincinnati had a population of 24,831, and Cleveland had only 1,075 residents. Many of the new bishop's visits to the remote places were made on horseback. In 1834 there were 30 clergymen on the diocesan records, and the new bishop reported 285 confirmations for the conventional year; the number of communicants was approximately 1,200.[15]

McIlvaine's energetic leadership ensured that the Diocese of Ohio grew along with the state. By 1859, travel had become easier, and the population of the state had tripled.[16] Cleveland was a city of over 40,000 inhabitants. McIlvaine had traversed his diocese again and again, and the diocesan lists in 1859 showed 84 clergymen canonically resident in Ohio. The diocesan journal reported that there were 5,680 communicants and that there had been 463 confirmations for the conventional year.[17] An assistant bishop was elected and was consecrated at the 1859 General Convention to assist with a growing need for episcopal services throughout the diocese.

At the General Convention in Philadelphia in the fall of 1838, six years after McIlvaine had become a bishop, his friend Leonidas Polk was named missionary bishop for Arkansas and the Southwest.[18]

## Leonidas Polk in Episcopate

### Missionary Bishop

One of Polk's consecrators at his elevation to the episcopate in Cincinnati in December 1838 was Ohio bishop Charles Pettit McIlvaine. McIlvaine also preached the consecration sermon, near the end of which he told the story of Polk's baptism at West Point and reviewed some highlights of Polk's ministry. He noted that the church had witnessed Polk in his role of pastor to a "humble and obscure congregation of Negroes, whom he had collected together from neighboring plantations," where he was, in fact, "a servant of servants" and had shown "the true spirit for the highest of all vocations in the church." To that vocation he was now being called, to face "more eminent responsibility, severer trials, and greater difficulties." McIlvaine offered "unspeakable thankfulness to God" for witnessing Polk's consecration and charged his protégé with words from scripture: "Thou, therefore, my son, be strong in the grace that is in Christ Jesus" (2 Timothy 2:1).[19]

Bishop Polk's missionary jurisdiction was vast, encompassing the following areas:

*Arkansas,* which had become a state in 1836, but for which a diocese had not been organized.

*Alabama,* which had become a state in 1819 and a diocese in 1831.

*Mississippi,* which had become a state in 1817 and a diocese in 1826.

*Louisiana,* which had become a state in 1812 and a diocese in 1838.

*Texas,* which was neither a state nor a diocese, but rather a republic, having won its independence from Mexico in 1836.

*The Indian Territory,* which is now the state of Oklahoma.[20]

Polk's first visitation journey began in February 1839 and ended in June. He traveled by boat, stage, and horseback some five thousand miles, visiting places in Tennessee as well as in Alabama, Mississippi, Louisiana, Arkansas, and Texas. He preached forty-four sermons and officiated at fourteen baptisms and forty-one confirmations. His second trip lasted three months and was restricted to Alabama, Mississippi, and Louisiana. Polk's third tour lasted five months and included visits in Arkansas, the Indian Territory, Texas, and Louisiana. On this final expedition Polk visited with several Cherokee chiefs and discussed with them the possibility of a missionary effort by the church among their people. He seemed encouraged by the chiefs' response.[21]

Many of his visits during his tenure as missionary bishop were heartwarming, and he felt that he was needed wherever he went, but it did not take Polk long to conclude that if parishes, those extant and those to come, in the vast area he was serving were to receive adequate episcopal services, more bishops would be needed. Given the territory to be covered and the modes of transportation available, he recognized and recommended that more missionaries be employed; he saw as well that neither he nor any bishop alone could devote the time required to establish and nurture missions and parishes on the scale that was needed.

### Bishop of Louisiana

Polk accepted the call to be the first bishop of Louisiana when, at General Convention in 1841, the request of the diocese for a diocesan bishop was honored by the convention.[22] Before being translated to the episcopate of Louisiana, Polk made what proved to be a serendipitous purchase when he bought Leighton, a large plantation in Louisiana, and moved there from Tennessee with his family and slaves. At Leighton, Polk became a sugar-cane planter and soon his income from producing sugar exceeded his expenses. The work was done by the slaves, more than two hundred of whom were owned by Bishop Polk. Polk held Sunday services to which all family members, plantation staff, and slaves, including children, were invited. Some sixty to eighty slaves generally were in attendance. During part of the service the slaves were divided into three groups—men, women, and children—and religious instruction was provided within each group. One of Polk's daughters served as catechist for the children. Polk emphasized the family in his teachings, and slave marriages were performed by the bishop. Wedding ceremonies were followed by a supper and other festivities.[23] The bishop thus led by example, and he also made clear in communications to his diocese that he viewed offering worship services and religious instruction to slaves to be an integral part of the diocesan mission and that he expected the full cooperation of laity, including slave owners, as well as clergy in conducting that mission.

At the 1861 meeting of the diocese Bishop Polk reported that he had confirmed 411 persons during the conventional year, of whom 120 were black.[24] Thus, although the numbers were not large in comparison with the total slave population in the diocese, the Episcopal Church in Louisiana was bringing slaves into its communion steadily when the war commenced.

During the early to mid-1850s, hard times came to Leighton, and Polk's personal fortunes declined. The plantation had been managed well enough by the bishop and by Frances Polk during her husband's absence, but two events brought fiscal disaster to the Leighton venture. The first was a cholera epidemic that took the lives of some slaves and caused disruption of the work cycle; this was followed about a year later by a tornado that destroyed buildings and much personal property. These misfortunes came immediately after Bishop Polk had suffered a substantial fiscal loss when some of his funds were embezzled.[25] In total these losses were too much to overcome, and the bishop felt forced to sell Leighton in order to satisfy creditors.[26] The Leighton chapter closed in the fall of 1854, and the family moved to New Orleans. Fortunately, the diocese, which had been previously unable to provide monetary support, was at last able to pay the bishop an annual salary, and this alleviated his fiscal distress.[27]

In contrast with the decline in Polk's personal fortunes, the fortunes of the diocese improved under his capable leadership, with growth in communicants, clergy, and parishes. The seventeen clergy and fifteen parishes of 1846 had grown to thirty-four clergy and thirty-five parishes in 1860.[28] Polk's great passion during the second half of the 1850s was the creation of a church university, a "University of the South" that would be an outstanding institution of higher learning and that would yield an indigenous supply of Episcopal clergy for the Southern states. His vision of such a university had been partially formulated early in his ministerial career, but it was not until the middle of the decade before the war that he laid that vision before nine other Southern bishops and received their endorsement. Polk then coordinated the planning effort, and, with the able help of Bishop Stephen Elliott of Georgia, began the process of fundraising to secure an endowment. These efforts culminated in October 1860 at Sewanee, Tennessee, when the cornerstone for the proposed university was laid.

*A Prayer Covenant*

Polk and McIlvaine had remained friends after McIlvaine had become a bishop, and McIlvaine and Bishop James Hervey Otey of Tennessee, in whose diocese Polk was a presbyter at the time of his nomination, were instrumental in having Polk named in September 1838 missionary bishop for Arkansas and the Southwest. While in Cincinnati for Polk's consecration, Bishops Meade, McIlvaine, Otey, and Polk agreed to pray for each other every Sunday morning. Some of the prayers written by Meade and Otey were incorporated by John Johns into Meade's biography. One, written by Otey, begins: "Almighty and everlasting God, mercifully hear and graciously answer the prayers which thy servants are covenanted to offer for each other at this time, through the intercession of thy dear Son. Grant oh Lord, that we may never lose sight of the weighty responsibility resting upon us. May we ever realize an abiding and deep sense of the value of souls, and never relax our exertions to win them to Christ."[29]

## A Long Friendship

After Polk's consecration in December 1838, he and McIlvaine were colleagues in the House of Bishops. Polk was an evangelical and supported McIlvaine in his resistance to the high-church emphasis on ceremony and ritual, which was energized by the Oxford movement that began in the early 1830s. The two bishops enjoyed each other's company and the atmosphere of goodwill and hope that permeated national church conventions, including the 1859 gathering in Richmond, the last convention at which they were together. They parted from Richmond with their thirty-three year friendship intact. The growing controversy over slavery had not caused a rift in their relations. As we shall see in a subsequent essay, however, when secession and war came the two bishops made dramatic but very different decisions about their Christian duty that did affect their friendship.

Notes

1. William Mecklenburg Polk, *Leonidas Polk, Bishop and General*, 2 vols. (New York: Longmans, Green, 1893), 1: 70–78.

2. Ibid., 75. Both McIlvaine's peroration and Polk's emotional response are given in this account by Polk's son.

3. The following sources were used for the biographical information on Leonidas Polk in the period of his life before he became a presbyter in Tennessee: W. M. Polk, *Leonidas Polk, Bishop and General*; William Stevens Perry, *The Episcopate in America* (New York: Christian Literature Company, 1895); and Joseph Howard Parks, *General Leonidas Polk, CSA: The Fighting Bishop* (Baton Rouge: Louisiana State University Press, 1962).

4. W. M. Polk, *Leonidas Polk, Bishop and General*, 1: 94–95.

5. For additonal discussion of Polk's changing attitudes toward slavery, see Lines, Stiles B., "Slavery and Churchmen: The Work of the Episcopal Church among Southern Negroes," (Ph.D. thesis, Columbia University, 1960).

6. *Diocese of Tennessee, 1834* (Nashville: W. Hasell Hunt, 1834), 24.

7. *Diocese of Tennessee, 1837* (Nashville: S. Nye, 1837), 7, and W. M. Polk, *Leonidas Polk, Bishop and General*, 133.

8. *Diocese of Tennessee, 1838* (Memphis: *Enquirer* Office, 1838), 16–17.

9. W. M. Polk, *Leonidas Polk, Bishop and General*, 1: 135.

10. *Diocese of Tennessee, 1839* (Nashville: S. Nye, 1839), 13.

11. Perry, *Episcopate in America*, 65.

12. George Franklin Smythe, *A History of the Diocese of Ohio until the Year 1918* (Cleveland: Diocese of Ohio, 1931), 179.

13. Perry, *Episcopate in America*, 65.

14. Smythe, *History of the Diocese of Ohio*, 183.

15. Ibid., 311.

16. Historical Census Browser, Geostat Center, University of Virginia Library. http://fisher.lib.virginia.edu/collections/stats/histcensus/. (Accessed 2 November 2008)

17. Smythe, 310–11, and *Diocese of Ohio, 1859* (Cincinnati: Bradley and Webb, 1859), 3–6, 92.

18. *Journal of the General Convention, 1838* (New York: Swords, Stanford, 1838), 80.

19. Charles Pettit McIlvaine, *The Sermon at the Consecration of Right Reverend Leonidas Polk, D.D., as Missionary Bishop for Arkansas* (New York: T. A. Wright, 1906), 27–28.

20. Walter Herbert Stowe, "Polk's Missionary Episcopate," *Historical Magazine of the Protestant Episcopal Church* 7 (September 1938): 342–43.

21. *Journal of the General Convention, 1841* (New York: Swords, Stanford, 1841), 157–72.

22. *Journal of the General Convention, 1841*, 116.

23. W. M. Polk, *Leonidas Polk, Bishop and General*, 1: 168–71.

24. *Diocese of Louisiana, 1861* (New Orleans: Bulletin Book and Job Office, 1861), 28.

25. W. Polk, *Leonidas Polk, Bishop and General*, 1: 178, 180.

26. See Glenn Robins, *The Bishop of the Old South: The Ministry and Civil War Legacy of Leonidas Polk* (Macon: Mercer University Press, 2006), for a discussion of Polk's decision to sell Leighton. Robins, in a chapter entitled "The Planter Priest," argues that Polk could have structured his finances to retain Leighton and that other factors determined Polk's decision to sell.

27. W. M. Polk, *Leonidas Polk, Bishop and General*, 1: 181.

28. *Diocese of Louisiana* [journals], *1846* and *1860*.

29. John Johns, *A Memoir of the Life of the Right Reverend William Meade, D.D., Bishop of the Protestant Episcopal Church in the Diocese of Virginia, with a Memorial Sermon by the Reverend William Sparrow, D.D.* (Baltimore: Innes and Company, 1867), 239.

# Bishops in the Slave States

*≡ Their Beliefs about and Responses*
*to Slavery in the Antebellum Period*

There were fifteen states in 1860 in which the institution of slavery was legal. Based upon the words and actions of the bishops in those states, it is possible to formulate a series of statements about their beliefs concerning slavery during the antebellum era. These statements are presented in this essay, with an indication in each case of how widely the belief was shared.

## Statements of Belief

The Episcopal bishops in the slave states believed that slavery presented not only an opportunity but also an obligation to save souls. This statement reflects the primary, and by far the most intense, response of this group of Episcopal bishops to slavery, and it was subscribed to unanimously. The bishops varied in the intensity and creativity of their approaches to saving the souls of slaves, but among the devices employed across these states were the following: urging and cajoling diocesan clergy to provide worship opportunities and religious instruction for slaves; soliciting the involvement of the laity (men and women); and hiring missionaries, with whatever assistance could be secured from the national church. Some of the missionaries were newly ordained deacons assigned by their bishops to serve plantation clusters. Bishops supported these efforts by frequent visits and by holding confirmation services both in churches and at assemblies of slaves on plantations. Although Bishops Davis of South Carolina and Elliott of Georgia were particularly forceful in their efforts to take the gospel to plantation slaves, all bishops pursued this goal, from Bishop Meade in the Old Dominion of Virginia to Bishop Alexander Gregg in Texas, who had become that diocese's first bishop in 1859. These efforts reached only a tiny fraction of the slave population, but the Episcopal bishops in the South led their dioceses to devote a considerable share of limited resources and energy to slave outreach.[1]

Slavery was not viewed as an evil institution against which the bishops felt bound to speak or against which they felt they must try to mobilize the moral authority of the Episcopal Church. During the antebellum era this statement applied to the slave-state bishops without exception. No bishop in any slave state raised his voice at diocesan rostrum or in pulpit against an institution that, by 1860, held nearly four million human beings in bondage and considered those human beings as property. This stance on the institution of slavery derived from the bishops' perception of God's will.

It was, in fact, the belief of these bishops that slavery was sanctioned by Holy Scripture and therefore by God. The most vociferous and publicly passionate proponent of this position was not a Southern bishop, but John Henry Hopkins, bishop of Vermont. In his writings Hopkins noted that slavery is mentioned in numerous stories in the Bible as part of the daily life of the time and place described. These biblical stories, together with the absence of explicit condemnation of slavery in both the Old and New Testaments, Hopkins contended, suggested a scriptural sanction for slavery, and the exhortations of Paul and Peter for slaves to obey their masters removed any doubt.[2]

In the South, before the war, Bishop Meade of Virginia espoused this position, and during the war Bishop Elliott proclaimed this position vigorously. The words, actions—and especially inactions—of their Southern colleagues are strong evidence of their concurrence, and that agreement, for the bishops of dioceses in states that seceded, was reflected in a formal resolution of the Confederate Episcopal Church as it was being formed.

 The concept of divine approval based on scripture was reinforced by another element in the theology shared among the slave state bishops and by many of their Northern colleagues as well. That theological element is encapsulated in the following passage from the Book of Amos, an Old Testament prophet: "Shall a trumpet be blown in the city, and the people be not afraid? Shall there be evil in a city and the Lord hath not done it?" (Amos 3:6, King James Version). This passage was interpreted broadly to mean that nothing—good or evil—happened without God's consent. Bishop Otey of Tennessee, for example, stated flatly in a pastoral letter that cholera epidemics were sent by God to punish communities for their transgressions.[3] Disasters did not just happen—they were God's instruments. Applying this reasoning to slavery, that institution would not have been extant had God not sanctioned it. If it were a monstrous evil, God would remove it at a time and with instruments of his own choosing.

As noted above, Bishop Whittingham of Maryland did apply these principles to slavery, remarking that he had no doubt as to its "lawfulness" (meaning congruence with divine law or sanction) and then noting that, in spite of his observation that slavery was deleterious to all, attempts at abolition were grave mistakes because "the evils attendant on slavery . . . are only to be cured by the operation of the Gospel on the system as it is." Any evils caused by slavery, in other words, had to be corrected by improving slavery, not by abolishing it.

Bishop Elliott carried the belief that slavery had God's sanction a step even further, arguing that slavery was an integral part of God's plan to spread the Gospel. In fact, Elliott declared that slavery was part of God's grand design to bring the residents of the continent of Africa into the Christian faith.[4] In Elliott's view, slaves had been brought to the United States with God's blessing to be given vocational and educational skills, and, most important of all, to be brought into Christ's fold. Once they had been made Christians—and sufficiently "elevated," as Elliott put it, in other skills—they would be set free to return to Africa to Christianize that continent. Elliot proclaimed this insight into God's will during the war, and his view of the Lord's grand plan for slavery was shared by some, but not all, slave-state bishops. The resolution of the Confederate Episcopal Church alluded to earlier referred to "the race placed under our care by the providence of God."[5] This wording supported Elliott's view that slaves were brought to the United States by God's design, although it did not address the idea of the subsequent salvation of Africa through former slaves in the role of missionaries.

Among the members of the American Colonization Society (ACS), established to promote and facilitate the emigration of free black persons to Africa, there was a variety of underlying reasons for supporting the society. One of those was the thought that combining emancipation with emigration could lead to slavery's extinction and the removal of all black persons from the United States. There is evidence of this thinking and a foreshadowing of Elliott's grand vision both in Bishop Meade's early involvement with the ACS and in Leonidas Polk's brief involvement with the society before he was ordained. Both men, however, abandoned that approach, although both continued to devote time and energy to bringing the gospel to slaves and to supporting missions abroad.

The Right Reverend John Payne, who was consecrated bishop of Cape Palmas and Parts Adjacent in 1851, clearly saw his mission in West Africa as being part of a two-phase movement that (1) would emancipate slaves and bring them to Liberia, which ultimately would end slavery in America, and (2) would enable the growing population of former slaves in West Africa to "suppress the slave trade, repress lawlessness among their pagan neighbors, and prepare them for the gospel and civilization" and become the instrument for Christianizing Africa. Payne's vision, in a sense, was Elliott's model with an implementation plan. Bishop Otey of Tennessee did not endorse this vision explicitly, but in a communication to his diocese urging support for Payne's mission, Otey attached a letter from Payne that detailed the entire plan.[6]

Before examining a final statement, one that reflected the views of bishops across sectional lines, it is useful to examine a growing concern among slave state bishops. There was a budding recognition among some bishops that the practice associated with slavery of separating families by selling the husband or wife alone or by removing children from slave families in order to sell them was un-Christian. Concern about breaking up slave families through sales was not in fact voiced frequently at the diocesan level in the antebellum South, but, as we have seen in our discussion of Thomas Frederick Davis, it was debated hotly in Davis's Diocese of South Carolina for two consecutive years. Then, just after the antebellum era closed, Elliott of Georgia, at one of the founding meetings of the Protestant Episcopal Church in the Confederate States, called for the prompt cessation of sales of slaves in which families were separated.[7] As the Civil War began, therefore, at least some of the slave state bishops had begun to decry one of the cruelest practices of slavery.

The chief grounds for concern, though, was the narrow one that breaking up a marriage in this way violated a scriptural injunction governing marriage found in Matthew's Gospel: "Therefore what God has joined together, let no man put asunder." Marriages, slave or free, black or white, were not meant to break up or be broken up, period.

Slavery was a civil institution goverened by the laws of the land. As such, it was not a proper subject on which the Episcopal Church should take action. These two statements reflect a widely shared belief among bishops, South and North, about the roles of the church and the civil government with respect to slavery. This belief represents the application to slavery of a broader principle, namely that political and civil government issues were not under the purview of the Episcopal Church and should not be brought before its forums for action or discussion. This statement was much more significant for the Northern bishops with regard to their response to slavery than it was to the response of the Southern bishops, who were guided chiefly by their belief that slavery was sanctioned by Holy Scripture. The most dramatic illustration of the Northern bishops regarding slavery as solely a civil issue occurred at the triennial convention of the Episcopal Church slightly more than a year before secession began. That convention, at which the bishops of the church ignored the issue of slavery, is the subject of the next essay.

The viewpoints on this issue of the bishops in the slave states that did not secede were varied. In the cases of Bishops Cicero Stephens Hawks of Missouri, and Benjamin Bosworth Smith of Kentucky, both of whose ministerial experiences had been in Northern states before being elected bishop of a slave state, it is likely that both the belief that slavery had scriptural sanction and the belief that slavery was a civil institution (and hence not an issue for the church) influenced their actions on slavery.[8] Bishop William Rollinson Whittingham of Maryland, although his early life and experiences were in New York and New Jersey, made clear in his writings that he believed that slavery had divine approval. Alfred Lee of Delaware, bishop of a slave state, though one with fewer than 1,800 slaves in 1860, did not speak against slavery from the pulpit until late November 1862, but it was clear from his words then that it was not a belief in scriptural sanction for slavery that had restrained him from speaking earlier.[9]

## Postscript

The case of Missouri's Bishop Hawks illustrates well the general principle of excluding civil issues from church forums. Cicero Stephens Hawks was the first bishop of Missouri and served from the early 1840s until 1868. He, like other slave-state bishops, supported religious instruction of slaves and did not speak against slavery in any church forum. Hawks, though, had an additional issue with which to contend. As we have seen above, in "Slavery in the United States: A Brief History," the years 1854–1858 were ones of upheaval and bloodshed along the Missouri-Kansas border. The trouble began when the Kansas-Nebraska Act became law, stipulating "popular sovereignty" as the determinant of slavery's status for the future states of Kansas and Nebraska. Antislavery settlers and proslavery settlers, many of the latter and their supporters coming from Missouri, made the proposed state of Kansas a battleground.

Although this armed conflict raged in territory across from the western border of his diocese and involved many Missourians, Bishop Hawks in his diocesan addresses during the period concerned did not mention the savage internecine violence.[10] Hawks must have had a position on the issue, and certainly could not have favored settling the matter by bloodshed, but he did not bring it into the church forum.[11] The governance of Kansas and the legality of slavery therein were civil matters.

## Notes

1. Diocesan journal records show that in 1859 in ten of the soon-to-be Confederate states, there was a total of 25,563 communicants. (Arkansas, the eleventh of these states, had not yet been organized as a diocese.) Using diocesan records and data from Stiles B. Lines, "Slavery and Churchmen: The Work of the Episcopal Church among Southern Negroes" (Ph.D. thesis, Columbia University, 1960), it is possible to estimate that in 1859, in the same ten states, there were about 4,900 slave communicants, with perhaps two to three times that number served by episcopal worship services and religious instruction. South Carolina claimed more than half of the slave communicant total.

2. See Colossians 3:22, Ephesians 6:5, and 1 Peter 2:18 (KJV).

3. *Diocese of Tennessee, 1850* (Columbia: Mitchell and Rainey, 1850), 18–19.

4. See below, "The Wartime Episcopate of Bishop Elliott of Georgia," for a detailed discussion of the basis for this belief, which is delineated in Elliott's sermon *Our Cause in Harmony with the Purposes of God in Christ Jesus* (Savannah: John Cooper, 1862).

5. The formation of the Confederate Episcopal Church and this particular resolution are discussed below, in "Church Division Is Ratified: The First General Council of the Protestant Episcopal Church in the Confederate States."

6. *Diocese of Tennessee 1853* (Nashville: Roberts, 1853), 38–41. The referenced pages comprise Bishop Payne's letter, a quotation from which is included in this paragraph.

7. Stephen Elliott, *Pastoral Letter from the Bishops in the Confederate States of America 1862. Delivered Before the General Council, in St. Paul's Church, Augusta, Georgia, Saturday, Nov. 22d, 1862* (Augusta: Steam Power Press and Chronicle, 1862).

8. Cicero Stephens Hawks was born in North Carolina, but his quest for orders and his early ministry took place in New York.

9. Bishop Lee's response to slavery is treated below, in the essays entitled "Episcopates in States Divided" and "Aftermath in Former Slave States in the Union."

10. A poignant and very grim account of life as a missionary during these years is given by Episcopal priest John McNamara in *Three Years on the Kansas Border by a Clergyman of the Episcopal Church* (New York: Miller, Orton, and Mulligan, 1856). McNamara describes the great hardships suffered by his family, the constant hounding by proslavery settlers, and, the lack of support from the national church.

11. Bishop's addresses in the journals of the Diocese of Missouri for the years 1855 through 1861.

# Richmond, Virginia, 1859

## ⊹⫤ *Ceremony, Church Affairs, and an Issue Ignored*

In the year 1859, from 5 October through 22 October, the triennial convention of the Protestant Episcopal Church in the United States was held in Richmond, Virginia. Delegates assembled in two houses, the House of Bishops and the House of Clerical and Lay Deputies, the latter composed of the clerical and lay deputies who had been elected by their respective diocesan conventions. The bishops and bishops-elect who were present totaled thirty-seven and included four assistant bishops and two missionary bishops as well as all diocesan bishops except those of California and Connecticut.[1] The bishops' attendance roster is provided in the table below. There were 131 members of the clergy and 106 representatives of the laity in attendance.[2]

Abolitionist agitation and sentiment in the United States had increased sharply during the 1850s, and, by the time the convention opened, it was abundantly clear that there were "two Americas," one comprising slave states and the other free states. The signs of an impending civil crisis were equally clear. The Richmond convention provided an opportunity for all bishops in the United States, those from the North and those from the South, not only to discuss and debate matters of church governance and church expansion but also to confront slavery, the paramount moral issue of their day. The record of what happened and what did not happen at that convention gives a portrait of Episcopal leadership just before the Civil War.

### The Convention Opens

The city of Richmond was pleased to be the site of the convention and extended a warm welcome to the delegates, some of whom stayed in private homes as guests of clergy or laypersons who lived in the city. An indication of the convention's importance locally was the publication of its proceedings in the city papers; the *Richmond Daily Dispatch* gave lead space on the front page to its convention reports.[3] There were welcomes on editorial pages, some general and some to particular delegates.[4]

## Protestant Episcopal Church in the United States General Convention of 1859 in Richmond, Virginia—Bishops in attendance

| Bishop | Diocese |
| --- | --- |
| William Meade | Virginia |
| John Henry Hopkins | Vermont |
| Benjamin Bosworth Smith | Kentucky |
| Charles Pettit McIlvaine | Ohio |
| James Hervey Otey | Tennessee |
| Jackson Kemper | Wisconsin |
| Samuel A. McCoskry | Michigan |
| Leonidas Polk | Louisiana |
| William H. DeLancey | Western New York |
| William Rollinson Whittingham | Maryland |
| Stephen Elliott | Georgia |
| Alfred Lee | Delaware |
| John Johns* | Virginia |
| Manton Eastburn | Massachusetts |
| Carlton Chase | New Hampshire |
| Nicholas H. Cobbs | Alabama |
| Cicero Stephens Hawks | Missouri |
| Alonzo Potter | Pennsylvania |
| George Burgess | Maine |
| George Upfold | Indiana |
| William Mercer Green | Mississippi |
| John Payne† | Africa–Liberia |
| Francis Huger Rutledge | Florida |
| John Williams* | Connecticut |
| Henry John Whitehouse | Illinois |
| Thomas Frederick Davis | South Carolina |
| Thomas Atkinson | North Carolina |
| Thomas F. Scott | Oregon & Washington Territory |
| Henry W. Lee | Iowa |
| Horatio Potter | New York |
| Thomas March Clark | Rhode Island |
| Samuel Bowman* | Pennsylvania |
| William H. Odenheimer‡ | New Jersey |
| Alexander Gregg‡ | Texas |
| Gregory T. Bedell*‡ | Ohio |
| Henry B. Whipple‡ | Minnesota |
| Henry Champlin Lay†§ | Arkansas and Southwest |

*Sources: Richmond Daily Dispatch*, 6 October 1859, 1; official listing in *Journal of the General Convention, 1859* (Philadelphia: King and Baird, 1860).

*Notes:* Bishops are listed in order of consecration. Diocesan bishops Thomas C. Brownell of Connecticut and William I. Kip of California were absent.

*Assistant bishop

†Missionary bishop

‡Consecrated during the convention

§Consecrated immediately after the convention

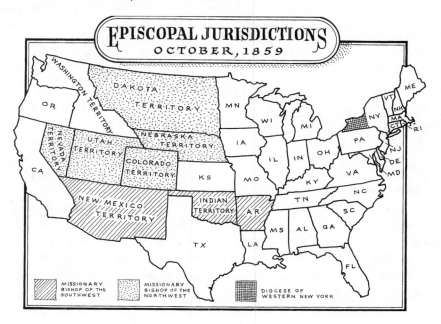

The opening ceremony and proceedings for the convention at the host church, St. Paul's, were eagerly anticipated and, as a reporter noted, not just by the delegates: "Although the hour of 10 was appointed for the commencement of the exercises, the throng began to gather in the Church before 8 o'clock, and it was with much difficulty that the seats reserved for delegates were kept vacant until their arrival. By 10 o'clock, every seat in the house was filled, the galleries were densely crowded, and many persons . . . were compelled to stand during the exercises." At 10 o'clock, the bishops entered from the vestry room, clad in full canonicals, and took their seats within the chancel.[5]

The opening sermon was given by James Hervey Otey, bishop of Tennessee. His message focused on the religious education of the young. The bishop proclaimed that instruction in moral values must be a part of a child's education if the principles on which our nation was founded were to remain. He went on to say that the family circle is the nursery for heaven, where the heart is molded for God for eternity. One's role is that of teacher, appointed by God. "The little plaything which we dawdle on the knee has a thinking soul, destined for heaven or hell. God has appointed the teachers—to their hands committed its destiny. If the duty is neglected, how shall we answer to God for it?"[6] When the two houses acted to admit two new dioceses, Kansas and Minnesota, into union with the Protestant Episcopal Church in the United States, everything was in place to proceed with the ceremonial highlight of the convention. This occurred on 13 October, when four bishops-elect were consecrated in three separate rites held simultaneously.

## A False Start

The first impulse of Bishop William Meade of Virginia, acting at the convention as presiding bishop in the absence of Thomas Brownell of Connecticut, was to hold a single service on the capitol grounds, a site large enough to accommodate the expected large attendance, and he secured the permission of state officials to do so. His colleagues in the episcopate apparently did not object, at least initially, but when the plan was communicated to the House of Deputies, a wave of protests erupted from both clerical and lay delegates. The appropriateness of holding this solemn ritual anywhere but in a church and the validity of administering Holy Communion in such a setting were challenged. The most colorful, if not the most theological, note was struck by a Mr. Hill from California, who thought the arrangement altogether improper. "Boys would be firing crackers, dogs fighting, old women selling cakes, and all manner of other accompaniments of a mass meeting would be encountered."[7]

While the deputies were debating how to cast their concerns in the form of a resolution, Bishop Meade reconsidered, and word arrived from the House of Bishops that arrangements had been made to hold consecration services simultaneously in three Richmond churches.

## A Day of Ceremony: 13 October 1859

When St. Paul's Church, located at the corner of 9th and Grace Streets across from the capitol grounds, opened its doors at 9:00 A.M., the crowd that had gathered on the steps and sidewalk moved into the church. All the pews not reserved for delegates were almost instantly filled.[8] At 10 o'clock Presiding Bishop Meade, fourteen other bishops, and the four attending presbyters entered. The bishops took seats in the chancel, the assisting clergy in the front of the nave. The Reverend William Henry Odenheimer, D.D., bishop-elect of New Jersey, and Gregory Thurston Bedell, D.D., assistant bishop-elect of Ohio, both wearing the rochet,

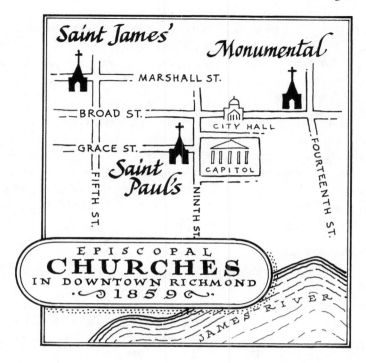

took seats at the front as well. The ceremony then proceeded in the following order: Service of Morning Prayer; the sermon by Bishop Alfred Lee of Delaware; the consecration service. A reporter from the *Richmond Daily Dispatch* gave an account of the proceedings:

> [The consecration service] is very solemn and imposing and on this occasion was rendered unusually so by the presence of a large number of the fathers of the church. The Bishops elect were presented to the Presiding Bishop (Right Reverend William Meade of Virginia) by Bishops Whittingham of Maryland, A. Potter of Pennsylvania, Eastburn of Massachusetts, and H. Potter of New York. The Presiding Bishop then demanded the testimonials of the persons presented for consecration, and they were read. After prayers and the Litany, the usual examination "in certain articles" was conducted by Bishop Meade. This having been concluded, the Bishops were robed in the full Episcopal habit, in which they were assisted by the Revs. R. B. Croes and W. C. Doane of New Jersey, Rev. C. M. Butler of Maryland, and Rev. R. B. Claxton of Ohio. (The Rev. Mr. Doane is the son of the late Bishop Doane of New Jersey, who is succeeded by Bishop Odenheimer). Veni, Creator, Spiritus was then said by the Presiding Bishop and others present and prayer was offered

in behalf of the elected Bishops. The imposition of hands by Bishops Meade, Lee, McIlvaine, McCoskry, Upfold, Johns, Payne, Chase, Rutledge, Hawks, Williams, and others, was an exceedingly solemn ceremony. Bibles were presented to the newly-consecrated Bishops, the communion was administered, and the congregation was dismissed with the benediction.[9]

At the other two churches chosen by Bishop Meade, the doors also were opened at 9:00 A.M., and the order of service was identical to that at St. Paul's. Large congregations were present at all three services. St. James's Church, located just six blocks from St. Paul's at 5th and Marshall, was the site for the investiture of Henry Benjamin Whipple, bishop-elect of Minnesota.[10] The Monumental Church, located five blocks from St. Paul's at 14th and Broad, was the host church for the consecration of Alexander Gregg, bishop-elect of Texas.[11]

## Two Missionary Bishoprics

In October 1859 there were thirty-three states in the United States, including California and Oregon on the west coast. Kansas, although admitted as a diocese at the convention, did not become a state until 1861. Every state except Arkansas was served by a diocesan bishop. New York State had two dioceses. North of Arkansas, Missouri, Iowa, and Minnesota made up a westernmost tier of noncoastal states, each served by a bishop.[12] There was a vast area of land between this tier and the west-coast states of Oregon and California, where Bishop Scott held episcopal authority both in the state of Oregon and in the Washington territory and where Bishop Kip was diocesan for California. Similarly, across the Southwest, although a bishop for the Diocese of Texas had been consecrated at the convention, there was considerable territory between Arkansas and California that was not served by a bishopric. Within these vast areas were Indian tribes and some pioneer settlements. Both the deputies and bishops saw these territories as fertile soil for the gospel and as the consummation of a "Manifest Destiny" for the Episcopal Church. Two missionary bishoprics therefore were created, and Henry Champlin Lay was elected missionary bishop for Arkansas and the Southwest and Joseph C. Talbot missionary bishop for the Northwest. Just after the House of Deputies voted unanimously to appoint two missionary bishops, the convention reporter observed that

> the members arose and sang *Gloria in Excelsis,* commencing
>> Glory be to God on high
>> And on earth peace, good will to men.
> This spontaneous outpouring of joy was followed by a prayer, the President officiating; . . . the spectacle was a remarkable one, even for a religious body.[13]

The Reverend Henry Lay was present at the convention, accepted the call, and was consecrated immediately after the convention on 23 October at St. Paul's Church. The Reverend Joseph Talbot also accepted his call and was consecrated in January 1860.

## Other Convention Business

### Consideration of Canons

Much convention time involved consideration of new canons. Of those proposed, twelve were adopted, fifteen were "negatived," and six were referred to the next convention. One of those passed was a substitute for Canon IX of 1853 and was entitled "Officiating of Ministers within the Cures of Others." The first point in the new canon read as follows: "No minister belonging to this Church shall officiate either by preaching, reading prayers, or otherwise, in the Parish or within the Parochial Care of another Clergyman, unless he has received express permission for that purpose from the Minister of the Parish, or Cure, or, in his absence, from the Churchwardens and Vestrymen, or Trustees of the Congregation, or a majority thereof."[14]

### Stewardship

Both the bishops and the deputies put upon the convention record their conviction that it was "the duty of every member of the Church to consecrate a definite percentage of his income to the advancement of the cause of Lord and Savior."[15]

### Domicile for the Bishop of Illinois

At one point Henry John Whitehouse, bishop of Illinois, was admonished by his fellow bishops to relocate promptly his family residence from New York to Illinois. This action was taken following receipt of a communication Bishop Whitehouse had brought before the bishops at the request of the clerical and lay deputies from his diocese. Whitehouse advised his fellow bishops of his intention to comply.[16]

### Pastoral Letter

An issue that generated controversy was the matter of how the pastoral letter, normally issued by the House of Bishops at a convention's close, was to be written. Bishop Whittingham on the second day of the convention made a motion to the effect "that this house regarding its assemblage as an especial call and opportunity for diligent labor for the edification of churches committed to the charge of our members, finds in the present condition of the church and of our country, urgent reasons why that opportunity should be turned to the utmost possible account . . . the issual of a pastoral letter, on canonical request of the House of Clerical and Lay Deputies, be carefully prepared by all members of the House."[17]

The resolution went on to call for two specific procedures, to wit: (1) that each bishop consult with his clerical and lay delegates and report back to the House of Bishops on the issues discussed and (2) that a committee of five bishops be designated to draft the letter, which should reflect the matters identified by broad consultation. Whittingham's entire proposal was laid on the table but called up the next day and referred to a committee of three. When that committee reported with a resolution to adopt the Whittingham resolution with only minor changes, Bishop Elliott made a substitute motion that there be no change in the method of preparation of the pastoral letter. Bishop McIlvaine moved to table the substitute motion, but the tabling motion was defeated. The substitute motion was adopted, and a committee of three was appointed by the presiding bishop to draft a pastoral letter. Then, on the fifteenth day of the convention, the House of Clerical and Lay Deputies passed a resolution asking the House of Bishops to prepare a pastoral letter that incorporated issues set forth in the report of the Committee on the State of the Church, which was forwarded with the resolution.[18] This report was a long one, with a diocese-by-diocese report appended to a general statement about the state of the church. The key general issues identified were the lack of candidates for holy orders and an apparent neglect of infant baptism.

The bishops responded by advising the House of Deputies that there was not enough time remaining to prepare a pastoral letter on the basis delineated by the deputies and that there would be no pastoral letter following the convention. The bishops did resolve, however, to call the report of the Committee on the State of the Church to the attention of all dioceses and parishes. Bishop Polk asked the presiding bishop to address a few pastoral words to the convention in his closing address.

The Whittingham resolution appeared designed to move the pastoral letter away from lofty platitudes and into addressing grassroots concerns within the church. There was, in fact, at least a hint in the wording of his resolution that Bishop Whittingham was moving toward a position that pastoral letters might address major societal issues. In spite of the "present condition of our church and of our country" that Whittingham noted, however, the House of Bishops apparently did not find compelling the opportunity for "diligent labor" to edify the wider church.[19]

## The Institution of Slavery: The Unspoken Issue

### Religious Instruction and Missionary Work

The religious instruction of slaves was described in the written reports of several Southern dioceses that were appended to the general report on the state of the church. The other mention of slavery occurred in an address by Missionary Bishop Payne, who was invited to speak about his work in Africa. Part of his remarks were devoted to the needs of the former slaves living in or near Monrovia, Liberia, all of whom were emigrants from the United States.[20] He reminded his audience that England had supported colonists when the new world was being settled and urged that the United States now do the same for the residents of Monrovia, who were in dire need.[21] In the course of his remarks, he commended the Old Dominion (the state of Virginia) for being the first to take measures to suppress the Atlantic slave trade.[22]

Bishop Payne did not point out, however, that slave markets and private slave sales in Virginia were a major source of the "internal slave trade," slaves taken south by traders for resale in the cotton belt along the Gulf Coast. This activity as a whole, and the specific fact of the existence in Richmond of the notorious Lumpkin Jail, a holding facility for slaves awaiting sale, did not come before the convention.[23]

### The Tumult Beyond

Outside the convention in the city of Richmond and in all points North and South, the controversy over slavery was in full cry. Richmond papers reported on this growing crisis and offered their opinions on editorial pages. An editorial in the *Richmond Whig* praised the Honorable Washington Hunt, former governor of New York and a delegate to the convention, for his position on the issue: "he believes that the North and South, if each section will mind its own business and cease pernicious interference with the purely domestic affairs of the other, may live happily and peacefully together, to the end of time."[24]

In an earlier editorial the *Whig* had blasted "Anti-Slavery Preaching," linking the use of the pulpit for that purpose to a drop in conversions to Christ in Northern churches. "It is a sign that the ministers of the gospel have neglected their duties most shamefully. But above all, it proves the utter wickedness of the present anti-slavery crusade. . . . Preachers of the gospel have no time to attend to the salvation of souls—they have no time to preach the word of God."[25] The *Richmond Daily Dispatch,* for its part, praised the "Episcopal Church of the North" for remaining aloof from the "anti-slavery agitation" and reported with satisfaction that a resolution introduced by Mr. John Jay at a convention of the Diocese of New York aimed at disapproval of the reopening of the slave trade was ridiculed and then "annihilated by a universal no vote."[26]

### John Brown's Raid

While the convention was in full swing, the controversy outside its walls over the existence of slavery in the United States became an uproar, sparked by an incident some 165 miles away. John Brown led a raid by a group of antislavery activists on the United States arsenal at Harper's Ferry, Virginia.[27] Brown commanded a band of twenty-one men, five of whom were free blacks. In the early morning hours of 17 October, Brown and eighteen of his men achieved success in their first objective—seizing control of the U.S. armory and the nearby Hall's Rifle Works that housed a large cache of rifles.

During the period that Brown controlled the arsenal complex, he took hostage prominent citizens of Harper's Ferry and environs, including the government officials in charge of the armory. Hostages also included two slaveholders who were brought with their slaves to the engine room, Brown's headquarters, at the armory. The slaves were armed with pikes and assigned guard duty by Brown. Brown, a militant antislavery crusader who had fought and gained notoriety during the struggle over slavery in Kansas, was confident that his daring raid would serve as a catalyst for a general uprising, both by slaves and by white persons opposed to that institution. According to his scenario, he and his men could depart the arsenal and hide in the countryside as soon as the rebellion gained momentum.

His hopes of a general uprising, however, were not realized. The armory soon was surrounded by a contingent of Virginia militia, and militia from Maryland came as reinforcements. Sporadic fighting occurred, and Brown attempted to negotiate a truce under which he and his men would leave and the hostages would be set free. These efforts failed; the men surrounding the armory, in fact, did not honor the white flags raised by Brown's emissaries. Two of his sons and other members of the band were killed.

When the arsenal was stormed Brown and four other conspirators were its only defenders. Of the twenty-two men involved in the raid, ten were killed, five escaped, and seven, including Brown, were captured. The marines who overcame Brown and his men were commanded by Brevet Colonel Robert E. Lee, who had been dispatched from Washington by President James Buchanan and Secretary of War John B. Floyd to retake the armory. Brown and the other captured members of his band were hanged for treason in December.[28]

All Richmond papers gave Brown's raid extensive coverage—the incident knocked the convention report from the front page of the *Daily Dispatch*, which characterized the raid as an "Abolitionist Invasion."[29] First reports were sketchy and greatly overstated the strength of Brown's raiding party, but once the basic outline of the raid was clear, the editorials began. The excerpt below from the *Whig* was typical.

Not an Insurrection!

The recent outbreak at Harper's Ferry was in no sense an insurrection! The slaves had no part nor lot in the matter, except in so far as some of them were forced to take part by the menaces of "Old Brown." . . . There were five free negroes engaged in this affair but not a single slave! . . .

The slaves of the South are contented with their lot, peaceably disposed, loyal to their masters, and hate a meddling northern intruder Abolitionist with a perfect hatred.[30]

The Brown raid caused a strain in some of the personal interactions of Northern and Southern delegates and probably led to awkwardness in the mealtime conversations between many Northern guests (bishops and delegates) and their hosts in private homes around Richmond. Years after the convention, the son of Bishop Gregg of Texas put it this way: "The general warmth of friendly intercourse which had previously prevailed between churchmen from different sections of the country suddenly chilled, and it is a great wonder that the General Convention was able to continue its sessions without the exhibition of deeper feelings of an opposite nature."[31] Thus this tension and its causes did not play out on the convention floor. Neither the Brown incident nor the public outcry it generated received official notice.

## An Optimistic Closure

In his closing remarks Acting Presiding Bishop Meade thanked the clergy and laypersons of Richmond for their hospitality and praised the visiting bishops and ministers for their sermons. The *Richmond Daily Dispatch* summarized the message of the presiding bishop's remarks as follows: "The discussions [during the convention] had been of the most harmonious character and favorable to the cause of religion. Charity—the best of all things—had been increased among us. Bishops were drawn nearer to bishops, ministers to ministers, and laymen to laymen. The bonds of the Union had been strengthened. Voices from the North and South, the East and West . . . had all been heard in unison, speaking and singing the praise of God."[32] The convention thus closed with no direct reference to slavery as an issue for the church. In fact, neither in its proceedings nor in the closing remarks from the acting presiding bishop was there mention of slavery as a moral issue. Also ignored was the growing civil controversy over slavery and the rapidly deepening rift between North and South spawned by that controversy—a rift that soon was to tear the nation apart.

## Postscript

Prior to the Civil War, the silence of the Episcopal Church on slavery reflected in part an effort to preserve unity in the church; Northern churchmen who opposed slavery, especially the bishops, were reluctant to offend their Southern brethren. This desire for unity was reinforced by the fact that there were close friendships in the House of Bishops that transcended sectional boundaries. On a deeper level, however, the silence reflected the traditional stance of the Episcopal

Church on political and societal issues, which was to leave those matters to the government—to the civil authorities. The mission of the church was to preach the gospel.

Having said this, it should be explicitly noted that the Northern bishops did not yet regard slavery as an evil in a religious or moral sense, or at least not an evil sufficient to break silence and speak against the institution in a church forum. As a civil or political evil, it was not a proper topic for the church's agenda. Although the Southern bishops would not have faulted these positions, many, as noted previously, regarded slavery not as an evil institution but as one sanctioned by Holy Scripture.

Before secession, and even in the early stages of war, the general view that the church should remain separate from state and from political issues (such as slavery, governance, government structures, and war) prevailed among bishops, North and South. As the war progressed, however, that view eroded as both Union and Confederate bishops began to see their cause as God's cause. Subsequent events, however, did not tarnish the memories; the 1859 convention was long remembered by bishops, North and South, for its fellowship, brotherly love, and unity.[33]

## Notes

1. At the start of the convention, thirty-two bishops were present; four more were consecrated during the proceedings. Henry Lay, although elected missionary bishop by the convention, was not consecrated until after adjournment. Although Kansas was admitted as a diocese, a diocesan bishop was not consecrated until December 1864.

2. William Stevens Perry, *A Handbook of the General Convention, 1785–1874* (New York: Thomas Whitaker, 1874), 202.

3. There was a reporter at the sessions of the House of Clerical and Lay Deputies; proceedings of the House of Bishops were not observed directly, but some actions and discussions were reported.

4. On its editorial page on 7 October 1959, the *Richmond Whig* noted that "hotels, boarding houses, and private residences were pretty well filled with delegates and visitors to the Episcopal convention. . . . 'Big Richmond' welcomes them all."

5. *Richmond Daily Dispatch,* 6 October 1859, 1.

6. Bishop Otey quoted in the *Richmond Daily Dispatch,* 6 October 1859, 1.

7. *Richmond Daily Dispatch,* 13 October 1859, 1.

8. Ibid.

9. Ibid.

10. St. James's Church relocated in 1913 to its present site at 1205 W Franklin Street.

11. *Richmond Daily Dispatch,* 14 October 1859, 1.

12. As noted, Henry Benjamin Whipple, the first bishop of Minnesota, was consecrated at this convention.

13. *Richmond Daily Dispatch,* 15 October 1859, 1.

14. *Journal of the General Convention, 1859* (Philadelphia: King and Baird, 1860), 204.

15. Ibid., 205.

16. Ibid., 161. Whitehouse had become bishop of Illinois in September 1852 but still maintained residence in New York. By 1859 the issue of his residence was a source of great tension between him and members of his diocese, especially the clergy. Whitehouse did move his residence to Illinois and remained bishop until his death.

17. *Journal of the General Convention, 1859*, 149. Prior practice had been that the pastoral letter was drafted by a small committee of senior bishops.

18. The report of the Committee on the State of the Church is appended to the journal of the 1859 convention.

19. *Journal of the General Convention, 1859*. The actions of the bishops and deputies following Whittingham's original motion may be found on pp. 156–213.

20. The colonization of Liberia by former slaves is discussed in the essays on Meade and Otey, above.

21. Bishop Payne's report may be found in the appendix to the *Journal of the General Convention, 1859*.

22. *Richmond Daily Dispatch,* 10 October 1859, 1.

23. The internal slave trade was active in Richmond from 1808, when the Atlantic trade was proscribed by Congress, until the Civil War, but was especially active in the two decades just before the war. Conditions at the Lumpkin jail are described on a website sponsored by the Smithsonian, "Digging Up the Past at a Richmond Jail," http://www.smithsonianmag.com/history-archaeology/Digs-Devils-Half-Acre.html. (Accessed 7 January 2013).

24. *Richmond Whig,* 7 October 1859, 2.

25. *Richmond Whig,* 17 September 1857, 2.

26. *Richmond Daily Dispatch,* 5 October 1859, 2. John Jay, a delegate from St. Matthew's Church in Bedford, also introduced an anti-slave-trade resolution at the 1860 convention of the Diocese of New York, a resolution that also was defeated. Diocese of New York (New York: Published for the Convention, 1860), 75.

27. Harper's Ferry became part of West Virginia when that state was formed in 1863 by separation from Virginia.

28. This brief summary of the raid on Harper's Ferry relies primarily on comprehensive works by Jules Abels, *Man on Fire: John Brown and the Cause of Liberty* (New York: Macmillan, 1971), and Truman John Nelson, *The Old Man: John Brown at Harper's Ferry* (New York: Holt, Rinehart and Winston, 1973).

29. *Richmond Daily Dispatch,* 19–24 October.

30. *Richmond Whig,* 24 October 1859, 2.

31. Wilson Gregg, *Alexander Gregg: First Bishop of Texas,* ed. Arthur Noll (Sewanee, Tenn.: University Press, 1912), 69.

32. *Richmond Daily Dispatch,* 24 October 1859, 2.

33. This observation is borne out in diocesan journals, North and South, for subsequent years.

# PART 3

# Secession and Church Division

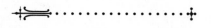

# Preamble

In spite of the pall cast by John Brown's raid, the Episcopal bishops left the Richmond convention with a sense of unity and accomplishment, feeling particularly pleased over the new dioceses, new bishops, and the commitment to the westward expansion of the church's missionary thrust. Across the South generally, however, concerns about attacks from the North on the institution of slavery were growing exponentially. One of the clearest—and most shocking— expressions of that concern appeared in an Episcopal Church publication in Virginia.

Slavery: The Causes of Our Troubles

Let us suppose that the Northern States were in great measure dependent upon the labor of horses for their prosperity; that apart from this species of labor, the Northern States would be ruined. Let us next suppose that a few persons in the South, were opposed to this kind of labor, believing it to be a political, social, and moral evil; that they began to agitate the question . . . until . . . newspapers and books and pamphlets all filled with complaints about this subject; that soon the few opponents grew into a large party; that societies were organized for the purpose of running off horses from the North; that when the owners went South to obtain their property, it could not be effected without danger to their lives, and but seldom they obtained their property. Let us suppose that soon a vast and overwhelming majority of Southern men began to look upon Northerners as little better than pirates; that Southern pulpits should echo the popular feeling, until at last the sentiment against "horse labor" became so engrossing, that in the South a political party should be raised up, whose one rallying cry was "down with horse labor" and that soon so strong the feeling should become, that on this one only ground they elected magistrates, and judges, and governors, and congressmen, and at last a President of the United States. Now, what would the North think? Their safety, their property, their welfare, their families, nearly their earthly all, dependent upon the labor of horses, and yet their fellow countrymen, citizens of the same country, who were not in the slightest degree injured by their horses, yet all agreed that they should not have horses. . . . What would they do? Would it not be the prevailing feeling among the vast majority, if we cannot carry out our own labor in the way which we think right, we had better separate and become two people?

Now, if our Northern readers will strike out the word "horse" and insert the word "slave" [We are not arguing as if we looked upon slaves in the light of brutes; far from it; they are heirs with us in the blessed promises], . . . they have the causes which have led to the most unhappy state of affairs we see around us. Only, this analogy does not convey one tithe of the wrong that has been done the South. Horses have no souls, no wills to be aroused by evil men. Pikes cannot be placed in their hands and they taught to make war against their masters. But slaves can be; so that this ceaseless agitation for five and twenty years, which has at last culminated in the erection of a party opposed not merely to the property of the South, but endangering the very lives of its citizens.[1]

The political leaders of the South began to feel that the time for verbal responses had passed; they were ready to take action, and the November 1860 presidential election provided the incentive to do just that.

### Secession Chronology

Abraham Lincoln was elected president of the United States in November 1860, and six weeks after the election the state of South Carolina passed an ordinance of secession. The United States began to break apart as other states followed South Carolina's lead. By early February 1861 seven states had seceded, and the Confederate States of America was established. On 18 February, Jefferson Davis was inaugurated as its provisional president. By early June four more states had left the Union. The seceding states are listed below, in order of secession date.[2]

| | |
|---|---|
| South Carolina | 20 December 1860 |
| Mississippi | 9 January 1861 |
| Alabama | 11 January 1861 |
| Florida | 11 January 1861 |
| Georgia | 19 January 1861 |
| Louisiana | 26 January 1861 |
| Texas | 1 February 1861 |
| Virginia | 17 April 1861 |
| Arkansas | 6 May 1861 |
| North Carolina | 20 May 1861* |
| Tennessee | 8 June 1861* |

*Legislative action on 7 May, but not approved by voters until date given.

Hostilities started in April at Fort Sumter; skirmishing began to occur immediately, and war preparations intensified North and South.

Notes

1. Editorial: "Slavery: The Causes of Our Trouble," *Southern Churchman*, 28 December 1860, 2. The reference to pikes probably is an allusion to the fact that a few slaves were commandeered near Harper's Ferry by John Brown and armed with pikes to serve on guard duty for hostages taken by Brown's men. The *Southern Churchman* was an Episcopal newsletter, published in Richmond.

2. There were secession attempts in Kentucky, Maryland, and Missouri but all were unsuccessful. These three states and Delaware were the slave states that remained in the Union.

# Prelude to Montgomery

## +≡ Southern Bishops Confront Secession, Threat of War, and Talk of Church Division

As the crises of 1860–1861, first political and then ecclesiastical, unfolded, there were sharp divisions among the Southern bishops. Bishops Otey, Meade, and Atkinson all originally had serious reservations about secession and remained hopeful even after Fort Sumter that civil war could be avoided. Leonidas Polk of Louisiana and Stephen Elliott of Georgia, in contrast, appeared to welcome the decision by their respective states to secede, although neither actively promoted secession. At the two extremes were Bishop Cobbs of Alabama, who remained committed to the Union until his death, and Francis Huger Rutledge of Florida who strongly and publicly advocated secession.

As states began to secede, the Southern bishops began to ponder the ecclesiastical implications of secession and the options open to their dioceses. The different views—and actions—of the bishops on the course the church should follow caused disagreements and controversy. The first four months of the year 1861 were ones of uncertainty and lack of unanimity among the Southern bishops.

### Nicholas Hamner Cobbs

In 1858 Edmund Ruffin of Virginia, an avowed and tireless advocate of Southern secession, was on a tour to promote his cause. While visiting the state of Alabama, he spoke briefly after a church service with Mrs. Nicholas Hamner Cobbs, wife of the Alabama bishop who was not present that Sunday. The editor of *The Diary of Edmund Ruffin*, William Kauffman Scarborough, offered the following comment on this encounter: "It is probably fortunate that Bishop Cobbs was absent during Ruffin's visit, for he [Cobbs] was the most noted opponent of secession in Alabama."[1]

Cobbs was proud to be a citizen of the United States, and two years later, in spite of the mounting fervor for it, he remained opposed to secession. Cobbs knew his country and his region, however, and he saw all too clearly the future when Lincoln was elected in November 1860. The bishop became ill shortly thereafter and was not told by his family when South Carolina seceded on 20 December. Exactly how much awareness he had of the details of the growing crisis in his last days is not clear, but he foresaw the sad outcome. His biographer gives this account of his death: "He prayed that he might not live to see the dissolution of the Union, and he died on the Eleventh of January, 1861, a very few minutes before the meridian gun boomed out the news of the passage of the ordinance of secession of Alabama."[2]

His friend Georgia bishop Stephen Elliott conducted funeral services at St. John's Church in Montgomery, preaching on the scripture verse "So He giveth His beloved sheep." Elliott incorporated some words of farewell to his clergy that Cobbs had dictated during his last illness: "Tell them that their dying bishop exhorts them to strive to be MEN OF GOD—men of peace, men of brotherly-kindness, men of charity, self-denying men, men of purity, men of prayer; men trying to perfect holiness in the fear of God, and laboring and preaching with an eye single to his glory and the salvation of souls."[3]

These farewell words are consistent with his biographer's view of the Bishop Cobb's attitude toward war: "Bishop Cobbs loved the Union fondly. He loved the flag, and believed in claiming it and fighting under it if necessary, but he deprecated, with all the force of his gentle spirit, the thought of bloodshed. Herein he was absolutely at one with his fellow Virginian Otey."[4] There is no doubt that Cobbs opposed secession, but he was spared the choice that Otey and Atkinson had to make when war came, a choice that probably would have been even more agonizing for him than for his two colleagues.[5]

### Francis Huger Rutledge

Among his colleagues in the House of Bishops, and even among his clergy, Francis Huger Rutledge, diocesan of Florida, was seen as quiet and unassuming.[6] For a brief period in January 1861, however, Rutledge exhibited neither of these characteristics when he took a public position that the state of Florida should secede from the United States.

During the last half of the 1850s, as tension between North and South over slavery escalated, talk of secession in Florida became frequent. Bishop Rutledge owned a small number of slaves, but he was not outspoken on the secession issue until South Carolina seceded in December 1860 and the state of Florida called a "people's convention" for early January 1861 to consider withdrawal from the Union. As the convention prepared to meet in January 1861, Bishop Rutledge met with Edmund Ruffin, the fiery secessionist from Virginia who had come to lend his support to Floridians who favored leaving the Union. Ruffin gave an account of their meeting in his diary: "After tea, Bishop Rutledge came in to visit the family. I was very much pleased with the venerable old minister, & with his ardent & active patriotic sentiments. He is a native of S.Ca., & said he had himself already seceded, with his native state, & in advance of Florida. We had agreeable conversation on this & various subjects until he left."[7]

On the first day of the convention, 3 January 1861, before the business began, there was a motion that Bishop Rutledge be invited to a seat by the side of the presiding officer and that the convention be opened with prayer. The delegates gave unanimous consent, and Rutledge, who had come to observe the proceedings, came forward to the rostrum to ask God to bless "the delegates in convention now assembled" and to guide them on the right path to fulfill their solemn duty to the people of Florida.[8]

On 10 January, at twenty-two minutes past noon, the convention passed an ordinance of secession by a vote of 62 to 7.[9] The bishop offered the opening prayer on 11 January, calling for God's blessing on the work of the convention, which he was certain was in accord with the divine will.[10] Finally, later that day he offered prayer before the governor-elect, convention delegates, and the members of the Florida House and Senate at the ordinance-signing ceremony.[11]

Among the convention spectators on both 10 and 11 January 1861 were the teenage Susan Bradford and her father, plantation owner Dr. Edward Bradford, who wanted his daughter to be aware of the historic nature of the times. Susan Bradford was impressed by Bishop Rutledge's prayers and recorded her excitement in her diary.[12] The bishop's participation in these significant moments certified his approval of the convention's action. The intensity of his feeling was best given expression early in the convention, however, when on 8 January, a communication was read to the convention: "The undersigned promises to pay the Treasury of the State of Florida, on demand, the sum of five hundred dollars, toward defraying the expenses of government for the year eighteen hundred and sixty-one, whenever by ordinance she shall be declared an independent republic. Frs. H. Rutledge."[13] In sending this letter Bishop Rutledge placed himself squarely and publicly on the side of secession and what soon would become the Confederate cause. Rutledge joined other Southern bishops later in the year, first at Montgomery and then in Columbia, in efforts to create a separate organization for the Southern church.

### William Meade

Unlike Rutledge, Bishop Meade of Virginia, the South's senior bishop, opposed the rush to secession that occurred after Lincoln was elected. On 15 December 1860 he wrote in a letter to his friend Bishop Charles P. McIlvaine of Ohio: "I am told that our clergy in Charleston and New Orleans speak and preach in favor of disunion. I fear some of our Bishops consent, or why have we heard no remonstrance?"[14] Meade felt that his fellow bishops, the "Ministers of Peace," should be dampening secession fever, not fanning its flames.

In January 1861 the Bishop of Virginia saw a glimmer of hope and wrote McIlvaine accordingly: "I believe that good sense, self interest, and religion, with God's providence, will arrest the calamity of disunion."[15] By early May, after his state had seceded in mid-April, his optimism had evaporated, and he wrote McIlvaine: "I have slowly and reluctantly come to the conclusion that we must separate."[16]

After concluding that separation was inevitable, Meade adopted the position that division could be accomplished peacefully—although by the time he accepted secession there was considerable momentum for war. In truth, Meade and others who had read carefully Lincoln's inaugural address, delivered in March 1861, after the inauguration of Jefferson Davis, knew that Lincoln was on record not to accept any acts of secession proclaimed by states in the South. The new president of the United States was conciliatory about slavery, unequivocally recognizing the right for it to exist in Southern states and conceding that the return of fugitive slaves was constitutional. Lincoln's views on the constitution and secession, however, were neither conciliatory nor ambiguous:

> No State upon its own mere motion can lawfully get out of the Union; that resolves and ordinances to that effect are legally void, and that acts of violence within any State or States against the authority of the United States are insurrectionary or revolutionary, according to circumstances.
>
> . . . I shall take care, as the Constitution itself expressly enjoins upon me, that the laws of the Union be faithfully executed in all the States. . . .
>
> In your hands, my dissatisfied fellow-countrymen, and not in mine, is the momentous issue of civil war. The Government will not assail you. You can have no conflict without being yourselves the aggressors. You have no oath registered in heaven to destroy the Government, while I shall have the most solemn one to "preserve, protect, and defend it."[17]

Bishop Meade had a different view of the constitution, believing firmly in "states rights," including the right to secede. In his address to the diocesan convention on 17 May 1861, Meade made clear his position that if civil war came the South would be in the right—and that the objective sought was worth whatever price had to be paid.

> It has pleased God to permit a great calamity to come upon us. Our whole country is preparing for war. Our own State, after failing in her earnest effort for the promotion of peace, is perhaps more actively engaged in all needed measures for maintaining the position which she has, after much consideration, deliberately assumed, than any portion of the land.
>
> A deeper and more honest conviction that if war should actually come upon us, it will be on our part one of self defense, and, therefore, justifiable

before God seldom, if ever, animated the breasts of those who appealed to arms. From this consideration, and from my knowledge of the character of our people, I believe that the object sought must be most perseveringly pursued, whatever sacrifice of life and comfort and treasure may be required. . . .

I have clung with tenacity to the hope of preserving the Union to the last moment. If I knew my own heart, could the sacrifice of the poor remnant of my life have contributed in any degree to its maintenance, such sacrifice would have been cheerfully made. But the development of public feeling and the course of our rulers have brought me slowly, reluctantly, sorrowfully, yet most decidedly, to the painful conviction, that not withstanding attendant dangers and evils, we shall consult the welfare and happiness of the whole land by separation.[18]

Still, in the same address he appeared to hope for the alternative of peaceful separation, giving the example of the "two venerable patriarchs" of old who found room enough in the "little pent-up land of Judea to live together in peace, by going the one to one hand and the other to the opposite."[19]

Even on 13 June, three weeks after federal forces had taken over Alexandria, Meade still had hope that civil war could be halted. He preached at the church in Millwood, at which he had previously served as rector. Armies from the two sides were forming and preparing for battle, and Meade told his listeners that although "poets and historians" spoke of the pomp and circumstance and the glory of war, the word of God spoke otherwise. He berated North and South for sectional hatred, blasphemy, and other sins that had led to the current impasse. He then made an appeal to the North.

I am no politician, but only an humble preacher of the Gospel; but could I be permitted to speak a word in the ear of the Administration and Congress, which rule over an almost boundless territory, with millions of people, . . . I would say, in the name of God and humanity, throw not away the noblest opportunity true patriotism and philanthropy ever gave to the rulers of the nations; . . . let the separation be one of friends and not of enemies. What monument ever erected to the greatest generals of earth, for subduing and recovering revolted provinces . . . can be compared to the peaceable settlement of the great controversy now about to deluge the land with blood?[20]

## Leonidas Polk and James Hervey Otey

According to his biographer son William Mecklenburg Polk, Bishop Leonidas Polk of Louisiana was not involved in any movement to promote secession, but the bishop did sense immediately after Lincoln's election that the Southern states would secede. His main concern, when his view was reinforced by South

Carolina's secession, was to avoid a civil war. On 26 December 1860, six days after South Carolina acted, he wrote to the president of the United States, James Buchanan.

Polk began by giving his reason for writing, which was to apprise the president of the true state of mind and determination in Louisiana and five other Southern states regarding secession. Polk was absolutely convinced, he advised President Buchanan, that those states were "deliberately and inflexibly resolved to cut themselves off from the Union" and that an attempt to prevent secession by force of arms would unleash a carnage that would desolate the land. He predicted (accurately) that a Southern Confederacy would be formed by 1 March and that other states would join it soon thereafter. It was his hope that the president's policy of moderation would continue and that bloodshed would be avoided by allowing the Southern states to depart peacefully.[21]

In commenting on this letter, William Mecklenburg Polk remarks that he did not find that "beyond this effort [the letter to Buchanan] to avert a danger which he saw more clearly than most other men, Bishop Polk did no more, before the adoption of the ordinance of secession by the convention of the State of Louisiana, than observe the course of events and consider what his duty as a bishop might require of him in view of facts as they occurred." [22]

In September 1860, before the crisis precipitated by Lincoln's election, in response to a letter from Commander M. F. Maury, who expressed concern over the growing rumblings about secession, Bishop James Hervey Otey of Tennessee spoke for the Union: "Surely there is enough of the conservative element left among us—enough of virtue, love of order, and enlightened patriotism, among our people—to form a wall of fire around the citadel of our liberties, if it could be prevailed upon to step out, and boldly avow itself on the side of the constitution and laws of the land."[23]

When Otey heard after the election that a convention to consider secession had been called in South Carolina, his sharp reaction was expressed in a letter to Edward Calohill Burks, a colleague in Virginia: "The course of South Carolina I look upon as infamous. There is not a redeeming trait about the movement to save it from the just and deep condemnation of posterity. . . . Leave the question of union or disunion to the people tomorrow morning and I verily believe that a majority in S.C. and in all the Southern States will vote for Union."[24] Bishop Polk had not taken the public partisan position proclaimed by Rutledge in Florida, but Bishop Otey, Polk's friend, mentor during Polk's early years as a priest, and one of his consecrators, felt that Polk's views, and those of Bishop Elliott of Georgia, were sadly wanting. He sent a stinging letter of rebuke:

Until a few days past, my confidence was strong that there was left among the people at large an abiding love of country, and a respect for order and the supremacy of law, that would resist the madness and the arts of those who are moving all the baser passions of our nature to plunge this nation into a gulf of horrors and sufferings to which the past history of the world furnishes no parallel. . . . To what quarter shall we look, when such men as you and Elliott deliberately favor secession? What can we expect, other than mob-law and violence among the masses, when the men of peace, the fathers of the land, the Ministers of the Gospel of peace, are found on the side of those who openly avow their determination to destroy the work which our fathers established?[25]

Bishop Otey's agony deepened as secession spread, but he was pleased in January 1861 that Tennessee was holding firm to the Union. He wrote his friend McIlvaine: "On my arrival at home last week, in reading your letter of January 5th my first impulse was to write you at once and assure you that Tennessee would be found in the right place and on the right side in favor of liberty and Union. Not only one and inseparable, but cemented by law and order, now and forever. I am well satisfied that a majority of the people in the seceding states if their view could be fairly heard would speak loudly in favor of union."[26]

On 9 February he made a diary entry: "In company with the Rev. Dr. Hines, deposit my vote for the Union candidate."[27] In March 1861 Otey wrote his friend Edward Calohill Burks a letter that excoriated secessionists, denouncing their motives and predicting dire consequences of their actions:

I look upon dissolution of the Union or the organization of two governments North and South, dividing upon the question of slavery, not only as setting the seal to the ruin of both, but especially as settling the destiny of slavery to speedy inevitable extinction. . . . It will deprive the institution of the moral support which it now derives from its being upheld by a government of over 30 millions of people.

How is it with the secessionists? Denunciation—defiance and menace dwell upon their lips. One would think that men engaged in breaking up a great government . . . and in constructing a new one out of its fragments, they would feel themselves burdened by the weight of responsibility that would make them serious—nay, tremble and fear.[28]

Instead, Otey felt, secessionists were convinced that cotton was king and its power would make their way smooth: "Depend upon it, this is the pride that goes before a fall. God will make our own passions—our covetousness, pride and ambition the executioners of his wrath. The day of vengeance I verily believe is at hand."[29] The secession movement succeeded, however, and Otey, who was horrified by war even more than he was by disunion, next argued for a peaceable separation. Even after President Lincoln called on 15 April 1861 for seventy-five thousand troops to put down the rebellion, Otey continued to try to get the North to let the South go in peace.[30] On 10 May 1861 Otey wrote a long letter to Secretary of State William H. Seward, outlining what he saw as the consequences of a civil war and questioning what the United States government would do with a prostrate South if the North's "war of subjugation" was successful: "Will you from these ruins reconstruct the *Union*? Will the children of the South who have escaped butchery, grow up. . . dutiful and obedient subjects of a Government whose foundations have been lain in the blood of their slaughtered parents? . . . Will you, after your work of subjugation and of vengeance is accomplished, make provision for the four millions of Africa's children, whose ancestors, your forefathers brought over the sea, and when their labor on Northern soil proved unprofitable, they sold them to the planters of the South?"[31] Otey concluded by pleading with Seward to urge President Lincoln to "desist from all hostile measures and efforts to compel an unwilling obedience to his Government."[32]

When all hope of a peaceful resolution was gone, Bishop Otey supported the Confederate government, believing that it was fighting a war to repel aggression by the North. He explained in a letter to one of his daughters on 24 May 1861: "And now, my dear child, you ask me if I think that the cause of the South is just, and that God will favor and defend us. I answer: *In very deed, I do.*"[33] Otey told his daughter that the attack on Fort Sumter had been made the "pretext" for declaring the South in a state of "outlawry" and that Lincoln had usurped powers belonging to Congress in order to make war on the South. Further, he was aware that in the North religion was being used to sanction the Union course and that the federal Union flag was "raised on the towers and spires of Christian temples." Thus, "I will no more stand up for a Union whose supporters desecrate all that is holy, and, in the madness and blindness of their rage, forget that they are men, and bear the name of Christians."[34] During the period he was tormented with the question of secession, another issue arose, equally dear to Otey, namely that of church unity.

Immediately upon the secession of Louisiana, Bishop Leonidas Polk had issued a pastoral letter to his diocese.

To the Clergy and Laity of the Protestant Episcopal Church in the Diocese of Louisiana

MY BELOVED BRETHREN—The State of Louisiana having, by formal ordinance through her Delegates in Convention assembled, withdrawn herself from all further connection with the United States of America, and constituted herself a separate Sovereignty, has, by that act, removed our Diocese from within the pale of "The Protestant Episcopal Church in the United States." We have, therefore, an Independent Diocesan existence.

... Our separation from our brethren of "The Protestant Episcopal Church in the United States" has been effected because we must follow our nationality. Not because there has been any difference of opinion as to Christian Doctrine or Catholic usage.

Leonidas Polk, Bishop of the Protestant Episcopal Church
in the Diocese of Louisiana
New Orleans, January 30th, 1861[35]

Polk also used the letter to advise clergy that he had appointed the following change in the Prayer for the President of the United States and all in Civil Authority, found in the Morning Prayer service. "Replace 'President of the United States' with 'Governor of this State.'" A similar change was delineated for the Prayer for Congress. Polk then noted that "the time had not arrived for entering fully into the discussion of questions suggested by this occasion" but that it was important to announce the change in diocesan status and the required liturgical adjustments.[36]

This pastoral letter was circulated to other Southern bishops, as well as within the Diocese of Louisiana, and the most vehement criticism came from Bishops Otey and Atkinson, who did not concur with Polk's reasoning. The criticism was directed at Polk's basic premise that withdrawal of the Diocese of Louisiana from the Protestant Episcopal Church in the United States was required, and, in fact, had been effected, by the secession of the state of Louisiana from the Union.

Otey wrote his friend Bishop McIlvaine of Ohio after receipt of Polk's pastoral letter: "But how is this movement called secession, if perfected, to affect our beloved church, the dear church of the Savior for which he shed his blood? Have you seen what Bishop _____ has written in his pastoral letter?"[37] Otey then quoted Polk's pastoral letter containing the reasoning on which its author based his vindication of the withdrawal of the Diocese of Louisiana from the national church and then asked McIlvaine:

Does that cap the climax of all that you have ever fancied as likely occurrence in the future of our church? By like reasoning, if Louisiana were reduced to the condition of a conquered province by Great Britain or France, the Protestant Episcopal Church in her territory would pass with all the soil. Is not rebellion as the sin of witchcraft? My dear brother, what are we to make of all these things? To think of such men [naming certain colleagues in the House of Bishops] avowing the doctrine of secession. Am I indeed so blinded that I can see no wisdom nor good cause, no practical utility, none of the spirit of the gospel, neither its charity nor humility nor patience nor kindness nor gentleness nor brotherly love in a thing in which it is claimed they all exist. Do write me fully and frankly and show me where I am in error when I suppose and hold that the church is above all arrangements and changes of human government, submissive to them only under the law of Christ thankful for protection and claiming that as a right under all circumstances.[38]

Otey wrote Polk directly on 18 March, sharply reminding his colleague that he was not made Bishop of Louisiana by "its civil convention or its Legislature" and that the ministry of the church in Louisiana "does not act under or by" the civil authority of the state.[39]

## Thomas Atkinson

Bishop Atkinson did not initially favor secession, believing that a less drastic solution could be found to the slavery issue. In fact, as noted above, in the essay on Bishops Atkinson and Whittingham, he had served notice while under consideration for bishop of South Carolina that he favored retention of the Union over retention of slavery. Less than a month after the fall of Fort Sumter, however, he argued that North Carolina had no choice but to support her sister states in their resistance to restoration of the Union by force of arms.[40] Atkinson would not have favored starting a war to protect slavery, but he believed that the Southern states had the right to secede.

Although he was in support of the Southern cause politically, the argument for separation from the Protestant Episcopal Church in the United States put forth by Polk in his January 1861 pastoral letter disturbed Bishop Atkinson and continued to rankle him even after hostilities commenced. As noted earlier, he shared with Otey the belief that secession of the state of Louisiana from the United States did not dictate withdrawal of the Diocese of Louisiana from the Episcopal Church in the United States. Atkinson presented at the meeting of his diocese on 10 July 1861 a sharp and detailed argument against Polk's analysis.

> If Political separation do, without any action of the Church, produce Ecclesiastical Disruption, we lose all control over ourselves, in our Church Relations, for the future. Suppose the Dioceses in the Confederate States form an United Church, as, no doubt, they will, and that one of these States should afterwards secede from the Confederacy, then the Diocese, in that State, will be cut off, whether she wish it or no, from the Southern Church. Then the Church, throughout all time, will have her relations settled for her by men not necessarily of her Communion, perhaps, by men hostile to her, and anxious to destroy her. Was it ever heard before, that the Church of Christ was under such bondage! . . . Church and State, although both are appointed by God, and both necessary for man, are yet entirely distinct organizations; distinct in the authority which frames them, the one being Human, the other Divine; distinct in the power which secures the execution of their laws, the one being

Force, the other Conscience; distinct in their objects, those of the one being Temporal Happiness, those of the other Eternal Felicity.[41]

Atkinson made the additional point that there were missionary bishops (John Payne in Africa and William Boone in China) in the American church whose purview was not within any state or territory of the United States, so that a diocese not being within the territory of the United States did not preclude its membership in the Protestant Episcopal Church in the United States.

Finally, Atkinson argued that though it did appear desirable to change the organizational structure of the church in the South, action on that matter should reflect a consensus among the Southern dioceses. By this time, July 1861, steps that had been proposed by Polk and Elliott to facilitate having the Southern dioceses act in concert already were in progress, and Atkinson was soon to join his fellow Southern bishops in that effort.

## Notes

1. Edmund Ruffin, *The Diary of Edmund Ruffin*, ed. William Kauffman Scarborough, 3 vols. (Baton Rouge: Louisiana State University Press, 1972–1989), 1:185.

2. Greenough White, *A Saint of the Southern Church: Memoir of the Right Reverend Nicholas Hamner Cobbs, with Notices of Some of His Contemporaries* (New York: James Pott, 1897), 173.

3. Stephen Elliott, *"So He giveth His beloved sheep": The farewell message from Bishop Hamner Cobbs to his clergy, the address delivered by Elliott at Cobbs' funeral; and obituary notices for Bishop Cobbs* (Montgomery: Barrett, Wimbish, 1861).

4. White, *Saint of the Southern Church*, 171.

5. See the sections on Otey and Atkinson, below.

6. The Reverend Jackson Scott praised Rutledge's humility in a memorial address that was attached to proceedings of the Diocese of Florida's 1867 convention.

7. Ruffin, *Diary of Edmund Ruffin*, 1:524. See also Lee L. Willis III, "Secession Sanctified: Bishop Francis Huger Rutledge and the Coming of the Civil War in Florida," *Florida Historical Quarterly* 82 (Spring 2004): 432.

8. *Journal of the Proceedings of the Convention of the People of Florida, 1861* (Tallahassee: Office of the *Floridian* and *Journal*, 1861), 4–5.

9. Ibid., 32.

10. Ibid.

11. Ibid., 40. The governor-elect participated in this ceremony instead of the governor, who was ill.

12. Susan Bradford Eppes, *Through Some Eventful Years* (Macon: J. W. Burke, 1926), 144.

13. *Journal of the Convention, People of Florida*, 20.

14. Meade to McIlvaine, 15 December 1860; reproduced in John Johns, *A Memoir of the Life of the Right Reverend William Meade, D.D., Bishop of the Protestant Episcopal Church in the Diocese of Virginia, with a Memorial Sermon by the Reverend William Sparrow, D.D.* (Baltimore: Innes, 1867), 492.

15. Meade to McIlvaine, 12 January 1861; cited in Philip Slaughter, *Memoir of the Life of the Right Reverend William Meade* (Cambridge: John Wilson and Son, 1885), 30.

16. Meade to McIlvaine, 6 May 1861; cited in Slaughter, *Memoir of Meade*, 30.

17. Abraham Lincoln, Inaugural Address, 4 March 1861.

18. *Diocese of Virginia, 1861* (Richmond: Chas. Wynne, 1861), 27–28.

19. Ibid., 27. Meade's reference in these remarks is to the biblical story in which Abraham and Lot separated.

20. Slaughter, *Memoir of Meade*, 34.

21. William Mecklenburg Polk, *Leonidas Polk, Bishop and General*, 2 vols. (New York: Longmans, Green, 1893), 1:263–65.

22. Ibid., 265–66.

23. Otey to M. F. Maury, 3 September 1860; cited in William Mercer Green, *Memoir of the Life of the Rt. Rev. James Hervey Otey, D.D., LL.D., First Bishop of Tennessee* (New York: J. Pott, 1885), 92.

24. Otey to Edward C. Burks, 23 November 1860, in James Elliott Walmsley, "Documents: The Change of Secession Sentiment in Virginia in 1861," *American Historical Review*, 31 (October 1925): 98.

25. Otey to Polk, 8 December 1860; cited in Green, *Memoir of Otey*, 91.

26. Otey to McIlvaine, 16 February 1861; quoted by McIlvaine in his address to the Diocese of Ohio in June 1863. *Diocese of Ohio, 1863* (Columbus: Richard Nevins), 18.

27. Otey's diary entry for 9 February 1861; excerpts of the diary are included in Green, *Memoir of Otey*. This diary note refers to an election in Tennessee in which voters rejected a proposal to call a secessionist convention.

28. Otey to Edward C. Burks, 12 March 1861, in Walmsley, "Documents," 98–100.

29. Ibid., 99–100.

30. See Shelby Foote, *The Civil War: A Narrative*, vol. 1, *Fort Sumter to Perryville* (New York: Random House, 1958), 51–53.

31. Otey to William H. Seward, 10 May 1861, *Memphis Daily Appeal*, 26 May 1861, 1.

32. Ibid.

33. Otey to his daughter, 24 May 1861, in Green, *Memoir of Otey*, 93–94.

34. Ibid.

35. Extracts from *Diocese of Louisiana, 1861* (New Orleans: Bulletin Book and Job Office, 1861), 9–10.

36. The "praying for the president" issue became a contentious issue during the war and immediately afterwards. See the essays below on the episcopate of Richard Hooker Wilmer.

37. Otey to McIlvaine, 16 February 1861; quoted by McIlvaine in his address to the Diocese of Ohio in June 1863, *Diocese of Ohio, 1863*, 18.

38. Ibid. When he had Otey's letter reprinted, McIlvaine omitted the names of fellow bishops identified by Otey, but the bishops named almost certainly were Polk and Elliott.

39. Otey to Polk, 18 March 1861; excerpt from a letter cited in Donald S. Armentrout, *James Hervey Otey: First Episcopal Bishop of Tennessee* (Nashville: Episcopal Diocese in Tennessee, 1984), 87.

40. Thomas Atkinson, *Christian Duty in the Time of Present Trouble: A Sermon Preached at St. James' Church, Wilmington, N.C., on the Fifth Sunday After Easter, 1861* (Wilmington: Fulton and Price, 1861).

41. *Extract from the Annual Address of the Rt. Rev. Thomas Atkinson, D.D., to the Convention of the Diocese of North Carolina, July 10th, 1861* (Raleigh: Church Intelligencer Office, 1861), 5–6.

# A Separate Church for
# a Separate Nation

✠══ *The Southern Bishops Choose Church Division*

**Montgomery, Alabama, July 1861:** *Nulla Vestigia Rotrorsum*
*The Call to Montgomery*

Although nonplussed by the reactions to his pastoral letter following the secession of Louisiana from the Union, Leonidas Polk knew immediately the course that had to be followed, namely the formation of a Confederate Episcopal Church. He enlisted the help of his friend and co-leader of the church in the seceded states, Stephen Elliott. The two bishops met at Sewanee, Tennessee, where they composed and circulated on 23 March 1861 a call to their fellow bishops in the states that had formed the Confederacy:

Rt. Rev. and Dear Brother:

The rapid march of events and the change which has taken place in our civil relations, seem to us, your brethren in the church, to require an early consultation among the Dioceses of the Confederate States, for the purpose of considering their relations to the Protestant Episcopal Church of the United States, of which they have so long been the equal and happy members. This necessity does not arise out of any dissension which has occurred within the Church itself, nor out of any dissatisfaction with either the doctrine or discipline of the Church. We rejoice to record the fact, that we are to-day, as Churchmen, as truly brethren as we have ever been; and that no deed has been done, nor word uttered, which leaves a single wound rankling in our hearts. We are still one in Faith, in purpose and in Hope; but political changes, forced upon us by a stern necessity, have occurred, which have placed our Dioceses in a position requiring consultation as to our ecclesiastical relations. It is better that those relations should be arranged by the common consent of all the Dioceses within the Confederate States, than by the independent action of each Diocese. The one will probably lead to harmonious action; the other might produce inconvenient diversity.

We propose to you, therefore, Rt. Rev. and dear Brother, that you recommend to your Diocesan Convention, the appointment of three clerical and three lay deputies, who shall be delegates to meet an equal number of delegates from each of the Dioceses within the Confederate States, at Montgomery, in the Diocese of Alabama, on the third day of July next, to consult upon such matters as may have arisen out of the changes in our civil affairs.

We have taken it upon ourselves to address you this Circular because we happen to be together, and are the senior Bishops of the Dioceses within the Confederate States.

Very truly yours in Christian bonds,
Leonidas Polk, Bishop of Louisiana
Stephen Elliott, Bishop of Georgia[1]

## Results of the Call

The invitation by Bishops Polk and Elliott resulted in the following attendance at the Montgomery meeting:

| Diocese | Bishop present | Clerical deputies | Lay deputies |
|---|---|---|---|
| Florida | Yes–Francis Huger Rutledge | Yes | Yes |
| Georgia | Yes–Stephen Elliott | Yes | Yes |
| Mississippi | Yes–William Mercer Green | Yes | Yes |
| South Carolina | Yes–Thomas Frederick Davis | Yes | Yes |
| Alabama | No | Yes | Yes |
| Louisiana | No | Yes | Yes |
| Texas | No | No | No |
| Tennessee | No | Yes | No |
| North Carolina | No | No | No |
| Virginia | No | No | No |
| Arkansas | No | No | No |

*Source: Proceedings of a Meeting of Bishops, Clergymen, and Laymen, of the Protestant Episcopal Church in the Confederates States, at Montgomery, Alabama on the 3d, 4th, 5th, and 6th of July 1861, 5–7.*

The first seven states listed had seceded by the time of the Polk-Elliott letter, and six of these had full or partial representation at Montgomery. Neither Alabama nor Louisiana had the services of a bishop, Alabama because of the death of Bishop Cobbs in January 1861 and Louisiana because, as we shall see in the next essay, Bishop Polk had taken a leave from his bishopric to enter the Confederate army. Both dioceses sent delegations that included clergy and laity. The four dioceses represented by bishops were strongly in favor of sending delegations to Montgomery, as was illustrated by the response from the Diocese of South Carolina.

At his diocesan convention held on 19 and 20 June 1861 in Abbeville, South Carolina, Bishop Thomas Frederick Davis brought the call by his two fellow bishops before the convention and recommended, after a long preamble, the election of delegates to the Montgomery meeting.

> It is my duty to call to your attention particularly to the condition in which we are now placed as a Church. The principles of association and union, than which none are more influential, impelled us into the General Convention of the United States. With these brethren we have lived long in Christian harmony and advancing Christian life . . . but we are compelled to consider and act upon our present relations. . . . Being myself convinced that our best interests, I think I may fairly say, our actual necessities require of us an independent Southern organization as a Church, I recommend the election of three clerical and three lay delegates, as has already been done by our sister dioceses to meet in convention in Montgomery on the third day of next month.[2]

After considerable discussion, the convention passed a series of resolutions, the key one of which was the following: "*Resolved* That this convention, responding heartily to the brotherly greetings of other Southern Conventions, do elect by ballot forthwith three (3) clerical and three (3) lay deputies to attend the proposed convention in Montgomery, and to report to the next Convention of this Diocese for consideration, confirmation or rejection."[3] The only one of the original seven Confederate dioceses without representation in Montgomery was Texas. The state of Texas had seceded at the beginning of February. During the next meeting of the Diocese of Texas, 11–13 April 1861, the bombardment and surrender of Fort Sumter occurred, and at that convention, Bishop Gregg laid before the delegates the March 1861 letter from Bishops Polk and Elliott calling for the meeting of the Southern dioceses in Montgomery.

Gregg had supported the acts of secession by South Carolina and the states that followed, including Texas.[4] However, there was certainly no clarion call for independence of the church in the South in his remarks to the April 1861 diocesan convention. He appeared hesitant and seemed to be mulling over the options; he approved the idea of a meeting for consultation but apparently was ambivalent about any change in ecclesiastical relations.

> Of the propriety, too, of such consultation [among the Southern dioceses], at this grave juncture in our ecclesiastical as well as our civil history, it appears to me no doubt should be entertained; and I heartily concur in the recommendation here made. It will devolve upon this body, if it should agree in this opinion, to take the action proposed.

If there are elements of change which can not be overruled or controlled, a fraternal interchange of views and harmonious action will doubtless give to these changes a right direction.

If again the general sentiment of the Church, North and South, should ultimately be found to tend to the expediency of the severance of the ecclesiastical union heretofore existing, the friendly consultation on our part as preparatory to the final action of the General Convention, would be every way desirable.

Or, if there may be ecclesiastically a Union, as there is unquestionably, in doctrine and feeling, a unity of the Church Catholic, which is above all nationalities, the course here suggested, under the peculiar circumstances in which we are placed, will be most likely to lead to its recognition.[5]

The matter was referred to a committee made up of three clergy and two laypersons. The committee submitted a majority report signed by four members and a minority report signed by one clerical member. The majority report repudiated the idea that secession of a state mandated dissolution of the diocese's relationship with the national church, indicated that the call by Polk and Elliott was "premature," and, although it recommended the election of the deputies requested by Polk and Elliott, stipulated that the delegates be instructed to oppose any effort to alter the relationship with the Protestant Episcopal Church in the United States.[6] The minority report called for the election of deputies to the proposed Montgomery meeting and explicitly provided that the representatives be sent without binding instructions. Both reports called for the actions in Montgomery to be submitted to the Texas convention for approval.[7]

After an extended debate the convention elected the delegates on the terms stipulated in the minority report.[8] Ironically, though, a misunderstanding (described below in Gregg's words) prevented their attendance at Montgomery.

Upon my arrival at Austin [on 23 June 1861], a communication was found from Bishops Meade and Atkinson, addressed to the bishops of the Confederate States, suggesting—in view of the addition, at an early day, of other states to the Confederacy—that the proposed convention at Montgomery should meet at some other time and place. It being too late to communicate with the others, and thinking it probable that the change would be made, I forthwith notified our delegates of the fact. Had it been otherwise, the journey to Montgomery would have been attended with heavy expense and great difficulty, in consequence of the blockade.[9]

The elected Texas delegates also failed to attend the adjourned session in Columbia in October, but Bishop Gregg did attend and participated fully in convention deliberations.

At the time of the Polk-Elliott letter in March, the states of Arkansas, North Carolina, Tennessee, and Virginia had not seceded. Given the need for diocesan action before sending deputies to Montgomery, this created logistical problems in those states. Bishop Otey of Tennessee did appoint a clerical deputy, but Otey himself was ill at the time of the Montgomery meeting. The bishop of North Carolina, Thomas Atkinson, and the bishop, William Meade, and assistant bishop, John Johns, of Virginia, wrote the other Southern bishops on 16 May 1861, requesting both a delay of "a month or two" and a change of place to Ashville or Raleigh, North Carolina or Sewanee.[10] Elliot replied that this would not be possible but invited the bishops of those states to attend an adjourned meeting that Elliott felt would be inevitable. Meade replied on 20 June, expressing the hope that the adjourned session would meet at a closer locale than Montgomery. He offered Richmond as the meeting site. At the time of the May request for a delay, North Carolina had not yet seceded from the Union, and its 1861 diocesan convention would not convene until July. Virginia had seceded in April; Bishop Meade wrote the request for a delay when the diocesan convention convened on 16 May. Delegates were elected on a basis such that they could attend any meeting of the Southern dioceses, but Bishop Meade was troubled both by the impact of the war on his diocese and the long journey to Montgomery. His June letter included the paragraph: "I am also now in the midst of scenes and duties which I ought not to forsake for any other. The contending armies are all around me, and in daily expectation of deadly conflicts, and I must not be far distant from those numerous and dear relations, friends, fellow citizens and brethren in Christ, who may suffer and die on the battle fields."[11]

Before secession, Episcopal parishes in Arkansas were part of the Missionary District of the Southwest, which the Right Reverend Henry Champlin Lay served as missionary bishop. After the state of Arkansas seceded in May 1861, Arkansas was in the Confederacy and the remainder of the district was in the United States. On 26 July 1861 Bishop Lay transmitted his resignation as missionary bishop to the presiding bishop of the Protestant Episcopal Church in the United States. He then offered to perform episcopal acts in Arkansas on behalf of the Confederate church.[12]

### A Plea from Bishop Hopkins

Long before the meeting in Montgomery, Bishop John Henry Hopkins of Vermont began pleading and remonstrating with his Southern brethren against taking actions that would destroy the unity of the American Episcopal Church. He wrote Polk immediately upon learning that the Diocese of Louisiana intended to use the secession example set by the state of Louisiana. He also wrote Bishop Meade of Virginia. Both sent courteous and affectionate replies, but neither gave Hopkins any hope. From New Orleans, on 30 April, Polk wrote: "This great city is one military camp, and so is all my Diocese, and the whole South. May God have mercy on us all, for, I fear, vain is the help of man."[13] Meade answered on 10 May: "Had our friends at the North only approached to the just views on the subject in dispute set forth in your late letter, the South would never have convened the work of secession. . . . But the die is cast, and our ecclesiastical and civil union is sundered, and, I fear, never to be restored."[14]

In spite of these discouraging responses, Hopkins composed a letter to "The Right Reverend Bishops of the Protestant Episcopal Church, and to the Clerical and Lay Delegates now Assembled at Montgomery" with the salutation "My Beloved Brethren." The letter was fourteen pages long and included twenty-one numbered points. The bishop had it printed in pamphlet form in New York and sent a package of pamphlets to a clergyman in Louisville, Kentucky, who arranged the delivery to Montgomery, where it arrived before the convention opened.[15]

Hopkins wrote that he understood the issue to be considered at Montgomery was the ecclesiastical relationship of the Southern dioceses to the other dioceses in the United States, given the current crisis in civil affairs. He said that he understood that the delegates considered themselves as citizens of the Confederate States of America and bound with a new allegiance to that government. The question, however, was "Must the Church be divided because the Union is rent asunder?" Hopkins noted that the purpose of his letter was to prove conclusively that the answer was a firm "No." Hopkins's basic premise was that any separation without a godly reason is schism—and hence a sin. He quoted much scripture, including: "I beseech you brethren, by the name of our Lord Jesus Christ, that ye all speak the same thing, and that there be no divisions among you, but that ye be perfectly joined together in the same mind and in the same judgment" (1 Corinthians 1:10, KJV).

Hopkins argued that the separation of the Church of England from Rome during the reformation was not a schismatic act, because the English church rejected the "perilous error and superstition" that had corrupted the Roman church. Under those circumstances separation was, in fact, a duty. The separation of the church in the United States from the Church of England after the Revolution also was not a schism. The Church of England was tied to the throne, and the authority of the church's actions was dependent on government sanction—clearly a situation not acceptable for the church in America. These were the only two cases of separation that Hopkins could justify as nonschismatic.

He then turned to the reasons for separation put forward by Polk and others. His argument was lengthy, but the thrust of every point was that the particular difficulty noted could be resolved within the structure and canons of the church in the United States. To the argument that the Southern dioceses did not belong in the Protestant Episcopal Church in the United States because those dioceses were not within the boundaries of that nation, Hopkins offered a solution:

change the name of the church. He offered the Protestant Episcopal Church in North America or simply the Protestant Episcopal Church. The name of the church, he labeled a "trifling matter," but "the unity of the church was a bond upon us by the authority of our Divine Redeemer." Hopkins also indicated that changes in prayers to name the president of the Confederate States (rather than the president of the United States) reflected "reasonable necessity and good judgment"—and presented no difficulty in a church that remained unified. He urged the delegates to "put away from your minds all thoughts of division, at least until our meeting in the next convention when it may be fairly expected that every change which you may deem necessary in our title, our constitution, our canons, or our Liturgy, will be arranged in a wise accommodation to circumstances."[16] He concluded by reminding his brethren that during the bloody conflicts that accompanied dissolution of the old Roman Empire, the bishops continued to come "together from every land, and hold their councils, and maintained the high and Holy Unity of the Kingdom of Christ."[17]

*Meeting Organization and Solitary Item of Business*

The first day of the Montgomery convention, 3 July, was taken up with receipt of credentials from delegates and organizing for business. The attendance was small, and the bishops and deputies sat as one body rather than dividing into separate houses. The senior bishop present in point of consecration, Stephen Elliott of Georgia, assumed the chair as presiding officer. After appointment of a Committee on Rules of Order, the convention adjourned for the day.

The next morning, 4 July, some thirty participants assembled in St. John's Church for the service of Morning Prayer at 10 o'clock. After services the substantive business of the convention began. The recommendation of the Committee on Rules of Order was accepted. Upon motion, a committee comprising three bishops, three clergymen, and three laymen was appointed to prepare and present for consideration "such subjects as may properly come within the purpose for which this convention has been assembled."[18]

When the convention opened at 9:00 o'clock the next morning, the committee was ready to report. In a preamble the committee report stated that a decision had been made to submit the "single question . . . of forming an Ecclesiastical organization among the Confederate States, independent of the Protestant Episcopal Church in the United States, and to suggest the mode in which this new organization shall be created." There followed a series of resolutions, the first two of which were the following:

> *Resolved*    That the Secession of the States of Virginia, North Carolina, South Carolina, Georgia, Florida, Alabama, Mississippi, Louisiana, Texas, Arkansas, and Tennessee, from the United States, and the formation by them of a new

Government, called the Confederate States of America, renders it necessary and expedient, that the Dioceses of the Protestant Episcopal Church within those States should form among themselves an independent organization.

*Resolved*    That it be recommended to the Ecclesiastical authorities within such States as are now, and as may hereafter become members of the Confederate States, to recommend to their Annual Conventions next ensuing the appointment of four clerical and four lay deputies from each diocese, who, with their respective Bishops, shall meet in Convention, at Columbia, S. C., on the first Wednesday in June 1862, for the purpose of arranging such organization.[19]

There followed a series of other resolutions, all focused on arrangements for an interim period prior to formal separation.

A minority report by three members of the committee was presented, and debate began. There was no disagreement about the first resolution—either in the minority report or from the floor. The crux of the discussion was whether or not the convention should take further action to facilitate the "independent organization" of the Church in the Confederate States. The committee called for deferral of "arranging such organization" until June 1862—almost a year in the future. The report cited the fact that four additional states had joined the Confederacy since the call to convention and that only one representative from the dioceses within those states was represented at this convention.[20] In the opinion of the majority, work on shaping a new church organization should not move forward without full representation from all dioceses. The minority countered that secession of the Southern states had left the Episcopal Church in the Confederacy without any general organization and that prompt action was required. Supporters of this view pointed out that any action by this convention on such an organization would require ratification by the individual dioceses—and hence that the convention would be facilitating progress, not dictating to absent members. The key elements in the new organization would be its constitution and canons, and some deputies wished to proceed as rapidly as possible with preparation and circulation of draft forms of these documents to the constituent dioceses for review.[21]

After considerable debate, a compromise was achieved. The first resolution of the committee was passed unanimously. A second resolution was adopted, namely:

*Resolved*    That as preliminary to the organization declared necessary in the foregoing resolution, a committee of three Bishops, three Presbyters, and three Laymen, be appointed by this Convention to propose and to report to an adjourned meeting of the Convention, to be held in Columbia, S.C. on the third Wednesday of October next, a Constitution and Canons, under which such an organization may be effected: and that the Ecclesiastical Authorities of all the Dioceses within the Confederate States, not now represented in this Convention, be invited by the Right Rev. President of the Convention to take the requisite steps for the representation of said Dioceses at the adjourned Convention.[22]

This outcome was closer to the position taken in the minority report, but it provided the opportunity for all diocesan representatives to meet together to discuss the drafted constitution and canons before forwarding those documents to the dioceses. The two-month hiatus was to be used to draft the documents. The drafting committee was constituted, and the convention had finished its work.

*Adjournment*

Before adjournment Bishop Elliott addressed the assembly: "I cannot but thank God in your behalf and in behalf of the Church, for the complete unanimity which has accompanied the assertion of the necessity and expediency of an independent organization. While we have differed upon some details of time and place, we have not differed at all upon this point."[23]

On 10 July, the *Montgomery Weekly Post* included a front-page article about the convention. The piece reproduced the two major resolutions that had passed, commended the deputies for a job well done, and then concluded: "The first resolution, we learn, passed unanimously and without debate; thus showing that the Episcopal Church in the Confederate States, which, though always a conservative body, nevertheless stands up always to the motto, 'nulla vestigia rotrorsum,' evidently regards the Southern Confederacy a fixed fact, and does not so much as dream of a reconstruction of the old Union."[24]

## Columbia, South Carolina, October 1861

*An Organization Is Proposed*

"I do believe the Holy Scriptures of the Old and New Testaments to be the Word of God and to contain all things necessary to salvation; and I do solemnly engage to conform to the Doctrines and Worship of the Protestant Episcopal Church in the Confederate States of America."[25]

*Council Attendance and Organization*

Bishop Elliott's invitation to participate in the adjourned convention went to all bishops in the eleven Southern states that had seceded, including the assistant bishop of Virginia. Polk's military duty again precluded his attendance, and

Alabama remained without a bishop, but all the others were able to come. Although he had continued to oversee parishes in Arkansas, after submitting his resignation as missionary bishop of the Southwest, Henry C. Lay technically came to Columbia as bishop without portfolio.

Given the war and concomitant travel disruptions, the meeting was remarkably well attended by clerical and lay deputies, as well as by bishops.

**Attendance at the Adjourned Convention of the Protestant Episcopal Church in the Confederate States, Columbia, South Carolina, 1861**

| Diocese | Bishop present | Clerical deputies | Lay deputies |
|---|---|---|---|
| Virginia | Yes–William Meade;<br>Yes–John Johns, assistant bishop | Yes | Yes |
| North Carolina | Yes–Thomas Atkinson | Yes | Yes |
| South Carolina | Yes–Thomas Frederick Davis | Yes | Yes |
| Georgia | Yes–Stephen Elliott | Yes | Yes |
| Florida | Yes–Francis Huger Rutledge | Yes | Yes |
| Alabama | No–No diocesan | Yes | Yes |
| Mississippi | Yes–William Mercer Green | Yes | Yes |
| Louisiana | No–Leonidas Polk in CSA army | Yes | No |
| Texas | Yes–Alexander Gregg | No | No |
| Arkansas (Southwest) | Yes–Henry Champlin Lay | No | No |
| Tennessee | Yes–James Hervey Otey | Yes | No |

*Source: Journal of Proceedings of an Adjourned Convention of Bishops, Clergymen, and Laymen of the Protestant Episcopal Church in the Confederate States of America, held in Columbia, South Carolina, October 1861, 3–5.*

The convention opened in Columbia on 16 October, and after services in Christ Church, Bishop Elliott took the chair to oversee presentation and certification of credentials for the deputies. That matter completed, Bishop Elliott declared the convention organized and called to the chair the Right Reverend William Meade of Virginia, the senior bishop present.

## Adoption of a Constitution

Bishop Elliott then presented to the convention on behalf of the committee elected in Montgomery a constitution proposed for the Protestant Episcopal Church in the Confederate States of America. There were twelve articles, and the document was taken up article by article. The document was similar in many ways to the constitution of the Protestant Episcopal Church in the United States. The two basic changes were simple—replacement of "United States" with

"Confederate States" and "Convention" by "Council." In its final form Article III stipulated the General Council of the Confederate church would meet on the second Wednesday in November, in 1862, in Augusta, Georgia, and "on the same day in every third year thereafter, in such place as to be determined by the Council."[26] Most articles generated little discussion before adoption—but a sharp debate occurred over wording for the very first article.[27]

*Article I. This Church shall be called "*THE PROTESTANT EPISCOPAL CHURCH IN THE CONFEDERATE STATES OF AMERICA.*"*

The Reverend Mr. Hines, clerical deputy from Tennessee, moved that the words *Protestant Episcopal* be struck and replaced by *Reformed Catholic*. Discussion occupied most of the time between 10 A.M. and 1 P.M. on the fourth day of the convention. The motion failed by a substantial margin in all orders when the vote was taken. Three of the ten bishops, Otey of Tennessee, Green of Mississippi, and Atkinson of North Carolina, favored the change. It was then moved simply that the word *Protestant* be struck; this, too, failed by a large margin. Only two bishops, Otey and Green, voted for this amendment.

These attempts at changing the name of the new church reflected a division between the "high-church" party and the "low-church," or evangelical, party in the American Episcopal Church that had existed long before secession—and had nothing to do with the question of forming an organizational structure separate from that of their Northern brethren.[28] The intensity of feeling over the underlying doctrinal issues is clear from the fact that, even under the stress of forming a separate organization in the midst of a civil war, there were attempts to change the name of the church to highlight the high-church position.

Article IV permitted a state that contained more than one diocese, with the consent of all dioceses within the state, to form an "Ecclesiastical Province," and gave rubrics for provincial organization and governance. Any actions by the provincial body affected only the dioceses within the province. The constitution drafted by the Montgomery committee of nine had stipulated a provincial structure that was more sweeping, but the committee's proposal was altered during debate. This article was the only case in which something substantive not found in the constitution of the church in the United States was introduced.

On the eighth day, a copy of the draft constitution, with all changes approved by the convention incorporated, was presented to the convention for final action. The constitution was adopted. The Committee on Constitution and Canons was instructed to circulate for consideration the constitution just adopted for consideration by the dioceses. A call to meeting in Augusta was to be issued after seven dioceses had ratified the constitution. The committee also was to prepare and circulate a draft set of canons that would be acted upon at the Augusta meeting. In the interim it was recommended by the convention to the dioceses in the

Confederate States that the canons of the Protestant Episcopal Church in the United States continue in force, "so far as they are not in conflict with the political relations of the Confederate States, and do not interfere with the necessities of our condition."[29]

## A Request from the Diocese of Alabama

The convention then returned to a petition made earlier by the Alabama delegation. Their diocese had been without a diocesan since Bishop Cobbs's death in January, and the delegation wished to know if a bishop could be consecrated before the diocesan conventions in the Confederate States ratified "any constitution or canons adopted by this convention."[30] This request had been referred on the sixth day to a committee of the three senior bishops present: Meade, Otey, and Elliott. After the constitution was adopted by the convention, the committee made a report beginning with a long and convoluted preamble that concluded: "While, therefore, we propose no change in the doctrine, discipline, and worship of the Church in the organization which has existed among us for eighty years past, we think that no alterations should be made in our forms and offices, further than shall be found indispensable in consequence of the political changes which force them upon us."[31]

The committee then offered its advice to the Diocese of Alabama: "We would therefore advise, that the Diocese of Alabama proceed under such regulations as have heretofore existed and still exist in the Diocese for the election of a Bishop, and as the canons now prepared for the government of the Church in the Confederate States require, to lay the evidences of election before the Standing Committees of the several Dioceses in the Confederate States, which shall be transmitted to the Senior Bishop in the same, who shall take order for the consecration of the Bishop elect according to the usages and canons of the Church."[32] The minutes do not reflect any discussion of or action on this report, but, when the Diocese of Alabama subsequently proceeded in accord with the advice given by the senior bishops, there was not unanimity, even among the three bishops who signed the report.[33]

## Resolution on Duty toward the African Race

The Reverend Dr. Richard Hooker Wilmer of Virginia offered the last resolution to come before the convention: "Resolved That this convention in view of the present circumstances of the country, recognize with peculiar solemnity the duty of the Church towards the people of the African race within our borders, and earnestly urges upon the ministry and laymen of the Church increased effort for the spiritual improvement of this people. Adopted."[34]

## Notes

1. *Proceedings of a Meeting of Bishops, Clergymen, and Laymen, of the Protestant Episcopal Church in the Confederates States, at Montgomery, Alabama on the 3d, 4th, 5th, and 6th of July 1861* (Montgomery: Montgomery, Barrett, Wimbish, 1861), 3–4.

2. *Diocese of South Carolina* (Charleston: A. E. Miller, 1861), 19–20.

3. Ibid., 25.

4. Wilson Gregg, *Alexander Gregg: First Bishop of Texas*, ed. Arthur Noll (Sewanee, Tenn.: University Press, 1912), 73.

5. *Diocese of Texas, 1861* (San Antonio: Herald Job Printing Office, 1861), 29.

6. Neither Tennessee nor North Carolina had seceded from the United States at the time of the 1861 Diocese of Texas convention.

7. Charles Gillette, *A Few Historic Records of the Church in the Diocese of Texas During the Rebellion, together with a Correspondence between the Right Reverend Alexander Gregg, D.D., and the Reverend Charles Gillette* (New York: John A. Gray and Green. 1865), 9–11.

8. *Diocese of Texas, 1861*, 32.

9. *Diocese of Texas, 1862* (Houston: Telegraph Book and Job, 1862), 13.

10. *Proceedings of a Meeting of . . . the Protestant Episcopal Church in the Confederates States*, 27. Meade's letter is included in the appendix.

11. Ibid., 28.

12. Edgar Legare Pennington, "The Organization of the Protestant Episcopal Church in the Confederate States of America," *Historical Magazine of the Protestant Episcopal Church* 17 (December 1948): 308–336, and Henry T. Shanks, "Documents Relating to the Diocese of Arkansas, 1861–1865, and Bishop Henry Lay's Papers," *Historical Magazine of the Protestant Episcopal Church* 8 (March 1939): 67–90.

13. J. H. Hopkins, Jr., *Life of the Late Rt. Reverend John Henry Hopkins, First Bishop of Vermont and Seventh Presiding Bishop* (New York: F. J. Huntington, 1873), 322.

14. Ibid.

15. Ibid., 324.

16. John Henry Hopkins, *A Letter to the Bishops and Delegates Now Assembled at Montgomery* (New York: 1861).

17. Ibid.

18. *Proceedings of a Meeting of . . . the Protestant Episcopal Church in the Confederates States*, 8.

19. Ibid., 11–12.

20. This was the Reverend David Pise, a clerical deputy appointed by Bishop Otey of Tennessee; *Proceedings of a Meeting of . . . the Protestant Episcopal Church in the Confederates States*, 7.

21. Ibid., 12–18.

22. Ibid., 18.

23. Ibid., 21.

24. *Montgomery Weekly Post*, 10 July 1861, 1.

25. *Journal of Proceedings of an Adjourned Convention of Bishops, Clergymen, and Laymen of the Protestant Episcopal Church in the Confederate States of America, held in Columbia, South Carolina, October 1861* (Montgomery: Montgomery Advertiser Job Printing Office, 1861), 14. This declaration is from Article IX of the constitution approved at the Columbia meeting; the article stipulated that any person ordained as deacon or priest must subscribe to that declaration.

26. Ibid., 35.

27. Ibid., 11–19.

28. The "high-church / low-church" issue, the Evangelical Party, the Oxford Movement, and the rise of ritualism all were matters that caused increasing controversy in the Episcopal Church during the nineteenth century, but the divisions that resulted were not along sectional lines.

29. *Journal of Proceedings of an Adjourned Convention* , 40.

30. Ibid., 25.

31. Ibid., 41.

32. Ibid.

33. See the essay entitled "A Controversial Consecration and a Bishop's Death."

34. *Journal of Proceedings of an Adjourned Convention,* 44.

# A Tale of Two Bishops Redux

⟻⟼ *A Friendship Ruptures*

### Polk's Personal Response to Secession and Impending War

Once secession occurred, Bishop Polk of Louisiana, a graduate of the U.S. Military Academy, became greatly concerned about the ability of the Confederacy to maintain control of the part of the Mississippi River that ran through the Southern states. Polk had known Jefferson Davis when both were cadets at West Point, and he proceeded to write President Davis to urge him to supply troops and a commander of stature to strengthen the river defenses. Davis was impressed with Polk's concern, but indicated in his reply that there was no immediate danger to the Mississippi Valley. The Confederate president did, however, request that Bishop Polk come to see him, and Polk obliged. Polk was greatly chagrined when President Davis offered him a commission as brigadier general in the Confederate army, with a command in the West along the Mississippi. Polk's immediate inclination was to refuse, but Davis persisted, and not long after their interview, sent the bishop a letter commissioning him as a major general. Soon afterward a delegation of Memphis citizens called upon Polk, urging him to accept both a commission and an assignment in the West to head a defense force.[1]

Polk agonized over the decision. He sought the opinions of Bishop Meade and Bishop Elliott, although he made clear that he would make the decision. Polk was torn between his belief that taking up arms was not a role for a bishop in the house of God and his growing belief that the offer from President Davis might represent a "call from Providence" to serve a cause that was morally right. The North-versus-South issue to Polk was simple; the Southern states had the right to secede—and the North was invading the South to prevent exercise of that right. He had received military training at public expense, and his immediate duty might be to use that training in defense of the South against unwarranted aggression.[2] On 22 June 1861 he wrote his wife concerning his struggle to decide and the decision that he had reached.

My beloved wife, . . . I told you in my last letter that I had been urgently solicited by many persons of consideration to lend the aid of my influence—my
name and my personal services—to this great cause. . . .

You know that my heart is in it and that I would do anything that was not
*wrong* to serve it; and yet I believe I have a low estimate of my ability, and
should fear to attempt what I could not well execute—supposing all that was
questionable as to the propriety of the matter out of the way. As to the latter
phase of the question, I had a long talk with Bishop Meade. His reply was,
under all circumstances of the case, taking my education, history, and natural
character into the account, he could not *condemn* it. He was not expected to
*advise* it. . . .

I have now had this matter before me a week, and have thought and prayed
over it, and taken counsel of the most judicious of my friends, and I find my
mind unable to say No to this call, for it seems to be a call of Providence. I
shall, therefore, looking to God for his guidance and blessing, say to President
Davis that I will do what I can for my country, our hearth-stones, and our
altars, and he may appoint me to the office he proposed.[3]

He accepted the commission because in his judgment there seemed to be a
niche in defending "country, our hearth-stones, and our altars" that only he could
meet at the moment. He requested a promise from President Davis, however,
that he be released from this duty as soon as a competent replacement could be
secured. He remained bishop of Louisiana, "buckling the sword over the gown"
to do his duty as a soldier.[4] On the same day that he wrote his wife, Polk wrote his
friend Bishop Elliott of Georgia that he would be unable to attend the meeting
in Montgomery, scheduled for 3 July, less than two weeks away.[5] Polk's activity
in and influence on the governance of the Southern church ceased immediately.

The initial reaction, South and North, to Polk's acceptance of a military commission was one of shocked surprise. In the North his action was condemned
by the press, by the clergy, and vehemently by some of by his fellow bishops.
After the initial surprise wore off, some Southern clergy remained dubious and
thought the action inappropriate; others unequivocally supported Polk's decision. His Southern colleagues in the episcopate, however, were not divided. These
men, including those who had originally opposed secession, understood and
accepted his decision to undertake a Confederate command. He entrusted the
episcopal services required by his diocese to Bishops Elliott, Lay, and Otey, all of
whom offered to assist.[6] As the months and years passed, Polk did not regret his
decision, but it pained him when he came to realize both that relief from what
he had hoped to be a temporary leave from his duty as bishop would come only
when the war was over and that the war was going to be a long one. Polk's feelings
come through in a poignant letter written to Elliott in the middle of the war. The

letter was delivered by Charles Todd Quintard, serving as a chaplain attached to Polk's command. "How I should like to be with you!—but I cannot yet. Quintard will tell you how things are with us, and how we long to see you and commune with you and our dear brethren generally; but we cannot yet. And what a relief it would be! Can you not come and see me? My feet are fast in the stocks, and I cannot get to see you! . . . Come and preach for us, and visit us, and administer the communion to us, and confirm our people young and old."[7]

Bishop-General Polk was assigned command of a force charged with defense of the Mississippi River north of Memphis. He served from his appointment in June 1861 until his death in June 1864. During that period, he tendered his resignation twice to President Davis but was told on both occasions that his services could not be spared. Polk's military career will be described below, in "Polk, Lay, and Quintard: The War Up Close and Personal."

### Charles Pettit McIlvaine: Stalwart for the Union

*Christian Duty to the Union*

When the Diocese of Ohio met in convention in June 1861, the Civil War had broken out and Polk was an officer in the Confederate army. McIlvaine used his address to the Ohio convention to lay before the diocese his views on the conflict. Two excerpts from this long, eloquent address are given below. The first is an exhortation to his diocese that makes clear his position on the Union cause. To McIlvaine, the overriding issue clearly was preservation of the Union—and support of the effort to preserve it was the *Christian* duty as well as the civic duty of every member of his flock. The second quotation shows a deep longing for restoration of church unity, but there can be no doubt that his priority was keeping the nation together, regardless of the cost to unity within the church.

> In these times it behooves every conscientious man to have a well-considered and decided answer to the question, What is my duty as a citizen and a Christian towards the constitution and government in the present crisis? . . . Our duty in this emergency is steadily, bravely, earnestly to sustain our government and its administration, in the use of all lawful means to preserve the integrity of the Union.
>
> We do not look upon the present unhappy contest as one chosen by the government. We believe that it has been forced upon the government. . . . The question that takes precedence now over all others is, Shall we preserve the government as now established? But not only *that*; but shall we have any social compact in which the name of government can with any propriety be given; or shall we submit to principles and measures which in their logical results and practical tendencies are essentially lawless and anarchical? A more momentous crisis never came upon a nation's counsels. Questions of mere

policy are unspeakably inferior. The greatest, deepest, most conscientious and sacred interests of the social state are involved.[8]

There are those with whom I never differed before; with whom I have been identified many, many years in all those common labors for the Gospel, and those affectionate sympathies of Christian brethren, which bind the heart so tenderly and yet so strongly. They are on the other side in this conflict. They see right, where I can see nothing but wrong. They see grievous sin, where I see only solemn duty. The gulf between us in this respect is wide indeed. I love them nevertheless, and with undiminished affection as most dear brethren in Christ, with whom I hope to have my inheritance forever in the common kingdom of our Lord and savior, and between whom and all with whom they stand, and us, I long and pray that peace, honorable and full of blessings to both, may soon be established.[9]

### The Unofficial Commission

McIlvaine's words reflect a strong commitment to the Union cause, and soon after his address to the Ohio convention in June 1861, he was confronted with an opportunity for action that caused him to reflect on where his duty lay. He was asked by President Lincoln in the presence of Secretary of State William H. Seward and Secretary of the Treasury Salmon P. Chase to undertake a mission on behalf of the United States government; the mission was to help prevent England from giving diplomatic recognition to the Confederate States and from entering the war on the side of the Confederacy.[10] The assignment required that the bishop go to England, where he would attempt to influence public opinion to see the rightness of the Union cause. His mission was not official in that he was not to be a member of the diplomatic corps or to have any powers, special or otherwise, to negotiate on behalf of the United States, but this was nonetheless an activity in support of the United States in the Civil War—undertaken on behalf and at the behest of the federal government. He would not be bearing arms, but he would be buckling an emissary's wartime commission over his bishop's gown in the same sense that his estranged colleague Polk had buckled the sword over the vestments of his episcopacy. Two questions troubled McIlvaine. First, was this an appropriate role for a Right Reverend Father of God? Second, in that this would be a long mission, was it proper to neglect his diocese to serve his country? His thinking on these questions was reflected in his addresses and letters.

There is no such thing as being neutral in this controversy unless we would live in a land over which the constitution of the United States claims no authority. There is no middle ground between loyalty to its government and disloyalty. Rightfully the supreme law over all the states, every inhabitant must choose in regard to it the one side or the other. And that choice is not a mere political or secular question. It involves the most sacred consideration of con-science and of religious duty, as well as the most important interests of the social state.[11]

McIlvaine refers here to a simple choice of commitment to the Union, but the words *most sacred consideration of conscience and of religious duty* stand out, suggesting that if he were asked to help his country he would feel that it was his *religious* duty to do so. Evidence that is more direct is found in the following ex-cerpt from a letter in which he reflected on the government's request: "My great doubts have been as to the aspect of secularity it may wear. But it strikes people, to my surprise as just what, as a Bp., I should do for the country. I do not want to go abroad when our dear land mourns—nor to meet foreigners when our faces are bowed down & them often so different from what they have been towards us. But if I *can* serve the country I will go."[12] In these remarks Bishop McIlvaine acknowledges with pleasure that both his assistant bishop and many clergy in his diocese felt strongly that he should accept this challenge, which these colleagues felt could be of paramount importance to the war effort. He thought carefully about the decision, but in his mind the cause of the Union and his Christian duty were bound together.

McIlvaine accepted and became part of what was known as the "Unofficial Commission." His role was to explain and advocate the cause of the Union before those affiliated with the Church of England. Other members were Archbishop John Hughes of the Roman Catholic Archdiocese of New York and Thurlow Weed, New York newspaper owner and political figure. Archbishop Hughes was a Roman Catholic prelate well known on the continent of Europe as well as in New York, where he had overseen the planning and building of St. Patrick's Cathedral. He was to be an unofficial spokesman and use his influence in Ro-man Catholic France and in Italy and perhaps in other countries as the mission developed. Weed was to focus on press relations, in both England and France, and on the political leadership in England.[13] The commission members sailed in November, but McIlvaine left later than the other two; he arrived in England on 7 December 1861.[14] Bishop McIlvaine did not undertake any task, be it delivering a sermon or establishing a schedule of Episcopal visits, without careful prepara-tion, and when he accepted his commission, he no doubt started work immedi-ately on his methodology and message.

## McIlvaine's Methodology

Although he was an American cleric, Charles Pettit McIlvaine was well known and respected by many in the Anglican Church for his writings and his promi-nence as a leader in the evangelical wing of the Episcopal Church.[15] He also was known personally by many in the Anglican Church, having visited England a number of times. His first two trips were in the 1830s, both for reasons of health. Twenty years later he had become celebrated in England, and, while on a visit in 1853, he was awarded an honorary degree by Oxford University. Cambridge conferred on him the LL.D. degree in December 1858. He always enjoyed being in England, which was his favorite place in which to restore his health when it broke down.[16]

McIlvaine's personality, his social graces, his status in England, and his commitment to the Union cause made him an ideal choice for this assignment. He decided that his chief approach would be talking—and listening—at both formal and informal gatherings and sometimes one-on-one after church or at dinner parties. He planned to visit clergy and lay leaders, getting their views on the conflict in America and to include when appropriate summaries of their concerns in his reports that would be read by Secretaries Chase and Seward and President Lincoln. Bishop McIlvaine hoped to be invited to preach and to meet with church leaders and ranking government officials. Although he would welcome the chance to attend functions at which attendance was by invitation only, he would decline to make speeches at public meetings because he wished to avoid the appearance of a propaganda tour.[17] Finally, McIlvaine decided to bring with him two of his daughters, Nain (Margaret), who was thirty years old, and Anna, who was nineteen.[18] Both were poised young women who were capable of holding their own in society—and in political argument. They proved to be great assets to his mission.[19]

### McIlvaine's Message

Britain had outlawed slavery earlier, and, on that point, the English public favored the Union side in the American Civil War; this was an advantage that McIlvaine intended to press. There were, however, commercial interests in England that depended upon importation of Southern cotton, and a long blockade of Southern ports might prove detrimental to those interests. There was some sentiment in England, in fact, that the North should simply let the South go in peace, avoiding bloodshed and the inconvenience of a blockade. Of these considerations, however, slavery was the more important, especially to the clergy and laypeople in the Anglican Church with whom McIlvaine would be interacting. A difficulty was that at this stage of the war the stated objective of the North was solely to preserve the Union; there was no commitment to the abolishment of slavery. This stance attenuated the moral advantage of the North in the English public eye. Nevertheless, the Union position retained a moral edge over that espoused by those who encouraged England to side with the Confederacy, which was committed explicitly to the perpetuation of slavery. Getting the British public, at least the middle and upper class church-going people whom he would seek to influence, to see that the cause of the North was just and on moral high ground, therefore, was to be McIlvaine's focus.[20] He would use the argument that without preservation of the Union there certainly could be no emancipation. The bishop would also express his personal belief that, once the secession crisis was over, a united country would find a way to free the slaves.

## The *Trent* Incident

After the Unofficial Commission was appointed—but before McIlvaine reached England—what became known as the Trent Affair injected a sense of urgency into the work assigned to McIlvaine and his fellow commissioner Weed. On 8 November 1861 a United States sloop, the *San Jacinto,* under the command of a Captain Wilkes, was in the Florida Channel off the coast prepared to take action against privateers. The *San Jacinto* stopped an English steamer by firing a shot across its bow. The English vessel, the packet ship *Trent,* was boarded, and two Confederate agents, James Murray Mason, formerly a U.S. senator from Virginia, and John Slidell, formerly a U.S. senator from Louisiana, both bound for England, were removed and put aboard the *San Jacinto* as prisoners. The news of the story first broke in the United States when the *San Jacinto* stopped at Fortress Monroe on 15 November, and newspapers began carrying the story the next day.[21] The *San Jacinto* continued on to Boston harbor, where Mason and Slidell were incarcerated at Fort Warren. Initial reaction in the Union States was that Captain Wilkes was a hero. Secretary of the Navy Gideon Wells sent him a letter of commendation; he was honored at a banquet in Boston; and he was lauded in newspaper accounts of the incident.[22] The theme of these accolades seemed to be that he had used initiative to prevent Confederate envoys from reaching England—which more than compensated for the fact that he was acting without orders to board a British ship.

When the *Trent* and news about the incident reached England on 27 November, the reaction was quite different. An American vessel had dared to violate a British ship with a boarding party. The British flag had been insulted. Anger in England intensified when American newspapers arrived that featured articles reflecting a "widespread rejoicing and glorification [of Captain Wilkes' action] in the Northern press."[23] A groundswell of opinion favoring entering the war on the side of the South began to build.[24] The British government channeled its anger into serious preparation for war, calling up thousands of naval reservists and sending eight thousand soldiers to Canada.[25]

McIlvaine learned of the outrage brewing in England on 6 December, when English newspapers were brought aboard his steamship at Queenstown.[26] By the time he disembarked the next day, he was therefore aware that his initial focus would have to be to try to help defuse the rising war sentiment. Even before setting foot on land, McIlvaine wrote Chase expressing confidence that the United States would concede if there were "valid grounds" for "remonstrance" by England. In the meantime McIlvaine would "arm" himself as best he could regarding international practice governing seizure at sea.[27]

After studying the newspapers on Saturday, 7 December, McIlvaine devoted Sunday and Monday to assessing the mood in England. On Sunday he and his daughters gathered information by attending three church services, hearing three sermons, and having informal conversations at each church after the service. He reported in a letter to his brother that "all [three sermons] were in a good, moderate, and very Christian spirit, especially the last two. I heard that every pulpit in the land was speaking on the same theme that day."[28]

McIlvaine also did not detect a desire to rush to war in after-church conversations but rather a fervent hope that the crisis could be resolved. On Monday he "began to go about, to hear, and learn, and feel." He spoke at length with Charles Francis Adams, the U.S. minister. He spoke as well with Thurlow Weed and some businessmen.[29] Assessing these conversations and the newspaper coverage, McIlvaine reached a conclusion—barely two days after his arrival—that releasing the Confederate envoys Mason and Slidell was prerequisite to any progress in calming English public opinion and then swaying that opinion to the Union side. In fact, freeing the envoys promptly was critical to avoiding a British declaration of war. In a letter to his brother on 10 December, he reported: "The Mason and Sidell affair is now so engrossing, that secession and all its connections, except as assisted by *that* [affair], are little discussed. . . . Lord Shaftesbury in answer to my remark that I had found the country in a great excitement, said: '*Not excitement.*' He did not see *that*. It was a deep, determined, unanimous feeling. He had never seen anything to be compared with it in that respect. The feeling in the Crimean War was nothing like it. Then there was some differences of view; here, none."[30] McIlvaine therefore advised the Lincoln Administration that the two prisoners simply had to be released—or else war most certainly would come and come soon. War, he noted, would bring the British people together in support of their government; the clergy and their congregations did not want war, but if their leaders determined that a peaceful resolution were not possible, they would unanimously be behind their government. Preparations for war, McIlvaine warned his government, already were underway.[31] Weed also advised Washington that the captives should be given up. Minister Adams had sent a similar message earlier and was pleased that the unofficial commissioners concurred.

Soon after becoming aware of the action of Captain Wilkes, the British government had delivered a sharp note to the United States government. Anger mounted in England while the United States considered a response. A formal demand was certain to come, and it appeared to McIlvaine that war was a real possibility if the British terms were not met. The bishop was not optimistic concerning a two-front war; "the Confederates will get all they want; their ports will be opened; their government acknowledged; the secession consummated; our navy crushed; our towns in danger; probably division of our forces; Washington taken; our commerce destroyed; we humiliated—for how can we contend with a power such as England, while taxing all our energies another way."[32]

McIlvaine, though, was quick to add: "But God reigns, and I pray—and thousands and thousands pray here—that war may not come."[33] Having sent his government his recommendation, McIlvaine turned his attention to the original concept of the mission, but with a message adapted to the circumstances created by the *Trent* incident. As soon as it became known that he was in England, he was invited to fill pulpits and attend a variety of functions. He preached by invitation "nearly every Sunday" which gave church members a chance to make a judgment about him and gave him a chance afterwards to listen to their thoughts and to talk one-on-one or in small groups about the North's position in the Civil War.[34] Throughout December, McIlvaine also attended receptions and dinners at which he emphasized that the United States did not want war with England and had meant no disrespect to the British flag.[35] He also explained that Captain Wilkes was not acting under U.S. government orders when he took the envoys into custody. He was received cordially and his explanations were respected, but he knew that release of Mason and Slidell remained the only real solution. Just before Christmas he wrote his assistant bishop, Gregory T. Bedell, who had episcopal authority in Ohio while the bishop was away. In this long letter McIlvaine recounted his experiences since arriving in England and repeated his key message sent earlier to the government in Washington. "They look on the Trent matter as an insult to their flag. . . . I do hope that our Govt. will not suffer any mistaken national honour nor any rising of unwise pride, or offense to prevent the *righting* of relations which have been so seriously endangered; . . . if there be no surrender of the prisoners then war *will be declared*."[36]

Events culminated when Lord Richard Bickerton Lyons, the British ambassador, delivered to Secretary Seward a formal communication advising the secretary that unless the envoys were released by 31 December, seven days from the date of the note, Lyons would be withdrawn by his government. Withdrawal of an ambassador was the step that immediately preceded a declaration of war. The British government also placed an embargo on several boatloads of saltpeter from India, an act which would soon force a drastic cut in production of munitions by the DuPont Company. Lincoln and his cabinet met on 24 and 25 December, and, prudently but reluctantly, agreed to the English demand. Lyons was notified by Seward that Captain Wilkes had acted independently and that Mason and Slidell would be "cheerfully released." Lyons arranged to have the envoys put aboard a British steamer at Fort Warren on 1 January 1862.[37]

McIlvaine was greatly relieved when he learned that the United States had agreed to the British demand. The bishop attended a large gathering of clergy that was held shortly after that news was received, along with the information that Mason and Slidell were on their way to England aboard a British ship. McIlvaine sent to the federal government a positive report of this gathering, indicating that there was a great sense of relief among those present that further escalation had been avoided—and that the feelings toward the North were ones of kindness and gratitude. There was no sense of jubilation that England had forced the United States to back down. Although the crisis was over, there were many in England with sympathy for the position of the South, and McIlvaine felt that he was still needed and that it now was possible to make headway in his original mission.[38]

### The Mission Post-*Trent*

The bishop continued to receive requests to preach, and he and his daughters continued their whirlwind round of attendance at receptions, dinner parties, and private meetings during January, February, and March. His sermons were attended by members of the upper and middle classes, with a preponderance of the latter. Those who came to the various functions generally were clergy, nobility, and other people prominent in ecclesiastical or governmental affairs. On 16 January he preached under the great dome at St. Paul's Cathedral in London which had been designed by Christopher Wren.[39] The bishop of London, however, was not friendly to the Union, and McIlvaine remarked, "I must try and do something with him."[40] Just over a week after making this observation, McIlvaine reported to his wife that the bishop of London, the bishop of Carlisle, and he had met to have "some effective talk about our matters."[41] The duke and duchess of Argyll invited the McIlvaines to a dinner at which many "notable persons" were present, giving the bishop a forum to discuss his views. He was warned that a debate in Parliament would ensue over whether or not England should lend support to the South, but was told also that those at the dinner felt that no action would be taken. McIlvaine listed among his contacts Sir William Heathcote, Lady Gainsborough, Lord Raleigh, the bishop of Winchester, Mr. Kinnaird (member of the House of Commons), and three cabinet members (not named).[42]

Most of the people who came to the functions attended by McIlvaine and his daughters were predisposed to favor the position of the North, but they benefited from McIlvaine's explanations when they discussed the issues with others. There were people invited, however, whose views were contrary to those of McIlvaine, and occasionally lively (sometimes heated) exchanges occurred. McIlvaine wrote his wife about such a meeting. As a preamble, he provided a stereotype of the kind of person who irritated him.

> I meet with . . . so many with whom, as a deep dyed American, it is most annoying to meet, and talk, and see their ignorance, and half concealed superciliousness, and cold selfishness under profession of a wonderful zeal to

see us proclaim instant abolition of slavery as the price of their sympathy with us. . . .

We had a great meeting last Friday night week at Mr. Kinnaird's to "ventilate" American affairs. Two drawing rooms were filled. . . . I carried the war unto the enemy's country and charged horse and foot. I was up. My spirit was provoked and I administered a dose. . . . Mr. Kinnaird cried *hear—hear.* He is most zealously with us. When it was over a clergyman, Mr. Winton, came over to me and said, "*I am wholly with you.*" I turned to the most "fractious" of the others, a clergyman named Gemiay [sp?] and said, "Are you not satisfied now?" He answered, "That was just what I wanted to hear."[43]

Lord Shaftesbury had told McIlvaine on 10 December that there was at the time no real need of Southern cotton because English manufacturers had "glutted" the markets, and, further, that England could wait until a supply could come from elsewhere. He advised the bishop that there were sixty thousand bales waiting in Calcutta to be bought when needed. Hence McIlvaine should not worry about pressure building for the blockade to be broken by British ships.[44] On 13 February, however, McIlvaine wrote to Bishop Bedell: "There is a desperate effort working here and will be in Parliament to get this Government to break the blockade or acknowledge the independence of the Confederate States but the Ministry is considered sure against it and Mr. Russell says privately, *it will not be done.* That means *now,* as things are. In other words *we will wait.*"[45]

After a speech in Parliament in the middle of March by Sir Roundel Palmer, which was favorable to the Union, McIlvaine felt that the issue of blockade-busting and intervention on the side of the South generally had been put to rest, barring any dramatic downturn in the fortune of Union arms.[46] Furthermore, McIlvaine knew that his assignment was scheduled to end by June, and he was exhausted from his practice of "unofficial diplomacy." In April he began a six-week tour of the continent to rest and restore his strength. He returned to England briefly and by 19 June his ship, the steamer *Glasgow,* was in the Port of New York.[47]

## Evaluation of the Mission

The Unofficial Commission was conceived and McIlvaine and Weed appointed to it for the broad purpose of helping to sway public opinion in England regarding the Civil War away from the South and toward the Union. The *Trent* incident occurred after the commission members were appointed and was not part of the motivation to establish the commission. When McIlvaine stepped ashore at Liverpool, however, the uproar over the seizure of Mason and Slidell was in full cry, and he and fellow commissioner Weed immediately refocused their energy to deal with that crisis. The result was probably the most significant impact of the commission: helping the Lincoln administration decide that preventing the Confederate envoys from reaching England—and upholding national pride— was not worth risking war with England, which would entail immediate hos- tile action by the British Navy and the end of the blockade of Southern ports. Britain no doubt also "helped" the U.S. government reach that decision when she signaled her intention to withdraw her ambassador, and there were certainly advisors to the president and his cabinet in Washington who urged release of the emissaries. The advice of the U.S. ambassador in England, and the two com- mission members, however, to release the envoys had to have carried special weight—Adams, McIlvaine, and Weed were on site, Adams with a feel for the pulse of the English government and McIlvaine and Weed with a feel for the pulse of the English people. In particular, McIlvaine and Weed (1) had been appointed specifically to assess and influence English public opinion; (2) formulated their recommendations based on firsthand knowledge of the English reaction to cap- ture of the envoys; and (3) made their recommendations to Washington before the United States government reached a decision.

Books written about the *Trent* Affair often either omit the Unofficial Commis- sion or give little weight to its role.[48] This treatment of the work of the commis- sion in general and McIlvaine, in particular, is unfortunate and inaccurate. After the Trent affair was concluded, McIlvaine remained in England until April 1862 to do the work for which the Unofficial Commission was originally appointed.[49] To what degree he was successful in that endeavor cannot be measured quantita- tively, but there is significant testimony that McIlvaine's work was of importance in building trust and good will among the English public. Secretaries Seward and Chase went on record that the two commission members in England deserved some of the credit for that country's course.[50] The archbishop of Canterbury, John Sumner, and Charles Francis Adams, United States minister to England, both felt that McIlvaine's efforts were of great value in promoting good relations between the two countries.[51] It seems fair to conclude that this grassroots ap- proach to influencing British opinion was, in fact, a success. It is difficult to deter- mine, however, if the efforts by McIlvaine and Weed after the *Trent* Affair was resolved greatly influenced the decision of the British government to keep out of the American civil conflict.[52] Other factors, such as the success of the Union army at key points and the Emancipation Proclamation certainly were more important as the war progressed, but the work of the commission may have had a role in blunting interventionist activity before those factors came into play.

McIlvaine was not overly optimistic when he accepted the assignment, and his personal evaluation was that he accomplished more than he had expected. The bishop saw his mission not as that of a lobbyist but as part of his Christian duty, an attitude that must have enhanced his effectiveness among the people with whom he interacted.[53]

## Back in the United States, June–September 1862

After his return from England, McIlvaine went first to Washington to report to the president, Secretary Seward, and Secretary Chase.[54] He got to Ohio in time to attend only the final day of the three-day June 1862 diocesan convention, but he received a hearty welcome from Assistant Bishop Bedell and the clerical and lay delegates assembled. The following resolution was adopted when the senior bishop took the chair on Friday morning: "That we welcome with great feelings of satisfaction the return among us of our beloved senior bishop: and that in consideration of interests affecting Church and Country which he left us to subserve, we have been well content to forego for the time the pleasure and benefit of his presence and labors among us."[55]

McIlvaine attributed his effectiveness on the mission to the goodness of God and the kindness of the English people. He read the letter that accompanied the set of episcopal vestments given to him by English clergy as a parting gift. He chaired the morning and afternoon sessions, but the assistant bishop presided at the final session that evening. Bishop Bedell had opened the convention and had presided over the major business sessions. That he was proud of McIlvaine and shared his diocesan's views was evident in Bedell's address to the convention.

> In a war for national existence, between loyalty and rebellion, Christianity should be a synonym for patriotism. Loyalty to Christ is loyalty to that civil authority which Christ, as head over all things to the church, has established for us. When, moreover, that loyalty is demanded by the most perfect of human governments, and that rebellion is the most unjustified outbreak of sinful prejudice and passion, the spirit of the gospel should find duty to be consonant with public law, and the maintenance, at every hazard, of those national rights, and safeguards and privileges which we have inherited with our constitutional liberty.
>
> The duty of Christian people at such a crisis is unwavering devotion to the government, outspeaking loyalty, unhesitating obedience, unshrinking self-sacrifice, a consecration of time, means and life, limited only by the necessity; and a determination that no effort shall be spared, under the blessing of God, to vindicate constitutional law.[56]

In mid-September, McIlvaine visited the battlefield in the aftermath of Antietam and saw General George B. McClellan briefly.[57] The sights on this visit very likely had an impact on his actions at the October 1862 triennial convention of the national church, where his influence resulted in the taking of a controversial pro-Union position on the Civil War by the Protestant Episcopal Church in the United States. Shortly after Antietam, on 22 September 1862, President Lincoln issued the Preliminary Emancipation Proclamation, which decreed that all slaves in states in rebellion against the United States government as of 1 January 1863 would be forever free. For a foreign power, supporting the South now meant supporting slavery, and for Great Britain, which had abolished slavery in 1834, such support would not be tenable.

## Irreconcilable Differences

Thus when secession and war came, the two bishops McIlvaine and Polk made dramatic but very different decisions about their Christian duty. Their choices put them not just on separate paths, but truly on opposite sides of a gulf that widened as each moved forward. The actions of McIlvaine and Polk on their respective pathways were forceful, and, while their colleagues in the episcopacy trod with one or the other on the Northern or Southern side of the gulf, McIlvaine was at the most aggressive end of the spectrum on his side, as was Polk on the other side. At issue was the matter of Christian duty in the crisis at hand, and their friendship was broken. McIlvaine soon would strongly condemn his protégé's actions.[58]

### Notes

1. Joseph H. Parks, *General Leonidas Polk, C.S.A.: The Fighting Bishop* (Baton Rouge: Louisiana State University Press, 1962), 165.

2. William Mecklenburg Polk, *Leonidas Polk, Bishop and General*, 2 vols. (New York: Longmans, Green, 1893), 1:322–23.

3. Ibid.

4. In his biography of his father, William Mecklenburg Polk relates an incident that occurred soon after Leonidas Polk accepted a commission as major general: "A friend exclaimed to the Bishop: 'What! you, a bishop, throw off the gown for the sword!' No sir, was the instant reply, 'I buckle the sword over the gown'" (*Leonidas Polk, Bishop and General*, 1:326).

5. Ibid., 327.

6. Ibid., 327–33.

7. Polk to Elliott, 4 May 1863, reproduced in W. M. Polk, *Leonidas Polk, Bishop and General*, 1:328.

8. *Diocese of Ohio, 1861* (Columbus: Richard Nevins, 1861), 20–22.

9. Ibid., 23–24.

10. Although this mission was under Seward's portfolio, Secretary Chase was an influential member of the cabinet and a strong advocate of Bishop McIlvaine for membership on the commission. Mr. Chase, a nephew of Philander Chase who had preceded McIlvaine as bishop of Ohio, and Bishop McIlvaine had been friends for many years, having come to know and respect each other during their years together in Ohio, during which Chase served a term in the U.S. Senate and two terms as governor. Chase was involved in negotiations concerning the length of and remuneration arrangements for McIlvaine's mission. Chase and McIlvaine communicated throughout the mission. Concerning the mission, see Loren Dale Pugh, "Bishop Charles Pettit McIlvaine: The Faithful Evangel"

(Ph.D. diss., Duke University, 1985), 114. Pugh quotes from a letter (available at the Kenyon College Library Archives) written by McIlvaine to his son-in-law, George W. DuBois, dated 31 October 1861, which indicates that the four men (Lincoln, Seward, Chase, and McIlvaine) met together.

11. *Diocese of Ohio, 1861,* 20.

12. Charles P. McIlvaine to George W. DuBois, 10 November 1861, McIlvaine Personal Correspondence, Kenyon College Library.

13. Jay H. Schmidt, "Mission to Europe, 1861–1862," *Michigan Alumnus Quarterly Review* 62 (August 1956): 311–16.

14. Ann Heathcote Stevens, "The Unofficial Commission to England in 1861" (M.A. thesis, Occidental College, 1937), 58.

15. Two of McIlvaine's published works known in England were *Evidences of Christianity* and *Oxford Divinity.*

16. William Carus, ed., *Memorials of the Right Reverend Charles Pettit McIlvaine,* 2nd edition (London: E. Stock, 1882), 45, 102, 146, 185.

17. Stevens, "Unofficial Commission to England," 65.

18· Carus, *Memorials of McIlvaine,* 131.

19. Kara M. McClurken, "Charles Pettit McIlvaine and the Civil War: The Public Crusades of an Evangelical Episcopal Bishop" (Honors thesis, Kenyon College, 1999), 36–37.

20. Pugh, "McIlvaine: Faithful Evangel," 112–14.

21. A series of articles in the *Washington Star* concerning the Trent Affair, including the initial story that ran on Saturday, 16 November 1861, may be found at http://www.civil warhome.com/washstartrent.htm (accessed 15 February 2009). These articles were not as gloating in tone concerning the capture as were those in many other papers.

22. Jay H. Schmidt, "The *Trent* Affair," *Civil War Times Illustrated* 1 (January 1963): 11.

23. Ephraim Douglas Adams, *Great Britain and the American Civil War,* 2 vols. (New York: Russell and Russell, 1924), 1:205.

24. For a detailed treatment of the *Trent* incident, see Norman B. Ferris, *The Trent Affair: A Diplomatic Crisis* (Knoxville: University of Tennessee Press, 1977), or Theodore Roscoe, *The Trent Affair, November 1861: U.S. Detainment of a British Ship Nearly Brings War with England* (New York: Franklin Watts, 1972).

25. Schmidt, "*Trent* Affair," 11.

26. McIlvaine did not sail until 23 November and was at sea when news of the incident reached England. The story was still breaking when he arrived at Liverpool. See McClurken, "Charles Pettit McIlvaine and the Civil War," 38–39.

27. McIlvaine to Chase, 6 December 1861, McIlvaine Personal Correspondence, Kenyon College Library. McIlvaine did devote time to study of maritime law and concluded, as did Thurlow Weed and ambassador to England Charles Adams, that the United States could not justify the seizure of Mason and Slidell. The bishop's reasoning was delineated in a long letter dated 30 December 1861 to Bishop Bedell, which may be found in Stevens, "Unofficial Commission to England," 107–13. Although there were arguments on both sides, which were expressed strongly in newspapers in England and in the United States, it was clear that the action of Captain Wilkes violated the position on the rights of neutrals at sea that the United States had previously defended.

28. Charles P. McIlvaine to Bowes R. McIlvaine, 10 December 1861, reproduced in Carus, *Memorials of McIlvaine,* 221–25.

29. Weed and Hughes had stopped in England in late November but had then gone to Paris. Weed had returned to England as the *Trent* brouhaha began to unfold. John Hassard, *Life of the Most Reverend John Hughes, First Archbishop of New York* (New York: Appleton, 1866), 455–62, provides a series of letters written by Archbishop Hughes in Paris during the period 28 November–10 December 1861. Hughes noted in a 10 December letter to Weed (who was in London) that he was lonely now that Weed had departed.

30. Charles P. McIlvaine to Bowes R. McIlvaine, 10 December 1861, reproduced in Carus, *Memorials of McIlvaine,* 221–25.

31. Stevens, "Unofficial Commission to England," 60–62.

32. Charles P. McIlvaine to Bowes R. McIlvaine, 10 December 1861, reproduced in Carus, *Memorials of McIlvaine,* 221–25.

33. Ibid.

34. Stevens, "Unofficial Commission to England," 58–60.

35. Carus, *Memorials of McIlvaine,* 226.

36. McIlvaine to Bedell, 23 December 1861. A complete copy of this letter is included in Stevens, "Unofficial Commission to England," 107—13.

37. Schmidt, "*Trent* Affair," 13.

38. Stevens, "Unofficial Commission to England," 62–63.

39. Charles P. McIlvaine to Mrs. G. W. DuBois (his daughter), 5 January 1862, McIlvaine Personal Correspondence, Kenyon College Library.

40. Charles P. McIlvaine to Bowes R. McIlvaine, 5 February 1862, quoted in Carus, *Memorials of McIlvaine,* 228–29.

41. Charles P. McIlvaine to Emily McIlvaine (his wife), 13 February 1862, McIlvaine Personal Correspondence, Kenyon College Library.

42. During this period between resolution of the *Trent* Affair and his sojourn on the continent, McIlvaine wrote several letters to his brother Bowes Reed McIlvaine, which may be found in Carus, *Memorials of McIlvaine.* Letters to other family members during the same period are in McIlvaine's personal correspondence at Kenyon College Library. These letters describe interactions with many members of the nobility and with civil and ecclesiastical leaders.

43. Charles P. McIlvaine to Emily McIlvaine, 13 February 1862, McIlvaine Personal Correspondence, Kenyon College Library.

44. Charles P. McIlvaine to Bowes R. McIlvaine, 10 December 1861, reproduced in Carus, *Memorials of McIlvaine,* 221–25.

45. Charles P. McIlvaine to Gregory T. Bedell, 13 February 1862, quoted in Stevens, "Unofficial Commission to England," 74.

46. Charles P. McIlvaine to Bowes R. McIlvaine, 14 March 1862, quoted in Carus, *Memorials of McIlvaine,* 230. McIlvaine told his brother that Weed attended the Parliament session when Sir Roundell gave his address and that members of Parliament advised Weed afterwards about the chance of intervention to open the blockade by saying: "It is all dead."

47. Charles P. McIlvaine to (son-in-law) George Washington DuBois, 18 June 1862, McIlvaine Personal Correspondence, Kenyon College Library.

48. See Ferris, *Trent Affair*; Roscoe, *Trent Affair, November 1861*; Gordon H. Warren, *Fountain of Our Discontent* (Boston: Northeastern University Press, 1981); and Hassard, *Life of the Most Reverend John Hughes* as examples.

49. Pugh, "McIlvaine: Faithful Evangel," 120–21.

50. Stevens, "Unofficial Commission to England," 77, 87.

51. Pugh, "McIlvaine: Faithful Evangel," 120. See also Henry Brooks Adams to Frederick William Steward, 30 January 1862, reproduced in *The Letters of Henry Adams,* ed. J. C. Levenson, 6 vols. (Cambridge: Belknap Press of Harvard University Press, 1982), 1:274–75.

52. Thurlow Weed's work with British newspapers is described in Glyndon G. Van Deusen, *Thurlow Weed, Wizard of the Lobby* (Boston: Little, Brown, 1947). Reading Van Deusen's book also shows that Weed and McIlvaine cultivated some of the same influential people. A more detailed but unconventionally organized account of Weed's activity during the mission period can be found in Harriet A. Weed, *Autobiography of Thurlow Weed,* 2 vols. (Boston: Houghton, Mifflin, 1883). Hassard, *Life of the Most Reverend John Hughes,* describes the work of Hughes on the continent, including his interview with the French emperor.

53. Carus, *Memorials of McIlvaine,* 234–36. These pages comprise a note written to his friend Carus in August 1862, in which McIlvaine penned his thoughts about the success of the mission.

54. Charles P. McIlvaine to (son-in-law) George Washington DuBois, 18 June 1862, McIlvaine Personal Correspondence, Kenyon College Library. A note on this letter indicates that the bishop had to go at once to Washington to report on his mission to England.

55. *Diocese of Ohio, 1862* (Columbus: Richard Nevins, 1862), 64.

56. "Address by Bishop Bedell," *Diocese of Ohio, 1862,* 20.

57. George B. McClellan to Charles P. McIlvaine, 18 November 1862, McIlvaine Personal Correspondence, Kenyon College Library.

58. That McIlvaine still regarded Polk as a brother in Christ may be inferred from his 1861 address to the Diocese of Ohio, from which excerpts are quoted above under the subhead "Christian Duty to the Union," but the earthly friendship broke apart when the secession crisis broke apart the country. For McIlvaine's condemnation of Polk's actions, see the essay below entitled "Assembly under Most Afflicting Circumstances."

# A Controversial Consecration
# and a Bishop's Death

✢ *Richard Hooker Wilmer and William Meade*

## The Alabama Consecration

The Diocese of Alabama had been without a diocesan since Bishop Cobbs died in January 1861. In November of that year the diocese began the process of seeking a new leader in accord with the advice given by the three senior bishops present at the council of Episcopal dioceses in the Confederate States that had met in Columbia the month prior.[1] The first step was to hold an election. Richard Hooker Wilmer, then serving as rector of Emmanuel, a country parish in his native Virginia, was chosen by the diocese.[2] Since his ordination to the priesthood in 1840, Wilmer had served several churches in Virginia as well as a parish in Wilmington, North Carolina. He had been educated at Yale University and Virginia Theological Seminary and recently had been awarded the degree of Doctor of Divinity by the College of William and Mary.[3] Wilmer also had served as a lay deputy from Virginia at the 1859 triennial convention of the Protestant Episcopal Church in the United States of America (PECUSA) in Richmond.[4]

A majority of the standing committees in other dioceses in Confederate states gave their consent to his nomination. In anticipation of a prompt consecration, Wilmer resigned as rector at Emmanuel Church effective 31 December 1861.[5] When the senior bishop, William Meade, "took order" for the consecration, however, there was opposition.

Bishop Thomas Atkinson of North Carolina, a friend and supporter of Wilmer, was invited to participate in the consecration ceremony, but Atkinson declined. He took the position that proper provision for consecration of a bishop under the Protestant Episcopal Church in the Confederate States of America (PECCSA) did not yet exist. Consecration, he argued, should await not only the formal ratification by the dioceses of the constitution for the Confederate church but also the adoption of canons at the scheduled November 1862 general council of PECCSA. He offered the following explanation.

Wilmer has expressed to me the wish that I should act, as one of his consecrators, a duty which I would gladly perform, both because of our long-standing friendship, and because of my high estimate of his qualifications for the office about to be conferred on him. But as the canons of the Church in the United States are not to be followed, and as the Church in the Confederate States has adopted no canons, I see no law or rule by which he is to be consecrated, and I must therefore decline to take part in what seems to me an irregular transaction. If there were a necessity for its being done at present, that necessity might in the place of law, but I see no such necessity, as canons can and will be passed at our meeting, and the Diocese might in the meantime be served by neighboring Bishops. I must therefore reluctantly request not to be named as one of his consecrators.[6]

Bishop James Hervey Otey of Tennessee, next in seniority after Meade among the Southern bishops, also declined to participate in the ceremony, writing that he lacked the funds to journey to Richmond. His lack of money and his failing health no doubt influenced his decision, but Otey clearly was not comfortable with Meade's choice to proceed with this consecration, which was evident in March 1862 when Otey gave his consent to the consecration of William Bacon Stevens as assistant bishop of Pennsylvania. By giving consent to the Stevens consecration, Otey was taking the stance that until PECCSA was in place, with the Diocese of Tennessee as a member, he was still a bishop in PECUSA and would act under its rubrics. Giving consent to Stevens's consecration in Pennsylvania, therefore, was proper.[7] The same chain of reasoning led to the conclusion that Otey's participation in the consecration of Wilmer would have constituted a canonical violation, because PECCSA was not yet established, and, his own diocese had not approved the PECCSA constitution.[8]

Bishop Atkinson followed his refusal to participate in the Wilmer consecration by also giving consent to the Stevens consecration on the grounds that until the Diocese of North Carolina was a member diocese in PECCSA, he, Atkinson, was still a bishop of PECUSA.[9] Other Southern bishops, however, felt that circumstances necessitated the prompt institution of a bishop for Alabama and that the consent of bishops or standing committees in the Confederate States was the only requirement that needed to be met.[10]

Meade's health was fragile, and John Johns, assistant bishop of Virginia, had hoped to spare the Confederate States' senior bishop the effort of participating in the actual service. The most promising location for assembling the canonical number of bishops had appeared to be Richmond, but now, with Otey and Atkinson unwilling to come and Davis unable to participate, Johns reluctantly communicated to Meade in a letter written 12 January 1862 that Meade's presence was needed. Meade immediately assented, and arrangements were made for the consecration and for his travel from Millwood to Richmond. The consecration of Richard Hooker Wilmer was scheduled for 6 March 1862, with Meade, Elliott, and Johns as the consecrators.[11]

The *Richmond Daily Dispatch* reported on the service.

St. Paul's was filled yesterday by a large audience, on the occasion of the consecration of the Rev. Richard Wilmer, D.D., to the Episcopate of Alabama. The Bishops present and officiating were Bishops Meade and Johns of Virginia, and Bishop Elliott of Georgia. The sermon, an able and eloquent one, was preached by Bishop Johns. The solemnity of the time hallowed services, the impressiveness of those august words in which, for so many centuries, the servants of Christ have been commissioned to go forth and disciple all nations, and the peculiar respect and affection universally entertained for the Bishop elect, made this consecration a scene long to be remembered. . . . Bishop Wilmer carries with him to Alabama the heartfelt love of all Virginia.[12]

Richard Hooker Wilmer departed immediately to begin his episcopate in Alabama.[13] He was the only bishop consecrated by the church in the Confederate States.

## Death of the Senior Confederate Bishop

As March 1862 began, Meade was "laboring under a deep-seated cold" and had hoped to remain until his condition improved at his beloved Millwood home in the valley at the western base of the Blue Ridge Mountains. When he learned, however, that his presence was essential if the consecration of Wilmer on 6 March was to proceed, he packed a "single change of raiment" and departed for Richmond. The journey in inclement weather exacerbated his condition, weakening him further, leaving him able, but just barely, to be present at the service.[14]

At the consecration in St. Paul's Church, Meade participated, in Bishop Johns's words, "only when his presence could no longer be dispensed with." Meade had struggled slowly up the aisle to his seat in the chancel, and, when it came time for the act of consecration, Elliott and Johns helped him to stand, supporting him while the three of them performed the imposition of hands, "whilst that voice, once of so much sweetness and compass, now tremulous and broken, enunciated with difficulty the apostolic commission—whose heart was not saddened by the spectacle?"[15]

A reporter for the *Richmond Daily Dispatch* wrote that Meade "was then in such feeble health that he could with difficulty get through that portion of the services which fell to his lot. It was evident that while the consecrating hands of the Presiding Bishop in this country were laid on the head of a new leader of the Christian host, the consecrating hands of the Angel of Death were descending upon his own white locks, and preparing them to receive that crown of glory

The Right Reverend William Meade, D.D.

which is the reward of him who is faithful to the end."[16] The consecration was Bishop Meade's last official act, and he did not attempt to return to Millwood after the event. He went instead to the home of Mr. J. L. Bacon, a friend in Richmond, where he spent the last eight days of his life, watched over by his grandson William and by Bishop Johns and other clergy. One of his visitors was General Robert E. Lee, whose catechism Meade had heard many years prior.[17] At one point Meade advised one of his diocesan clergy: "Speak boldly to your people. Tell them to persevere in sustaining their country in this struggle. The war against us is iniquitous. I am persuaded that God is with us and will give us success."[18]

Bishop Johns was at his bedside when Meade died. In his funeral sermon Johns told his listeners: "If the gift which I covet for you and myself, 'a double portion of his spirit,' depended on the condition named to Elisha—that blessing would be ours—for I witnessed his departure, and cried from my heart: 'My Father! My Father! The chariot of Israel, and the horsemen thereof!'"[19] Bishop

Meade's funeral was held on 17 March at St. Paul's, and Johns's sermon included a special message from Meade. Near the end Meade had asked to speak alone with his assistant bishop, at which time he gave Johns his final testimony for the church in Virginia. Johns wrote down the spoken words and then went over the text with Meade. The man on whom Meade's mantle had devolved then delivered that testimony as part of the funeral sermon.

> The views of evangelical truth and order, which I have advocated for fifty years, I approve and exhort my brethren, North and South, to promote more than ever. My course in civil affairs I also approve; resistance to secession at first, till circumstances made it unavoidable. I trust the South will persevere in separation.
>
> I believe there are thousands in the North who condemn the course of their administration towards us, and in time will express themselves openly.
>
> The prospect of rest from sin and suffering is attractive, though I am willing to remain and take my part in the labor and trials which may be before us.
>
> My hope is in Christ, the "Rock of Ages." I have no fear of death, and this is not from my courage but from my faith.
>
> The present seems a proper time for my departure. I am at peace with God through Jesus Christ my Lord, and in charity with all men, even our bitterest enemies.
>
> All that has been said in commendation of me, I loathe and abhor, as utterly inconsistent with my consciousness of sin.
>
> I commend you and all my brethren to the tender mercies of Christ, and pray for his blessing on the Church in Virginia.[20]

After having communicated these words of his predecessor, Johns said simply: "The message is duly delivered. The weighty words of the wise leader—his legacy of love—are with you."[21]

By the time of his funeral, Meade's homestead and the surrounding valley had been overrun by Union forces and transportation and communication in that part of Virginia disrupted, but the bishop was spared that knowledge. Bishop Meade was laid to rest in Hollywood Cemetery in Richmond.[22] In 1876, when the Virginia Theological Seminary established a cemetery, his remains were translated to that site.

### Notes

1. See above, "A Separate Church for a Separate Nation," for the election and consecration rubrics advised by the senior bishops.

2. Bishop Cobbs had expressed his wish to be succeeded by Henry C. Lay, who had been consecrated following the Richmond convention in 1859 as missionary bishop for Arkansas and the Southwest. Lay's name was presented and, though strongly supported

by some, he was not nominated. Had he been chosen, he could simply have been translated to the Diocese of Alabama. Wilmer's biographer Walter C. Whitaker felt that the manner of Lay's actions while assisting Bishop Cobbs had offended some Alabama clergy and derailed Lay's election prospects. See Walter C. Whitaker, *History of the Protestant Episcopal Church in Alabama, 1763–1891* (Birmingham: Roberts and Son, 1898), 155–57. See also Stephen E. Row, *Emmanuel Church—Brook Hill, 1860–1985: A Parish History* (Richmond: Emmanuel Church History Committee, 1988), 10–14.

3. William Stevens Perry, *The Episcopate in America* (New York: Christian Literature Company, 1895), 155.

4. Walter C. Whitaker, *Richard Hooker Wilmer, Second Bishop of Alabama* (Philadelphia: George W. Jacobs, 1907), 80–81.

5. Row, *Emmanuel Church,* 14.

6. Marcus Benjamin, *The Consecration of Bishop Wilmer of Alabama in 1862* (Philadelphia: Church Historical Society, 1927), 3.

7. William Mercer Green, *Memoir of Rt. Rev. James Hervey Otey, D,D,, LL.D., First Bishop of Tennessee* (New York: J. Pott, 1885), 100–101. In these pages of the memoir Green provides entries from Otey's diary regarding (1) his decision to decline to participate in the Wilmer consecration and (2) a conversation between Otey and Green regarding Otey's consent for the Stevens consecration. Green felt that, with the consent "viewed as a legal or canonical question," Otey "was clearly in the right."

8. The Diocese of Tennessee met in 1861 but did not meet during the war years, so that the diocese never ratified the PECCSA constitution, and Otey technically was never a bishop of the Confederate church.

9. An analysis of the canonical issues surrounding the Wilmer consecration may be found in John Fulton, "The Church in the Confederate States," in William Stevens Perry, *The History of the American Episcopal Church,* vol. 2 (Boston: Osgood, 1885), 571–72. The report of the three senior bishops in October 1861 was ambiguous at best, in that it did not state explicitly that Meade should proceed before the PECCSA canons were adopted. Fulton believed that the Columbia convention did not modify the report out of deference to Meade, who was thought to be the author.

10. Regardless of the arguments within the Southern dioceses, most Northern bishops viewed the "Alabama consecration" as irregular and noncanonical, in that they did not recognize the validity of separation of any dioceses from PECUSA.

11. The 12 January 1862 letter from Johns to Meade is reproduced in Benjamin, *Consecration of Bishop Wilmer,* 3.

12. "Consecration of Dr. Wilmer," *Richmond Dispatch,* 7 March 1862, 2.

13. Whitaker, *Richard Hooker Wilmer,* 91–96; Fulton, "Church in the Confederate States," 561.

14. John Johns, *Sermon on the Occasion of the Funeral of the Rt. Rev. William Meade, March 17, 1862* (Baltimore: Entz and Bash, 1862), 8–10.

15. Ibid., 9.

16. *Richmond Daily Dispatch,* 15 March 1862, 2.

17. Philip Slaughter, *Memoir of the Life of the Right Reverend William Meade* (Cambridge: John Wilson and Son, 1885), 44. Six weeks after his visit to Meade, following the

Battle of Seven Pines, Lee was given command of what became the Army of Northern Virginia.

18. Johns, *Sermon on the Occasion of the Funeral of Meade*, 12.

19. Ibid., 14.

20. Ibid., 12.

21. Ibid., 13.

22. Meade actually left explicit instructions regarding the site of his burial. He stipulated the burying ground in Hanover if he were to die east of the mountains. If he were to die west of the mountains, then he was to be interred in the old graveyard in Clarke. Given the conditions in wartime Virginia, the family opted for a temporary repose in Hollywood Cemetery, with the intent to rebury the bishop later in Hanover. For whatever reason, the second step did not occur, and Meade's remains joined those of Bishop Johns and Bishop Payne at the cemetery at Virginia Theological Seminary. See Johns, *Sermon on the Occasion of the Funeral of Meade*, 5.

# Assembly under Most Afflicting Circumstances

*≁≋ The Northern Bishops in General Convention in 1862*

### Attendance and General Business

The General Convention of the Protestant Episcopal Church in the United States assembled at St. John's Chapel in New York City on 1 October 1862. The Right Reverend John Henry Hopkins, Bishop of Vermont, acted as presiding bishop in the absence of Presiding Bishop Thomas Church Brownell, who was absent due to extended illness. The Right Reverend Samuel Allen McCoskry, bishop of Michigan preached at the service that opened the convention. McCoskry acknowledged with sorrow the rebellion and the division of the church, but he eschewed exploration of political causes. He spoke instead of the absence of the name of Jesus in "National Councils" and decried the "pride and vain boasting" that characterized the nation instead of a true religious belief. The *New York Times* reported that McCoskry administered a "severe rebuke to the irreverence of the times, and the tendency displayed by too many ministers of the Gospel to convert the pulpit into a political rostrum."[1]

By the second day twenty-three bishops were present, but no bishop or deputy, clergy or lay, attended from a diocese in a seceded state.[2] The secretary of the convention called the roll, including the Southern dioceses, a clear signal that the Northern states did not recognize a separation. There were matters of ongoing business conducted at the convention, including the adoption of twelve new canons, the rejection of fifteen other proposed canons, and the referral of six proposed canons to the next triennial convention.

This was an era of missionary work, at home and abroad, and the House of Bishops received reports from the following missionary bishops: Thomas Fielding Scott, Oregon and the Washington Territory; Joseph Talbot, Northwest; John Payne, Cape Palmas and Parts Adjacent (West Africa); and William J. Boone, at Shanghai (Bishop Boone also reported briefly on missionary work in Japan).[3] No report was received from Henry C. Lay for the Southwest, however. Bishop Lay had resigned his affiliation with the Episcopal Church in the United States.[4]

The House of Bishops passed a resolution introduced by William Bacon Stevens, assistant bishop of Pennsylvania, that called for a committee of three bishops to "consider and report upon the subject of the best manner of calling out more fully and incorporating more formally in the working economy of the Protestant Episcopal Church, the services of women whose hearts God has moved to devote themselves to works of piety and charity; that said report be made to this House at the next Triennial Convention."[5] The chair appointed Stevens, Bishop William Rollinson Whittingham of Maryland, and Bishop Horatio Potter of New York.[6]

### A Special Service

Although the bishops and deputies attended to these and other matters, the war and the action in progress by the Southern dioceses to form a separate organization were the two topics uppermost in the minds of everyone in both houses. A special committee was named in the House of Bishops "relating to the present state of the Country." On the third day Bishop Cicero S. Hawks reported for that committee: "The House of Bishops in consideration of the present afflicted condition of the Country, propose to devote Wednesday, the 8th day of October, instant, as a day of fasting, humiliation, and prayer, and to hold in Trinity Church a solemn service appropriate for the occasion."[7]

The bishops adopted this proposal and "affectionately requested" the House of Clerical and Lay Deputies to join them in the observance. The five senior bishops were given the task of making arrangements for the service. The service was one of Morning Prayer, and its tone is embodied in the following excerpts from a special confession and a prayer that followed the General Thanksgiving.

> We, thine unworthy servants, desire most humbly to confess before thee, in this time of sore afflictions in our land, how deeply as a nation, we deserve thy wrath. . . . We beseech thee so to sanctify unto us our present distresses, and so to make haste to deliver us, that war shall be no more in all our borders, and that all opposition to the lawful government of the land shall utterly cease. May our brethren who seek the dismemberment of our National Union, under which this people by thy Providence have been so signally prospered and blessed, be convinced of their error and restored to a better mind. Grant that all bitterness, and wrath, and anger, and malice, may be put away from them and us and that brotherly love and fellowship may be established among us to all generations.[8]

Another prayer beseeched God to guide those who led the nation and to protect and bring success to those who bore arms for the United States.[9]

There was no mention of slavery in the service. President Lincoln had issued his Preliminary Emancipation Proclamation nine days before the convention opened, which stipulated that all slaves would be free within those states (or parts of states) in rebellion against the United States as of 1 January 1863. This action and the abolishment of slavery in the District of Columbia were steps that suggested that slavery's days in the United States were limited, but the Lincoln administration was not yet formally committed to complete abolition.[10] The issue was complex and plagued by uncertainty; should a state "in rebellion" have abrogated its act of secession before 1 January 1863 and returned to the Union, the slaves in that state would not have been freed by the proclamation. The bishops planning the special service chose not to confront the question of slavery.

### The Pastoral Letter

The most serious controversy in the House of Bishops erupted over the pastoral letter that it was customary for the House of Bishops to distribute to all dioceses at the close of a convention. The task of preparing the letter was referred to the five senior bishops, who were, in order of consecration seniority, Hopkins of Vermont, Smith of Kentucky, McIlvaine of Ohio, Kemper of Wisconsin, and McCoskry of Michigan. Bishop Potter of New York introduced a long resolution, replete with five *whereas* clauses before the "*Therefore be it resolved*" resolution statement, the burden of which was that the church was concerned with matters spiritual, not secular, and that all matters not purely ecclesiastical and spiritual be excluded from the pastoral letter.[11] This motion was tabled upon motion of Bishop Alfred Lee of Delaware, and Bishop Henry W. Lee of Iowa immediately submitted the following resolution: "Resolved: That in the preparation of the Pastoral Letter the five senior bishops be requested to introduce the subject of the sinfulness of the present rebellion against the constituted authorities of the United States, and also to express the deep regret of this House that any diocese of this church has attempted a separation from the same during the existing civil difficulties."[12] On motion of Bishop Whittingham of Maryland, this resolution was laid on the table. The five senior bishops were free to do their work, unencumbered by directions from the house.

At the first meeting of the committee, Bishop Hopkins determined that no other member had prepared anything and proceeded to read a draft that he had written.[13] Hopkins took notes on the suggestions for changes, and at the next meeting the modified draft was approved, on motion by Bishop McIlvaine, for submission to the House of Bishops. Nothing political was in the draft, but Bishop Hopkins called for allegiance to the Union, anchoring his call to the mandatory allegiance to the "powers that be" delineated by St. Paul. Hopkins began his draft by noting that the pastoral letter was being issued while a national tragedy was unfolding:

Your Bishops are called on to issue a pastoral Address, under very mournful and depressing circumstances. Our Country, so lately flourishing in prosperity and peace, lies bleeding under the terrible affliction of the bitterest national warfare. Thousands upon thousands have fallen upon the field of battle, and no one can estimate the desolated homes, the broken hearts, the misery of the widows and orphans, the poverty and the wretchedness, the woes and the agonies, which have marked this awful conflict.[14]

Hopkins felt that the pastoral letter should not address the worldly or "secular" causes of the conflict, which were not the concern of the body of Christ. "Of the political questions which have been, in the eyes of the world, the instrumental causes of this mournful conflict, your Bishops have no wish to enter. . . . We address you as the chief officers of the Kingdom of Christ, which is not of this world . . . Leaving therefore the secular aspects of this awful war to statesmen and politicians, to whom they may properly belong."

Instead, the bishops should recognize and condemn the human conduct that had caused God to punish the nation by permitting war.

We confine ourselves to the religious character of our natural afflictions, and proceed to place before you the primary cause to which, according to the principles of our sacred faith, we are compelled to ascribe the distracted condition of our Country. . . .

Bribery in our elections, bribery in our legislatures, bribery in Congress itself; frauds in public contracts, falsehoods and deceits for party purposes, the rapidly increasing recklessness of human life, and the fearful growth of youthful licentiousness,—all concur to prove our mournful degeneracy. Alas! rebellion against the government of God has been at work for years in our once-favored Country, and we have no reason to wonder that it has at length brought down upon us the judgment of his righteous indignation.

Hopkins's draft explicitly stated that Christians owed loyalty to the government under which they were placed and risked incurring the wrath of God by resisting that government: "The doctrine of the Church proclaims complete and unswerving allegiance, first, to the divine Redeemer who has all power in heaven and in earth, and secondly, to the government under which his Providence has placed us. . . . 'Let every soul be subject to the higher powers, for there is no power but of God: the powers that be are ordained of God. Whosoever, therefore, resisteth the power, resisteth the ordinance of God, and they that resist shall receive to themselves damnation.'"[15]

Hopkins's draft, in accord with his position that the immediate secular causes of the civil conflict were not in the purview of the church, cautioned against bringing the subject of war to the pulpit. The letter concluded with the thought that God's favor, not military might, would bring peace to the clergy. "You cannot, reverend brethren, maintain your proper influence over your flocks, by descending from your high and sacred position as the ministers of Christ, in order to gratify the political feeling of the day, or by lowering the spiritual dignity of the sacred desk, under any pretext, to the level of a secular platform; . . . let no earthly strife . . . draw you away from the great warfare against sin, the world, and the devil. . . . Happy if we remember that fleets and armies can be no effectual substitute for the favor of the Lord of Hosts. . . . He alone can preserve our Country in the enjoyment of peace and unity."

Later, but before Hopkins's letter was transmitted, McIlvaine had second thoughts about its suitability. The bishop of Ohio requested in writing that the committee reconvene. Hopkins obliged by calling the committee together, and McIlvaine then said that it was his conviction that the current draft was inadequate in the present crisis. He read a letter that he had drafted. The approach and tone of his draft were very different from that of the Hopkins document. McIlvaine opened his draft letter by bemoaning the fact of rebellion and the role of Southern churchmen therein.

> We have been assembled together in the Triennial Convention of our Church under most afflicting circumstances. . . . We look in vain for the occupants of seats in the Convention, belonging to no less than ten of our dioceses, and to ten of our bishops. And whence such painful and injurious absence? The cause stands as a great cloud of darkness before us, . . . concentrated in a stupendous rebellion . . . for the dismemberment of our national Union— . . . . We are deeply grieved to think how many of our brethren, clergy and laity, in the region over which that dark tide has spread, have been carried away by its flood, . . . to a sad extent, sympathizing with the movement, and giving it their active co-operation.[16]

McIlvaine's harshest words were in a peroration directed at his protégé Polk:

> When the ordained Ministers of the Gospel of Christ, whose mission is so emphatically one of peace and good will, of tenderness and consolation, do so depart from their sacred calling as to take the sword and engage in the fierce and bloody conflicts of war; when in so doing they are fighting against authorities which, as the "powers that be," the scriptures declare are "ordained of God," . . . when especially one comes out from the exalted duties of an Overseer [bishop] of the flock of Christ, to exercise high command in such awful work,—we cannot, as Overseers ourselves of the same flock, consistently with duty to Christ's Church, His Ministry, and people, refrain from placing on such example our strong condemnation. We remember the words of our

blessed Lord, uttered among his last words, and for the special admonition of his ministers—"They that take the sword shall perish with the sword."[17]

At this point Bishop McIlvaine took pains explicitly to separate God and men as agents of cause for the calamity that gripped the nation. McIlvaine saw the hand of God at work in using the war to punish the country for its sins.

> Just as the personal affliction of any of you is God's visitation to turn him from world and sin, unto Himself; so is this national calamity most certainly His judgment upon this nation. . . . Marvelously have we been prospered in everything pertaining to national prosperity, riches, and strength. God has loaded us with benefits; and with our benefits have grown our ingratitude, our self-dependence, and self-sufficiency, our pride, our vain-glorying. . . .
>
> Dear brethren, can we consider these things, so palpable to every eye, and not acknowledge that we deserve God's anger, and need, for our good, His chastening Providence?[18]

McIlvaine then returned to the agency of man in causing the war, a theme implicit in his opening remarks. He noted that silence on the war was not an option, and that the bishops felt compelled to speak in this time of national crisis. He equated rebellion with sin and equated support of the Union with the cause of Christ.

> Ever since the Church had her Litany, we have been praying for deliverance from "sedition, privy conspiracy, and rebellion." And now that all the three are upon us, and in a depth of scheme, a force of action, a strength of purpose, and an extensiveness of sway such as the world never saw before united for the dismemberment of any government, shall we refuse to tell you in what light we regard that gigantic evil? . . .
>
> What say the Scriptures touching the subject before us? We have no need to go beyond the words of St. Paul, in the thirteenth chapter of the Epistle to the Romans—"Let every Soul be subject to the higher powers. For there is no power but of God. The powers that be are ordained of God. Whosoever, therefore, resisteth the power, resisteth the ordinance of God; and they that resist shall receive to themselves damnation."
>
> . . . Where, then, do we find those powers and ordinances to which . . . we . . . are bound, for His sake, to be subject? We answer, IN THE CONSTITUTION AND GOVERNMENT OF THE UNITED STATES.[19]

McIlvaine went on to proclaim that refusal of allegiance to the government of the United States was a sin and that rebellion was a great crime before the laws of God as well as of man. He then made clear that God's kingdom should be the primary concern of his flock and that emotions in the crisis at hand should not divert members of the church from God's commands.

> Let not the love of Country make your love to God and your gracious Savior the less fervent. Immense as is this present earthly interest, it is only earthly. The infinitely greater [interests] of the soul and of the kingdom of God remain as paramount as ever; . . . watch and pray lest during this unhappy strife you should allow any bitterness of spirit to dwell in you toward those who . . . have brought on this war, with its great injuries and calamities. . . . To hate rebellion, so uncaused, is duty; but to hate those engaged therein, is the opposite of Christian duty.[20]

In the discussion that followed, Hopkins argued for a majority recommendation and a minority report, but McIlvaine objected to that approach. Hopkins left the meeting, not wishing to "push his own draft." McIlvaine remained. The result was a tie vote, with McIlvaine and Smith for the McIlvaine letter, and Kemper and McCoskry for the Hopkins letter. Having no choice, the committee brought forward to the House of Bishops both letters with a brief explanation: "The committee to whom was referred the preparation of a pastoral letter to be presented for the consideration of the House, beg leave to say that they have not fully agreed as to the two letters read before them. They would therefore present them both for the action of the House."[21]

After both documents were presented, Bishop Whittingham of Maryland moved that, after any alterations resulting from suggestions from the floor, the second (McIlvaine) letter "be the Pastoral Letter of the House to the members of the Church."[22] Many bishops were silent during the voice vote, but the motion passed.[23] The next day Bishop Hopkins read a letter to the House of Bishops in which he entered his "solemn protest against the political aspect of the pastoral letter that had been adopted" and gave notice that he would not participate in its dissemination to the public. He gave the following explanation that was based on his view that the letter flagrantly violated the principle of separation of church and state.

> This action, in my judgment, involves a fundamental principle in our ecclesiastical position. We stand opposed, in this country, to any union between church and state. In our individual capacity, as citizens, we are bound by the plain precepts of the inspired apostles, to bear true allegiance to "the powers that be"—the earthly government under which the providence of God has placed us. For that, our system sets forth an ample arrangement, in the homily against rebellion, in the catechism appointed for the instruction of youth, in the lessons of the scripture, in our Litany, and in the prayers for the president

and congress, to say nothing of the special supplications set forth for the present national troubles, all uniting in the most positive testimony to the duty of Christian loyalty. But beyond this, I cannot allow that this House of Bishops, assembled in our official relations to the church of God, has a right to go, by expressing any judgment on the measures of secular government. Under the American Constitution, the State has no right to declare its sentence on the legislation of the Church, so long as we do nothing to impair this duty of loyalty. And, under our apostolic constitution, the Church has no right to utter her sentence upon the legislation of the State, so long as it forebears to assail our Christian liberty. The respective functions are distinct. The almighty ruler of the world has committed to the State the wide sphere of temporal interests, and He has committed to the Church the far higher sphere which embraces the interests of eternity. Each has its own allotted orbit, and I cannot comprehend how any reflecting and intelligent man in our Communion should desire that these orbits, in the present condition of mankind, should come together.[24]

He then explained how this separation of church and state applied to him.

I desire to say that I yield to no man in my loyalty as a citizen, in my attachment to the Federal Union of the states, or in my deep sorrow that any event should have occurred by which that Union could be endangered or destroyed. But my duty as a citizen is one thing, and my duty as a Bishop is another. By the first, I hold a relation to the State, under the laws and the Constitution. By the second, I hold, however unworthy, a high office in the kingdom of Christ, which is not of this world.

Bishop Hopkins concluded by acknowledging that his position on the pastoral letter reflected his beliefs concerning where his duty lay and noted that he respected the "conscientious sincerity" of brethren who differed with him. His withdrawal from participation in the pastoral letter was with "the kindliest feelings of fraternal affection towards all my colleagues without exception."[25] Hopkins asked that his protest be entered in the minutes, but the bishops adopted a motion that stipulated that it be filed "among the documents of the House."[26] It was also resolved that Bishop McIlvaine be appointed to sign the pastoral letter. The pastoral letter was read at the convention in place of a sermon. The presiding bishop's chair, which Hopkins occupied at the convention, was vacant. When it came time for the Eucharist, however, the acting presiding bishop emerged to assist with its celebration.[27]

This controversy did not end with the convention. In some churches the pastoral letter was not read. In others the date on which it was to be read was published, "so that all who did not want to hear it would stay away." In other cases the letter read was the rejected draft by Bishop Hopkins, which Hopkins had released to the newspapers. In the *New York Times,* the protest letter was printed along with an explanation from the *Church Journal,* written by John Henry Hopkins Jr.[28] The sequence of events by which the pastoral letter emerged was presented factually, but young Hopkins praised Bishop Horatio Potter for attempting to get the House of Bishops to proscribe a political tone or political messages.[29] In referring to the two letters, he contended: "But the real and only difference between the two, was, that the Bishop of Ohio's letter was a political manifesto, and the Bishop of Vermont's was not."[30]

The church-and-state issue was further exacerbated when McIlvaine sent a copy of the official pastoral letter to his friends in the cabinet, Treasury Secretary Salmon Chase and Secretary of State William H. Seward, and the latter's reply appeared in newspapers.[31] In his response Seward informed McIlvaine that the pastoral letter had been submitted to President Lincoln, who then authorized Seward to assure the bishop that he, the president, "receives with the most grateful satisfaction the evidences which that calm, candid and earnest paper gives to the loyalty of the very extended religious communion over which you preside to the Constitution and Government of the United States. I am further instructed to say, that the exposition which the highest ecclesiastical authority of that Communion has given in the Pastoral Letter of the intimate connection which exists between fervent patriotism and true Christianity, seems to the President equally seasonable and unanswerable."[32]

Both McIlvaine and Hopkins believed that Christian citizens were bound, by the words of St. Paul, to be loyal to the United States government, but McIlvaine also felt that the Episcopal Church was obligated to support openly the war to restore the Union and to condemn the rebellion explicitly. Hopkins felt that the latter actions were appropriate for statesmen and for church members as citizens but were inappropriate actions to be taken by the church. The difference between the loyalty to the state that Hopkins supported and the public advocacy of the Union cause that McIlvaine urged was not mere hair-splitting. Hopkins was a literalist, believing that the church should not go beyond the exact words of either the relevant Bible passages or the authorized prayers. McIlvaine felt that those biblical words and the prayers justified a strong pro-Union stance for the Episcopal Church in the extant national crisis.

Both bishops felt that God was using the war as punishment of the country for sin. Hopkins was categorical that political preaching was to be shunned; McIlvaine did not address this matter in his draft of a pastoral letter but on other occasions did advise his clergy not to bring the war to the pulpit.[33] McIlvaine was careful to distinguish between hating rebellion (which was appropriate) and hating those who rebelled (which was un-Christian). Both men, as well as all their Northern colleagues in the episcopate, wished to see an early triumph of

Union arms, with the United States again united. The Northern bishops also were unanimous in their belief that the Southern dioceses should not have separated from the American church.

Neither Hopkins nor McIlvaine mentioned slavery in his draft of a pastoral letter, even though slavery and slavery-related disagreements were the root cause of the Civil War. Its steps had been deliberate and incremental, but by October 1862 the Lincoln government was out in front of the Episcopal Church, North as well as South, on the issue of slavery.[34] As we shall see in later discussion, individual bishops in the North soon began to confront the slavery issue openly, but consideration by the bishops in assembly did not come until the postwar 1865 General Convention, by which time slavery had ended in the former Confederate states, and the resultant action was oblique, divided, and timid. Again, Hopkins and McIlvaine were on opposite sides.

### In Conclusion

The positions held by the Episcopal bishops in the states that remained in the Union during the Civil War on the major issues facing the United States at the outset of that great conflict are reflected in the discussions and actions recorded at the 1862 triennial convention of the Protestant Episcopal Church in the United States. It is clear from conference records that the bishops present did not feel that the church in the South should have separated from PECUSA. Although there was controversy over the pastoral letter written by McIlvaine (based on the church-and-state issue), most Northern bishops no doubt shared his disappointment over the apparent concurrence of their Southern colleagues in the decision by the states in the South to secede and agreed with him that Polk's action in taking up arms was wrong.

In the prayers written for the special service held to seek divine relief from "the present afflicted condition of the Country," there were explicit calls for the success of Union arms and for those seeking to dismember the Union to cease and desist. There was, however, no mention of slavery in the special service and none in the pastoral letter. Slavery was a civil issue that did not belong on the floor of a church convention.

### Notes

1. *New York Times,* 18 October 1862, 2.

2. *Journal of the General Convention, 1862* (Boston: E. P. Dutton, 1863), 17, 111, and day by day attendance changes listed throughout the convention journal.

3. Ibid., 236–53.

4. Ibid., 119, 135–36.

5. Ibid., 142.

6. The committee was unable to report in 1865 and was granted leave to report in 1868.

7. *Journal of the General Convention, 1862,* 116.

8. Ibid., 349.

9. Ibid., 350.

10. "The District of Columbia Emancipation Act." http://www.archives.gov/exhibits/featured_documents/dc_emancipation_act/. (Accessed 13 January 2013).

11. *Journal of the General Convention, 1862,* 140–41.

12. Ibid., 141.

13. Hopkins, J. H., Jr. *The Life of the Late Right Reverend John Henry Hopkins, First Bishop of Vermont and Seventh Presiding Bishop by One of His Sons* (New York: F. J. Huntington, 1873). The descriptions of proceedings within the committee of the five bishops are based upon accounts given by J. H. Hopkins, Jr.

14. John Henry Hopkins, *The Bishop of Vermont's Protest, and Draft of A Pastoral Letter* (N.p.: 1862). This excerpt, and the following four, are from the draft of the pastoral letter.

15. Epistle to the Romans 13: 1–2 (KJV).

16. Charles Pettit McIlvaine, *Pastoral Letter from the Bishops of the Protestant Episcopal Church, Delivered Friday, October 17, 1862, at the PECUSA Annual Convention* (New York: Baker and Godwin, 1862), 3–4.

17. Ibid., 4.

18. Ibid,. 4–6.

19. Ibid., 8–9.

20. Ibid., 11–12.

21. *Journal of the General Convention, 1862,* 144.

22. Ibid., 145.

23. J. H. Hopkins, Jr., *Life of John Henry Hopkins,* 328.

24. Ibid., Appendix 2, 461–65. This and the following excerpt are from his letter of protest.

25. Ibid, 465.

26. *Journal of the General Convention, 1862,* 152.

27. J. H. Hopkins, Jr., *Life John Henry Hopkins,* 328.

28. *New York Times,* 26 October 1862, 5.

29. J. H. Hopkins, Jr., *Life of John Henry Hopkins,* 329–30.

30. *New York Times,* 26 October 1862, 5.

31. J. H. Hopkins, Jr., *Life of John Henry Hopkins,* 329.

32. *Western Episcopalian,* 13 November 1862. The *Western Episcopalian* was published at Kenyon College in Gambier, Ohio, by the Theological Seminary Press from 1853–1868. Ohio Bishop Charles P. McIlvaine was a frequent contributor to its pages.

33. *Diocese of Ohio, 1861* (Columbus: Richard Nevins, 1861), 20–29.

34. See discussion above of the special service held at the convention.

# Church Division Is Ratified

## *⊹⊨ The First General Council of the Protestant Episcopal Church in the Confederate States of America*

Augusta, Georgia, 12–22 November 1862

Believing with a wonderful unanimity, that the providence of God had guided our footsteps, and for His own inscrutable purposes, had forced us into a separate organization. . . . We are all satisfied that we are walking in the path of duty, and, that the light of God's countenance has been wonderfully lifted up upon us. (From the pastoral letter read by Bishop Elliott at the 1862 Council of the Protestant Episcopal Church in the Confederate States)[1]

### Summons and Attendance at the Council

Following the adjourned convention in Columbia in October 1861, the constitution approved by the delegates was circulated to the ecclesiastical authorities in all the seceded states. On 19 September 1862, Bishop Stephen Elliott of Georgia reported by letter to those ecclesiastical authorities that he had received "satisfactory evidence" from seven dioceses, the number stipulated in Columbia, that each had adopted the constitution. In the same letter, therefore, Bishop Elliott proclaimed the formation of the Protestant Episcopal Church in the Confederate States of America (PECCSA) and announced that the constitution of that church now was binding on the seven dioceses concerned. The role of senior bishop among those who led dioceses affiliated with the PECCSA had devolved to Elliott upon the death of Virginia's Bishop Meade in March. On 27 September, Elliott issued a call to the First General Council, asking that bishops and clerical and lay delegates assemble on 12 November 1862 at St. Paul's Church in Augusta, Georgia.[2]

Elliott's summons to attend was answered as follows.[3]

The first seven dioceses listed comprised the new PECCSA, and six bishops and thirty delegates from those states were present. The federal presence along the Mississippi kept Bishop Gregg and most of the Texas delegation away, but given the state of transportation in the South, the overall attendance was remarkably

Attendance at the First General Council of the Protestant Episcopal Church in
the Confederate States of America, Augusta, Georgia, 1862

| Diocese | Bishop present | Clerical deputies | Lay deputies |
| --- | --- | --- | --- |
| Alabama | Yes–Richard Hooker Wilmer | Yes–3 | Yes–2 |
| Georgia | Yes–Stephen Elliott | Yes–3 | Yes–3 |
| Mississippi | Yes–William Mercer Green | Yes–3 | No |
| North Carolina | Yes–Thomas Atkinson | Yes–3 | Yes–2 |
| South Carolina | Yes–Thomas Frederick Davis | Yes–2 | Yes–3 |
| Texas | No | Yes–1 | No |
| Virginia | Yes–John Johns | Yes–3 | Yes–2 |
| Arkansas | Yes–Henry Champlin Lay | Yes–1 | No |
| Florida | No | No | No |
| Louisiana | No | No | No |
| Tennessee | No | No | No |

*Source: Journals of the Protestant Episcopal Church in the Confederate States of America,
Facsimile Edition*, ed. William A. Clebsch, 11ff., 125–26.

good. Arkansas was not a diocese when the council convened, but that status
would be granted during the council session. The Diocese of Florida was not represented but would join her sister dioceses in 1863, bringing to nine the number
of dioceses affiliated with the Confederate church.

Wartime disruptions, including occupation of key areas by Union troops,
prevented diocesan councils from being held in Louisiana and Tennessee until
after the war, so that these two dioceses were never formally part of the PECCSA
organization. Hence, although Otey of Tennessee and Polk of Louisiana were senior to Elliott in years in the episcopate, neither was eligible to serve as presiding bishop—nor even to have a seat with vote in the House of Bishops. Had he
been able, Bishop Otey might have attended the Augusta meeting anyway, and
would have been welcome, but he was in a stage of declining health that would
lead to his death in April 1863. Bishop-General Polk was involved in a military
campaign.

## Work of the Council

The item of business at the meeting that consumed by far the most time was the
consideration and adoption of a body of canons for governance of the Confederate church.[4] The canons that emerged reflected the new church organization,
replacing "United" with "Confederate" and replacing "Convention" with "Council" throughout, but the PECCSA canons were basically the same as those of the
church in the United States. Some of the deviations from this general rule were

debated with intensity and at length—but given the short lifetime of the Confederate church these changes turned out to be of no real significance.[5]

After receipt of a report from a committee that had considered documents brought forth by Bishop Lay, the House of Deputies passed a resolution that Arkansas be admitted as a diocese in union with the Protestant Episcopal Church in the Confederate States. The House of Bishops concurred and then confirmed the election of Henry Champlin Lay as diocesan of Arkansas, an action in which the House of Deputies promptly concurred. After the council admitted the Diocese of Arkansas, the Reverend Dr. J. T. Wheat was seated as a clerical delegate.[6]

The Joint Committee of Bishops and Deputies presented proposed revisions to the Book of Common Prayer (BCP). Although the committee identified places in which the BCP might benefit from substantive revision, the only modifications recommended to and approved by the council reflected the new ecclesiastical bond among the dioceses—the name of the church—and the existence of the Confederate States, which was acknowledged in changing *United* to *Confederate* in the Prayer for the President of the United States and all in Civil Authority. Publication of a BCP for the church in the Confederate States, to include the approved changes and a new preface, was authorized, as was the printing of a shortened version of the BCP for use by military personnel. The joint committee, chaired by Bishop Atkinson, was continued, with instructions to report in 1865.

Bishops and deputies clearly wanted to continue the work of missions, both within the confines of the Confederate States, notably in Texas and Arkansas, and abroad—although the council recognized that the Union blockade made success in any effort to communicate with foreign missions highly unlikely. A resolution of the Committee on the State of the Church in the House of Deputies addressed directly the church's mission to slaves: "Resolved: That this church desires specially to recognize its obligation to provide for the spiritual wants of that class of our brethren, who in the providence of God have been committed to our sympathy and care in the national institution of slavery."[7] The report of the committee, including this resolution, was forwarded to the House of Bishops, along with a recommendation that the bishops prepare and disseminate a pastoral letter at council's end.

Memorial resolutions for Bishop Cobbs of Alabama and Bishop Meade of Virginia were adopted, and, after initially designating Huntsville as the site of the 1865 meeting, the action was rescinded, and Mobile was selected. The council voted to send copies of its journal of proceedings to the ecclesiastical authorities in Florida, Louisiana, and Tennessee.

## Closing Service and Pastoral Letter

As the bishops followed the secretary of their house down the aisle of the St. Paul's Church at the start of the closing session, the secretary announced: "The

House of Bishops." The deputies stood at that point, and remained standing until the bishops were seated in the chancel.[8] The most memorable part of the 1862 council was the pastoral letter read at the close of the convention on 22 November.[9] Its author was not recorded in the council proceedings, but Bishop Elliott is generally credited with having written it. Elliott began the letter by declaring that "seldom has any council assembled in the Church of Christ under circumstances needing His presence more urgently than this which is now about to submit its conclusions to the judgment of the Universal Church."[10] Elliott noted that, with civil strife in progress, the council members had been forced "by the providence of God" to separate from a church with which they were in "entire harmony" on matters of doctrine and worship. He pointed out that the only changes in the Book of Common Prayer that had been made in council reflected those dictated by the change in the civil government to which member churches of the council now owed allegiance. His two exhortations to clergy and laity concerned the spiritual needs of slaves and the need to cleanse the institution of slavery from "unchristian features."

> The time has come when the Church should press more urgently than she has hitherto done upon her laity, the solemn fact, that the slaves of the South are not merely so much property, but are a sacred trust committed to us, as a people, to be prepared for the work which God may have for them to do, in the future. While under this tutelage He freely gives to us their labor, but expects us to give back to them that religious and moral instruction which is to elevate them in the scale of being. And while inculcating this truth, the Church must offer more freely her ministrations for their benefit and improvement. Her laity must set the example of readiness to fulfill their duty towards these people, and her clergy must strip themselves of pride and fastidiousness and indolence, and rush, with the zeal of martyrs, to this labor of love. . . .
>
> It is likewise the duty of the Church to press upon the masters of the country their obligation, as Christian men, so to arrange this institution as not to necessitate the violation of those sacred relations which God has created and which man cannot, consistently with Christian duty, annul. The systems of labor which prevail in Europe and which are, in many respects, more severe than ours, are so arranged as to prevent all necessity for the separation of parents and children and of husbands and wives, and a very little care upon our part, would rid the system upon which we are about to plant our national life, of these unchristian features. It belongs, especially, to the Episcopal Church to urge a proper teaching upon this subject, for in her fold and in her congregations are found a very large proportion of the great slaveholders of the country. . . . Hitherto have we been hindered by the pressure of abolitionism; now that we have thrown off from us that hateful and infidel pestilence, we should

prove to the world that we are faithful to our trust and the Church should lead the hosts of the Lord in this work of justice and of mercy.[11]

Elliott thus was unequivocal that, in his view, the separate sale of a wife or a husband—or of minor children—violated Christian principles and should not be tolerated. His reference to abolitionist pressure followed by an admonition that the church now should prove faithful to its trust was an unsubtle way of stating that anti-abolition anger should no longer serve as an excuse for inaction.

From the perspective of a century and a half later, what appears remarkable is that, although Bishop Elliott recognized the inhumanity and violation of God's will in breaking up slave families on the auction block, he also felt comfortable in having a system that held people in bondage and deprived them of hope both for their future and the future of their children to be the system upon which the national life of the Confederate States was to be planted.

After reading the pastoral letter, Bishop Elliott offered concluding prayers and the benediction. The bishops retired to the lecture room, where the House adjourned, *sine die*. The Protestant Episcopal Church in the Confederate States of America was organized and ready to assume its role as a national church. Before the next scheduled triennial council, however, the nation under whose aegis the new church had been founded had ceased to exist.

### Notes

1. Stephen Elliott, *Pastoral Letter from the Bishops in the Confederate States of America 1862, Delivered Before the General Council, in St. Paul's Church, Augusta, Georgia, Saturday, Nov. 22d, 1862* (Augusta: Steam Power Press and Chronicle, 1862), 7.

2. *Journal of the Proceedings of the General Council of the Protestant Episcopal Church in the Confederate States of America, November 1862* (Augusta: Steam Press of Chronicle and Sentinel, 1863). The journal is included in William A. Clebsch, ed., *Journals of the Protestant Episcopal Church in the Confederate States of America, Facsimile Edition* (Austin, Tex.: Church Historical Society, 1962). Elliott's communications of 19 and 27 September are reproduced on pages 5–9 of these proceedings.

3. When the council opened, there were only nineteen deputies present, but delegate arrivals continued through the fifth day.

4. The summary comments in this section reflect the proceedings for the House of Bishops (pp. 125–188) and the House of Deputies (pp. 11–123) in *Journal of the General Council of the Episcopal Church in the Confederate States.*

5. For example, the House of Bishops wished to amend a particular canon entitled "The consent necessary for officiating" by adding a section 2 that stipulated: "Any Bishop may, at his discretion, license any suitable person to act as lay-reader." The House of Deputies did not concur. The House of Bishops also spent time debating several amendments to a canon pertaining to degrading or deposing a minister. *Journal of the General Council of the Episcopal Church in the Confederate States,* 156 and 72, 171–72.

6. Ibid., 161 and 104. On the latter page it was reported that when action was taken to admit Arkansas as a diocese, a six-member Arkansas delegation was certified. Only one deputy from the new diocese, however, the Reverend Dr. Wheat, was present to take his seat.

7. Ibid., 102.

8. Ibid., 119.

9. The Reverend John Fulton in his monograph "The Church in the Confederate States," included in William Stevens Perry, *The History of the American Episcopal Church, 1587–1883*, 2 vols. (Boston: Osgood, 1885), 2:574, wrote that this pastoral letter "will never cease to be precious to the Church of God. . . . It is the noblest epitaph of the dead, and, if they needed such, it is the noblest vindication of the living, that their dearest friends could wish."

10. Elliott, *Pastoral Letter from the Bishops in the Confederate States*, 3.

11. Ibid., 3–12.

# PART 4

# Slave State Bishops and Civil War

# A Tragic Ending

*⚔ The Wartime Episcopate of*
*James Hervey Otey of Tennessee*

## A Change of Heart

As we have seen, Bishop Otey of Tennessee was opposed to secession when the crisis began in December 1860 and remained hopeful that Tennessee would remain in the Union even as the Confederacy was being formed. Otey not only believed that the Union could and should be preserved, but he also feared that secession could result in civil war, plunging the country "into a gulf of horrors and sufferings to which the past history of the world furnishes no parallel."[1] During the spring of 1861, however, it became clear first that the group of seceded states that had proclaimed a new nation in February would be joined by several other states, including Tennessee, and second that the Lincoln administration was making plans to preserve the Union by force of arms.[2] Faced with these circumstances, Otey devoted his energy to an attempt to prevent civil war by taking the position that the Southern states should be allowed to depart in peace. Once he understood that the North was committed to prosecute the war until the Union was made whole, Otey saw the war as one of subjugation and supported the South.

In July 1861 Otey wrote in a letter to his friend Edward C. Burks in Bedford County, Virginia: "Our duty is clearly and unequivocally to repel force by force, and to make every sacrifice rather than submit to an administration that tramples down every barrier raised by our Forefathers for the protection of personal, social, and public rights."[3] By early August, an Otey to Burks letter indicated that the bishop's support had become imbued with personal passion:

> I am rejoiced to learn that that our native county has acquitted herself so well in the persons of her sons at Manassas. She has never been found wanting when the call was made on her for either head or heart and I trust she never will be. . . .

I do hope that another battle such as Manassas will put an end to the war. The idea of an invader treading on soil within sight of the peaks of Otter makes my blood hot. I think if I heard that he was at [the town of] Liberty [Virginia] I should go to the army anyhow. I hope that I may not hear it. Our Bedford boys I think will be a match for every Buckeye that crosses the Blue Ridge. O if I were only 20 years of age![4]

In November 1861 Otey visited near Columbus, Kentucky, with his old friend Bishop Leonidas Polk, now a Confederate major general, with whom Otey had disagreed sharply over secession. Otey slept in the general's tent and made a diary entry while there: "I slept with General Polk last night, and had much interesting and gratifying conversation with him, especially concerning his position and his earnest desire to be relieved from it. We had sweet communion in prayer morning and night. He stands higher in my esteem than ever."[5] After returning home from the visit, Otey received a packet of correspondence that included a letter from Polk to President Davis resigning his commission and a copy of the response to Polk from the president, declining to accept Polk's resignation from military service.[6] Otey promptly wrote to Polk.

If a doubt lingered in your mind as to the propriety of your retaining the position into which you have been called by the providence of God, it seems to me that it should be removed by the statements and reasonings of those letters. Your letter of the 6th of November, tendering the resignation of your commission as Major General, of which I have just made a copy, will triumphantly indicate the purity of your motives, and the high and noble considerations which have influenced your course; . . . if examples of men who have been called to take up arms for the defense of the altars of God and their country, be called for, they can readily be furnished from the records of Holy Writ; . . . did not Samuel, the minister of God from his very infancy, lead forth the hosts of Israel to battle, and with his own hand slay the king of Amalek?[7]

## Church Organization

Although from the latter part of May 1861 on, Otey supported the Confederate war effort, his thoughts about church unity remained conflicted. By the end of 1861 he had arrived at the position that the word *Confederate* should replace *United* in the prayer for the president and other civil authorities.[8] In January 1862, however, he declined to participate in the consecration of Richard Hooker Wilmer as bishop of Alabama that was scheduled for Richmond in March, and, also in March 1862, gave his consent to the consecration of William Bacon Stevens as assistant bishop of Pennsylvania, a diocese of the Protestant Episcopal

Church in the United States.[9] When the church in the Confederate States was fully constituted in the fall of 1862, Otey's ambivalence might have been dissipated, but a canonical barrier to his participation in the Confederate church remained; the Diocese of Tennessee did not meet in the years from 1862 to 1864 and hence never voted to give its allegiance to the new Confederate church. Neither Otey nor diocesan delegates attended the November 1862 meeting of the newly formed Protestant Episcopal Church in the Confederate States. Otey thus remained head of a diocese still technically affiliated with the U.S. church, although he supported both the Confederacy and the Episcopal Church in the Confederate States. Before the end of 1862 another complication, his state of health, became the dominating factor in his life.

## Declining Health

Otey's health declined early in 1862, and he was unable to fulfill a promise to Polk to make an episcopal visit to Louisiana. He also did not have sufficient strength to go to Hot Springs, Arkansas, as his physicians had recommended. He went instead to Cooper's Well in Mississippi, where the "sulphured" water was reputed to have health benefits. In the bishop's case, his stay of a few weeks did not seem to help. He then moved to nearby Jackson where he was cared for by old friends for four months.[10] Dr. Charles Todd Quintard, formerly a minister in Otey's diocese, was on leave from his chaplain's duties in the Confederate army and visited Otey while he was recovering. While in Mississippi, Otey reaffirmed his support and concern for Polk, writing to him on 15 July 1862: "My dear brother: I have endeavored to be with you daily and nightly in spirit, invoking God's protection in all dangers, his guidance in all difficulties, his support under all your trials, his grace to comfort you in all your sorrows. I can do no more."[11]

## Wartime Memphis

Otey returned to his home in Memphis on 4 October 1862, where he found the city under the control of federal troops commanded by William T. Sherman. During 1862 a large part of Tennessee, including Memphis and Nashville, had been yielded to the Union. Otey was treated with courtesy by Sherman, who allowed the bishop freedom of movement about the city, and Otey secured an unrestricted pass from the provost marshall to visit Confederate prisoners and wounded.[12] Two diary entries from December reflect his activity:

> Dec. 10 . . .Went to the Irving Block Prison, and found one (Crisp) very ill, too much so for me to converse with him: and another (Russell) with a sore throat and great hoarseness. Begged officer to remove Crisp to the hospital.

> Dec. 12 Visited a wounded man (Captain Jones of Texas) at the Overton Hospital, and gave him a prayer book. Also visited the prisoners at the Irving

The Right Reverend James Hervey Otey, S.T.D.

block, and was glad to find that Russell had obtained medicine for his throat and cough, and that Crisp had been taken to the hospital.[13]

At one point General Sherman decreed the removal from Memphis of a number of prominent citizens as retaliation for partisan, or "bushwhacker," activity on the part of irregular Confederate volunteers. Otey succeeded in having the order suspended—and then wrote General John C. Pemberton, Confederate commander at Vicksburg, asking him to "disclaim and as far as possible restrain" this activity, which had included some atrocities—and which exposed the citizens of Memphis to reprisals. Sherman attended church services held by Otey, and, when his forces left the city, the general wrote Bishop Otey a kind letter.[14]

## Death of a Bishop

Otey's last illness began in late December, and he ceased writing in his diary on 3 January 1863. His wife had died in 1861, near the start of the war, but some of his six surviving children were with him in his last days. His slaves left him soon after they were freed.[15] Otey died at home in Memphis on 23 April 1863.

Although still more battles were to occur in Tennessee in 1863 and 1864, Otey's state and diocese already were devastated. The state and the church would recuperate, as would the many other areas in which Otey had labored as a missionary or provisional bishop—and much good would come of his labor. That was not clear when Otey died, however, for, as a church historian wrote nearly one hundred years later: "The lives of few men have ended so tragically. His home overrun by invading armies, his churches in ruins, and his people scattered like sheep upon a thousand hills, had he been able, Bishop Otey would have looked back across hundreds of miles from the river to the Smokey Mountains, from which he first looked at Tennessee, and seen nothing but devastation. The Church which he had labored so hard to establish seemed farther than ever from achievement of its appointed task."[16]

Bishop Otey must have had something akin to this vision of his diocese when, during what he knew was his terminal illness, he wrote his friend the bishop of Ohio. McIlvaine spoke of that letter in his 1863 diocesan address, saying that "during his last illness he wrote me a long and most affectionate and touching letter evidently from a heart broken from the distresses of the times . . . He expressed the highest joy at being very near his time of departure and the strongest consolation in Christ."[17]

## Notes

1. Otey to Polk, 8 December 1860, cited in William Mercer Green, *Memoir the Life of the Rt. Rev. James Hervey Otey, D.D., LL.D., First Bishop of Tennessee* (New York: J. Pott, 1885), 91.

2. On 15 April, just after Fort Sumter fell, Lincoln issued a call for seventy-five thousand volunteers to put down what he saw as rebellion.

3. James H. Otey to Edward C. Burks, 17 July 1861, in James Elliott Walmsley, "Documents: The Change of Secession Sentiment in Virginia in 1861," *American Historical Review* 31 (October 1925): 100.

4. James H. Otey to Edward C. Burks, 7 August 1861, in Walmsley, "Documents," 100. Liberty, Virginia, to which Otey refers, was in 1861 a town in the center of Bedford County, Otey's birthplace. Liberty was renamed and is now the city of Bedford. The Library Services Department of the Bedford County Public Library provided the information that Bedford was incorporated in 1890. See also Saul B. Cohen, ed., *The Columbia Gazeteer of the World* (New York: Columbia University Press, 1998).

5. William Mecklenburg Polk, *Leonidas Polk, Bishop and General*, 2 vols. (New York: Longmans, Green, 1893), 1:331.

6. These letters are discussed below, in "Polk, Lay, and Quintard: The War Up Close and Personal."

7. Green, *Memoir of Otey*, 96.

8. Otey's position, stated in response to a query from a presbyter, was that ministers in churches governed by the United States were bound to pray for the president of the United States and that ministers in areas governed by the Confederacy were obligated to pray for the Confederate president. See Donald S. Armentrout, *James Hervey Otey: First Episcopal Bishop of Tennessee* (Nashville: Episcopal Diocese in Tennessee, 1984), 94.

9. The matters of these consecrations and the failure of Tennessee to join the PECSSA are discussed above, in "A Controversial Consecration and a Bishop's Death."

10. Green, *Memoir of Otey*, 101.

11. W. M. Polk, *Leonidas Polk, Bishop and General*, 1:331.

12. Green, *Memoir of Otey*, 102.

13. Ibid., 169.

14. Ibid., 102–3.

15. At the start of 1863 Tennessee was a state "in rebellion" against the government of the United States, and hence all Tennessee slaves were "forever free" under the Emancipation Proclamation. In areas under federal control, such as Memphis, the proclamation was effective de facto as well as de jure on 1 January 1863.

16. Frank McClain, *James Hervey Otey of Tennessee* (New York: National Council, 1956), 18.

17. *Diocese of Ohio, 1863* (Columbus: Richard Nevins, 1863), 16–24.

# The Wartime Episcopate
# of Bishop Elliott of Georgia

+≒ *A Chronicle of Christian Patriotism*

## 1861

*Diocesan Convention*

Bishop Stephen Elliott opened his May 1861 diocesan convention address with sadness and determination: "Hitherto we have assembled as an Ecclesiastical Council, with no cares resting upon our hearts save those which concerned the Church of Christ. To-day we feel most painfully, in addition to these, the sorrow which arises from the severed ties of friendship and of country. Hitherto peace has ever smiled upon our meetings with her bright face of prosperity and security. To-day the whole land is resounding with the preparation for war—war with those who, until a few months since, were our countrymen and our brethren."[1]

Elliott was concerned that full-scale war was likely, but he was focused at this convention on what he saw as the necessity of forming a separate church in the Confederate States. He argued that separate ecclesiastical structures for the North and South were necessary because the Episcopal Church in the South was no longer in the United States. Elliott seemed especially anxious that colleagues in the Northern church should understand both that necessity and also the concern of their Southern colleagues for the religious welfare of the slaves.

> It is due to those with whom we have been so pleasantly united as a Church, that they should understand this matter. . . . It [secession] has been done with a lively sense of our duty to God, to our children, and above all to the race whom He has committed to our guardianship and Christian nurture; . . . we conscientiously believe it [slavery] to be a great missionary institution—one arranged by God, as he arranges all the moral and religious influences of the world. . . . We believe that we are educating those people as they are educated no where else; that we are elevating them in every generation; that we are working out God's purposes, whose consummation we are quite willing to

leave in his hands, . . . being determined, meanwhile, by the grace of God, to defend with the sacrifice of everything, if need be, this sacred charge which has been committed to us. We can not permit our servants to be cursed with the liberty of licentiousness and infidelity, but we will truly labor to give them that liberty wherewith Christ has made us all free.[2]

The diocese proceeded to elect delegates to the meeting called by Polk and Elliott to assemble in Montgomery in July. Beginning at that meeting, as we have seen, Elliott guided his fellow bishops, the clergy, and the laity during the process that led to establishment of the Confederate Episcopal Church and approval of its constitution.

### Sermon: Victory at Manassas Junction

By July, war had broken out in earnest, and Elliott preached on Sunday, 28 July, a stirring sermon crediting God with the Confederate victory at Manassas a week earlier. Elliott first described in some detail the Union's preparation for battle, which resulted in the assembly "over three long and weary months" of a mighty host under "the most experienced warrior of our land," presumably General Winfield Scott, the ranking Union commander, though the army being assembled was under the immediate command of General Irving McDowell. Elliott painted a picture of this well-equipped mighty army streaming out of Washington with pomp and pride to march to Richmond, certain that it would crush the Confederate force that dared to intervene. He lauded the South's leadership and the courage of its soldiers for being the "secondary" cause for the stunning success of Confederate arms, but he concluded that, given the superiority in men and equipment of the Northern armada, God had to have been on the side of the Confederacy.[3]

> The newspapers from Washington to Maine on the one hand and to Minnesota on the other, held, with one or two honorable exceptions, one unchanging tone of exultation, boasting of the power, of the strength, and the invincibility of the North, and saying, in the very language of Pharaoh: "We will pursue, we will overtake, we will divide the spoil; our hands shall destroy them." Not a word about God and his justice and power that we could hear; not a moment's distrust of themselves and reliance upon God! When their churches were entered it was to desecrate their altars with star-spangled banners, and to spread over the very communion table, the symbol, not of Christ's sacrifice, but of their national pride. (10)

Elliott then reviewed the leadership, strength, and readiness of the two armies, giving the edge in the first one to the South, but in the last two to the North by a wide margin, suggesting that predictions of a Union victory were justified. He proclaimed that when the battle raged, however, God had watched over the Confederate soldiers:

> Could the eyes of our fainting, dying children, have been opened that day
> to see spiritual things, I feel sure that they would have seen horses and chariots
> of fire riding upon the storm of battle, and making those that were for them,
> more than those that were against them. . . .
>
> It is but seldom, in the annals of war, that so signal a victory has been
> granted to the arm of valor and the prayer of faith; . . . he [God] has permitted
> us totally to destroy that insolent army; to drive them back in shame and con-
> fusion, . . . to strip them of their batteries which they boasted to be invincible,
> to despoil them of the stores which they had been so painfully gathering for
> so long a time—snatch from them the prestige of power which their partisan
> writers had given them abroad. (13–14)

Elliott added, however, an admonishment:

> If we continue humble and give the glory to God, we shall go on from vic-
> tory to victory, until our independence shall be acknowledged and our home
> be left to us in peace. But if we suffer ourselves to be elated and to ascribe our
> success to ourselves—if our heart be lifted up and we forget the Lord our God
> and say in our heart, "My power and the might of mine hath gotten me this
> victory," then shall our peril be imminent, for the Lord hateth the proud and
> smiteth those who would rob him of his glory. This victory is, we firmly be-
> lieve, an answer to prayer, and while we would detract nothing from the skill
> of our leaders or the bravery of our troops, which are the secondary causes of
> success, we can see enough in its circumstances to satisfy us of the presence
> of God. Let us not lose this advantage, . . . let us lay all the glory at the feet of
> Jesus and acknowledge him to be our saviour and mighty deliverer. (19–20)

## 1862

### Sermon: New Wine Not to Be Put in Old Bottles

28 February 1862 was designated by President Jefferson Davis as a day of "solemn humiliation before God," and Elliott preached that day in Christ Church, Savannah.[4] By this time, there were signs that a long war, replete with reverses as well as victories, was going to ensue; two such signs in Tennessee were the fall of Fort Henry and the surrender of Fort Donelson earlier in February. Elliott, though, did not use his sermon to prepare his flock for a lengthy struggle. His sermon, "New Wine Not to Be Put into Old Bottles," focused on the religious principles that should undergird the government of the new nation and guide its people; principles, Elliott insisted, that had to avoid certain egregious errors made in the founding document of the United States.

The Right Reverend Stephen Elliott, D.D.

The bishop conceded that political dispute between the North and South was the immediate cause of the conflict that led to separation, but he argued that the fundamental cause was that the United States had been established on principles that were seriously flawed. Those flaws were built into the founding documents and led to a moral decay that would have doomed the Union, even had the "political necessity" (the slavery dispute) not arisen. Elliott identified the flaws:

> The reason of man was exalted to an impious degree, and in the face not only of experience, but of the revealed word of God, all men were declared to be created equal, and man was pronounced capable of self-government.
> Two greater falsehoods could not have been announced—falsehoods, because the one struck at the whole constitution of civil society as it had ever existed, and because the other virtually denied the fall and corruption of man.

. . . Man is not capable of self-government because he is a fallen creature, and interest, passion, ambition, lust, sway him far more than reason or honor. As for equality among men, whether by creation or birth or in any other way, it is a miserable *ignis fatuus*, not worthy to be followed, even for the purpose of exposure. Upon principles as false and as foolish as these was our late Government founded. (10–11)

These principles, Elliott claimed, eventually undermined the moral fabric of the government. The "new bottles" into which the "new wine" of the Confederacy needed to be poured had to be a set of principles that acknowledged God and the need for God's guidance. Elliott was pleased that the Confederate constitution in its preamble invoked the "favor and guidance of Almighty God" in ordaining and establishing the constitution.[5] The United States constitution did not include such an invocation. Referring to this omission, Elliott remarked: "Thank God, we have washed out that stain, and if we have not yet distinctly proclaimed ourselves a Christian nation, we are at least a nation of Theists—men who recognize the presence of God in the affairs of the world . . . and for that He may bless us and give us more light" (16).

The Confederate States, in other words, had taken a formal step toward becoming a Christian nation—which it must become in spirit as well as in law if it was to persevere. The war might help achieve that goal. "War is a fearful scourge, as God's word plainly tells us; but it may sanctify as well as chasten. . . . The infidel principles which I have been discussing have, even in a century, struck deep root into the minds and hearts of our countrymen, and it requires an equally deep cautery to burn them out" (17).

### Diocesan Convention

By the time of the diocesan convention on 8 May 1862, Nashville, as well as much of middle and western part of Tennessee was in Union hands, and the bloody stalemate at Shiloh had resulted in more than ten thousand Confederate casualties. Elliott's message on the war was to trust in God and fight to the finish.

Civil war—the most cruel of all wars—has already become familiar to us, and is leaving in its track hatred and mourning, and desolation. Fighting as we are, in absolute defense of our rights, our homes, and our freedom of thought and action, we have nothing to do but to struggle and to bear, and if need be, die upon our thresholds and before our altars. We are powerless to make peace, except at a sacrifice which will make peace more terrible than any war. God alone can rule the hearts of the children of men, and we must bide his time, and be satisfied to wait until He shall choose to give us the inestimable blessing of peace.[6]

Elliott then asked the convention to put aside war issues and to focus on the church. He reported on the meeting of representatives of the Episcopal Church in the Southern states at Montgomery and on the provisional convention of the Protestant Episcopal Church in the Confederate States of America held in Columbia. The diocesan representatives accepted Elliott's recommendation that the constitution proposed in Columbia for the Confederate church be ratified.

Elliott mentioned his sorrow in having to withhold a response to Bishop Thomas C. Brownell's request for concurrence or objection with regard to the consecration of William Bacon Stevens as assistant bishop of Pennsylvania, because he, Elliott, was no longer a bishop within the Protestant Episcopal Church in the United States. Dr. Stevens had resided in Georgia for a number of years, and Elliott had ordained him to the diaconate and to the priesthood.[7]

A report of the diocesan Committee on the State of the Church lamented that the work of the diocese among the "colored people" had been interrupted by the "unnatural war" now in progress. The report blamed the North for this distressing side effect of the war.[8]

### Sermon: Our Cause in Harmony with Purposes of God in Christ Jesus

President Jefferson Davis appointed Thursday, 18 September 1862, a "Day of Prayer and Thanksgiving, for Our Manifold Victories, and Especially for the Fields of Manassas and Richmond, Ky." Both victories had occurred in late August. "Second Manassas" was a stunning Union defeat, and the Confederate victory at Richmond, Kentucky, was a hopeful sign for a Kentucky campaign by Confederate forces. Elliott preached at Christ Church, Savannah, a sermon entitled "Our Cause in Harmony with the Purposes of God in Christ Jesus." Elliott bestowed praise on the rank-and-file Confederate soldiers, but he primarily used this sermon to set forth his view of God's purpose for the slavery system of the South.[9]

Bishop Elliott began his discussion of the institution of slavery by noting that the peoples of all continents were on the way to being converted to Christianity, except the peoples of Africa. He then offered a litany of unsuccessful missionary efforts on that continent and attributed those failures to the fact that the white race was unsuited to the climate and conditions found there. Elliott saw the solution to this difficulty in the African slaves who were living in the South. In fact, it was God's plan that from this group would come those who could function in Africa and be the instruments to bring the light of Christ to its shores and innermost regions. Elliott was careful to emphasize that this would happen on God's timetable and pointed out that the Hebrews were held in bondage in Egypt for hundreds of years before God sent forth his chosen people.

God, Elliott was certain, had appointed the Southern people as guardians of these enslaved members of the black race. The job of slave masters and their families, he told his congregation, was to bring their charges to culture and to Christianity. This was a trust from the Almighty, and slave owners must act not only as masters but also as teachers and missionaries; masters were accountable to God for that trust. God's purpose for the slaves could not be consummated until the South had done its duty, and God, Elliott noted explicitly, would not permit his purpose to be derailed by those seeking to use the war as an instrument of emancipation. The South, therefore, Elliott was convinced, ultimately would prevail if it met its obligation to lead the slaves to Christ.

> The great revolution through which we are passing certainly turns upon this point of slavery, and our future destiny is bound up with it. . . . The responsibility is upon us, and if we rise up, in a true Christian temper, to the sublime work which God has committed to us of educating a subject nation for his divine purposes, we shall be blessed of him as Joseph was. . . . But if contrariwise, we shall misunderstand our relations and shall assume the dominion of masters without remembering the duties thereof, God will "make them pricks in our eyes and thorns in our sides, and shall vex us in the land wherein we dwell." (11)

The bishop then summarized the history of slavery in the United States. His discussion began with the slave trade, which he referred to as "hateful," and pointed out that when it was abolished by worldwide consent, it was thought that ending the trade would be a "fatal blow" to slavery. That did not happen, however, because the slave masters were forced to pay greater heed to the "comforts and morals" of their charges and to "foster" marriage and family relations among slaves. Further, when diminished profits from indigo and rice reduced the need for slaves, God "permitted" the introduction of cotton, which greatly increased the need. God also preserved the institution in the border states by seeing that wheat and tobacco experienced a "sudden and unexpected" increase in value. These actions had been responsible for an increase in slaves in America from eight hundred thousand in 1808 to four million in 1862.[10] Having thus established God's interest in and providential care of the institution of slavery, Elliott continued:

> Most of you are looking to other causes for our success and our preservation, to the valor of our troops, to the skill of our generals, to the extent of our territorial surface, to foreign influence, to the power of commerce and of trade. I am looking to the poor despised slave as the source of our security, because I firmly believe that God will not permit his purposes to be overthrown

or his arrangements to be interfered with. . . . God has made us the guardians and champions of a people whom he is preparing for his own purposes. . . .

We are moving forward, as I firmly believe, as truly under his direction, as did the people of Israel when he led them with a pillar of cloud by day and of fire by night. (10–15)

## 1863

### Sermon: Samson's Riddle

On 27 March 1863, a Day of Fasting, Humiliation, and Prayer appointed by President Davis, Bishop Elliott preached a sermon entitled "Samson's Riddle" at Christ Church, Savannah. Since his sermon there in September 1862, on the Day of Thanksgiving for victories in the battles of Second Manassas and Richmond, Kentucky, there had been much bloodshed. The Confederacy had triumphed under Stonewall Jackson in September at Harper's Ferry, and the Fredericksburg / Marye's Heights battle in December had been a Union debacle. A major battle in September at Antietam Creek, however, had been a costly draw with heavy casualties, which had brought to a halt Lee's Maryland campaign. The war in the West had not gone well. A Confederate campaign into Kentucky led by General Braxton Bragg had been checked at the Battle of Perryville in October, and Bragg's army had retreated back into Tennessee, where it suffered severe casualties in a winter battle near Murfreesboro. In an act that changed the avowed war objectives of the Union, Lincoln had issued his Preliminary Emancipation Proclamation immediately after Antietam, and the Emancipation Proclamation itself was promulgated on 1 January 1863, declaring that all slaves in states then in rebellion against the United States were free.

Both sides were gearing up for campaigns in 1863, but Elliott sensed a great war-weariness and yearning for peace across the South. His chief concern was that this yearning for peace not shake the Southern people's resolve to achieve independence. Elliott began by recognizing the deep desire for peace, a time when the sun did not cast its setting rays upon fields of blood and carnage.[11]

> Peace, however, must come only in God's time—and must come with honor. It was natural to wish for an end to a cruel strife, but peace for the South must come with "entire independence and complete nationality" and without concession of territory, goods, or principle.
>
> Every thing forbids us to be too solicitous for peace. Our consecrated cause—consecrated by the blood of our children—the aid and comfort it would give our enemies—the permanent welfare of our posterity. If God sends it to us, then welcome, bright-eyed Peace! but woe to us if, for its sake, we sacrifice one jot or one tittle of our duty and of eternal justice! (9)

At the present time, Elliott argued, peace was not possible because of the Confederate territory now under Union control. This included half of Tennessee, sections of Virginia, Louisiana, and nearly all of the coast. In addition, the right to self-determination of future status in Kentucky, Maryland, and Missouri had been usurped by federal forces. Elliott demanded of his listeners:

> Would you consent to peace upon the terms of the *uti possidetis*, each party holding what it possesses? Your own solemn legislative pledges cry out against it. Virginia would blush for shame at such a proposition, and would weep, as Rachel, for her children, refusing to be comforted. Louisiana would lift her saddened eyes and fettered arms and plead for mercy and deliverance. The home of Jackson would burn with indignation that the ashes of her unconquered hero should be trampled upon by hirelings and slaves. Old ocean would murmur curses against you upon her wailing winds, and would lash your shores in fury at their degradation. (10)

It was God's will, in fact, that the war be continued and it was the duty of the faithful to accept that will.

> It may be a bitter disappointment to us that the dove has returned to the ark without the olive leaf in her mouth, thus notifying us that the waters of strife have not yet subsided, but the ark is still in safety and under the guidance of Him whose eye never sleepeth and whose love never faileth! Let us, then, resume our sacred work of stern resistance; let us pray for fortitude, for patience, for endurance, for faith; let us be satisfied that there are lessons of deep moral import which are yet to be evolved from the continuance of this struggle, and we shall discover in God's own time that "out of the eater came forth meat and out of the strong came forth sweetness." (7)

The main theme of this sermon was thus "staying the course in accord with God's will," but Elliott incorporated other messages aimed at the hearts and behaviors of his flock. One concerned profiteering, which he perceived as damaging the war effort and, of more importance, as a moral problem that would bring down the wrath of God—and thereby delay the successful conclusion of the war. He was particularly offended by those whose excessive profits came at the expense of soldiers in the field.

The bishop also told his listeners that hope should not be wasted or efforts expended on attempts to bring about foreign intervention; if God wanted to intervene by fomenting insurrection against the war in the North or by having the North attacked by a great naval power, God would act on his divine timetable. If not, or until that time, this war was the South's to fight. Ultimately, with or without external assistance, the enemies of the South would suffer a "deep and bitter humiliation," and independence would result.

Near the end of his address Elliott spoke about slavery, noting that before hostilities began the nations of the world and even many people in the Confederacy felt that there would be a slave uprising when war came. This had not happened, and Elliott saw this fact both as a vindication of the way slaves were treated in the South and as a tribute to the loyalty of the slaves, which he felt should be rewarded: "I sincerely hope that when this war is over, we shall, in token of their fidelity and good will, render their domestic relations more permanent, and consult more closely their feelings and affections" (21). Elliott's certainty that the South would triumph is implicit in this remark.

### Diocesan Convention

In May 1863 Elliott addressed the diocesan convention. It was the first meeting since the initial council of the Protestant Episcopal Church in the Confederate States, and Elliott, now its presiding bishop, was pleased to announce that the Confederate church was ecclesiastically organized and witnessing for Christ. He also reported that diocesan affairs in Georgia were in order.

Elliott expressed his gratitude that the church in Georgia, along with that in Alabama, had been spared the terrible destruction of church property and scattering of congregations that had occurred in other Confederate states. He noted that in Arkansas and Tennessee, "the Church has been utterly destroyed," and that in Florida, Louisiana, North Carolina, South Carolina, and Virginia many congregations had been broken up and scattered—and their buildings desecrated or destroyed: "Terrible as has been the war which has raged around us, our Lord and Master has not permitted this portion [Georgia] of his heritage to be further devastated, and we have not been called to mourn over newly-scattered parishes, or church edifices left in their ashes. We have been most graciously preserved, and our first duty is to ascribe the praise and glory of our preservation to him who has the power to control our enemies and to say, 'thus far shalt thou go and no farther.'"[12]

Elliott reported that on Sunday, 29 March, he had visited the Ogeechee Mission. Because of the proximity of Union ships, many slaveholders had moved their servants back to the interior, but some slaves remained near the mission between the rivers, and the bishop held a service for them. He reported on his feelings: "I could not but conjecture, as I performed this service within sight of the blockading fleet, . . . which was doing God's work most acceptably, the Church in the South, which was laboring to train the children of Africa in the way of righteousness and truth, or he who was sending marauding expeditions up every river and creek in the South to interrupt those efforts and to demoralize the subjects of those missions."[13]

*Sermon: Ezra's Dilemma*

Elliott's sermon "Ezra's Dilemma" was delivered at Christ Church, Savannah, on 21 August 1863. In May the South had won a great but costly victory at Chancellorsville in which General Stonewall Jackson had been mortally wounded. Since then the military situation had changed drastically for the worse. The Army of Northern Virginia had suffered a defeat, with many casualties, at Gettysburg, ending Lee's invasion of the North, and, in the West, General Pemberton had surrendered his army to Grant at Vicksburg. The Vicksburg surrender was soon followed by a surrender of Confederate forces at Port Hudson, Louisiana, leaving the entire Mississippi River open for Union water traffic. Finally, General Bragg's army was continuing to retreat eastward across Tennessee. This array of defeats had begun to erode public confidence that the South would win the war. To Bishop Elliott, however, there was no cause for panic—and the Confederacy's root problem was not military, but moral. God would bless his people, but only if their commitment to him was absolute.

Elliott reminded his hearers of their mindset at the war's beginning and chastised them for their wavering in the face of the current adversity: "Did any of us ever doubt, in the first years of this conflict, that God was on our side? ... Did we not proclaim it from the house tops, that our God was manifesting himself to us almost as palpably as he had done to his own chosen people?"[14] Elliott then reviewed the first victory at Manassas and other triumphs, the "propitious" arrival of arms from abroad, the changes in generals and indecision in the North, and other factors that "were to us what the miracles at the Red Sea and in the wilderness were to the Israelites. Have we forgotten all these things? Have they faded from our hearts and from our memories because of a few reverses?" (16). Elliott cited the loyalty of slaves to their Southern masters during the war as evidence against the "calumnious" charges of cruelty that the "fanatics" of the North had brought against Southern slaveholders. Elliott's thesis that slavery was God's instrument for bringing Africans to Christ was implicit in his remarks.

The main message of this sermon, however, was that the South would triumph when—and only when—the commitment of the Southern people to God and to his purposes for the war was absolute. Elliott denounced the profiteering that had grown in scope after the early Confederate victories. The enrichment motive had even resulted in avoidance of military service: "Men were seen skulking in every way to avoid service in the army, not from cowardice, not from any doubt about the value of the conflict or the certainty of its success, but that they might be at liberty to mingle in this mad hunt after money." What was needed now of each and every person was giving of oneself—one's entire self—to God. When God was satisfied, independence and peace would come.

Elliott used a Roman legend to drive this point home. He began with these words: "In the early history of the Roman Republic, there yawned in the centre of the Forum a deep and dark abyss—an abyss that had opened of its own accord, and had hourly grown wider and wider and threatened to engulph all Rome" (19). The Romans, Elliott continued, were told that all their city would be swallowed by the abyss unless the gods were appeased by a sacrifice cast into the gaping hole in their midst. The offering had to be "most precious," but what it was to be was being left to the people to decide. The people first poured their "hoarded wealth of glittering coin" into the abyss, with no result. The matrons of Rome then poured their jewels into the huge crevice, but again to no avail. Finally, the noble warrior Curtius rode his steed through the crowd to the brink of the gulf and turned to face the people.

"Romans," said Curtius, "ye have offered sacrifice of your possessions, of your treasures, of your affections, but who has offered the sacrifice of self? Trust me, Romans, it is the sacrifice of self that is the most precious." "With these words, rider and steed plunged into the unfathomable abyss. There was a moment of dreadful feeling—a moment that seemed an age. Slowly the abyss closed; the self sacrifice was received, and Rome was delivered" (20).

It was not just that sins of commission, such as profiteering, had to cease; God required total commitment of *self* from each person. Elliott asked this question of his listeners: "Have we determined to give up everything, if need be, for the cause of our country? . . . It is far easier to cast into this gulf such things as property, money, treasures, gems, and even sons, than it is to strip ourselves of vanity, of self-conceit, of pride of opinion, of ambition, of evil habits, of those things which make up our identity; . . . let us truly humble ourselves and beseech Him to show us our own hearts and to convict us especially of those sins which are offensive to him" (21).

Elliott concluded with a vivid description of what he saw as the fate that awaited the South should it not regain God's favor—and fail to win the war:

> Forward, my hearers, forward, with our shields locked and our trust in God, is our only movement now. It is too late even to go backward. . . . It is now victory or unconditional submission; submission not to the conservative and Christian people of the North, but to a party of infidel fanatics, with an army of needy and greedy soldiers at their backs . . . and they will sweep down upon the South as the hosts of Attila did upon the fertile fields of Italy. . . . You will have an ignoble home, overrun by hordes of insolent slaves and rapacious soldiers, . . . yourselves degraded, your delicate wives and gentle children thrust down to menial service, insulted, perhaps dishonored. . . . The language of Scripture is alone adequate to describe it—"The earth mourneth and languisheth: Lebanon is ashamed and hewn down: Sharon is like a wilderness.

They that did feed delicately are desolate in the streets: they that were brought up in scarlet embrace dunghills. They ravished the women in Zion and the maids in the cities of Judah."

Let us turn then this day to the Lord our God with all our heart and soul and mind, believing that His hand is upon all them for good that seek him. (24–25)

## 1864

In September 1863 the retreating army of Braxton Bragg won a victory at Chickamauga Creek in Georgia, just below Chattanooga. The Union forces retreated to Chattanooga and were surrounded by the Confederates, but in November, under Grant's supervision, Union forces broke out, routing the Confederates from the high ground around the city. The South took up defensive positions in North Georgia. There were skirmishes and probing actions early in 1864, but there was no significant military activity in Georgia until May.

### Diocesan Council

The diocesan council of Georgia met from 5 to 7 May 1864 at Trinity Church in Columbus. Elliott attributed to God the fact that his diocese had been spared the devastation wreaked in other Southern dioceses, that had included desecration of churches and scattering of congregations. Elliott again thanked God for his mercy in stopping Union forces at Georgia's borders with the command "Thus far shalt thou go and no farther."[15]

The bishop then described his activities for the past twelve months. He noted that St. Paul's Church in Augusta was in "very flourishing condition" and helping with needed diocesan resources. More generally, he reported that "in no year since the commencement of my Episcopate, have I confirmed so many persons, nor admitted to the communion of the Church so many young and active men, preparing, I trust, for future usefulness in her work upon earth" (10).

In late 1863 he had received notice that the Diocese of Florida had adopted the Constitution and Canons of the Confederate Episcopal Church, and on 4 January 1864 he had issued, as presiding bishop of the Confederate church, a declaration of union of that diocese with that church. He also reported on his efforts on behalf of Confederate soldiers, including his two-week stay with the Army of the Tennessee near Shelbyville, Tennessee, where he preached to the troops and also baptized and confirmed many, including their commander General Bragg.

In April he had preached at the Ogeechee Mission and then in Rome, from where he departed for the Confederate army headquarters in Dalton, Georgia. Dr. Charles Quintard collaborated with the bishop on a service held at the Methodist church there. The service included the baptism of a general officer and then a confirmation of eleven persons presented by Quintard, including three general officers. "The church was crowded to the utmost capacity, and the services were received with the most quiet and earnest attention. Such scenes give me the most cheerful hope, not only for our present success but for the future of our Confederacy" (19). There is a tone of optimism throughout Elliott's report, and that optimism is reflected in the charge at the end of his report: "God seems once again to have lifted the light of his countenance upon us, and to be aiding our counsels and leading our armies. Let us evince our gratitude to Him by a solemn Thanksgiving during the present session of our Council, and let us propitiate the continuance of His favor to us during the remainder of the year, by setting apart one day in every week, upon which, at the same hour, we shall, as a church, supplicate him for his mercy and support" (25).

### May–August

As the council ended on 7 May, however, General William T. Sherman's forces confronted General Joseph E. Johnston's army at Rocky Face Ridge in North Georgia. Johnston fell back to Resaca, then to Adairsville, and continued to retreat, attempting unsuccessfully to force Sherman to attack on terrain and under conditions favorable to the South. The Union suffered the more casualties in May and June, but Sherman was driving inexorably toward Atlanta. Elliott had attributed to God the command "Thus far shalt thou go and no farther" given at the Georgia border to Union forces, but God apparently had lifted that proscription.

Elliott was devastated in mid-June when news of Polk's death reached him. His eulogy at the funeral in Augusta included a scorching peroration aimed at bishops and clergy in the North who supported the Union cause.[16] On 24 July Elliott visited the Ogeechee Mission to slaves at New Hope Church, on which occasion he confirmed "fifty-four persons, all colored." This visit, at such a critical stage of the war in Georgia, showed the priority that Elliott gave to ministry to slaves.

### Sermon: Patience

In late August, when he must have been prepared for Atlanta to fall, he preached a sermon in Savannah entitled "Patience." His rhetoric was muted.

> The grace which we exercise in times like these upon which we have fallen is patience. . . . As faith gives us the possession of Christ, so does this patience give us possession of ourselves. An unbelieving man has no hold upon Christ: so an impatient man has no hold upon himself. . . . The Lord has promised us that "it shall come to pass, that at evening time it shall be light" but evening time may yet be distant; and meanwhile we must cultivate patience and

possess our souls. . . . We can do no more than we are doing to change our condition, except wait upon God in cheerful submission. . . .

Even though all his will will be to bless and prosper us—which I firmly believe it will be—He may not be able, consistently with his mode of action, to bring his purposes to pass at once.[17]

There was no suggestion in these words that defeat should be anticipated or accepted, but he had no predictions or exhortations for his flock other than to await God's will.

### Sermon: Vain Is the Help of Man

Three weeks later, on 15 September 1864, in a sermon entitled "Vain Is the Help of Man," the muted tone had vanished, replaced by predictions that although even harsher times were ahead, the Confederacy would triumph and the Union would self-destruct. These predictions, though asserted with confidence, came with the proviso that the Southern people submit completely to God's will. The occasion was a Day of Fasting, Humiliation and Prayer appointed by the governor of Georgia. Atlanta had fallen, and refugees were coming south. The worst, for rural southern Georgia and Savannah itself, where the bishop preached this sermon, was yet to come, but Elliott seemed resolved to face it. The sermon opened with an acknowledgement that the war was at their doorstep—and the thought that perhaps it should be: "For months past has it been steadily advancing toward us; we have heard its hoarse and cruel murmuring as it came nearer and nearer; the spoils of its destructive progress have been brought to our feet in the exiled women and children who have fled to us for refuge, and in the dead bodies of our noble young men which have come back to us for Christian burial.[18]

The trouble was now at hand in spite of the best efforts of Confederate arms, and appeals for help "unto man" bore "no fruit." "We have nothing left but to follow the example of the Psalmist and crying unto God to 'give us help from trouble,' to acknowledge that 'vain is the help of man'" (3–4). Elliott noted that this was no new state of affairs. It had been known from the beginning of the conflict that for the South to prevail, God had to be on its side. In the past God had answered distress calls for the Confederate cause, but "we now are in bitterness for our own fair heritage, and for the sufferings of our personal friends, and for the slaughter of those who are near and dear to us" (4). The prayers being offered were for personal deliverance.

It was proper to ask God to alleviate their distress, but at the same time the people of Georgia had to recognize that they were in the midst of a time of trial that already had afflicted their sister states: "Why should we, of all the States of the Confederacy have hoped to be exempt from suffering? Are we better than they? Have we a higher tone of morality and religion than that proud mother of

States [Virginia] for example, who has for three years been the battle ground of
the revolution?" (5). It would be better, Elliott argued, if Georgia bore its share
of the suffering wrought by the invaders. The state's fields were being strewn
with "blood and desolation," but the struggle should produce a "national character" that "would bless us for long generations" (6).

Elliott then reprised a theme from prior sermons that, although only God
could deliver his people, his people had to supply the instruments of deliverance,
namely food, supplies, and men for the army—and too many of his people had
failed in their duty: "What can our State expect but subjugation, if her citizens
will not consent to supply our armies with food and with men?" (7). The bishop
then turned to the issue of slavery and the black race:

> In this conflict, more perhaps than in any the world has seen, must it be
> God who shall tread under foot our enemies. It is a conflict involving the
> future of a race, whose existence or extinction depends upon its result. The
> white race of the South, even though subjugated might continue to exist, to
> live on for a time in shame and degradation, and at last to commingle, as the
> Anglo-Saxons did, with their Norman conquerors. But the black race perishes
> with its freedom. They will die out before the encroaching white labor of Eu-
> rope, which will be poured in upon them, as the Indians have died out before
> the progress of civilization, or they will be banished to other lands to perish
> there, forgotten and unlamented. (8–9)

Having stipulated this consequence for the black race should the North prevail,
Elliott went on to reaffirm that God had allowed black people to be brought to
the South as slaves "to be preserved, to increase, and to be civilized" and that the
freedom sought for them by their "pretended friends" was at odds with God's
purposes. God therefore would ensure that the North was not victorious.

Elliott also restated his belief that the Civil War served two divine purposes,
to wit: punishment from God for America's sin of "ascribing to their institutions"
rather than to God's kindness and mercy their success and power and the "dis-
comfiture" of "short-sighted philanthropists" who had chosen among their missions the abolition of slavery. On the latter point Elliott contended that already
"the bitterest disappointment of this war [to the abolitionists] has been the quiet
contentment of the slaves. They have never gone to our enemies in any numbers"
(10). He added that the fate of slaves who had fallen under the aegis of the Union
armies was a sad one, and estimated that one-half of those who had thus been
"deprived of the protection of their masters had already perished" (11).

Elliott presents the entire course of the war, especially the defeats and sufferings of the South, as punishment for its sins, but notes that "when God is satisfied
with our chastisement, and we, in humble penitence and submission have said,

'Give us help from trouble; for vain is the help of man,' then will He permit our sufferings to cease and theirs [the people of the North] to begin. They need not boast that they do not feel the war; they need not exult in their wealth and luxury; they are only fattening in a large place as a lamb for the slaughter. Their feet shall slide in due time" (12).

What had to be feared most, Elliott proclaimed, was not the power and cruelty of the Union; it was that the people of the South might waver: "What we have most to fear in our exhausted and depressed condition, is an administration which would come with kindness on its lips, and reconstruction with our ancient privileges in its hand. I fear our people would not have virtue to resist it, and we should be linked once more to that 'body of death'" (12–13). He closed with a defiant peroration: "We must make the choice between a perpetual resistance, if necessary, and a condition of serfdom, in which we and our children shall be made 'hewers of wood and drawers of water,' to the paupers of Europe, the negroes of Africa, and last and lowest of all, to the Black Republicans of the North. If any of you are ready for that, I am not, and therefore I cry unto God to help me in trouble, 'for He it is who is to tread down our enemies'" (13). In this sermon Elliott thus mixed a prediction of dramatic reversal of fortune for the North with exhortations to the South and with graphic description of the consequences of Southern defeat.

## Hiatus and Disaster

There was a hiatus in the war in Georgia after this sermon; after regrouping, General John B. Hood took his army north to Tennessee in what proved to be a disastrous attempt to recapture Nashville and draw Sherman from Georgia. Sherman rested his army until November, but then began his march to the sea. Bishop Elliott left Savannah with a Confederate army under General William J. Hardee on 20 December, after which Union forces under Sherman occupied the city. Elliott wanted to be free "to communicate with my clergy, and to move in and out among my people as necessity should require."[19] The bishop spent Christmas in the home of William Bostick in Allendale, South Carolina, and officiated at a Methodist church while there. He then made his way to Augusta, arriving on 29 December, and remained there during the last months of the war.

### Notes

1. *Diocese of Georgia, 1861* (Savannah: John M. Cooper, 1861), 13.

2. Ibid., 19–20.

3. All excerpts are taken from Stephen Elliott, *God's Presence with Our Army at Manassas Junction. A Sermon Preached on 28 July 1861, in Christ Church, Savannah* (Savannah: W. Thorne Williams, 1861). Page references are in parentheses in text following each excerpt.

4. Excerpts that follow are from Stephen Elliott, *New Wine Not to Be Put into Old Bottles: A Sermon Preached in Christ Church, Savannah, on Friday, February 28th, 1862* (Savannah: John M. Cooper, 1862). Page references are in parentheses in text following each excerpt.

5. The Constitution of the Confederate States is provided online by Lillian Goldman Law Library of Yale University Law School: http://avalon.law.yale.edu/19th_century/csa _csa.asp (accessed 15 April 2009). The Constitution of the United States is provided on the Internet at http://www.usconstitution.net/const.html (accessed 15 April 2009).

6. *Diocese of Georgia, 1862* (Savannah: John M. Cooper, 1862), 8.

7. Ibid., 21.

8. Ibid., 37.

9. Excerpts taken from Stephen Elliott, *Our Cause in Harmony with the Purposes of God in Christ Jesus. A Sermon Preached in Christ Church, Savannah, on Thursday, September 18th, 1862* (Savannah: John Cooper, 1862). Page references are in parentheses in text following each excerpt. The published sermon includes a letter to Elliott from the wardens and vestry of Christ Church, Savannah.

10. According to the Historical Census Browser, Geostat Center, University of Virginia Library, there were 1.1 million slaves in the United States in 1810.

11. Excerpts taken from Stephen Elliott, *Samson's Riddle. A Sermon Preached in Christ Church, Savannah, on Friday, March 27th, 1863* (Macon: Burke, Boykin, 1863). Page references are in parentheses in text following each excerpt. The published version of the sermon includes correspondence between Elliot and the vestry of Christ Church, Savannah, and instructions and prayers for special service on 27 March 1863.

12. *Diocese of Georgia, 1863* (Savannah: E.J. Purse, 1863), 10.

13. Ibid., 19–20.

14. Stephen Elliott, *Ezra's Dilemma. A Sermon Preached in Christ Church, Savannah, on Friday, 21 August 1863* (Savannah: George H. Nichols, 1863), 15. Quotations that immediately follow are from this source; page references are given in parentheses in text following each quotation.

15. *Diocese of Georgia, 1864* (Savannah: E. J. Purse, 1864), 9. Page references for quotations that follow from this source are given parenthetically in text.

16. See below, the essay entitled "Polk, Lay, and Quintard: The War Up Close and Personal."

17. "Patience," in *Sermons by the Right Reverend Stephen Elliott, D.D., Late Bishop of Georgia, with a Memoir,* ed. Thomas Hanckel (New York: Pott and Amery, 1867), 490–94.

18. Stephen Elliott, A Sermon: *Vain Is the Help of Man. A Sermon Preached in Christ Church, Savannah, on Thursday, September 15, 1864* (Macon: Burke, Boykin, 1864), 3. Subsequent page references to this sermon are given parenthetically in text.

19. *Diocese of Georgia, 1865* (Savannah: Purse and Sons, 1865), 22.

# John Johns of Virginia

⊰⊱ *A Wartime Episcopate in a Battleground State*

## Church and State in Virginia, 1862

In Richmond on 22 February 1862, while serving as assistant bishop of the Diocese of Virginia, John Johns participated in the inauguration of Jefferson Davis as president of the Confederate States of America. As reported in the *Richmond Daily Dispatch*, "the exercises there were opened by a fervent, eloquent and patriotic prayer, from the Rt. Rev Bishop Johns, in which he earnestly invoked the guidance of Providence and protection of Heaven, in our struggle. The prayer of the Bishop . . . caused many a tear to trickle from eyes unused to weep."[1] Just under three weeks later, Bishop Meade died, and John Johns became bishop of Virginia.[2]

Jefferson Davis was reared as a Baptist, but after moving to Richmond decided to join the Episcopal Church, a decision that much pleased his wife, Varina Howell Davis.[3] President Davis was baptized by the Reverend Dr. Minnigerode, rector of St. Paul's, and confirmed later by Bishop Johns in a private ceremony.[4]

At the diocesan convention in May 1862, Johns urged the Diocese of Virginia to adopt the Constitution for the Protestant Episcopal Church in the Confederate States that had been approved at the provisional convention in Columbia in October 1861. The diocese accepted Johns's recommendation, and the Diocese of Virginia became part of the Confederate church.

### Ministry to the Soldiers

Although the Civil War was a major factor in the episcopates of all Southern bishops, its impact was particularly strong on Bishop Johns, essentially defining the first three years of his episcopate. Virginia was the battleground for the war in the East with nearly 140 engagements, including some of the major battles of the war, being fought on its soil. When his episcopate began, Johns was faced with the need to help supply a ministry to troops in Southern armies based in Virginia. Such a ministry involved helping to care for, spiritually and physically, a flood of wounded soldiers. As Johns saw it, this ministry also entailed helping to keep morale and support for the Confederate cause high. Johns also confronted disruption and destruction in parishes within his diocese and the concomitant need to maintain services and pastoral care for the affected congregations.

At Wheeling in April 1861, while still the assistant bishop, Johns was in the midst of episcopal visitations when word of Fort Sumter reached him. He had no official news and received no reply to a telegram, but he was "strongly inclined to return" and did so, reaching Seminary Hill in Alexandria at 10 P.M. on 26 April. Some students from the North had decided that they must leave the seminary, and Johns ordained three of them to the diaconate before they departed.[5] On 24 May, federal forces seized Alexandria, and Johns did not wish to be confined behind Union lines (and cut off from much of his diocese), so the Johns family departed, spending nights with friends as they traveled. During July 1861 Johns conducted religious services for Confederate soldiers at Manassas a few days before the great battle and was deeply moved by the experience at the time and later by its memory when he realized that it had been the final religious service for many soldiers.[6] After the battle he visited the wounded and preached at funeral services for those who had fallen, one service being at Warrenton for four soldiers. He reported to his diocese in 1862 that "many hearts were severely affected by this bereavement and deeply felt that the miseries of war are inseparable from its most brilliant victories."[7] Johns also recalled a poignant visit to a wounded Confederate colonel from Alabama. The officer was aware that he would not survive and told Johns that he "felt the need of a savior."[8]

When Johns became diocesan, it was clear from his remarks at his first meeting of the diocese that he expected a long struggle: "How long the eventful struggle in which we are engaged is to continue, or to what sacrifice and suffering it may expose us in its progress, it is for God, in his wise and merciful providence, to determine. It is our part and place to be at his feet in sincere humiliation for our sins—with filial trust in his mercy."[9]

In late June 1862 the series of battles known as the Seven Days took place, and Bishop Johns was there, as he reported to the diocese in May 1863:

> The battles in front of Richmond which had now begun, left me in no doubt as to the place of duty. Suspending all other services I hastened to the city to unite with my brethren of the Clergy in such ministrations as might be needed by the wounded and the dying.
>
> The signal successes with which it pleased Almighty God to crown our arms, effectually relieved our beleaguered metropolis, and the menacing hosts were driven into a position where, from the demoralization of defeat and the fatal malaria of the region, their remaining numbers were so reduced that their formal withdrawal was hardly noticeable. In the midst of our joy and

The Right Reverend John Johns, D.d., LL.D.

gratitude for such deliverance there was great cause for lamentation. Many noble men had fallen in our defence, and . . . wounded were conveyed to the hospitals in and around Richmond.

. . . These sufferings furnished occasion for the manifestation of some of the finest phases of character, in the uncomplaining spirit with which they were borne and the grateful, tender and efficient sympathy and care which they promptly received. Nothing seemed too much to be done for those to whom, under God, we owed so much, and whilst ministering to their bodily sufferings their spiritual welfare was not forgotten.[10]

Bishop Johns knew and admired General Thomas J. "Stonewall" Jackson, and the general respected the bishop.[11] Early in the spring of 1863 Jackson sent via a young chaplain a message to Johns, advising the bishop that there were forty vacant chaplaincies in the Army of the Rappahannock and begging that clergy be sent to the camp to provide ministerial services. Shortly thereafter Jackson was wounded at Chancellorsville and died on 10 May, less than two weeks before the convention began. Johns brought Jackson's appeal to the convention: "This last appeal for the spiritual benefit of a command which he blessed by his consistent example and wholesome influence as a Christian, and inspired with fearless energy by his own noble heroism, I cannot suppress, and you would not neglect. Though dead, he yet speaketh—'Send faithful ministers to the army.'"[12]

The council did respond with a resolution asking Bishop Johns to request clergy without parochial cures "to render religious services to the army, in such way and for such length of time as he may designate." It was also suggested that parishes with ministers would be willing to have their clergy assigned to the army for short stated periods, and the clerical members of the council volunteered to accept such assignments.[13]

In June, Bishop Johns accompanied General William N. Pendleton on a visit to General Richard S. Ewell's headquarters.[14] Ewell had replaced Jackson, and Johns was much encouraged by the visit, feeling that Ewell was a Christian commander and that "the grace of God had prepared the way most invitingly for the extension of the Gospel in the Army." Johns preached that same day to a regiment of Virginia soldiers.[15]

### Diocesan Visits in Wartime

Bishop Johns's calendar during the war years also was filled with episcopal visits to parishes throughout his diocese, preaching, confirming, and ordaining as he went. His record of visitations and confirmations reflected his concern for slaves. Impediments faced by the bishop, in addition to normal weather delays, were caused by the war. In May 1863, for example, he missed an appointment at Hicksford because travel on the Richmond and Fredericksburg Railroad was first halted briefly and then reserved for the military. As the war wore on, his visits became more unpredictable and difficult. The following account, from Sunday, 7 August 1864, is illustrative:

> We . . . proceeded through a desolate and apparently deserted county to Shepherdstown, into which . . . we entered with some anxiety, uncertain by which army it was occupied. We found it to be in the possession of a few Confederates, but as the Union troops in large numbers were known to be only a few miles distant, and their advance expected, it was suggested that we might be interrupted in our proposed services and subject to inconvenient detention. We concluded, however, to venture upon the experiment. The bell was rung, and the congregation assembled. The Reverend Mr. James read prayers.

Whilst I was preaching, a note was handed to the Rector informing him that the Federal forces were approaching the town. I was not willing to leave the church without confirming those who were desirous to ratify their baptismal vow. Descending to the chancel and calling them around me, I administered the apostolic rite to ten persons. The service was of peculiar interest, and I'm sure will not soon be forgotten by those whom it specially concerned, or by those by whom it was witnessed.[16]

### Desecration and Disruption

The greatest impediment to parish life during the war, however, was directly caused by acts of federal forces against churches. Many churches were desecrated. Some disruptive acts served a legitimate purpose, including those cases in which church buildings were used as field hospitals. There were documented cases of wanton destruction, however, including those in which churches were converted, by ripping out the pews, to horse stables. Other churches were utterly destroyed. In a few cases the federal commanders simply seized a church and brought in Episcopal clergy from outside the diocese to conduct services and manage the church building. Finally, Union officers decreed in some instances that the Prayer for the President of the United States and all in Civil Authority be used during services of Morning and Evening Prayer. Clergy refusing to use the prayer had their churches closed. At least three Episcopal ministers were arrested for declining to comply; in one case the minister, the Reverend Dr. J. H .D. Wingfield, was sentenced to serve on the chain gang, cleaning up the streets of Portsmouth.[17]

The "Parochial Reports" section of 1863 *Journal of the Annual Council* for the Diocese of Virginia includes reports of the disruption experienced by diocesan clergy, one of which is provided below:

Spottsylvania County, St. George's Church, Fredericksburg,
A. M. Randolph, Rector.

The Federal forces occupied Fredericksburg about the middle of April 1862. In consequence, the Rector was prevented from attending the Convention of that year, or from sending the usual report. The public are familiar with the sad history of Fredericksburg from the 17th of November last. Since that time no services have been held in the church by the Rector. He has been occupied during the winter and spring, in visiting the few families of his congregation which remain in the neighborhood of the town, and in distributing funds so generously contributed for the relief of the Fredericksburg sufferers. He is about to enter upon the duties of a chaplain in the Confederate army. During the bombardment of the town the church was struck twenty-five times. The communion service was stolen—the building desecrated by the enemy.[18]

In his 1863 address to the diocese, Johns asked for other parts of the diocese to come to the aid of the sections damaged by the war: "In those sections of our State which have been invaded and devastated by the enemy, parishes and congregations previously flourishing and efficient, have been sadly impoverished and disabled. . . . These devastated parishes are now, in a measure missionary ground, and rendered so by a painful dispensation which must endear them exceedingly to their more favored brethren."[19] At the time they occurred, these acts by Union soldiers made it difficult for the Diocese of Virginia to provide religious services. The more lasting effect, however, was the bitterness engendered. These bitter feelings resulted in the Diocese of Virginia, which had been among the last of the dioceses to separate, and then with reluctance, from the Protestant Episcopal Church in the United States, becoming the very last diocese to reunite with that body after the war.

## Notes

1. *Richmond Daily Dispatch,* 24 February 1862, 3. Jefferson Davis was inaugurated as provisional president in Montgomery, Alabama, on 18 February 1861. After the State of Virginia joined the Confederacy, the capital was moved to Richmond. Following his election to a six-year term on 6 November 1861, Davis was inaugurated as president of the Confederate States of America on 22 February 1862. The ceremony was on the capitol grounds.

2. See above, the essay entitled "A Controversial Consecration and a Bishop's Death: Richard Hooker Wilmer and William Meade."

3. Ishbel Ross, *First Lady of the Confederacy: The Life of Mrs. Jefferson Davis* (New York: Harper, 1958), 146. Ms. Ross relates that Varina Davis, who had been reared as an Episcopalian, had asked the Reverend Dr. Charles Minnigerode, rector of St. Paul's Church in Richmond, to speak with Jefferson about joining the Episcopal Church. Dr. Minnegerode did so, and Varina Davis was happy with the outcome.

4. Elizabeth Wright Weddell, *St. Paul's Church Richmond Virginia: Its Historic Years and Memorials,* 2 vols. (Richmond: William Byrd Press, 1931), 1:160–61.

5. *Diocese of Virginia, 1861* (Richmond: C. Wynne, 1861), 41–42.

6. *Diocese of Virginia, 1862* (Richmond: MacFarlane and Fergusson, 1862), 14.

7. Ibid., 14.

8. Ibid., 15.

9. Ibid., 20.

10. *Diocese of Virginia, 1863* (Richmond: MacFarlane and Fergusson, 1863), 16.

11. Sumner Wood, *The Virginia Bishop: A Yankee Hero of the Confederacy* (Richmond: Garrett and Massie, 1961), 36.

12. *Diocese of Virginia, 1863,* 23–24.

13. Ibid., 27.

14. At the outbreak of the war, the Reverend William N. Pendleton was a priest serving as a church rector in the Diocese of Virginia. Pendleton was also a West Point graduate, however, and accepted an artillery command in the Confederate army. He continued his

diocesan connection, conducting services while in the army, but he resigned his rectorship at the end of 1862. General Pendleton served for a long period as chief of artillery for
General Lee.

15. *Diocese of Virginia, 1864* (Richmond: Farlane and Ferguson, 1864), 14.

16. *Diocese of Virginia, 1865.* (Richmond: Gary and Clemmitt, 1866), 17.

17. G. MacLaren Brydon, "The Diocese of Virginia in the Southern Confederacy," *Historical Magazine of the Protestant Episcopal Church* 17 (December 1948): 384–410. See also
John Fulton, "The Church in the Confederate States," in William Stevens Perry, *The History of the American Episcopal Church, 1587–1883*, 2 vols. (Boston: Osgood 1885), 2:577–78.
The Reverend Dr. Wingfield's sentence to the chain gang was soon revoked. This and
other examples of acts, motivated by the "prayer issue," against Episcopal Churches by
federal forces are described in these two references.

18. *Diocese of Virginia, 1863*, 81–82.

19. Ibid., 22–23.

# The Impact of War
# on an Episcopate

✛═ *Thomas Frederick Davis of South Carolina*

At the time of the June 1861 meeting of the Diocese of South Carolina the Civil War was two months old, and Bishop Thomas Frederick Davis had this to say about it to his clergy and laity:

> We are in the midst of war and its consequences. We are looking out every day for exciting events.— Our hearth-stones are up-turned. Our brothers and our children are in the field. Our youths with whom hitherto we have only sported have sprung up into armed men. This is not confined to a few; it is spread throughout the land. There is not a hamlet where it is not heard; there is not a heart which it does not reach. . . . But this is no time for weakness or for fear. A country was never so saved. . . . Our cause is right and our God is true. Let us show the world that we can trust both. . . . We are not dependent upon circumstances or combinations or numbers for our inward strength, but can stand erect in personal character, in the sense of integrity and the fear of God. Before Him indeed let us humble ourselves, confess our sins, implore his pardon, and supplicate his grace and spiritual benediction.[1]

The convention fully supported Bishop Davis's position on the war, passing four resolutions with regard to it. The fourth resolution expressed disappointment in their Northern Episcopal brethren: "Resolved, That . . . we cannot but express our great surprise and bitter mortification, that none of those who have been united with us in the household of faith, have, so far as we have known, either individually or through an ecclesiastical body, raised their voice against the measures now in progress for our subjugation—all having with one consent united in the endeavor to throw the sanctions of religion around a government which has violated the most fundamental principles of its own constitution and of civil liberty."[2] The fundamental point in this statement, that churchmen in the South were greatly disappointed in the stance of their colleagues in the North on the war, was shared widely by other Southern bishops and churchmen. Bishops

North and South sharply disagreed as to which side of the conflict deserved the "sanctions of religion" or, in plainer terms, as to which side God favored.

In July, Davis participated in the Montgomery meeting of delegates from dioceses in the seceded states, and Trinity Church in Columbia hosted the adjourned session in October. The South Carolina delegation and its bishop supported the establishment of a separate organizational structure for a church in the Confederate States. In spite of these two extended meetings, Davis continued his visitation schedule. On 28 July 1861, for example, the Day of Thanksgiving for Victory at Manassas, he preached "on the state of the country" at Holy Trinity in Grahamville. That afternoon he consecrated the nearby Bethel Chapel, which "had been erected chiefly for the accommodation of the colored people," then preached and confirmed sixteen black persons.[3]

At the diocesan meeting in February 1862, the deputies voted to approve the proposed constitution for the Protestant Episcopal Church in the Confederate States of America that was circulated following the Columbia meeting, and delegates were elected to the new church council to be held in Augusta in November 1862.

### Role of the Church in Wartime

Davis concluded his diocesan convention address in 1862 with the following words:

> Beloved brethren, the times that try men's souls are upon us. We are visited with a war, cruel and unnatural. Those who were our brethren are invading our soil and desolating our homes. Every day brings with it increased intelligence of their encroachments, ravages, and bloodshed. But let none of these things move us. Let us "not be afraid of their terror, neither be troubled; but sanctify the Lord God in our hearts." . . . Let us submit to His Holy will; rest upon His mercies, and pray to him to strengthen our confidence in his mighty power and righteous judgment.[4]

Davis attended the first PECCSA council in Augusta, meeting in November 1862, and reported at the 1863 diocesan council. He congratulated those at the diocesan session "upon the regular and permanent organization of the Protestant Episcopal Church in the Confederate States of America." The bishop was pleased with the canons approved in Augusta and clearly felt that there was now a proper administrative structure for the Southern church.[5]

Davis's remarks about the war at the 1863 diocesan council were confined to expressing concern and exhorting the delegates about an aspect dear to his heart.

> The number of confirmations among the colored people for the past year is less than one-sixth part of the annual confirmations of each year for the last preceding nine; and the confirmations are tolerably fair exponents of ministerial

operations among these people. Why is this? The cause is only too apparent. Along our entire coast, including its islands and adjacent territories with rare exceptions, the voice of our ministers is no longer heard among them nor their footsteps seen. Who is answerable for this loss and moral wrong to these unoffending people? But we do not expect to make any impressions upon our enemies; nor is it for us to condemn; the judgment is above and there we must all give account. But this seems clear; that the Southern people must alone be looked to for the religious instruction of the negro population.[6]

The bishop was speaking here of federal activities along the South Carolina coast, which involved excursion raids and Union seizure of some ports and coastal land. These activities supported the Union blockade of the Southern coast, and the first foray in South Carolina had been the Union takeover of Port Royal, Beaufort, and surrounding lands in the fall of 1861. These outposts and raids posed the threat of liberating slaves or causing them to run for freedom. Many slaves were moved inland to avoid this danger, and the missionaries who were serving the affected plantations no longer could function effectively. The blame, Davis was certain, for this terrible consequence of war lay with the Union, the aggressor. The bishop called for an increase in effort by clergy and laity to reach the black population in order to overcome this problem. South Carolina clergy served as chaplains to units on the front lines in Virginia and to soldiers stationed along the coast of South Carolina. Vacancies left by clergy who accepted assignment as chaplains were among the dislocations caused by the war that reduced the missionary effort among slaves or deprived white congregations of pastoral care.

On 10 May 1864 Bishop Davis consecrated the Church of the Advent in Spartanburg, and the next day the diocesan council convened in the same church. The Confederacy's military situation was grim by that time. Defeats at Gettysburg and Vicksburg had occurred the prior summer, and even as the convention opened Sherman was beginning the campaign that would result in the capture of Atlanta. Still, most of Davis's address had a business-as-usual tone. The period covered by Davis's report was from 14 February 1863 to 10 May 1864, and he listed many visits and confirmations. From 3 through 17 April 1864 Davis had visited chapels on eight separate plantations, during which time he had confirmed 128 slaves. In his closing exhortation, however, he appeared to acknowledge the situation that the South faced: "And now, brethren, surrounded as we are by dangers and pressed by our enemies, let us gird up the loins of our minds, and strengthen our faith in the righteous and overruling Providence of God. Let us so truly seek to do His will that, in all our works, 'begun, continued, and ended in Him, we may glorify His holy name; and finally, by his mercy, obtain everlasting life, through Jesus Christ our Lord.'"[7]

The Right Reverend Thomas Frederick Davis, D.D.

The explicit message of 1861, "Our cause is right and our God is true," had carried over to 1864 only partially. God was still true, and Southern churchmen should have faith in his "overruling Providence," but the sure result, Davis seemed to be saying, was that God would decide righteously, not necessarily, for a Southern victory.

## Devastation and Defeat: 1863–1865

Two federal campaigns wreaked havoc in South Carolina as the war wound down. Both Union efforts, by design, impacted heavily on the civilian population. Many churches were damaged, and ten were destroyed; congregations were scattered; and ministers were driven out of their homes or dislocated by the disruption of their parishes. Parishioners and priests alike were impoverished.

### Bombardment of Charleston

The first campaign started in the late summer of 1863, when Union artillery began a bombardment of Charleston that continued at intervals until the city was evacuated by the remaining Confederate defenders and surrendered to Union forces by the mayor in February 1865. The first big Union gun was located in a muddy area by Morris Island, and later batteries were set up on Black Island and at Cummings Point; all locations were approximately five miles from the city. In the early months of the bombardment the steeple of St. Michael's Episcopal Church was used by Union artillery gunners as a target, which in effect guided the shells into the lower part of the city. On Christmas night 1863, just after midnight, a barrage began that landed 134 shells in that area. In a nine-day period in January 1864 some 1,500 shells hit the city. As the shelling continued for nearly a year and a half, the daily intensity varied greatly, but incendiary shells were used and there were fires almost every day that bombardment occurred. The gunners over time shifted their aim toward upper Charleston; the range of the guns ended around Calhoun Street.[8]

The bombardment disrupted life in lower Charleston, and businesses and residents moved uptown or out of town. Churches were affected also, including the two best-known churches in the city, as indicated by a diocesan damage-assessment committee report.

> St. Michael's. The grave yard was ploughed, and its monuments scarred by the balls so remorselessly rained upon it. . . . Several shells penetrated the Church, destroying portions of the interior. The roof, pews, and floor suffered from the dangerous missiles. One struck the centre of the chancel wall and burst just within, tearing in pieces the carved panels of English oak, with its exquisite paintings, and massive rails. . . .

> St. Philip's. St. Philip's Church suffered more than St. Michael's, or any other in the city. The marks of twelve shells were visible, which had penetrated the roof and walls. The costly organ was irreparably damaged.[9]

On Sunday, 19 November 1863, before this damage occurred, both churches had decided to discontinue services for the duration of the war. The decision was based on a bombardment that began during church services. St. Michael's cut its service short. At St. Philip's the rector, the Reverend William Bell Howe, who was to succeed Davis as bishop, did not interrupt his sermon; he conducted the service as usual, and the congregation remained with him. Both of these congregations were invited by St. Paul's, located in the city but beyond range of Union missiles, to worship there. The invitation was accepted, and the ministers shared the services until the two downtown churches could reopen.[10]

Other churches in the city were damaged by the bombardment, and some in the environs were damaged by federal forces that occupied the area after Charleston was evacuated by the Confederates. Some examples: at the 1864 council the Reverend J. G. Drayton, minister of St. Andrew's Parish, reported that "the congregations during the past winter and spring have been large, but made up principally of the troops quartered in the parish, and so constantly fluctuating. Many of the parishioners are still away, and in their places refugees from the islands have come. Under these circumstances, no accurate list of congregation or communicants can be given."[11] At the 1866 council Drayton reported that soon after the evacuation of Charleston his parishioners all departed and "there was no longer a field for the exercise of my ministry."[12]

In May 1864 the Reverend Christopher Gadsden reported that many from his congregation at St. Luke's in Charleston were refugees in other parts of the state. He was continuing services at St. Luke's, however, including a weekly prayer meeting for the black members. He was also holding services for soldiers and officiating at other churches when asked. In 1866 he reported simply that, on 11 October 1864, he had left, "my congregation having been driven from the church by the bombardment."[13] In 1866 the Reverend Henry L. Philips reported that in January 1864 he had been driven from St. Luke's Chapel in Charleston by "the sacrilegious missiles of the enemy."[14]

The Reverend Charles Cotesworth Pinckney, rector of Grace Church in Charleston, reported at the 1864 council that, as of 1 January 1864, "the Siege of Charleston has suspended our services . . . , our church being within range of the enemy's fire. Thus far it has mercifully escaped all injury. . . . Our congregation is still scattered over the state, our Sunday-school closed, and our good works hindered by the war. The attendance at the church has been chiefly from the military and members of other congregations."[15] After the surrender of Charleston, Grace Church reopened and Pinckney at first did not offer the prayer for the president of the United States. When federal soldiers were sent with an order for him to do so, he complied, saying, "I know of no one who needs praying for more than the President of the United States."[16]

In January 1865 Bishop Davis visited Charleston, preaching at St. Paul's, which, in addition to those congregants from St. Michael's and St. Philip's, was attracting communicants from other congregations that had been dispersed as the war enveloped coastal South Carolina. The bishop also preached or officiated on James Island, Sullivan's Island, and at Mount Pleasant. Many of his listeners were soldiers.

### Sherman's March through South Carolina

The second federal campaign of destruction began in January 1865, when Union general William Tecumseh Sherman's forces entered South Carolina from near Savannah, Georgia, to undertake a march of two months' duration that would lay waste to a swath of land some one hundred miles wide as the marchers moved from the lower western part of South Carolina up to Fayetteville, North Carolina. Several columns of Sherman's army spread apart to follow a route that moved from near Savannah to encompass Orangeburg, then Columbia, then Cheraw, finally to end at Fayetteville. The best-known incident in Sherman's South Carolina march is the burning of Columbia, but the torching and other destructive acts, especially by Sherman's "bummers," who were responsible for foraging to feed and supply the army, left ruin all along the march's route. The march began in the southwestern part of the state. A sampling of reports from the aftermath is provided below:

> St. Peter's Church, Robertsville . . . was a new church, built in 1859, of wood. It was burnt by the Federal army in January, 1865, together with the residences of every member of the congregation. The small congregation has been entirely dispersed. There is neither building, nor minister, nor people. The church may be considered dead.
>
> Christ Church, Columbia, shared the fate of that beautiful city when burnt by General Sherman's army in February 1865. . . . The Church with its organ, carpets, books, and all that it contained, was destroyed that fearful night . . . and the removal of many of their members in the depopulation of Columbia has reduced to its lowest ebb this once flourishing congregation. . . . The few survivors . . . unable to support a minister. Their services are maintained by the aid of the Domestic Board of Missions.
>
> St. John's Church, Winnsboro. This church was wantonly burnt by Sherman's troops, on their march through Winnsboro. The public square was destroyed, but the church was not touched by that fire. It was on the outskirts of the town in a large lot, and was deliberately set on fire by the soldiers. . . .
>
> St. David's, Cheraw was the last church in the eastern part of the State in the line of the Federal invasion. It was seriously damaged by an explosion of ammunition near it, and doors, windows, and part of the wall shattered. The Church plate was stolen, with books and furniture, and its enclosure torn down. But the Church is habitable, and its worship continues.[17]

The Reverend J. H. Quinby, who had returned to the Diocese of South Carolina from Texas in 1861, was providing services for a small group in Lexington and teaching to earn an adequate income when Sherman's troops came through: "After Sherman had desolated the Country . . . my school was so broken up and scattered, that I could barely eke out a subsistence. . . . At last I was compelled to abandon the place, and the hopes of the Church's future there. . . . Since my return [to Charleston], I have been officiating for the congregation at Calvary Church, and have celebrated the Holy Communion once and baptized three colored adults and two children."[18] Destruction was not limited to places of worship serving largely whites, and the resultant disruption of slave congregations was accentuated by emancipation which began de facto as the Confederate cause was dying late in the war and then became general and *de jure* as federal troops assumed the role of occupation forces after the war. Examples from a diocesan committee report of damage are cited below.

> The Church on Hilton Head, a chapel of ease to St. Luke's Parish, has entirely disappeared. It was a wooden structure, not of much value. The materials, it is believed, were removed by the negroes in order to build homes for themselves on that island.
>
> This appears to have been the fate with many of the chapels built by the planters all around Beaufort, for the religious benefit of their people. Chapels and materials have both disappeared, probably with the same destination.
>
> The Mission Chapel, . . . built by Rev. S. Elliott for the negroes on the Combahee, was taken down by Sherman's troops in order to build a bridge over that river. . . .
>
> It was Mr. Elliott's design to revive his church among the colored population, to whom he had been preaching the gospel for thirty years . . . but his unexpected death deprived the diocese . . . of one of the most experienced African missionaries of our Church; . . . his work has ceased, his congregation is scattered, and his Church destroyed.
>
> Waccamaw . . . : the prostration of the once flourishing Churches on Waccamaw is complete. . . . There were the homes of the largest rice planters on this continent. Their provision for the temporal and spiritual welfare of their slaves was a standard to other planters. Numerous chapels, built by the proprietors for the use of their people, adorned the estates. . . . The faithful labors of their revered pastor, Rev. A. Glennie, for thirty years, had brought blessed results, aided by the systematic teachings of the planters and their families. Hundreds of the colored race were communicants of our Church—thousands of colored children recited the catechism. . . . Alas . . . poverty has overtaken these desolated homes. The rice fields . . . lie desolate; their former laborers can scarcely be induced to work. . . .
>
> Their religious deterioration is painful. They have forsaken the way which they had learned, and taken to themselves teachers of their own color. . . . There are no religious services re-established in the three churches on Waccamaw. The planters are bankrupt; their houses despoiled.[19]

## A Diocese in Chaos

The Episcopal Church in South Carolina during the last year of the war thus suffered desolation and impoverishment, with many of its congregations scattered and ministers displaced. The ministry to black people suffered also from a turning away of former slaves from the Episcopal Church. When peace came Bishop Davis would confront the monumental challenge of restoring and revitalizing the church's mission in South Carolina.

## Notes

1. *Diocese of South Carolina, 1861* (Charleston: A. E. Miller, 1861),18.

2. Ibid., 24.

3. *Diocese of South Carolina, 1862* (Charleston: A. E. Miller, 1862), 20.

4. Ibid., 25–26.

5. *Diocese of South Carolina, 1863* (Charleston: A. E. Miller, 1863), 27–28.

6. Ibid., 28.

7. *Diocese of South Carolina, 1864* (Columbia: Evans and Cogswell, 1864), 27.

8. E. Milby Burton, *The Siege of Charleston, 1861–1865* (Columbia: University of South Carolina Press, 1970), 255–59.

9. "Destruction of Churches and Church Property," *Diocese of South Carolina, 1868* (Charleston: Joseph Walker, 1868), 79–92.

10. W. Chris Phelps, *The Bombardment of Charleston, 1863–1865* (Gretna, La.: Pelican Publishing, 2002), 46–47.

11. *Diocese of South Carolina, 1864,* 43.

12. *Diocese of South Carolina, 1866* (Charleston: Joseph Walker, 1866), 55.

13. Ibid., and *Diocese of South Carolina, 1864,* 45.

14. *Diocese of South Carolina, 1866,* 58.

15. Diocese of South Carolina, 1864, 57.

16. Phelps, *Bombardment of Charleston,* 141.

17. *Diocese of South Carolina, 1868,* (Charleston: Joseph Walker, 1868), 79–92.

18. *Diocese of South Carolina, 1866,* 61.

19. *Diocese of South Carolina, 1868,* 79–92.

# Thomas Atkinson of North Carolina

✠ *Wartime Episcopate*

### Civil War in North Carolina

The war came early to North Carolina, with fighting in August 1861 at Hatteras Inlet, followed by engagements in February and March 1862 at Roanoke Island and New Bern. These were Union successes that helped to tighten the Union blockade of the Southern coast. About twenty engagements occurred in the state, nearly all relatively minor, but the last battle at Bentonville from 19 to 21 March 1865 between forces led by Confederate general Joseph E. Johnston and Union general William Tecumseh Sherman resulted in an estimated 4,700 casualties. After being defeated Johnson retreated toward Raleigh and in late April surrendered his army to Sherman. There were very few Confederate successes on North Carolina soil.[1]

### War Overview 1861

As noted above in "Prelude to Montgomery," Thomas Atkinson had not advocated secession. He abhorred the thought of civil war, however, and saw the North as the aggressor for not letting the South depart in peace. He clarified—and justified—his dedication to the Southern cause in a sermon given on 5 May 1861. He outlined first the catastrophic storm starting to burst upon the South, then made plain his belief that God was directing the track of the storm and that it was by repentance and adherence to God's will that the storm's fury could be abated:

> We stand today, face-to-face with civil war, a calamity, which, unless the experience and universal testimony of mankind deceive us, is direr and more to be deprecated than foreign war, than famine, than pestilence, than any other form of public evil. The cloud we have all been so long watching, which we have seen, day by day, and month by month, enlarging its skirts, and gathering blackness, is now beginning to burst upon us.

It seems to me that no one but an Atheist . . . can doubt that it is God who rides in this storm, and will direct the whirlwind, and that He now calls upon us to look to Him, to consider our ways and our doings, to remember the offences by which we have heretofore provoked Him, and to determine on the conduct we will hereafter pursue towards Him, toward our fellowmen, and towards ourselves.[2]

Atkinson saw two grounds for God's favor, one of which was that North Carolina had no part in causing the conflict. The second was that the South, at this point, was indisputably in the right:

She [North Carolina] has sought, until the last moment, to avert it. . . . But when compelled to elect between furnishing troops to subdue her nearest neighbors and kindred, and to open her territory for the passage of armies marshaled to accomplish that odious, unauthorized and unhallowed object, or to refuse to aid, and to seek to hinder such attempts, she chose the part which affection, and interest, and duty seems manifestly, and beyond all reasonable question, to require.[3] . . . There is another consideration from which I derive great comfort. . . . It is that whatever we may think of some of the earlier steps in these disputes . . . we can calmly, conscientiously, and . . . conclusively, . . . maintain before God and man that *now* at least we of the South are in the right. For we are on the defensive, we ask only to be let alone. (6)

The "old Union" was "now dissolved," and the choices were (1) a voluntary and friendly separation or (2) an attempt at subjugation. These were choices between peaceful separation and civil war "with all its horrors," and Atkinson thought that the choice was clear. He marveled that anyone would hesitate at which to choose: "I cannot then doubt, and it seems a singular hallucination that any man should mistake, the righteous cause in this present most lamentable controversy, and I hope and I believe that God will bless with temporal success the righteous cause. He may not, however, for He does not always see fit to make right visibly triumphant.—But succeed or not, it is the cause on the side of which one would desire to be found" (7).

Atkinson thus believed that the South was on the right side in the war that had broken out, but he also believed that God would grant the South victory only if the Southern people turned to God and followed his ways. The terrible scourge of civil war Atkinson believed had resulted from the country's failure to withstand the trial of prosperity. Prosperity, in fact, had been accompanied by rapid moral deterioration. The Civil War was a time of trial for that deterioration and the accompanying plethora of sins. He advised his hearers to "believe and lay to heart, and keep constantly before your minds this most certain truth, that whoever may be the *instruments* of our present troubles, God is the efficient author of them. . . . The first requisite to success against our enemies is reverent obedience towards God. . . . Let us then earnestly and perseveringly seek the favor of Him without whom our enemies can do us no hurt" (11–12).

Atkinson cautioned against bitter feelings and language toward those "once our brethren" but now our enemies on the battlefield. He asked his listeners to recall the prayer of Christ on the cross and to follow that example.

## War Overview 1862–1864

At the May 1862 diocesan convention Atkinson's assessment of the war and its impact did not strike an optimistic chord, but he urged forbearance and faith in the God who was directing the war: "We suffer, not only as patriots, but as churchmen. The blood of our brethren of the household of faith has been shed on the field of battle. Our congregations have been dispersed, our ministers driven from their churches, public worship suspended, and the slender maintenance of the clergy diminished or taken away. . . . May we, by His grace, learn to bear [these calamities], and to inherit the blessing promised to those who suffer as Christians."[4] To the list of disruptions of church activities Atkinson might have added his visitation schedule, which had to remain flexible throughout the war. Damage to roads and rails augmented the damage to church property and the scattering and impoverishment of some congregations.

At the May 1863 council of the diocese Atkinson felt that the diocese had reason to thank God for being able to meet again. He noted that many of "the sad forebodings of the past year" were unfulfilled and that prospects for the future were "more cheering." The "tide of invasion had been stayed," and Atkinson felt that God was more likely to "vouchsafe" an honorable peace.[5]

Two months after his assessment at the May 1863 council, however, there came the defeats at Gettysburg and Vicksburg, and at the diocesan council a year later Atkinson's perspective had shifted: "Amid the scenes of worldly distress and confusion witnessed around us, we are led to look for encouragement and consolation, not so much to the hope of final, perhaps speedy success and deliverance to our country, although this too is right and reasonable, as to the remembrance of what He has done for His church, and the greater blessings, we trust, He has yet in store for her."[6]

## Ministry to the Soldiers

Throughout the high and low points of the war, Atkinson sought to provide for the spiritual welfare of Confederate soldiers. His personal ministry led him to spend the month of August 1861 in Virginia where he officiated at services in military encampments and also preached at Richmond churches.[7] He also encouraged his clergy to serve as chaplains to army regiments. In his 1862 diocesan address Atkinson reported that five clergy from the diocese were serving as

The Right Reverend Thomas Atkinson, D.D., LL.D.

chaplains, two of whom had remained parish rectors. As the war progressed and the demand for chaplains rose and the number of available clergy diminished, Atkinson proposed a plan for temporary military service by diocesan clergy: "To supply this lack of service, the most feasible and most equal plan seems to be to designate certain clergymen who should give a portion of their time to the Army without resigning their parishes, having their places during the period of service, supplied in some part by their neighboring brethren."[8]

In his treatment of the life of Bishop Atkinson, Marshall Haywood lists thirteen clergymen from North Carolina and their regimental or post assignments as chaplains.[9] Reports from two chaplains in the diocesan journal of 1864 are excerpted below, the first from the Reverend Joseph Murphy, rector of the Church of the Holy Innocents in Henderson: "From the date of my last report to Nov. 2, 1863, I continued my work as chaplain of the 32nd Regiment N.C.T., giving the soldiers under my care such attention as circumstances seemed to allow. During the month of July, after the Battle of Gettysburg, and at one of the field hospitals, I buried 23 soldiers." The Reverend George Patterson, Chaplain 3rd Regiment, N.C.T., had received various donations and used the funds to purchase Bibles and prayer books for the troops. He also reported: "I have been connected with this regiment since December 1862. On Sundays, services read from Prayer Book and as circumstances permit, Eucharist celebrated. On June 20th, 1863, at Sharpsburg, Maryland, I read the Funeral Office over the bodies of our soldiers who were killed in the battle near that place on September 17th, 1862."[10]

### Ministry to Slaves

Bishop Atkinson's primary charge in 1855 included an exhortation to attend to the religious instruction of slaves, and the new bishop had vigorously tried to pursue that objective before the war. He continued his efforts during the war, but his attempts to reach the slaves often were impeded along with the other phases of his ministry. Atkinson maintained as best he could his schedule of visitations to slaves and noted in his reports of episcopal acts when "colored persons" were confirmed or baptized. One visit with slaves in October 1863 apparently went well: "At Mr. P.W. Hairston's, I preached to a large body of his slaves, some of his family, and a few of his neighbors also being present, and administered the Holy Communion. The care bestowed by Mr. and Mrs. Hairston on the religious instruction of the slaves is much to be commended."[11]

Another visit that same month saddened the bishop, motivating him to offer a commentary on the household of Josiah Collins, a wealthy slaveholder and churchman who had died. The bishop praised Collins's efforts to bring "Christian culture" to a large body of slaves. Referring to the effect of the war on Collins's estate and his slaves, Atkinson said in his diocesan address:

> It is a painful thought that this household has been scattered, the master's days embittered, perhaps shortened, and the comfort and happiness, and the spiritual advancement, of these negroes hindered by the efforts of those who claim to be the especial friends of that race. Whatever they may have meant, they have evidently so far done the part of its worst enemies, and the probable issue of their success in this war would be the ultimate extermination of the race they profess to wish to serve. That God will avert this, and the innumerable other ills which would result from their success, is and ever has been my confident belief. That we may use success, if he vouchsafes it to us, rightly, wisely, beneficially to that race, as well as to our own, is one of my dearest earthly aspirations.[12]

During the early war years confirmations of both white and black communicants dropped. By contrast, the numbers reported at councils in May 1864 and

September 1865 rose, reflecting the bishop's determination to minister in increasingly adverse times.[13]

## Confirmations in the Diocese of North Carolina, 1862–1865

| Convention year | White communicants | Black communicants | Total |
|---|---|---|---|
| 1862 | — | — | 122 |
| 1863 | 163 | 15 | 178 |
| 1864 | 281 | 29 | 310 |
| 1865 | 225 | 50 | 275 |

### Incidents at War's End

As the war drew to a close Bishop Atkinson and his family had taken temporary residence in Wadesboro. Unfortunately this location was in the path of General Sherman's sweep up the Carolinas from Savannah.

> Early in March I had brought home to me some of the atrocities and losses which war entails on a community, and which I had witnessed in varied forms at a distance—
>
> At that time the army of General Sherman, in its advance through the Carolinas, had come sufficiently near to Wadesborough, where my family had a temporary residence, for some of the marauding parties to visit that village. I thought it right to remain, and not leave my household exposed to outrage, and without any protection. I supposed, too, that my age and office would secure me against outrage. In this, it turned out, I was mistaken. I was robbed of property of considerable value; and that it might be accomplished more speedily and completely, a pistol was held at my head. While I do not affect to be indifferent, either to the outrage, or to the loss I have sustained, I felt at the time, and still feel, that it is a weighty counterbalancing consideration, that partaking of the evils which the people of my charge have been called upon to undergo, I could more truly and deeply sympathize with them in their sufferings.[14]

By permission of the bishop, the Reverend A. A. Watson, rector of St. James' Parish, was prepared not to use the prayer for the president of the Confederate States after the federal occupation of Wilmington in February 1865, but the military authority insisted that he use the prayer for the president of the United States. Watson declined to comply:

> This, I felt, I had no canonical right to do; and for this reason, and because I would by its use have made myself a party to the infringement of the liberty of

the church, to direct her own worship, I refused compliance. The keys of the church then were seized by military orders, emanating, I believe, from Major Gen. Schofield. Subsequently, the church was seized by order of Brig. Gen. Jos Hawley (now Gov. of CT) for a military hospital . . . the pews were . . . torn out with pick axes. The pastor and people had quietly, however reluctantly, submitted to the change of authority. There was sufficient room elsewhere, more suitable for hospital purposes.[15]

Rector Watson was ordered to leave, but before he was forced to do so the war ended, and his application to use the church again was granted, contingent upon his use of the prayer for the president, which, at that point, the rector agreed was appropriate.

### Postwar Overview 1865

In September 1865 Atkinson told his diocesan council that "whatever else we may see in this result, we as Christians must see the finger of God in it. The Government of the United States is the Government He has appointed for us. These are the 'powers that be' ordained of God. Whoever resisteth the power resisteth the ordinance of God."[16] The bishop pointed out that the Southerners had appealed to the "God of Battles" and that he had decided against them. Atkinson went over different ways in which God might have intervened to alter the war's outcome, but the Almighty had chosen not to. God has spoken, the bishop proclaimed, and we must accept the result.[17] The war was over; it was time to confront the future. The bishop followed his own exhortation and looked forward, moving to what he saw as the important issues facing the diocese.

### Obligation to the Clergy

Civil War had brought destruction, disorganization, and great fiscal loss to the diocese, especially to the clergy. Atkinson had made pleas throughout the war years for support of parish clergy. His 1865 address included an urgent appeal. Even in prosperous times, he noted, the clergy had received "slender compensation." The current condition, however, was not one of prosperity. The laity had been stripped of almost all their property, and even men who had large prewar fortunes were wondering if what remained of their resources would be taken away. Under these circumstances the clergy were not being provided with the support necessary to sustain them. Recalling the story of the widow's mite, Atkinson said that, if parishes were to continue having ministers, proportionate sacrifices by all laypeople to support the clergy must be made, starting immediately.[18]

### Church Unity

The issue about which Atkinson felt the greatest anxiety was church unity. He began discussion of this matter by saying that the organization of the Protestant

Episcopal Church in the Confederate States of America (PECCSA) was the right thing to have done in 1861, and the church would have been indispensable had the war turned out differently. The issue now, however, was what to do in 1865. Atkinson's analysis of this issue took up seven pages of his address. He covered the pitfalls of remaining separate and, with considerable passion, the advantages of reunion. He urged consultation with other dioceses but pointed out that the time to act was at hand, given that "the interests are too momentous to be left to the hazards and uncertainties of time": "My earnest desire, then, and constant prayer, is that the church be restored again in the unity of its government, and the unfeigned love of its members."[19]

He was open about his concerns that some in the North might demand too high a price for reunion, including "repentance for what we do not see as evil." He felt confident, however, based on conversations with friends in the North, that the overwhelming sentiment there was for restoration of unity. Atkinson's remarks on this subject were referred to a committee. The committee report was appreciative of Atkinson's position and concluded with the following resolutions:

> Resolved That the Diocese of North Carolina is prepared to resume her position as a Diocese in connection with the PECUSA [Protestant Episcopal Church in the United States of America], whenever, in the judgment of the Bishop, after consultation with the Bishops of the other Southern Dioceses (which consultation he is hereby requested to hold) it shall be consistent with the good faith which she owes to the Dioceses with which she has been in union for the last four years.
>
> Resolved That, with a view to such a contingency, there be four clerical and four lay deputies elected, to represent the Diocese in the ensuing General Convention of the PECUSA.[20]

The first resolution specified consultation with other bishops but did not specify the manner in which that consultation was to take place. There was a minority report, however, that offered a much more restrictive resolution stipulating that a majority of Southern bishops must want to rejoin PECUSA before the Diocese of North Carolina did so. The minority report was rejected by vote of the council. Then, a lay delegate, E. J. Hale, offered a resolution with a preamble, the burden of the preamble being that the Northern church should issue an invitation to her Southern brethren after the October PECUSA meeting. The resolution called for the entire matter to be referred to the PECCSA meeting scheduled for November. Both the preamble and the resolution were defeated by vote. The committee report and resolutions therein were adopted. Delegates to the PECUSA triennial convention were elected on the contingency basis stipulated, and Bishop Atkinson now had what he felt was authorization to proceed on a course that he was confident was essential if reunion was to be achieved.[21]

## Notes

1. A list with brief descriptions of the military engagements can be found on the website "Civil War Battle Summaries by State,": http://www.nps.gov/hps/abpp/battles/bystate.htm (accessed 22 August 2007). A comprehensive account of the Battle of Bentonville is Mark L. Bradley's *Last Stand in the Carolinas: The Battle of Bentonville* (Campbell, Calif.: Savas Woodbury Publishers, 1996).

2. Thomas Atkinson, *Christian Duty in the Time of Present Trouble. A Sermon Preached at St. James' Church, Wilmington, N.C., on the Fifth Sunday after Easter, 1861* (Wilmington: Fulton and Price, 1861), 5. For the quotations immediately following from this source, page references are given parenthetically in text.

3. Shortly after the Confederate capture of Fort Sumter, Secretary of War Simon Cameron sent a telegram to all governors of states still in the Union asking each state to supply troops from its militia to the federal government to help put down the rebellion. The North Carolina ordinance of secession was not passed until 20 May 1861, so that Governor John Willis Ellis received this request; he gave a harsh negative reply, referring to the levy of troops as "in violation of the Constitution" and an "usurpation of power." See "The Call for Volunteers," *Harper's Weekly*, 27 April 1861, 253, http://www.sonofthesouth.net/leefoundation/civil-war/1861/april/call-for-volunteers.htm (accessed 22 August 2007).

4. *Diocese of North Carolina, 1862* (Fayetteville: Edward J. Hale, 1862), 11.

5. *Diocese of North Carolina, 1863* (Fayetteville: Edward J. Hale, 1863), 11.

6. *Diocese of North Carolina, 1864* (Fayetteville: Edward J. Hale, 1864), 10.

7. Hugh T. Lefler, "Thomas Atkinson, Third Bishop of North Carolina," *Historical Magazine of the Protestant Episcopal Church* 17 (December 1948): 428.

8. *Diocese of North Carolina, 1864*, 17.

9. Marshall Haywood, *Lives of the Bishops of North Carolina: From the Establishment of the Episcopate in that State down to the Division of the Diocese* (Raleigh: Alfred Williams, 1910), 164–65.

10. *Diocese of North Carolina, 1864*, 48–49.

11. Ibid., 12.

12. Ibid., 19–20.

13. *Diocese of North Carolina, 1862, 1863,* and *1864* and *Diocese of North Carolina, 1865* (Raleigh: J. C. Gorman, 1865).

14. *Diocese of North Carolina, 1865*, 13.

15. *Diocese of North Carolina, 1866* (Fayetteville: s.n., 1866), 50.

16. *Diocese of North Carolina, 1865*, 9.

17. Ibid.

18. Ibid., 24–25.

19. Ibid., 22.

20. Ibid., 31.

21. Ibid., 30–33.

# Richard Hooker Wilmer of Alabama

✦⟊ *An Episcopate Begun in Wartime*

## Background: Alabama in Wartime

According to the U.S. Census, Alabama had a total population of 964,201 in 1860. Slaves numbered 435,080 or 45 percent of the population, and there were 34 Episcopal churches in the state.[1] By the time Richard Hooker Wilmer arrived as bishop in March 1862, Alabama was part of the Confederate States of America, a nation at war. Alabama was not invaded during the first year of hostilities, but beginning in the early spring of 1862, after the Tennessee River had become a Union waterway, a swath of northern Alabama was occupied by federal forces; Huntsville, Decatur, Tuscumbia, and Athens were among the towns taken over.[2] These occupation forces were dislodged in the summer of 1862 by Confederate general Bragg's army on its way to Kentucky. Once war had come to northern Alabama, it was the site of many raids and skirmishes, and, unfortunately, civilian suffering, brutality, and reprisals were common as the war progressed.[3]

Of the seven significant military engagements in Alabama during the Civil War, three, including the two with the highest number of Confederate casualties, took place in April 1865 when the war was essentially over.[4] These formal engagements were only part of the story of the war in Alabama; as the conflict wore on, federal raids and the concomitant destruction of property and livelihoods extended to central and south Alabama.[5]

## A Episcopate Begins in Controversy

Soon after Wilmer's arrival in Alabama, several clergymen brought to the new bishop a matter that they felt must be confronted. The service of Morning Prayer in the Book of Common Prayer included a prayer for "all in Civil Authority" that specifically named the president of the United States.

> O LORD, our heavenly Father, the high and mighty Ruler of the universe, who dost from thy throne behold all the dwellers upon earth; Most heartily we beseech thee, with thy favour to behold and bless thy servant The President of

the United States, and all others in authority; and so replenish them with the grace of thy Holy Spirit, that they may always incline to thy will, and walk in thy way. Endue them plenteously with heavenly gifts; grant them in health and prosperity long to live; and finally, after this life, to attain everlasting joy and felicity; through Jesus Christ our Lord. Amen.[6]

Dioceses in the Confederate States had substituted alternate language, replacing "President of the United States" with "President of the Confederate States."[7]

In other states partially occupied by Union troops, some federal military commanders were demanding that the prayer for the president of the United States be used, and the clergy wanted guidance from their new bishop as to how they should respond.[8] Bishop Wilmer's position was unequivocal when he replied to the clergy who brought this matter to him:

> The Diocese of Alabama has, formally, as she has the right and reason to do, severed the legislative connection between herself and the Church in the United States. Her clergy, acting under the advice of her late Bishop, have, for more than one year, prayed for the President and other officers of the Confederate Government as "in authority" over them. The occupation of our soil by a hostile force does not absolve us from our allegiance to the Government of our affections, and of our deliberate choice. In the vicissitudes of war, we may, temporarily, be under the military power of a foreign Government; but one government only can have *"authority over us."* In my judgment, we can neither repudiate nor evade the obligation to maintain firmly our rights and convictions, without untruthfulness and dishonor.[9]

Although firm in his view that no civil or military authority had the right to order a particular prayer to be said—or to issue any instructions whatever regarding the worship service—Bishop Wilmer wished to avoid desecration of his churches by confrontations with occupation forces during the service and the possible arrest of priests in his diocese. He therefore directed his clergy in areas that were under occupation to proceed as follows. First, to ask the local military commander if he intended to interfere with public worship. Second, if the commander replied that he would either direct that the prayer for the president of the United States be used (or require that all reference to civil authorities be deleted), the minister should then close the church.[10] Wilmer made his reasoning explicit: "It can never be our duty to worship God at the expense of principle.... This war is not as ordinary wars, a conflict between governments merely. It is a struggle on our part for liberty of thought and speech. We, of the clergy, are not called to the field of combat; but we must meet the issue where the issue finds us—at our altars, and standing in our lot."[11]

The Right Reverend Richard Hooker Wilmer, D.D.

When Union occupation of the Tennessee Valley began, nearly all diocesan clergy followed Wilmer's direction. During 1862 and early 1863 federal troops occupied only parts of Alabama, and closings were not widespread. Federal raids and occupations spread during the latter stages of the conflict, though, and Wilmer reaffirmed his position at the 1864 diocesan meeting: "I then [in 1862] recommended that we should close our churches, rather than consent to worship according to military dictation. In reply to many inquiries which have reached me on this point, I take this opportunity to say, that I have seen no reason to modify the opinion then given, but, on the contrary, that time and experience have only tended to confirm my first impressions."[12] Wilmer also reminded the delegates that he had previously expressed the opinion that the "regular and ordinary forms of public worship should be so entirely catholic in character as to be adapted to all exigencies of time, place and circumstance." Prayers should not be specific to particular officeholders or current issues of politics or governance but should implore that civil rulers have the grace, wisdom, and understanding to execute justice and to maintain truth.[13] Bishop Wilmer went on to recommend that the Diocese of Alabama bring this matter to the next [1865] General Council of the Protestant Episcopal Church in the Confederate States and that diocesan delegates vote for changes that would make these prayers more catholic. The war ended before the council met, however, and that assembly was almost solely devoted to questions of church organization.[14]

## Ministries and Issues in Wartime

### Ongoing Mission of the Church

Wilmer confronted many tasks besides the prayer controversy when he came to Alabama in the spring of 1862. The bishopric of the diocese had been vacant since January 1861, and Wilmer began immediately a schedule of episcopal visits, administering confirmation to 136 persons before the 1862 convention opened on 1 May.[15] During the next conventional year, Wilmer confirmed 225 white and 45 black communicants.[16] In closing his 1863 address the new bishop laid out a framework for the work of the church in Alabama. Wilmer seemed to imply that the earthly context of civil war might be unusual, but the mission of the church remained clear: "A vast responsibility devolves upon us, brethren beloved, of the clergy. What a work opens to our view when we consider the relationship of the Church to the world and that of the ministry to the church. In this poor, sick, miserable, ignorant, fallen world, how vast a work is ours, when we learn, as good old Bishop Wilson tells us: 'The poor are designed to excite our liberality—the miserable our pity—the sick our assistance—the ignorant our instruction— those that are fallen our helping hand.'"[17]

Between the 1863 and 1864 conventions Wilmer confirmed 293 white individuals and 39 black persons, "the largest number of confirmations than ever recorded in Alabama."[18] Part of the increase, Wilmer noted, had been generated by refugees fleeing Union occupation in other states, and he added: "How earnestly we should endeavor to show our thankfulness to Almighty God, by sharing the blessings still vouchsafed to us with those who are seeking shelter and sympathy at our doors."[19]

## Work among the Slaves

Although Wilmer's journals reflect entries such as "confirmed seventeen at St. John's, Montgomery; two were Negroes," and "confirmed six, one of whom was a Negro," the majority of confirmations of blacks occurred in plantation chapels or at special services held for slaves.[20] Wilmer believed that "plantation evangelism" was most effective with slaves. He spent the summer of 1864 in Tuscaloosa, "preaching repeatedly," and while there he confirmed thirty-five persons, twenty-one of whom were slaves from one plantation. He credited this group of confirmands to a resident minister who was aided by the plantation owners. He added that he had never known an effort of this kind upon the plantation that had not been successful. By contrast, he noted, that "in our towns and villages, the Negroes are carried with the throng; and the efforts of our clergy have not, as a general rule, proved of much avail."[21]

On 10 April 1864, in the morning, Wilmer preached at St. Michael's in Marengo County, where he "confirmed six Negroes." That afternoon he preached at nearby Faunsdale Chapel and administered confirmation to twenty slaves. Wilmer spoke later about his thoughts on that occasion:

> This chapel constitutes one of the missionary points under the pastoral care of the Rev. William A. Stickney. I could but think as I beheld this beautiful house of worship crowded with an attentive congregation . . . how little they comprehended the mission of the Church, who doubted of the adaptation of her ritual to the necessities of this ignorant and much-neglected race. This chapel, with its band of earnest worshippers, is the fruit of much prayer and labor. May the day soon dawn when all the children of Africa shall worship God in the prayer of our blessed Lord, shall rehearse their faith in the primitive creeds, and shall be trained to walk in the ways of God's laws and the works of his commandments.[22]

Wilmer continued his work among slaves until the very end of the war, reporting at the 1865 meeting of the diocese that during the conventional year he had confirmed 185 white persons and 52 black Christians. His visitation schedule ended during April 1865, although his illness during the winter and travel delays related to the war had periodically disrupted his plans earlier.[23]

### Ministry to Soldiers

Bishop Wilmer felt a special obligation to Confederate soldiers and, assisted by clergy and laypersons in the diocese, devoted efforts and funds to securing and distributing tracts and other materials to soldiers in the field. He preached to encampments of soldiers when he was asked.[24] He did not feel, however, as some in the diocese suggested to him, that churches should be closed (or operated by lay leadership) and the clergy sent to the army or that a rotation system was feasible. As bishop he felt obligated to maintain a viable presence of the Episcopal Church in the diocese that he been consecrated to oversee.[25] Wilmer had made plans to visit the army commanded by General John Bell Hood while it was in Tennessee, but the shattering defeat in December 1864 at Nashville and the retreat of the Confederate army from Tennessee vitiated those plans.

In 1865 Wilmer reported to his diocese that he had invited five clergymen to go among the soldiers in hospitals and in the field in Georgia and that they had done so with "diligence." Bishop Henry C. Lay had advised Wilmer that he, Lay, would remain with the army and Wilmer asked the Alabama clergy on duty with the army to report to the Arkansas bishop and arrange for confirmations with him.[26]

## False Oaths

An issue that disturbed Wilmer was the taking of "false oaths," a practice to which some citizens succumbed when their area was taken over by Union forces. Wilmer addressed this matter at the 1864 diocesan council, taking a position similar to his stand on the issue of praying for the president. The bishop allowed that it was not part of his charge to tell others which government to choose or if, or when, to switch allegiance, but, he held, they should not take an oath that they intended to subvert, or worse, subscribe by oath to something that violated their true beliefs. "It is, however," he said, "incumbent upon me to premonish clergy and laity upon a great question of morals, and to urge them to take heed unto themselves, lest, through an unworthy timidity or an unholy greediness of gain, they make ship wreck of faith and a good conscience, and do dishonor to the name of the great God."[27]

## War's End

Until very near the war's end Bishop Wilmer remained optimistic that the South would prevail.[28] He accepted the outcome, but when Alabama became part of the Military District of Tennessee under the command of Major General George H. Thomas, the stage was set for a collision on the "praying for the president issue" that pitted the dictates of Bishop Wilmer's conscience against General Thomas's authority, a confrontation that also would provide a test of the principle of separation of church and state in America.[29]

## Notes

1. Historical Census Browser, Geostat Center, University of Virginia Library, http://fisher.lib.virginia.edu/collections/stats/histcensus/ (Accessed 10 April 2008). As noted on the website, all data provided by the Geostat Center are drawn from the U.S. Census of Population and Housing.

2. Walter L. Fleming, *Civil War and Reconstruction in Alabama* (New York: Peter Smith, 1949), 62.

3. Ibid., 63–69.

4. "Civil War Battle Summaries by State," http://www.nps.gov/hps/abpp/battles/bystate.htm. (Accessed 7 January 2013).

5. Fleming, *Civil War and Reconstruction in Alabama*, 68–78.

6. "Daily Order for Morning Prayer," Book of Common Prayer (Philadelphia: Protestant Episcopal Church, 1789).

7. Leonidas Polk, "Circular of February 20, 1861," in *Extracts from the Twenty-Third Annual Convention of the Protestant Episcopal Church in the Diocese of Louisiana* (New Orleans: Bulletin Book and Job Office, 1861), 12. This circular directed Louisiana clergy to make the change noted. Other Confederate dioceses made the same change.

8. John Fulton, "The Church in the Confederate States," in William Stevens Perry, *The History of the American Episcopal Church, 1587–1883*, 2 vols. (Boston: Osgood, 1885), 2:576–77.

9. *Diocese of Alabama, 1862* (Montgomery: Montgomery Advertiser Book and Job Office, 1863), 16. Walter C. Whitaker in *History of the Protest Episcopal Church in Alabama, 1763–1891* (Birmingham: Roberts and Son, 1898), 148–49, noted that Bishop Cobbs's "last official act" was to direct his clergy to refrain from using the Prayer for the President of the United States "so soon as the state and diocese of Alabama were no longer within the limits of the United States." Greenough White, in *A Saint of the Southern Church: Memoir of the Right Reverend Nicholas Hamner Cobbs* (New York: James Pott, 1897), 172, reported that a circular was issued to that effect on 29 December 1860 but that the corresponding entry in the bishop's journal was "made in a strange hand." Regardless of the circumstances, however, the circular came from the bishop's office.

10. *Diocese of Alabama, 1862*, 16.

11. Ibid., 16–17.

12. *Diocese of Alabama, 1864* (Mobile: Farrow and Dennett, 1864), 16.

13. Ibid., 16.

14. See below, the essay in part 6 entitled "Closure with Dignity."

15. *Diocese of Alabama, 1862*, 14.

16. *Diocese of Alabama, 1863* (Montgomery: Montgomery Advertiser Book and Job Office, 1863), 65.

17. Ibid., 70.

18. *Diocese of Alabama, 1864*, 14.

19. Ibid., 13.

20. *Diocese of Alabama, 1863 and 1864* and *Diocese of Alabama, 1865* (Mobile: Farrow and Dennett, 1865).

21. *Diocese of Alabama, 1865*, 8–9.

22. *Diocese of Alabama, 1864*, 12–13.

23. *Diocese of Alabama, 1865*, 10.

24. Ibid., 8.

25. *Diocese of Alabama, 1864*, 13.

26. *Diocese of Alabama, 1865*, 13.

27. *Diocese of Alabama, 1864*, 18.

28. Walter C. Whitaker, *Richard Hooker Wilmer, Second Bishop of Alabama* (Philadelphia: George W. Jacobs, 1907), 118–21.

29. See below, the essay entitled "Confrontation in Alabama: The Bishop and the General."

# Bishops in the Confederate States in Wartime

## +≡ *Some General Observations*

### Uniting to Support the Southern Cause

When it was clear that there was to be war, the Episcopal bishops in the Confederate States closed ranks and unreservedly supported the South's effort to win independence. They felt that the North was using force to prevent the Southern states from exercising their right to secede, which amounted to waging a war of subjugation. Bishops William Meade of Virginia, James Hervey Otey of Tennessee, William Mercer Green of Mississippi, Thomas Atkinson of North Carolina, and perhaps others had clung to the hope, even after the battle at Fort Sumter, that a peaceful separation between North and South could be arranged, avoiding all-out war. When that hope died, however, the Confederate bishops were certain that their side was the right side and the side that God favored. Events had rendered moot the earlier concerns voiced by some bishops during the secession crisis that the Union should be preserved, as illustrated by Atkinson's words in May 1861: "whatever we may think of some of the earlier steps in these disputes . . . we can calmly, conscientiously, and . . . conclusively, . . . maintain before God and man that *now* at least we of the South are in the right."[1]

### Building and Maintaining Morale

Religious sanction—and the hope that came with it—was bestowed upon the Southern cause by Episcopal bishops across the Confederate States throughout the Civil War. This was accomplished by sermons, by addresses at diocesan conventions, by pastoral letters, and by calls to special services. The religious blessing laid upon the Confederate war effort by the bishops served two important functions, to wit: (1) it provided assurance and reinforcement for the belief that the South's cause was right, serving to assuage any doubts that laypersons might have, and (2) it offered words of comfort to help strengthen the resolve of people during the low points of the war after major defeats or when a loved one was killed or one's community was laid waste by Union soldiers. The sermons and addresses of Stephen Elliott provide the most eloquent illustrations of this activity by the bishops.

## Meeting the Ongoing Missions

The impact of the Civil War on daily living was severe in much of the South, where the overwhelming majority of battles were fought and where the vast destruction of property included not only fortifications and ordnance but also transportation networks, commercial and farm buildings, and private homes. Some churches were destroyed and others desecrated. These and other factors, including the interruption of business and agriculture, led to scattering of congregations. These consequences of the war impeded the work of the Episcopal Church to some degree in every Southern diocese, including worship and pastoral services in parishes and mission stations, episcopal visits, and diocesan communications. The scope and timing of the devastation in Virginia, Georgia, the Carolinas, and Tennessee has been described briefly in previous essays.

Providing worship opportunities and religious instruction for slaves remained a high priority for Episcopal bishops during the war, and these efforts were hindered or halted by destruction of slave chapels, disruption of transportation, and, as the war progressed, by emancipation. When Union forces impeded the work of bringing the gospel to slaves—whether intentionally or as a by-product of military actions for other purposes—it was seen by the bishops as interference with God's plan for Christianizing the slaves. In spite of the difficulties just described, all bishops in Confederate states strove to see that the Episcopal Church provided ministry to all within the bounds of their dioceses.

## The Prayer Issue

When during the war Union forces occupied a city, town, or other area in which an Episcopal church was located, the use of the Prayer for the President of the United States and all in Civil Authority during the Morning Prayer liturgy very often became a contentious issue. Confederate bishops had authorized the substitution of "President of the Confederate States" for "President of the United States," but the prayer in this form was intolerable to Union commanders. As described above, in "Thomas Atkinson of North Carolina: Wartime Episcopate," this issue was most pronounced in Alabama, but it surfaced in many Southern states before the war ended. Some clergy refused to use the version of the prayer with the phrase "President of the United States" and were ejected from their parishes. One priest in Virginia was put in prison for his refusal. After the war the matter should have become a nonissue, but, as we shall see, it spawned a major confrontation in Alabama.

## Note

1. Thomas Atkinson, *Christian Duty in the Time of Present Trouble. A Sermon Preached at St. James' Church, Wilmington, N.C., on the Fifth Sunday after Easter, 1861* (Wilmington: Fulton and Price, 1861), 6.

# Episcopates in States Divided

*≠≡ Bishops in Slave States in the Union*

## William Rollinson Whittingham of Maryland

*An Unusual Silence*

Because of wartime disruptions the annual convention of the Diocese of Maryland was not held in 1861. In his address to the convention in 1862, excerpted below, Bishop William Rollinson Whittingham did not sound forceful:

> Under the first head which the law of the Church assigns for treatment in the address of a Bishop to his Convention—the affairs of the Diocese since the last Convention—I should have much to say, were my unaided private sense of duty to dictate my course.
>
> But I defer to the judgment of respected brethren of both orders when I waive all discussion of the reasons why so long an interval has elapsed since last we were assembled, and forego, together with the exercise of my official privilege of discoursing to my brethren of the clergy in the delivery of a charge touching their duty and mine in our present trials, the gratification of my own earnest longings to set before the people of my Diocese views which seem to me of great concernment, in relation to our common obligations as Christian men in the conjunctures which have been and still are so seriously pressing on us.
>
> I remit to Him who knows the heart and its issues the judgment of my course, and submit to the counsels of those who have the right to speak in behalf of what they deem to be the interests of the Diocese, while in the rest of this address I limit myself to the most succinct mode of presenting what information I have to give under the particular heads recounted in the Canon.[1]

In brief and in plain words the bishop of Maryland was telling his clergy and laity that, rather than laying before them what he thought needed to be said about the war and the duties of the diocese and individual Christians to the government of the United States in the crisis at hand, he was remaining silent in deference to advice that he had received from "respected brethren." He would report only on the state of the diocese.

This forbearance continued throughout the war years; he made this terse observation in 1864: "In adherence to the course of which I announced the adoption, with its reasons, in this place two years ago, I shall limit myself, in what I am about to lay before you, to the mere details of what has occurred since the last Convention requiring mention in fulfillment of the canonical direction for securing an accurate view of the state of the Church."[2] Even in 1865, after the war had ended, Whittingham's remarks to his diocese on the Union victory and on church and state issues continued to be restrained. This series of diffident and controlled remarks in diocesan addresses not only masks Whittingham's strong pro-Union views, but also obscures the aggressive stance the bishop had taken at the outset of the war to help keep Maryland in the United States and ignores subsequent actions he took in support of the Union.

### Views on the Union

Bishop Whittingham's dedication to the Union from the start of the secession crisis was without qualification. In his view rebellion against constituted authority or the "powers that be" was contrary to God's ordinances and therefore a great sin. Whittingham felt that the Southern states were entitled to seek relief from real or perceived injustices through the means available under the constitution, but he also believed that secession defied God's will, and that it was his duty, and the duty of all Christians, to oppose secession strongly and openly. In 1861 the time came for him to put that belief into practice.

### Correspondence with the Governor

The Maryland legislature was not scheduled for session in 1861 when the crisis began, but Southern loyalists demanded that the governor, Thomas Hicks, convene a special session to consider the issue of secession. Hicks refused, and, as the pressure mounted, addressed his constituency with a plea for moderation and patience, namely to wait until the regular session to deal with the matter, when the proper course might be clearer. Delay, as both sides knew, would work in favor of the Union.[3]

Upon reading Hicks's address, Bishop Whittingham sent him on 9 January 1861 a letter of high praise. The bishop related that since 1 November he had been in ten counties, having had conversations with influential men in each county. These discussions, and his own assessment, after living in Maryland for twenty years, made him certain that the governor's course was the right one.

> May I be allowed to say that in my own opinion your forcible, frank, manly, and true-hearted statement of your policy, and the grounds on which it has

been adopted and will be maintained, must but be attended (under the Divine blessing) with the happiest results? . . .

My humble efforts, therefore, shall not be wanting in my sphere to back your noble persistency in keeping Maryland in her only true, right, safe attitude of dignified and quiet expectation of legitimate redress of past wrongs, and provision against contingent dangers in the regular workings of the constitutional government of the United States.[4]

Whittingham closed with an expression of "warm admiration and heartfelt thanks" for the governor's stance. Governor Hicks responded promptly, thanking the bishop and requesting Whittingham's permission to publish the letter. The bishop's courageous reply leaves no doubt regarding his views on secession or his support of the governor, but the supposition in his first paragraph was a serious misjudgment:

I should hesitate about acceding to your proposal to publish what I wrote did I suppose that it would, by any possibility, be understood as mingling in political discussion. As a minister of Christ, I serve a master who disclaims interference in secular affairs beyond the line of enforcing individual duty and general peace.

But obedience to constituted civil government, and observance of contract even to one's own hurt, are clearly laid down in His word as duties to be enforced on His authority. . . .

The purpose, therefore, to keep Maryland out of strife and true to recognized relations and engagements, is one that I am bound to further if I can.

If my testimony as to the opinion of others . . . and expressions of my own personal convictions . . . tend to further such a purpose, I have no right to withhold them.[5]

## Consequences for the Bishop

The correspondence between the governor and the bishop was published in the newspapers, and, though there were some in the diocese who agreed with the bishop's stand and those who admired his courage, the overall reaction in the diocese and throughout Maryland was negative. Those critical of Whittingham included Southern sympathizers, but also included were Northern sympathizers who felt that the bishop had stepped out of his role and that his letter was an intrusion of the church into affairs of state. It was predicted that his reputation would be tarnished and the effectiveness of his role as a spiritual leader diminished by his involvement in what was clearly a political issue. That prediction proved to be painfully accurate. At times some members of the congregation

The Right Reverend William Rollinson Whittingham, S.T.D., LL.D.

protested by walking out of the church during an episcopal visit when the bishop began to conduct a part of the worship service.[6]

Maryland Episcopalians alienated by the bishop's action included friends of long standing, people who in other circumstances would have been prompt to offer support and solace. Whittingham did not recant or waiver, however; he continued to act on his belief that it was his Christian duty to support the federal government regardless of the personal cost to him.

### Other Issues during the War Years in the Diocese

*Views on Slavery*

Whittingham's antebellum positions on slavery and abolition, delineated above in "Thomas Atkinson of North Carolina and William Rollinson Whittingham of Maryland," did not change with the onset of war; he was opposed to slavery, but he also opposed imposing abolition on the South. In May 1862 he advised a colleague, "I am no abolitionist, and have not the slightest sympathy for any who are."[7] He supported the Lincoln administration's decision to restore the Union by force of arms, however, and that support remained firm after the Emancipation Proclamation was issued, even though that document was in effect an abolition order for states in rebellion. During 1863 a change in Whittingham's thinking did occur, and that shift is sharply delineated in a letter that he wrote to Dr. George Shattuck, his friend and physician in August of that year.

Dr. Shattuck had returned from a trip south and had written the bishop from Boston regarding abolition of slavery. The bishop responded: "I am delighted with your testimony as to the result of your observations in your late trip, convincing you that if rightly borne the abolition of slavery will be worth all the suffering. It is my own deepest conviction, and I cannot sufficiently admire the admirable train of providentially governed and overruled events by which, without end, as it were, in spite of human planning and execution, the absolute and final release of our young nation from the horrible incubus so long brooding over it, has been brought about."[8] Whittingham had thus moved from a prewar position that "the calumny of abolitionism must be carefully guarded against" to embrace abolition by armed force. Buried in phrases such as "providentially governed and overruled events" was his belief that God was using Lincoln and the war to shed the "incubus" of slavery.

*Contingency Plans*

Whittingham was visiting parishes away from Baltimore when, on 19 April 1861, a regiment of Union army soldiers from Massachusetts arrived at the President Street train station and marched to the Camden Station in order to board a train for Washington. The marchers were attacked by Southern sympathizers, and the ensuing violence resulted in sixteen fatalities, including four soldiers.

When he returned Whittingham met with several of his clergy to assess the intensity of pro-Southern feeling. Although the bishop was a strong Unionist, he felt obligated to prepare for passage by the legislature of a secession ordinance, and he drafted a circular letter to clergy for that contingency.[9] He shared his plans by letter with some of his concerned clergymen, advising them that, in the event that the state legislature should vote for secession, he would authorize the alteration of the prayer in the Morning Prayer service "for the President of the United States, and all in Civil Authority" so that it would read only "behold and bless thy servants in civil authority." Bishop Whittingham thus planned to authorize omission of "the President of the United States" from the prayer but he did not decide to substitute "the President of the Confederate States." He expressed the hope that the modified prayer was a more catholic petition that he hoped "all can join in" in the event secession occurred.[10]

*Adherence to the Liturgy*

In spite of the secession fervor that Whittingham observed in Baltimore, the legislature did not pass an ordinance of secession when it met in Frederick on 27 April, and the bishop did not send a directive to clergy for modification of the prayer for those in civil authority.[11] Southern sentiment remained strong in parts of the state, especially Baltimore and the Eastern Shore, however, and federal soldiers occupied Baltimore on 13 May and maintained a presence there throughout the war. Some clergymen elected to omit the prayer without the bishop's permission, and Whittingham reacted strongly, sending a letter on 15 May 1861 to diocesan clergy in which he reminded them that Maryland had remained in the United States and that there were severe consequences for omitting a part of the liturgy. Such omission, the bishop wrote, made "the clergyman liable to presentment for willful violation of his ordination vow," and Whittingham added that he would feel "bound to act on any evidence of such offense."[12] The bishop did proceed with presentments based upon evidence received, but the Standing Committee of the diocese, to which these cases were brought, was comprised of pro-Southern members, and no action was taken on the bishop's charges.

*Presidential Proclamations*

Another matter that brought the bishop into conflict with some of his clergy and laity involved the calls throughout the war issued by President Lincoln for special days of prayer or thanksgiving. The first such proclamation was issued on 12 August 1861 to designate 26 September as a Day of Public Humiliation, Prayer, and Fasting. The proclamation required that the various faiths offer prayers and petitions in accord with their creeds and modes of worship. All people of the United States were called "to confess and deplore their sins and transgressions...,  and, whereas our beloved country, once, by the blessing of God, united, prosperous, and happy, is now afflicted with factious and civil war, it is peculiarly fit for us to recognize the hand of God in this visitation, and, in sorrowful remembrance of our faults and crimes, as a nation and as individuals, to humble ourselves before Him and to pray for his mercy; to pray that we may be spared further punishment, though most justly deserved; that our arms may be blessed and made effectual for the re-establishment of law, order, and peace throughout the Country."[13]

Bishop Whittingham sent his clergy a copy of the president's proclamation along with a pastoral letter dated Baltimore, 14 August 1861. Whittingham noted that setting aside such a day was especially appropriate in that the "land was now red with best blood of its inhabitants." He also noted that it was clear that the legislature and the governor had decided that Maryland was to remain part of the United States and that "there our allegiance must lie." Finally, he observed that when Marylanders pray "to deliver us from sedition, privy conspiracy, and rebellion," they mean by "us" the United States of America.

It was clear from his remarks that the bishop thought that those in sympathy with secession were at best misguided, but he took a paragraph to explain that he had attempted to construct a prayer that anyone in Maryland could offer to God without reservation.

> Being painfully sensitive how largely even honest and pious men, in the pitiable weakness of human judgment, hoodwinked by natural affection, social relations and surrounding influences, may be hindered from the perception of the strongest obligations of religious duty, . . . I have taken care to prescribe no petition in which all who believe in the just government of God and truly desire the accomplishment of his righteous will, may not from the heart consent. . . . If there be any among us still disposed to cast their lot with those who are in arms against their government, my office concerns itself not with their political tenets or their social bias, further than to warn them to take good heed they be fostering in themselves a delusion.[14]

Excerpts from the prayer prescribed show his efforts:

> Restore peace in our time, O merciful Lord, and cause us so to agree in endeavor to thy glory and the welfare of all people. . . .
> . . . Give us grace seriously to lay to heart the great dangers we are in by our unhappy divisions. Take away all hatred and prejudice and whatever else may hinder the restoration of Godly union and concord: that, as there is but one body, and one spirit, One Hope of our calling, One Lord, One Faith, One Baptism, One God and Father of us all; so may we once again be made of one heart, and of one Soul, united in one holy bond of truth and peace, of Faith and Charity, and may with one mind and mouth glorify thee, through Jesus Christ Our Lord. Amen.[15]

In spite of the bishop's attempts to make the prayers palatable to everyone, his accompanying letter and the proclamation by Lincoln left no doubt that the purpose of the day was to pray either for a peace achieved by suppression of the rebellion by the Union military or for a peace effected through a change of heart, in which the South, seeing the error of its ways, would abandon rebellion and voluntarily return to the Union fold. The bishop's invitation to a day of prayer and fasting, therefore, was not seen as a generic or catholic call to pray for peace, for deliverance from the tumult and agony of war, and for healing of the bitterness engendered by the conflict; it was viewed as a summons to pray for peace on Union terms. Further, Whittingham's language, such as "pitiable weakness of human judgment" and "hoodwinked," in his transmission letter was condescending to anyone with the slightest sympathy toward the Southern cause.

Whittingham was criticized, even by his supporters, for issuing a call that many parishioners inevitably would protest or simply ignore, leading to more discord, not healing, across the diocese. The bishop's response to these criticisms was firm, if not harsh, and can be summarized as follows:

1. The war involved the very existence of civil government and of submission to constituted authority as ordained by God.
2. The Lincoln proclamation carried the full weight of the president and Congress and therefore commanded obedience of all citizens.
3. He, as a bishop, was thus unable to remain silent.[16]

During the war, there were many more days appointed by President Lincoln. Parishioners in some Baltimore churches largely shunned the calls to observances by President Lincoln but observed days proclaimed by the Confederate president. This was but a symptom of the fundamental problem in the Diocese of Maryland with calls to days of prayer; loyalties were divided within both clergy and laity. Some churches had a preponderance of Unionists and others had a majority of Southern sympathizers, but in both types of parishes the reality was that a call to prayer by President Lincoln, and the bishop's endorsement thereof, was divisive.

Nevertheless, as the war progressed, Bishop Whittingham commended every day appointed by the president to his clergy, and the wording of his prescribed prayers became more direct than it was in 1861, as these excerpts show. For a Day of Thanksgiving on 6 August 1863, for Union Victory at Gettysburg and Confederate surrender at Vicksburg: "For . . . signal and effective victories . . . we render thee thanks and praise; beseeching thee to continue thy gracious protection to our armies and fleets, and to use them as thy instruments for the restoration of peace, good order, and Godly quietness in the land."[17] For a Day of Humiliation and Prayer on 4 August 1864: "Grant to our armed defenders by land and sea, and to the masses of the people, the courage and power of resistance and endurance, needful to secure. . . our unity as a people. . . and permanently to establish the national constitution and laws in their due supremacy."[18]

## Loyalty Oath and the Clergy

Still another issue divided the bishop and his clergy, and this one was potentially the most explosive. A state legislator introduced a bill that would require the taking of a loyalty oath by members of selected occupations and professions. Those refusing to take the oath would be deprived of license to practice their trade or profession in Maryland. A loyalty oath for anyone was anathema to some Episcopal clergy, but it came to light that Bishop Whittingham had actually advised the sponsor to include clergymen in the bill. This action angered not only the already alienated pro-Southern clergy but also some of the bishop's strongest supporters, including the Reverend William Francis Brand, a favorite student of Whittingham's at General Theological Seminary. Brand and six colleagues banded together to protest the proposed action and the bishop's part in it. These men, and others, felt that such an action violated the principle of separation of church and state, could lead to a state role in selection and control of clergy, and would make politicians of ministers. Brand's letter of protest also noted that attenuation of the bishop's influence and further dissension would result. Whittingham was unmoved, responding that a minister by virtue of his "privileged position" should be subject to the oath—and that the state had the right to impose it. The bishop's position reflected his belief that the Episcopal Church's obligation to support the state in time of crisis was paramount. Whittingham requested that the group of seven protesting the bishop's action refrain from further protests until the fate of the bill in the legislature was decided. The bill establishing the loyalty oath did not pass. Brand, in his biography of Whittingham, expressed his belief that nothing could have allayed the feeling against Bishop Whittingham had the bill passed. As it was, although the furor died down, this issue did leave residual feelings of bitterness.[19]

From the beginning of the war, clergymen were arrested in Maryland by the federal government on suspicion of disloyalty. Bishop Whittingham did not formally protest these arrests, a fact that did not enhance his standing with his clergy. Arrests were made for "treasonable language" and similar charges. One rector was released on condition that he would "conduct services as prescribed by Bishop Whittingham."[20]

### An Attempt at Damage Control

The exception to Bishop Whittingham's aggressive confrontation of the issues connected with the Civil War was found in his diocesan addresses from 1862 to 1865, in which he made a deliberate decision to avoid stirring up controversy. His convention remarks, some excerpts from which are given at the beginning of this essay, stand in stark contrast to his actions and other statements, especially early in the war.

In a letter to a colleague, the Reverend Elisha Mulford in South Orange, New Jersey, written in January 1864, Whittingham seemed to feel that he had shown great restraint in not "publishing pastoral letters and charges inculcating loyalty" and that by doing so he had helped prevent division within the diocese and "open disloyalty of too many of its members." He noted that his strategy was followed at the sacrifice of his own prestige.[21]

Whittingham's charges in convention addresses certainly were bland, and after the exchange of letters with Governor Hicks and the loyalty-oath controversy, the bishop maintained a much lower public profile. He did not disseminate pastoral letters to "inculcate loyalty," but his calls to observe presidential days of fasting and humiliation or days of thanksgiving were direct and unambiguous—including a call at war's end that generated an unfortunate incident (described below) involving the date of the 1865 diocesan convention. These calls and the accompanying prayers left no doubt as to where he stood on the issues of loyalty to the Union and Christian duty to the state in crises. His ability to lead was damaged severely early in the war, and that damage was not repaired by his communications and actions as the war progressed.

## A Discordant Convention

In the closing months of the war Lee surrendered at Appomattox on 9 April 1865, and President Lincoln was assassinated five days later, on Good Friday, 14 April. President Andrew Johnson called for 25 May to be a Day of Fasting, Humiliation, and Prayer for the mourning of Lincoln's death. Whittingham immediately wrote the new president that 25 May was Ascension Day, a feast day of the church, and respectfully pointed out that he and many other Christians could not subordinate a church feast to a day appointed by the president. Whittingham also noted his support of the Union throughout the war and his efforts to have all days proclaimed by President Lincoln observed in Maryland. The bishop then suggested designating instead 26 May. President Johnson honored Whittingham's request for deferral, but proclaimed 1 June the date for the day of mourning.[22] This solved one problem for the bishop but created another, in that 1 June was the second day of the annual convention of the Diocese of Maryland. Whittingham therefore notified the parishes of his intention to move, on the first day of the convention, 31 May, that the meeting be adjourned to 27 September in order to permit observance of President Johnson's proclamation. He then issued on 11 May a letter in which clergy were "respectfully and affectionately entreated" to observe the day of "national humiliation and mourning on the occasion of the sudden and violent end of our late Chief Magistrate."[23] His appointed prayer included a petition "for the speedy restoration of public peace, and the establishment throughout all the land of the supremacy of the constitution and laws of the United States."[24]

In view of the bishop's notice to seek adjournment, many delegates stayed home from the convention on 31 May, as Whittingham expected, but approximately fifty did attend. To the bishop's great chagrin, his motion for adjournment was defeated by a narrow vote. Stung and disappointed, Whittingham vacated the chair and departed from the convention. The delegates then voted to adjourn, but added the indignity of choosing 13 September instead of the 27th as the date to reconvene.[25]

By 31 May, the date these events occurred, the war truly was over, but the time for the healing process had not come.[26] A majority of the delegates at the convention—and many who remained at home—felt that President Andrew Johnson's appointed day was just the last in a series of such days that deserved to pass unobserved. Anger toward the "partisan" bishop enhanced that feeling and motivated the action by the rump convention.

When the convention reconvened in September, the bishop mentioned in his address neither his shabby treatment in May nor, in any direct way, the war's end. He opened his remarks with recognition of God's mercy in permitting an assembly in "such strength" to proceed with the work "committed to us," especially after the "convulsions" the diocese had experienced.[27] He thus acknowledged the upheaval caused by the war and gave thanks for the condition of the diocese, but he did not offer, or lead the delegates in, thanks for peace or the restoration of the Union.

## Ministry to Soldiers

A topic not mentioned in Whittingham's wartime addresses or in biographical sketches is that of ministering to sick and wounded soldiers and their families. This is a puzzling omission, in that there was fighting on Maryland soil. Many other bishops visited battlefields, and Bishops Henry Whipple of Minnesota and Charles Pettit McIlvaine of Ohio visited Maryland after the Battle of Antietam. Whittingham's health could have precluded battlefield visits, even to those in Maryland, but health problems cannot account for his silence on ministry to soldiers. Marylanders fought on both sides during the war, and the bishop certainly would have wanted those soldiers, whether in blue or gray, and their loved ones comforted in times of sorrow or anxiety. The bishop's son, Dr. Edward T. Whittingham, served for three years as a surgeon in the eastern theater in the U.S. Army and attended wounded after many battles. He served at first under New Jersey general Philip Kearney until Kearney's death on 1 September 1862.[28]

## A Day of Thanksgiving

The end of the Civil War was commemorated on 7 December 1865, which had been proclaimed a National Day of Thanksgiving by the president of the United States. Bishop Whittingham did his duty by summoning the diocese to observe this final special day of prayer related to the Civil War. In accord with the theme of the day, the bishop prepared a prayer to thank God for his goodness "in relieving our beloved country from the fearful scourge of Civil War, and permitting us to secure the blessings of peace, unity, and harmony, with a great enlargement of civil liberty."[29] All were grateful for the blessing of peace, but gratitude for the enlargement of civil liberty (that is, the end of slavery) was not shared by all, and Bishop Whittingham was already aware that unity and harmony were ideals not yet achieved in the Episcopal Church or in civil polity.

*Observations on Bishops in Other Slave States in the Union*

Alfred Lee of Delaware, Benjamin Bosworth Smith of Kentucky, William Rollin-son Whittingham of Maryland, and Cicero Stephens Hawks of Missouri had in common the fact that all were bishops of slave states that remained in the Union during the Civil War. Delaware had only 1,798 slaves according to the 1860 census, and the state was not the site of fighting during the Civil War.[30] Kentucky, Mary-land, and Missouri, however, all had the experience of having engagements dur-ing that conflict fought on their soil. One of the seven engagements in Maryland was the battle at Antietam Creek in 1862, as a result of which General Lee halted his Maryland campaign. Also in 1862 the battles at Munfordville, Richmond, and Perryville in Kentucky comprised Confederate general Braxton Bragg's foray into that state, which ended with Confederate forces withdrawing to Tennessee. Of the three states, the most military engagements were fought in Missouri, but all were relatively small battles or skirmishes. Missouri, however, was plagued with vio-lence involving civilians, especially guerilla-type raids on the civilian population, led by men such as Bloody Bill Anderson. These raiders favored the Confederate cause, and their actions and the reprisals by Union commanders were harsh and generated widespread misery in Missouri. In a state with a citizenry of divided loyalties, these raids and reprisals created anger and mistrust among neighbors and exacerbated divisiveness in areas where there were both Union and Confed-erate sympathies. Although there was little partisan violence, the populations in Kentucky and Maryland also were divided, as illustrated by the reaction to Bishop Whittingham's stance in favor of loyalty to the Union. Kentucky was a state with nearly one-quarter of a million slaves and many ties to the South, but for a long period it had been the western salient beyond the original thirteen colonies, and many of its citizens were proud of being part of the United States. All four states contributed soldiers to both the Union and Confederate armies.

Bishops Smith and Hawks shared Bishop Whittingham's belief that all Chris-tians, Episcopal Church members included, were bound by the injunction of the apostle Paul to be subject to "the powers that be," which in their situation meant being loyal to the United States. Smith and Hawks certainly were loyal in their hearts, but their public declarations during wartime focused on seeking God's kingdom and then on asking God's help in restoring peace, not on praying for Union success in battle. Both Smith and Hawks, in spite of wartime conditions, attempted to maintain diocesan efforts to provide religious instruction and wor-ship opportunities for slaves.

*Benjamin Bosworth Smith*

Bishop Smith told his convention delegates in May 1861 that "whatever may hap-pen, the Church is safe; and so are all they who put their trust in Him. As dangers thicken, and men's hearts fail them more and more, for fear of those things which may be coming upon our unhappy country, let us all be found more true to our duty to God and His Church; and cleaving for shelter more closely than ever to the cross of Christ, and to the hopes of the Gospel."[31]

By the 1862 convention Smith was distressed that concerns about the war were leaving no room for consideration of religious matters. He advised his diocese, therefore, that, "admonished by many prudential considerations," he was going to "omit all outside questions." Smith therefore mentioned neither the causes nor the current state of the war.[32] He closed his address by expressing the hope that "peace may speedily be restored to our deeply afflicted country, and with it that prosperity and quietness of mind." In 1863 Smith again referred to the "prudential consideration" that led him to abstain in 1862 from "any allusion to the sad condition of our country" and closed with a prayer for the gospel to bring wisdom, betterment, and happiness to all the earth's people. His public utterances throughout the war did not deviate from this approach.

In spite of his position when facing his diocese, however, Bishop Smith voted in committee with Bishop McIlvaine of Ohio at the 1862 triennial convention to recommend the McIlvaine pastoral letter to House of Bishops, a letter that gave explicit support to the Union cause and condemned the action of Bishop Leonidas Polk of Louisiana in accepting a position of high command in the Confederate army.[33]

### Cicero Stephens Hawks

Bishop Hawks began his response to the incipient conflict at his May 1861 diocesan meeting by noting that "in these unhappy times of civil discord and distraction, when our beloved country is convulsed from the center to the circumference," the "hearts of all good men are oppressed with sorrow and foreboding." Hawks's primary message for such times was that when communicants gather for services, when ministers preach, and when the diocese meets, the kingdom to seek is Christ's kingdom—one not of this world. He went on to urge that all pray for peace on earth, and seek God's forgiveness for the sins that had brought this catastrophe upon the country. He acknowledged the day of prayer called by the president of the United States but made plain that the pulpit was not the place to call for the success of Union arms—or the place to rail against the South. He appended the text of two prayers that he wrote for the 4 January Day of Fasting and Humiliation appointed by the president; an excerpt from one is given below:

> Thy mercy, guidance, and protection gave us a national existence; Thy mercy, guidance, and protection alone can secure us in the same. Heal the land, for it is divided; . . . help us to repent of past ingratitude. Give grace to our Chief

Magistrate, the President of the United States; to the Governor of this commonwealth, . . . that they may faithfully and truly perform their duties. And to all citizens give the spirit of soberness, righteousness, and truth, that they "may both perceive and know what things they ought to do, and may also have the grace and power faithfully to fulfill the same." O let all bitterness, wrath, pride, and prejudice be put away from us. . . . Amid the stormy billows that surround us, let us not our afflicted country be wrecked, but let us hear thy voice speaking to the angry waves, "Peace be still."[34]

Throughout the war, Hawks was saddened by the destruction and disruption wrought by the conflict. Except in St. Louis and environs, diocesan activity crumbled. In 1864 he told his diocese: "You are already aware that most of our country parishes are closed, the demands of the war causing loss of men and means, making some of them too feeble to act; and I fear many of them will continue helpless for a long time."[35] He then listed fifteen parishes and missions that lacked clergy.

Bishop Hawks strongly disapproved of the pastoral letter written by Charles Pettit McIlvaine and so advised his diocese.[36] He pointed out that the Episcopal Church already was committed to loyalty to the "powers that be" and had in its liturgy prayers for those in civil authority and against rebellion. The convention had concerned itself with matters "foreign to its work." Consistent with this viewpoint, Hawks made mention in his public remarks neither of the 1863 massacre at Lawrence, Kansas, launched from Missouri and led by William Quantrill nor of the brutal "scorched earth" response by Union forces that uprooted thousands of families near the Missouri-Kansas border.[37]

## Alfred Lee

From the onset of hostilities Delaware bishop Alfred Lee took an aggressive public stance in favor of the Union. In a sermon entitled "Thanksgiving Discourse" on 27 November 1862, Lee honored Lincoln's intent to proclaim emancipation on 1 January 1863.

> If in the providence of the Almighty, the issue of this struggle shall be the end of an institution which has borne these pernicious and baleful fruits, the fountain of the bitter streams, the one great source of strife among those whom so many bonds and interests conspire to draw together; of that which has been our reproach among the nations of the civilized world, a glaring contradiction to our boasts of liberty, the blot upon our Christianity; if such shall be the issue, then I do believe there will be praise among the angels of God and joy in heaven.
>
> I cannot doubt then on which side of this contest is a holy God.[38]

## Notes

1. *Diocese of Maryland, 1862* (Baltimore: Published by the Convention, 1862), 15.

2. *Diocese of Maryland, 1864* (Baltimore: Published by the Convention, 1864), 10.

3. A few months later, after the war had begun and the April 1861 Baltimore riot had occurred, Union soldiers began occupying Baltimore and other parts of Maryland.

4. William Francis Brand, *Life of William Rollinson Whittingham, Fourth Bishop of Maryland*, 2 vols. (New York: E. and J. B. Young, 1883), 2:10.

5. Ibid., 11.

6. Nelson Waite Rightmeyer, "The Church in a Border State—Maryland," *Historical Magazine of the Protestant Episcopal Church* 17 (December 1948): 414.

7. Letter from Whittingham to the Reverend Mr. Billop, May 1862, quoted in Brand, *Life of Whittingham*, 1:264.

8. Brand, *Life of Whittingham*, 2:46–47.

9. Bishop Atkinson told the congregation in his sermon commemorating Whittingham's life that "if Maryland had become one of the Confederate States, Bishop Whittingham would have greatly regretted it; but I believe he would not have hesitated to obey, not from fear, not from force, but for conscience sake, the government of the Confederate States. But as Maryland to his great contentment remained under the government of the United States, he, with heart and head and power and influence, did what he could to sustain that government." Thomas Atkinson, *A Sermon Commemorative of the Rt. Rev. William Rollinson Whittingham, D.D., LL.D., Late Bishop of the Diocese of Maryland* (Baltimore: William Boyle, 1879), 8.

10. William Rollinson Whittingham, "Various Pastoral Letters and Prayers, 1861–65," Keller Library Archives, General Theological Seminary (GTS). In a letter in this collection dated 23 April 1861 and addressed "Rev. and Dear Brother," Whittingham revealed this contingency plan and cited a canonical reference to support such a change.

11. The legislature met in Frederick because Annapolis, the capital, was occupied by federal troops. Although the legislators did pass a "neutrality" resolution and vote to reconvene in September, the real outcome was that Maryland remained in the Union. Federal troops occupied Baltimore in May, and the proposed September meeting of the legislature did not occur. Marylanders fought for both the Union and the Confederacy.

12. Whittingham to diocesan clergy, 15 May 1861, Whittingham Papers, Keller Library Archives, GTS.

13. President's proclamation for the day of prayer on 26 September 1861, Whittingham Papers, Keller Library Archives, GTS.

14. Whittingham to Maryland clergy, 14 August 1861, Pamphlet Collection, Whittingham Papers, Keller Library Archives, GTS.

15. Whittingham, Prayer forms for 26 September 1863, Whittingham Papers, Keller Library Archives, GTS.

16. Richard Duncan, "Bishop Whittingham, the Maryland Diocese, and the Civil War." *Maryland Historical Magazine* 61 (December 1966): 335.

17. Whittingham, "A Form of Prayer and Thanksgiving appointed for 6 August 1863," Whittingham Papers, Keller Library Archives, GTS.

18. Whittingham, "A Form of Prayer appointed for a Day of National Humiliation and Prayer, 4 August 1864," Whittingham Papers, Keller Library Archives, GTS.

19. Brand, *Life of Whittingham,* 2:29. The views expressed in Rightmeyer, "Church in a Border State," and in Duncan, "Bishop Whittingham, the Maryland Diocese, and the Civil War," are reflected in the treatment of the loyalty-oath issue.

20. Duncan, "Bishop Whittingham, the Maryland Diocese, and the Civil War," 341–45.

21. Rightmeyer, "Church in a Border State," 418.

22. Ibid., 419.

23. Whittingham to clergy in Diocese of Maryland, 11 May 1865, Pamphlet, Whittingham Papers, Keller Library Archives, GTS.

24. Whittingham, "A Form of Prayer appointed for a Day of Humiliation and Prayer, 1 June 1865," Whittingham Papers, Keller Library Archives, GTS.

25. *Diocese of Maryland, 1865* (Baltimore: Published by the Convention, 1865), 1.

26. Joseph E. Johnston had surrendered to Sherman in North Carolina in late April, which left only scattered Confederate units in the western theater. These units had surrendered or were in the process of doing so by the end of May.

27. *Diocese of Maryland, 1865,* 15.

28. Marian Keefe Meisner, "1857–1870," in *History of Millburn Township.* (Millburn, N.J.: Millburn / Short Hills Historical Society and Millburn Free Public Library, 2002).

29. Whittingham, "A Form of Prayer for a Day of National Thanksgiving appointed for 7 December 1865," Whittingham Papers, Keller Library Archives, GTS.

30. See above, "Slavery in the United States: A Brief History," for a table showing the number of slaves by state in 1860.

31. *Diocese of Kentucky, 1861* (Frankfort: S. I. M. Major, 1861), 28.

32. *Diocese of Kentucky, 1862* (Louisville: Hanna, 1862), 15.

33. See above, the essay entitled "Assembly under Most Afflicting Circumstances: The Northern Bishops in General Convention in 1862."

34. *Diocese of Missouri, 1861* (St. Louis: George Knapp, 1861), appendix.

35. *Diocese of Missouri, 1864* (St. Louis: George Knapp, 1864), 8.

36. See essay above, "Assembly Under the Most Afflicting Circumstances: The Northern Bishops in General Convention in 1862."

37. See Carl Breihan, *Quantrill and His Civil War Guerrillas* (New York: Promontory Press, 1959), 116–34. See also *The War of the Rebellion: A Compilation of the Official Records of the Union and Confederate Armies,* Series 1, Vol. 22, Part 2 (Washington, D.C.: Government Printing Office, 1888), 470–73. A copy of General Order 11 issued by General Thomas Ewing is provided, along with correspondence relative to the massacre at Lawrence. See also Jay Monaghan, *Civil War on the Western Border, 1854–1865* (Boston: Little Brown, 1955), 289–349.

38. Alfred Lee, *Thanksgiving Discourse: A Sermon Delivered in St. Andrew's Church, November 27, 1862* (Wilmington: Henry Eckel, 1862), 13.

# Polk, Lay, and Quintard

+≒ *The War Up Close and Personal*

### War Comes to a Bishop

The devastation caused by war described in previous essays affected all Southern bishops, but sometimes the war came a bit too close to a particular bishop, as was the case for Mississippi bishop William Mercer Green on the two occasions described below. One of these incidents occurred early in the Union's Vicksburg campaign, before that city fell, and the other happened just afterward.

On 14 May 1863 Union forces attacked and captured Jackson. Green gave this account: "As my residence [just outside of Jackson] was immediately in front of the fortifications thrown up for the defense of the city, and was likely to receive the missiles of friends as well as foes, I left it when the roar of musketry indicated that my peaceful home was in a few moments to be converted into a field of battle."[1] The federal forces took Jackson, cut the rail connection between there and Vicksburg, burned some of the town, and departed, the objective being to prevent Jackson from being used as a staging area for relief of Vicksburg. When Green returned to his home, it was standing and, in his words, had been "spared the stain of blood," but every room had been trashed and pillaged. He had hidden the diocesan records, but his personal papers and book collection had been damaged. Green asked God to forgive the evil that the Union soldiers had wrought.

After Vicksburg fell on 4 July 1863, the Union forces returned to Jackson, and this time there was a brief siege during which an artillery barrage was directed at the city. The bishop and his family fled a second time, at first into Jackson, where they spent the first night, and then, the next day, they departed, according to the bishop: "Amidst the roar of battle, and under a shower of shot and shell, I set out with my family, to seek a safe retreat at a distance from the then seat of war."[2] This time Jackson was burned to the ground before being abandoned by Union troops. Green and his family took refuge in Demopolis, Alabama, for several weeks, and after their return were guests of friends until they found a

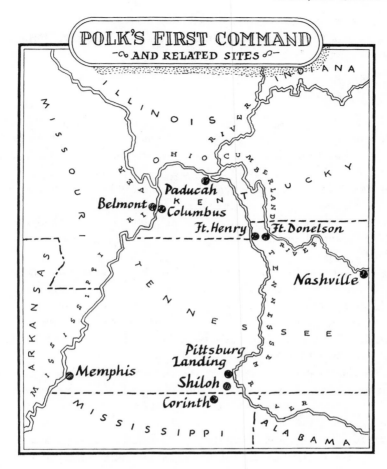

POLK'S FIRST COMMAND
―∞ AND RELATED SITES ―

home in Columbus near the Alabama border. Green then resumed his efforts to provide episcopal visits for the balance of the war.

Bishop Green's suffering occurred because the war came to him. Two other bishops and one bishop-to-be endured the privations of the war because they went where the war was. Bishop Leonidas Polk of Louisiana "buckled the sword over his bishop's gown" to lead troops into combat; Bishop Henry Champlin Lay of Arkansas, whose new diocese was disrupted by the war, served as a missionary bishop to a Confederate army and interacted with several Union generals; and the Reverend Dr. Charles Todd Quintard served as a Confederate chaplain throughout the war and shortly after its close became bishop of Tennessee. The experiences of these three church leaders as participants in as well as observers of the war are the subject of this essay. Their paths intersected at times throughout the war and had a confluence under tragic circumstances in Georgia during June 1864.

## June 1861—Early February 1862

### Leonidas Polk

After Leonidas Polk accepted his commission as a major general in the Confederate army, he was first assigned the responsibility of protecting from federal encroachment the northern segment of the Mississippi River that ran through the Confederate States.[3] He assumed command of Department No. 2 with headquarters in Memphis on 13 July 1861.[4] The initial core of Polk's command was six thousand soldiers led by Brigadier General Gideon Pillow, who had come with these troops to the Confederate army from the Tennessee militia.[5] Major General Polk set about the business of securing more troops and supplies as well as organizing for action.

Polk felt that with the Union defeat at Manassas, the focus of the federal war effort would be in the East and that it was imperative to seize the initiative along the Mississippi before the Union was geared to send reinforcements to the West. Polk's most significant act while exercising independent command was to occupy Columbus, Kentucky, a controversial move that he felt was absolutely necessary to preempt an anticipated occupation by Union forces.[6] From the bluffs at Columbus, Confederate shore batteries could effectively prevent federal gunboats from going down the Mississippi. In spite of this military advantage, some in the Confederate government, Secretary of War Leroy P. Walker among them, believed that the move would help tip the balance of the then neutral Kentucky toward the Union—and was therefore a grave political error.[7] Confederate president Jefferson Davis supported Polk, as did General Albert Sydney Johnston, to whom the matter was referred when he assumed overall command in the West, but Polk's action caused a major controversy within the Confederacy.[8]

Polk had urged the appointment of West Point classmate General Albert Sydney Johnston to take over the entire western theater. President Davis concurred, and Johnston arrived from California in the early fall.[9] While serving under Johnston, Polk devoted his energies to supervising construction of fortifications along the Mississippi River, including artillery emplacements on the Columbus bluffs. Then, on 6 November 1861, feeling that he had fulfilled his promise to serve in an interim capacity while his services were sorely needed, Polk submitted his resignation to President Davis. Because Johnston had taken charge, Polk felt that the leadership vacuum was filled and that he could—and should—resume his role as a bishop of the church.[10]

Polk dispatched from his staff his son Hamilton to deliver the letter to Davis in Richmond, but the very next day Union forces under Brigadier General Ulysses

S. Grant attacked Belmont, Missouri, almost directly across the Mississippi from Columbus. Polk ordered Pillow to move his forces across the river to meet Grant. Polk briefly watched from the bluffs an exchange of fire between artillery and Union gunboats that had appeared on the Mississippi. He was concerned that there might be another attack on the Columbus side of the river. He established his command post on the riverbank in order to observe the battle and to monitor any other threats to his forces.[11] No threats materialized, and in the afternoon Polk accompanied reinforcements across the river.[12] By sunset the battle was over. Grant, after success early in the day, had been repulsed. Both sides claimed victory, and both commanders received both plaudits and blame in their respective countries. Lincoln and Davis each thought that his side had triumphed based upon battle reports by Grant and Polk. Although Grant left the field to the Confederates, the attack highlighted the threat to Southern control not only of its part of the Mississippi but also on the Tennessee and Cumberland Rivers—navigable waterways of immense value in the Confederate heartland.

President Davis firmly and promptly declined Polk's resignation, declaring that Polk's "continuance in the army" was "imperiously demanded." Davis advised the bishop-general that General Albert Sydney Johnson's success depended upon "the efficiency of the division commanders" and then cited Polk's experience with defense of the Mississippi River, including his recent victory at Belmont.[13] On 8 December, Polk wrote to Davis expressing appreciation for his confidence and indicating that he had determined "to retain my office so long as I may be of service to our cause."[14] By the end of January 1862, however, Polk submitted his resignation for a second time, and his son was again sent to Richmond with a letter for Davis. Polk and other officers in the West, including the commanding general, realized that there were too few troops to defend the vast territory and river networks under General Johnston's purview. Neither this problem nor friction with subordinate Gideon Pillow (who had resigned earlier that month) seemed to be the issue with Polk, however. Polk also did not seem to mind the expected arrival in the West of General P. G. T. Beauregard who might oversee Polk's work at Columbus; he appeared to view this assignment as helpful to his objective of returning to his calling in the church.[15]

Timing worked against him again, however, in that news of Grant's capture of Fort Henry on the Tennessee River on 6 February reached Davis before he replied to Polk. In his 7 February response Davis asked that Polk "abandon for the present all thought of resigning," pointing out that Polk's knowledge was of "great importance to the defense of the Mississippi Valley" in the grim struggle ahead.[16] Although the words *abandon for the present* were used in Davis's letter, Polk, when he accepted Davis's decision, knew that he was placing his services at the disposal of the Confederate military for the duration. The president's letter did not end on an optimistic note. He was aware that two large armies, one commanded by Grant and the other by Don Carlos Buell, were about to launch a western offensive—and his letter implicitly admitted that the wherewithal to meet that offensive was not yet in hand.

Polk's exchanges with President Davis were not his only communications during this period. Even before the Battle of Belmont, he had corresponded with General Grant on the matter of prisoner exchanges, and after the battle the two agreed upon means for care and exchange of the wounded. In one instance Polk granted visitation privileges to the wife of a wounded Union colonel who was a Confederate prisoner. There were face-to-face meetings, including one instance in which the two generals and some staff officers shared a meal.[17]

Polk also corresponded with his wife regularly. His letter of 25 November acknowledged her report that the family was "comfortably settled" in Nashville and expressed a longing to be with her again, "with nothing pressing upon me."[18] A month later he wrote again. "It is Christmas Day! A day on which angels sang 'Glory to God in the highest, peace on earth, and good will toward men,' and oh! How my heart yearns to join in the same song, if our enemies would let us. Indeed, I may say with truth, I can and do feel the full force of the sentiment of the song toward them. . . . But we trust now as ever that the Lord will deliver us out of their hands."[19]

### Charles Todd Quintard

Charles Todd Quintard was born in Stamford, Connecticut, on 22 December 1824, was educated in New York City, and was awarded the degree of doctor of medicine in 1847 from the University of the City of New York. After spending a year at Bellevue Hospital in Manhattan, he moved to Athens, Georgia, to practice medicine. In 1851 he accepted appointment as professor of physiology and pathological anatomy on the faculty of the College of Medicine in Memphis, Tennessee. Dr. Quintard began to consider changing his vocation soon after meeting the Right Reverend James Hervey Otey, bishop of Tennessee. Quintard was ordained by Otey to the sacred order of deacons at Calvary Church in Memphis in January 1855 and one year later was ordained priest at the same church. Following a brief period of service in Memphis, he became, at the request of Bishop Otey, rector of the Church of the Advent in Nashville, where he remained until the start of the Civil War.[20]

Quintard was elected chaplain by the Rock City Guard, a Tennessee militia unit, and at a Thanksgiving service held by the group in 1860 he preached the sermon—and spoke in favor of the Union. After Tennessee seceded in May 1861, however, the Reverend Dr. Quintard accepted the chaplaincy of the First Tennessee Regiment, formed from the Rock City Guard and other militia units in the state. In July the regiment was ordered to Virginia.[21]

The new chaplain first moved his wife and children to Georgia, then went to Virginia to join his regiment in August.[22] Although the soldiers of the First Tennessee Regiment did see some limited action while in Virginia, they spent much time marching and maneuvering, and Quintard's personal narrative of the months from September 1861 to February 1862 focuses on the privations and hardships the men endured—and which he shared. These began immediately: "Our first night out, after I had traveled twelve miles on foot, . . . we halted at 10 o'clock. Soon it began to rain heavily."[23] Quintard was carrying his blankets and those of a Lieutenant Joe Van Leer, with whom Quintard had become friendly during the march. The two of them made a bed in a hollow on the mountainside, with blankets on the ground and over them for cover. "Shortly after midnight a little river began running down my neck. The rain was pouring in torrents . . . so I spent the night as did the Georgia soldier who said that he had slept in the bed of a river with a thin sheet of water over him. This was not altogether a unique experience."[24]

Quintard described his evening repast of a few days later: "I had no provisions, but various persons gave me what made up a tolerably good supper, to wit,—a roasting ear, a slice of bacon and a biscuit; and, in the morning I found on a log a good sized piece of fresh meat, not strikingly clean, but I sliced off a piece and cooked it on a long stick. The fire, I reckon, removed all impurities."[25] After the next march Quintard noted that many of the soldiers were barefooted. Soldiers died, some in or after skirmishes from wounds but more from illness exacerbated by the conditions of the campaign. Quintard held the burial services.

## Henry Champlin Lay

Henry Champlin Lay was born in Richmond, Virginia, on 6 December 1823. He was graduated from the University of Virginia in 1842 and completed his studies at Virginia Theological Seminary in 1846. Lay was ordained to the diaconate by Bishop William Meade in Christ Church, Alexandria, on 10 July 1846 and served for six months as a deacon at Lynnhaven Parish, Virginia. He then moved to Huntsville, Alabama, where he began serving the Church of the Nativity, and where Bishop Nicholas H. Cobbs ordained him priest on 12 July 1848. Lay continued there as rector until he was consecrated as missionary bishop of the Southwest (Arkansas and the Indian Territory) on 23 October 1859, the day after the 1859 triennial convention.[26]

In 1847 the Reverend Mr. Lay married Elizabeth Withers Atkinson, daughter of Roger B. and Mary Atkinson. Roger was the brother of the Reverend Dr. Thomas Atkinson, then rector of St. Peter's Church in Baltimore who became bishop of North Carolina in 1853.[27] The Lay family had moved to Fort Smith, Arkansas, in 1859 and was living there when Arkansas seceded from the Union in May 1861, hostilities having already begun. Lay did not attend the July 1861 Montgomery meeting called by Bishops Polk and Stephen Elliott, but late in that month he resigned his bishopric in the Protestant Episcopal Church in the United States. On 1 October 1861 he crossed the Mississippi River and traveled to Columbia, South Carolina, for the adjourned session of that provisional convention of the Protestant Episcopal Church in the Confederate States.[28]

After the convention, the bishop returned home by way of Huntsville, where he preached on 3 November, and Little Rock. He reached home on 15 November and remained there during the winter, conducting church services at places in northwest Arkansas. In late December, Lay received a request from the presiding bishop of the Episcopal Church in the United States for canonical consent to the consecration of William Bacon Stevens as assistant bishop of Pennsylvania. Lay did not respond, because he no longer considered himself a bishop in that church.[29]

### February 1862—September 1862

*Leonidas Polk*

The Union's capture of Fort Henry on the Tennessee River was followed within a few days by an attack on Fort Donelson on the Cumberland River. This Confederate fort surrendered also, and this time many Confederate prisoners were taken. Both rivers were now accessible to the Union for movement of troops and supplies, a great logistical benefit for the North. The garrison at Columbus, Kentucky, was ordered evacuated, an order that chagrined and disappointed Polk, who had spent months making Columbus a key part of the Mississippi River's defense system. Nevertheless, he carried out the order competently.

At the same time a large part of Tennessee, including Nashville, was abandoned. Polk's wife and two daughters were part of the civilian hegira from Nashville prior to its fall on 25 February; they were assisted by Hamilton Polk, who was visiting his family on his return trip from delivering his father's resignation request.[30] Polk's wife and daughters relocated to New Orleans, where the family had lived before the war. In June 1862 Memphis, already vacated by the Confederate army, fell to a flotilla of Union gunboats.[31]

Confederate forces led by Generals Albert Sydney Johnston and P. G. T. Beauregard consolidated at Corinth, Mississippi, near the site of one of the war's major battles, Shiloh, was fought on 6 and 7 April 1862. General Polk commanded a corps comprising two divisions in this battle, in which there were more than 23,500 casualties, about 10,500 of which were suffered by the Confederacy.[32] Confederate commanding general Albert Sydney Johnston was wounded and died during the battle. On four occasions, Polk personally led battle charges of troops under his command.[33] One of these charges was witnessed by General Beauregard, who described General Polk arriving on the field with one of his divisions;

then "dashing forward with drawn sword, at the head of Cheatham's fine division, he soon formed his line of battle at the point where his presence was so much needed, and, with unsurpassed vigor, moved against a force at least double his own, making one of the most brilliant charges of infantry made on either day of the battle. He drove back the opposing columns in confusion, and thus compensated for the tardiness of his appearance on the field."[34]

Although the Union casualties were higher, and the Confederates appeared to have victory in hand at the close of the first day, the federal forces pushed the rebels back on the second day, and Beauregard, upon whom command devolved at Johnston's death, withdrew.[35] Soon after Shiloh, General Braxton Bragg became the new leader of the western theater.[36] After a period of recuperation and reorganization, Bragg decided to take his forces to Chattanooga and then to launch in cooperation with General Edmund Kirby-Smith's army, which was based near Knoxville, a campaign into Kentucky. Polk commanded a corps under Bragg as the army moved into Kentucky.

### Charles Todd Quintard

In February 1862 the first Tennessee Regiment was ordered back to Tennessee. After a hiatus Quintard rejoined that regiment in Chattanooga. He was welcomed by his old comrades and by Bishop Leonidas Polk of Louisiana, now a major general and commander of the corps to which Quintard was assigned.

### Henry Champlin Lay

Personal tragedy visited Bishop Lay in late winter, and it was juxtaposed with the coming of the Civil War to Arkansas. On 13 February 1862 the bishop noted in his diary that "at 4 and ½ p.m. fell on sleep our saintly child Thomas Atkinson."[37] On 15 February, Lay preached two sermons, one in Fort Smith and one in Van Buren, and that night he and Mrs. Lay closed the coffin of their son. On 18 February the bishop read the funeral service in his garden, witnessed by his wife, two servants, the gravedigger, and a friend, Mrs. Sandels, whose husband was a clergyman.

On the day that he buried his son Lay learned that federal forces were near Fort Smith and that Confederate general Benjamin McCullough was planning to confront them only thirty miles away.[38] The bishop was anxious to relocate his family away from the path of hostilities. The very next day, the Lay family attempted to leave on a chartered stagecoach, but the vehicle could not accommodate them. In his diary on 23 February, Lay recorded that he preached in Fort Smith a sermon entitled "The Disciples in a Storm"—and that the "enemy is within 50 miles of us." Finally, on 5 March, the bishop and his family left home and reached Memphis on 1 April.[39] The bishop did not return to western Arkansas until after the war.

When they left Memphis, Lay had hoped to visit Louisiana to perform episcopal acts for the absent Polk but decided against it based on war reports. They passed Corinth, Mississippi, just after the Battle of Shiloh. The morning after arrival in Huntsville, Lay learned that Union forces under General Ormsby M. Mitchell had occupied the town; the Lay family was confined to Huntsville for the five months of federal occupation. In his journal and subsequent writings Lay was harshly critical of the treatment of Huntsville citizens by the Union military during the occupation, citing "the injuries done to our defenseless people," and referring to the occupying forces as a "mailed hand."[40]

At one point in May the bishop was arrested and kept under guard with eleven other prisoners in the courthouse; they were unaware of the reason for their arrest until Lay and two other prisoners were brought before General Mitchell. The general was upset over the "unfriendly spirit" and the hostile actions of citizens against his soldiers. Citizens were not authorized to engage in warfare, he pointed out—and he thought it "incumbent" on those arrested to help stop acts of violence by civilians. After some negotiation, Bishop Lay and his fellow prisoners drew up and signed the following document.

Huntsville, Ala.
May 4th, 1862

We the undersigned, citizens of Northern Alabama, do hereby solemnly pledge ourselves that so long as our state north of the Tennessee is in the possession of the armies of the United States, we will not only abstain from any act of hostility, but will do our utmost to persuade *other citizens* to do the same.

We disapprove and abhor all unauthorized and illegal war: and we believe that citizens who fire upon railway trains, attack the guards at bridges, destroy telegraph lines and fire from concealment upon pickets, deserve and should receive the punishment of death.

We even disapprove all guerilla warfare *by citizens* as calculated to embitter feelings already too much excited, as destructive of the best interests of the community in which such war is waged, and as is no degree calculated to bring to a close the great contest now existing between the North and the South, to settle which a legitimate war should alone be waged.[41]

Bishop Lay does not indicate in his journal what part he played in the composition of—and agreement to sign—this remarkable document, but in view of his position and the fact that he was one of the three persons who met directly with General Mitchell, it seems safe to assume that his role was significant. Given the rules of war for the period, there was nothing disloyal to the Southern cause in the paper, but the bishop and the others must have struggled with the propriety of preparing and signing such a document under duress.

After Lay and the others who had been arrested were released, church services were resumed, and Bishop Lay assisted on a number of occasions the Reverend Mr. Bannister, who was now rector of the Church of the Nativity, where Lay had been minister before being elected bishop in 1859. Lay noted that in the Service of Morning Prayer the Prayer for the President and all in Civil Authority was "disused" to avoid antagonizing the occupation authority.[42]

On 29 June, Lucy, Bishop and Mrs. Lay's seven-year-old child, became ill with dysentery. Within a week their only daughter had died; she was buried at 6 P.M. on 5 July, with Mr. Bannister officiating. Lucy had been born in Huntsville during Lay's tenure as parish priest, and his diary records that the tears of parishioners "mingled with our own."[43]

During the week of 24–31 August, the Union forces evacuated Huntsville, and Confederate troops entered town immediately. About one hundred sick and wounded Union soldiers were left behind in the hospital, many of whom feared retaliation by the Confederates for the treatment of the townspeople. Lay and Bannister did their best to assuage those fears, telling the patients that no harm would come to the "prostrate." The bishop paid regular visits to the Union soldiers in the hospital, and, on one occasion, baptized a young man from Ohio. In mid-September, Lay preached on the Day of Thanksgiving for the recent Confederate victories at Manassas and Richmond. Soon thereafter Bishop Lay and his family departed Huntsville for Richmond.[44]

## October 1862–December 1862

### Henry Champlin Lay

By 20 October the Lay family was in Richmond. The family took residence in Virginia and resided there or in North Carolina for the duration of the war. After getting the family settled, Lay departed for Augusta by way of Charleston to attend the first General Council of the Protestant Episcopal Church in the Confederate States, held from 12 to 22 November. While in Charleston, he preached at St. Michael's Church and paid a call on General Beauregard. He arrived in Augusta in time to preach at the opening of the council a sermon entitled "God That Hideth Thyself."[45]

In the meantime the primary convention for the Diocese of Arkansas had convened on 1 November. Twelve parishes and six presbyters were present at the call of the Standing Committee. Lay learned during the meeting in Augusta of the petition to admit Arkansas as a diocese of the Confederate church—and learned as well that he had been elected unanimously as diocesan bishop. The messenger was the Reverend Dr. J. T. Wheat who had come to represent Arkansas at the council. Dr. Wheat also advised the diocesan-elect of the following resolution: "RESOLVED: That the present condition of the Diocese of the country makes it impossible for us to pledge with confidence a sufficient support to a Bishop"[46] Lay's response in accepting his election was that "I want you, not yours." The council admitted Arkansas as a diocese and confirmed Lay's election as bishop.[47] After the council Lay returned to Arkansas, crossing the Mississippi River at Vicksburg and reaching Pine Buff on 28 December. He did not return to Fort Smith but established his base in Little Rock. From there he made episcopal visits across the state to wherever wartime conditions permitted.[48]

## Leonidas Polk

The initial engagement of Braxton Bragg's Kentucky campaign was a Confederate victory at Munfordville on 17 September 1862. Next came the bloody Battle of Perryville, in which the Confederates, including Polk's corps, fought bravely but suffered heavy casualties. The battle did not have a clear victor, but in the aftermath Bragg decided that he had to withdraw from Kentucky, abandoning the state to the Union.

Bragg's army retreated into Tennessee, and the Union army, now led by Buell's replacement, General William S. Rosecrans, pursued, halting at Nashville.[49] Bragg's forces stopped at Murfreesboro. The Confederate war department was not pleased with this outcome, and Polk actually led the army's retreat while, at President Davis's request, Bragg visited Richmond to give an accounting. After Bragg's return, Polk was summoned before the president to give his perspective. Polk delayed his return to duty in order to visit his family in Raleigh; they had left New Orleans to relocate in North Carolina. While he was away Polk's promotion to lieutenant general became effective on 26 November 1862.

During the battle at Perryville, Polk's disobedience in the form of a modification (in which his division commanders concurred) of a direct order from Bragg initiated a rift between the two generals that festered and widened over the next year.[50]

While the Confederates camped at Murfreesboro, Tennessee, in December Bishop-General Polk performed the wedding ceremony for John Hunt Morgan and Martha Ready. Brigadier General Morgan was a dashing cavalry leader who specialized in raids that disrupted Union army supply lines. Polk officiated with a bishop's vestment draped over his uniform and wrote his wife that the two were united in Holy Matrimony by "a lieutenant-general, a select company present—Generals Bragg, Hardee, Breckenridge, Cheatham, etc. It was an historic event."[51]

Rosecrans began moving out of Nashville in late December. There was a battle at Stone's River (near Murfreesboro) from 31 December 1862 to 3 January 1863. This was a major engagement that resulted in some 23,500 casualties; the Confederates left the field first but Rosecrans did not give pursuit. Both armies then went into winter quarters.[52]

*Charles Todd Quintard*

Quintard served with General Polk during General Bragg's Kentucky campaign. He witnessed the early success at Munfordville, but the baptism of chaplain and physician Quintard into the harsh reality of a major battle and its aftermath came in October 1862 at Perryville.

> When the wounded were brought to the rear, at 3 o'clock in the afternoon, I took my place as a surgeon on Chaplain's Creek and throughout the rest of the day and until half past five the next morning, without food of any sort, I was incessantly occupied with the wounded. It was a horrible night I spent, God save me from such another. I suppose excitement kept me up. About half past five in the morning of the 9th, I dropped,—I could do no more. I went out by myself and leaning against a fence, I wept like a child. And all that day I was so unnerved that if any one asked me about the regiment, I could make no reply without tears. Having taken off my shirt to tear into strips to make bandages, I took a severe cold.[53]

A few days after the battle Polk asked Quintard to accompany him to St. Philip's Church in Harrodsburg, a church for which Bishop Benjamin Bosworth Smith had overseen the construction and purchased stained glass windows.[54] The two men entered the church, and Polk suddenly was deeply moved, probably by the contrast between the beauty of the church and the peace it represented and the horror in which he had just participated. He requested Quintard to have prayer, and the chaplain held a brief service. General Polk knelt at the railing and wept.[55] Quintard accompanied the army during its retreat into Tennessee, did his duty as surgeon and chaplain after the fight at Murfreesboro, and joined the other officers and men in winter quarters.

### January 1863–February 1864

*Leonidas Polk*

In spite of exhortations from President Lincoln, it was five months before Rosecrans moved to engage the Confederates again. Near the end of this lull, in May 1863 an observer from Great Britain, a Lieutenant Colonel Arthur Fremantle of the Coldstream Guards, visited the Confederate camp in Shelbyville, Tennessee, and was given a week's hospitality by the corps commanders Polk and William J. Hardee.

> I slept in General Polk's tent, he occupying a room in the house adjoining. Before going to bed, General Polk told me an affecting story of a poor widow in humble circumstances, whose three sons had fallen in battle one after the other, until she had only one left, a boy of sixteen. So distressing was

her case that General Polk went himself to comfort her. She looked steadily at him, and replied to his condolences by the sentence, "As soon as I can get a few things together, General, you shall have Harry too." The tears came into General Polk's eyes as he related this episode, which he ended by saying, "How can you subdue such nation as this!"[56]

Fremantle's visit overlapped that of Bishop Stephen Elliott of Georgia, who had come at Polk's invitation to preach and to perform rites of baptism and confirmation. At one service, according to Fremantle, Elliott preached "most admirably" to a congregation of nearly three thousand soldiers, including many generals, who listened with "profound attention."[57] Fremantle also witnessed the baptism of General Braxton Bragg by Bishop Elliott: "The bishop took the general's hand in his own (the latter kneeling in front of the font), and said, 'Braxton, if thou has not already been baptized, I baptize thee' &c. Immediately afterwards he confirmed General Bragg, who then shook hands with General Polk, the officers, their respective staffs, and myself, who were the only spectators."[58] When Rosecrans finally resumed the offensive, there followed a long Confederate retreat beginning in June 1863 that was punctuated by skirmishes across Middle Tennessee and that culminated with battles at Chickamauga Creek in September and at Chattanooga in November.

Polk—and the other generals reporting to Bragg—had been critical of the way Bragg had led the army during the Kentucky-Tennessee campaign, and things came to a head after the Battle of Chickamauga. Orders from Bragg to Polk to launch a major dawn attack on 20 September by the army's right wing commanded by Polk were not carried out. The attack at daylight was to have been initiated by Lieutenant General D. H. Hill under Polk's command. An order from Polk to Hill was prepared just before midnight and dispatched by courier, but the courier could not locate General Hill. Polk became aware of the problem at dawn and took steps to get the attack moving, but Hill, having no advance warning of the attack plans, was unprepared and argued that he could not proceed immediately. Polk and Hill blamed each other for the delay. Bragg's anger over the delay, regardless of where the fault lay, no doubt was exacerbated by his resentment over Polk's failure to obey an order at Perryville, and Bragg refused to accept Polk's explanation.[59]

After the battle, Bragg relieved corps commander Polk of duty and directed Polk to wait in Georgia while charges were drawn up. To complicate matters, near the end of the battle when the Union forces had withdrawn and the Confederates were clearly victorious, Polk and other general officers had come to Bragg at different times to urge a full-scale pursuit that offered the opportunity to shatter Rosecrans's army. Bragg refused and had his forces surround Rosecrans in Chattanooga, to which the Union army had retreated. Polk, D. H. Hill, and other officers, especially General Nathan Bedford Forrest, felt that a golden opportunity had been allowed to slip away.[60]

Jefferson Davis intervened in the Bragg-Polk dispute, dismissed the charges against Polk, and restored Polk's status in the army, although Polk elected assignment to Mississippi rather than resuming service under Bragg.[61] After the Union forces routed the Confederates on Missionary Ridge and thereby broke the siege of Chattanooga in November, Davis relieved Bragg—at Bragg's request.[62] Polk's decision to choose duty in Mississippi reflected his determination to avoid serving any longer under General Bragg, not a desire to serve in the department centered in Mississippi, a locus which was hardly a plum assignment for a lieutenant general. His major task, in fact, when he began in Enterprise, Mississippi, in November 1863 was to collect and organize for service in the army the Confederate troops who had been paroled and exchanged at Vicksburg and Port Hudson, where Southern defeats had occurred some four to five months prior.[63]

Nevertheless, when the department commander, General Joseph E. Johnston, was reassigned to Georgia and Polk replaced him, the first general order issued by the new commander was a ringing endorsement of the Confederate cause, the importance of the department, and the quality of the troops now under his command.[64] Polk quickly involved his new command in a problem faced by some Mississippi counties, namely that "deserters, draft dodgers, and renegades in general" were spreading terror by violent and disruptive behavior, including the seizure of government property. General Polk felt he should be given authority to bring in deserters and draft dodgers and arrange for integration of those who were fit for service into the army. That authority was centralized in Richmond, however, and there, over Polk's objections, it remained. Polk interpreted a response from Secretary of War James A. Seddon, however, to allow him at least to go after deserters.[65] Before his tenure in Mississippi was over, Polk was able to report to President Davis that he had "returned more than 1000 deserters to their commands."[66]

## Charles Todd Quintard

Unlike his friend Bishop-General Polk, who was constantly at odds with his commanding general, Quintard respected General Bragg, and the respect was mutual. When Quintard learned that Bishop Elliott was coming to visit, he not only exhorted the soldiers and officers in his charge to come forward with a profession of faith, but he also made a special appointment with the commanding general to urge him, Braxton Bragg, to take that step. Bragg's initial reception of his chaplain was curt, but after Quintard stated his mission the general seemed deeply moved—and consented to being instructed in the faith by Quintard.[67] Thus it was because of the efforts of Chaplain Quintard that General Bragg came forward as candidate for baptism and confirmation when Bishop Elliott visited during May 1863.

### Henry Champlin Lay

Having arrived in Arkansas by the first of the year, Bishop Lay opened and presided at the Second Annual Council of the Diocese of Arkansas, held at Christ Church in Little Rock from 13 to 17 May 1863. In his address to the diocese the bishop advised that no clergyman should permit himself to be detained behind enemy lines, if escape was possible—but if detention was unavoidable, he should omit from services the Prayer for the President and all in Civil Authority, as had been done in Huntsville. This action, the bishop felt, was preferable to closing the churches because a "mailed hand" (the Union military) proscribed the one prayer.[68]

After Polk made his decision to accept a commission in the Confederate army, he had written his fellow Bishops Otey and Lay requesting that they supply episcopal services to his diocese. Both agreed, but Otey's health failed, and Lay was detained behind federal lines for months in Huntsville. In June and July 1863, however, Lay undertook visitations in Louisiana, which he officially reported to the Standing Committee of the diocese after the war: "June 16 In the Church of the Redeemer, Morehouse Parish, preached and confirmed three persons. At night, at Harrison and Duval's Plantation, I preached to a large well-trained Negro congregation. The chants were sung, and the whole evening service used. I confirmed on this occasion nineteen Negroes."[69] In July he spent a week in and near Shreveport, preaching six times and confirming sixteen persons. He also facilitated a subscription effort to retire a $2,500 debt. Lay was impressed "with the cordial hospitality of Louisiana Churchmen—their warm interest in the religious welfare of the Negro race, and with the universal veneration and love entertained for their Bishop. His message, when delivered, elicited the response of tears and loving replies."[70]

At the end of July he reached "debatable" country (where skirmishing often occurred) and after crossing first the Atchafalaya River and then the Mississippi River by skiff he decided that further visitations were not feasible. Because federal forces were taking control in Arkansas, he also decided not to return there. He began the long journey to Virginia that would enable him to rejoin his family.[71]

### February 1864–June 1864

### Leonidas Polk

In early February 1864, during the "Mississippi Interlude" in Polk's military service, General William Tecumseh Sherman departed with twenty thousand infantry out of Vicksburg and began moving east across Mississippi toward Meridian, where a large store of supplies was located as well as considerable rolling stock.[72] A few days later, under Sherman's orders a cavalry force of ten thousand commanded by General Sooy Smith left Collierville, Tennessee, also headed to Meridian.[73] Sherman's objectives were to destroy the railroads at Meridian along the way and then to capture Mobile or Selma, again destroying railroads. Polk's smaller cavalry force led by Major Generals Nathan Bedford Forrest and Stephen D. Lee harassed Smith during his advance, and Smith stopped short of his planned juncture with Sherman. Polk's infantry under Major Generals William Loring and Samuel French was greatly outnumbered by Sherman's force, and Polk withdrew from Meridian without giving battle. He did, however, send safely away nearly all of the supplies and rolling stock as well as the shop tools for railroad repair.[74] Sherman took over Meridian and destroyed railroads and other property, but the failure of Smith to join him and the arrival (from Johnston's army in Georgia) of reinforcements for Polk, led by General Hardee, caused Sherman to abandon plans to move on Mobile. Both Sherman and Smith withdrew. Thus Polk did not risk his army against a much larger force in order to try to save Meridian, but his delaying tactics were a factor in dissuading Sherman from pushing into Alabama to wreak more destruction.

When Sherman was called to Chattanooga to assume command of Rosecrans's former army, it was clear that the Union was about to move on Atlanta. Polk was recalled to Georgia, and he brought most of his force, some ten thousand infantry and four thousand cavalry, with him.[75] Lieutenant General Polk arrived in Resaca, Georgia, on 11 May 1864.

## Henry Champlin Lay

In February 1864 Bishop Lay and his friend, a Judge Perkins, visited two sites in the Richmond area where Union prisoners of war were being held. The first was Libby Prison, at which Lay found one thousand Union officers, in quarters that were not crowded, who had tasks to occupy them. The prisoners were in "good spirits. At Belle Isle, however, the 7,500 inmates were confined in too small an area, had an inadequate diet, and had little to do. They looked "sour."[76] On Sunday, 6 March 1864, Bishop Lay preached to a Confederate unit, the Powhatan Troop, in Emmanuel Church. The sermon was entitled "The Devout Soldier." One of the themes was that the profession of arms was sanctioned by the Almighty and that there were three conditions under which blood might be shed lawfully and hence with God's blessing. The conditions were (1) in self defense; (2) in the protection of the helpless; and (3) when directed by the civil power. Lay spoke passionately about these conditions, using each one as a vehicle to bolster and exhort the troops, telling them first that they were defending their own hearthstones against invasion, second that they were protecting helpless citizens from a ruthless foe and preventing overthrow of the divine guardianship of slaves

entrusted to the South, and third that they were fighting for their country, the legitimate civil power.[77]

In the late spring Bishop Lay traveled south to meet Bishop Stephen Elliott to discuss the need for revision of the Book of Common Prayer as used in the Confederate States, and while there he was diverted for the sad duty of attending the funeral service for Bishop Polk. Lay then remained in Georgia, ministering to the troops falling back before Sherman's army as it advanced on Atlanta.[78]

### Leonidas Polk

By mid May 1864 General Sherman was in command of the Union army at Chattanooga, and Joseph E. Johnston commanded the opposing Confederate forces. General Polk, who had been recalled to Georgia, and Generals William Hardee and John Bell Hood were Johnston's three corps commanders. The Southern army was deployed near Dalton, Georgia, some eighty miles north of Atlanta. Sherman's move out of Chattanooga toward Dalton signaled the start of a Union campaign to try to take Atlanta. Polk arrived on 11 May, and he and Hood traveled together for a strategy meeting with Johnston. Hood, who had recently returned to duty after recuperation from loss of a leg at Chickamauga, told Polk that he wished to be baptized. Bishop-General Polk was delighted. He wrote his wife afterward: "The scene was a touching one, he with one leg, leaning on his crutches—a veteran in the midst of his & my officers & I the officiating minister. His heart was fully in it."[79]

A sharp engagement with 5,500 casualties then occurred at Resaca from 13 to 15 May before Johnston decided to retreat. For the next month Sherman forced Johnston south toward Atlanta with flanking movements. Johnston attempted without success to maneuver Sherman into having to attack strong defensive positions. Some six engagements in which Polk participated were fought during the month from mid-May to mid-June. Union losses were slightly higher than Confederate losses during this period. One of Johnston's attempts to lure Sherman into a fight on Confederate terms was at Cassville, but Sherman's flanking strategy forced a Confederate withdrawal. The night before the battle near Cassville was to have occurred, General Johnston was baptized by Polk—who had been asked in a letter from Mrs. Johnston to administer this sacrament to her husband: "You are never too much occupied I well know to pause to perform a good deed and will I am sure, even whilst leading your soldiers on to victory, lead my soldier nearer to God. . . . I have written him on the subject & am sure he only waits your leisure."[80] Polk performed the rite on 18 May, with Generals Hood and Hardee in attendance. In Polk's words, "It was a deeply solemn scene & what a passage for history! God seems to be drawing our hearts to him."[81]

Polk's experiences with General Bragg in Tennessee and his own Mississippi command had done little to lift his spirits, but he always praised his soldiers by whom he was beloved and respected. The Atlanta campaign, although a series of Confederate retreats, seemed to revive Polk's optimism. He felt that the men were healthy and wrote his wife that they were confident and in good spirits—and that both Polk and his troops had confidence in Johnston and would be ready to fight when the time came.[82]

## Charles Todd Quintard

After the Confederate defeat at Missionary Ridge and the subsequent change in command for the Army of Tennessee, with Braxton Bragg being replaced by Joseph E. Johnston, Quintard remained with the army with the title of chaplain-at-large. During the lull in the fighting between the fall of Chattanooga in November 1863 and the Union push toward Atlanta that started in May 1864, Quintard established St. Luke's parish in Atlanta. Services began in a Methodist church, but a new building was erected in about six weeks' time. The new church was consecrated by Bishop Elliott on 22 April 1864. Quintard presented five people to the bishop for confirmation. Chaplin Quintard was busy with his military duties as well, presenting at services in Marietta a group of officers and other soldiers for confirmation. He also produced religious booklets: "It was about this time that I prepared some little books adapted to the use of the soldiers as a convenient substitute for the Book of Common Prayer. I also prepared a booklet, entitled, 'Balm for the Weary and Wounded.' The first four copies of the latter booklet that came from the press were forwarded to General Polk, and he wrote upon three of them the names of General J. E. Johnson, Lieutenant-General Hardee and Lieutenant-General Hood, respectively, and 'With the compliments of Lieutenant-General Leonidas Polk, June 12, 1864.'"[83] On 14 June, only two days after Polk inscribed these booklets, Quintard received a telegram from a member of Polk's staff stating that "Lieutenant-General Polk was killed today by a cannon ball."[84]

*Leonidas Polk*

On 14 June, Johnston and two of his commanders, Hardee and Polk, ascended a large hill known as Pine Mountain for a position assessment before Johnston decided on his next move; the Union lines were clearly visible from the summit, which was dominated by a Confederate battery, but the hilltop was also within range of Union artillery. General Sherman was doing some reconnoitering of his own opposite Pine Mountain, on which he later reported: "In plain view, stood a group of the enemy, evidently observing us with glasses. General Howard, Commanding the Fourth Corps, was nearby, . . . and [I] ordered him to cause a battery close by to fire three volleys. . . . General Polk, in my opinion, was killed by the second volley."[85] A Union shell landed nearby while the three officers were in consultation, and the conference ended as the generals sought safer ground. Polk, however, for reasons known only to him, lingered at the crest to have a last look. A cannon ball entered one arm and went through his body, killing him instantly. After his body had been moved from the field of fire, an ambulance carried it to headquarters. According to Polk's son and biographer William Mecklenburg Polk, "'Jerry,' the noble roan he had ridden in nearly all his marches and battles was led riderless in front."[86] The three blood-stained copies of Quintard's *Balm for the Weary and Wounded* were removed from General Polk's breast pocket and transmitted to the fellow generals for whom he had inscribed the booklets. General Johnston issued a proclamation to the army:

HEADQUARTERS, ARMY OF TENNESSEE
IN THE FIELD, June 14, 1864
General Field Orders No. 2.

The Right Reverend Leonidas Polk, D.D.

Comrades: You are called upon to mourn your first captain; your oldest companion in arms. Lieutenant-General Polk fell today at the outpost of this army,—the army he raised and commanded, in all of whose trials he shared, to all of whose victories he contributed.

In this distinguished leader we have lost the most courteous of gentlemen, the most gallant of soldiers.

The Christian, patriot, soldier has neither lived nor died in vain. His example is before you; his mantle rests with you.[87]

J. E. Johnston, General
Kimlock Falconer, A.A.G.

General Sherman's notice of Polk's death was briefer: "We killed Bishop Polk yesterday and have made good progress today."[88]

### Charles Todd Quintard

The telegram from army headquarters requested that Quintard meet General Polk's body at the train depot in Atlanta. Quintard wrote: "I was never more shocked and overwhelmed; . . . the body of the dead Bishop and General was escorted to St. Luke's Church, and placed in front of the altar. He was dressed in his gray uniform. On his breast rested a cross of white roses and beside his casket lay his sword."[89]

Polk's body lay in the church until noon on 15 June, enabling soldiers and the citizens of Atlanta to pay their respects. One citizen, Sarah "Sallie" Conley Clayton, recorded her observations:

> I do not remember at what hour, but quite early, that the church was opened, and thousands who thronged the streets waiting for this were permitted to pass in. . . . All were required to enter the [front] door at the left, continue up the left aisle, pass in front of the casket and down the right hand aisle to the door on that side. I could not begin to say how many, many thousands marched through the little church on that occasion or how sad their mien.
>
> The good old Bishop's death seemed a personal loss to everyone who looked upon his bloodless face that day. Tears were shed by hundreds of those present, but very silently, not a sound was heard in the entire church but that of footsteps as the crowd passed through. Many, very many, of the throng paused long enough when the casket was reached to stoop, for it was quite low, and take a leaf or flower or twig. There was no cessation of the stream of humanity; except for a short religious service.[90]

Quintard held funeral services and gave a eulogy; the bishop's body was then taken from the church to go by train to Augusta for the burial service. In Clayton's words, "The crowd made way in the street for the passing of the hearse and the carriages of the pall bearers, then fell quietly in line, and with bowed heads followed in their wake, while all the time the beauty of the morning seemed a mockery to the gloom and sorrow of Atlanta that day."[91]

### Henry Champlin Lay

The final service was held at St. Paul's Church, Augusta, on 29 June. Bishop Elliott of Georgia had consulted with the Polk family, and it had been decided to commit Leonidas Polk's remains to the care of the Diocese of Georgia until the Diocese of Louisiana was able to "claim them as her rightful inheritance." Elliott issued a funeral notice:

> The Bishops, Clergy, and Laity of the Protestant Episcopal Church in the Confederate States, the officers of the Army and Navy of the Confederate States, and the citizens generally, are invited to attend the funeral services of

the Rt. Rev. Leonidas Polk, D.D., from the City Hall of Augusta, Georgia, on Wednesday, the 29th of June. The procession will move from the City Hall to St. Paul's Church. His remains will be deposited in the church-yard of St. Paul's until the war closes.

Stephen Elliott
Senior Bp. Of Prot. Epis. Ch. In C.S.A.[92]

Bishop Lay and Bishop William Mercer Green of Mississippi joined their colleague Elliott in the conduct of the service. Lay read the lesson. Elliott's sermon was a moving tribute to his friend Polk, with whom he had collaborated on the initial steps that led to the formation of the Protestant Episcopal Church in the Confederate States. Near the close of his address, he turned his attention to his Northern brethren:

> And now, ye Christians of the North, and especially ye priests and bishops of the Church who have lent yourselves to the fanning of the fury of this unjust and cruel war, do I this day, in the presence of the body of my murdered brother, summon you to meet us at the judgment-seat of Christ—that awful bar where your brute force shall avail you nothing: where the multitudes whom you have followed to do evil shall not shield you from an angry God; where the vain excuses with which you have varnished your sin shall be scattered before the bright beams of eternal truth and righteousness. I summon you to that bar in the name of that sacred liberty which you have trampled under foot; in the name of the glorious constitution which you have destroyed; in the name of our holy religion which you have profaned; in the name of the temples of God which you have desecrated; in the name of a thousand martyred saints whose blood you have wantonly spilled; in the name of our Christian women whom you have violated; in the name of our slaves whom you have seduced and then consigned to misery; and there I leave justice and vengeance to God. The blood of your brethren crieth unto God from the earth, and it will not cry in vain. It has entered into the Lord God of Sabaoth, and will be returned to you in blood a thousand-fold. May God have mercy upon you in that day of solemn justice and fearful retribution!

Bishop Elliott closed his sermon with the following words:

> And now let us commit his sacred dust to the keeping of the Church in the Confederate States until such time as his own diocese shall be prepared to do him honor. That day will come: I see it rise before me in vision, when this martyred dust shall be carried in triumphal procession to his own beloved Louisiana. . . . And he shall then receive a prophet's reward! His works shall rise up from the ashes of the past and attest his greatness! A diocese

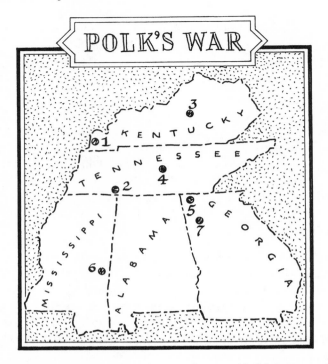

(1) Columbus, KY (Battle at Belmont): November 1861  (2) Shiloh, TN: April 1862
(3) Perryville, KY: October 1862  (4) Stones River, TN: December 1862–January 1863
(5) Chickamauga, GA: 18–20 September 1863  (6) Meridian, MS: 14–20 February 1864
(7) Pine Mountain, GA (General Polk killed): 14 June 1864

rescued from brutal dominion by the efficacy of his blood!—a church freed from pollution by the vigor of his counsels!—a country made independent through his devotion and self sacrifice!—a university sending forth streams of pure and sanctified learning from its exuberant bosom—generations made better and grander from his example and life, and rising up and calling him blessed![93]

After the service the coffin was lowered into a grave behind the chancel window. As Bishop Elliott said "Earth to earth, ashes to ashes, dust to dust" at graveside, Lieutenant-General James Longstreet, Army of Northern Virginia, Bishop Lay, and Bishop Green of Mississippi cast dirt upon the coffin.[94]

### July 1864–August 1864

For nearly two months after Polk was killed, the Atlanta campaign was conducted, with engagements ranging from Kennesaw Mountain, some twenty-five miles north of Atlanta, to Jonesboro just south of Atlanta. Sherman led the Union forces throughout the campaign. Johnston was replaced as the Confederate commander by John Bell Hood on 17 July. Hood's tactics were more aggressive and resulted in staggering casualties without stemming the Union advance. On 1 September, after a Union victory at Jonesboro, Hood evacuated his army from Atlanta.

### Henry Champlin Lay and Charles Todd Quintard

While they were in Augusta for Polk's funeral, Stephen Elliott, senior Confederate bishop, asked Bishop Lay to assume responsibility for the chaplains in the Army of Tennessee and offered a stipend that would be paid "as long as the churches in Georgia remain open." Lay accepted and considered the work to be a missionary assignment. On 1 July, Lay and Chaplain Quintard met over tea to discuss their work for the soldiers. Lay preached, baptized, and confirmed while the Atlanta campaign continued.[95]

There was a brief hiatus in Quintard's chaplaincy service during this period. Bishop Elliott arranged for him to go to Macon to serve a parish in which the rector was recovering from illness. By August, however, Quintard had resumed his military responsibilities: "I was with Bishop Lay of Arkansas in Atlanta, and with the army again, though compelled to go on Sundays to Macon to officiate for the sick rector at that place."[96]

While he was in Atlanta, Bishop Lay held an outdoor confirmation service at General Hood's headquarters; Chaplain Quintard presented the confirmand class. Among the class members were General John B. Hood and officers from his staff. The bishop and the chaplain also visited St. Luke's Church, built earlier that year under Quintard's supervision. The church had been shelled. According to Quintard, "One of the largest shells had torn through the side of the building and struck the prayer desk on which the large Bible happened to be lying. The prayer desk was broken and the Bible fell under it and upon the shell so as apparently to smother it and prevent its exploding. I lifted up the Bible and removed the shell and gathered up all the prayer books I could find for the soldiers in the camps. . . . This was the last time I visited St. Luke's Church. . . . It was destroyed in the 'burning of Atlanta.'"[97]

Quintard and Lay remained under stressful conditions at Hood's headquarters until the Atlanta campaign ended. "The city was being shelled by the Federals," Quintard recalled, "and some of the shells fell very thickly about the General's Headquarters. I thought the locality seemed very unhealthy, but as the General and his staff did not seem in the least disturbed, Bishop Lay and I concluded that everything was going on all right according to the art of war and we stood it with the best of them."[98]

**September 1864–June 1865**

*Henry Champlin Lay*

After the Confederate army evacuated Atlanta, it was several weeks before any significant movements or military actions occurred.[99] Hood's army was recuperating, and both commanders were thinking through their next moves. Bishop Lay decided that this hiatus offered an opportunity to visit close friends in Huntsville—but he would need authorization to cross the Union lines. "About the middle of September [1864]," Lay recalled, "I paid a visit to General Hardee at Jonesboro, his headquarters. There was a standing truce to allow the transit of citizens exiled from Atlanta by General Sherman's order, and all through the night we heard the noise of the long wagon train conveying these unfortunates. It occurred to me . . . that I might under the cover of this truce find an opportunity to visit some very dear and much afflicted friends in Huntsville."[100]

Lay then wrote the following letter:

> The undersigned respectfully suggests to Major General Sherman that he greatly desires to enter his lines, spend two or three days in Huntsville, and return.
>
> His object is to visit an old lady who has been as a mother to him, and whose situation is such as to require an interview. He is well aware how unusual is such a request and urges it with great deference. He can say only that the permission, if accorded, shall not be abused by any covert word or deed.

Very Respy
Henry C. Lay
Bishop of Arkansas
Address care of Gen. Hardee[101]

The bishop's request was endorsed by General Hardee and sent to General Sherman, who responded promptly.

Atlanta Sept. 17th 1864
General Hardee

Dear Sir,
Bishop Lay may come to Atlanta where the necessary papers will be given him to visit the city of Huntsville and return. I will not exact of the Bishop any specific promise, but will presume on his character to observe the war secrecy.

W. T. Sherman
Major General[102]

On 28 September a prisoner exchange occurred at a railroad station named Rough and Ready, and arrangements were made for Lay to accompany to Atlanta the federal prisoners who were being exchanged. While waiting for the process to finish, Lay talked with some of the Confederate soldiers who were handed over by the federals. It must have been a discouraging conversation, because he was told that some Confederate prisoners had taken an oath of allegiance to the Union and gone north to live; others had even accepted a bounty to enlist in the Union army, and, that very morning, many Confederates had refused the option of being returned. Along the way to Atlanta, the train carrying the 149 officers being sent back to the Union stopped to pick up a Southern deserter.

Upon arrival in Atlanta, General Sherman spoke at a ceremony to welcome the returnees. Lay then met with the general, who invited him to supper. They discussed the Atlanta campaign and the charge that Sherman's order forcing the residents of Atlanta to evacuate the city was inhumane—a charge that Sherman rejected. His position was that he could not feed them, and therefore it was best that they depart in good weather rather than straggle out later. The general also argued that reunion of the North and South was inevitable and that there would be no lasting enmity once it was effected. Lay disagreed, saying that "there was now a deep-seated alienation which would render it impossible for them to live together on terms on intimacy."[103]

The next day Bishop Lay was provided with a paper that stated authorization to visit Huntsville and return, specified courteous treatment, and entitled him to free passage on the railroads. Lay's trip—both ways—was an adventure. On the way the train from Chattanooga to Huntsville was delayed by the need to repair the tracks and because General Nathan Bedford Forrest was threatening Huntsville. On the return trip Bishop Lay attempted to leave on 7 October but could get no farther than Stevenson, Alabama; he returned to Huntsville. On his second try a month later he got through to Chattanooga on 8 November. Then, after a train trip south of seventy miles that required two days, he arrived at Kingston, Georgia, some fifty miles north of Atlanta. Sherman, it turned out, had his headquarters there, and the bishop located the general.

### Hood and Sherman: Their Final Campaigns

General John Bell Hood, in consultation with President Jefferson Davis who had visited the general soon after the fall of Atlanta, decided that his strategy would be to march his army north into Tennessee to retake Nashville. Sherman's supply lines would be cut in the process, and, Hood thought, Sherman would be lured north to the chase. The Confederate Army of Tennessee therefore abandoned Georgia to begin what one author has called "the last great campaign of the Civil War."[104]

Sherman, however, had other plans. He dispatched a part of his army under General George Henry Thomas to deal with Hood.[105] With Hood gone, the way was open for the "March to the Sea," a "campaign" that would entail using some sixty-two thousand soldiers to cut a swath of destruction sixty miles wide for the three hundred miles to the sea at Savannah, at which point the march would turn north through the Carolinas.[106]

### Henry Champlin Lay

When Bishop Lay found him at Kingston, Sherman was ready to begin his march to Savannah and did not wish to send Bishop Lay through the Confederate lines south of where they were. Sherman indicated that he trusted the bishop but thought that it would be difficult for Lay to talk about his return without betraying something about Sherman's plans. They agreed that Lay would return to Confederate lines via Richmond, which suited Lay well in that it would permit a visit with his family. Lay was given an authorization that allowed him to travel to Baltimore by way of Louisville, and then to reenter Confederate lines. Bishop Lay watched General Sherman's departure: "Between eight and nine o'clock the troops began to move. They were splendidly equipped, with bands playing and colors flying. I observed them from the window with no small pang of sorrow. . . . General Sherman. . . mounted his horse, rode away, . . . and I saw him no more. . . . Thus on the morning of the 12th of November, General Sherman marched from Kingston on his way to lay waste the homes of my people, while I turned my face to pass through the North Country."[107]

When Bishop Lay watched General Sherman's armada begin to depart on that November morning, his "pang of sorrow" no doubt reflected a premonition of the coming devastation that Herman Melville later evoked in his poem, "The March to the Sea."

> For behind they left a wailing
> A terror and a ban,
> And blazing cinders sailing,
> And houseless households wan,
> Wide zones of counties paling,
> And towns where maniacs ran,
> Was it Treason's retribution—
> Necessity the plea?
> They will long remember Sherman
> And his streaming columns free—
> They will long remember Sherman
> Marching to the sea.[108]

The Right Reverend Henry Champlin Lay, D.D., LL.D.

The bishop reached Baltimore on 18 November after a journey partly by rail and partly by steamboat. He found General Ulysses S. Grant at City Point on 25 November and was invited to spend the evening with the Union commander. In conversation Grant and Lay agreed that diplomatic discussions between North and South should be held at once, but Grant cautioned that the North would never agree to separation. Grant also discussed some of the changes that were happening in the art of warfare, especially the vanishing of open-field fighting.[109]

The next morning Lay met General George Meade at Grant's headquarters, and Meade, as Grant had done, pressed upon the bishop the argument that the resources, and especially the number of soldiers available to the North, made the cause of the South hopeless, and he asked why the Confederacy did not recognize this. Lay replied that God "givest not always the battle to the strong." Meade rejoined: "Both parties, I doubt not, very sincerely expect divine interference; but I have yet to find reason for expecting that interference to be on your side."[110] By the evening of 25 November the bishop was in Confederate territory and within a week he was at the headquarters of General Robert E. Lee, speaking with the general.

Bishop Lay summarized in his diary his impressions of the time that he had spent behind federal lines. His first three points reflected a comparison of the armies. Union men were "ruddy and beefy"; Confederates "sinewy and brown." Soldiers in the United States were provided with everything—military supplies were abundant. Comforts of all sorts were available to federal troops. Lay also commented on the luxury, extravagance, and money of the North. There was no "seeming dependence" on God in the North, "the national vainglory inexpressible." He preferred "our Confederate poverty, ennobled as it is by patience." The bishop gave his impression of the character of the Union generals as men who were courteous and well mannered—and who thought themselves honorable and kind—but who, "in the best conscience," though with regret, behaved like Torquemada. Turning to the "masses," Lay noted the "universal horror of rebellion." "They consider rebels outside the pale of humanity" and "deem it no harm to commit any outrage on a rebel." "I brought home with me one deep and abiding conviction. We must, at whatever cost, win our independence. There is no other alternative open to us which can for one moment be considered."[111]

### Charles Todd Quintard

On 6 September, soon after the Confederates had relinquished Atlanta, Chaplain Quintard was issued a general pass by Hood's chief of staff, Brigadier General F. A. Shoup. The pass entitled Quintard to travel within Confederate lines, and Quintard went to attend to his family. He located a suitable place just two miles from Columbus, Georgia. Quintard assumed the duties of rector for Trinity Church in Columbus, acting for the Reverend Mr. Hawks, who was ill. He also began to conduct services at Carnes Hospital, where he found a "good congregation of surgeons and convalescents with a number of ladies from the town."[112] Although he was certainly not idle, Quintard felt strongly pulled to return to what he saw as his duty in the army—especially when he learned that Hood was taking the army back to Tennessee. He expressed this pull in his diary with the entry: "The Path of Duty is the Path of Happiness."[113]

Quintard soon got his wish, departing Columbus on 9 November to join Hood's army. The journey was mostly by rail, but there were times when he walked; it was not an easy trip. His diary entry on 15 November begins "Ye Rats! Ye Rats! For size and multitude the Okolona rats cannot be excelled. All the night long they played the most fantastic tricks in the room we occupied. Once I got up and lighted the fire to drive them off."[114] On 22 November he walked seventeen or eighteen miles, then spent a restless night. Finally, on 23 November, he caught up with the army. Quintard's spirits rose as he met old friends, including many generals. He marched some twenty-two miles with the army on 24 November.

The next day Quintard was welcomed cordially by General Hood at Hood's headquarters, and the general seemed in good spirits and optimistic about the outcome of the campaign that he had undertaken. The anticipation of battle—and success therein—heightened in the next several days, and Quintard became swept up in it. On 27 November Quintard conducted the service of Morning Prayer at the home of Lucius J. Polk, on which occasion he baptized two persons: "This was my first full service in Tennessee since entering the State and my heart went up in gratitude to God for all his great goodness in delivering us from the snare of the fowler. The lessons for the day—the Psalms—were full of comfort and warmed my hope into a trusting faith."[115] Quintard's optimism evaporated on the morning of 1 December when, on the way to Franklin, Tennessee, he met a Confederate captain who was bringing the bodies of three officers back to Columbia. All three were known to Quintard; two he had baptized the prior spring during the lull between the Battle of Chattanooga and the opening of the Atlanta campaign. One, his friend General Otto F. Strahl, was among the six Confederate generals to die in the battle for Franklin, where there were 6,261 Confederate casualties.[116] In spite of this, Hood pressed on with his army to Nashville, which he intended to recapture for the Confederacy. Quintard attended to the spiritual and physical needs of the wounded and conducted burial services for the dead.

Hood's Tennessee campaign ended with a disastrous battle at Nashville. The Confederates suffered nearly 4,500 casualties, and Hood's troops broke and ran; the battle was a decisive Union victory. General Hood gathered his army together as best he could—being pursued and harassed by General George H. Thomas's army—and retreated to Tupelo, Mississippi—where in mid January 1865 his request to be relieved from command was granted by President Davis.[117]

Quintard stayed with or close to the army during the retreat, which he describes in his diary under the heading "The Darkest of All Decembers." His entry into Mississippi was noted in his short diary entry on 26 December: "Crossed Tennessee River at 9 a.m. God's Holy Will be done." After parting from General Hood at his headquarters in Tuscumbia on 27 December, Quintard, after stopovers in Aberdeen and Columbus, Mississippi, made his way home to Columbus, Georgia, to reunite with his family. He resumed his work in Columbus with Trinity Parish, essentially serving as rector for the Reverend Mr. Hawks, who was seriously ill. Quintard's contacts with the military were maintained through the many officers who came to services or to see their old comrade. He preached on the Day of Fasting, Humiliation, and Prayer appointed by President Davis for 10 March. On Palm Sunday, 9 April, the very day that Generals Lee and Grant were meeting to arrange terms for the surrender of Lee's army, Quintard preached at services attended by soldiers and officers. At noon federal artillery began firing on the city. By noon the next day the defenders had retreated from Columbus. Quintard, as did many others, hid the family's valuables in anticipation of the arrival of Union soldiers. Quintard and his family were unscathed by the brief federal occupation, managing even to keep their horses, but the town was not so fortunate. The destruction focused on military and government property, but bridges, stores of cotton, and other material also were destroyed.[118]

Word soon came that the war was over, and Quintard and his family started their return journey to Tennessee, stopping in Atlanta. While he was there, Quintard conducted on 21 May services at the Central Presbyterian Church.

> There was an immense congregation present. It was made up of about an equal number of Federals and Confederates. Before beginning the service, I made brief address in which I expressed my views as to the duties of all true men in the then present condition of the country. I said that every man should do his utmost to heal the wounds and to hide the seams and scars of the fratricidal war that had just closed. I told the congregation that I would not use the prayer for the President of the United States at that service, simply because it had not yet been authorized by the Bishop of the Diocese whose ecclesiastical jurisdiction in the matter I recognized. I then proceeded with the service.[119]

## September 1865–November 1865

### Charles Todd Quintard

The congregation of the Church of the Advent, where Quintard had officiated before the war, was no longer intact, and, upon reaching Nashville, Quintard began assisting with services at Christ Church. He also served the spiritual needs of the federal army in Nashville, from the wife of the provost marshal to the soldiers in hospitals and camps. Then with his family he visited New York, where he was invited to preach at St. Thomas' Church. About a week after his return from New York, a special convention of the Diocese of Tennessee assembled at Christ Church, Nashville, elected the Reverend Charles Todd Quintard, M.D., bishop of the diocese.[120]

### Henry Champlin Lay

In September and October Bishop Lay and his colleague and kinsman Bishop Thomas Atkinson of North Carolina met to decide upon a course of action that resulted in their playing a crucial role in negotiations for reunion of the Northern and Southern branches of the Protestant Episcopal Church.[121]

## Notes

1. *Diocese of Mississippi, 1864* and *1865*, attached to *Diocese of Mississippi, 1867* (Jackson: Clarion Steam Printing, 1867), 53–54.

2. Ibid., 54.

3. On Polk's commission as major general, see above, "A Tale of Two Bishops Redux: A Friendship Ruptures."

4. Department No. 2 "embraced the whole of what was known as West Tennessee; the town of Cornith, Miss., with the adjacent country; a small strip of Alabama extending from the town of Waterloo on the west to that of Stevenson on the east; the counties of the states of Mississippi and Arkansas adjacent to the Mississippi River; the riparian parishes of Louisiana north of the Red River; and a section of the state of Arkansas, including the counties bordering the Mississippi and the districts lying to the north and east of the White and Black rivers." William Mecklenburg Polk, *Leonidas Polk, Bishop and General,* 2 vols. (New York: Longmans, Green, 1893), 2:1.

5. Joseph H. Parks, *General Leonidas Polk, C.S.A.: The Fighting Bishop* (Baton Rouge: Louisiana State University Press, 1962), 174.

6. W. M. Polk, *Leonidas Polk, Bishop and General,* 2:17–20.

7. Walker, in fact, wired Polk to withdraw his forces from Columbus immediately. Polk had sent a communication to President Davis, however, and Davis upheld Polk. Parks, *General Leonidas Polk,* 182.

8. Ibid., 184–86. See also W. M. Polk, *Leonidas Polk, Bishop and General,* 2:21–29.

9. Parks, *General Leonidas Polk,* 186–87.

10. W. M. Polk, *Leonidas Polk, Bishop and General,* 1:334–35.

11. Nathaniel Cheairs Hughes, Jr., *The Battle of Belmont* (Chapel Hill: University of North Carolina Press, 1991), 67.

12. W. M. Polk, *Leonidas Polk, Bishop and General,* 2:40.

13. Ibid., 1:337–38.

14. Ibid., 343.

15. Pierre Gustave Toutant Beauregard was a four-star general. Earlier, he had commanded the forces that forced the evacuation of Fort Sumter and had played a major role in the Confederate victory at First Manassas. Polk wrote of his goal of returning to the church in a letter to his wife dated 31 January 1862. See W. M. Polk, *Leonidas Polk, Bishop and General,* 2:67.

16. Ibid., 1:348.

17. Ibid., 2:47–50.

18. Ibid., 2:51.

19. Ibid.

20. William Stevens Perry, *The Episcopate in America* (New York: Christian Literature Company 1895), 163, and Charles Todd Quintard, *Doctor Quintard, Chaplain C.S.A. and Second Bishop of Tennessee: The Memoir and Civil War Diary of Charles Quintard,* ed. Sam Davis Elliott (Baton Rouge: Louisiana State University Press, 2003), 10.

21. Quintard, *Doctor Quintard,* ed. Elliott, 16.

22. The Quintards had two children die as infants in the 1850s. Three, George William (1856–1908), Edward Augustus (1860–1903), and Clara Eliza (1861–1915), survived to adulthood. Quintard, *Doctor Quintard*, ed. Elliott, 10–11.

23. Charles Todd Quintard, *Doctor Quintard, Chaplain C.S.A., and Second Bishop of Tennessee: Being His Story of the War*, ed. Arthur Howard Noll (Sewanee: University Press, 1905), 20.

24. Ibid., 21.

25. Ibid., 26.

26. Perry, *Episcopate in America*, 147.

27. Introductory biographical sketch of Henry Champlin Lay, Bishop. Henry C. Lay Papers, Southern Historical Collection, University of North Carolina at Chapel Hill Library, and "Death of Bishop Lay," *Baltimore Sun*, 18 September 1885, 4.

28. When the Confederate church was formed, Lay resigned his jurisdiction as missionary bishop of the Southwest and offered his services to Bishop Stephen Elliott as missionary bishop to Arkansas. See above, the essay entitled "A Separate Church for a Separate Nation: The Southern Bishops Choose Church Division."

29. Henry C. Lay, "Private Journal, 1861–1863," entries from October to December 1861, Henry C. Lay Papers, Southern Historical Collection, University of North Carolina at Chapel Hill Library.

30. Parks, *General Leonidas Polk*, 212.

31. "Civil War Battle Summaries by State." http://www.nps.gov/hps/abpp/battles/bystate.htm. (Accessed 15 January 2013).

32. Ibid.

33. Margaret Warner, Gary W. Gallagher, and Paul Finkelman, eds., *Library of Congress Civil War Desk Reference* (New York: Simon and Shuster, 2002), 420.

34. W. M. Polk, *Leonidas Polk, Bishop and General*, 2:107. Bishop Polk's son cites Beauregard's *Military Operations*, vol. 1, 313, as the source for this quotation.

35. Some historians have argued that the South lost an opportunity through hesitation and inaction at the end of the first day. See Parks, *General Leonidas Polk*; W. M. Polk, *Leonidas Polk, Bishop and General*; and James Lee McDonough, *Shiloh, in Hell Before Night* (Knoxville: University of Tennesee Press, 1977), for detailed accounts and perspectives on this battle.

36. Braxton Bragg was a West Point graduate (class of 1837) who had remained in the U.S. Army until 1856, when he became a planter in Louisiana. He had an outstanding record in the war with Mexico and was serving as a brevet lieutenant colonel when he left army service. He first joined the Louisiana militia as a colonel before hostilities began, then rose rapidly in rank to lieutenant general. He commanded a corps at Shiloh and was promoted to general after that battle. See Grady McWhiney, *Braxton Bragg and Confederate Defeat*, vol. 1, *Field Command* (New York: Columbia University Press, 1969).

37. Lay, "Private Journal 1861–1863."

38. Ibid., entry for 18 February 1862.

39. Ibid., entries from February to April 1862.

40. Henry T. Shanks, "Documents Relating to the Diocese of Arkansas 1861–1865, and Bishop Henry C. Lay's Papers," *Historical Magazine of the Protestant Episcopal Church* 8 (March 1939): 82.

41. Lay, "Private Journal 1861–1863," entry for 4 May 1862.

42. Shanks, "Documents Relating to the Diocese of Arkansas," 81–82. The issue of the prayer for the president during federal occupation of Southern states is addressed in detail below, in "Confrontation in Alabama: The Bishop and the General" and "Confrontation in Alabama: The Bishop and the General, Redux."

43. Lay, "Private Journal 1861–1863," entry for July 1862. See also Shanks, "Documents Relating to the Diocese of Arkansas," 82.

44. Lay, "Private Journal, 1861–1863," entries from June to September, 1862.

45. Ibid., entries from October to November 1862.

46. Ibid., entries that recorded proceedings of primary convention, Diocese of Arkansas, held in November 1862.

47. Shanks, "Documents Relating to the Diocese of Arkansas," 83.

48. Lay, "Private Journal, 1861–1863," entries from November 1862 to June 1863.

49. Rosecrans was in the class of 1842 at West Point. He had commanded at Rich Mountain, Virginia, and at Corinth and Iuka in Mississippi before being brought in to replace Buell as commander of what became known as the Army of the Cumberland.

50. W. M. Polk, *Leonidas Polk, Bishop and General*, 2:147 and Parks, *General Leonidas Polk*, 270. Polk was ordered to attack at a particular place and time, but he was concerned that neither he nor Bragg had correct intelligence regarding the strength of the enemy position they were to attack. After consulting his staff, he positioned his forces for "offense or defense" depending upon what the enemy did.

51. Parks, *General Leonidas Polk*, 282.

52. W. M. Polk, *Leonidas Polk, Bishop and General*, 2:189.

53. Quintard, *Doctor Quintard*, ed. Elliott, 55.

54. W. Robert Insko, *Kentucky Bishop: An Introduction to the Life and Work of Benjamin Bosworth Smith* (Frankfort: Kentucky Historical Society, 1952), 15–18.

55. Quintard, *Doctor Qunitard*, ed. Elliott, 56.

56. James Arthur Lyon Fremantle, *The Fremantle Diary*, ed. Walter Lord (Boston: Little, Brown, 1954), 116–17.

57. Ibid., 123.

58. Ibid., 129.

59. This incident and the context in which it occurred are described in Peter Cozzens, *This Terrible Sound: The Battle of Chickamauga* (Chicago: University of Illinois Press, 1992), 303–10. An account of the incident by Polk's son is given in W. M. Polk, *Leonidas Polk, Bishop and General*, 2:244–52.

60. Brigadier General Nathan Bedford Forrest, cavalry commander, on 21 September sent two letters, one through Polk, to Bragg, and paid the commanding general a visit during which he urged Bragg to attack the retreating Union forces. Bragg refused. See Cozzens, *This Terrible Sound*, 519–20.

61. W. M. Polk, *Leonidas Polk, Bishop and General*, 2:283–85.

62. After being relieved of command, Bragg first spent time in Warm Springs, Georgia, from where he was recalled to duty in Richmond by President Davis. Bragg served as chief of staff of the Confederate armies, under the direction of Davis. As the ranking officer after Bragg was relieved, General Hardee assumed command of the Army of the Tennessee, but he declined a permanent appointment. In December, Davis appointed General Joseph E. Johnston to that position.

63. Parks, *General Leonidas Polk,* 353.

64. Johnston was summoned to Georgia in December 1863 to take command of the army that Bragg had commanded. *The War of the Rebellion: Official Records of the Union and Confederate Armies,* Series 1, Vol. 31, Part 3 (Washington, D.C.: Government Printing Office, 1888), 835. Polk's command was designated in January 1864 as the Department of Alabama, Mississippi, and East Louisiana. Ibid., 857n.

65. Secretary of War Seddon concluded a lengthy response on 16 March 1864 to Polk's request for such authority with the words "while I do not say that if on reflection the authority you request is still thought to be advisable it will not be granted, I prefer, for the present at least, to request your serious reconsideration of the matter, with the hope that fuller information may convince your judgment of the inexpediency of such power." *The War of the Rebellion: A Compilation of the Official Records of the Union and Confederate Armies.* Series I, Vol. 32, Part 3. (Washington: Government Printing Office, 1891), 646.

66. Parks, *General Leonidas Polk,* 370.

67. Quintard, *Doctor Quintard,* ed. Elliott, 69–71.

68. Shanks, "Documents Relating to the Diocese of Arkansas," 70–76 and 81–82.

69. Henry C. Lay to the Reverend W. T. Leacock, 24 March 1866, printed in *Diocese of Louisiana, 1866* (New Orleans: Isaac T. Hinton, 1866), 28.

70. Ibid., 29.

71. Shanks, "Documents Relating to the Diocese of Arkansas," 78.

72. A detailed account of Polk's time in Mississippi may be found in Parks, *General Leonidas Polk,* 348–80. See also the letter from Polk in Meridian to General Maury in Mobile, 13 February 1864, *Official Records,* Series 1, Vol. 32, Part 2, 733–34.

73. Parks, *General Leonidas Polk,* 360.

74. Letter from Sherman in Memphis to Hallack in Washington, 12 January 1864; Letter from Grant in Nashville to Hallack in Washington, 15 January 1864, *Official Records,* Series 1, Vol. 32, Part 3, 75 and 100.

75. Parks, *General Leonidas Polk,* 373.

76. Lay, "Private Journal 1864–1865," entry for 26 February 1864.

77. Henry C. Lay, *The Devout Soldier: A Sermon Preached by Request to the Powhatan Troop at Emmanuel Church, March 6, 1864* (N.p: n.d).

78. Lay, "Private Journal, 1864–1865," entries for June and July 1864.

79. Leonidas Polk to his wife, 21 May 1864, quoted in Parks, *General Leonidas Polk,* 374.

80. Mrs. Joseph E. Johnston to Leonidas Polk, 16 May 1864, ibid., 377–78.

81. Leonidas Polk to his wife, 21 May 1864, ibid., 378.

82. Parks, *General Leonidas Polk,* 379–80.

83. Quintard, *Doctor Quintard,* ed. Elliott, 85.

84. Ibid., 86.

85. William Tecumseh Sherman, *Memoirs of General William T. Sherman* (New York: Library of Classics of the United States, 1990), 523–24.

86. W. M. Polk, *Leonidas Polk, Bishop and General*, 2:350.

87. Ibid., 350.

88. Communication from General Sherman in Georgia to General Hallack in Washington, 15 June 1864, quoted on "About North Georgia." http://ngeorgia.com/history/polk .html. (Accessed 7 January 2013).

89. Quintard, *Doctor Qunitard*, ed. Elliott, 86.

90. Sarah "Sallie" Conley Clayton, *Requiem for a Lost City: A Memoir of Civil War Atlanta and the Old South*, ed. Robert Scott Davis, Jr. (Macon: Mercer University Press, 1999), 114–15.

91. Ibid., 115.

92. Stephen Elliott, *Funeral Services at the Burial of the Right Reverend Leonidas Polk, D.D., together with the Sermon Delivered by Bishop Elliott in St. Paul's Church, Augusta, GA, on June 29, 1864* (Columbia: Evans and Cogswell, 1864), 8.

93. Ibid., 17.

94. General Longstreet was in Georgia recuperating from a wound.

95. Lay, "Private Journal, 1864–1865," entry for 1 July 1864.

96. Quintard, *Doctor Quintard*, ed. Elliott, 87.

97. Ibid., 88.

98. Ibid., 87. Bishop Lay, in his "Private Journal, 1864–1865," entry for August 9, 1864, noted that he was in Atlanta with Quintard and that "shells are imploding all around headquarters."

99. The narrative in this section is based upon the Henry C. Lay Papers. Two articles derived from those papers, to wit, Lay's "Sherman in Georgia," *Atlantic Monthly* 149 (February 1932): 166–72, and his "Grant before Appomattox," *Atlantic Monthly* 149 (March 1932): 333–40, provide the basis for describing Lay's interactions with Generals Sherman and Grant.

100. Lay, "Sherman in Georgia," 166.

101. Ibid., 166.

102. Ibid.

103. Ibid., 169.

104. Winston Groom, *Shrouds of Glory, from Atlanta to Nashville: The Last Great Campaign of the Civil War* (New York: Atlantic Monthly Press, 1995).

105. Union Major General George Henry Thomas, Virginian by birth and the "Rock of Chickamauga," is best known for his heroic stand in that battle, but he also decisively defeated Hood in Tennessee. His postwar role as governor of the Military District that included Alabama is significant to this narrative and will be treated in the essays below, "Confrontation in Alabama: The Bishop and the General" and "Confrontation in Alabama: The Bishop and the General, Redux."

106. Sherman, *Memoirs*, 649.

107. Lay, "Grant before Appomattox," 335. The date of Sherman's departure from Kingston is confirmed in Sherman, *Memoirs*, 644.

108. Herman Melville, "The March to the Sea," original published in *Battle-Pieces and Aspects of the War,* (New York: Harper and Brothers, 1866).

109. Lay, "Grant before Appomattox," 337–38.

110. Ibid., 339.

111. Ibid., 340. Bishop Lay's "Private Journal, 1864–1865" has an entry at the end of April showing the dates of Lee's surrender, Lincoln's assassination, and Johnston's surrender.

112. Quintard, *Doctor Quintard,* ed. Elliott, 167.

113. Ibid., 171.

114. Ibid., 175.

115. Ibid., 183.

116. "Civil War Battle Summaries by State." http://www.nps.gov/hps/abpp/battles/bystate.htm. (Accessed 15 January 2013). Union casualties were reported as 2,326.

117. Groom, *Shrouds of Glory,* 274.

118. Quintard, *Doctor Quintard,* ed. Elliott, 124.

119. Ibid., 126. Given the reaction of federal authorities in Alabama, in particular, and in some other states as well, when he omitted this prayer, Dr. Quintard was either very skillful in his remarks —or very fortunate—because no incident was precipitated. See below, the essay entitled "Confrontation in Alabama: The Bishop and the General."

120. *Proceedings of a Special Convention of the Protestant Episcopal Church in the Diocese of Tennessee, 1865* (Memphis: Daily Commercial, 1866), 11.

121. The convention of 1865 in Philadelphia, including the role of Bishops Atkinson and Lay, is discussed in detail below, in "What Price Reunion?"

PART 5

# Northern Bishops and Civil War

# A Tale of Two Northern Bishops

+≡ *John Henry Hopkins and Alonzo Potter*

## An Early Friendship

*A Joyful Consecration*

On 23 September 1845 Presiding Bishop Philander Chase officiated at a service held at Christ Church, Philadelphia, to consecrate the new bishop of Pennsylvania, the Reverend Dr. Alonzo Potter. The previous bishop, Henry Ustick Onderdonk, had resigned in 1844 under painful circumstances, having been charged with "habits of intemperance." Onderdonk did not deny the charges and was suspended by his fellow bishops from the "exercise of his office and ministry."[1] Election of a new bishop had been further complicated by agitation, especially among the clergy, to select a bishop of a particular affiliation (either "high-church" or "low-church"), but Alonzo Potter was viewed across the diocese and in the national Episcopal hierarchy as someone who could unite the Pennsylvania church. Bishop John Henry Hopkins of Vermont preached the consecration sermon and had high praise and a fervent blessing for the man being elevated to the episcopate.

> To you, my long known and beloved brother, whose election to be the Bishop of this extensive and powerful Diocese has called forth so strong and general an expression of the Church's approbation and gratitude to God. . . . May you have boldness without temerity, firmness without obstinacy, zeal without rashness, and meekness without fear. May the spirit of prayer keep your heart in constant communion with the Holy one of Israel, and bring down upon all your admonitions the blessing of his love. May our brethren who united in your election, be always united in sustaining you. And may you and they go forward in the cause and strength of God, until you shall all be enabled to render up your stewardship, and receive the gracious sentence, "Well done, good and faithful servant, enter ye into the joy of your Lord."[2]

Some eighteen years later, Bishop Hopkins and his "beloved brother" Bishop Potter became embroiled in an acrimonious dispute that destroyed their personal relationship.

## John Henry Hopkins

John Henry Hopkins was born in Ireland in 1792 and moved with his parents to America, where the family settled in Philadelphia in 1800. Hopkins was a multi-talented individual. He began work in a counting house and then accepted an assignment from Alexander Wilson to color plates for Wilson's book *American Ornithology*,[3] after which he became an "iron master," first managing a blast furnace north of Pittsburgh and then a furnace in the Ligonier Valley south of that city. The ventures in iron production failed, but soon afterward he studied law while teaching drawing in a school operated by his mother. He became a successful lawyer in Pittsburgh. Another skill that he developed early in life was playing music, and the rector of struggling Trinity Episcopal Church in Pittsburgh asked Hopkins to be church organist on a gratis basis. Hopkins accepted and soon became active and a leader in church affairs. Although he was neither priest nor deacon, nor even in the process of seeking Holy Orders, the Trinity vestry called Hopkins to the rectorship when their rector departed in July 1923. In September, Hopkins contacted Bishop William White, who authorized the young lawyer to begin conducting services immediately as a lay reader, and in December Hopkins was admitted to the sacred order of deacons. In May 1824 Bishop White ordained him to the priesthood.

The new rector of Trinity Parish served as the architect for its new building, plans for which the vestry had approved the very night Hopkins had accepted their offer to become rector. Much of his energy went into bringing people into the fold at Trinity, and when Bishop White visited in June 1825 the bishop confirmed 150 persons, making Trinity the third largest parish in the diocese.[4]

During his tenure at Trinity, Hopkins also did evangelical work in western Pennsylvania; he helped establish seven churches in the Pittsburgh environs. In 1826 and 1829 he served as a delegate to General Convention.[5] In 1831 the Reverend Mr. Hopkins accepted an invitation to become assistant minister at Trinity Church in Boston.[6] After a brief tenure in that position, Hopkins was elected the first bishop of Vermont. He was consecrated in 1832.

## Alonzo Potter

Alonzo Potter was a native of New York State, born in July 1800 in Duchess County. Potter was graduated in 1818 from Union College in Schenectady, New York, was called to serve as a tutor at Union in 1919, and, at age twenty-one, became professor of mathematics and natural philosophy. Soon after assuming this post, he became a candidate for Holy Orders and was ordained deacon by Bishop

John Henry Hobart on 1 May 1822. He was elevated to the priesthood on 16 September 1824.[7] In 1826 the Reverend Alonzo Potter accepted a call to be rector of St. Paul's Church in Boston, where he was instituted on 26 August and where he was serving when John Henry Hopkins was called to become assistant minister at Trinity Church. Potter remained at St. Paul's for five years, and his service there proved to be his only experience as a parish priest. In 1831 he returned to Union College, this time as professor of moral philosophy.[8] He became the vice president, and, as the health and energy of Dr. Eliphalet Nott, his father-in-law and the college president, declined, Potter assumed much of the administrative responsibility at the college.[9] He was serving in that position when he was consecrated in 1845 and became bishop of Pennsylvania.

## Labor of Love

In the spring of 1858 Bishop Alonzo Potter was stricken with a stroke that temporarily prevented him from exercising his responsibilities. Absent an assistant bishop, the Standing Committee of the diocese felt that it was imperative to invite another bishop to act on Bishop Potter's behalf, at least until the annual diocesan convention. The invitation went to Bishop Hopkins of Vermont. Although the bishop of Vermont was occupied with his own diocese, including his efforts to establish a diocesan institute, he graciously accepted. He reported his activities to the annual convention of the Diocese of Pennsylvania in late May of that year and noted that those activities had been a labor of love.[10]

During the period 28 March–23 May, Bishop Hopkins confirmed 1,331 persons in 63 churches within the Diocese of Pennsylvania. He ordained four men to the priesthood, three candidates to the diaconate—and preached fifty-five sermons. He concluded his report by urging the diocese to select an assistant bishop who would be an "assistant indeed" who possessed the same "enlarged views," "conservative wisdom," and "freedom from party spirit" that their beloved diocesan had.[11]

## Civil War Exhortations

### Alonzo Potter

Potter had two assistant bishops during his episcopate, first Samuel Bowman, who was elected following Potter's illness in 1858. Bowman died, apparently from heart failure in 1861. In 1862 William Bacon Stevens was elected and served for the remainder of Potter's tenure—and became the diocesan upon Potter's death. These men were united in their support of the Union and in their belief that, though they were bound to uphold the federal government, malice, anger, and an unforgiving spirit—even toward the rebellion—had no place in the churches of the diocese. What needed to be strengthened was obedience to and reliance upon Almighty God, from whom would come deliverance from the agony that now engulfed the nation. Bishop Potter's words rang through the diocese as the war progressed, at diocesan conventions and in pastoral letters, and Bishop Stevens spoke when illness prevented Potter from attending the convention held as the war was ending.

*From his June 1861 address to diocesan convention:* "We assemble, brethren, at a time of portentous difficulty and danger. The dire necessity of appealing to arms to withstand forcible disintegration of our Republic, and to maintain within proper limits the supremacy of the national will, seems to be laid upon us.... Let us pray for ourselves that we may be found wanting in none of the characteristics of good and loyal citizens... Let us guard anxiously against all bitterness, and wrath, and anger, and revenge."[12]

*From a pastoral letter to clergy and congregations in support of President Lincoln's designation of 26 September 1861 as a Day of Humiliation, Prayer, and Fasting:* "Our greatest sin is forgetfulness of God—our greatest peril presumptuous trust in our own wisdom and might. Institutions, in which we exulted with impious confidence, are in jeopardy; a Union, which we boasted that nothing could destroy, totters to its fall; material resources with which we thought to defy the world, take to themselves wings and fly away. Our reliance on the God of nations and of battles needs to be revived and strengthened; and where can this be done but at the footstool of the Divine Mercy."[13]

*From an 1863 pastoral letter:* "Let us think less of the sins of those who are arrayed against us, and more of our own."

*From an 1864 pastoral letter:* "We need by earnest repentance and continued prayer, to invoke his presence and aid, who alone can deliver from sedition, privy conspiracy, and rebellion, or restore us to that solid, abiding and righteous peace, for which we long. 'Unless the Lord keep the city the watchman waketh but in vain.'"

*From the May 1865 diocesan convention address by Assistant Bishop Stevens:* "While as citizens we unite in our rejoicings over the crushing out of this rebellion, it becomes us, as Churchmen and Christians, to look up, most earnestly, to God, and implore His blessing on all in authority over us, that they may be guided to do that which shall best heal the wounds of this nation, which shall soonest re-unite our severed portions."[14]

## John Henry Hopkins

Although he regretted the decision to go to war to bring the Southern states back into the Union, Hopkins also unequivocally supported the armed forces of the United States. He called for repentance as a necessary step to end the scourge of

The Right Reverend John Henry Hopkins, D.D., LL.D.

war. He focused sharply, however, on his belief that any discussion of the war or war-related issues did not belong in the councils of the church—or in pulpits. Some excerpts from his addresses at diocesan conventions are given below.

*June 1861:* "I believe that this civil conflict, awful as it is, has been appointed as a wholesome chastisement for our sins of pride and irreligion, by the wise judgment of God who is the almighty ruler of nations. I believe that it is designed to humble us for our good, and trust, that the mourning and sorrow which it must produce will be the means of turning multitudes to righteousness. I believe that it will rouse the dormant virtues of our people, and force them to acknowledge their dependence upon that merciful and long-suffering Lord, who has been, in the faithless presumption of our prosperity, so sadly forgotten. . . .

"Now as to the War itself, its causes, its policies, or its results, this is not the place for the discussion. Political questions have no proper field in the Church of Christ for, 'his "kingdom is not of this world.' Political preachers and political preaching have always been firebrands in the community, and it is the glory of our church that she has thus far continued, and will always continue, free from these two popular abuses of the house of God. . . .

"[Following the apostle Paul, Christians have] the plain duty of allegiance and support to the constitution, the laws, and the authorities, under which the providence of God has placed us. Rebellion against these is thus made a sin against heaven, however the politicians of this world may justify it."[15]

*June 1862:* "We would fain hope that he who is the Almighty Disposer of things will mercifully incline our misguided brethren [in the South] to peace and duty."[16]

## The Controversy over Slavery and the Bible

In 1861 John Henry Hopkins expressed his views on the slaves:

For every candid observer agrees that the Negro is happier and better as a slave than as a free man, and no individual belonging to the Anglo-Saxon stock would acknowledge that the intellect of the negro is equal to his own.[17]

But no reflecting man can believe that the great mass of slaves, amounting to nearly four millions, are qualified for freedom. And therefore it is incomparably better for them to remain under the government of their masters, who are likely to provide for them so much more beneficially than they could provide for themselves.

### A Pamphlet

Bishop Hopkins was requested in December 1860 "by several gentlemen of New York" to furnish in writing his opinions on "the Biblical argument on the subject of Negro slavery in the Southern States."[18] Hopkins responded by letter in January 1861, attaching a pamphlet entitled *Bible View of Slavery* that set forth his views. Hopkins noted later that the document was provided "purely as a service to what I deemed to be the truth at a time when the secession of the Southern States had invested that truth with the highest importance to the peace and safety of our country."[19]

In this pamphlet Hopkins's central thesis was that slavery had existed from the earliest biblical times and was accepted by Abraham, Jesus, and Jewish religious leaders in between, as well as by the apostle Paul, so that there was clear *biblical sanction* for the practice.[20] Hopkins began his analysis by noting that the word *servant* in our English-language Bible often means *slave* and offered a definition of slavery as "servitude for life, descending to the offspring" (6). He pointed out that by this definition slavery had existed throughout the ages. In reference to the question as to whether or not slavery was a moral evil, Hopkins then noted: "If it were a matter to be determined by my personal sympathies, tastes, or feelings, I should be as ready as any man to condemn the institution of slavery. . . . But as a Christian, . . . I am compelled to submit my weak and erring intellect to the authority of the Almighty" (6–7).

The bishop then proceeded to examine the biblical position on slavery. He started with Noah, who decreed: "Cursed be Canaan [the son of Ham], a servant of servants shall he be to his brethren."[21] This assertion was followed by "proof that slavery was sanctioned in the case of Abraham" (7). Hopkins noted first the large number of bond servants in Abraham's possession and then called attention to Sarah's slave Hagar, who, after fleeing, was commanded by an angel to return to her mistress. The next element of "proof" submitted came from the Ten Commandments: "Thou shalt not covet thy neighbor's house, thou shalt not covet thy neighbor's wife, nor his *man-servant,* nor his *maid servant,* nor his ox, nor his ass, nor anything that is thy neighbor's."[22] Hopkins then explained his view of the significance of this commandment: "Here it is evident that the principle of property—'anything that is thy neighbor's'—runs through the whole. I am aware, indeed, of the prejudice which many good people entertain against the idea of property in a human being. . . . I am equally aware that the wives of our day may take umbrage at the law which places them in the same sentence with the slave, even with the house and the cattle. . . . But whatever, whether person or thing, the law appropriates to an individual, becomes of necessity his property" (8). The last Old Testament "proof element" was taken from the Exodus, chapter 21, in which rules governing Hebrew servants (slaves) who have been purchased are set forth. A male servant thus obtained was to be set free after six years, but, in the case in which the master has given the slave a wife, the slave's wife and their children shall remain with the master, and the slave shall go free by himself. The slave may choose, however, to serve his master permanently and thereby avoid separation from his family. Hopkins concludes this section by asking, "With this law before his eyes, what Christian can believe that the Almighty attached immorality or sin to the condition of slavery?" (9).

Hopkins then turned to the New Testament for more supporting evidence.

First, then, we ask what the divine redeemer said in reference to slavery. And the answer is perfectly undeniable: HE DID NOT ALLUDE TO IT AT ALL. Not one word of censure upon the subject is recorded by the Evangelists who gave His life and doctrines to the world. Yet slavery was in full existence at the time, throughout Judea; and the Roman Empire, according to the historian Gibbon, contained sixty millions of slaves, on the lowest probable computation!

How prosperous and united would our glorious republic be at this hour, if the eloquent and pertinacious declaimers against slavery had been willing to follow their Saviour's example! (12)

Hopkins then cited several statements from St. Paul, all of which appear to give sanction to slavery as an institution. One example will suffice, from Colossians 3:22 and 4:1: "Servants [that is, bond servants or slaves], obey in all things your masters according to the flesh, not with eye-service, as men-pleasers, but in singleness of heart, fearing God"; "Masters, give unto your servants that which is just and equal, knowing that ye also have a master in heaven" (13). Hopkins concluded that the biblical evidence clearly showed that the gospel did not call for abolition of slavery. He delivered a peroration directed at antislavery preachers and politicians, in which he described Christ's actions (1) in cleansing the temple, (2) in censuring the Jewish practice of divorce for the "slightest cause," and (3) in rebuking other sins; he then notes that Christ did not utter a word against the practice of the slavery that was in plain view all around him.

Hopkins summarized his biblical arguments and turned to the "various objections which have been raised in the popular mind to the institution of Southern Slavery": "First on this list stand the propositions of the far-famed Declaration of Independence, 'that all men are created equal; that they are endowed by their creator with certain inalienable rights; that among these are life, liberty, and the pursuit of happiness.' These statements are here called 'self-evident truths.' But with due respect to the celebrated names which are appended to this document, I have never been able to comprehend that they are truths at all" (18–19).

After this opening, Hopkins devoted ten pages to arguing that these claims in the Declaration of Independence crumble when tested against reality, asking questions such as: "Where is the equality in mind between one who is endowed with talent and genius, and another whose intellect borders on idiocy?" (19). All men, in fact, Hopkins argues, are born unequal—in body, in mind, and social privileges. Further, when the signers of the Declaration of Independence subscribed to the premise that "all men were created equal," they did not include the black race. To support this claim Hopkins notes that Jefferson was a slaveholder as was the great majority of other signers. The dogma of human equality, Hopkins argued, "was never intended to apply to the question of negro slavery. And it never can be so applied without a total perversion of its historical meaning, and an absolute contrariety to all the facts of humanity, and the clear instruction of the word of God" (28–29).

Hopkins then proceeded to state and, to his satisfaction, demolish objections to slavery besides the equality argument. The objection on grounds of cruelty was refuted by pointing out that in the North children and apprentices were disciplined with "corporal correction" and that this form of punishment had been administered in the armed forces and in Massachusetts in recent times—and Christ had used a whip fashioned of small cords to cleanse the temple. The fact that slavery separated husbands from wives and children from their parents was conceded, but Hopkins argued that among the lower classes economic necessity often required such separations. Children were sent away, husbands and wives went into service with different families, for example. Further, many European husbands seeking fortunes in the United States or Australia abandoned their families. Finally, such separations were necessary—and state-sanctioned—among soldiers and sailors. If this practice existed and was tolerated among freemen, its existence under slavery should not serve as an objection to that institution.

Hopkins concluded by giving his view of how slavery had elevated the black race and was a vehicle for God's plans. His argument was almost identical to that proclaimed by Bishop Elliott:[23] "The slavery of the negro race, as maintained in the Southern States, appears to me to be fully authorized, both in the Old and New Testament, which, as the written word of God, afford the only infallible standard of moral rights and obligations. That very slavery, in my humble judgment, has raised the negro incomparably higher in the scale of humanity, and seems, in fact, to be the only instrumentality through which the heathen posterity of Ham have been raised at all" (39–40). Far more black people had been brought to Christ through the system of slavery in the South than by all the white missionaries to Africa. Hopkins then pointed to the settlement of former slaves in Liberia, from which he felt confident that black missionaries would go forth to win that continent to Christianity.

The *Bible View of Slavery* appeared in New York City newspapers and was published in the form of a pamphlet comprising thirty-five printed pages.[24] In addition to these distributions, which were arranged by the "gentlemen from New York," Hopkins circulated this work to some of his friends among the bishops and clergy. Hopkins received replies, some published and some by private communication, dissenting from the views expressed in this pamphlet, but the real torrent of negative reaction came more than two years later, when the pamphlet was reissued.

## Distribution in Pennsylvania, 1863

Hopkins received on 15 April 1863 a letter from six men in Philadelphia who had read his 1861 document with "much satisfaction and profit." The writers expressed the opinions that "false teachings" on the "scriptural aspects" of slavery had greatly contributed to the onset of the current civil strife and that a "lamentable degree of ignorance" existed concerning the Bible and slavery. They felt that dissemination of a statement from a "Christian bishop" might dispel some of that ignorance, and asked that Hopkins's views be sent to them with permission to make those views public.[25] Hopkins's reply on 2 May 1863 began: "The pamphlet

published in January, 1861, to which you have so kindly referred, is at your service." A copy of the pamphlet was attached.[26] Mr. Wharton and the others who
made the request proceeded to give that document wide circulation across Pennsylvania.

### Protest by Bishop Potter and Pennsylvania Clergy

The republication and circulation of this pamphlet ignited a firestorm among
Episcopal clergy in Pennsylvania. Their response came in the form of a broadside
signed by Bishop Potter and 164 of his clergy. This document, entitled PROTEST *of
the Bishop and Clergy of the Diocese of Pennsylvania against Bishop Hopkins' Letter
on African Slavery,* did not attempt to refute Hopkins's arguments but summarized the substance of his key points and then referred the reader to Hopkins's
pamphlet, clearly with the thought that simply reading the document would
serve to refute it. The closing of the *Protest* was sharply worded:

> But the document itself should be read to appreciate its character. This letter
> was scattered and broadcast over the State of Pennsylvania. As coming from a
> Bishop who is widely known throughout the Diocese, the Bishop and Clergy
> of Pennsylvania felt constrained to enter against it the following protest.
>
> The subscribers deeply regret that the fact of the extensive circulation
> through the Diocese of a letter by "John Henry Hopkins, Bishop of the Dio-
> cese of Vermont," in defense of Southern Slavery, compels them to make this
> public protest. It is not their province to mix in any political canvass. But, as
> ministers of Christ, in the Protestant Episcopal Church, it becomes them to
> deny any complicity or sympathy with such a defense.
>
> This attempt not only to apologize for slavery in the abstract, but to ad-
> vocate it as it exists in the cotton states, and in the States which sell men and
> women in the open market as their staple product, is, in their judgment, un-
> worthy of any servant of Jesus Christ. As an effort to sustain, on Bible prin-
> ciples, the States in rebellion against the government, in the wicked attempt
> to establish by force of arms a tyranny under the name of a Republic, whose
> "Cornerstone" shall be the perpetual bondage of the African, it challenges
> their indignant reprobation.
>
> PHILADELPHIA, September, 1863[27]

### Bishop Hopkins's Reply

Hopkins was chagrined and hurt by this response: "I had anticipated the prob-
ability that the republication of the foregoing pamphlet would bring down upon
me a liberal share of abuse and contumely from the abolition press, . . . but I was
not prepared for the extraordinary sentence of 'indignant reprobation' which the
Bishop of Pennsylvania and a majority of his clergy saw fit to fulminate against

The Right Reverend Alonzo Potter, D.D., LL.D.

my course."[28] He immediately wrote a six-page response to Potter, the first sentence of which highlighted the phrase "*unworthy of any servant of Jesus Christ,*" and charged Potter with a "gross insult against his senior" and with false accusation. He regarded the "protest" and "indignant reprobation" as "the idle wind that passes by." Hopkins noted that the original pamphlet was published three months before the outbreak of hostilities and therefore could not have been in support of the Southern war effort.

He promised to publish within a few months a detailed demonstration of the truths in his January 1861 thesis. His son, J. H. Hopkins Jr., did his best to dissuade his father from undertaking that task. Young Hopkins saw slavery as doomed and hated to see effort put into a work that would have negligible impact on that institution and would result only in bringing more personal grief to his father.[29] Bishop Hopkins, however, was tenacious, and during 1864 his *Scriptural,*

*Ecclesiastical, and Historical View of Slavery,* addressed to the Right Reverend Alonzo Potter, D.D., appeared in print, a book of more than 350 pages, each chapter of which began with the salutation "Right Reverend Brother," highlighting the fact that the work was addressed to his colleague in the episcopate.

Hopkins's chief purpose was to expand and clarify the Bible view of slavery; chapter 1 served as a preamble:

> Before I enter on the main subject of this volume, I must take the liberty of premising a brief statement of my own position in relation to the controversy. I am no lover of slavery and no advocate for its perpetuity any longer than circumstances may seem to require; ... all my habits, sympathies, and associations are opposed to slavery, and in favor of abolition. But I hold abolition can only be accomplished on the grounds of a just and wise expediency, with a sacred regard for the Holy Scriptures, ... in accordance with the real welfare of the colored race, in harmony with the best interests of the Southern States, and with a full recognition intended to be secured to them by the Federal Constitution.[30]

He devoted chapters to topics such as Hebrew slavery, the Decalogue, slavery under the apostles, Aristotle, and the English poor. Although much more detailed, the arguments supporting scriptural sanction for slavery reflected those in his January 1861 pamphlet.

### Issues, Feelings, and Outcome

"May God forgive it [Potter's insult], as I most freely do, not withstanding the personal results which I presume to be irreparable."[31] There was deep disagreement between the two bishops over the biblical view of slavery presented by Hopkins, but the real heat and hurt between Hopkins and Potter were generated by other factors. Pennsylvania was not Hopkins's diocese, and circulation of the pamphlet was viewed by many clergy and lay Episcopalians as a discourteous intrusion. To others in the citizenry generally, the distribution was unwarranted and disruptive meddling. Given the unrest in the state legislature over the war, the Emancipation Proclamation, conscription, federal infringement on individual rights, and related issues, the Hopkins document certainly was seen by many as political—an attempt to fuel anti-(Lincoln) administration and antiwar sentiment in Pennsylvania. These issues were at the forefront of the campaign that would culminate with the October 1863 gubernatorial election.[32]

Independent of the issue of diocesan turf, Alonzo Potter, an admirer of Abraham Lincoln, made clear his stand for the Union at every wartime diocesan convention. Any document that even hinted—or could be construed to hint— that the Union war effort might be misguided would have offended Potter. Because Hopkins had acted as presiding bishop at the General Convention the prior

October, Potter and the Pennsylvania clergy feared that the document could be taken as the position of the Episcopal Church in the United States on the matter of slavery.[33] These factors added outrage to the sharp disagreement Potter and the Pennsylvania clergy had with Hopkins's view of slavery. Still, M. A. DeWolfe Howe, a close friend of Potter, notes in his memoir of Potter that his friend found it "painful" to send such a strong response to Hopkins.[34]

For Hopkins's part, he was deeply wounded by the harsh nature of the response, coming from Potter, a friend whose diocese Hopkins had served faithfully during Potter's illness in 1858. The words *unworthy of any servant of Jesus Christ* offended him particularly, as did the implication that he gave aid and comfort to the rebellion to produce a "tyranny in the name of a republic." Hopkins, in fact, had been clear and consistent in his support for the Union—support that extended to members of his diocese serving in the United States Army, including his son, the Reverend William Cyprian Hopkins who was serving as a Union chaplain. The bishop's diocesan addresses, from which excerpts were given above, stressed the need to stand firmly behind the United States, and so Hopkins viewed as unfair and distorted the implication that he was giving aid and comfort to the rebellion. A particular matter that stung Hopkins was that he had sent Potter in 1857 a copy of *The American Citizen: His Rights and Duties,* a book published by Hopkins that year. In this work of 459 pages Hopkins had set forth his views on the constitution, politics, religious rights, marriage, the pitfalls of common professions and businesses—and on the institution of slavery and abolition, topics that comprised six chapters and forty-four pages. Although the topic coverage in the two works was not identical, there was considerable overlap, and the essence of Hopkins's 1861 biblical defense of slavery was stated explicitly. In his immediate reply to the protest by the Pennsylvania bishop and clergy, Hopkins wrote:

> I do not know whether your band of indignant reprobationists ever saw my book published in 1857, but you read it, because I sent you a copy, and have your letter of acknowledgement, in which, while you dissented from some of my conclusions, you did it with the courtesy of a Christian gentlemen. In that letter there is nothing said about my opinion being "unworthy of any servant of Jesus Christ," and nothing of "indignant reprobation." But tempora mutantur, et nos mutamur in illis [times are changing and we are changing with them].[35]

In his 1864 book, *A Scriptural, Ecclesiastical, and Historical View of Slavery,* Hopkins gave explicit expression to his personal feelings: "For you are still my brother in Christ, notwithstanding you are so thoroughly alienated by your course of public and libelous denunciation, that I cannot look forward to any future association with you on earth, however I may hope to meet you in his heavenly kingdom. But this is of small importance. . . . I can finish my humble course in the Church below, without any renewal of my former fraternal intercourse with the Diocesan of Pennsylvania."[36] John Henry Hopkins succeeded Thomas Church Brownell as presiding bishop and played a significant role at the 1865 General Convention, as described below in "What Price Reunion: The Philadelphia Convention." Alonzo Potter died prior to the General Convention; the two bishops never reconciled.

### Reflection on Hopkins's View of Slavery

Before making some general observations on Hopkins's writings about slavery, it is useful to examine one of his actions that predated those writings—an action that seems incongruous with views that he later expressed. The Reverend Alexander Crummell was a black clergyman whose initial efforts to enter the Episcopal ministry had been hindered by prejudice. The first roadblock he encountered was being denied admission to General Theological Seminary because of his race. He studied in Boston and after being ordained to the diaconate there undertook assignments in Massachusetts, Rhode Island, and New York. He was ordained priest by the bishop of Delaware, and by 1847 he had decided to spend some time in England and sought a letter of introduction. Bishop Hopkins provided him with a warm letter, addressed to the Reverend William Carus, a prominent churchman in Cambridge. Hopkins wrote that Crummell stood high in "the opinion of our most distinguished evangelical clergy" and added: "I think our brethren in your country, who feel so warmly in the case of injured Africa, will welcome his arrival, as affording them a visible proof of the rank to which her sons may attain, when favored with reasonable advantages of education."[37] This letter seems startlingly out of place with Hopkins's expressed belief that black individuals had an inferior intellect and with a belief that an entire race would be better off enslaved than free.[38]

Hopkins wrote four major pieces that addressed the issue of slavery, the first being a lecture given in 1851, the second a book, *The American Citizen: His Rights and Duties, According to the Spirit of the Constitution of the United States,* published in 1857, and the third and fourth the 1861 and 1864 works discussed above.[39] The first two works included Hopkins's views about slavery but were not exclusively devoted to that topic. These early works also focused on what Hopkins saw as the civil dangers of slavery, such as a massive insurrection when the slave population reached unsustainable numbers. He included a plan for gradual emancipation and relocation through colonization that would take twenty-five years to accomplish but would eliminate slavery in the United States. He called upon South and North to confront the problem together and to share the costs of an emancipation/colonization program. He urged the South to abandon consideration of secession and urged the abolitionists in the North to cease and desist while a joint effort proceeded. In all four of the works, however, he was clear in his belief that slavery was sanctioned by the Bible. The last two publications had a more narrow focus. The 1861 work was written during the secession crisis, and the 1864 work was colored by his chagrin and anger over the broadside from the bishop and clergy of Pennsylvania.

In an examination of Hopkins's January 1861 lecture and his 1864 book, his failure to take into account the context of the biblical incidents that he cited and his rigid literalism stand out as major faults. Given that Hopkins was a scholar and a prolific author on theological topics, this narrow literalism is difficult to understand—and it apparently prevented him from accepting and articulating the crucial point related to what he acknowledged as the major social issue of his time.[40] This point was made succinctly by one of his critics.: "For the *malum in se* of slavery consists . . . in its animus and essential purpose. This purpose, the very life, and only vital principle of the thing, which is to make the slave the mere instrument, *tool*, of the master—an instrument *exclusively* for the ends of the master, the slave having no legal claim or rights whatever in relation to the ends for which he is used. . . . He is a thing, a chattel."[41] Hopkins was against war as a means of ending slavery, but he never wavered in his support for the Union. He was personally opposed to slavery, but his belief that slavery in America had biblical sanction was never shaken. For that belief he not only ignored personal abuse, ridicule, and attenuation of his effectiveness but also was oblivious to the sheer enormity of the wrong of four million human beings in bondage.[42] He stubbornly wrote his 1864 book, *Scriptural, Ecclesiastical, and Historical View of Slavery,* even against the advice of the Reverend J. H. Hopkins, Jr., his eldest son. Bishop Hopkins struggled publicly with the issue for more than a decade, but he never came to grips with the root evil of slavery. It was his greatest failure.

## Impact of the 1864 Book

Events soon dwarfed any national impact that Hopkins's book, published in April 1864, might have had. Although the Civil War would continue another year, Sherman's Atlanta campaign and march to the sea, Thomas's defeat of Hood at Nashville, and Grant's war of attrition in Virginia ensured Union victory and meant that Hopkins's book addressed an issue of neither current import nor relevance. After the war, how to respond to the economic, social, and educational needs and problems created by the sudden existence of four million freed slaves became an issue, as did—North and South—the civil rights and social acceptance of freed slaves, but a biblical view of slavery, especially a defense of that institution, was not a topic that mattered in the postwar America that ratified the Thirteenth Amendment on 6 December 1865.

## Notes

1. William Stevens Perry, *The Episcopate in America* (New York: Christian Literature Company, 1895), 49.

2. John Henry Hopkins, *Episcopal Government: A Sermon Preached at the Consecration of the Rev. Alonzo Potter, D.D., as Bishop of the Diocese of Pennsylvania* (Philadelphia: King and Baird, 1845), 23–24.

3. The reference is to Alexander Wilson's nine-volume work *American Ornithology; or The Natural History of Birds in the United States* (Philadephia: Bradford and Inskeep, 1808–1824). In John Henry Hopkins, Jr.'s *Life of the Late Right Reverend John Henry Hopkins, First Bishop of Vermont and Seventh Presiding Bishop by One of His Sons* (New York: F. J. Huntington, 1873), Bishop Hopkins's son wrote that his father had "no equal" as a colorist.

4. J. H. Hopkins, Jr., *Life of John Henry Hopkins*, 69–83.

5. Perry, *Episcopate in America*, 59.

6. J. H. Hopkins, Jr., *Life of John Henry Hopkins*, 133–39.

7. Perry, *Episcopate in America*, 105.

8. Ibid.

9. M. A. DeWolfe Howe, *Memoirs of the Life and Service of the Right Reverend Alonzo Potter, D.D., LL.D., Bishop of the Protestant Episcopal Church in the Diocese of Pennsylvania* (Philadelphia: J. B. Lippincott, 1871), 58, 60, 99.

10. *Diocese of Pennsylvania, 1858* (Philadelphia: J. S. McCalla, 1858), 33.

11. Ibid., 33–34.

12. *Diocese of Pennsylvania 1861* (Philadelphia: J.S. McCalla, 1861), 39–40.

13. Copies of this pastoral letter and those that follow for 1863 and 1864 are in the Keller Library Archives, General Theological Seminary.

14. *Diocese of Pennsylvania, 1865* (Philadelphia: McCalla and Stavely, 1865), 60.

15. *Diocese of Vermon,t 1861* (Burlington: Danforth and Hoyt, 1861), 24–25.

16. *Diocese of Vermont, 1862* (Burlington: Danforth and Hoyt, 1862), 7. See above, the essay entitled "Assembly under Most Afflicting Circumstances," for Hopkins's role at the 1862 General Convention.

17. John Henry Hopkins, *Bible View of Slavery* (1861; reprinted in Hopkins, *A Scriptural, Ecclesiastical, and Historical View of Slavery, from the Days of Patriarch Abraham, to the Nineteenth Century, Addressed to the Right Reverend Alonzo Potter, D.D.* [1864; repr., New York: Negro Universities Press, 1969), 5–41]). This passage appears on page 21; the one immediately following in text is found on pages 32–33.

18. John Henry Hopkins, *A Scriptural, Ecclesiastical, and Historical View of Slavery, from the Days of Patriarch Abraham, to the Nineteenth Century, Addressed to the Right Reverend Alonzo Potter, D.D.* (1864; repr., New York: Negro Universities Press, 1969), 3.

19. Ibid.

20. John Henry Hopkins, *Bible View of Slavery*. Page references to this document are given parenthetically in text.

21. Genesis 9:25

22. Hopkins translated *servant* as *slave* and added the emphasis.

23. See the discussion of Elliott's sermon *Our Cause in Harmony with the Purposes of God in Christ Jesus* above, in "The Wartime Episcopate of Bishop Elliott of Georgia."

24. Leonard Marsh, *Review of Bishop Hopkins' "Bible View of Slavery," by a Vermonter* (Burlington: Burlington Free Press, 1861). According to the preface of this review, twenty

thousand copies of the pamphlet were being printed for distribution by the American Society for the Promotion of National Unity.

25. Hopkins, *Scriptural, Ecclesiastical, and Historical View of Slavery,* 4.

26. Ibid., 5.

27. PROTEST *of the Bishop and Clergy of the Diocese of Pennsylvania against Bishop Hopkins' Letter on African Slavery* (Philadelphia: Diocese of Pennsylvania, 1863).

28. Hopkins, *Scriptural, Ecclesiastical, and Historical View of Slavery,* 42.

29. J. H. Hopkins, Jr., *Life of John Henry Hopkins,* 336.

30. Hopkins, *Scriptural, Ecclesiastical, and Historical View of Slavery,* 51.

31. Ibid., 60.

32. See Philip S. Klein and Ari Hoogenboom, *A History of Pennsylvania* (New York: McGraw-Hill, 1973), 257–58, for discussion of the 1863 gubernatorial election in Pennsylvania.

33. Howe, *Memoirs of the Life and Services of Alonzo Potter,* 239.

34. Ibid.

35. Hopkins to Potter, 5 October 1863. This letter is included with the prefatory material in *A Scriptural, Ecclesiastical, and Historical View of Slavery.*

36. Hopkins, *Scriptural, Ecclesiastical, and Historical View of Slavery,* 345.

37. John Henry Hopkins to William Carus, 10 December 1847, John Henry Hopkins Collection, Special Collections, University of Vermont Library.

38. See the quotation from Hopkins at the start of the section in this essay entitled "The Controversy over Slavery and the Bible." After his stay in England, Alexander Crummell went on to become a missionary to Liberia. He later returned to the United States where he became well known as a black nationalist and an advocate for the rights of black people.

39. Hopkins's lecture is *Slavery: Its Religious Sanction, Its Political Dangers, and the Best Mode of Doing It Away: A Lecture Delivered Before the Young Men's Associations of the City of Buffalo, and Lockport, on 10 and 13 January 1851* (Buffalo: Phinney, 1851); his 1857 book *The American Citizen: His Rights and Duties, According to the Spirit of the Constitution of the United States* was published in New York by Pudney and Russell.

40. Hopkins, *Slavery: Its Religious Sanction, Its Political Dangers, and the Best Mode of Doing It Away,* 3.

41. Marsh, *Review of Bishop Hopkins' "Bible View of Slavery,"* 14.

42. Henry Charles Lea, a publisher in Philadelphia, published a parody of Hopkins's reasoning that featured a justification of polygamy (Henry Charles Lea, "Bible View of Polygamy," S.l., s.n., 18xx). This paper is available in Special Collections at the University of Vermont Library. A petition from laypersons was circulated among the Vermont clergy in January 1864 asking clergy "to publicly deny any complicity or sympathy with Bishop Hopkins' defense of slavery." (This petition is in the archives of the Diocese of Vermont.)

# Henry Benjamin Whipple
# of Minnesota

+⟞⟝ *A Bishop Confronts War on Two Fronts as well as
the Institution of Slavery and the Rights of Indians*

### Background and a Unique Challenge

Henry Benjamin Whipple, who was born in New York in 1822, decided to seek
Holy Orders at age twenty-six. He was ordained priest in 1850 and served churches
in Rome, New York, and in Chicago before being elected in 1859 as bishop by
the new Diocese of Minnesota.[1] When Whipple was barely twenty-one, just after
he and his wife Cornelia had their first child, he was ordered by his physician to
spend the winter in the South. During the months October 1843 to May 1844,
Whipple left his wife and child in New York while he undertook a southern tour
to restore his health.[2] During the year 1853 he was granted a leave of absence by
the vestry at Zion Church in Rome, New York, so that he and his family could
again spend time in a warm climate. This time it was Cornelia Whipple's health
that required a change of residence. The family spent the time in Florida, and
Whipple served as cure for Trinity Church in St. Augustine and worked as a
missionary under the guidance of the diocesan bishop, Francis Huger Rutledge.
These two sojourns in the South gave the bishop-to-be opportunity to observe
slavery directly.[3] He also had the chance to discuss the Seminole conflicts in Florida, including the fate of Osceola.[4] Whipple had been fascinated by American
Indians since his childhood, and his time in Florida strengthened his belief that
they were being mistreated by the U.S. government.

Whipple assumed the bishopric of Minnesota after his consecration at the
Richmond convention in October 1859. The new bishop saw the Chippewa and
Dakota Sioux resident in Minnesota as part of the missionary responsibility of his
diocese and soon began work with these Native Americans. Whipple's first visit
to a settlement was to a Chippewa village by the Episcopal mission at Gull Lake,
located not far north of Crow Wing, and he was greatly distressed at the poverty
and squalid living conditions he observed. He was also distressed at the greed of

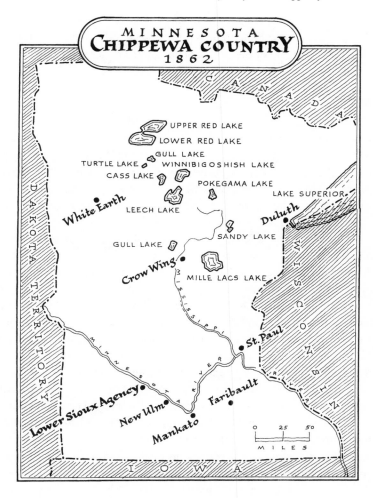

those agents, traders, and other white men who treated Indians shabbily in order to amass personal wealth. The sale of whiskey by traders and others incurred his particular wrath.[5]

At the same time Whipple felt encouraged that the gospel could be spread among the American Indian population. The bishop baptized, confirmed, preached, administered communion, and visited individual wigwams. On his initial visit the new bishop resolved that he would make the welfare of these people, physical as well as spiritual, a priority of his episcopate. Whipple's initial impressions were strengthened as he continued work among the Chippewa. He remained convinced that efforts to spread the gospel would be successful, but his distress at the wrongs suffered by the Indians intensified, and he came to believe that the policies of the United States toward them were responsible. It was not until he visited a Dakota Sioux reservation, however, that he became fully convinced of the culpability of the United States government for the plight of these individuals.

## War in Minnesota

### Before the Outbreak

When Bishop Whipple came to Minnesota in 1859, the Dakota reservation was a strip of land averaging ten miles wide that was bounded on the north by the Minnesota River.[6] The reservation began near Big Stone Lake on the Dakota Territory border and jutted through the advancing frontier of white settlers approximately 140 miles to the southeast, where the eastern terminus was near a white settlement at Milford; the town of New Ulm was less than ten miles downriver. The white settlers were farmers, and agrarian communities dotted the area north and south of the reservation.

The long narrow finger of land south of the river was all that was left of the huge expanse—millions of Minnesota acres—that the Sioux once roamed to hunt for their livelihood.[7] The rest of the lands had been ceded to the United States by various treaties. Under the terms of the treaties the United States gained title to the lands and the Dakota (Sioux) bands were promised annuity payments. They also were promised assistance in relocating and adjusting to their new homelands.[8] Annuity payments, however, were often late and depleted by payment of debts owed traders for goods purchased on credit by individuals or by reimbursements to traders or others who had submitted claims for damages against individual tribe members. Such a diversion of funds was permitted by the treaties, but the Indian chiefs felt that their agreement to this treaty provision was secured by deception of government negotiators—and the matter continued to infuriate the Sioux. Together with the exorbitant prices frequently charged by traders, the ability to divert funds paved the way for collusion between Indian agent and trader—and hence for fraud and corruption. Many Sioux had come to believe that treaty agreements meant little to the white man.

The land onto which the Sioux were compressed actually included two reservations, with each reservation served by a U.S. government agency. The Upper Agency was located on the west bank of the Yellow Medicine River, and the Lower Agency was located about thirty miles to the southeast. Each agency had an office for the Indian agent and accommodations for other government workers, as well as storehouses and other out-buildings needed for the agency's operation. Traders' stores were located nearby.[9]

In June 1860 at the Lower Agency Bishop Whipple paid his first visit to the Dakota Sioux. Conditions there were better than those at the Chippewa villages he had visited, but the three leaders with whom he met, Chief Wabasha, Chief

Taopi, and Good Thunder (Tapoi's head soldier and chief advisor), presented to their visitor a list of needs as well as a litany of grievances against the U.S. government. The latter included, in addition to late and depleted annuity payments, the fact that they had been promised a school, but there was neither a building nor a teacher.

Soon after returning to his home in Faribault, Bishop Whipple ordained Samuel D. Hinman to the diaconate and assigned the Reverend Mr. Hinman as missionary to the Lower Sioux. Hinman established a mission with a school and began conducting services in September 1860. On a visit in June 1861 Bishop Whipple confirmed seven individuals and was delighted that there were fifty children in the school.[10] After the bishop's first visit to the Lower Agency, Wabasha, Taopi, and Good Thunder became his friends. The bishop was pleased that these three Sioux leaders had encouraged their followers to take up farming, because he believed that giving up a life "in the wild" was key to Indian survival.

By the spring of 1862, although still pleased with progress of Hinman's mission, Whipple was becoming worried about the mood of the Sioux. He expressed his concerns about government policy regarding American Indians in an open letter to President Lincoln in March 1862.[11] In July 1862 when Whipple visited the Lower Sioux Agency, his misgivings deepened. He recalled his feelings in his remarks at the 1863 meeting of the diocese: "There was a dark cloud lowering on the border, which even then filled us with fear. . . . You will bear me witness, brethren, that for three years I have tried to awaken the people and their rulers to the enormities of an Indian system which I believed, if there were any truth in history, would desolate our land with blood. I never left the Indian Country with a heavier heart."[12]

## The Outbreak

Later in the summer of 1862, ongoing resentment and frustration on the Sioux reservations over treatment by the U.S. government and by the traders who siphoned off annuity payments was intensified when an expected annuity payment was two months overdue. Protests by the Sioux chiefs and braves at the Lower Agency became increasingly angry. The uprising was triggered on 17 August, when five white settlers were killed near Acton by a small Sioux hunting party. These killings were spontaneous, not authorized by the tribal leaders, but after hurried councils that night, the Lower Sioux bands made a decision to go to war. The wrongs that they had suffered, the fact that the ranks of "bluecoats" (U.S. soldiers) in Minnesota had been thinned by the war with their brethren, and the inevitability of white reprisals for the Acton murders were among the factors considered. Under Chief Little Crow's leadership they made a brutal surprise attack on their agency the next morning. Twenty deaths resulted, of traders and Lower Agency personnel, including the agency physician, his wife, and two children. This uprising continued from mid-August to mid-September and claimed the lives of more than four hundred settlers.[13] Many women and children were taken prisoner, and others were massacred along with the men—entire families being killed in some cases. Dakota attacks occurred on settlements over a wide area, including those at or near Acton, Hutchinson, Litchfield, Lake Shatek, Milford, and New Ulm. In the panic that ensued, twenty-three counties in Minnesota were depopulated as the settlers fled toward the east. Some families never returned.[14]

The governor of Minnesota, Alexander Ramsey, responded by asking Henry Sibley, a former governor, to lead a force of volunteers to quell the outbreak. While Colonel Sibley was organizing his volunteer force, a small contingent of U.S. Army soldiers at Fort Ridgely engaged the Sioux warriors. In early September Union major general John Pope, who had been relieved as commander of the Army of the Potomac after its defeat in the second battle at Manassas Junction, was assigned command of U.S. Army units in the Northwest and given overall responsibility for the war in Minnesota. Battles occurred at New Ulm, Fort Ridgely, and Birch Coulee. Finally, at Wood Lake on 23 September, with Sibley's forces reinforced by Minnesota troops that had seen action in the Civil War, the Sioux were defeated decisively and the uprising ended, although many Sioux continued to surrender in the weeks ahead—and others fled to the Dakota Territory or Canada. As the fighting wound down, some Dakotas who were friendly and had not taken part in the massacres took charge of a large number of white prisoners, nearly all women and children, captured by the warring Sioux. The captives were kept in safety and turned over to U.S. government troops when the fighting ended. The site at which the turnover occurred was given the name Camp Release.

### A Bishop's Involvement

Bishop Whipple was in St. Paul when he heard of the 1862 outbreak, and his first action was to ride at Colonel Sibley's request some fifty miles to Faribault where he sent a boy as a town crier to announce the news and to summon the citizens to a meeting. At the meeting Whipple called for volunteers to join Sibley's force at St. Peter, taking guns and horses. A few days later the bishop, who had a surgical kit and some rudimentary skills in dealing with wounds and injuries, went to St. Peter to assist the lone surgeon who was caring for the wounded settlers arriving in great number. Subsequently the bishop ministered spiritually to Indian prisoners as well as to settler families affected by the massacre.

### Military Justice

Immediately after the fighting ceased, the Sioux braves who had been taken prisoner and were believed to have participated in the uprising were put on trial

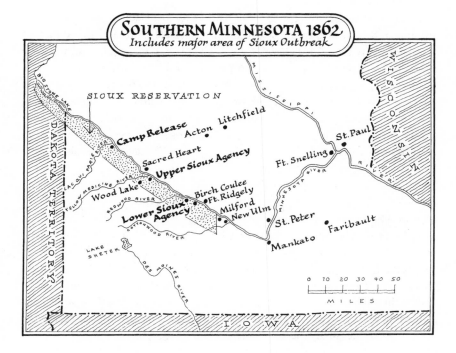

SOUTHERN MINNESOTA 1862
Includes major area of Sioux Outbreak

before a military commission composed of five members appointed by Colonel Sibley. The trials proceeded rapidly, and, by their conclusion six weeks later, 303 Sioux had been condemned to death by hanging. President Lincoln, however, after a review of the trial proceedings and outcomes with his cabinet, issued a directive through General Pope that no executions were to proceed without his explicit order.

### Cry for Vengeance

The 303 prisoners who had received death sentences, as well as a smaller number who had received lesser sentences, were moved from the trial site to a camp near Mankato. White outrage over the massacre of settlers was boiling, and a mob attacked with stones and bricks as the column moved through New Ulm, leading to some serious injuries among the prisoners and guards.[15] At Lincoln's request, General Pope forwarded to the president the names and trial records for the condemned. Appended to these documents was an appeal from Pope urging that all the executions proceed forthwith. General Pope's wish was shared not only by the public at large but also by most newspaper editors, politicians, and other public figures across the state. There was a public outcry not only for swift execution of the condemned prisoners, but also for the removal of all other Sioux from Minnesota, including those who had no role whatsoever in the uprising. In view of the massacres, public sentiment also seemed to be demanding that any prior treaty provisions guaranteeing the Sioux a homeland in Minnesota be voided. The governor concurred, and from 1,500 to 1,700 Indians in the latter group were removed by Colonel Sibley's forces from the reservation area to an encampment at Fort Snelling. These Indians were victims of mob violence along their route, being attacked in Henderson with a variety of weapons and hand-hurled projectiles. There were injuries, including one sustained by an infant who died soon thereafter.[16] *Indian sympathizer* was a sobriquet to be avoided at all costs in Minnesota.

## A Voice of Dissent

Bishop Whipple did sympathize with the plight of the Indians and had done so since his 1859 arrival in the state. Although his heart went out to the families who had lost loved ones in the Sioux attacks and although he supported death sentences for those Indians who could be proved to have massacred settlers, Whipple did not favor summary trials and mass executions. He wanted to be sure that each individual condemned truly deserved the death penalty.[17] Whipple also had a burning concern that went beyond the need for fair trials of those accused of complicity in the August-September massacre.

In spite of the outbreak Whipple remained focused on the longstanding injustices that American Indians had suffered and the need for corrective measures. This was the proper Christian response, he felt, and it was also a response that would prevent additional violence by removing the factors that had motivated the uprising. Bishop Whipple pleaded his case before the president of the United States and before his colleagues in the episcopate—and from the outset he made his views public in Minnesota.

## Appeal to President Lincoln

In mid-September 1862, while the fighting in Minnesota was still in progress, Whipple went to Washington, D.C., where, accompanied by his cousin, Major General Henry Halleck, he conveyed his concerns in person to President Lincoln. Bishop Whipple recounts in his book about his episcopate that he gave Lincoln an account of the outbreak, its causes, and the "sufferings and evil" that followed in its wake. The bishop felt that the president was deeply moved. Not long afterwards it was reported to Whipple that Lincoln had remarked to a visitor that Bishop Whipple "came here the other day and talked with me about the rascality of this Indian business until I felt it down to my boots. If we get through this war, and I live, this Indian system shall be reformed!"[18] Lincoln's decision regarding the fate of the Sioux who had been sentenced to death in Minnesota may well have been influenced by Whipple's report.[19]

## An Appeal to the Convention

From 1 to 17 October 1862 Bishop Whipple attended the triennial convention of the Episcopal Church in the United States in New York and used the opportunity to solicit the support of his fellow bishops in asking the federal government to adopt a humane policy toward the American Indians. Whipple had drawn up a letter for transmission to the president over the signatures of those present at convention. The letter began by stating that the poor record of the United States in administration of Indian affairs was due to a flawed policy, went on to outline areas in which the system needed improvement, and concluded with a recommendation that a commission be appointed by the president to revamp the entire system for administration of Indian affairs.

Whipple was rebuffed by the first bishop he approached at General Convention. This colleague expressed the hope that Whipple would not bring "politics" to the House of Bishops. Bishop Alonzo Potter of Pennsylvania, however, was supportive and assisted with circulation of the petition. Signatures of nineteen of the twenty-four bishops present as well as those of twenty deputies were secured.[20]

## Public Statements and Letters

Whipple's position that the underlying causes for the Sioux attacks were the policies of the United States government was made known through addresses and conversations and stated bluntly in communications that appeared over his signature in Minnesota newspapers.[21] In one long letter entitled "The Duty of Citizens Concerning the Indian Massacre," the bishop noted at the outset his heartfelt sorrow for the victims of the uprising and for the devastation that had been wreaked, and he made clear his belief that the guilty should be punished. It was also clear, however, that he felt that not all Indians, not even all Sioux Indians should suffer for the crimes of those who had planned and those who had carried out the massacre.

In this letter Whipple noted that the tribal government structures had been rendered ineffective by treaties and that "the only being in America, who has no law to punish the guilty or protect the innocent, is the treaty Indian." He discussed the sale of "fire water" to Indians and the deception and fraud by white traders and Indian agents that was permitted and facilitated by government policy. He cited several instances of unpaid or overdue payments promised by the government. He said flatly that the Department of Indian Affairs was known to be the most corrupt agency in the United States. The bishop then assigned blame for the uprising: "Who is guilty of the causes which desolated our border? At whose door is the blood of these innocent victims? I believe that God will hold the nation guilty."[22]

It was clear from the tone of the letter that Whipple did not favor removal from Minnesota of all Dakota Sioux, but he pleaded that if that action was to be taken it should be carried out with justice and in a way that guaranteed that this time the land given them would be theirs forever. He also stipulated that they should be given a "strong government," fair conditions for trade, and honest agents. He made a special appeal for fair treatment of those, including Taopi and Good Thunder, who had not been part of the outbreak and had in fact intervened to protect the lives of captive settlers until they were released.

*Reponses to the Bishop*

Whipple's letter made clear his sympathy with settlers affected by the massacre, but the litany of U.S. government actions as the root causes of the outbreak and the appeal to exercise caution in the administration of penalties did not elicit positive responses among the populace. The bishop found a storm of denunciation and abuse swirling around him. Stories from settlers who felt his ministrations —physical and spiritual—after being wounded in the massacre helped mitigate the angry backlash. Whipple recalled in his autobiography published years later the praise of a German woman he had helped: "Dat bishop is no pad man; he haf sewed up my wounds and made me well; he is one goot Christian man."[23]

Still, the overwhelming public sentiment was simply to rid Minnesota of the Sioux by whatever means was most expeditious—and what happened to them during and after the move was not a concern. That approach, in the public view, was the one sure way to prevent another Sioux outbreak in Minnesota.

## Consequences of the Uprising for the Sioux

### The Hangings

"Citizens and visitors are requested to occupy the sand bar in the river, from which the best view can be had. The ceremony will necessarily be brief, and we hope good order will prevail."[24] While tensions mounted in Minnesota, President Lincoln arranged an independent review within his administration of (1) the trial records for the 303 Sioux who had been sentenced to death and (2) the statements forwarded by General Pope that indicated the culprits with the highest degree of guilt. The president then made a decision based on his personal review of the independent analysis. On 6 December 1862, a month after the trial records were forwarded to him, Lincoln issued an order that listed the thirty-nine executions that could proceed. One of the persons listed was reprieved (based on a review of the evidence at his trial) before the execution date. On 26 December thirty-eight Sioux dressed in white muslin were hanged in Mankato, Minnesota. The hanging platform was constructed such that all the prisoners could be fitted with nooses before anyone was hanged. Cutting a single large rope with an axe then caused the floor to drop from under all, resulting in a simultaneous hanging.

Onlookers cheered when the rope was cut. It was the largest mass execution in U.S. history.[25]

## Relocation Authorized

Public demands continued in Minnesota for punishment of the remaining convicted Sioux, who were incarcerated at Mankato, and for banishment beyond the state border for all the other Minnesota Sioux, who were interned at Fort Snelling. This matter remained in abeyance until April 1863 when an act of the U.S. Congress provided the authorization for removal of all Sioux from the state. During this interim Bishop Whipple, in spite of intense anti-Sioux public sentiment, worked to provide ministries to both groups of American Indians.

Those Sioux interned at Fort Snelling, mostly women and children, were compelled to spend the winter in a fenced-in enclosure where they endured the severe winter of 1862–1863. Bishop Whipple appointed the Reverend Samuel Hinman as a resident missionary to minister to their spiritual needs and, as best as he could, to their physical needs as well. Bishop Whipple came at intervals to confirm those who were ready; he laid hands on one hundred confirmands in the Sioux camp during the internment period.[26]

Whipple was greatly saddened when in early May 1863, following the congressional authorization, the Sioux at Fort Snelling were removed to Crow Creek, a desolate site in the Dakota Territory on the Missouri River. Whipple knew that removal from Minnesota was inevitable, but the unsuitability of the new site was distressing.[27] The Sioux removed to the Crow Creek reservation in the Dakota Territory found life there wretched. Hinman, with Bishop Whipple's approval, remained with his charges as their missionary, and his 1864 report to the diocese included a chilling statistic that reflected conditions on the removal journey and at Crow Creek: there had been 300 burials since the approximately 1,300 Indians had left Minnesota.[28] The inadequacy of the site was confirmed by a government commission in the fall of 1865. In 1866 these Indians were moved to a mission at the mouth of the Niobrara River in Nebraska, where conditions were an improvement over those at Crow Creek.

The prisoners at Mankato who had been reprieved from hanging by President Lincoln (and a smaller number of others who had received prison sentences) were removed in April 1863 to an incarceration site at Camp McClellan near Davenport, Iowa.[29] In March 1866 these prisoners were freed by President Andrew Johnson and sent to live at the Niobrara site in Nebraska, where a reunion occurred when their families arrived from Crow Creek.

## Fate of the "Friendly Indians"

Some Sioux who were known to have protected and then released the white captives or known to have opposed the outbreak were allowed to remain in

The Right Reverend Henry Benjamin Whipple, D.D.

Minnesota.[30] Some of these became scouts for Sibley, who had been promoted to brigadier general, in his campaigns against the Sioux warriors who had fled into the Dakota Territory following the defeat at Wood Lake. Whipple requested that the federal government provide land in Minnesota and relocation expenses for these "friendly Indian" families. This proposal was inhibited, however, by objections from white settlers; no one wanted a Sioux neighbor. Whipple's distress over these objections came through in his 1863 address to his diocese: "The people will not now listen to any condemnation of the wicked system which has nurtured savagery, lest it should seem to shield the wretches who had perpetrated such awful crimes. Nor are they willing to admit, on the plainest testimony, that there is an Indian, whose hands are not red with blood, even when that testimony is from white captives, who openly declare that they owed their lives to these men."[31]

At Bishop Whipple's urging, Taopi and a small group of Indian families were allowed to remain on Alexander Faribault's property near Faribault for a time, but this arrangement proved difficult in that the families had no satisfactory means of supporting themselves. Mr. Faribault, with help from Bishop Whipple, provided support for them. Whipple took note of this problem in an address to his diocese after the Civil War: "There are a small number of Christian Sioux in the State, who have been left without clothing, annuities, or homes. It is a sad instance of our ingratitude and neglect to our hapless wards."[32] In spite of opposition from seemingly every quarter, the cause of Native Americans remained one of Bishop Whipple's priorities, however, and he continued to work on their behalf throughout his life.

## Bishop Whipple and the Civil War

### A Bishop's Perspective

Although bishop of a large frontier diocese far from the battlefields of the Civil War and constantly involved—often embroiled—in attempting to ameliorate the local conflict between the United States and the Sioux, Whipple, a staunch Unionist, was active for the Union cause during the war. He made his position clear to his diocese before the conflict began in a pastoral letter issued 26 December 1860, calling on his flock to keep 4 January 1861 as a Day of Fasting, Humiliation, and Prayer as recommended by President James Buchanan. South Carolina had just seceded and, Whipple wrote,

> Fearful dangers threaten our beloved Country: With our storehouses full, there is a cry of sorrow in the streets, "men's hearts failing them for fear." Business disaster and commercial ruin are forerunning signs of strife and civil war. . . . The nation has forgotten God. Irreverence for law, disloyalty to government, and disrespect to rulers, have made us unmindful of our obligations to each other. . . . We are reaping what we have sown. . . . Let us make the fervent words of our Liturgy the outpouring of our hearts; that we may be delivered from envy, hatred, malice, and all uncharitableness: from sedition and rebellion: that God may bless all Christian rulers and Magistrates: that he may give to us unity, peace, and concord. . . . May he . . . preserve our land to be a heritage for our children's children, forever.[33]

On 17 April, four days after Fort Sumter fell, the bishop issued another letter to his diocese and mandated a prayer to be used after the General Thanksgiving in the services of Morning and Evening Prayer. His pastoral had two themes:

> Everything seems to foreshadow the most awful strife which has ever darkened our land. The duty of the Christian is plain. He must be loyal to the Government. . . . The lessons of our holy religion teach loyalty—first, loyalty to God; and, second, loyalty to those whom the providence of God has made the guardians of our country.

The duty is no less plain, as followers of Jesus Christ, to seek and pray for peace. Let us, therefore, be careful that no word or deed of ours fans the flame of discord. Let us ever have the olive branch in our hands, and the love of God in our hearts.[34]

On 12 May 1861, he preached to the First Regiment of United States Volunteers from Minnesota. These men comprised the first regiment in the U.S. Army to be mustered in for a three-year term after the war began, and they were soon to see action. "It was," he recalled, "one of the most solemn services of my life. I knew many of the men, and as I looked into their faces I knew that it would be the last time that I should tell them of the love of Jesus Christ."[35] Although his diocesan responsibilities required that he decline, Whipple was honored by his election as chaplain of the regiment. At the time of the June 1861 diocesan convention, Whipple gave a moving address built on two themes: loyalty to country and loyalty to Christ. The latter theme urged no malice toward errant brethren in the South. "The blood which waters the earth is the blood of brethren; . . . while Christian men have no right to falter a hair's breadth in their duty as citizens [of the United States], we may not forget for an hour that we are also citizens of that kingdom which was heralded by the angel's song, 'Peace on earth, good will to men.' . . . I . . . pray God that He will make us one again in love."[36]

## Ministry to the Soldiers

While Bishop Whipple was in Washington to give to federal officials his account of the Sioux uprising raging in Minnesota, the battle at Antietam Creek occurred in Maryland. Fighting took place from 16 to 18 September 1862, with the bloodiest action beginning at dawn on 17 September. Total casualties exceeded 23,000, and more than 2,100 Union soldiers were killed. Having just left the aftermath of the massacres in Minnesota, Whipple went immediately to the battlefield and came upon the First Minnesota Regiment, which had been in the midst of the heaviest fighting. The bishop surveyed a field covered with dead soldiers and ministered to the wounded and dying who had been taken to a nearby barn. He listened to messages that those in the barn wished to be given to loved ones in Minnesota. He then held a service for the surviving members of the regiment who were able to attend.[37]

In his diocesan address the following June, Whipple recalled being on the battlefield where the terrible carnage had just occurred—and also recalled his prescription for ending the conflict: "In these awful scenes, I realized as I never had before, the nature of that fiery ordeal through which we were passing, and that our only hope is in such a repentance as will bring to us again the blessing of God."[38] Before leaving the field Whipple received a note from an old friend, George McClellan, now a major general commanding at Antietam. Whipple had known McClellan in Chicago where Whipple had served as rector of a church and McClellan was chief engineer for a railroad. The general asked the bishop to hold a service that night in the general's camp. McClellan felt that the victory was due to God's mercy and asked Whipple to be "the medium to offer the thanks I feel due from this army and the country."[39] The bishop held the service and afterwards spent the night in McClellan's tent, where the two had a lengthy talk. Whipple also visited hospitals between the battlefield and Washington, where he "had the opportunity to commend some dying men to God, and to whisper to them the Saviour's name for the last journey." He told the sick and wounded soldiers of their general's concern for them and reported by letter to McClellan the love that the wounded soldiers expressed for their commander.[40]

Whipple felt a special obligation to the Union army and made visits each year of the war to soldiers in the eastern theater. He came to know several Union generals, and on Easter Sunday 1864 Bishop Whipple held a service of Holy Communion in General George Gordon Meade's camp, which Meade described in a letter home that evening: "We have had most interesting services today by Bishop Whipple, who administered the Holy Communion to quite a number of officers and soldiers. . . . The Bishop brought down with him a magnificent bouquet of flowers, with which our rude altar was adorned. The Bishop is a most interesting man, about forty years of age, but full of life and energy. He preached two most appropriate and impressive discourses, well adapted to all classes of hearers."[41] When Meade died in 1872, Whipple preached the funeral sermon, recalling that Easter service: "It was a strange place for Easter flowers and Easter songs, and the story of the Resurrection, but I do not recall a sweeter service or one more redolent of the peace of heaven. . . . That day I knew that we had in our camps centurions who feared God and prayed always."[42]

## Bishop Whipple and Slavery

During a physician-ordered year in the South at age twenty-one, five years before seeking Holy Orders, Henry Whipple recorded his impressions of slaves and slave owners. His diary entries denounced slave traders and expressed revulsion at slave auctions but also were critical of abolitionists and recorded his perception of kind treatment of slaves by their owners. He did not condemn slavery as an institution.[43] These ambivalent impressions of a young man, however, altered radically as the years passed, and he became deacon, priest, and bishop.

Concern for Indian rights dominated Henry Whipple's social-justice agenda, and his own diocese was a laboratory for that agenda from the time of his arrival in Minnesota until the last days of his life. By contrast, the black population in Minnesota during his lifetime was not substantial, and local opportunities for hands-on intervention in the issues faced after the Civil War by freed men and women were limited. At the national level, however, Whipple made his voice heard against slavery and for actions by church and by government that he felt were necessitated by emancipation. After the war, for example, the Episcopal Church sponsored a program to help meet the educational and spiritual needs of the former slaves, and Whipple was one of that program's strongest supporters.[44]

In his autobiography Bishop Whipple recalled a scene at a slave auction in Mobile that he had witnessed on his southern tour. This simple and poignant story expresses concisely the wrong of slavery as experienced by one subjected to it—and exposes sharply the blind spot in a slave buyer's perspective:

> A buyer said to an old slave—
> "Where do you want to go, Uncle?"
> "Ise done want to go to Africa."
> "Africa? This is a better country than Africa!"
> "It's a mighty good country for white men," the slave answered, "but dreffful bad for a nigger."[45]

Whipple also offered in his autobiography a reflection on the fact that General McClellan was faulted for not bringing the war to an early, victorious conclusion—a criticism that Whipple believed was not justified, because "our people did not know that this was God's war. North and South were reaping a harvest of their own seed-sowing. Had the war been closed then, slavery would have been fastened on the Republic."[46]

### Notes

1. William Stevens Perry, *The Episcopate in America* (New York: Christian Literature Company, 1895), 145.

2. Phillips Endecott Osgood, *Straight Tongue* (Minneapolis: T. S. Denison, 1958), 32.

3. Whipple's first southern tour is documented in Lester B. Shippee, ed., *Bishop Whipple's Southern Diary 1843–44* (Minneapolis: University of Minnesota Press, 1937). Whipple's recollections of time in Florida assisting Bishop Rutledge are recorded in Henry Benjamin Whipple, *Lights and Shadows of a Long Episcopate* (New York: Macmillan, 1899).

4. Osceola was a Seminole leader who led the fight against displacement of the Seminole Indians from Florida. He was captured in 1837 in violation of a white flag and died of malaria while in captivity.

5. A recollection of this first visit is given by Bishop Whipple in *Diocese of Minnesota, 1884* (Minneapolis: Johnson, Smith, and Harrison, 1884), 39. The mission at Gull Lake was founded in 1852 by missionary James L. Breck.

6. The following account of the Dakota uprising is based upon the following works: Kenneth Carley, *The Sioux Uprising of 1862* (St. Paul: Minnesota Historical Society, 1961); William Watts Folwell, *A History of Minnesota*, vol. 2 (1924; rev. ed., St. Paul: Minnesota Historical Society, 1961); William E. Lass, *Minnesota: A History* (New York: W.W. Norton,

1997); Whipple, *Lights and Shadows of a Long Episcopate* ; and Douglas O. Linder on the website "The Dakota Conflict Trials," http://law2.umkc.edu/faculty/projects/ftrials/dakota/Dak_account.html. (Accessed 7 January 2013).

7. Carley, *Sioux Uprising*, 12.

8. Paila Giese, "Treaties with Minnesota Indians," http://www.kstrom.net/isk/maps/mn/treaties.html. (Accessed 7 January 2013).

9. Carley, *Sioux Uprising*, 19.

10. Whipple, *Lights and Shadows of a Long Episcopate*, 61–62.

11. Whipple to President Lincoln, 6 March 1862. Reproduced by Linder, "Dakota Conflict Trials," http://law2.umkc.edu/faculty/projects/ftrials/dakota/Light&Shadows.html#TO%20THE. (Accessed 8 January 2013). The Whipple letter may be reached from the Linder website by clicking on the link to "Bishop Whipple's Discussion of Causes of the War," and scrolling down to the letter.

12. *Diocese of Minnesota, 1863* (St. Paul: Pioneer Printing, 1863), 9.

13. Lass, *Minnesota*, 109. Lass reports that 413 white civilians were killed during the 1862 Sioux conflict. Earlier writers had given estimates of 800 to 1,000.

14. Folwell, *History of Minnesota*, 124.

15. Roy W. Meyer, *History of the Santee Sioux* (Lincoln: University of Nebraska Press, 1967), 127–28.

16. Ibid., 128.

17. In Whipple's view Sioux who participated in massacres of settlers clearly deserved execution, but individuals who fought in battles against government forces did not. Once the leadership of a tribe or band had chosen war, the individual men were obeying their leaders and should be treated as enemy soldiers. President Lincoln subsequently adopted a similar position in his decision regarding the trial verdicts.

18. Whipple, *Lights and Shadows of a Long Episcopate*, 137. Whipple makes no mention of a response from President Lincoln to his letter of 6 March 1862, a time when the president was preoccupied with the Civil War (that was not going well, at least in the eastern theater). The disaster in Minnesota, coupled with Whipple's personal visit, apparently got Lincoln's attention.

19. President Lincoln authorized execution for only 39 of the 303 braves sentenced to death. See the section in this essay entitled "The Hangings," below.

20. A copy of the petition signed by bishops and other convention delegates is reproduced in Whipple, *Lights and Shadows of a Long Episcopate*, 138–41. Whipple did not name the bishop who was concerned about bringing politics into the House of Bishops, but given Bishop Hopkins's position on church-and-state issues and the fact that he was acting presiding bishop, it is likely that it was Hopkins. The journal of the 1862 General Convention has no record of this affair. Only matters of official business were recorded in the minutes.

21. *St. Paul Press*, 4 December 1862, 1.

22. Ibid.

23. Whipple, *Lights and Shadows of a Long Episcopate*, 122.

24. *St. Paul Press*, 24 December 1862, 1.

25. Linder, "Dakota Conflict Trials," http://www.law.umkc.edu/faculty/projects/ftrials/dakota/Dak_account.html. (Accessed 8 January 2013). Scroll down for a description of the executions and the reaction of onlookers.

26. Whipple, *Lights and Shadows of a Long Episcopate*, 133.

27. *Diocese of Minnesota, 1864* (Shakopee, Minn.: Argus Office, 1864), 15–16. It also distressed Whipple that when the Sioux from Fort Snelling were put on board a steamboat to relocate them they were pelted with rocks thrown by onlookers. (*St. Paul Press,* 24 April 1863, 1.)

28. *Diocese of Minnesota, 1864,* 38.

29. *St. Paul Press,* 24 April 1863, 1.

30. For these individuals the issue was twofold: (1) those who resisted the uprising should not be punished; (2) to exile them with the others who had supported the outbreak would be a death sentence, at least for the males.

31. *Diocese of Minnesota, 1863,* 20.

32. *Diocese of Minnesota, 1867* (St. Paul: Ramsey and Clark, 1867), 16.

33. *Diocese of Minnesota 1861* (St. Paul: Pioneer Printing, 1861), 14.

34. *Diocese Minnesota 1861,* 17.

35. Whipple, *Lights and Shadows of a Long Episcopate*, 96.

36. *Diocese Minnesota, 1861,* 22.

37. Whipple, *Lights and Shadows of a Long Episcopate*, 96–97.

38. *Diocese Minnesota, 1863,* 11.

39. Whipple, *Lights and Shadows of a Long Episcopate*, 97.

40. William Starr Meyers, *General George Brinton McClellan* (New York: Appleton-Century, 1934), 363n.

41. George Meade, *The Life and Letters of George Gordon Meade*, vol. 2 (New York: Charles Scribner's Sons, 1913), 184.

42. Whipple, *Lights and Shadows of a Long Episcopate*, 304.

43. Shippee, *Bishop Whipple's Southern Diary.*

44. See essay below, "The Freedman's Commission."

45. Whipple, *Lights and Shadows of a Long Episcopate*, 411.

46. Whipple, *Lights and Shadows of a Long Episcopate*, 98. Whipple's view of the relationship between the Civil War and slavery might be compared with McIlvaine's postwar view, presented in the next essay, "Charles Pettit McIlvaine: The War Years between National Conventions."

# Charles Pettit McIlvaine

## +⩱ *The War Years between National Conventions*

### 1861

In his diocesan address in 1861 Bishop Charles Pettit McIlvaine had been explicit that in the North preservation of the Union was the sole issue in the war that was beginning to unfold.

> Nor do we consider that the peculiar institution of the South has any place in this struggle, so far as our side is concerned. While, on one side, the cause of slavery and of secession for its sake, accounts for all their movements; and though, until some seven weeks ago, the main question with us was, what can conscientiously be done to satisfy the slave states in regard to slavery; *that* subject has now been driven out of sight, to come back only when a greater and more fundamental interest is settled. The question that takes precedence now over all others is, Shall we preserve the government as now established? . . . It is very far from anything like enmity to our brethren of the seceding states, or a desire to interfere with the protection which the constitution has thrown around their peculiar institution—protection which they united in enacting, and with which they have professed to be satisfied.[1]

### 1862

When the Ohio diocese convened in June 1862 President Lincoln had not made emancipation a war issue, and Bishop McIlvaine, just back from England, did not give a diocesan address. In his address Assistant Bishop Gregory T. Bedell noted that there was in progress a "war for national existence, between loyalty and rebellion," in which "Christianity should be a synonym for patriotism" and that "loyalty to Christ is loyalty to that civil authority which Christ as Head over all things to the Church has established for us."[2] Slavery was not mentioned.

## 1863

When the Diocese of Ohio met in June 1863 the momentum of the war in the East appeared to be with the Confederacy. McIlvaine acknowledged in his address the terrible toll that the war was exacting and said: "We long for such peace as the permanent interests of law and order, of justice and right, will permit our government to seek and accept."[3] In spite of the high price in blood and treasure, however, McIlvaine was convinced that the Union had followed the proper course. He reaffirmed the position on the war that he had taken at the outset, namely that the North was in the right and deserved the support of all members of the church. McIlvaine also noted, though, that being on the right side in the current conflict did not absolve the North from its share of the sins that had brought on a national calamity. War was God's instrument, and it was being used to punish North and South. His colleague Bishop Bedell said this explicitly and suggested how people should respond: "In the school of affliction, the Lord disciplines national as well as individual character. Recognizing his purpose, let us still possess our souls in peace; waiting in faith for his good time, when out of trials our beloved country shall come forth in the maturity of its vigor."[4] What is puzzling about the 1863 convention is that McIlvaine did not use the bully pulpit of the diocesan address to speak against slavery as an institution. When the diocese met in June of that year the Emancipation Proclamation, which after 1 January 1863 made abolition of slavery a consequence of Union victory, had been in effect more than five months.[5] Although McIlvaine shared with nearly all bishops of that era a reluctance to speak on issues that were purely political or involved only social policy, he had been moving for years toward a stance that slavery was incompatible with his religious beliefs and that the institution should be abolished.[6]

This position had not been taken publicly, but similar sentiments had been expressed in two of McIlvaine's letters from England, both dated 27 March 1862, one to President Lincoln and the other to Secretary of the Treasury Salmon P. Chase.[7] In his letter to Lincoln he advised the president that "Americans have rejoiced in the steps you have taken towards Emancipation" and cited in particular the move in progress to abolish slavery in the District of Columbia.[8] Slavery was abolished in the District of Columbia in April 1862, but it is not clear precisely what other "steps toward emancipation" McIlvaine had in mind.[9] The significance of these letters, however, is in the exposure of McIlvaine's attitude toward the institution of slavery, at a time months before a draft of the Preliminary Emancipation Proclamation was revealed by Lincoln to his cabinet. Still, at the diocesan convention more than a year later (and after the Emancipation Proclamation had been issued), McIlvaine did not address the issue from the bishop's chair. The state of the war in the East, with General Robert E. Lee moving his army north, may have been a factor, or McIlvaine may have wanted to keep his message the single one that the federal government deserved the unqualified support of the church. For whatever reason, it was to be 1864 before McIlvaine addressed slavery at diocesan convention.

McIlvaine devoted a substantial part of his 1863 address to a tribute to James Hervey Otey of Tennessee, his longtime colleague in the episcopate who had died in April 1863. He gave a moving tribute to Bishop Otey, quoting at length from an 1861 letter in which Otey had expressed opposition to secession. McIlvaine also alluded to a recent letter written by the bishop of Tennessee near his death which reflected Otey's distress over the war and the state of the church.[10] Although Otey had remained loyal to the United States during the secession crisis, in the end he had not supported the use of force to restore the Union and had sustained Louisiana bishop Leonidas Polk in his decision to accept a commission in the Confederate army. The bishop of Ohio had supported the use of force by the Lincoln administration and had excoriated his protégé Polk for taking up arms, but McIlvaine sympathized with Otey's agony over the war and had a deep affection for him.

Of the four bishops who had made a covenant at Polk's consecration as missionary bishop for Arkansas and the Southwest in 1838, Otey was the second to die. McIlvaine, Virginia's William Meade, Otey, and Polk had agreed while together for that service to pray for each other every Sabbath morning.[11] McIlvaine had been traveling in Italy during the spring of 1862, after completing his "unofficial mission" tour in England when he learned that his friend Bishop Meade had died.[12] McIlvaine had been saddened on that occasion, and later recalled it by writing that his love for Meade had "not changed in the least." There was great pain over the issue that divided them, but McIlvaine, in spite of their disagreement, had never doubted Meade's "rectitude of purpose and motive."[13] The thought must have struck McIlvaine that the two remaining members of the covenant were truly poles apart, Polk a general in the rebel army and himself a strong advocate of the Union who had served the federal government on a diplomatic mission.

## 1864

In the spring of 1864 General Ulysses S. Grant began his Overland Campaign, moving General George Meade's Army of the Potomac south toward Richmond. Although capture of the Confederate capital was indeed an objective, Grant's primary goal was the destruction of the Army of Northern Virginia, which was commanded by General Lee. Toward that end Grant did not retreat when his troops were bloodied or defeated but simply withdrew and continued moving south, forcing Lee to move his forces to set up a new defensive line farther south. Battles that raged in the Wilderness, around Spotsylvania Courthouse, and at Cold Harbor were especially bloody.[14] The Union suffered more casualties, but its pool of replacement manpower enabled it to sustain its losses. The losses by the South, though considerably fewer than those of the North, were devastating to the Army of Northern Virginia. The Union advance halted only when a long siege at Petersburg began, which would culminate in the spring of 1865 in the loss of that city and of Richmond.

The wounded from the battles around Spotsylvania from 8 to 21 May were taken to Fredericksburg, about twelve miles distant. Bishop McIlvaine joined a delegation from the United States Christian Commission at Fredericksburg while the fighting at Spotsylvania was in progress. The Christian Commission had been formed by the Young Men's Christian Association to furnish help, spiritual and physical, to sick and wounded soldiers. McIlvaine furnished observations and reflections on his trip, both to his wife while he was there and to his diocesan convention when he returned.[15]

Before leaving Belle Plain on the Potomac River, McIlvaine sat on horseback to address and pray with eight hundred rebel prisoners: "I began with saying that when I preached the Gospel, I knew no man as an *enemy*, but only as a sinner for whom Christ had died. From that starting point, I went on to '*Preach Christ unto them*,' making no allusion to war or their circumstances. They received it with manifestations of respect and thankfulness."[16] When McIlvaine reached Fredericksburg, he was staggered by the scope of the suffering he saw and by the enormity of the tasks that fell to army surgeons and volunteers. There already were in Fredericksburg some ten thousand wounded soldiers, with more expected from another battle in progress. In the bishop's words, the wounded were

> lying on floors of every sort of house, from the church to the humblest private dwelling. None had more than a blanket between him and the hard board. Not a mattress was there to any. Only a week or ten days before, the town had been in possession of the rebels. The accumulation of that mass of suffering was too sudden to be provided for. Transportation of the wounded to hospitals elsewhere, where every comfort was provided, was going on as fast as possible.
>
> Meanwhile, the surgeons were vastly overworked. Ten times as many were needed. Chaplains there were none, for army chaplains were with the army.[17]

Another battle occurred while McIlvaine was there, and, as the wounded were brought in, amputations were performed on the very tables on which he and others had been having their meals. In the course of describing the suffering McIlvaine vented his feelings about rebellion: "Oh! The impression I got from all those scenes, of what they must answer for, whose selfish conspiracy to fasten the bonds of slavery brought on this war!"[18]

McIlvaine noted that both the U.S. Sanitary Commission (USSC) and the U.S. Christian Commission (USCC) were on hand to help with the overwhelming task at hand.[19] The chief aim of the USCC, he noted, was to "furnish spiritual care to our armies, in such circumstances as the Government provision of Chaplain-cies cannot meet," and the vast number of wounded being brought together in makeshift hospitals during Grant's 1864 campaign had created just such circum-stances.[20] Commission delegates, as its workers were called, were not compen-sated; they received transportation to their worksite and the same food as the soldiers. At Fredericksburg the delegates had been assembled

> suddenly from their distant homes—minute-men, having set off with a few minutes' warning, plunged into all that work, obeying orders with the dis-cipline of soldiers, and taking every sort of work—the most loathsome, the most trying that human sufferers could demand.
>
> I shall never forget their morning and evening worship, before they went to their day's work, and when they came in from it. There were no seats but for some ten or twelve out of the hundred and seventy. There was no shelter but for a very few. In the garden of the house where their stores were given out, they stood, and sang, and prayed, and spake to one another.[21]

McIlvaine observed that the workers of the USCC made no distinction between wounded Union soldiers and wounded Confederate prisoners; he cited an exam-ple on the streets of Fredericksburg when delegates took food and drink to wait-ing ambulances without regard to the affiliation of the occupants. The bishop rejoiced that clergymen and laymen of the Episcopal Church were among the "most devoted laborers."[22]

In June 1864 there was no doubt that the fortunes of war favored the Union. Emancipation in Southern territory under federal control had been in progress for some time. For the first time McIlvaine used his diocesan address to con-front the institution of slavery. He stated his belief that the institution had been a "curse" and "dishonor" to the United States. His statement was comprehensive and strong, and, given his remarks about the issue in 1861 and his silence at the 1863 convention, represented a change in official position.[23]

> I trust the cause of the freedmen engages, brethren, your strongest sympa-thies. An emancipation, which we trust will not cease until every slave is free, must necessarily, in its progress, produce a great deal of want and suffering, at the same time that it opens the door for the education of ignorant thousands, and their claim for self support and reliance. Thus a great responsibility is thrown upon all of us. I trust God will raise up some wise and mighty system of cooperation, by which the friends of the freedmen, seeking their highest welfare, may be united in such measures as may be best adapted to present exigencies . . . . God be praised for what, in his good providence, has been wrought in the past year, in turning the rebellion of the slave holding states

into a great instrument for the destruction of slavery. God has made a way in the sea, and a path in the mighty waters of this awful war—this deep tribulation of the whole land—a way in which no human foresight anticipated, for the ultimate deliverance of the whole land, as I most earnestly hope and pray, from that which has been so long its curse and dishonor, and the fruitful parent of the chief political dissentions of our country. May the same kind providence nourish in all the people of the free States, and especially in all the churches, the spirit ... to meet the duties and necessities which so great a social change will demand.[24]

McIlvaine's call for his diocesan brethren to accept responsibility for helping the freedmen become educated, self-supporting, and self-reliant showed a grasp of the problems that would arise as emancipation proceeded. In a letter a few months before the convention, the bishop had written about the needs of the liberated slaves who were streaming to the North and urged a generous response by the nation and by the church. He called for "a great and combined organization" that would be "as wide and as powerful, as well-managed, and as earnestly supported as the Sanitary and Christian Commissions." He also focused on the role of the church. Referring to the freedmen as "the colored men, women, and children who have been liberated from slavery ... and who are now exposed to so much suffering and want," he noted that

God has brought them to our hands, and placed them under the care of the people of the loyal States. He will require an account of our stewardship. There is no operation of benevolent zeal arising out of the war which I feel more anxious to see vigorously and universally taken up all over the States, than this of attention to the physical, intellectual and spiritual wants and improvement of these poor people....

I hope most earnestly that the Freedman's cause will engage the hearts of the people throughout our Church.[25]

## 1865

At the 1865 diocesan convention McIlvaine reaffirmed the theme that the war had been used by God to abolish slavery. He was certain that God's mighty power had been at work during the entire four years of the war, "the Red Sea and the wilderness" through which the nation had passed. It was indeed God's hand that had permitted the war to continue so much longer than the statesmen and others in the North had anticipated and which had sustained the people of the country during the prolonged struggle.[26] Now the plan of the Almighty was clear.

When could it have been sooner ended? How could it have been otherwise ended? How could our anxieties for the termination of a conflict so terrible,

The Right Reverend Charles Pettit McIlvaine, D.D., D.C.L., LL.D.

have been sooner gratified, and yet all that we now rejoice in, especially the end of slavery, with such universal acknowledgement and general satisfaction, have been so well accomplished? Whatever else man had in view, God had that great deliverance in view from the beginning, and he would not let peace come till that had come, so surely as to make resuscitation impossible. That gain is worth the war, though the country would never have ventured on the war for the sake of that gain.[27]

Bishop McIlvaine noted in his address one blot on the happiness that had come with the end of the conflict. The assassination of Lincoln, a man for whom McIlvaine had great admiration, saddened and "revolted" the bishop.

McIlvaine offered eulogies for those in the church who had died in the conventional year just ended. The bishops noted were Thomas Church Brownell, the presiding bishop, whose health had limited his activity for years; William Jones Boone, who had served as missionary bishop for China; and William Heathcote

Delancey, who had served as bishop of Western New York.[28] Missing from the necrology was McIlvaine's protégé and longtime friend Leonidas Polk, whose death had occurred shortly after the 1864 diocesan convention. McIlvaine's failure to mention Polk's death was in stark contrast to his eulogy of Otey in his 1863 convention remarks and to his remarks when he learned in 1862 that Bishop Meade had died.

The bishop of Ohio reminded his listeners at the 1865 convention of his 1861 charge: "Our duty is, steadily, bravely, earnestly, to sustain our government and its administration in the use of all lawful means to preserve the integrity of the Union."[29] That duty, McIlvaine noted, had been fulfilled; the Union was preserved and furthermore the curse of human slavery had been given a death sentence. McIlvaine hoped that the entire church would express gratitude for these blessings, but in that hope he was to be disillusioned—by his Northern colleagues—at the national convention in October.

### Notes

1. *Diocese of Ohio, 1861* (Columbus: Richard Nevins, 1861), 21–22.

2. *Diocese of Ohio, 1862* (Columbus: Richard Nevins, 1862), 20.

3. *Diocese of Ohio, 1863* (Columbus: Richard Nevins, 1863), 16.

4. Ibid., 25.

5. The Emancipation Proclamation applied to those states in rebellion against the United States; a Union victory was necessary if the proclamation was to be effective. Slavery was not legally abolished nationwide until the Thirteenth Amendment to the U.S. Constitution became effective in December 1865, more than six months after the war ended.

6. Kara M. McClurken, "Charles Pettit McIlvaine and the Civil War: The Public Crusades of an Evangelical Episcopal Bishop" (Honors thesis, Kenyon College, 1999), 74–82.

7. Charles P. McIlvaine, London, to President Lincoln, Washington, 27 March 1862, and Charles P. McIlvaine, London, to Salmon P. Chase, Washington, 27 March 1862. Both letters are in the McIlvaine's personal correspondence at Kenyon College Library.

8. McIlvaine to Lincoln, 27 March 1862.

9. Slavery was abolished in the District of Columbia on 16 April 1862 when President Lincoln signed a bill that had been passed by both houses of Congress. See "The District of Columbia Emancipation Act," http://www.archives.gov/exhibits/featured_documents/dc_emancipation_act/. (Accessed 7 January 2013).

10. *Diocese of Ohio, 1863*, 18–19. See above also, "A Tragic Ending: The Wartime Episcopate of James Hervey Otey of Tennessee."

11. See above, "A Tale of Two Bishops: An Intersectional Friendship."

12. One of the prayers used by Meade in accord with the covenant was published in John Johns, *A Memoir of the Life of the Right Reverend William Meade, D.D., Bishop of the Protestant Episcopal Church in the Diocese of Virginia, with a Memorial Sermon by the Reverend William Sparrow, D.D.* (Baltimore: Innes, 1867), 239. An excerpt from this prayer was included above in "A Tale of Two Bishops: An Intersectional Friendship."

13. William Carus, ed., *Memorials of the Right Reverend Charles Pettit McIlvaine,* 2nd edition (London: E. Stock, 1882), 238–39.

14. For summaries of these battles, including casualty figures, see "Civil War Battle Summaries by State," a website maintained by the National Park Service: http://www.nps .gov/hps/abpp/battles/bystate.htm#va. (Accessed 2 January 2013).

15. Charles P. McIlvaine, Fredericksburg, to Emily C. McIlvaine, Ohio, 19 May 1864. McIlvaine Personal Correspondence, Kenyon College, and *Diocese of Ohio, 1864* (Columbus: Richard Nevins, 1864), 28–32.

16. *Diocese of Ohio, 1864,* 32.

17. Ibid., 29–30.

18. Ibid., 32.

19. The United States Sanitary Commission was founded in 1861. Its purpose was to promote sanitary conditions in the U.S. military camps. The USSC provided staff for field hospitals and secured supplies necessary for the care of the sick and wounded.

20. *Diocese of Ohio, 1864,* 28.

21. Ibid., 30–31.

22. Ibid., 32, 28.

23. In the diocesan newspaper, *Western Episcopalian,* of 14 January 1864, McIlvaine had expressed a similar viewpoint to that presented in his diocesan address.

24. *Diocese of Ohio, 1864,* 28.

25. Letter of Charles Pettit McIlvaine in *Western Episcopalian,* 18 February 1864.

26. *Diocese of Ohio, 1865* (Columbus: Richard Nevins, 1865), 16–18.

27. Ibid., 18.

28. Ibid., 21–22.

29. Ibid., 17.

# Overview of Issues Faced by
# Northern Bishops during the Civil War

### Words and Actions: An Overview

All Northern bishops believed that the tenets of their Christian faith required that they and their flocks be loyal to the Union. This belief reflected the call for allegiance to the "powers that be" by the apostle Paul. A corollary belief was that secession was in defiance of God's will and hence a sin. Along with the belief that loyalty to the Union was required, however, there was a professed belief in the separation of church and state and a general agreement that the pulpit and diocesan addresses were not to be used for patriotic sermons. These beliefs and principles were not entirely compatible, and the emphasis put on each varied from bishop to bishop. The two excerpts below illustrate the two ends of the spectrum of pronouncements on the church and state issue.

#### George Burgess of Maine

As Christians, we must not in act only honor and obey the civil authority, and render to Caesar the things which are Caesar's, but also must uphold with warm affection and steadfast allegiance of heart the safety of this great Christian republic. Our Church has never been accustomed to seek neutral ground, when treason and revolt were on one side, and on the other side was fidelity to rulers, laws, oaths, and the common rights of human beings. We must not say that our religion has no concern with things like these. A religion which should permit its servants to look silently on while conspirators set fire to a magazine, and after the explosion should bid them take tender care for the mangled limbs and dead bodies of the multitude of sufferers, would be a heartless, miserable mockery. It is a stronger duty to sustain our Country now than it could be to rescue from its ruins such remains of peace and happiness, truth and justice, religion and piety, as might be left when privy conspiracy, sedition, and rebellion should have fully done their work.[1]

*Jackson Kemper of Wisconsin*

We are assembled from various parts of the diocese for high and Holy purposes; and especially to exert ourselves to spread far and wide the consolation and blessings of the Gospel of Peace. Let us, during this short period, withdraw from the world and its transactions, and deliberate with calmness and brotherly love upon those concerns which are so intimately connected with an eternity of bliss. You are all deeply interested in the welfare of our Country. Now prove that the patriot can be a Christian, and that while faithful to the constitution and laws of our Country, you can with your whole souls serve, honor, and obey that adorable redeemer, who has called us out of darkness to the marvelous light and liberty of the Gospel.[2]

Bishop Burgess clearly considered it vital that the church be vigorous and public in support of the Union effort to put down a sinful rebellion. To Bishop Kemper it was appropriate for Christian citizens to stand with their government, but when they were assembled as part of the body of Christ they should dwell exclusively on the spiritual matters that were the only concern of Christ's church. The war and related matters were not within the purview of the Episcopal Church as an institution. In between Burgess and Kemper were bishops who made an explicit declaration that they and their flocks should be loyal to the Union but felt that the details of the war effort and the progress of the war should not be brought into the pulpit or church meetings. This issue was addressed by the Northern bishops as a body at the 1862 convention, in the context of the debate over the content of the pastoral letter.[3]

A twist in the Burgess-Kemper spectrum concerned the matter of explicit condemnation, especially of Bishop Leonidas Polk. Concerning Polk, the words of John Williams, who served for a long period during Bishop Thomas C. Brownell's tenure as assistant bishop and became bishop of Connecticut upon Brownell's death in January 1865, provide a good example: "My brethren, there are things more distressing to record than death; . . . for a Bishop in the Church of God to abandon the proper labors of his function, and take up arms of earthly warfare . . . in aid of an insurrection against legitimate authority, is an act which shocks every religious sentiment, as it also violates every vow of consecration, and every obligation of most sacred duty."[4] Several bishops made statements condemning Polk's course, feeling that the church was obligated to dissociate itself from what Polk had done, but most felt that such pronouncements, which added to the ill feeling between churchmen North and South, had no place in councils of the church. Iowa's Bishop Henry W. Lee in 1861 expressed the hope that the war would lead to the end of slavery in the United States, but his statement was unique.[5] In general, slavery was not an issue addressed by bishops in the North during the war until it became clear that emancipation was becoming a reality and the need for the church to play a role in assisting the freed people was recognized.

### Thomas March Clark—Diocese of Rhode Island

Thomas March Clark was an 1831 graduate of Yale. He studied theology at Princeton from 1833 to 1835 and received a license to preach from a Presbyterian church. He then sought Holy Orders and was ordained deacon on 3 February 1836 and ordered priest in November of the same year. Clark served as priest for eighteen years in parishes in Massachusetts, Pennsylvania, and Connecticut. During that time the future bishop of Rhode Island served for four years as the assistant minister of Trinity Church in Boston where Manton Eastburn, bishop of Massachusetts, was the rector. Clark was consecrated on 6 December 1854 at Grace Church, Providence, Rhode Island.[6]

*Perspective on the Crisis*

When he spoke about secession, war, and church separation at his June 1861 diocesan convention, Clark's words were perhaps the most stinging of any Northern bishop. Clark began with the matters of church separation and the role of Southern bishops in the crisis:

> We have cherished the integrity of our national Church, as a treasure to be preserved at almost any cost; we have known no North and no South, no East and no West; and while other religious bodies have, one after another, been sundered by sectional differences, we have endeavored "to keep the unity of the spirit in the bond of peace."
>
> In the present solemn juncture of the nation, we felt that we had a right to expect that our bishops and clergy at the South would have done their best to avert any open rupture of the body of Christ; that men, who have been praying all their lives to be delivered from "sedition, conspiracy, and rebellion," would have vigorously exerted themselves to stay the tide of delusion which threatens to sweep away all that we hold most precious and sacred; that they would have yielded to the popular clamor only so far as they felt themselves obliged to do by the stern necessity of the case; that they would have hesitated long, before yielding to a policy which must . . . actually alienate those who have, all their life long, been accustomed to live and labor together as brethren. In all these respects, with some signal and noble exceptions, we have been sadly and sorely disappointed. In certain instances, the action of rebellious politicians has been anticipated by the authorities of the Church, and such a course has been pursued as must of necessity seriously embarrass and complicate the reunion of the church, whenever the nation is restored again to a condition of peace and unity.[7]

Clark then condemned the rebellion itself.

> Never, in the history of the world, has there been a rebellion of such awful magnitude, involving such frightful possibilities, and putting in peril so many precious interests, for which there is so meager an apology to be made. It is treason against the most beneficent and prosperous government ever vouchsafed by God to man; and it has broken upon us at a time when the most perfect security to all the rights of man, consistent with human institutions, prevailed in every section of the land. . . . It is a crime against civilization; and one year ago it would have seemed impossible that good men, and Christian men, in such vast multitudes, could ever have been drawn into this vortex of delusion.[8]

The cause of the Union was right, Clark proclaimed, and it had to triumph: "It is an awful but stern necessity which has forced us to make armed resistance to this foul treason. There never has been an emergency summoning men to the deadly strife, in which there has been manifested a deeper sense of the moral grandeur of the work to be accomplished, or more absolute reliance upon the right, and a more real and faithful trust in God. . . . There is no release in this war; no retreat, until the question is settled for which we now contend."[9]

*A Soldiers' Bishop*

From the outset Clark was a "soldiers' bishop," blessing and sending off Rhode Island troops to battle, visiting camps and battlefields, and playing an active role in promoting the welfare of the troops. On Sunday, 21 April 1861, he spoke from a flag-draped chancel to an overflow crowd at Grace Church, Providence, which included a contingent of departing soldiers: "Soldiers, in the name of the citizens of this state, I now bid you farewell. God bless you and protect you! God bring you safely home to us again! But if it be otherwise ordered, if . . . you should never return, we will hallow your memory; we will cherish your name in our hearts, and we will provide for those you may leave to our care as brothers and fathers."[10]

The previous day the bishop had addressed the First Rhode Island Regiment, a "ninety-day volunteer" regiment which was departing for Washington.[11] In June the bishop went with the Second Rhode Island Regiment to Washington, where he spent an entire week in the regiment's camp, "determined to see the whole of military life." Clark did indeed get a feel for camp life, eating soldiers' fare, observing the cooking arrangements, watching dress parades, and participating in a "grand round" in which the encampment was circled and the sentinels were tested.[12]

After the First Battle of Bull Run (First Manassas) in July 1861, a depleted First Rhode Island Regiment returned home. Its men had served their ninety days honorably; the troops were mustered out. The regiment was disbanded although its soldiers were free to reenlist.[13] The returning troops were greeted warmly by the townspeople. This time, though, the chancel in Grace Church was draped in black, and the service commemorated all the Rhode Island soldiers who had been casualties. Clark paid honor and offered sympathy to the wounded and missing and their families, as well as offering sympathy to the families of those who had died, but his remarks on the war had a defiant tone: "Our brothers' blood cries to us from the ground. We do not mean that it shall be shed in vain. . . . We have given so much to save the nation that we must give more. Our next movement will be the roll of a mighty avalanche, and it will crunch the forests where the rebels lurk, as if they were a bundle of reeds."[14]

Clark reported in 1862 that he had been chosen a member of the U.S. Sanitary Commission, an agency of the United States government established 18 June 1861 when Lincoln signed the legislation. The Sanitary Commission provided funds, supplies, and personnel to improve sanitary conditions in army camps and to help sick and wounded soldiers. The commission also helped families locate wounded soldiers, and, after the war, until it was disbanded in May 1866, assisted soldiers returning home. The decision-making board comprised some ten men, including Bishop Clark, who met at intervals in Washington. The fieldwork of the commission was carried out mostly by volunteer women, who raised funds, secured supplies, served as nurses and aides in field hospitals, and performed other work as needed.[15] In her biography of Bishop Clark, her father, Mary Clark Sturtevant refers to the Sanitary Commission as the most "gigantic charity the world had ever known."[16]

Bishop Clark, however, did not simply go to commission meetings; he wrote from Washington on 6 September 1861: "I find that our duties on the commission are no sinecure. We meet at 10 a.m. and adjourn at 10 p.m., with short intervals for meals. This evening, I have an appointment with General McClellan in order to arrange with him for an inspection of the whole army."[17] Clark's session with McClellan must have been productive, because during the winter of 1861–1862 the encampments of the regiments around Washington were inspected by the Sanitary Commission and each regimental commander apprised of the findings.[18] Bishop Clark visited the Second Regiment on 4 September 1861 and came again on 8 September to preach. On 10 September the regiment received an official visit from the Sanitary Commission, with the visiting team led by the Reverend Dr. H. W. Bellows, president of the commission.[19]

The Second Regiment fought in many of the major battles in the eastern theater of the war and suffered many casualties from combat and from disease.[20] Bishop Clark followed its progress throughout the war.[21] Late in the war, over two thousand wounded soldiers in varying states of recovery were brought to a hospital at the site where Bradford, RI, is now located. Sanitary Commission member Clark helped with oversight of the facility and spent much time visiting the soldiers. The bishop also helped to arrange for some Confederate prisoners who were with the Union soldiers to be exchanged for federal prisoners in the South. This arrangement gave Clark satisfaction, because prisoner exchange had been on his mind throughout the war. Much earlier, on an occasion when he was in Washington, the bishop had met with President Lincoln and urged him, without success, to arrange for an extensive exchange of prisoners.[22]

### Clark's Thoughts at War's End

Bishop Clark's joy at the ending of the war was greatly dampened by the assassination of President Lincoln, but by the time of his diocesan convention in June 1865 he had thought through some postwar issues that he felt the Episcopal Church should address. He articulated these thoughts in his diocesan address and planned to attend the October 1865 General Convention of the Protestant Episcopal Church in the United States, prepared to raise or speak to these and any other important issues that might arise.

One vital matter was church reunification. Clark pointed out that the Northern church had never acknowledged "a rupture in the organic unity of our communion." All that was necessary was for the Southern dioceses to "ignore" the actions they had taken to create a separate organization and for the church in both sections to "lay aside all bitterness, wrath, clamor, and evil speaking" and reunite in peace.[23] Two other issues identified by Clark were the needs of freedmen and aid to the Southern church. With regard to the first, he said:

> Three or four millions of human beings have been suddenly called to the exercise of their faculties and duties as freedmen, the great body of which are uneducated and unenlightened in the real truths of Christianity. When we have given them their freedom, our whole duty is not discharged. We owe them something beyond this, and inasmuch as they are destined to become a power in the State, policy demands that we should do all that we can do to qualify them for the discharge of their duty as citizens. I know of no way in which this can be done more effectively than by raising up an intelligent, earnest, and faithful ministry of colored persons in our Church to carry on the work of the Gospel among their brethren. A colored clergyman of the Diocese of Connecticut has already been called to the charge of a church in Savannah, with the prospect before him of a wide field of usefulness. Hundreds might be employed in the same good work, if only we had the men properly trained for this important mission.

And he noted, with regard to the second issue of support for the Southern church, that "the Church in that region must be to a great extent a desolation, and our aid will be needed in order to build up the walls of Jerusalem, and lift up the stones out of the heap of rubbish. We trust that this aid will be as cheerfully received as we are sure it will be generously rendered."[24]

Clark did not go into the particular issues of church reunion that would confront the October 1865 General Convention, but it was clear from his remarks that complete reunion of the church, spiritual as well as organizational, was his priority. His statement of the needs of the former slaves was clear and on target, but his solution ("hundreds of colored ministers") was long-term and did not address the immediate needs of the freed people.[25] Although the evidence is implicit, Clark seemed to favor separate educational and religious facilities for white citizens and the newly freed slaves.

### Horatio Potter—Diocese of New York

Horatio Potter, younger brother of Bishop Alonzo Potter of Pennsylvania, was an 1826 graduate of Union College in New York. He was ordained to the diaconate by Bishop John Henry Hobart of New York on 15 June 1827 at Christ Church, Poughkeepsie. Horatio Potter was ordered priest by Bishop Thomas C. Brownell of Connecticut at Christ Church, Hartford, on 14 December 1828. While he was a deacon, he served Trinity Church in Saco, Maine. He was the chair of the Department of Mathematics and Natural Philosophy at Washington (which became Trinity) College until 1833, when he became rector of St. Peter's Church in Albany, New York, where he served until being elevated to the episcopate. He was consecrated at Trinity Church, New York, on 22 November 1854, and served as provisional bishop of the Diocese of New York until 1861. Bishop Benjamin Treadwell Onderdonk died in that year, and Horatio Potter became the diocesan, serving until his death in 1887.[26] From his consecration in 1854, Potter was the de facto bishop of New York, because Bishop Onderdonk had been suspended from his duties as a result of a trial by his fellow bishops.

Horatio Potter was an unequivocal supporter of the Union during the Civil War, but he believed that politics, government affairs, war, and other worldly matters were not fit subjects for the pulpit and had no place on the agenda of diocesan meetings. At the end of the war, restoration of a unified Protestant Episcopal Church in the United States, in his judgment, dwarfed all other objectives at the General Convention.

The strength of Potter's conviction that the church should focus solely on spiritual matters came through clearly before the war, when at the 1860 diocesan convention John Jay, a lay delegate, introduced a three-part resolution preceded by a lengthy preamble with four *Whereas* clauses.[27] The preamble stated that convincing evidence existed that the (Atlantic) slave trade, abolished by the United States in 1808, was flourishing in New York City, the very "seat of our Episcopate, ... in violation of the laws of God and the statutes of the Republic." The preamble also implied that it was a church responsibility to enlighten the community about the "great wickedness of the slave trade" and stated that the church should act to establish "justice, religion, and piety" among church members in the Diocese of New York.

The proposed resolution called, in summary, for the following:

1. That Bishop Potter respectfully be asked to make denunciation of the slave trade the subject of a pastoral letter.
2. That the clergy be asked to preach on occasion against the wickedness of the slave trade being conducted within the diocese.
3. That the laity be asked to exert their influence to try to halt slave trafficking within the diocese.

This resolution was promptly tabled, and, when reintroduced in a modified form, tabled again, each time by decisive votes of both the clerical and lay delegates.[28]

At the next (1861) convention Potter devoted a long segment of his address to his view of the role of the church in troubled times. He contrasted the "serenity and vigor" of life within the church with the "turbulence and disaster" in the secular world. The goodness of God still flourished in the "luxuriant ripening harvest" in rural New York and in other good works, standing in contrast to the violence of man. He then congratulated his clergy on keeping "the House of God a holy place, a sanctuary from the passions of the world . . . and the Minister of God a holy person, unspotted from the world, undisturbed by the noise of political strife, serene and heavenly in the elevation of his spirit."[29]

The bishop offered a prayer and commentary: "God most merciful, grant that our Holy things may be kept Holy, so that in the sanctuary no disturbing thoughts, no profane, no merely temporal objects may be permitted to come between our souls and the unsearchable riches of Christ's truth, grace, and salvation."[30] Potter expressed his hope ("in conformity to this prayer") that the convention would consider only "strictly ecclesiastical" matters. He added that "any attempt to introduce in this body, at this time, questions connected with the political conditions of the Country, or speculative propositions in regard to the rights and duties of dioceses would be, it seems to me, at once irregular and injurious."[31] Reading his 1861 prayer and message leaves no doubt where Potter stood on resolutions such as the one against the slave trade introduced in 1860 or on any effort to have the Diocese of New York condemn the Southern dioceses for forming a separate organization. He attempted to hold to the stance that the war per se was not a matter suitable for sermons or ecclesiastical meetings, but his feelings about the Union and the sacrifices of its soldiers did come into his prayers and public utterances as the war progressed.

In September 1862 there is almost no mention of the Civil War in Potter's address to the diocese. At the September 1863 meeting Bishop Potter spoke on behalf of his country: "if we have virtue and magnanimity enough to rise in this crisis above party passions and personal ends, seeking before all meaner things the good of our country, the maintenance of its rightful authority, the restoration in it of unity, order, and peace, we shall be blessed of heaven."[32] For the last Thursday in November 1863, the Day of National Thanksgiving, Praise, and Prayer to Almighty God, Potter set forth a prayer blessing God's name "on account of the signal favor recently vouchsafed to the efforts put forth in defense of our beloved country." The prayer gave God the glory for the victories of Union arms.[33]

At the diocesan convention in September 1864, Potter reported on private conversations that he had held with men in the army and navy over the course of the war. Some were headed to battle, others were on a temporary respite or recovering from wounds, and others were dying. The bishop then gave a summary of these conversations, and his words on the Union cause and patriotism were passionate:

> They believed that every question of the day, however magnified by excited minds, was utterly insignificant compared with the one, present, vital, supreme object of beating down the unhallowed sword of rebellion, and reinstating an insulted and distracted Country in her place of strength and glory. God give us all a like spirit. I fully appreciate the evils of war. I sigh and pray for peace—peace in that there is one place where patriotism—devoted love of country—may survive and burn brightly even though it should perish everywhere else! And that is among the heroic men who daily face death rather than see that country dismembered, dishonored, and ruined.[34]

Horatio Potter greeted his diocesan delegates in September 1865 with great joy. The war was over, and swords were being turned into ploughshares as soldiers resumed their peaceful pursuits: "It would be unworthy of us as Christians and patriots to reassemble after the lapse of a year, to re-enter upon the work of an annual synod, . . . without a grateful recognition of the Merciful Providence which has delivered us from the horrors of civil war, shed over all our land the blessings of peace, and restored to us, as a nation, unity, strength, and honor."[35] Potter was certain that the "speedy reappearance" of the Southern dioceses in the Protestant Episcopal Church in the United States soon would occur, and he "fervently hoped and prayed" that no reproach or expressions of bitterness would mar the anticipated reunion. He cautioned against any "ill-timed words" that would "break the charm of Christian unity." Any ecclesiastical actions taken by the church in the former Confederate States, Potter felt, should and would be ratified by the General Convention. The bishop then asked the diocese to stand ready to assist their Southern brethren in the task of rebuilding churches and reinvigorating parishes that was necessary as a result of wartime destruction. Potter noted that two bishops, Elliott of Georgia and Johns of Virginia, had expressed intentions not to solicit or accept aid, but felt that eventually aid offered in the right spirit would be received gratefully.[36]

A high point of the diocesan convention for the bishop occurred when the bishop-elect of Tennessee, the Reverend Dr. Charles T. Quintard was introduced. The delegates rose "as one body" to receive him. This action, coming from the great Diocese of New York, Potter felt, had a "great and salutary effect" upon both the church and the country.[37] Bishop Potter went on to play a significant role in the General Convention the following month in Philadelphia.

## Notes

1. *Diocese of Maine, 1861* (Bangor: Wheeler and Lynde, 1861), 16.

2. *Diocese of Wisconsin, 1861* (Delafield: Nelson C. Hawks, 1861), 46.

3. See the essay above, "Assembly under Most Afflicting Circumstances: The Northern Bishops in General Convention in 1862."

4. *Diocese of Connecticut, 1862* (Hartford: Case, Lockwood, 1862), 16.

5. *Diocese of Iowa, 1861* (Davenport: Luse, Lane, 1861), 22–26. In his remarks Lee was out in front of McIlvaine.

6. William Stevens Perry, *The Episcopate in America* (New York: Christian Literature Company, 1895), 135.

7. When Clark spoke of the sundering of religious bodies by sectional differences, he was referring to the division of the Baptist, Methodist, and Presbyterian churches along sectional lines. *Diocese of Rhode Island, 1861* (Providence: Cooke and Davidson, 1861), 13.

8. Ibid., 14.

9. Ibid.

10. Mary Clark Sturtevant, *Thomas March Clark: Fifth Bishop of Rhode Island*, ed. Latte Griswold (Milwaukee: Morehouse, 1927), 84.

11. An account of the actions of the First Rhode Island Regiment, commanded by Colonel Ambrose E. Burnside who rose to the rank of major general, is given in Augustus Hunter, *A Narrative of the Campaign of the First Rhode Island Regiment* (Providence: Sidney S. Rider, 1862).

12. Sturtevant, *Thomas March Clark*, 91.

13. Hunter, *First Rhode Island Regiment*, 140.

14. Sturtevant, *Thomas March Clark*, 87–88.

15. Katharine Prescott Wormeley, *The Cruel Side of War: With the Army of the Potomac. Letters from the Headquarters of the United States Sanitary Commission during the Peninsular Campaign in Virginia in 1862* (Boston: Roberts Brothers, 1898).

16. Sturtevant, *Thomas March Clark*, 92.

17. Ibid., 94.

18. Wormeley, *The Cruel Side of War*, 12–13.

19. Sturtevant, *Thomas March Clark*, 96.

20. See Augustus Woodbury, *The Second Rhode Island Regiment: A Narrative of Military Operations* (Providence: Valpey, Angell, 1875), for a detailed account of the campaigns of this regiment.

21. Sturtevant, *Thomas March Clark*, 91.

22. Ibid., 99 and 93–94.

23. *Diocese of Rhode Island, 1865* (Providence: H. H. Thomas, 1865), 27–28.

24. Ibid.

25. It would take several years to prepare a cadre of black ministers, and there were immediate educational needs for the former slaves.

26. Perry, *Episcopate in America*, 133.

27. *Diocese of New York, 1860* (New York: Daniel Dana, 1860), 75.

28. Ibid., 87.

29. *Diocese of New York, 1861* (New York: F. D. Harriman, 1861), 79.

30. Ibid., 80.

31. Ibid., 80–81.

32. *Diocese of New York, 1863* (New York: James Pott, 1863), 111.

33. Ibid., appendix, 280.

34. *Diocese of New York, 1864* (New York: James Pott, 1864), 103–4.

35. *Diocese of New York, 1865* (New York: James Pott, 1865), 98.

36. Ibid., 99–102.

37. *Diocese of New York, 1866* (New York: Pott and Amery, 1866), 100.

PART 6

# Aftermath—The Perspective of the National Church

# Confrontation in Alabama

## ✦══ *The Bishop and the General*

### George Henry Thomas: The General

On 31 July 1816, about three and one-half months after the birth of another Virginia native, Richard Hooker Wilmer, who became bishop of Alabama in 1862, George Henry Thomas was born on a farm in Southampton County, Virginia. By the time he became of age, Thomas knew that he did not want to be a farmer. He was working in an uncle's law office when he was offered an appointment to West Point. Young Mr. Thomas accepted and was graduated from the U.S. Military Academy in 1840. After being commissioned, he served in the Seminole War in Florida and in the Mexican War. Unlike many other West Point graduates from the South, Thomas remained loyal to the United States when it was clear that there would be a war to preserve the Union. When he notified his two sisters of his decision, his portrait in their Virginia home was turned to the wall, and no reconciliation ever took place.[1]

Thomas rose to the rank of major general, commanded Union forces in battles in Kentucky, Mississippi, Tennessee, and Georgia. His leadership on the second day of the Battle of Chickamauga prevented a rout of the Union army and earned him the nickname Rock of Chickamauga. His devastating defeat of General John Bell Hood at Nashville late in the war resulted from a meticulously planned and carefully executed strategy.

After the war, in June 1865, military divisions for the United States were created, and the command of one, the Division of the Tennessee, was placed under General Thomas. The five departments (corresponding to states) in this division included Tennessee (where Thomas's headquarters were located in Nashville), Alabama, Georgia, Kentucky, and Mississippi. Alabama was among the former Confederate states occupied by federal troops, with governance by military, not civil, rule. Richard Hooker Wilmer, Episcopal bishop in Alabama, had called General Thomas a "renegade," for siding with the Union against Thomas's (and

Wilmer's) native state of Virginia, and General Thomas was in no mood to tolerate what he perceived as disloyal activity on the part of Bishop Wilmer.[2]

## A Confrontation over Prayer

The initial step toward the postwar confrontation between these two natives of Virginia was Wilmer's 20 June 1865 pastoral letter to the clergy and laity of the Diocese of Alabama. Wilmer conceded at the outset of this letter that the disappearance of the Confederate government required that the Prayer for the President of the Confederate States and all in Civil Authority be omitted from the liturgy. The demise of that government, however, Wilmer contended, did not dictate the "immediate substitution" of another form of that prayer. Wilmer noted further that the duty to pray for those in authority was of religious, not political, origin. The right to determine how that duty was discharged, therefore, rested solely with ecclesiastical authority, and the church must be left "free and untrammeled" in making that determination, as she must in all matters spiritual. "Any attempt on the part of a civil or military power to dictate to the Church in this matter cannot but be regarded as unauthorized and intrusive."

He then delivered his central message:

> Now the Church in this country has established a form of prayer "for the President and all in civil authority." The language of that prayer was selected with careful reference to the subject of the prayer—"All in civil authority"; and she desires for that authority prosperity and long continuance. No one can reasonably be expected to desire a long continuance of military rule. Therefore the prayer is altogether inappropriate and inapplicable to the present condition of things, when no civil authority exists in the exercise of its functions. Hence, as I remarked in the Circular (of May 30th), "We may yield a true allegiance to, and sincerely pray for grace, wisdom, and understanding in behalf of a government founded upon force, while at the same time we could not, in good conscience, ask for it "continuance, prosperity," etc., etc. . . . .
>
> My conclusion is, therefore, and my direction which I hereby give, that when civil authority shall be restored in the State of Alabama, the Clergy shall use the form entitled, "A Prayer for the President of the United States and all in Civil Authority," as it stands in the Book of Common Prayer.[3]

The bishop's action and his supporting reasons brought a delayed but long and severe response from Major General Thomas, the military commander under whose jurisdiction Alabama was housed.[4] The response was not sent to Bishop Wilmer; it was published in September in the daily papers of Mobile as "General Orders No. 38" from the Headquarters of the Department of Alabama, over the signature of Major General Charles Woods, military commander for Alabama. The preamble to General Orders No. 38 began with a review of the fact that the

Prayer for the President and all in Civil Authority was being omitted from services at the recommendation of Bishop Wilmer. Wilmer's reason for this was quoted from his letter, beginning with "Now the Church in this country has established" and ending with "continuance, prosperity, etc., etc." It was then stated that the prayer in question was not one for continuance of military rule, but a prayer to the "High and Mighty Ruler of the Universe" to bless and "replenish with the grace of his Holy Spirit" the president and all others in authority. It was a prayer that "any heart not filled with hatred, malice, and uncharitableness" could offer. In addition to violating church canons, Wilmer's advice to omit this prayer and the act of doing so by the clergy showed a "factious and disloyal spirit" and was an "insult to every loyal citizen." In the judgment of the issuing authority, such men should not be in "places of power and influence over public opinion."

> It is therefore ordered, pursuant to the instructions of Major General Thomas, commanding the military division of Tennessee, that said Richard Wilmer, Bishop of the Protestant Episcopal Church of the Diocese of Alabama, and the Protestant Episcopal clergy of said diocese be, and they are hereby forbidden to preach or perform divine service, and that their places of worship be closed, until such a time as said Bishop and clergy show a sincere return to their allegiance to the Government of the United States, and give evidence of a loyal and patriotic spirit by offering to resume the use of the prayer for the President of the United States and all in civil authority, and by taking the amnesty oath prescribed by the President.
>
> This prohibition shall continue in each individual case until special application is made through the military channels of these headquarters for permission to preach and perform divine service, and until such application is approved at these or superior headquarters.[5]

After reading this edict in his morning paper, Bishop Wilmer considered the matter carefully, and then sent the next day, 22 September, the following communication to the local military commander Major General Charles Woods.[6]

> Dear Sir:
>
> I see in the morning paper of this city an order, issued under your authority, forbidding the Bishop of Alabama and his clergy "to preach or perform Divine Service," etc.
>
> The object of this note is to inquire if it is your purpose, by the intervention of military force, to obstruct me, or any of my clergy, in the performance of ministerial duties.
>
> I do not, for a moment, recognize the right of any Civil or Military Officer to dictate to me in the performance of my duty in the Church of God. At the same time, I have neither the wish nor the power to resist military force.

The expression, on your part, of a determination to oppose the celebration of Divine Services by force of arms will be regarded by me as equivalent to a forcible ejection from the precincts of the Sanctuary.

In making the above inquiry, I wish clearly to define my position:

I have issued a Pastoral (a part of which is quoted in your "General Orders") to the Clergy and Laity of the Diocese of Alabama. The positions stated therein were taken with great deliberation, and I see no cause . . . other than the intervention of a higher Ecclesiastical authority, to reconsider them.

Standing upon the provisions of the Constitution which I have sworn faithfully to defend, and also upon that inherent independence and supremacy of the Church (in all matters pertaining to her doctrine, discipline, and worship), . . . I do most respectfully, but most firmly, enter my solemn protest against the interference expressed in your "General Orders."[7]

General Woods "curtly" responded that if his orders were disobeyed he would "certainly" use force to close the churches. Wilmer again wrote Woods saying that he was about to issue a pastoral letter "to his flock" and requested permission to quote the "General Orders" and the related correspondence. Woods not only refused permission but "forbade" issuance of the pastoral letter. Wilmer ignored the general's response and issued a pastoral letter that did include quoted material from the orders and the correspondence that delineated why Episcopal churches in Alabama were being closed.[8]

Wilmer's next step was to write, before the October General Convention of the Protestant Episcopal Church in the United States, three of his Northern colleagues, Bishops John Hopkins of Vermont (presiding bishop), Thomas Clark of Rhode Island, and Arthur Coxe of Western New York, in order to summarize the state of things in Alabama as he saw them. He began his letter as follows:

Rt. Rev. and Dear Brethren:

I send you a statement of the condition of things here at this time, thinking that it would interest you as churchmen. As to the use of the prayer in question, I presume that you would take issue with me. That is not the point to which I call your attention. As a dutiful son of the Church, I will submit myself unquestioningly to her decisions and hear thankfully her admonitions, even when contrary to my private judgment. But, as I hope to receive mercy at the last day, I will not move in matters pertaining to the supremacy of the Church within her sphere, at the dictation of any secular power, civil or military,[9]

Wilmer went on to argue that the military intrusion into worship in Alabama was a violation of the United States Constitution. He did not explicitly ask for help from the PECUSA bishops, but it was his hope that, given the facts of the case, the General Convention would make a "solemn protest" against the "secular interference" with Episcopal worship services that was extant in Alabama.[10]

## Notes

1. Freeman Cleaves, *Rock of Chickamauga* (Norman: University of Oklahoma Press, 1948), 4–5, 7–9, 16–42.

2. Janie M. Moore, "Praying for the President," *Alabama Heritage,* no. 24 (Spring 1992): 37.

3. Richard Hooker Wilmer, "Pastoral Letter to Clergy and Laity in the Diocese of Alabama," 20 June 1865, reproduced in Walter C. Whitaker, *Richard Hooker Wilmer: Second Bishop of Alabama* (Philadelphia: George W. Jacobs, 1907), 123–127.

4. Wilmer's pastoral letter was brought to Thomas's attention in September by William Brownlow, then "reconstruction" governor of Tennessee. See Moore, "Praying for the President."

5. *Mobile Advertiser and Register,* 23 September 1865, "By Telegraph" section, 2.

6. Whitaker, *Richard Hooker Wilmer,* 133.

7. Ibid., 133–34.

8. Ibid., 134.

9. *Diocese of Alabama: Proceedings of a Special Council, held 17 January 1866* (Mobile: Farrow and Dennett, 1866), 6–7.

10. Ibid., 7.

# What Price Reunion?

⊹⊱ *The Philadelphia Convention, 4–24 October 1865*

### Atkinson and Lay: A Fateful Decision

At the end of the war, Bishop Henry C. Lay, missionary bishop for Arkansas and the Southwest, was in temporary residence in Lincolnton, North Carolina. He described his circumstances as follows: "The railroads were broken up throughout the South; we could not visit each other, for few of us had a dollar. One could do little but think and wait and pray."[1]

When North Carolina bishop Thomas Atkinson came to Charlotte, near Lincolnton, the two old friends met on 1 June to talk about how they should proceed with respect to the church's organization.[2] They were in agreement and immediately dispatched a letter, dated 2 June 1865, to Stephen Elliott, presiding bishop of the Protestant Episcopal Church in the Confederate States of America (PECCSA), pointing out that the reason for a separate church in the Southern states no longer existed. In fact, they argued, the principle that there should be one national church in each country dictated that reunion with the Northern church was the proper course of action. They urged Bishop Elliott to call a meeting of the PECCSA council. In that the General Convention of the Protestant Episcopal Church in the United States of America (PECUSA) was scheduled for October, they suggested that the PECCSA council meet in September. The Southern dioceses then would be in a position "to make proper representations to the General Convention of the Church in the United States." Atkinson and Lay emphasized that the Southern dioceses should act "in concert" and expressed a particular concern that the bishop of Alabama not be "embarrassed" by the circumstances of his consecration. Even if time considerations precluded a full council meeting, Bishops Atkinson and Lay felt that it would be "competent" if the bishops met to reach a consensus on this vital issue.[3]

Their letter did not reach Elliott until July, and although he agreed with the concept of reunion, he wished to proceed differently and on a different timetable. He began his response as follows: "I do not see how we can avoid returning into connection with the Church in the Union, but I think that it should be done with great deliberation, with proper self respect, and only with the hearty cooperation of the church and laity, as well as the Bishops of the church."[4] Elliott felt, in fact, that the initiative should come from the stronger of the two parties (the church in the United States), and that PECUSA would have the opportunity to take that initiative when it met in October. He also noted that the sad state of transportation across the South would make an early meeting of the PECCSA council difficult. Nevertheless, because Alabama bishop Richard Hooker Wilmer also had requested a meeting of the bishops, Elliott indicated that he would ask the bishops to convene. Elliott also expressed his deep concern for the former slaves. The white Southerners, he wrote, "would rise above our evils," but the freed slaves would "melt away before civilization and competition, as the Indians have done."[5] The inclusion of these pessimistic remarks in his response suggests that Elliott had not really come to terms with the outcome of the Civil War.

A call was issued to the PECCSA bishops to meet in Augusta on 27 September, but several bishops indicated that it was unlikely that they could attend. Atkinson then requested that Elliott change the place of meeting to Winchester, Virginia, in order that the attendees might have the option of going from Winchester directly to the PECUSA convention in Philadelphia, but the PECCSA meeting was aborted.[6] Bishop Atkinson met with his diocese in September and secured its endorsement to use his judgment on the matter of reunion of the Diocese of North Carolina with PECUSA.[7]

Bishop Lay and Bishop Atkinson met in Baltimore on 2 October. They agreed to attend the Philadelphia convention, but, at Lay's initiative, not to take their seats in the House of Bishops until first determining how they would be received. Bishop Atkinson proceeded to attend the convention on the first day but seated himself in the congregation. Bishop Lay arrived on the second day.[8] The action of Atkinson and Lay was contrary to the wishes of Bishop Elliott, who felt that Southern bishops should not attend PECUSA's October 1865 General Convention, but that the Southern diocese should act in concert after that meeting at the November 1865 council of PECCSA. Elliott's position was shared by Bishops Francis Huger Rutledge, Thomas Frederick Davis, William Mercer Green, and Richard Hooker Wilmer. Bishop John Johns very much wanted to attend the October PECUSA convention, but his diocese voted to defer action on the reunion issue until after the November meeting of PECCSA. At Bishop Alexander Gregg's urging, the Diocese of Texas had already withdrawn from PECCSA and reaffiliated with PECUSA. This action by the Texas Diocese was taken without consultation by Gregg with Elliott, which offended the PECCSA senior bishop.[9] Although Texas sent delegates to the PECUSA General Convention, Bishop Gregg did not attend. He therefore did not share in the work of Atkinson and Lay that facilitated church reunion. The episcopates in Tennessee and Louisiana, neither of which had formally affiliated with PECCSA, were vacant when PECUSA convened.

## Preconvention Atmosphere

The *Episcopal Recorder,* a church periodical based in Philadelphia, published an editorial on 6 May 1865 entitled "Clerical Rebels."[10] General Lee had surrendered a few weeks prior, the last engagement of the Civil War, at Palmito Hill, Texas, was just over a week away, and the nation was in mourning over the assassination of President Lincoln. A crisis in Alabama over the Prayer for the President and all in Civil Authority, although brewing, had not yet developed, but the issue had arisen elsewhere in Southern cities that were occupied by Union troops. The editors of the *Recorder* felt that many prominent Southern clergy, including some bishops, not only had escaped being held accountable for their role in the rebellion but also were being allowed to continue to exhibit disloyal behavior. These bishops and clergy, in fact, were still "among the most determined, bitter, and most mischievous of all the enemies of the Government." A distinction, the editorial noted, was being made by the public between rebel leaders and those who were led, or deceived, by those in authority and influence.

> Now, where can be placed many of the bishops and leading clergy of our Church in this movement but among the leaders? . . . Next to the most prominent leaders of secession such as DAVIS and TOOMBS, and RHETT, we must place, in point of influence, such men as Bishops ELLIOTT and DAVIS, and WILMER, and a host of clergymen of like mind with them. Without their influence, secession could not have succeeded. Against it, secession would not have been undertaken; . . . their sanction and advocacy were essential, in order to satisfy the moral and religious portion of the community of the righteousness of the contemplated rebellion. And they have done the work which the rebel leaders have desired at their hands—done it with a will. They have preached the Divine right of slavery, and the Divine duty of upholding it by a Divine rebellion.[11]

The editors noted that even though the rebellion had been broken, the clerical rebels were "among the last to yield and preach submission" and added that "to refuse to pray for the President of the United States is to refuse to recognize government at all—for there is now no other government but the Federal Government in Richmond."[12] The concluding paragraph of the editorial urged that bishops and other clergy who continued to advocate resistance "be sent out of the country," and added that clergy who persisted in disloyalty should "not be the last to suffer the penalties of treason."[13] In the next issue of the *Episcopal Recorder,* a sermon preached in Highgate, Vermont, by the Reverend Edward Winthrop was reprinted. Winthrop did not single out bishops or clergy, but he denounced the rebellion and called for "executing the leaders at the hands of the common hangman."[14] Throughout the summer and early fall, the editors took the position that it would be best if the Southern bishops and deputies did not attend the October General Convention—on the grounds that more time was needed to sort out the issues and—especially—feelings involved. The paper also issued periodically sharp criticisms of Southern bishops such as Wilmer, Elliott, and Green.

In making the decision to attend the General Convention, therefore, Bishops Atkinson and Lay knew that they faced opposition from their Southern colleagues who preferred delay until after the November General Council of the Confederate Church, and they must have been apprehensive about their reception in Philadelphia, given the hostility shown by the Episcopal paper housed in the city of brotherly love. The two bishops might have been even more concerned had they been privy to certain letters written recently by Northern bishops. On 22 June 1865, John Henry Hopkins, presiding bishop since January 1865, had proposed (and drafted for review) an invitation to all bishops in the former Confederate states to be signed by all Northern bishops.[15] After receipt of the draft, Bishop Alfred Lee of Delaware wrote Bishop Charles Pettit McIlvaine of Ohio

> May I ask for a free statement of your opinion on this movement? However desirous of peace and unity, I confess that I entertain a strong reluctance to affix my name to such a paper. It will be sent, among others, to the Bishop of Georgia. You, I presume, have seen his funeral address at the burial of Bp. Polk (Published in the Xn Witness of June 2/65) in which, in the strongest terms, & with full deliberation, he justifies the course of our unfortunate brother in taking the sword—and wherein he hurls against the loyal Bishops and Clergy of the U.S. denunciations unsurpassed in any Papal Bull of Anathema. Is the author of such a vituperation to be welcomed back to his place in our councils without retracting or apologizing for his abusive and slanderous accusations? Is he not really more culpable than Bp. Polk himself?[16]

Lee then noted that Hopkins, in his draft, had absolved the church in both North and South from any responsibility for causing the war, a position that Lee thought was false: "The Church at the South, by her current teachings on the subject of slavery, by promoting sectional hatred, and by rushing with indecent haste into the assumption of Southern independence, had a great deal to do with producing and sustaining the conflict. Next to the leaders of the conspiracy no class of men have a heavier responsibility than those Bishops and Clergy."[17]

At least five other bishops declined to sign the proposed communication. The others were less harsh, but there was a reluctance to issue an invitation that might imply that the wartime support of the Confederacy and the support of slavery were condoned.[18] Hopkins sent the letter over his signature, telling his Southern colleagues that he felt authorized to say that they would be greeted warmly by their Northern brethren.[19] As it developed, the strong desire for unity that motivated Atkinson and Lay to risk censure by their Southern colleagues and rebuff by their Northern colleagues was shared by most of the bishops who attended the Philadelphia convention.

## A Cordial Reception

Bishop Atkinson attended on the first day, but, in spite of friendly overtures from his Northern colleagues to join them in his rightful place in the chancel, Atkinson seated himself in the congregation. During a pause after the prayer for the church militant, however, the secretary of the House of Bishops came for Bishop Atkinson; Atkinson yielded and took his place with the other bishops, who welcomed him cordially, some with tears. The impromptu welcoming had an impact on the entire assembly.[20]

The next day, however, both Bishop Atkinson and Bishop Lay were in attendance, and they were reluctant to take their seats in the House of Bishops for the formal meetings of that house. Atkinson and Lay had come to facilitate reunion and hoped to be able after the convention to tell their fellow bishops and churchmen in the South that they would be welcome. If their Northern colleagues desired to reunite only on terms unacceptable to the Southern dioceses, however, the two Southern bishops did not want to separate themselves from those with whom they had been in union in the Confederate church. Finally, Bishop Horatio Potter of New York discussed with his colleagues the feelings of the two Southern bishops who did not wish to move forward with steps toward reunion if irreconcilable differences were going to surface. In this connection they mentioned explicitly the Wilmer consecration. Maryland bishop William Rollinson Whittingham advised Bishop Potter to ask Bishops Atkinson and Lay "to trust to the honor and love of their brethren." The two Southern bishops did give their trust and promptly entered the House of Bishops to a warm welcome.[21]

## Three Potential Barriers to Reunion

Potentially, there were three major stumbling blocks to reunion of the former PECCSA dioceses with the Protestant Episcopal Church in the United States, as follows.

### 1. Confederate Military Service by Leonidas Polk

It is highly unlikely that a majority of the Northern bishops and churchman could have brought themselves to welcome to resumption of an episcopate in the Protestant Episcopal Church in the United States a lieutenant general of the Confederate army—someone who had put aside his responsibilities in the House of God to bear arms and, in the view of many in the Northern church, to lead troops into battle to support "privy conspiracy, sedition, and rebellion." His returning as bishop had become a nonissue with Polk's death, but condemnation of or even a slur on Polk at the convention could have dealt a lethal blow to reunion

The Right Reverend Horatio Potter, D.D., LL.D., D.C.L.

sentiments in the Southern church. Bishop Stephen Elliott put the matter this way, in response to an inquiry from the *Episcopal Recorder.*

> I think that it is our duty to guard the memory of our deceased Bishops Meade, Otey, and especially our beloved Polk. Not that we should expect any endorsement from the General Convention of their views and actions, but that we should feel assured that no reproach, either direct or implied will be cast upon their graves. About ourselves, the living, we care but little; we are here and can defend ourselves; but the reputation of the dead is in our keeping, and we can fraternize with nobody who would willingly disturb their ashes. They have lived and died for us, and however wrong others may think them, we revere their memories and weep over their graves.[22]

No reproach, in fact, was cast by the convention on the deceased Polk. There were motions—with debate—to proscribe military service by any member of the clergy, but although Polk was the only bishop to bear arms, there were clergy, North and South, who fought in the war, and the resolution that finally passed looked to the future: "It is the sense of the Protestant Episcopal Church in the United States of America, that it is incompatible with the duty, position, and sacred calling of the clergy of this church to bear arms."[23]

### 2. The Diocese of Arkansas and the Status of Bishop Lay

Arkansas had been elevated to diocesan status in 1862 by the General Council of the Confederate Church. Henry C. Lay, who had resigned as missionary bishop for the Southwest, was then confirmed as bishop of the Diocese of Arkansas by the General Council. Neither of these actions was viewed as canonical by some in the North. Refusal by the Northern dioceses to recognize either the validity of the status of the Diocese of Arkansas or the validity of Lay's status as its bishop would not have been acceptable to the Southern dioceses.

The bishops and deputies appeared ready to receive both Arkansas as a diocese and Lay as its bishop, but Bishop Lay made matters easy for the convention. Although there had been twelve active parishes in Arkansas in 1862, there were only two in October 1865, and in Lay's judgment the church in Arkansas was in no condition to function as a diocese. Lay proposed that the state revert to missionary territory and, in fact, once again become part of the Missionary District of the Southwest, for which Lay would resume episcopal responsibility. In that his resignation of that bishopric had never been accepted and Arkansas had not been made a diocese by the church in the United States, this approach required no action by the convention. Although this solution met with favor at the convention, subsequent reaction was mixed in the South, where some churchmen felt that Lay had no right to abandon a diocese validly established by the church in the Confederate States, and, in fact, that what took place was not canonical. This feeling surfaced later on two occasions when Lay was being considered for the office of diocesan bishop.[24]

### 3. The Bishop of Alabama

The thorniest issues were those that surrounded Richard Hooker Wilmer, who had been elected bishop of the Diocese of Alabama and was consecrated in March 1862 by three Southern bishops. As Bishop Elliott had stated in the *Episcopal Recorder*, the stakes in consideration of the validity of Wilmer's consecration involved not only Wilmer's title but also the validity of his official acts for the three years that he had served as bishop.[25] In addition to the consecration issue, the controversy over the Prayer for the President of the United States and all in Civil Authority was raging in Alabama. Wilmer had not retreated from the position taken in his June 1865 pastoral letter, in which he had refused to direct clergy in Episcopal churches in Alabama to use the prayer for the president of the United States on the grounds that there was military rule and no real civil authority in Alabama. As a result Episcopal churches in Alabama were closed by a military order published on 20 September.

When it came time to consider this matter on 6 October, Bishop Whittingham offered a detailed motion that provided for the House of Bishops to accept the Wilmer consecration. Bishop Alfred Lee moved to lay the motion on the table, but Lee's motion failed. After discussion the Whittingham resolution was adopted, and on 7 October the following message was sent to the House of Clerical and Lay Deputies:

> Resolved That this House is satisfied that the Rev. Richard Hooker Wilmer, D.D., has been validly consecrated to the office of a Bishop, having been elected to the exercise of that office in the vacant Diocese of Alabama; and that, without examination of the circumstances occasioning certain canonical irregularities in the election and consecration and expressly declaring that its present action shall never be construed or accepted as a precedent, this House hereby accepts the Right Reverend Dr. Wilmer as Bishop of Alabama, and consents to his Episcopate as such, providing that the House of Clerical and Lay Delegates is willing to signify its concurrence in such acceptance and consent; and that thereafter the Bishop of Alabama shall transmit in writing to the Presiding Bishop . . . , the promise of conformity comprised in the office for the consecration of a Bishop in the ordinal.[26]

The deputies referred the bishops' message to a committee on consecrations. This committee reported with a resolution that the House of Clerical and Lay Deputies concur in the action taken by the House of Bishops. After extended discussion and three amendments, the House of Clerical and Lay Deputies did concur in the action by the House of Bishops. The amendments (1) made it explicit that a condition of Wilmer's acceptance as bishop of Alabama be that all papers be transmitted in advance to the presiding bishop; (2) required that the letters from the consecrating bishops (or equivalent documentation) be among the papers provided; and (3) made it explicit that the written promise of conformity noted in the resolution of the House of Bishops be signed by him in the presence of three bishops. In the end, therefore, Wilmer's consecration was recognized, and he was asked only to furnish documentation equivalent to that required of any bishop consecrated in the American church. The resolution of concurrence and its amendments were sent to the House of Bishops.[27]

Bishop Whittingham then offered the following resolution, which was adopted: "Resolved That we do hereby express to the Bishop of Alabama our fraternal regrets at the issue of his late pastoral letter, and assured confidence that no further occasion for such regrets will occur."[28] Whittingham asked that the resolution be entered in the minutes of the House of Bishops as having passed NEM.

CON., unless objection be taken. There was no objection. Following passage of this resolution, the House of Bishops concluded its actions taken on the Wilmer consecration by passing a motion that Bishop McIlvaine might go to Washington "if necessary" to confer with the president regarding the suspension of clerical functions in Alabama by military authority.[29] The resolution of this church-and-state crisis in Alabama did not come until mid-January 1866.[30]

### Consecration of Charles Todd Quintard as Bishop of Tennessee

Although it was a diocese within a Confederate state, the Diocese of Tennessee had not met during the Civil War and had not separated from PECUSA to join the Confederate church; the diocese had been without a bishop since James Hervey Otey's death in April 1863. Bishop-elect Charles Todd Quintard accompanied the Tennessee delegation to the Philadelphia convention. In the House of Clerical and Lay Deputies, the Committee on Consecration of Bishops accepted the testimonials provided by the Diocese of Tennessee and proceeded to recommend that the House of Deputies sign and forward to the House of Bishops the proper certification. There were questions from the floor concerning the validity of the diocesan convention at which Quintard was elected, and a clerical delegate voiced his opinion that Quintard should not be consecrated as bishop because of his "having taken part in the army services." The delegate also noted that Quintard's name had been linked with that of Bishop Polk. When the vote was taken, however, very few dissenting voices were heard.[31] After his election was confirmed by the convention, Quintard spent the evening of 10 October in meditation and prayer at the Church of St. James the Less in preparation for his consecration the next day at St. Luke's Church.[32]

In his consecration sermon Bishop William Bacon Stevens noted that Quintard, then a young physician, came to Stevens when he was minister for a congregation in Georgia. Stevens received Dr. Quintard, who became a "most useful and faithful" member of his communion. Quintard now stood before him, ready to build up a diocese "despoiled by a cruel war." Stevens charged his new colleague: "You are to perpetuate Christ's ministry, to build up Christ's Church, to maintain Christ's truth."[33]

The ceremonial hiatus was over; the convention turned to two items that would prove to be the most contentious, namely the theme for a service of thanksgiving and the subject for a pastoral letter.

### Resolutions for a Day of Thanksgiving

Although emotional wounds in the North from the war and separation of the Southern dioceses certainly were not healed, the one matter which might have been expected to proceed without great discord was arranging a service of thanksgiving for the restoration of peace. There was, in fact, unanimity for the act of holding a service—but the wording of the thanks to be offered generated maneuvering—both on and off the house floor—and considerable controversy.[34]

Bishop George Burgess of Maine brought the issue before the house. He first recalled the Day of Fasting, Humiliation, and Prayer held at the 1862 convention and reminded his colleagues of the afflicted condition of the country at that time. He proposed appointing Thursday, 12 October, as a Day of Thanksgiving, now that God had delivered his people from those afflictions. He proposed that thanks be offered for the universal establishment of the authority of the national government, for complete restoration of peace, and for extension among all classes of men the condition of freedom and social improvement—in other words the abolishment of slavery. His motion was laid on the table.

Sensing that the tabling action reflected a desire in the House of Bishops not to offend the Southerners in attendance, Bishop Burgess visited during a recess with Bishop Lay at the latter's desk. Burgess asked Lay what there was in the resolution that could "possibly grieve you." Lay pointed to the "extension of freedom" provision and answered: "I trust in God that freedom may bring to the colored race all the blessings you anticipate; but wiser men than I, and Northern men at that, honestly doubt whether freedom will prove to them a blessing or a curse. Why should this House commit itself in a matter wherein it has no authority?"[35]

Burgess subsequently was granted leave to amend his motion, even though it was on the table. His amending action removed the wording that called for the extension of freedom to all classes of men and added thanks for the "kindness of the Lord to this Church in the re-establishment of unity throughout the land, as represented in its National Council." Bishop Whittingham then made a substitute motion that was much more general, but Rhode Island bishop Thomas Marsh Clark moved, and it was adopted that both motions be referred to a committee of the five senior bishops charged with the responsibility for developing the form and content of the service. Bishops Hopkins, McIlvaine, Smith, Kemper, and McCoskry comprised the committee.

On the eighth day, Presiding Bishop Hopkins gave a report for the committee that referred first to a service at the 1862 PECUSA convention at which God had been asked that the nation be delivered from war, that opposition to the lawful government cease, and brotherly love be established among the faithful. He noted that those prayers had been answered and that the time had come to thank the Almighty for that blessing. It should be "Therefore Resolved That this House appoint Tuesday, the 17th day of October, to be observed by the same, in appropriate public services as a day of thanksgiving and praise for God's manifold services to our Country and his Church, especially in giving us deliverance from the late afflicting war, in re-establishing the authority of the National Government over all the land, in restoring to our Country the blessings of union and concord, and in bringing back the unity of the Church as represented in this convention."[36]

The House of Bishops suspended its order of business to consider and to adopt the report, after which the House of Clerical and Lay Deputies was invited to participate in the service.

The two Southern bishops, Atkinson and Lay, had not participated in either the formal actions of the house on this matter or in the intense discussions that preceded the votes. Atkinson, in particular, felt that it would be best if he and Bishop Lay did not hear the debate, some of which he felt would be painful to anyone who had believed in the Southern cause. Once the House of Bishops had adopted the report of the five senior bishops, though, the Southerners were asked to join their colleagues in the thanksgiving service. Bishop Atkinson responded calmly and with neither rancor nor apology that the Southern bishops could not join in that celebration. Bishops North and South could thank God for the restoration of peace and for the renewal of unity in the church, but those from the South could not be thankful for the restored national authority over the entire country. They had, in fact, fought and prayed for a different result. They acquiesced in the result and would accommodate themselves to it as citizens, but they could not offer thanks to God for that outcome. They were grateful for the restoration of peace to the country and unity to the church.

The next day, on motion of Bishop William Odenheimer of New Jersey, the bishops resolved to reconsider the action of the House "respecting a Day of Thanksgiving." Bishop William Bacon Stevens of Pennsylvania then offered the following motion to replace the report of the five senior bishops: "Resolved That the House of Bishops, in consideration of the return of peace to the Country, and unity to the Church, propose to devote Tuesday, the 17th day of October instant, as a Day of Thanksgiving and Prayer to Almighty God for these His inestimable benefits, and that an appropriate service, prepared under the direction of the five senior bishops, be held in St. Luke's Church."[37]

Bishop Burgess quickly moved to lay on the table the motion of Bishop Stevens. The tabling motion lost by a 16 to 7 vote. Bishops McIlvaine (Ohio), A. Lee (Delaware), Eastburn (Massachusetts), Burgess (Maine), H. Lee (Iowa), Bedell (assistant bishop., Ohio), and Vail (Kansas) voted to table; Bishops Hopkins (Vermont, presiding bishop), Smith (Kentucky), Kemper (Wisconsin), McCoskry (Michigan), Whittingham (Maryland), Chase (New Hampshire), Hawks (Missouri), Whitehouse (Illinois), Kip (California), Potter (New York), Clark (Rhode Island), Odenhemer (New Jersey), Whipple (Minnesota), Talbot (Indiana), Stevens (Pennsylvania), and Coxe (Western New York) voted nay. The Stevens motion then was adopted.

Following passage of this resolution, the committee of senior bishops prepared an order of service that was circulated among the members of the House of Bishops. This led to a final attempt by the dissenting bishops to modify the service. Bishop Manton Eastburn of Massachusetts moved the following resolution:

"Resolved That to the subjects of Thanksgiving contained in the service reported by the five senior bishops to this house, there be added two others, VIZ, the establishment of the authority of the National Government throughout the land and the extension of the blessings of freedom and social improvement."[38]

Bishop Horatio Potter of New York immediately moved to table the Eastburn resolution, "the resolution of the Bishop of Massachusetts being inconsistent with the understanding with which the preparation of the service for the DAY OF THANKSGIVING was referred to the five senior Bishops be laid on the table."[39] The motion to table passed by a 15 to 7 vote, and the special service of thanksgiving proceeded on the morning of 17 October at St. Luke's Church. The special thanksgiving prayer included the following general or catholic wording: "thou hast healed our divisions and restored peace to our land and the fellowship of thy church."[40]

The issue was not closed, however. On the evening of the 17th, another service, arranged by the dissenting bishops, was held at the Church of the Epiphany. Both services were described in the *Philadelphia Inquirer*, the evening service on page one and the official service on page two. The offering at both services was dedicated to the relief of freedmen.

The words at the evening service were not general; they focused on the matters that been excluded from the official thanksgiving in the morning. Bishop McIlvaine opened the service and was the first speaker after other bishops who had joined him as sponsors had read lessons and prayers. He noted that three years earlier at their last General Convention, "they did not pray for any peace but such as would restore the national authority, concord, and peace throughout the land." This had come, and they were assembled to give thanks for it. McIlvaine also noted the "deliverance of the land from involuntary servitude" and added: "We must thank God for this. But great blessings bring great responsibilities. These four millions of freedmen call for our help and support. We must never forget our duty to them for their sorrows of the past. Do not forget the Freedman's Aid Society of our Church. Aid them tonight in the collection."[41] After the two delegates, Mr. Binney and Dr. Vinton, who had led the move in the House of Deputies for a stronger resolution had spoken, Bishop Burgess addressed the congregation. He concluded by expressing his fear that freedmen would be "perpetually treated" as freedmen and called for freedmen to be recognized on the "same level as those who were once their masters."[42]

The thanksgiving service arrangements caused a split among the Northern bishops and among the Northern deputies. In the House of Bishops, McIlvaine led those who wanted to thank God for the victory in the two great causes for which the North had fought—restoration of the Union and abolition of slavery—and in the eyes of McIlvaine and his supporters, these were Christian causes, not just Union objectives. They were also concerned about how the church would be perceived if a watered-down version of thanks was offered. The majority of the bishops no doubt favored a stronger wording for the service, but they valued unity in the church highly, and they felt that the chance for almost immediate reunion could slip away for the sake of the wording in a service. Everyone was thankful for peace—and the preservation of the Union and the demise of slavery had been achieved. Why, they reasoned, risk alienation over a religious service at the convention?

### Pastoral Letter Redux

On motion of Bishop Whittingham, the preparation of the pastoral letter was assigned to a committee made up of the five senior bishops. Remembering his experience in 1862, Bishop Hopkins, now the presiding bishop, indicated that he did not want anything to do with the pastoral letter unless it was committed to his charge. McIlvaine, however, was ready with a draft of a letter that was approved for reading to the House of Bishops. It included a eulogy for Lincoln and the paragraph below.

> Blessed be God—our prayers and those of Christian brethren in other communions, were not in vain. God has not dealt with us after our sins. His compassions have not failed. War has ceased. Precious peace has come. The National Union is preserved. The authority of the National Government is universally restored. Bitterness and anger are wonderfully passing away. That great source of dissension and evil feeling, involuntary servitude, is considered on all hands as having found its end. The means of education and improvement are being extended among those who have been delivered from that yoke of bondage.[43]

After the letter was read to the house, Whittingham moved that the letter not be the pastoral letter, and the motion passed.[44] In discussions off the floor a number of bishops agreed that there should be no pastoral letter. Horatio Potter was chosen to make the appropriate motion. He did so, but, upon learning that Hopkins wished to read a draft, yielded the floor. Hopkins's draft included a tribute to Alonzo Potter, Horatio Potter's brother. It apparently was eloquent and especially moving in view of the bitter dispute in which Alonzo Potter had engaged with Bishop Hopkins. Kemper moved that the Hopkins letter be accepted as the pastoral letter, but the other bishops were already committed, and there was no second. The resolution not to have a pastoral letter was adopted.[45]

### Mission Accomplished

The Southern bishops were pleased with the convention outcomes, and, near the end of the meeting—on Friday, 20 October—Bishops Atkinson and Lay sent a letter "to our brethren in the Southern dioceses." The new bishop of Tennessee,

Charles Todd Quintard, appended an endorsement saying that "in all the statements and conclusions of the Bishops of North Carolina and the Southwest, I most heartily concur." The letter was sent to the Southern bishops and to clerical and lay leaders in the South and was released to church papers when the convention adjourned.[46] The letter opened with a rationale for their attendance in Philadelphia, followed by general comments on their interaction with other bishops.

> In resuming our seats in the General Convention of the Church in the United States, we have taken a step in advance of those with whom we have been for some years associated. We are aware that we ventured much: but we were prepared to venture much in order to secure the reunion of the church, and to obviate the evils which were likely to grow up in the absence of frank and personal conference. . . .
>
> We demanded no formal guarantees: the assembled Bishops offered us no pledge save that of "their honor and their love.". . . they welcomed us with cordial greeting.[47]

The letter included a one-page summary of convention "results," including those on the matters of Bishop Lay and the status of the church in Arkansas, the Wilmer affair, the consecration of Bishop Quintard, and the official service of thanksgiving. "In celebrating a thanksgiving," the summary said, "the convention abstained from disputed topics, and confined its expression of gratitude to the mercies which we recognize in common, viz., peace in the country and unity in the Church."[48]

Atkinson and Lay also noted that their advice was solicited and "Episcopal authority duly respected" when the convention developed a system for instruction of the freedmen. The instruction system to which Atkinson and Lay referred was to be administered by the Protestant Episcopal Freedmen's Commission, an entity established by the convention within the Board of Missions. The new commission gave the Episcopal Church a vehicle to provide secular and religious instruction for the former slaves.[49] The bishops and other convention participants, Atkinson and Lay continued, "have in no wise denied or concealed their sentiments on the questions political and social brought by the war to a practical solution," but no agreement or even expression of opinion was required of the Southern bishops on those topics. Atkinson and Lay stated their conviction that the convention outcomes were "the doing, not of man but of God." Further, they noted, "we see nothing now to hinder the renewal of the relations formerly existing in the church."[50]

## Closing Services

The now three Southern bishops at the convention and the majority of Northern bishops present were greatly pleased with what had been accomplished. The joy of some Northern prelates, though, was marred. In the House of Clerical and Lay Deputies, a closing resolution gave the appearance of restored harmony: "Resolved, unanimously, That this House recognizes the singular unanimity of all its deliberations and actions; the absence of all spirit of discord; that, with one heart and one voice, we, the clergy and laity, offer thanks and praise to the Great Head of the Church for this manifestation of his presence and love. 'Not unto us, O Lord, not unto us, but unto thy name be the praise.'"[51] Following passage of this resolution, the bishops joined the deputies, Evening Prayer was read, and the presiding bishop pronounced the Blessing of Peace. Members of the House of Bishops returned to their room, and both houses adjourned *sine die.*

### An Uneasy Parting

There was no resolution or prayer of unity in the House of Bishops before or after the closing service. Although all the Northern bishops were no doubt pleased that church reunification now seemed a certainty, the lingering ill feelings caused by the sharp disagreements over the special service of thanksgiving and the pastoral letter were captured in this editorial published in the *Episcopal Recorder*: "On the breaking up of the session of the House of Bishops, one of them angrily refused to shake hands in parting with another. It was found impossible for the House of Bishops to agree upon a Pastoral Letter. For the first time, a portion of the House of Bishops have considered that the action of the Convention so compromised the Church, and committed it to principles utterly at variance with all its past history, that they felt constrained to issue a solemn document of dissent!"[52]

### A Statement of Dissent

Church unity, an outcome that all Northern bishops had hoped for, had been achieved, but for some the price of that outcome had been too high. The seven bishops who dissented from the majority on the rubrics for the thanksgiving service read a statement near the end of the convention and then made it public. The *Episcopal Recorder* published the statement, with the introduction that it would "go far to relieve the Church of the obloquy to which it has been subjected by its refusal to return thanks for the restoration of the National authority and the destruction of slavery." The statement is reproduced below.

> In the decisions of the House of Bishops with reference to the Day of Thanksgiving for the restoration of peace and to other important subjects, the ground has been taken, that, for the sake of more complete conciliation, no sentiment should be expressed by this House, or this convention, or this Church, in any collective capacity, on subjects of such importance and so dear to all of us as the re-establishment of the National union and the emancipation of the slaves.

The House of Bishops unquestionably loved its Country and its unity, and they could not approve the system of human bondage; but they will seem to have adopted as the position henceforth occupied by this Church, one which is consistent with indifference to the safety and unity of the Nation, and to the freedom of the oppressed.

This is a position which, as the undersigned believe, should not be maintained by any branch of the Christian Church in the United States, whether in the present or any future generation. To signify that it was not accepted by all on this occasion, and that those who did not accept it believed it to have been accepted at all, only because an extreme desire for conciliation and unanimity prevailed for the hour, the undersigned have prepared this document, with perfect and cordial respect for their brethren, but under the consciousness of a great duty to the inseparable interests of their beloved Church and Country.

Philadelphia, October 24, 1865

| | |
|---|---|
| Charles P. McIlvaine | Bishop of the Diocese of Ohio |
| Alfred Lee | Delaware |
| Manton Eastburn | Massachusetts |
| George Burgess | Maine |
| Henry W. Lee | Iowa |
| Gregory T. Bedell | Asst. Bishop Ohio |
| Thomas H. Vail | Kansas[53] |

## Notes

1. Henry C. Lay, "The Return of the Southern Bishops to the General Convention of 1865: A Sketch, with Sundry Letters and Documents," *Churchman* 47 (21 April 1883): 422–23.

2. Lay's wife was the daughter of Atkinson's brother, and the two men had enjoyed a close relationship for many years.

3. Lay, "Return of the Southern Bishops," 423..

4. Henry C. Lay, continued, "The Return of the Southern Bishops to the General Convention of 1865: A Sketch, with Sundry Letters and Documents," *Churchman* 47 (5 May 1883): 478–79.

5. Ibid., 478–79.

6. Ibid., 479.

7. *Diocese of North Carolina, 1865* (Raleigh: J. C. Gorman, 1865), 31. The resolution empowering Atkinson to attend the 1865 convention is discussed above in "Thomas Atkinson of North Carolina: Wartime Episcopate."

8. Henry C. Lay, "Private Journal, 1864–1865," Henry C. Lay Papers, Southern Historical Collection, University of North Carolina at Chapel Hill Library, entries for 2 and 5 October 1865.

9. *Diocese of Texas, 1865* (Houston: E. H. Cushing, 1865), 9–10, and *Church Intelligencer* 6, no. 2 (25 January 1866). The *Church Intelligencer* was published in Raleigh, N.C. After the war, it published letters by bishops relating to church issues, especialy reunion with the Northern Church.

10. *Episcopal Recorder* 43, no. 6 (6 May 1865): 44.

11. Ibid.

12. Ibid.

13. Ibid. In J. H. Hopkins, Jr.'s book *Life of the Late Right. Reverend John Henry Hopkins, First Bishop of Vermont and Seventh Presiding Bishop by One of His Sons* (New York: F. J. Huntington, 1873), 345, it is reported that an editorial in the *Episcopal Recorder* demanded that some leading bishops and clergy be hanged; the same report may be found in Joseph Blount Cheshire's *History of the Church in the Confederate States* (New York: Longmans, Green, 1912), 210. Although the *Episcopal Recorder* editorial certainly excoriates the bishops and clergy in the Confederate States, there is no explicit demand for them to be hanged.

14. *Episcopal Recorder,* 43, no. 7 (13 May 1865): 50.

15. J. H. Hopkins, Jr., *Life of John Henry Hopkins,* 345.

16. Alfred Lee to Charles P. McIlvaine, 29 June 1865, "Letters of the Northern Bishops of the Protestant Episcopal Church on Reunion with the Bishops of the South after the Civil War," Kenyon College Archives.

17. Ibid.

18. "Letters of the Northern Bishops of the Protestant Episcopal Church on Reunion with the Bishops of the South after the Civil War," Kenyon College Archives. This packet of eight letters, some addressed to McIlvaine, some to Hopkins, reveals the reluctance of several Northern bishops to sign a blanket letter of welcome as proposed by Hopkins. William Rollinson Whittingham of Maryland did write to Hopkins that he would support Hopkins's sending a letter on his own.

19. J. H. Hopkins, Jr., *Life of John Henry Hopkins,* 345.

20. *Episcopal Recorder* 43, no. 28 (7 October 1865): 221.

21. Henry Lay, "Private Journal 1864–1865," entry for 5 October 1865.

22. *Episcopal Recorder* 43, no. 22 (28 August 1865): 169.

23. *Journal of the General Convention, 1865* (Boston: William A. Hall, 1865), 195.

24. In May 1866 Lay was nominated by the clergy as bishop of Louisiana, but the laity failed to confirm his selection. Resentment over his action at the 1865 convention may have been a factor. See *Diocese of Louisiana, 1866* (New Orleans: Isaac T. Hinton, 1866), 37. In 1869, when Lay was elected bishop of Easton, two bishops, Johns of Virginia and Wilmer of Alabama, refused consent on the grounds that canonically Lay was still bishop of Arkansas. Under the canons, a missionary bishop could be elected to and assume a diocesan bishopric; there was no provision for a diocesan bishop to move to become bishop of another diocese. A majority of bishops consented to Lay's appointment, however, and he was translated to be bishop of Easton. See *Diocese of Virginia, 1870* (Richmond: Clemett and Jones, 1870), 23–26, and *Diocese of Alabama, 1870* (Mobile: Henry Farrow, 1870), 37.

25. *Episcopal Recorder* 43, no. 22 (26 August 1865): 169.

26. *Journal of the General Convention, 1865,* 45.

27. Ibid., 45, 47, 53, 57, 166–67.

28. Ibid., 157.

29. Ibid., 217. The author was unable to locate a record of such a visit.

30. See below, "Confrontation in Alabama: The Bishop and the General, Redux."

31. *Philadelphia Inquirer*, 12 October 1865, 2.

32. Charles Todd Quintard, *Doctor Quintard, Chaplain C.S.A. and Second Bishop of Tennessee: The Memoir and Civil War Diary of Charles Todd Quintard,* ed. Sam Davis Elliott (Baton Rouge: Louisiana State University Press, 2003), 131. The consecration service was held on Wednesday morning, 11 October, at St. Luke's Church in Philadelphia, and a detailed account appeared in the *Philadelphia Inquirer*, Thursday, 12 October 1865, 1–2.

33. *Philadelphia Inquirer*, 12 October 1865, 2.

34. *Journal of the General Convention, 1865.* The record of proceedings regarding the Day of Thanksgiving is based upon this journal. The off-floor maneuvering descriptions reflect material in Henry C. Lay's "Private Journal, 1864–1865."

35. Henry C. Lay, *Sermon Delivered 18 May 1881 in Christ Church, Raleigh, at the Diocesan Convention of North Carolina, Commemorating the Late Thomas Atkinson, D.D., LL.D., Bishop of North Carolina* (New York: James Pott, 1881), 35–39.

36. *Journal of the General Convention, 1865,* 165.

37. Ibid., 168–69.

38. Ibid., 176.

39. Ibid.

40. William Stevens Perry, "The Reunion of the North and South," in *The History of the American Episcopal Church, 1587–1883* (Boston: Osgood, 1885), 2:344.

41. *Philadelphia Inquirer*, 18 October 1865, 1.

42. Ibid.

43. *Episcopal Recorder* 43, no. 36 (2 December 1865): 284.

44. McIlvaine's draft also included a section on "rationalism" which he saw as a disturbing trend, but this was not the issue that led to the rejection of the letter by his fellow bishops. McIlvaine was asked, in fact, to prepare a paper on that topic for circulation to clergy and theological students.

45. This discussion reflects the actions in the House of Bishops at the General Convention of 1865, as reported in the *Journal of the General Convention, 1865,* and the commentary on those actions by J. H. Hopkins, Jr., in his *Life of John Henry Hopkins.*

46. Cheshire, Joseph Blount. *The Church in the Confederate States* (New York: Longmans, Green, 1912). The letter is reproduced on pages 253–56.

47. Ibid., 253.

48. Ibid., 254.

49. *Journal of the General Convention, 1865,* 87, 188. See the next essay, "The Freedmen's Commission," for a discussion of the work of this body authorized by the 1865 General Convention.

50. Cheshire, *Church in the Confederate States,* 255.

51. *Journal of the General Convention, 1865,* 143.

52. *Episcopal Recorder* 43, no. 32 (4 November 1865): 252

53. *Episcopal Recorder* 43, no. 31 (28 October 1865): 245.

# Closure with Dignity

**Augusta, Georgia: November 1865**

> The states, which from 1861–1865, were confederate as a political government, and which included the dioceses that connected themselves together and formed the Protestant Episcopal Church in the Confederate States of America . . . will become, once more, integral parts of the United States.
>
> This condition of things, brought about by the providence of God, removes any political or canonical hindrance to our reunion with the Protestant Episcopal Church in the United States.
>
> Stephen Elliott, May 1865[1]

On 8 November 1865 a remnant of four bishops, twelve clerical deputies, and four lay deputies gathered for Morning Prayer and celebration of the Eucharist at St. Paul's Church in Augusta, Georgia. After services, they divided themselves into the House of Bishops and the House of Clerical and Lay Deputies and proceeded to arrange for the proper demise of the Protestant Episcopal Church in the Confederate States.

By the time this second triennial council convened, the Confederate states no longer existed as a governmental entity, and there were only six dioceses associated with the Confederate council. The Dioceses of North Carolina and Texas, without waiting for action by their governing council, had reaffiliated with the Episcopal Church in the United States; the dioceses of Tennessee and Louisiana had never formally joined the Confederate church; and Arkansas had ceased to exist as a diocese. Church buildings had been destroyed or damaged across the South. Many congregations had no minister, and many congregations were scattered, disorganized, and in extreme financial distress.

The attendance roster for the member dioceses was as follows:

**Attendance at the General Council of the Protestant Episcopal Church in the former Confederate States, Augusta, Georgia, 1865**

| Diocese | Bishop present | Clerical deputies | Lay deputies |
|---|---|---|---|
| Georgia | Yes–Stephen Elliott | Yes–3 | Yes–1 |
| Virginia | Yes–John Johns | Yes–3 | Yes–3 |
| Mississippi | Yes–William Mercer Green | Yes–1 | No |
| Alabama | Yes–Richard Hooker Wilmer | Yes–3 | Yes–1 |
| South Carolina | No | Yes–2 | Yes–1* |
| Florida | No | No | No |

Source: *Journals of the Protestant Episcopal Church in the Confederate States of America, Facsimile Edition,* ed. William A. Clebsch, IV-7, IV-10, and IV-28.

*The lay deputy arrived on the second day.

## Church Organization

After housekeeping preliminaries, the two houses each addressed the primary issue of the future of the council and the Episcopal Church in the dioceses comprising it. A lengthy resolution was offered by a joint committee, which, after much discussion and several amendments was adopted by both houses. The committee report began by noting that the dioceses assembled had been impelled by political events to form a separate legislative body and had done so in accord with "Holy Scripture and Primitive Antiquity." That body, as a branch of the One Catholic and Apostolic Church, had the right to continue, or its constituent dioceses could form any other "Synodical association." The key sections of the "Preamble and Resolutions" finally adopted are given below:

> *Whereas,* In the opinion of several of the Dioceses which co-operated in the formation of this independent branch of the Church Catholic, the exigency which caused its arrangement no longer exists; and
>
> *Whereas,* The spirit of charity which prevailed in the proceedings of the General Convention of the Protestant Episcopal Church in the United States, at its late session in Philadelphia, has warmly commended itself to the hearts of this Council; therefore,
>
> *Resolved,* I. That, in the judgment of this Council, it is perfectly consistent with the good faith which she owes to the Bishops and Dioceses with which she has been in union since 1862, for any Diocese to decide for herself whether she shall any longer continue in union with this Council.[2]

Other resolutions in the motion that was adopted included (1) a provision to replace *Confederate* with *United* in all church documents and (2) rubrics through which a diocese could withdraw from the council simply by giving formal noti-fication to the dioceses remaining in the council.[3] The heart of this report was in the two excerpted *Whereas* statements, from which flows not only the option to choose provided in the first *Resolved*, but also a clear recommendation of what choice to make. The second of the *Whereas* statements reflects the postconven-tion report sent from Philadelphia by Bishops Atkinson and Lay.

Later in the meeting, a resolution initiated in the House of Deputies and to which the House of Bishops concurred changed the name of the church, speci-fied in Article I of the constitution from Protestant Episcopal Church in the Confederate States to Protestant Episcopal Church of Associated Dioceses in the United States.[4]

### Protest against Military Intrusion into Worship Services

The second major item on the council agenda was the issue of military intrusion into divine worship services in the Diocese of Alabama. This matter had been at impasse since the Episcopal churches in that state had been closed since Septem-ber by order of Major General George H. Thomas. The report of a joint com-mittee appointed to draft a resolution to protest that order was considered and adopted by both houses. Stephen Elliott and William Mercer Green represented the House of Bishops on the committee, but they no doubt consulted with Richard Hooker Wilmer before helping to formulate the committee recommendations.[5]

The committee report began with two *Whereas* clauses, the first of which stipulated that Bishop Wilmer had been consecrated by the Protestant Episcopal Church in the Confederate States of America (PECCSA) and had never been a bishop in the Protestant Episcopal Church in the United States (PECUSA). That church had recently declared that he would not be a bishop therein unless and until he had made a "promise of conformity" to its constitution and canons. The second clause stated that he was therefore under no ecclesiastical obligation to use the prayer in the PECUSA prayer book for the "President of the United States, and all in Civil Authority." The report continued:

> Whereas, The independence of the Church, in matters purely spiritual, is held to be of Divine Authority, and has been the doctrine of the Church since the foundation of Christianity, and is at this day universally conceded by the pow-ers of this world, wherever the Church has been true to itself; therefore,
>
> We, the members of this Council, do, in our own behalf, and in behalf of the Christian Church throughout the world, solemnly protest against the Order issued September 20th, 1865, from the Headquarters of the Department of Alabama, that the Bishop and Clergy of that Diocese "be suspended from their functions, and forbidden to preach or perform Divine Service, and that their places of worship be closed."[6]

## Final Actions of the PECCSA Council

There were other items of business. The site of the 1868 triennial meeting was designated as Charleston, South Carolina. A joint resolution lamenting the deaths of Bishops Otey and Polk and praising both for their contributions to the church was adopted. Noting that the major resolution of the present council had provided for each individual diocese to determine its relation to the council, the members of the House of Bishops resolved that it was "inexpedient to enter upon any questions, which, in their bearings, may be legislative, until such time as the dioceses shall have determined those relations." The deputies disagreed, and a conference committee on the matter was constituted, but no report from that committee came back to the floor.

On Friday, 10 November, the third and final day of the council, both houses held evening sessions. When the House of Deputies had completed its business, "the Secretary was requested to inform the House of Bishops that the House of Deputies is now ready to adjourn, *sine die.*" The House of Bishops immediately communicated to the lower house that its members would unite with the deputies for closing devotional services. The bishops were escorted to their places in the chancel, and after they were seated, the presiding bishop made a few "exceedingly appropriate" remarks before the assembly, read closing prayers, and pronounced the Apostolic Benediction.[7] When the bishops had retired, the House of Deputies adjourned. The House of Bishops returned to the Lecture Room of St. Paul's Church, where the minutes of the day were read and approved. The last act of the Protestant Episcopal Church in the Confederate States occurred when the House of Bishops adjourned, *sine die.*

## Convention Aftermath

The action to change the name of PECCSA and choose a site for a future meeting aroused considerable ire in the North. Bishop McIlvaine expressed his anger over the matter in a letter to Bishop Whittingham,[8] and the *Episcopal Recorder* in its 25 November issue aimed a two-pronged diatribe entitled "The Protestant Episcopal Church of the Associated Dioceses of the United States" at (1) the "Associated Dioceses" and (2) the actions taken by the October General Convention in Philadelphia. The *Recorder* editors felt that the welcome extended to the two bishops and the Southern delegates who attended the Philadelphia convention was so enthusiastic as to be "a little excessive and absurd" and that concessions had been made by the Northern bishops and deputies at the expense of a "loss of dignity and self-restraint." The litany of concessions listed by the *Recorder* included the following: (1) acceptance of Wilmer's consecration and arranging for his admittance as a PECUSA bishop; (2) rescinding a resolution for a day of thanksgiving to God for the restoration of the national authority over the

The Right Reverend William Mercer Green, D.D.

country; (3) rejection of a pastoral letter by Bishop McIlvaine because the letter included praise for President Lincoln and thanks to God for both restoration of the national authority and the destruction of slavery. These concessions had been made in order to achieve reunion of the church, but now the Southern dioceses had made a deliberate decision to "retain their separate organization."[9] The editorial concluded:

> Through the unwise haste for external reunion . . . we have divided the South . . . and put it into a position from which there is reason to fear that a real schism will ensue.
>
> . . . Long—long will it be before the Church will recover from the inner evils and the outer obloquy to which the proceedings of this convention have exposed us![10]

In spite of the name change there is no evidence that, upon their return to their home dioceses, any of the bishops planned to urge that their diocese remain separate from PECUSA. Elliott and Johns had declared their intentions to seek reunification before the meeting, and any bishop who may have preferred a separate organization faced administrative separation not only from his Northern brethren but also from nearly all of his Southern colleagues. This latter point was clear to the two bishops who had earlier announced for continued separation: William Mercer Green, who was present in Augusta, and Thomas Frederick Davis, who was not. What was at issue was merely having an appropriately named organization for the time required for action at the diocesan level.

The *Episcopal Recorder* editorial therefore reflected an incorrect interpretation of the action to change the name of the Southern church. Bishop Whittingham reassured his Ohio colleague on this point, and predicted correctly that reunion soon would occur.[11]

Before PECCSA met in November, Bishop Elliott at his 1865 diocesan council, which had assembled in both May and August, had arranged for reunion between the Diocese of Georgia and PECUSA.[12] At that first postwar meeting of the diocese, Elliott advised the delegates that he saw no reason why reaffiliation with PECUSA could not occur as soon as civil government was restored in Georgia. As he stressed in communicating with Bishops Atkinson, Lay, and Gregg, however, Elliott felt strongly that the Diocese of Georgia should act only in concert with other dioceses of the Confederate church. In Elliott's judgment, therefore, it would be best for the two conventions, of PECUSA and PECCSA, to meet separately, in October and November respectively, so that the PECUSA delegates could work out any issues alone—and the PECCSA churchmen would not have to endure what could be painful discussion at the meeting of their Northern brethren. The delegates at the diocesan meeting in August passed resolutions in exact accord with their bishop's wishes, authorizing reunion and leaving it to him to decide the timetable.[13]

In January 1866, in accord with the PECCSA resolutions of November 1865 and the views of Atkinson and Lay after attendance at the PECUSA convention, Elliott notified Presiding Bishop John Henry Hopkins of the Diocese of Georgia's action to authorize reunion with PECUSA. The five other dioceses remaining in union with the Associated Dioceses followed Georgia's lead and reunited with PECUSA within the next seven months. The reunion dates by diocese are shown below.

| Diocese | Date rejoined PECUSA |
|---|---|
| Georgia | 3 January 1866 |
| Alabama | 17 January 1866 |
| South Carolina | 16 February 1866 |
| Florida | 22 February 1866 |
| Mississippi | 9 May 1866 |
| Virginia | 16 May 1866 |

*Source:* Joseph Blount Cheshire, *The Church in the Confederate States* (New York: Longmans, Green, 1912), 252.

The Diocese of Arkansas was reborn in 1871 and became a part of PECUSA.[14] The resolution of the crisis over the Prayer for the President and all in Civil Authority will be described in the next essay.

## Notes

1. From an address by Stephen Elliott, in *Diocese of Georgia, 1865* (Savannah: Purse and Sons, 1865), 28.

2. "Journal of the Proceedings of General Council of the Protestant Episcopal Church in the (late) Confederate States of America, 1865," in *Journals of the Protestant Episcopal Church in the Confederate States of America, Facsimile Edition*, edited by William A. Clebsch (Austin: Church Historical Society, 1962), 32–33.

3. Ibid.

4. Ibid., 38.

5. Ibid., 20.

6. Ibid., 35–36.

7. These remarks were delivered without notes, and the secretary of the House of Deputies was unable to secure a written version to enter in the journal.

8. Whittingham to McIlvaine, 25 November 1865, McIlvaine Personal Correspondence, Kenyon College Library.

9. *Episcopal Recorder* 43, no. 35 (November 25, 1865): 276.

10. Ibid.

11. Whittingham to McIlvaine, 25 November 1865, Archives, Kenyon College Library.

12. Edgar Legare Pennington, "Bishop Stephen Elliott and the Confederate Episcopal Church," *Georgia Review* 4 (Fall 1950): 243–46.

13. *Diocese of Georgia, 1865*, 38–39.

14. *Primary Convention of the Protestant Episcopal Church of the State of Arkansas for the Purpose of Organizing a Diocese* (Little Rock: The Gazette, 1873). The convention was held at Christ Church, Little Rock, 24 August 1871.

# Confrontation in Alabama

## ✛══ The Bishop and the General, Redux

As noted above in "What Price Reunion?," the Northern bishops at the October 1865 convention of the Protestant Episcopal Church in the United States proceeded to accept Richard Hooker Wilmer's consecration and to recognize him as bishop of the Diocese of Alabama. However, the bishops in convention did not support the Alabama bishop's position on the criteria for resumption of use of the Prayer for the President and all in Civil Authority. The bishops, in fact, communicated to Wilmer their "fraternal regrets" over his pastoral letter of 20 June 1865 and expressed confidence that they would have no further occasions for regret. Apparently the bishops felt that the distinction made between civil and military authority in Wilmer's June letter was "hair-splitting" that had precipitated an unnecessary crisis, especially given that no other Southern bishop had taken the position that Wilmer set forth.

Regardless of the Northern bishops views on Wilmer's judgment as expressed in his June pastoral letter, they were confronted with the facts that (1) a military officer had in September ordered the Episcopal bishop and clergy in Alabama not to conduct services in their churches, and Bishop Wilmer had been advised that the order would be upheld by armed force, if need be, and, further, (2) the same military officer had mandated use of a particular prayer from the church's liturgy as a condition for allowing public worship to resume. Nevertheless, the "solemn protest" that Wilmer had hoped for when he advised his Northern colleagues of the situation in Alabama did not occur; no resolution directly protesting General Order 38 was introduced in either house. Probably the bishops who understood the issue did not want to press it because it involved Wilmer. In any event the resolution that was adopted by the House of Bishops, stating the "desire" of the bishops that Bishop McIlvaine go, "if necessary," to Washington "to confer with his Excellency, the President of the United States in relation to suspension of clerical functions by military authority" was a tepid and inadequate response to a blatant intrusion of government into worship.[1] No record of a meeting between President Johnson and Bishop McIlvaine on this topic was located, but Bishops

Atkinson, Lay, and Quintard did attempt to see the president soon after the convention. They were unable to secure an audience with him, but did arrange for a document to be sent to President Johnson's attention.[2]

Then, in early November, with Wilmer present, the council for the Episcopal Church in what had been the Confederate States met. This body confronted the issue directly and adopted a strong resolution protesting the action of General George Henry Thomas in closing the Episcopal churches in Alabama.[3] Wilmer also appealed to Governor Lewis E. Parsons to have the military order lifted. Parsons had been appointed provisional governor of Alabama by President Andrew Johnson on 21 June 1865.[4] Wilmer outlined his case and asked the governor to consider the "larger principle" (presumably, the supremacy of the church in matters of faith, morals, and conduct of worship services), even though the governor might differ with Wilmer's decision to omit the prayer for the president. The bishop noted that he had "made no appeal to the military authorities because I could not consent to seem to acknowledge their right to make inquisition into things ecclesiastical." Besides, the "orders" were couched in terms so offensive as to preclude all discussions and explanations.[5] Governor Parsons answered "with courtesy," promising to transmit Wilmer's appeal and the accompanying documentation to President Johnson. Later the Governor wrote to say that the case had been "laid before the President" and that "there was no prospect of the order being rescinded."[6] Finally, on 27 November 1865, Bishop Wilmer wrote directly to the president:

> The undersigned trusts that he will not be regarded as transcending the limits of propriety in venturing to bring to the attention of the President the following considerations: that the constitution of the United States is supreme in all secular law; that it prohibits Congress from interfering with religious worship; and that no military power can properly do by orders what the supreme legislative power is prevented from doing.
>
> . . . For the high reason that the secular power has no authority in the Church of God, either in framing her creed, or in prescribing her worship, or in any way interfering with her functions, the undersigned, in behalf as aforesaid, makes his solemn protest to your Excellency against said "General Orders," acknowledges no authority in them, and claims in equity and constitutional law that they be rescinded.[7]

After several weeks the president gave an order that General Orders No. 38 should be rescinded by the same authority that issued it.[8] General Thomas obeyed by issuing General Orders No. 40 from his headquarters in Nashville. This long document was devoted almost entirely to harsh criticism of Bishop Wilmer, which began with the charge that the bishop immediately attempted to undermine the president's Proclamation on Amnesty and invitation to all "lately in rebellion" to reconstruct and restore civil authority. Wilmer therefore forgot his mission to preach peace and good will to all men and, Thomas said,

> issued, from behind the shield of his office, his manifesto of the 20th of June last to the clergy of the Episcopal Church of Alabama, directing them to omit the usual and customary prayer for the President of the United States and all others in authority, until the troops of the United States had been removed from the limits of Alabama; cunningly justifying this treasonable course, by plausibly presenting to the minds of the people that, civil authority not yet having been restored in Alabama, there was no occasion for the use of said prayer. . . .
>
> This man . . . thus took advantage of the sanctity of his position to mislead the minds of those who naturally regarded him as a teacher in whom they could trust, and attempted to lead them back into the labyrinths of treason.
>
> For this covert and cunning act he was deprived of the . . . right to officiate as a minister of the Gospel, because it was evident he could not be trusted to officiate and confine his teachings to matters of religion. . . .
>
> As it is, however, manifest that so far from entertaining the same political views as Bishop Wilmer the people of Alabama are honestly endeavoring to restore the civil authority in their State, . . . the restrictions heretofore imposed upon the Episcopal clergy of Alabama are removed, and Bishop Wilmer is left to that remorse of conscience consequent to the exposure and failure of the diabolical schemes of designing and corrupt minds.[9]

The order was issued by General Thomas on 22 December 1865 and promulgated in Mobile by Major General Charles Woods on 10 January 1866.

Although supportive of the initial action (General Orders No. 38) taken by the military against Wilmer, the language of General Orders No. 40 was too much even for the *Episcopal Recorder.* In an editorial in early 1866 the editors called the rescinding order "diffuse, illiterate, abusive, unsuited to the occasion, and unworthy of the authority in whose name it was issued."[10] A few days after General Orders No. 40 was published, Bishop Wilmer issued his last pastoral letter on the matter, pointing out that the "revocation of the military orders" now rendered it proper for him to direct clergy to use the prayer for the president of the United States as it stood in the Book of Common Prayer.[11]

At a special convention of the Diocese of Alabama held on 17 January, Bishop Wilmer gave a detailed report on the issue of the prayer for those in civil authority, including an explanation of his actions. Copies of his letters and those of the military authorities were included in the convention records. The convention delegates responded with two resolutions commending their bishop, the first of which was as follows: "Resolved That the firm, dignified, and Christian manner in which the independence and dignity of the church in this Diocese has been maintained by its Bishop, the Right Reverend Richard Hooker Wilmer, D.D., during the trying ordeal of the last year has elicited our admiration and deserves our cordial thanks."[12] At this same convention the Diocese of Alabama placed itself under the aegis of the Protestant Episcopal Church in the United States. Richard Hooker Wilmer then traveled to New York, where, on 31 January 1866, he signed in the presence of three bishops the "Promise of Conformity," completing thereby the documents required for him to be accepted as a bishop in the Protestant Episcopal Church in the United States.[13]

### Notes

1. See above, "What Price Reunion? The Philadelphia Convention, 4–24 October 1865." For an excerpt from the letter Wilmer wrote to three Northern bishops before the PECUSA General Convention, see "Confrontation in Alabama: The Bishop and the General."

2. Henry C. Lay, "Private Journal, 1864–1865," Southern Historical Collection, Univ. of North Carolina at Chapel Hill Library, entry for November 1865.

3. See above, the essay entitled "Closure with Dignity."

4. Parsons was appointed at the beginning of "Presidential Reconstruction" and served until 13 December 1865. He was succeeded by Robert Miller Patton, who had been elected in November. See Samuel L. Webb and Margaret E. Armbrester, *Alabama Governors* (Tuscaloosa: University of Alabama Press, 2001), 77–83.

5. *Diocese of Alabama: Proceedings of a Special Council, 17 January 1866* (Mobile: Farrow and Dennett, 1866), 8.

6. Ibid., 8.

7. A copy of Wilmer's letter to the president is included in *Diocese of Alabama: Proceedings of a Special Council*, 9.

8. Walter C. Whitaker, *Richard Hooker Wilmer: Second Bishop of Alabama* (Philadelphia: George W. Jacobs, 1907), 144.

9. "General Thomas' Last," *Mobile Advertiser and Register*, 10 January 1866, supplement, part 1.

10. *Episcopal Recorder*, 43, no. 42 (13 January 1866): 332..

11. Wilmer's pastoral letter of 13 January 1866 is included in *Diocese of Alabama: Proceedings of a Special Council*, 12.

12. *Diocese of Alabama: Proceedings of a Special Council*, 13.

13. John Williams, bishop of Connecticut, was one of the three bishops before whom Wilmer made his promise at Trinity Chapel in New York. Williams reported on the ceremony to his diocese in the *Diocese of Connecticut, 1866* (Hartford: Case, Lockwood, 1866), 29.

# The Freedman's Commission

The 1865 General Convention of the Protestant Episcopal Church in the United States considered the steps and issues involved in church reunification, intensely debated the focus of a special service of thanksgiving, and failed to achieve consensus on the content of a pastoral letter. One significant accomplishment of that convention was achieved without the rancorous debates that surrounded those issues. The convention established, within the Board of Missions, the Protestant Episcopal Freedman's Commission, an entity that lasted a dozen years and had a positive impact on thousands of recently freed people. The bishops, North and South, were involved in the creation and funding of the commission and bore considerable responsibility for its successes and struggles during its brief lifetime.

### Birth, Organization, and Initial Projects of the Freedman's Commission

Emancipation created challenges for the Episcopal Church.[1] All dioceses in slave-holding states had programs in place to provide religious instruction and worship opportunities for slaves, but the destruction of war and the advent of emancipation had disrupted these efforts. Programs of evangelism and religious instruction patterns needed to be launched in the South to retain and attract free black people to the Episcopal Church. At the same time the economic problems confronting the freed people could not be ignored by the church; in some areas the need for adequate food, clothes, and shelter was desperate. Finally, there was an urgent need for basic education among both children and adults if the freed people were to take their places as citizens and were to participate effectively in the church. The figure varied from place to place and usually was different for former field slaves and former house slaves, but generally there was a 5 to 10 percent literacy rate among freedmen.[2]

Both the House of Bishops and the House of Clerical and Lay Deputies recognized these challenges for the church. Responsibility for initiating church action on behalf of the freedmen rested with the Board of Missions, and on the evening of 5 October, the second day of convention, a committee was appointed by that board to study the matter. The seven-member committee appointed by the board included two Southerners, Bishop Thomas Atkinson of North Carolina and Bishop-elect Charles Todd Quintard of Tennessee.[3] This committee recommended on 13 October that the constitution of the board be altered to provide for a special commission, named the Protestant Episcopal Freedman's Commission, to be established within the board to facilitate and coordinate the response of the Episcopal Church to the needs of the recently freed slaves.[4]

The Reverend Dr. Francis Wharton of Brookline, Massachusetts, presented the committee recommendation to the Board of Missions and included the remarks below in his preamble:

> The condition of the Freedmen, to which the attention of the Committee has been directed, is such as to demand the anxious care of the whole Church. Docile, amiable, and peculiarly susceptible to religious influence, they are now exposed, not only to those personal and social disasters which may result from their being thrown, without sufficient moral preparation, on their own resources, but to the still greater calamity of the withdrawal of the saving principles of the gospel of Christ. The religious associations by which they were formerly surrounded have been broken up. Not only are they in a large measure detached from their old homes, but, in the general disintegration of their particular society, religion has either ceased to be heard by them at all, or is heard in utterances the most fantastic and demoralizing. Religion, in its best sense, is needed to rescue them from the peril which their final debasement or extinction would produce; and yet, among themselves, religious institutions in almost any stable and orthodox sense have ceased to exist. The question, then, is how is this vital need to be supplied.[5]

Wharton went on to argue that meeting this need was not the responsibility of Southern churchmen alone and that the South, in fact, did not have the resources to undertake so massive a task. This was a matter for the entire church.[6] The actual resolution provided for a Freedman's Commission to whom "shall be committed the religious and other instruction of the freedmen." The Board of Missions accepted the committee recommendation, and both houses of the General Convention approved.[7]

The original Freedman's Commission appointed by the board did not include a Southerner among the bishops who served. Members were John Williams of Connecticut, William H. Odenheimer of New Jersey, Horatio Potter of New York, and William Bacon Stevens of Pennsylvania.[8] Bishop Henry C. Lay of the Southwest did become a member later, and both Atkinson and Quintard offered advice and support, but given the facts that only two bishops from the South attended the 1865 convention and that most Southern dioceses would not officially reunite with the church in the United States for some months, it was inevitable that the

Freedman's Commission would begin under Northern leadership with operational plans formulated at the North.[9] Funding also came from Northern dioceses, for the organizational reasons just given and because the Southern dioceses were in disarray and impoverishment from the war. The aims of the commission soon were assisted by state auxiliary societies, especially in Pennsylvania and New York. Formation of these societies was encouraged by the commission.[10]

After the convention and during the remainder of 1865, commission secretary Francis Wharton addressed many church groups to explain the purpose of the commission and to solicit financial support. Bishop Horatio Potter of New York, who chaired the commission, also held meetings with the same objectives, and appeals were issued through newspapers. Bishops of Southern dioceses were contacted to ask for their help in determining where assistance was most needed.

Wharton took the position in his addresses that action to educate the freedmen and to equip them for economic productivity and citizenship was essential not only for their well-being but also for the welfare of the nation as a whole. He stated unequivocally that the freed people were capable of being educated and that the institution of slavery had repressed that capability: "We cannot look at the schools where the children of both races are respectively taught, without seeing that the Negro child, so far as concerns the reception of the primary branches of education, is not behind those of our own color, whose home advantages have been as slight.[11]

On 5 December 1865 Bishop Potter presided at a meeting in Calvary Church, Manhattan, to gain support for the Freedman's Commission. One speaker noted that God had ordained lifting the bondage of four million slaves but that emancipation was only the first step. It was now necessary to raise them to the "high level of American citizenship"; freedmen must be changed to freemen. Other speakers called for immediate aid to alleviate pressing physical needs of the freedmen. The final speaker was Bishop Lay, who endorsed providing help "at once" for food and clothing as well as funds for educating the former slaves. Lay, however, cautioned discretion in providing relief, lest the recipients lose incentive to learn to support themselves. He also thought that it would be unwise to attempt to provide a "university course" for all freedmen.[12]

On 10 December an advertisement placed by the Executive Committee of the commission appeared in the *New York Times*. The notice included an urgent appeal to both clergy and laymen for clothing and money, calling on parishes to organize to solicit support for freedmen whose suffering would increase as winter descended. Plans to open schools for that population also were noted.[13]

## The Early Months of the Commission

In December 1865 the Executive Committee of the Freedman's Commission proceeded to authorize the first educational projects under its charge to provide "religious and other instruction of the Freedmen." One school was opened in Richmond, Virginia, where the Reverend T. B. Dashiell, who served as rector for a black congregation, offered to house a school in his church building. Another school was established in New Bern, North Carolina, upon the recommendation of Bishop Atkinson. Two teachers were sent by the commission to each location, and a fifth teacher was sent shortly to Petersburg. A minister, the Reverend M. E. Willing, was sent to Norfolk to explore the possibility of opening a school or schools in that city. A decision also was made to send a donation to the Memphis, Tennessee, Colored Orphans Asylum.[14]

By the time of the commission's March 1866 report, a school in Petersburg and a school in Norfolk were operational. The number of pupils attending at each site was reported as follows:[15]

| | |
|---|---|
| Richmond | 105 |
| New Bern | 105 |
| Petersburg | 107 |
| Norfolk | 116 |

The character and qualifications of the teachers sent out by the commission were praised highly in this report, and the feeling was expressed that the ladies concerned would have success not only in their instructional duties but also in disarming prejudice in the communities in which they served.[16]

## Other Freedmen's Aid Societies

In beginning to assist with education of the freedmen, the Episcopal Church became part of an effort already in progress. There were benevolent societies in the North that had begun this work during the war. In 1861, Union forces began to occupy parts of the Southern coast to facilitate a blockade. In November of that year the takeover in South Carolina of Port Royal and several nearby sea islands resulted in an exodus of the white population from those coastal islands. About 8,000 slaves were left behind. Abandoned by their owners, long before the Emancipation Proclamation, the slaves were considered "contrabands." Plantation superintendents were appointed by the Union military to keep the farmlands productive and the slaves busy. Teachers sponsored by benevolent organizations in the North were permitted to come to the islands to set up schools to teach adults as well as children reading, writing, and other basic subjects.[17]

By the end of the Civil War, branches of freedmen's aid societies in New England, New York, and Pennsylvania had established 216 schools, sent 455 teachers to staff those schools, and served 28,744 pupils, at a cost of $210,000.[18] From the beginning of the Civil War until 1872, several thousand teachers, mostly women known as Yankee schoolmarms, came to the South to teach the freed people. About fifty benevolent organizations in the North sponsored the teachers. The

average number of teachers per year, approximately 50, sponsored by the Episcopal Church's Freedmen's Commission when in full operation was only a small
fraction of the annual total.[19] The Freedman's Commission cooperated with the
Freedmen's Bureau of the United States directed by General O. O. Howard, who
on occasion was able to arrange for use of a building or to provide construction
funds.[20]

## Initial Objectives of the Commission

As we have noted, the Freedman's Commission began by opening three schools
in Virginia and one in North Carolina. Before responding to a request by Bishop
Atkinson of North Carolina to staff additional schools in Raleigh and Wilmington and to several other requests to open schools, the Executive Committee
paused to formulate the following operational principles based upon the charge
to the commission.

1. That the special object of the Commission was the proper instruction of the
   Freedmen, old and young, in useful elementary knowledge, religious and secular.
2. That in the establishment of schools, it should be done upon consultation
   with the Rector of the Parish, where there was one.
3. That the teachers should be of sound principles and approved character.
4. That the provision for the relief of the physical wants of the Freedmen should
   be subsidiary to the work of education, and that relief should be so judiciously
   distributed by competent agents, consulting with the clergy where practicable,
   and in such manner as to avoid as far as possible the evils of indiscriminate
   and unnecessary alms-giving.[21]

The committee also came to a "definite and decided conclusion" on two needs
that the commission would *not* address, to wit: (1) The commission would not
send out missionaries. This vital work was the province of the Domestic Committee of the Missions Board. Clergymen were eligible for commission appoint-
ments as school teachers or administrators. (2) The commission would not
provide schoolhouses.[22]

With some experience and a set of guidelines in place, the Freedmen's Commission was ready to expand its assistance to former slaves. That assistance would
take the form of education in a Christian setting, but would concentrate on secular education, with an initial focus on reading, writing, and basic math skills.
Commission activity proceeded to expand rapidly between the adoption of these
working guidelines reported in March 1866 and the late spring of 1868, when a
fiscal crisis occurred. The attitude of the various Southern bishops toward the
Freedman's Commission and their involvement in its work during its first two
years determined in which states the commission concentrated its initial efforts.

## Response of Southern Bishops

The responses by bishops in Northern dioceses to the Freedman's Commission were strong and positive, but the initial reception in the South was mixed. Bishop Elliott of Georgia urged the people of his diocese to accept the results of the Civil War and to move forward, but his own feelings about the war and abolition of slavery were conflicted and clearly influenced his stance on the Freedman's Commission. He proclaimed in his 1866 diocesan address: "The other practical point is that we have no need to change our system of instruction because of this emancipation, or to call any foreign help to our assistance. The Church in Georgia has always taught the colored race so far as the number of her clergymen and the rivalry with other denominations would permit her. We must simply carry on the same plan in the future."[23]

Bishop Elliott went on to say that in the Diocese of Georgia black people had always been welcome in churches and that they had been permitted to organize their own churches. If the freedmen now wanted to organize churches, then "we shall be glad to assist and cheer them and lead them in the way of true godliness. I see no necessity to change course for the present; nor do I see that we need any help from abroad [the North] in their religious culture."[24] Elliott was concerned that the instruction and other work among the recently freed slaves in Georgia be done by Georgians, lest the freed people be influenced by outsiders, however well meaning: "We have Christian men and Christian women in abundance among us, who will undertake any work for the Church. Organize them in your various parishes, and they will do the work more efficiently than any others can. . . . Every person imported from abroad to instruct or teach these people is an influence, unintentionally perhaps, but really, widening the breach between the races."[25]

Bishop Elliott noted that he had accepted and distributed within the diocese unsolicited donations from churches in Kentucky, Maryland, and New York and, after initially asking the Domestic Committee of the Board of Missions to "hold in abeyance" a two-thousand-dollar allocation for Georgia, had accepted the funds to help support clergymen coming into the diocese to serve in missionary stations. He made clear, however, his general position on soliciting outside support for either the freedmen or rebuilding the diocese. "In my address at Athens, in August last, I advised my clergy to abstain from going abroad for help to rebuild their churches or to renew the waste and desolate places of our Diocese. I am still of the same mind."[26]

The initial response of the bishop of Alabama, Richard Hooker Wilmer, to the Freedman's Commission was not welcoming. He opened the subject in his 1866 diocesan address with a discussion of the duties of the church toward the "colored population." Wilmer began by saying that the diocese had always recognized an obligation to minister to all persons and could not now "properly recognize the existence of any new obligation" to "this class of our people" resulting from their changed political and domestic status. Further, he was unwilling to swell the tide of sympathy that was flowing so strongly in their favor. With respect to the commission, he said: "In the correspondence which has passed between myself and the 'Freedman's Commission,' I have taken the ground that I was prepared, through instrumentalities of my own selection, to make use of any means which they might see fit to place in my hands. I see no propriety in departing from the usages of the Church, in accordance with which, the Bishop of a Diocese is charged with the selection of the instrumentalities which, in order to work properly, must work under his supervision."[27]

The responses from Bishops Elliott and Wilmer appear to ignore the scope of the challenges posed by emancipation. Elliott, in particular, had devoted much time, energy, and diocesan resources for nearly twenty-five years in trying to bring the gospel to slaves. Regardless of the success of those efforts, the delivery system for the gospel that included plantation missionaries and plantation chapels was not relevant in that the former slaves were no longer on the plantations and available for services at times approved by their masters. At minimum there needed to be a new vehicle for evangelism in the new social structure. The matter of church assistance with secular education, whether that education was to support participation in religious services or to help move the freedmen to informed citizenship and economic independence, was not addressed by the initial responses of either bishop. Overall, Wilmer's attitude seemed to be "Help me on my terms," and Elliott appeared to be saying "These are our problems, and we'll deal with them."

At the opposite end of the spectrum were Bishops John Johns of Virginia, Thomas Atkinson of North Carolina, and Thomas Frederick Davis of South Carolina, all of whom cooperated with the Freedman's Commission at or shortly after its creation and soon received for their dioceses substantial support. Although Virginia and the Carolinas continued to receive the greatest benefit from the Freedman's Commission, many dioceses in former Confederate states eventually received some support from the commission, as did the Diocese of Kentucky. Some examples of particular assistance rendered by the Freedman's Commission to former slave states will be given in essays below. The focus here is on the overall work of the commission during its brief lifetime.

## Commission Status 1868

The commission's teacher corps had fifteen teachers by June 1866. As shown in the table below, the number of teachers had quadrupled by April 1868. Twenty-three of these teachers were funded by the Pennsylvania branch of the Freedman's Commission.

**Freedman's Commission teachers and teaching sites, 1866 and 1868**

| | June 1866 | | December 1866 | | April 1868 | |
|---|---|---|---|---|---|---|
| Diocese | Sites* | Teachers | Sites | Teachers | Sites | Teachers† |
| Virginia | 3 | 8 | 4 | 12 | 7 | 21 |
| North Carolina | 3 | 5 | 3 | 7 | 4 | 12 |
| South Carolina | 1 | 1 | 4 | 4 | 3 | 15 |
| Georgia | 0 | 0 | 0 | 0 | 1 | 2‡ |
| Florida | 0 | 0 | 0 | 0 | 3 | 5 |
| Mississippi | 0 | 0 | 1 | 1 | 0 | 0 |
| Kentucky | 0 | 0 | 0 | 0 | 3 | 5 |
| Tennessee | 1 | 1 | 1 | 2 | —§ | — |
| Total | 8 | 15 | 13 | 26 | 21 | 60 |

*Sources:* The sources for these figures are *Spirit of Missions* 31 (1866): 351, 768, and *Spirit of Missions* 33 (1868): 60.

*A site is a city, town, or community; some sites had more than one school.

†The 1868 teacher complement includes teachers sent and supported by the Pennsylvania branch of the Freedman's Commission.

‡The two teachers in April 1868 in Georgia were affiliated with the Freedman's Commission but did not receive compensation from either the commission or its Pennsylvania branch.

§Although support of an orphanage in Memphis was not reported in the April 1868 *Spirit of Missions,* commission support of this institution was first reported in February 1866, and the orphanage and an associated school were still being supported in the 1870s.

At the 1868 General Convention in October, the figure of 5,500 was reported as the total students being served by schools sponsored by the Freedman's Commission (including its Pennsylvania branch).[28]

In accord with the commission charge as interpreted by its Executive Committee, these schools under the commission's aegis attempted to focus on instruction in "useful elementary knowledge, religious and secular." A major purpose was to develop the intellectual skills of those who attended, which was expected to improve their ability to function as citizens, to advance economically, and to read the Bible and participate in church services. In that these schools were under the umbrella of the Episcopal Church, the daily schedule generally included opening and closing exercises that were religious. In some cases the curriculum included explicit study of the Book of Common Prayer and practice with the parts of the liturgy calling for congregational responses.

## Community Resistance

Early on the Freedman's Commission encountered some resistance from bishops and rectors as well as laity, the last often viewing the commission as a Northern organization meddling in the affairs of the South, which already had been sufficiently disrupted by the war. As early as July 1866, however, an editorial in the *Spirit of Missions,* the national Episcopal Church journal for missions, stated that "the difficulties that were met before at every step have vanished; those we once asked to receive our teachers now are asking us."[29]

The resistance encountered by Freedman's Commission teachers was milder than that described by Allis Wolfe in her 1982 study of three hundred teachers sent by the American Freedman's Union Commission and the American Missionary Association to serve in Virginia, North Carolina, South Carolina, and Georgia. At one point Wolfe characterized the treatment of these teachers as follows:

> Most white Southerners saw the freedmen's educational movement as an attack on their way of life, especially on Southern race relations, and the Yankee schoolmarms received considerable attention as the movement's most visible symbol.
>     . . . Once the [Union] army [of occupation] withdrew, life often became so unbearable that the teachers were forced to leave, often in the wake of a school burning.[30]

Wolfe describes threats, harassment, and vandalism but indicates that physical violence against the women did not occur. She also observes that Southern women (or men) who taught in freedmen's schools often were ostracized and subjected to the same harsh treatment as their new Yankee colleagues. Teachers, Northern and Southern, who staffed the Episcopal Freedman's Commission schools had the advantage of sponsorship by a united Episcopal Church and had the support of a diocesan bishop and local clergy. Commission teachers were not sent into a community without the consent of the bishop.

## Financial Problems

Almost from the start, fiscal problems plagued the Freedman's Commission. In August 1866, some nine months into its existence, when the commission reported that twenty teachers were on its rolls, a fiscal warning signal appeared; income from contributions had been exceeded by expenses "for the past month or two."[31] In November 1866 Bishop Charles Pettit McIlvaine reported as chairman of a special committee appointed by the Board of Missions to evaluate the Freedman's Commission. The committee praised the work of the commission and concurred with the operational principles under which the commission had done its work.

McIlvaine then turned to fiscal matters: "For the millions of freedmen who, by the Providence that made them free, have been thrown with so many necessities, physical, intellectual, and spiritual with so much in their history, and so much in their special character, as a people, to call for the most earnest regard and the most vigorous assistance from us all, how much, as our share, has been contributed during the past year? A little more than $26,000, besides clothing estimated at $12,000. That is all! We grieve to state it."[32]

McIlvaine went on to note that at the last meeting of the Freedman's Executive Committee, there were requests for assistance from several dioceses as well as application from some fifteen potential teachers. The commission, however, had no funds and could not respond: "The Church did not give them the means. Alas! that the teachers were ready to go and the Church was not ready to send. . . . The Commission, in their report, indicated that to enter upon and occupy the fields open to them, in their particular sphere, they should receive at least $100,000 during the next year, and that twice or thrice that amount could be employed to advantage."[33] A January 1867 editorial in the *Spirit of Missions* reiterated the issue: "We have work for hundreds, and hundreds can be found willing and ready to engage in it, whom the Committee would gladly commission, if support could only be guaranteed."[34]

Although the Freedman's Commission was not funded at a level that enabled it to meet all the requests it received for assistance, the scope of the commission, as reflected in the table above, expanded steadily through the spring of 1868. By July 1868, however, a growing financial problem could no longer be ignored. It began with a high school that opened in Charleston, South Carolina, in July 1867. The school was originally funded by the commission for a principal and four teachers, but when it opened there was need of eight more teachers, based on the large enrollment. The commission decided to meet that need.[35] The high school was provided with the full complement of teachers needed at a cost of seven thousand dollars beyond what was projected based on the prior year's income, with the expectation that the church, through increased contributions, would cover this unexpected expenditure of funds.[36] This expectation was not fulfilled, though, and the resultant deficit translated into a poignant problem on the front lines of the commission's work.

When the Executive Committee decided in the spring of 1868 that it must take corrective action, the projected deficit for fiscal year was ten thousand dollars, and the commission treasurer had advanced four thousand dollars from personal funds to meet obligations to which the commission was committed. The Executive Committee decided to close the schools early and not to send any more money to the teachers after the new closing date. This sudden truncation of an annual income that they thought had been guaranteed placed a financial burden on teachers that in some cases was crushing.[37] Letters published in the *Spirit of Missions* revealed the plight of the teachers. The excerpts below from one letter were typical.

Your letter was like a thunderbolt to my associate and myself, . . . my grief is too deep at the thought of leaving this noble work of my master to admit of saying much. . . . I am many hundreds of miles from home, in a strange land, and at the end of this month when all expenses are met, I shall be without one penny. . . . When I came out here under the commission, it was with the stipulation that my expenses would be paid by the Commission to and from my residence. . . . To leave a teacher in a land of strangers, without means of staying, without means of helping herself, is beyond what I am able to fathom. Will you please be so kind as to send me sufficient to defray my expenses?[38]

Another teacher wrote that she was stranded without funds with unpaid bills in a strange land. She also expressed sadness and frustration that stopping her work so soon would result in "no lasting benefit" to the "poor children" with whom she had worked.[39]

The crisis did not end when the fiscal year closed; Augusta Hammond, a commission teacher in Charleston, South Carolina, expressed her dismay in an October 1868 letter with regard to the impact that the action of the Executive Committee was having on the school there: "October is here and our school is still closed to the hundreds who hunger and thirst after knowledge. Why is this? How must we account for the luke-warmness of the people of our Church in this important matter?"[40]

The frustration of the Executive Committee was understandable; the Freedman's Commission income was miniscule when compared to the scope of the task assigned by the church to the commission, and the Board of Missions had, in a November 1867 report, "heartily" approved the action of the Executive Committee with respect to both the high school at Charleston and a normal school at Raleigh.[41] Still, the committee appeared naïve, if not disingenuous, when it disclaimed any responsibility for a fiasco that had caused embarrassment and anguish to many teachers and had created disruption within the very schools that the commission was trying hard to nurture.

It has been stated before . . . that the Committee, acting for the Freedman's Commission, greatly moved by the urgency of the cases presented to them, in connection with the work which the Church called them to superintend and carry forward; undertook, in addition to what they did last year, a work requiring ten thousand dollars in additional means.

They did this, because they did not see how they could be true to their trust, *and not do it*. They did it because they thought the Church would come up to the work which God seemed to have assigned her in this part of his vineyard. . . .

The teachers had been employed for the year, or until the 1st of July. The Committee thought, as the Church had not given them the money, and four thousand dollars had been advanced through their Treasurer, that the fault of shortening the term must lie with the Church and not with them.

There has been a sad breach of faith. Teachers had been engaged and sent into the field for a year. With a very short notice they are dismissed before the year expires. Many of them had made no other arrangement, and could make no other for a support. The case was most trying and difficult.[42]

The shortening of the school year in fiscal year 1868 did not enable the central Freedman's Commission to liquidate its debt, and the commission carried a deficit into fiscal 1869; a diminishing debt, in fact, was on its books until finally cleared in 1872. Monthly receipt records of the commission, which were published in the *Spirit of Missions* show that for the fiscal years 1866 to 1877 the income for operation of the commission had a low of $16,707 in 1869 and a high of $29,022 in 1875, with most years between 21 and 23 thousand dollars. The primary source of Freedman's Commission income was contributions from parishes.[43]

In 1871 it was reported in the *Spirit of Missions* that 80 percent of parishes in the Protestant Episcopal Church in the United States did not contribute to the Board of Missions, and that board received from the church a sum equal to one dollar per year for each communicant.[44] Contributions designated for the Freedman's Commission always made up only a small share of the amount given to missions generally, and when a commission for missions among Indians was created, its income soon surpassed that of the Freedman's Commission by a wide margin.[45] Fiscal problems for the Pennsylvania branch of the commission as fiscal year 1869 began exacerbated the difficulties of the education program for freedmen. This branch, which had funded twenty-three teachers in 1868, experienced an income drop that forced it to reduce the number of teachers that it supported. Recently opened schools in Florida were victims of this retrenchment.[46]

### Changes in Name and Policy at the 1868 General Convention

The Freedman's Commission reported to the 1868 General Convention that its work was proceeding unimpeded, and, in fact, was being strengthened and guided by the bishops and assisted by communities throughout the South. To help alleviate any lingering concerns among the laypeople, however, the name of the Freedman's Commission was changed, by action of the convention, to Home Missionary Commission to Colored People. A shorter form, Home Missions to the Colored People, generally was used. The convention delegates apparently felt that the appellation Freedman's Commission had political overtones that would prejudice some Southern communities against the organization.[47]

In spite of the fiscal crisis that had occurred in the spring, and continuing financial difficulty, the Freedman's Commission convention report was enthusiastic about the work that it had done and the opportunities before the commission. The report recommended, however, a shift of policy from that established at the outset by the Executive Committee. The commission sought a change that would strengthen the missionary component of its work:

> While schools alone are valuable agents they will not accomplish their full purpose, nor realize the full intention of the church unless they are connected with permanent missionary work, and prosecuted under the supervision of the resident parochial clergy or of the duly appointed missionaries of the church. . . . The Church has no proper call to engage in the work of school teaching at all, except as she can make it subserve her dominant purpose, viz: the gathering into her fold for religious instruction and discipline of those whom she teaches in her schools. The school and the mission or the school and the parish should not, as a rule have been disconnected. The time has come when unless the Commission can be brought to subserve a strictly missionary use it may as well be abandoned as a work of the church. There is no lack of schools as such [in the Southern dioceses].[48]

This proposal was referred to the Board of Missions, and in November 1870 the board took action. First the importance of the commission's work in progress was reaffirmed.[49] The board then established a new policy for the commission. It was resolved that "the labors of the Commission for Home Missions among the Colored People be hereafter directed more largely to the support of Missionaries proper among this class of our population, who shall be nominated by the Bishops in whose jurisdiction they shall come, upon the same plan and principle adopted by the Domestic Committee of this Board."[50]

Whereas under the old guideline the first priority had been to establish schools and assign teachers, the priority now would be to support missionaries recommended by the bishop of the diocese concerned. Under the new approach, improving the intellectual skills of the black population remained a key objective, but now any school and its teachers were to be rooted in a parish or missionary station under the supervision of a clergyman, a change that explicitly recognized the authority of the diocesan bishop. It was, however, understood in the meeting of the Board of Missions at which the resolution passed that existing schools would not be abandoned and that the new policy being approved could only be made operational with funding above and beyond what was required to support existing schools.[51]

## Denouement

An approach to financing, using "honorary district secretaries" that Secretary Wellington E. Webb had inaugurated in 1871 at first enabled the commission to fund the extant schools and to undertake a modest level of activity under the new policy guidelines, but the vast increase in funds needed to expand significantly the scope of the Freedman's Commission never materialized. Moreover, at the same time that the new guidelines were adopted in November 1870, the Board of Missions passed a resolution that the commission's funding be increased from a minimum of twenty thousand dollars per year to fifty thousand annually, but this did not happen because the necessary increase in contributions from parishes was not forthcoming.[52] Then in early 1877 finances began to worsen, raising the specter of fiscal year 1868 redux. The Reverend Hugh Roy Scott was retained to canvass parishes across the church to raise funds to avoid "great personal inconvenience" to commission teachers and missionaries.[53]

The original special niche for the Freedman's Commission identified by the Executive Committee was eroded by changes in policy and structure within the Board of Missions. The 1870 decision to focus on missionaries was the first change, bringing to a halt the commission's unique focus on education. Then, the understanding that schools already in operation would be unaffected by the new emphasis began to fade. An editorial in the *Spirit of Missions* in October 1877 provided a status report.

> It was at length, however, deemed advisable by the Board (the want of secular education being largely met by the action of the respective states) to change the character of the work, and was accordingly resolved, at the earliest period, to elevate the mere school into the dignity of a mission, and, where practicable, the mission into a parish, and to this end the [Executive] Committee was instructed. Where this could not be done, *the schools were closed,* and the means at disposal devoted to the missionary or evangelist who could find openings in other localities of greater promise. This has been effected within the past year. [54] (Emphasis added.)

Next, a structural change in the Board of Missions at the October 1877 General Convention provided for a Board of Managers that had full power to act for the Board of Missions between General Conventions and was given authority to appoint from among its membership a Domestic Missions Committee, a Foreign Missions Committee, and any other committees deemed desirable to promote special missionary work.[55] The Board of Managers moved quickly to instruct the Domestic Missions Committee to appoint a special committee for missions among the black population.[56] This downgraded the status of the Commission for Home Missions among the Colored People (the Freedman's Commission) and adumbrated its demise. The Freedman's Commission as a separate unit survived until 12 February 1878, when its functions were absorbed by the Domestic Committee of the Board of Missions.[57] A special committee of the Board of Managers reported the board's action to the church at large as follows: "That the Department of Home Missions to the Colored People was discontinued and the work assigned to the care of the Committee for Domestic Missions; thus saving the salary of a Secretary and the rent of an office."[58]

The Reverend Wellington E. Webb, who was the last secretary and general agent for the Freedman's Commission, gave a statement of his views on the commission's declining importance in the September 1877 issue of the *Spirit of Missions,* only a few months before his position was phased out. Webb still believed in the educational mission of the commission, arguing that the schools then operating in the South were having an impact by subduing ignorance and reducing antagonism and emotionalism.[59] He was quite clear as to what he believed was the root cause of the commission's inadequate funding by the church.

> After all that can be said of the obstacles that retard the Christian education of the Freedmen, they all seem to hinge on the one ubiquitous hindrance of *race prejudice.* . . . It is race prejudice that causes so little to be done for the Colored People. It is race prejudice that makes the accomplishment of what is attempted so extremely difficult. It is race prejudice that prevents the Clergy in *all* sections from doing what they would. It is race prejudice that thrusts the Colored People aside, with unlettered and emotional teachers, and then jeers at their ignorant and ill-conducted devotional exercises.[60]

Webb's remarks were aimed more at Northern apathy, which he felt was rooted in racial bias, than at Southern obstructionism. Neither section was giving fiscal support to the commission's work at a level that Webb felt was adequate, but only a strong commitment by churches in the North, which had not suffered the wartime destruction and impoverishment that was widespread in the South, could have enabled a real expansion of the commission's work.[61] The apathy which Webb decried was evident in the Northern diocesan journals, in which, after 1866, there was a paucity of coverage of the needs of freedmen in Northern bishops' addresses, and little attention was given to that topic by church committees.

## Scope of Commission Work

In seven of the former slave states, Virginia, North Carolina, South Carolina, Kentucky, Florida, Tennessee, and Mississippi, all of which except Kentucky formerly were in the Confederacy, the Freedman's Commission participated in efforts not long after the war to provide secular and religious education for the freed people and in efforts to bring the gospel message to that population. The first three of these states received the biggest influx of commission support, but all indicated at an early date that they would welcome such support.

From the start the work of the commission was pursued with enthusiasm by its teachers, who found the work fulfilling, and the commission generally was received with enthusiasm by the students and communities it served. The work continued to expand until the fiscal crisis intervened in the spring of 1868, which led to painful financial readjustments and a policy shift to emphasize missionary work.[62] The commission continued to serve the freed people effectively after these changes, but the high point of the commission's existence came early in 1868, before the fiscal debacle halted its expansion and interrupted important work in progress.

### Notes

1. Most slaves were free by the time the General Convention met in October 1865. The institution was not completely eradicated by law in the United States, however, until the Thirteenth Amendment was ratified in December 1865.

2. Allis Wolfe, "Women Who Dared: Northern Teachers of the Southern Freedmen, 1862–1872" (Ph.D. diss., New York: Columbia University, 1982), 155. See also Edgar W. Knight, ed., "The Instruction of Negroes," *Educational Theories and Practices,* vol. 5 of *A Documentary History of Education in the South before 1860* (Chapel Hill: University of North Carolina Press, 1953), 459–515, which reviews the legislation that had been passed in Southern states to prohibit teaching slaves to read and write.

3. "Proceedings of the Board of Missions, Protestant Episcopal Church, Meeting of 5 October 1865," *Miscellanies 1815–1868, Protestant Episcopal Church in the United States of America,* undated, available at the library of General Theological Seminary; see also *Spirit of Missions* 30 (1865): 402–3.

4. "Proceedings of the Board of Missions, Protestant Episcopal Church, Meeting of 13 October 1865," *Spirit of Missions* 30 (1865): 411–12.

5. Ibid.

6. Ibid., 411.

7. *Journal of the General Convention of the Protestant Episcopal Church, 1865* (Boston: William A. Hall, 1865), 87, 175, 179, 188.

8. *Spirit of Missions* 30 (1865): 412.

9. H. Peers Brewer, "The Protestant Episcopal Freedman's Commission, 1865–1878," *Historical Magazine of the Protestant Episcopal Church,* 26 (December 1957): 366.

10. Ibid., 367–68.

11. "Address of the Reverend Dr. Francis Wharton, December 1865," in *Protestant Episcopal Freedman's Commission Occasional Paper, January 1866* (Boston: Rand and Avery, 1866), 6. Wharton's complete address also was published in *Spirit of Missions* 31 (1866): 43–48.

12. *New York Times*, 5 December 1865, 2.

13. *New York Times*, 10 December 1865, 8.

14. *Spirit of Missions* 31 (1866): 155.

15. Ibid., 156.

16. Ibid., 156–57.

17. Wolfe, "Women Who Dared," 25.

18. Ibid., 27–28.

19. Ibid., 16. See also the journals of General Convention for the years 1865 to 1874.

20. "Proceedings of the Board of Missions, Annual Meeting, New York, October 1867"; appended to the *Spirit of Missions* 32 (1867). See also *Spirit of Missions* 34 (1869): 237–41, in which reference is made to particular cases of assistance by the Freedman's Bureau.

21. *Spirit of Missions* 31 (1866): 156.

22. Ibid., 157.

23. *Diocese of Georgia, 1866* (Savannah: Purse and Sons, 1866), 26–27.

24. Ibid., 27.

25. Ibid., 27.

26. Ibid., 29.

27. *Diocese of Alabama, 1866* (Mobile: Farrow and Dennett, 1866), 11.

28. *Journal of the General Convention of the Protestant Episcopal Church, 1868* (Hartford: Printed for the Convention, 1869), 370.

29. *Spirit of Missions* 31 (1866): 411.

30. Wolfe, "Women Who Dared," 102.

31. *Spirit of Missions* 31 (1866): 463.

32. Ibid., 653.

33. Ibid.

34. *Spirit of Missions* 32 (1867): 86.

35. See *Spirit of Missions* 33 (1868): 162 for a listing of the teaching staff.

36. "Proceedings of the Board of Missions, October, 1867," 44.

37. *Spirit of Missions* 34 (1869): 557, and *Spirit of Missions* 33 (1868): 581.

38. *Spirit of Missions* 33 (1868): 582–83. This letter and one following were published without identification of the sender or the school in which she taught.

39. Ibid., 582.

40. Ibid., 920.

41. *Spirit of Missions* 32 (1867): 827. The normal school in Raleigh is discussed below, in the essay entitled "Aftermath in North Carolina: Thomas Atkinson."

42. *Spirit of Missions* 33 (1868): 581.

43. These figures do not include a large donation in 1877 dedicated to the Normal School in Raleigh, North Carolina. Source: Freedman's Commission sections, contribution acknowledgement pages, *Spirit of Missions*, 1868–1878. Fiscal data for the commission also may be found in Brewer, "The Protestant Episcopal Freedman's Commission," and in reports of the Board of Missions in the journals of the General Convention. The commission leadership based its planning and its reports to the Board of Missions on the data recorded in the *Spirit of Missions*.

44. *Spirit of Missions* 36 (1871): 143.

45. In fiscal year 1875, for example, the $29,022 in contributions to the Freedman's Commission may be compared to the $50,101 total for the Indian Commission.

46. *Spirit of Missions* 34 (1869): 755.

47. *Journal of the General Convention, 1868,* 277.

48. Ibid., 370–71.

49. "Report of the Proceedings of the Board of Missions, Annual Meeting, New York, October 1870" *Spirit of Missions* 35 (1870): 638.

50. Ibid., 644.

51. Ibid.

52. Ibid., 638 and 644.

53. *Spirit of Missions* 42 (1877): 92.

54. Ibid., 535–36.

55. "Missionary Canon of the General Convention, Title III–Canon 9, of the Constitution of the Domestic and Foreign Missionary Society of the Protestant Episcopal Church in the United States of America, Section I, Article V," *Spirit of Missions* 42 (1877): 616.

56. Brewer, "Protestant Episcopal Freedman's Commission," 380.

57. *Spirit of Missions* 43 (1878): 124.

58. Ibid., 185.

59. *Spirit of Missions* 42 (1877): 481.

60. Ibid., 479–80.

61. Webb's anger was not directed at the Freedman's Commission or the Board of Missions, both of whose actions were dictated by budgetary reality. He remained supportive even as it became clear that the commission's life was nearing its end. His frustration was with the lack of support across the church for the work of the commission.

62. See description of the work of the Reverend C. O. Brady below, in "Aftermath in North Carolina: Thomas Atkinson."

# PART 7

# Aftermath from the Diocesan Perspective and Concluding Observations

# Preamble

## Two Vignettes

### Dejection

When Florida was put under United States military rule while hostilities were drawing to a close, a Sunday service conducted by Bishop Francis Huger Rutledge in Tallahassee was witnessed by the same Susan Bradford who as a teenager four years earlier had heard his impressive prayers at the secession convention for the state of Florida.[1] Miss Bradford published what she observed:

> First came an order from [military] headquarters to the clergy of Talla-hassee; the President of the Confederacy must not be prayed for, but every minister in the city must pray for the President of the United States. We were in church when the venerable Bishop Rutledge was trying to obey this order. His long white hair, like spun silk, was gently stirred by the spring breeze, from the window at his back, his surplice falling about his aged and shrunken figure gave him an almost unearthly appearance. He was a Southerner of Southern-ers, and for four years his whole heart had gone up in prayers for Jefferson Davis, the South's adored President. Now with trembling lips and unsteady voice he began his prayer: "Oh, Lord, Our Heavenly Father, the High and Mighty Ruler of the Universe, Who doth from Thy Throne behold all the dwellers upon earth; most heartily we beseech thee with thy favor to behold and bless thy servant The President of the Confederate States." Realizing his mistake, the poor old head fell low on his breast as he retrieved himself, and in a faltering voice repeated: "Thy servant the President of the United States and all others in authority."[2]

Rutledge's pain was felt by diocesan leaders across the South. When the Civil War ended, the bishops in the former Confederate states became leaders of dioceses characterized by devastation and impoverishment combined with dejection and resentment.[3] Feelings in the latter two categories were exacerbated by Union oc-cupation forces that filled the civil vacuum left by the collapse of the Confederate government.

The bishops in the former Confederate states faced an immediate challenge to determine and to work to bring about the future organizational affiliation of their dioceses. This issue and its overall resolution are described above, in part 6. The other broad challenges confronting the Southern bishops were (1) to assist their flocks with the acceptance of the loss of the Civil War and thereby engage in the healing processes that would enable them to face their future objectively in a Christian spirit; (2) to begin the process of diocesan revival, including the physical rebuilding of destroyed or desecrated church edifices, the gathering together and spiritual rebuilding of scattered congregations, and the strengthening and proper allocation of diocesan and parish resources; and (3) a goal shared by those slave states that had remained in the Union, namely to provide worship opportunities, religious instruction, and other assistance to the former slaves. This last effort addressed the change in social structure concomitant with emancipation and was complicated and enlarged by the physical and educational needs of the freed people resulting from that social change. It was also complicated and made difficult by the attitude of many white parishioners. A case in point is the experience of Bishop Charles Todd Quintard as a result of a confirmation service in Memphis.

### An Incident in Memphis

At a service of confirmation conducted by Bishop Quintard of Tennessee on 21 March 1869 at Calvary Church, Memphis, there were seven candidates, one of whom was black.[4] Quintard thought that he had made clear that all candidates should come at the same time to kneel at the rail to receive the sacrament, but only the six white candidates came forward. After the confirmation was finished and his blessing had been bestowed, Quintard was "astonished" when "the Negro boy came forward."[5] By way of explanation before repeating the ceremony, Quintard told the congregation: "This person should have come forward with the other Candidates, because in the bestowal of her spiritual Blessings, 'Our mother the Church, have never a child to honor before the rest.'"[6]

The bishop's remarks were harshly criticized in the Memphis newspapers. An editorial in the *Memphis Daily Appeal* was typical: "We think he [Quintard] did that which may justly be regarded as a violation of the comity of manners that has always existed at the South, and we unite with our contemporaries in condemnation of it. We do not believe in negro equality in any shape—in or out of the church—and hope that Bishop Quintard will make haste to correct an impression growing out of his unfortunate *faux pas*, injurious to him and to the church over which he presides."[7]

In response, Bishop Quintard made clear his belief that the distinctions in the eyes of society based solely upon skin color "which have always been maintained" should not be "abrogated," but he strongly defended his position that because

God was "no respecter of persons" there should be no distinction made between white and black when candidates for confirmation knelt at the altar rail.[8] This "equal in God's eyes but not in the sight of man" paradox would haunt the Episcopal Church for the next century.

## Notes

1. See above, the essay entitled "Prelude to Montgomery: Southern Bishops Confront Secession, Threat of War, and Church Division."

2. Susan Bradford Eppes, *Through Some Eventful Years* (Macon: J. W. Burke, 1926), 341. The "order from headquarters" applied to all churches in Tallahassee, including those that did not have a prescribed form of prayer. Eppes also provided a description of the compliance of the Methodist and Presbyterian churches, observed on subsequent Sundays.

3. Of the eleven Confederate states, Texas, which was isolated during most of the war, suffered the least destruction.

4. *Diocese of Tennessee, 1869* (Nashville: Paul, Tavel, and Hanner, 1869), 39.

5. Ibid.

6. Ibid. The poem quoted by Quintard is Arthur Cleveland Coxe's "Churchyards," published in *Christian Ballads and Poems* (London: Parker and Parker, Oxford, 1859), 90. Coxe, who was serving in 1869 as bishop of Western New York, had written "Churchyards" in 1840.

7. "Placing Ourselves Right," *Memphis Daily Appeal*, 25 March 1869.

8. *Diocese of Tennessee, 1869*, 40.

# Aftermath in Georgia

✠ *Stephen Elliott*

Bishop Stephen Elliott's postwar episcopate began in a diocese ravished by the war.

> Our Diocese has been left . . . in a state of much depression. Churches have . . . to be repaired, in some instances to be rebuilt. Our clergymen are . . . without salaries, their people being scattered or else impoverished. Many of the funds which we had been collecting . . . have been lost entirely or very much impaired; and worse than all, our agricultural industry, which was the basis of our prosperity, is . . . at a standstill. All these things are against us, but I trust that there is still left to us a true and living faith, which will enable us to rise superior to these ills of fortune.[1]

In spite of the devastation and great need for resources to get the state and diocese back on their feet, Elliott was adamantly opposed to solicitation of help from outside the diocese. This was the "hour of trial" and churchmen should be at home determined to help themselves, not running "abroad" to beg for help."[2]

### Sermon: "Be Still and Know That I Am God"

Elliott's primary message to his flock after the war was to accept the South's defeat as the will of God and to turn to the challenges they now faced. He delivered this message eloquently on 15 October 1865 in his first sermon in Savannah since the war had ended. It was an emotional occasion for both pastor and congregation. His sermon was entitled "Be Still and Know That I Am God," and his theme was plain in his opening: "The trial of our faith is brought home to us, my beloved people, at this moment of our reunion, in a most striking manner; and my earnest prayer both for you and for myself is, that it may end in a triumph of that faith, and that we may have grace given to us to 'be still,' and to know that it is God who has overruled every thing to the purposes of His will, and that without his permission nothing could have happened which has happened."[3] Elliott expanded on this message, cautioning the congregation not to feel anger and bitterness toward "human agents" of God's will, presumably including Union soldiers, General Sherman, and President Lincoln. These feelings were counter-productive:

> So long as we fasten our thoughts upon secondary causes, upon human agents, upon earthly instruments, our most dangerous passions are kept alive: our anger, our wrath, our bitterness, our hatred, our uncharitableness;—the very feelings . . . inspired men have commanded us, as Christians, to put aside. It is not until God is permitted to fill our hearts, and to become—what he is—the Ruling Spirit of all worldly movements, and to shut out by his glorious presence the human instruments through whom he works and punishes, that these unchristian passions can be soothed and quelled by the magical words: 'Be still and know that I am God.' (478)

Elliott was telling his flock that it was not enough to be *outwardly* calm toward those men who had defeated their cause and wreaked destruction on their land. The swelling of indignation *in the hearts* of the Southern People must cease before they would be truly still before God. In words that certainly applied to himself as well as to many of his listeners, Elliott asserted that "man attempts to understand and interpret God's dealings: but it is not in his province 'to know the times or the seasons which the Father hath put in his own power.' Man's duty is, when he has labored as God intended him to labor and has thus acquitted his soul, to acquiesce in the results, to have faith that God is wiser and holier than himself, and to be still, in contemplation of His dealings and in waiting upon his will" (480).

Elliott knew that his understanding of God's plan for slavery and his belief in the ultimate triumph of the South had both been wrong, and that he, as well as his flock, needed to recognize that and move forward:

> We have done up to this time what we honestly and sincerely believed to be our bounden duty to God and therefore to man. Let us not now swerve from what is the continuation of that duty
>
> . . . We believed that we were Christians, while we labored for our cause; shall we not be Christians when called upon to acquiesce in God's decision upon that cause?
>
> Nothing which occurs upon earth is an end. It is only a means, leading on through antecedents and consequents to the greatest and final purpose of human redemption. (483)

Elliott knew when he delivered this sermon how hard it would be for his congregation to hear, because he sorely did not want to preach it—but he felt that its message had to be delivered. Elliott's choice of words in urging his flock to accept God's decision for the outcome of the war might be compared with those of his colleague Bishop William Mercer Green of Mississippi, who delivered the same message but in very different language.

The foe that prevailed against us by brute force seems determined, with like brutality, to trample us in the dust. Not content with breaking up the relation of master and slave, a relationship of God's own appointment, they would, if possible, reverse the whole order of society; and after robbing us of one-half of our wealth, would take from us also every incentive to love the Government which has subjected us to its power. To these orderings of All-wise Providence it is our painful duty to submit, because we know that it is *His* doing, and that "He doeth all things well," although he often sees fit to let the wicked triumph for a season.[4]

### Ministry to the Former Slaves

In 1865, at the first diocesan council after the war, Elliott was concerned about the essentially total disruption of ministry to those who had been slaves but who were now free; they remained brothers in Christ, and he felt that the ministry to them should continue. Given the upheaval in the social structure and chaos across the diocese, however, he appeared uncertain as to how to proceed. He mentioned specifically the Ogeechee Mission, where on 24 July 1864 he had confirmed fifty-four persons, all of whom were black. Since then, "the sweep of General Sherman's army has dispersed this noble mission, and what will be its future fate, God only knows. Mr. Williams [the resident missionary], upon the approach of the Federal forces, left the mission, with my consent. . . . In his separation from these people, he carries with him the satisfaction of knowing that he has labored most faithfully among them in his Master's service. . . . Whether he will ever minister to these people again, is a problem which cannot, at present, be solved."[5]

At the diocesan meeting in 1866 Elliott began a discussion of emancipation with a historical review of slavery that was, in effect, a passionate defense of how that institution had operated in the South. Slavery had been used to Christianize and otherwise elevate a savage race, a remarkable achievement in only two centuries. Never "in the history of the world had there been such a rapid and effective missionary work." The loyalty of the slaves to their owners during the war was offered as the "sublimest vindication" of how the slaves had been treated.[6]

Turning to the mission of the Episcopal Church to the now free black population, Elliott acknowledged that there had been social upheaval, but, he proclaimed, the church's mission of religious instruction and provision of religious opportunity had not changed—and Georgia's Episcopalians needed no outside help in continuing their ministry to the freed people.[7] Elliott called for diocesan efforts and resources to continue serving the black population, even though the war had left a legacy of poverty and chaos in Georgia.

Elliott, however, had conflicted feelings about the new order that emancipation would bring. This is implicit in his rejection of "imported" help on the grounds that Georgia's white residents "best understood" the former slaves, but his internal struggle went deeper than a concern that outsiders might promote tension between the races. Offering a context for the obligation to offer religious instruction and worship opportunities to the black people of Georgia, who now were "brethren beloved," Elliott noted that "love must go along with it [religious instruction]; gratitude for their past services; memories of our infancy and childhood; thoughts of the glory which will accrue to us, when we shall lead these people, once our servants, but not now as servants, but above servants, as brethren beloved, and present them to Christ as our offering of repentance for what we may have failed to fulfill in the past, of our trust."[8]

The very next paragraph in the same address, however, strongly suggests that Elliott believed that, in the long term, such an effort was futile.

> But it may be asked—do you regret the abolition of slavery? For myself and my race, No! I rather rejoice in it: but for them, most deeply. I sincerely believe it the greatest calamity which could have befallen them; the heaviest stroke which has been against religious advancement in this land. I would not, if I could, have it restored for any benefit to me or mine or my countrymen. . . . But for them I see no future in this country. Avarice and cupidity and interest will do for their extinction what they have always done for an unprotected inferior race. Poverty, disease, intemperance will follow in their train and do the rest. I say these things from no ill feeling against the race, for God is my witness I have loved them and do love them, and have labored for them all my life, but because at this moment I think it is my duty to put these opinions upon record, that the past may be vindicated and the future take none by surprise.[9]

Elliott's remarks reveal his paradoxical beliefs, first that there was a divine directive to white Christians to bring an emancipated race to Christ and, second, that the former slaves were doomed to extinction, in large part because of what Elliott perceived as their inherent characteristics.

### St. Stephen's Church

With all the disruption of the ministry to former plantation slaves, Elliott was glad to find stability after the war at St. Stephen's Church in Savannah, which was founded in 1856 to serve free black people.[10] The white minister had become seriously ill, and the worship services had been placed under the charge of James Porter, a well-educated black layman appointed by Elliott. There were seventy members of the congregation. Most worship services had been read by Porter, but he had secured the help of visiting ministers when possible, and the church was stable and strong. Elliott confirmed eight persons when he visited.[11] He was grateful to Porter and the vestry, but the tone and content of his report reflected a paternalistic view of black communicants as perpetual students under the tutelage of a white ministry—and a hope, if not a belief, that within the Episcopal Church, at least, emancipation would not alter the black–white relationship. He closed his report with the words: "May God watch over them and keep them in the grace of humility and free from all the wild delusions which are now cursing the land."[12]

Porter had been one of twenty black leaders who met with Secretary of War Edwin M. Stanton and General William Tecumseh Sherman in Savannah in January 1865 to share their vision on the future of a people freed by the war.[13] It is doubtful that he shared Elliott's perspective on the future of black–white relations. Porter's diocesan report, however, expressed pride in his congregation and the belief that a "good and efficient minister" sent to St. Stephen's could reap an "abundant harvest."[14] Elliott missed an opportunity to begin building a corps of black clergy by not urging Porter to seek Holy Orders immediately after the war.[15]

## Last Days

In a sermon on 22 November 1866, a day appointed by the Georgia legislature as a state fast day, Elliott put the still-stalled economy in biblical terms: "Our corn and our oil have failed of their abundance; our flocks and our herds are diminished. Their cry of want is heard in our land; the manna and the quails come not yet."[16] It was right, Elliott noted, that the legislators had called the people to humiliation and prayer, because the blessing of an abundant harvest, when it came, would come from God. God had decreed the outcome of the war, and only submission to God's will would convince God to relieve their economic plight.[17] Stephen Elliott never wavered in his belief that all human endeavor was subject to God's will and plan. Man might misread the plan, as he, Elliott, had done at times, but in his view submission to God's will was the foundation of Christian life.

Elliott's died suddenly on 21 December 1866. His work in facilitating church reunion on terms that he felt were honorable must have given him satisfaction, and he was a beloved figure throughout his parishes. When he died, however, his diocese was economically prostrate, and there had been little progress in retaining black congregants or bringing them into the Episcopal Church in Georgia. In 1868 a report from the Diocese of Georgia to the General Convention stated that "the Ogeechee and other missions along the coast, which at one time included one-fourth of the whole number of communicants within the Diocese, were broken up in 1865, and the people, for whose benefit they had been previously sustained, being deprived of pastoral supervision, have been for the most part separated from the Church. This result, unavoidable perhaps under the circumstances, forms a discouraging feature in the later history of the Church in Georgia."[18]

## Notes

1. *Diocese of Georgia, 1865* (Savannah: Purse and Sons), 26–27.

2. Ibid., 26.

3. Thomas Hanckel, ed., *Sermons by the Right Reverend Stephen Elliott, D.D., Late Bishop of Georgia, with a Memoir* (New York: Pott and Amery, 1867), 477. Excerpts immediately following from this sermon—"Sermon 43," preached 15 October 1865—are from this source; page references are given parenthetically in text following each quotation.

4. *Diocese of Mississippi, 1866*, appended to *Diocese of Mississippi, 1867* (Jackson: Clarion Steam Printing, 1867), 64.

5. *Diocese of Georgia, 1865*, 21.

6. *Diocese of Georgia, 1866* (Savannah: Purse and Sons, 1866), 25–26.

7. As described above in "The Freedman's Commission," Elliott was opposed to having Freedman's Commission schools established in Georgia. In her book *Soldiers of Light and Love: Northern Teachers and Georgia Blacks, 1865–1873* (Chapel Hill: University of North Carolina Press, 1980), Jacqueline Jones described the work of freedmen's aid societies including the American Missionary Association and the American Freedman's Union Commission, as well as the efforts of the U.S. Freedmen's Bureau. There was no mention of the Freedman's Commission.

8. *Diocese of Georgia, 1866*, 28.

9. Ibid., 28–29.

10. The founding of St. Stephen's Church is discussed above in "Stephen Elliott of Georgia and Thomas Frederick Davis of South Carolina."

11. *Diocese of Georgia, 1866*, 22.

12. Ibid.

13. Charles Lwanga Hoskins, *Yet with a Steady Beat: Biographies of Early Black Savannah* (Savannah: Gullah Press, 2001), 158.

14. *Diocese of Georgia, 1866*, 60–61.

15. This view is expressed by Charles Lwanga Hoskins in *Black Episcopalians in Georgia: Strife, Struggle, and Salvation* (Savannah: Hoskins, 1980), 56. Porter's acceptance as a candidate for ordination was reported in the diocesan journal of 1867, after Elliott's death, but the 1868 journal reported that he had withdrawn his name.

16. "Submission to God's Will," *Sermons by Stephen Elliott*, 499. The reference to manna and quails is from Exodus 16: 13–16.

17. "Submission to God's Will," *Sermons by Stephen Elliott*, 496–507.

18. *Journal of the General Convention, 1868* (Hartford: Printed for the Convention, 1868), 299. These missions for slaves by rivers and the coast had been disrupted as Sherman's forces marched from Atlanta to Savannah.

# Aftermath in South Carolina

✠ *Thomas Frederick Davis*

### A Diocese in Distress

There was not a quorum when the Diocese of South Carolina convened in May 1865. No official actions could be taken, but the proceedings, including Bishop Thomas Frederick Davis's address and a few parish reports, were published. The latter reflected the destruction, desolation, and economic chaos left in the wake of the Civil War in general and Sherman's army in particular. One of the parish reports was by a missionary who served the Church of the Redeemer in Orangeburg. He related that after Union soldiers took his horse, as well as most of his clothing and food, he had to walk the five miles from home to church to hold services, but recently his sister-in-law had arrived with a "broken-down mule," and he was grateful to have transportation to and from church.[1]

Conditions were little better when the diocese met in February 1866, but Davis saw the church as a pillar of strength: "We have passed through a season of extraordinary trial, necessarily drawing men's hearts to eternal considerations. At every place of their refuge, her dispersed children have met their church, and she has proved to them a solace and a power in the day of their calamity. Whatever else was taken away they still had left with them permission to worship God, . . . and I am persuaded that the Church is stronger than ever in the hearts of her people."[2]

Recovery in South Carolina continued to be slow; the parochial reports section of the 1867 diocesan journal listed twenty-two parishes without rectors, and five others were listed as having no report.[3] In 1868 ten churches were listed as needing to be rebuilt, and the State of the Church Committee listed fifteen churches as "without any ecclesiastical organization" and recommended that they be taken off the diocesan rolls until they were "again in active organization." There were ten other churches for which the committee had been unable to secure adequate information to make a judgment. The committee also recommended that a group of churches on the seaboard with dislocated congregations be put under the umbrella of a single mission station and assigned an itinerant missionary.[4]

Amid these reports of a diocese in tatters, Bishop Davis managed to strike an optimistic note at the 1868 diocesan convention. He must have recognized that with white people, the repair or rebuilding of churches and the restoration and expansion of the communicant base were problems that could be solved as the disruption quieted and the economy improved, and he was confident that recovery, however slowly, surely would come. With regard to black individuals, the restoration of the communicant base was complicated by other factors.

## A Framework for Missionary Work among Former Slaves

When he addressed the diocese in February 1866, Davis knew that "the colored population had been separated from us," and he felt that something needed to be done to reconnect the former slaves with the church. The Committee on the Relation of the Diocese to the Colored People was established by the convention to deal with the matter. The committee presented a report that began with a pejorative preamble that alluded to emancipation as "the calamitous change wrought in the present condition of the colored people." The preamble also attributed to fancy ideas put in former slaves' heads by "liberators" and the "intoxication" freedmen felt with their newly acquired freedom. This last statement no doubt reflected the fact many freedmen felt free not to listen to former authority figures, including Episcopal ministers. Having made these venting statements, the committee then stated its belief that the gospel would help in fitting freedmen for their new political and social status. The white people of the South, the committee felt, were best qualified to help freedmen and should do so; the destinies of the two races were "intertwined." The committee then gave a comprehensive set of recommendations.

(1) That a Board of Missions to the Colored People and Freemen of the Diocese be established and be entrusted with the "whole subject" of instruction of the freedmen (2) that the Board be asked to take early action to revive and sustain such missions to colored people exclusively, as existed before their emancipation (3) that this Board consider the expediency of organizing churches consisting in whole or in part of colored people (4) that the Board be urged to establish and maintain parochial schools for the secular and religious instruction of the colored people, . . . to be conducted by teachers . . . of our own communion, and under the supervision of the clergy within whose cures they may be established (5) that this Board be authorized and requested to search out and take by the hand any of this class who may be desirous of preparing for the sacred ministry of our own church . . . and to provide for their education and training at schools or seminaries, with the sanction and approval of

the Bishop. Recommendation (6) urged legal representatives of property no longer needed by white churches to consider donating that property to the Board. Recommendation (7) empowered the Board to receive and disburse funds. Recommendation (8) was that the Board consider appointing a missionary "to ascertain needs and wishes of Colored People" and to bring his findings to the Board.[5]

The bishop and the convention concurred, thus putting the diocese on record in support of allocating resources for providing black congregations with churches, for education (in parochial schools) of freed people, and for training black ministers. For several reasons this action by the diocese was surprising, given that the language in the preamble to the resolutions was condescending to blacks, and yet a truly comprehensive plan to help black people and bring them into the church was adopted; that during that time of fiscal adversity there existed no resources to support such a sweeping set of resolutions; and that evidence was mounting that many of the freed men and women who had been instructed in the Episcopal faith did not wish to continue that affiliation. Recommendations (2), (3), and (6), it should be noted, either permitted or explicitly called for separate churches for black communicants.

### Help from the Freedman's Commission: A Bright Spot

The diocese had rejoined Protestant Episcopal Church in the United States, and both Bishop Davis and the Diocesan Board of Missions for Colored People were enthusiastic about receiving help from the Freedman's Commission. The commission funded four schools in the state for the education of black individuals. Two, one at Charleston and the other at Winnsboro, thrived for a number of years. Davis praised both the commission and the schools at later diocesan conventions. A letter from a Miss Finney, a teacher at Winnsboro, showed the enthusiasm of one of the first commission teachers in South Carolina:

> My school could not be more pleasant. The pupils, amiable, and obedient. The most perfect order reigns, secured without any severity. . . . Not a day passes that I do not wish that you and all of our good Commission could look upon us, and see how happy and busy we are. My school is in my every thought, and I am happiest when with my scholars. You will not be surprised or think it strange when I tell you that, at the commencement of our work, there were many strong prejudices against it, and you will be grateful to learn that very few, if any, now exists. . . . Today there were present 56 pupils, who did nobly on all their exercises. You would love to hear them repeat, in concert, verses of Scripture, and answer questions I put to them. Tis wonderful how quickly and well they learn.[6]

The Diocesan Board of Missions secured a building in Charleston used during the war as a marine hospital, and one of the schools supported by Freedman's Commission was housed therein. The opening of this school at Charleston in 1867 was a leading factor in the fiscal crisis that culminated within the Freedman's Commission in the spring of 1868. The Charleston school reopened in November 1868 and by 1870 was operating smoothly, staffed by six teachers and serving 233 pupils.[7] A special visitor sent by the Freedman's Commission reported favorably on the performance of the school's pupils in December 1871 but noted that the scholars did not have warm clothes.[8]

### Outreach to Former Slaves: A Stalled Mission

In addition to a lack of resources, Davis's efforts to bring back former slaves to the church faced other difficulties. The volatility of the situation with black communicants is illustrated by the case of the Church of the Holy Cross, Claremont Parish, where the Reverend Robert Wilson was rector and the Reverend J. V. Welch served as deacon and missionary. The following excerpt is from the parochial report for the 1867 convention: "The spaces left blank in reference to the colored congregations, are so owing to the impossibility of even approximating figures. Besides those of the Freedmen who regularly attend services, there are large numbers who are occasional attendants, but who do not belong to the congregation. A colored Sabbath School is about to be organized under competent (colored) teachers. J. V. Welch, Missionary, also reports successful work. . . Welch has 134 pupils in a day school."[9]

The report from the same parish for the 1868 convention was quite different: "The large congregation reported last year disappeared, en masse, and without notice, on Whitsunday (Pentecost), 1867. They are now organized as the African Episcopal congregation, have a place of worship erected in sight of the church, and have never given me since the day they left, the slightest opportunity to minister among them. Of the 11 colored attendants now reported [that is, who remained at Claremont Parish], only two are freedmen; the rest being well-educated persons who were never slaves. None of this latter class have proved unfaithful to the Church."[10]

The Committee on the State of the Church reported in 1868 that in lowcountry parishes where black communicants had numbered in the hundreds there were now half as many in some cases, and in other cases the black communicants had simply vanished. Many of the chapels built for use by slaves had been destroyed during or just after the war, but the major problem faced by clergymen attempting to minister to freed men and women was that the organizational structure of plantation worship had disappeared. Slavery was over, and the freed persons no longer had to remain on the plantations. "Moving about" was common as the now emancipated people sought to restructure their lives, and there were other options for worship open to them. The surviving chapels that had been built for use by slaves stood in silent desuetude. Further, as the Committee on the State of the Church reported, for those freed people who did remain in or near their pre-emancipation homes, planters were no longer able to support worship and religious education programs—and in spite of the good intentions expressed at the 1866 convention, the diocese had insufficient resources to secure the number of missionaries needed. Finally, the factors of mobility and wider choice of worship options applied to all former slaves, not just to those who had lived on large plantations. Bishop Davis remained hopeful: "You are aware how large a proportion of the colored population have been lost to our church; we are not, however, without hope that a more established state of things, and a more mature judgment will bring many home again to their old fold."[11] His hope, however, was not realized, as is shown by the table below.

**Diocese of South Carolina: Total number of communicants reported by parishes, 1840–1880**

| Year | White communicants | Black communicants | Total |
|------|------|------|------|
| 1840 | 2,580 | 689 | 3,269 |
| 1850 | 2,669 | 2,247 | 4,916 |
| 1860 | 3,166 | 2,960 | 6,126 |
| 1861 | 2,979 | 2,973 | 5,952 |
| 1862 | 2,818 | 1,528 | 4,346 |
| 1864 | 2,660 | 1,200 | 3,860 |
| 1866 | 1,425 | 93 | 1,518 |
| 1868 | 2,614 | 395 | 3,009 |
| 1870 | 2,633 | 358 | 2,991 |
| 1871 | 3,359 | 784 | 4,143 |
| 1872 | 3,102 | 618 | 3,720 |
| 1880 | 3,932 | 617 | 4,549 |

*Sources:* Data for 1840, 1850, 1870, and 1880 are from Albert Sidney Thomas, *A Historical Account of the Protestant Episcopal Church in South Carolina, 1820–1957,* 702. Data for 1860 and the war years are from the journals of the Diocese of South Carolina.

This table shows the work of Davis's predecessors, Bishops Nathaniel Bowen and Christopher Gadsden, in evangelizing the slaves in the decade and a half before Davis came in 1853. During Davis's episcopate the peak communicant level was in 1860, a level that in 1861 held for black communicants but had begun dropping for their white counterparts. The decline in white communicants after 1860 may be attributed to the disruptions of the war and its aftermath. By 1862 the war was causing slaves either to be pulled back from or abandoned along the

Carolina coast, which, in turn, made it difficult to continue the church's ministry among them. Disruptions continued and became more common as the war progressed. The postwar data through the early 1870s reflect phenomena discussed in this essay. For white communicants the prewar peak in communicants had been reached by 1871 and by 1880 was significantly higher. For black Episcopalians, however, the communicant level that had plummeted with the war was in 1880 still at a fraction of its value in 1860.

## Epilogue

Bishop Davis died in 1871.[12] His successor, Bishop William B. W. Howe, supported at the 1876 convention the application of St. Mark's Church in Charleston, a black church that both Davis and Howe had nurtured, for union with the Diocese of South Carolina. The clergy voted approval, but the application failed because it was rejected by the laity. Howe was greatly disappointed, believing that the diocese had let prejudice subvert its mission. He made this clear in his 1877 convention address. Howe also viewed this action as a setback for diocesan outreach to black individuals.

> We see a congregation excluded, which comes up to every requirement of your constitution and canons, which can send four delegates, competent in point of intelligence to consult for the interests of their constituents, and we see them refused admission because of color, and for social reasons. . . .
>
> When our Diocese shall open its Convention to deputies who are qualified by our rules to sit here, and from congregations competent for union with us . . . we shall then have put our feet upon a rock, and shall become strong . . . as witnesses to the truth that the church belongs not to man, or to illustrate our social position, but to God.[13]

## Notes

1. *Diocesan Records of the Year A.D. 1865* (Charleston: Walker, Evans, and Cogswell, 1865), 25. This document recorded the proceedings of those clergy and lay persons who assembled in May 1865. It is not an official diocesan journal and is not bound with the records of the diocese.

2. *Diocese of South Carolina, 1866* (Charleston: Joseph Walker, 1866), 26–27.

3. *Diocese of South Carolina, 1867* (Columbia: W.W. Deane, 1867), 49.

4. See reports from the Committee on the State of the Church and Committee on the Destruction of Churches and Church Property in *Diocese of South Carolina, 1868* (Charleston: Joseph Walker, 1868).

5. *Diocese of South Carolina, 1866*, 48.

6. *Spirit of Missions* 31 (1866): 726.

7. *Spirit of Missions* 35 (1870): 63.

8. *Spirit of Missions* 37 (1872): 250.

9. Ibid., 54.

10. *Diocese of South Carolina, 1868,* 58–59.

11. Ibid., 50.

12. *Diocese of South Carolina, 1872* (Charleston: Walker, Evans, and Cogswell, 1872), 27.

13. *Diocese of South Carolina,* 1877 (Charleston: Walker, Evans, and Cogswell, 1877), 43. In 1965 St. Mark's was granted admission to the Diocese of South Carolina at last. A summary of the rich history of this church is provided on the church website: http://www .saintmarkschurch.com/2501.html (accessed 15 January 2013).

# Aftermath in North Carolina

✠ *Thomas Atkinson*

Although there were pockets of destruction, North Carolina had not suffered the widespread damage in wartime that occurred in Virginia and South Carolina. Nevertheless, when the Diocese of North Carolina convened in September 1865, Bishop Thomas Atkinson faced several "aftermath" issues of deep concern to him, including parishes that were struggling financially, inadequate clergy compensation, scattered congregations, and chaos in transportation. Adequate clergy compensation, in particular, which Atkinson felt was essential to the diocese's recovery from war, remained an issue that troubled him for several years.[1] The issue about which the bishop spoke the most forcefully, however, was bringing the gospel to the former slaves.

## Historical Context for Obligation to the Black Race

He began his discussion of how the diocese should proceed with respect to the religious life of the former slaves by placing the matter in historical context:

> Some of us have ever feared, while the colored people were in the condition of slavery, that the power and control which the white race possessed over them was not exercised in such a way as to make us acceptable to God, and faithful servants in His sight.
>
> . . . There was a good deal of care shown in providing for their bodily wants, but very insufficient attention was paid to their moral and religious improvement; . . . under the system of slavery in these States the African race made a progress, during the last hundred years, not only in numbers and physical comfort, but a progress from barbarism to civilization, from Heathenism to Christianity, to which the history of the world offers no parallel. . . .
>
> But the system was no doubt defective, better adapted to the early stage of a people's progress from the savage state, than to that which they have now reached, and, at any rate, God in his providence has definitely set it aside. The future of that people is very obscure. . . . What then must we do as Christian men and women? We must continue our care for them; we ought even to

increase it. We have surely, been in some degree, delinquent in the past; let us resolve in God's strength, not to be so for the future.[2]

Atkinson was saying that slave owners had not paid sufficient attention to religious instruction of slaves and that it was vital now that the slaves were free people that their religious needs be met. Moving from concept to practice, Atkinson urged that several actions be taken. First, because former slaves were now entitled by law to wages for their labor, they should be paid, "not grudgingly," and given not merely "what is just and equal," but something more. Atkinson believed that black people felt contempt or rudeness "more than a serious injury," and it was the duty of church members to avoid that behavior toward the now freed men and women. It was important to make them feel that white Episcopalians, in fact, are their "best friends," ready to give counsel, aid, and protection. Most of all, the bishop was concerned that they be provided (by the church) with sound religious instruction. He feared "false teachers" and "fanatics" who could lead the former slaves astray, causing "calamitous" results for both races. He concluded with this challenge: "Let us raise up colored congregations in our towns, and let all our clergy feel that one important part of their charge is to teach and to befriend the colored people, and especially to train, as far as they are permitted to do so, the children of that race."[3]

This section of Atkinson's address was referred to a special committee, which submitted a detailed report that was generally in harmony with the views of the bishop. In a thoughtful *Whereas* clause, the committee noted the "revolution" in society that had altered the relations between black and white people in the South had created confusion and was causing alienation, rooted in indifference on the part of former slave owners and distrust and suspicion on the part of former slaves. This alienation was hindering, sometimes halting, the religious education of the freedmen. The committee noted, however, that the status of freedmen was "providential" and urged that the church move to reduce the confusion and with all the "energy and wisdom at her command" work to "elevate the colored race." There followed five specific resolutions, calling for

1. separate houses of worship "as soon as practicable," with colored vestries which ultimately would have power to elect ministers, who could be white or black;
2. locating and providing instruction for colored men as catechists and Sunday school teachers;
3. inviting colored ministers in other dioceses to "come among their own people in this Diocese, and to labor in their sphere with us";
4. initiating steps to provide for the education of young colored men for the ministry;

5. "whenever practicable," to make provision for the mental training of colored children (that is, to begin day schools that would teach the basics of reading, writing, and mathematics).[4]

In winding down their report, the committee members expressed the need for "decisive and definite action," claiming that since emancipation there had been almost "universal deterioration in the moral condition" of the freedmen and claiming that the path outlined by the committee was "the most direct way of carrying to the colored man the blessing of our holy Christianity." That blessing, the committee contended, should be brought to "every soul committed to our care, whether its casket be Anglican or African." The diocesan council, however, did not share the committee's sense of urgency and voted to postpone action on the report until the next council meeting, scheduled for May 1866. The "temporal and religious interests of our colored population" in the meantime were commit-ted to the "benevolence and wisdom of the Diocese."[5]

Atkinson's address to the 1866 diocesan convention was read by someone else; the bishop was en route to Europe for a stay of six months, which he hoped would restore his health.[6] In that address Atkinson reaffirmed his commitment to reli-gious instruction and to education of the black population and reinforced the call of the postponed resolutions of 1865 for the diocese to provide for the prepa-ration of colored ministers who could lead colored congregations. This time the diocese responded favorably, without further delay, to the requests of the bishop, passing a series of resolutions. These resolutions, though offered by a different special committee from the September 1865 committee, reflected the views of that committee and of Bishop Atkinson.

The 1866 resolutions were shorter and less explicit than those proposed in 1865, but the key elements remained, including the provision that black and white congregations have separate churches. Progress was slow, however, as may be in-ferred from Atkinson's address in May 1867, in which he reiterated his conviction that the diocese should do what it could "for the education and religious instruc-tion of our colored population" and should proceed to admit into the ministry "well qualified persons of African descent." Yet another special diocesan commit-tee responded by offering resolutions that the diocese establish regular schools under the church aegis and arrange to educate and to admit black clergy. These passed the council, as did a resolution that the diocese would "accept aid to build churches and school houses for the colored people."[7]

## Obligation to the Black Race: Areas of Progress

After the war the Episcopal Church's Freedman's Commission, with the assis-tance of Bishop Atkinson, established schools in Wilmington, New Bern, Fayette-ville, and Raleigh. These schools were associated with churches, and the bishop, the rectors, and the parishioners supported the work of the schools. The presence of these schools, in turn, helped with establishment and growth of black congregations in the communities concerned.[8] All four were successful. Two of these ventures are described below.

## *Wilmington*

St. Paul's Church in Wilmington was founded just three years before the Civil War. When it suspended services in 1863, its communicant rolls showed thirty-four white and sixteen black members. There was a chaotic period near the end of the war and during its immediate aftermath, in which the use of the church building was controlled by Union occupation forces.[9] Soon after the war, however, both black and white communicants began returning to St. Paul's. By the 1867 diocesan meeting, the minister in charge, the Reverend Daniel Morrelle, reported on behalf of the "Colored Congregation Worshipping at St. Paul's, Wilmington" that there were forty-three black communicants. It was also reported that a day school with four teachers paid by the Freedman's Commission was operating in the church building and that there were 280 pupils. Minister Morrelle noted that "full choral services" had been commenced on Easter Sunday, with the expectation that, "under Divine Blessing," such services would help to build up a large congregation. In the autumn of 1869 the African American members separated from St. Paul's in order to form a new congregation, St. Mark's. In 1870 Bishop Atkinson received into the diocese the Reverend Charles O. Brady, a black man who had been ordained deacon in 1869 by Bishop John Williams of Connecticut.[10] Deacon Brady was put in charge of the St. Mark's congregation and opened a second mission school, at which he served as the teacher.

By the time Brady came, the first mission school had weathered the impact of the fiscal crisis that had struck the Freedman's Commission in 1868, but the school had only two teachers and a smaller enrollment than it had in 1867. The head teacher, Miss Hesketh, reported in April 1870.

> Our number of pupils continues the same, that is, from 100 to 120 every day. The children are doing very well indeed, with their studies, and are good, as well as industrious. Today we were favored with a visit from Bishop Payne in company with Bishop Atkinson. The former gave the children some account of the real Africans, with which they were very much interested. He also sang two little hymns (which all children know in our language) in one of the languages of Africa. Bishop Atkinson told the children that they might laugh at it now, but really it was the same language that perhaps their grandparents had spoken; this, they thought so very, very strange. On Wednesday, we hope to have Bishop Payne preach to the colored congregation, and will have a collection taken up for their brothers in Africa.

Rev. Mr. Brady's (our missionary) school is very good indeed. I believe it numbers 75.[11]

Deacon Brady reported a month later that his congregation, which still worshipped at St. Paul's, was increasing in numbers and that during a recent visit by Bishop Atkinson a full congregation had witnessed sixteen parishioners being confirmed. The "whole staff" of clergy of the city was present. He then noted that the average attendance at his school was from fifty-five to sixty pupils per day and that he was "happy to state that I have some well qualified for higher branches."[12]

Within a year of Brady's arrival, St. Mark's had secured sufficient funding to begin constructing a church building at a different site.[13] The residents of Wilmington and those of Boston, Brady's hometown, which he had visited on a fundraising trip, both responded generously to appeals for funds.[14] There were ninety-seven communicants when, in 1873, Deacon Brady wrote in the parochial report to convention: "Since my last report the congregation of St. Mark's Parish has applied for admission into union with the diocesan convention, and has been, I am happy to say, admitted by unanimous vote."[15] St. Mark's Church was consecrated on 18 June 1875 by Bishop Atkinson. The Reverend C. O. Brady remained until he announced his retirement on 15 April 1885.[16] St. Mark's celebrated its one-hundredth anniversary in 1969 and is still functioning today.

*Raleigh*

In October 1867 J. Brinton Smith, secretary of the Freedman's Commission, resigned and transferred to the Diocese of North Carolina from New Jersey. His primary duty in the diocese was noted in an announcement by Bishop Atkinson: "Since the last meeting of the convention, a Normal School for the education of colored teachers and a training school for the instruction of colored ministers, have been established in the city of Raleigh, under the superintendence of the Rev. J. Brinton Smith, D.D. and that there is every ground to hope for their success, and consequently, for great benefit to the colored people of the State and indirectly to the entire population."[17]

St. Augustine's Normal School and Collegiate Institute in Raleigh had been organized under the auspices of the Freedman's Commission, using as endowment a twenty-five-thousand-dollar bequest from the estate of Charles Avery of Pittsburgh, Pennsylvania. The Freedman's Bureau under General Oliver O. Howard also helped with the establishment of this institution. A charter for the school was obtained from the state of North Carolina, and Bishop Atkinson and members of the clergy and laity of the Diocese of North Carolina were named as trustees.[18] St. Augustine's endowment increased, and over time the institution evolved from a normal school to educate freed slaves into St. Augustine's College, which granted its first baccalaureate degrees in 1931.

*Analysis of Postwar Outreach to Black Population*

In the decade after the war there were efforts at several sites to educate the children of freed people and to bring black citizens into the Episcopal Church. A few of these efforts, with the help of the Freedman's Commission, were successful, resulting in black churches being established and growth in black communicants in those localities. Although there was some progress at other sites besides the four mentioned above, across the diocese as a whole progress was very slow, and the key elements of the Atkinson plan, namely separate churches to serve large numbers of freed people and a cadre of black ministers to staff those churches, were not materializing as the 1870s began.

In 1869 and 1870 the reported numbers of confirmations of blacks in the diocese were sixty-eight and seventy-six, respectively. These numbers exceeded only slightly those for the years just before the war. Overall growth in black membership was slow, climbing from a reported nadir of 177 communicants in 1866 to 278 in 1867, then dropping again and reaching 333 by the 1871 report.[19] The diocesan report to the 1871 General Convention projected a pessimistic outlook: "The efforts made in this Diocese for the spiritual improvement of the colored race are not as promising of good results as are desired by the friends of the freedmen; while in some few places they seem to appreciate the teachings and ministrations of the Church, in most cases they have separated themselves from the ministry of the Church, and given themselves to the guidance of ignorant teachers of their own race, who are leading them into the wildest excesses of delusion and fanaticism."[20]

The "excesses of delusion and fanaticism" were observed by Miss Sproat, a Freedman's Commission teacher at Wilmington who wrote a letter in which she first expressed her joy in being given the chance help her charges, who were "so anxious to learn," and then added: "Some of the colored people have had what they call a series of anxious meetings, in a building a very short distance from our house. They commenced them on a Saturday evening and have kept them up for three successive nights, beginning about nine o'clock in the evening and continuing all night or rather about three o'clock in the morning. It is almost frightful to listen to the groans and shrieks which they consider evidence that the 'Holy Spirit' is striving with them."[21]

The 1871 report to General Convention acknowledged the reality that the freed people in North Carolina generally were not responding to overtures from the Episcopal Church. The harsh language, however, seemed to reflect disappointment, if not some bitterness, at being rejected by the bulk of the black population. Attributing the rejection largely to the "guidance of ignorant teachers" was a generalization that ignored the complex reasons for that rejection, including both white paternalism and the variety of religious options being chosen by black individuals. In spite of this situation, the pockets of success at Wilmington, New Bern, Fayetteville, and Raleigh alluded to in the report were to result in enduring congregations of black Episcopalians.

## Notes

1. *Diocese of North Carolina, 1867* (Fayetteville: s.n., 1867), 65.
2. *Diocese of North Carolina, 1865* (Raleigh: J. C. Gorman, 1865), 22–23.
3. Ibid., 24.
4. Ibid., 36–37.
5. Ibid., 37–38.
6. The respite from his duties did have the desired effect. Atkinson served as bishop until January 1881, assisted from 1873 by Assistant Bishop Theodore B. Lyman.
7. *Diocese of North Carolina, 1867,* 48.
8. The examples of black congregations given below are taken from the journals of the Diocese of North Carolina for the years 1865 to 1870.
9. See William M. Reaves, *Strength through Struggle: the Chronological and Historical Record of the African American Community in Wilmington, North Carolina, 1865–1950,* ed. Beverly Tetterton. (Wilmington: New Hanover County Public Library, 1998), 125–26, for a brief history of St. Paul's prior to 1867.
10. *Diocese of North Carolina, 1870* (Published by the Convention, 1870), 22.
11. *Spirit of Missions* 35 (1870): 255.
12. Ibid.
13. *Diocese of North Carolina, 1871* (Published by the Convention, 1871), 50.
14. Reaves, *Strength through Struggle,* 127.
15. *Diocese of North Carolina, 1873* (Raleigh: Edwards, Broughton, 1873), 56.
16. Reaves, *Strength through Struggle,* 129, 131.
17. *Diocese of North Carolina, 1868* (Wilmington: Bernard's Printing, 1868), 31.
18. *Spirit of Missions* 32 (1867): 44–45.
19. See the Diocese of North Carolina journals for the years 1858 through 1871.
20. *Journal of the General Convention, 1871* (Boston: Printed for the Convention, 1872), 466.
21. *Spirit of Missions* 31 (1866): 526.

# Aftermath in Virginia

⇥ *John Johns*

### State of the Diocese

Far more Civil War battles occurred on Virginia soil than on that of any other state; fighting began there in May 1861 and lasted until General Robert E. Lee's surrender at Appomattox in April 1865. Many Episcopal churches in Virginia were damaged or destroyed during wartime, and destruction of personal property and impoverishment were widespread among communicants.

The following communications appeared in the parochial reports section of the May 1866 diocesan journal. George A. Smith, rector of Lexington Parish in Amherst County, reported that "the impoverished condition of the members of the church in Amherst County has prevented the collection of any money for church purposes."[1] J. H. Morrison, rector of St. Andrew's Parish in Brunswick County, gave a similar assessement: "This parish, formerly a wealthy one, is now so utterly impoverished, that it is almost useless to attempt to raise any money in it for any object whatever. Apart from this, the prospects of the church are decidedly encouraging."[2] The report from St. Mark's Church in Culpepper County was explicit with regard to the nature and scope of the devastation:

> Episcopal Churches [three] within the lines of the Union Army in this County were utterly destroyed by it . . . during the occupation of that army in 1863–1864. The whole county is widespread desolation as far as man could destroy.
>
> Families who stayed were stripped of everything but house and land . . . all their horses, mules, and stock of every description, with even the poultry of the County were swept away. Thus poor and peeled, they are now struggling for a bare subsistence, whilst those that fled and are now returned have come to see and partake of a like destitution. But poor as we are, we hope by the blessing of God to be revived again.[3]

When the war ended, Virginia bishop John Johns at first declined offers of assistance from Northern churches but soon relented, and the diocese did receive aid for clergy salaries and for help in rebuilding and restoring property.[4] The list of contributors reported by the bishop in May 1866 included the Board of Missions, "the ladies of a church in Louisville," and many other individual churches in states from Massachusetts to Maryland.[5] A report from Abington and Ware parishes in Gloucester County noted in 1866 that for the past year the rector had been supported by outside donations, most of which had been collected by the bishop.

During this economic crisis Johns spoke to his flock a message of hope, citing biblical examples of how great afflictions had been overcome, while at the same time urging the faithful to make "systematic efforts" to secure the funds to provide clergy with a living wage. The addresses given by the bishop from 1867 to 1869 and the various committee reports indicated that recovery was in progress.

### Prayer for the President

Union troops took control of Richmond on 3 April, and on 12 April 1865 the commander of the Union occupation force had the following document, headed "General Order, No. 29," published in the newspaper: "Protection is hereby extended to all churches and public worship. Religious services may be continued without interruption as in time of profound peace. This protection must not, however, be perverted for the utterance in any form of worship of treasonable sentiments or expressions. When this is perverted, it will be withdrawn. In all churches where prayers have heretofore been offered for the so-called President of the Confederate States, a similar mark of respect is hereby ordered to be paid to the President of the United States. By command of Major General G. Weitzel."[6] The "prayer issue" had come to the capital city of the Confederacy.

Episcopal churches in Virginia were under a directive from their bishop, disseminated after Virginia joined the Confederacy, to substitute "Confederate States" for "United States" in the prayer for "all in Civil Authority" and could not make the change stipulated in General Order, No. 29, without authorization from the diocesan bishop. Bishop Johns did authorize the change, but because both public transportation and mail service were disrupted, there was a delay in word getting to many parishes. After General Order, No. 29, was published, St. Paul's did not hold services until 30 April, the vestry having met on the previous day to approve the resumption of Sunday services.[7] Even though the bishop had authorized the change, and the vestry had approved holding services again, and the rector began implementing the change, many members of the congregation did not accept the prayer. Elizabeth Wright Weddell in her history of St. Paul's describes what occurred: "In those days the congregation got down on their knees with their backs to the chancel. . . . There were many people attending church who could not conscientiously pray for the President of the United States and got up off their knees when this prayer was said. The ladies then wore hoop-skirts and there was heard quite a 'rustle through the church' when they would rise, and a few minutes later, turn and kneel again!"[8]

In spite of acts of destruction by Union troops against Episcopal churches in Virginia and his unequivocal support of the Confederacy, Bishop Johns publicly accepted the South's defeat and did so gracefully and promptly. Johns's recommendation with regard to the Prayer for the President of the United States and all in Civil Authority was in sharp contrast to that of Bishop Richard Hooker Wilmer in Alabama. As soon as Johns had received "reliable intelligence" that the Confederate cause was lost and the authority of the United States reinstated, he felt that it was his duty and that of the clergy and laity of the Diocese of Virginia promptly to give "honest obedience" to the federal government. They also had the obligation to pray for those in authority, and he authorized use of the Prayer for the President and all in Civil Authority. The president and other officers of the United States were "in authority," and to them the prayer was applicable.[9]

Bishop Johns acknowledged that military orders proscribing omission of the prayer for the president had been criticized as being an infringement on religious liberty but noted that (1) his call for reinstatement of the prayer antedated any such orders and (2) use of the prayer was now a duty "clearly enjoined in scriptures"; hence any actions by military authorities, even improper interference, did not "absolve" the church from that duty.[10]

## Church Reunion

Johns then told his diocese that the proper course of action for the church in Virginia was to reunite as soon as possible with the Protestant Episcopal Church in the United States of America (PECUSA). The council, however, felt that the matter should be referred to the November 1865 meeting of the Protestant Episcopal Church in the Confederate States (PECCSA) in Augusta, Georgia, and passed a resolution to that effect.[11] Johns was disappointed but felt that under the circumstances he could not attend the October meeting of PECUSA. The PECCSA session in November provided a mechanism for withdrawal from PECCSA, and, by the time of the May 1866 diocesan council meeting for Virginia, all other dioceses originally in PECCSA had withdrawn to reunite with PECUSA. At that 1866 meeting, finally, the Diocese of Virginia declared itself by resolution to be under the aegis of PECUSA. The vote, however, was not unanimous, being 57 to 9 in the clergy order and 36 to 11 among the laity; the debate was acrimonious and "stormy" at times, with some participants no doubt influenced by the harsh treatment received by their churches during the war.[12]

## Ministry to Free Black Men and Women

The dominant issue requiring action at the 1866 diocesan convention was re-union with PECUSA, but Johns also urged diocesan action to try to retain those former slaves and free black persons who were communicants and to launch a missionary effort among the freed men and women: "The zeal which has sought the native African in the bush, and deemed it right that even life should be risked in preaching the Gospel to them under the scorching heat, and exposed to the fatal fevers of the unfriendly climate, cannot neglect the religious cultivation of those whom Providence has mysteriously domesticated amongst us."[13] Johns then suggested that this local missionary work be a permanent part of the agenda for the Committee on the Diocesan Missionary Society. A special diocesan Commit-tee on Colored Congregations was appointed with the expectation that it would report at the next meeting.

Schools supported by the Freedman's Commission had begun appearing in Virginia even before the diocese rejoined the national church.[14] A glimpse of one of these early ventures was provided in April 1866 by the Reverend M. E. Willing, who helped start and then taught in commission-funded schools at Norfolk.

> A day school, numbering one hundred and fifty children, and a night school numbering about fifty adults, have already been organized. . . . The colored people generally have manifested great interest in the enterprise from its very inception, and the kind, prudent, and conservative manner in which our operations have been conducted, have entirely silenced the somewhat for-midable opposition that we first met with; and all now seem to wish us suc-cess. . . . On Friday, March 16th [1866] the Right Reverend Bishop of Virginia, Mrs. Johns, and the Reverend Rector Bartine [rector of Christ Church, Nor-folk] favored our School with a visit. The Bishop made a most beautiful and impressive address, expressing the great interest he felt in our work, and his pleasure in being permitted to address us under such favorable circumstances. All who heard him were more than ever impressed with the fact that he feels the deepest concern in whatever tends to promote the best interests of the colored race. . . . Mrs. Johns exhibited much interest in the improvement of the scholars, kindly examining and commending first efforts at writing etc.[15]

Bishop Johns welcomed the support of the Freedman's Commission, and when the Diocese of Virginia reunited with PECUSA in May 1866, he was pleased to solicit the commission's assistance officially. Just over a year later, commission secretary Brinton Smith requested that Southern dioceses draw up plans for their work among the freedmen, begin implementation of those plans, and then seek assistance from the commission and other sources for that part of the needed support that the diocese could not supply. Johns acted on Smith's suggestion promptly, and a significant share of the Freedman's Commission resources were used to support religious and secular instruction of freed people in Virginia.[16]

At the 1867 diocesan meeting the Committee on Colored Congregations did submit a detailed report, introduced with a general observation: "Since the last annual meeting of the Council, the work among the colored population of the Diocese has progressed slowly indeed, but steadily, and on the whole with a reasonable degree of success. At five or six points only in this vast Diocese has the work been kept up among them since the change in their condition took place. And at all these points, notwithstanding the many difficulties which have been encountered, God seems to have blessed our efforts, at some of them, in a very great degree."[17]

The report then proceeded to describe some of the work among the freed people, much of which was being supported by resources and personnel supplied by the Freedman's Commission.

> In the City of Richmond, more obstacles to this work seem to present themselves than anywhere else in the Diocese. . . . Yet even here we have a separate congregation worshipping in its own church, the first, and as yet the only one in the Diocese, with a Sunday School averaging through the last year 150 scholars, and two day schools numbering 277. Three faithful teachers supported by the Freedman's Commission—one of them a highly cultivated lady of our own State—continue with zeal and perseverance their labors among them. A clergyman of our own Diocese now has charge of the congregation, and a candidate for orders has been received among them.[18]

Work in several other locations was discussed, including Petersburg, where a fire had just destroyed a chapel that was being used both for religious services and as a school building. The committee acknowledged that there were obstacles to overcome, but added that "by the change in their social condition, the Great Head of the church now offers to the Episcopal Church, advantages for instructing the colored people, which she has not had for many years before in the Diocese enjoyed."[19]

Before the 1868 diocesan meeting the new assistant bishop Francis M. Whittle consecrated a new building for St. Stephen's, a black congregation in Petersburg. Whittle incorporated into his address to the council in May an account of this collaborative venture that had begun right after the war, when a day school for black children had been established in a chapel built during the war. Funding for the school's operation had been furnished by the Freedman's Commission. The chapel, as noted in a diocesan committee report the prior year, had burned in April 1867, but a structure that gave the black communicants of St. Stephen's their own church and also served to house the day school was built quickly with funds secured from the Freedman's Bureau, the Pennsylvania and New York branches of the Freedman's Commission, and private donors. By the time of the 1868 report, there were more than forty communicants and more than four hundred scholars.[20]

## Status of Black Churches

The post-emancipation outreach to the black population in Virginia was built on a model of encouraging separate congregations for black communicants, which would be staffed by black ministers as soon as practicable. The status of these congregations within the Diocese was uncertain, however, as shown by the case of St. Stephen's Church in Petersburg, which in May 1869 submitted an application for union with the Diocese.[21]

The first signature on the application was that of the Reverend J. S. Atwell, who had just been ordained to the priesthood by Johns in a ceremony at St. Stephen's. The bishop, in reporting on the ordination, noted that "the Rector in a long and careful examination by the brethren who united in his ordination, gave satisfactory proof of his aptness for the work of the ministry, and, by his faithfulness, diligence and his irreproachable conduct as a deacon, has secured the respect and confidence not only of his own people, but of the Christian community by which they are surrounded."[22]

In response to the petition for membership in the diocese it was resolved that St. Stephen's be admitted to union with the diocese and be given representation and that the interests of St. Stephen's within the diocese be cared for by the Standing Committee on Colored People. What actually passed, however, was a three-part substitute motion that stipulated that the congregation of St. Stephen's Church, Bristol Parish, "be and hereby is taken under the care of this Council," and its interests with the council are "hereby entrusted to the aforesaid Standing Committee [on Colored People]." Hence St. Stephen's was "under the care of" the council but not a member of the council and would voice its "interests" to a standing committee, not directly to the council. After these motions had been adopted, another resolution was passed that established a committee of three clergy and two laymen to consider "a plan for . . . spiritual well being of the colored members of our church, more promotive of the respect to which they are entitled as Christians, and in every way more agreeable to themselves than any which has been submitted to our consideration heretofore."[23] More than a decade later the diocese proposed at the 1880 General Convention that the idea of an entirely separate organization for black communicants within the church be explored. The House of Bishops responded that it could not agree to consider a proposal that would divide the house of God, and the matter was dropped.[24]

Thus the Diocese of Virginia was committed to bringing African Americans into the church, but the issue of the status that African Americans would have within the Virginia church remained unresolved fifteen years after the Civil War.

### Postscript: A Different Approach in Texas

The model for postwar outreach efforts to black people described in this and the preceding three essays was not followed by Bishop Alexander Gregg of Texas. In Bishop Gregg's diocese there was no base of freed people who had been confirmed while they were slaves. He was the first bishop of Texas, having arrived a few months after his consecration in October 1859, and little had been done in way of religious instruction for the freedmen before his coming.

Nevertheless, Gregg shared the view of his fellow bishops in the former Confederacy that there should be a vigorous outreach to the freedmen. His first model for outreach, though, differed from that of his colleagues in that he favored worship services in the same building for the two races. At the 1866 meeting of his diocese he recommended that a portion of seats be set aside in churches for the freed people, unless limited capacity required separate facilities. Even then, he noted, in a statement that proved remarkably prescient, that "the principle of separation, further than is necessary or becoming, should not have place. If encouraged, it will be found the fruitful source of an antagonism which can but prove disastrous in the end."[25] A diocesan committee affirmed this approach by resolution at the 1867 convention.[26]

Efforts to bring black people into the church in Texas were not successful, however, and in 1874 Gregg changed course in a major way, embracing a proposal for a suffragan bishop in the diocese who would oversee outreach efforts to black people, treating them as a separate population. This proposal was rejected by General Convention.[27]

### Notes

1. *Diocese of Virginia, 1866* (Richmond: Gary and Clemmitt, 1866). 58.

2. Ibid., 62–63.

3. Ibid., 68–69.

4. G. MacLaren Brydon, "The Diocese of Virginia in the Southern Confederacy," *Historical Magazine of the Protestant Episcopal Church* 17 (December 1948): 404–5.

5. *Diocese of Virginia, 1866*, 25.

6. Elizabeth Wright Weddell, *St. Paul's Church Richmond, Virginia: Its Historical Years and Memorials*, 2 vols. (Richmond: William Byrd, 1931), 1: 248–49.

7. Ibid., 250.

8. Ibid., 250–51.

9. *Diocese of Virginia, 1865* (Richmond: Gary and Clemmitt, 1865), 21.

10. Ibid., 22.

11. Ibid., 38–39.

12. *Diocese of Virginia, 1866*, 29, and Brydon, "Diocese of Virginia in the Southern Confederacy," 408–9.

13. *Diocese of Virginia, 1866*, 22.

14. See above, the essay entitled "The Freedman's Commission," and *Spirit of Missions* 31 (1866): 156.

15. *Spirit of Missions* 31 (1866): 229, 231.

16. *Spirit of Missions* 33 (1868): 60.

17. *Diocese of Virginia, 1867* (Richmond: Medical Journal Press, 1867), 57.

18. Ibid., 58.

19. Ibid., 59.

20. *Diocese of Virginia, 1868,* (Richmond: Farmer's Gazette, 1868), 41–42.

21. *Diocese of Virginia, 1869* (Richmond: Gary and Clemmitt, 1869), 178.

22. Ibid., 28.

23. Ibid., 56.

24. *Journal of the General Convention, 1880* (Boston: Printed for the Convention, 1881), 33, 328.

25. *Diocese of Texas, 1866* (Houston: Gray and Smallwood, 1866), 27.

26. *Diocese of Texas, 1867* (Houston: A. C. Gregg, 1868), 12.

27. *Diocese of Texas, 1874* (San Antonio: Herald Printing and Binding, 1874), 60. See also *Journal of the General Convention, 1877* (Boston: Printed for the Convention, 1878).

# Aftermath in Former
# Slave States in the Union

⊬⇒ *Benjamin Bosworth Smith, William Rollinson*
*Whittingham, Alfred Lee, and Cicero Stephens Hawks*

When the war ended, the dioceses within the four slave states in the Union did not have to contend with the issues of civil and church reunion faced by dioceses in the former Confederate States. There was some degree of destruction and disruption, except in Delaware, and there was a legacy of internecine struggle, especially in Missouri, where the strife had been accompanied by considerable violence. This essay examines the war's aftermath in the Union slave states only with regard to the involvement of the diocesan bishops in steps taken by the dioceses to offer religious instruction, worship opportunities, and educational programs to the black people, all of whom were free by the end of 1865.

The states of Maryland and Missouri took action during the Civil War to grant freedom to the slaves within their borders. This action took the form of a constitutional change in Maryland in November 1864 and of an executive order issued by the governor of Missouri in January 1865. Slaves were legally freed in Kentucky and Delaware when the Thirteenth Amendment became effective in December 1865.

When the war ended, Kentucky, Maryland, and Missouri faced the issues raised by emancipation of significant numbers of slaves. The issue in Delaware, which had only 1,798 slaves in 1860, was the need to confront its abysmal record of dealing with the free black population. Maryland also had many black people who had been free at the start of the war.

## Benjamin Bosworth Smith of Kentucky

The Diocese of Kentucky, under the leadership of Bishop Benjamin Bosworth Smith and Assistant Bishop George Cummings, began immediately after the war to address the religious and educational needs of the freed slaves. The essence of the position taken by the two bishops can be summarized as follows:

1. There was a massive societal and educational problem among the free black citizens and there should be a commitment by the church to help solve it.
2. The Episcopal Church should be responsible for bringing at least a significant share of this population into the Christian fold.
3. A segregated approach should be followed for both educational programs and religious services.[1]

Immediately after the war Bishop Smith took a vigorous, hands-on approach to move toward achievement of these goals; one of his first steps was the ordination to the diaconate on 16 December 1866 of Joseph S. Atwell.[2] Atwell was a native of the island of Barbados who had studied at Codrington College and was one of several black men from the island who had been recruited by Smith to come to Kentucky. The Reverend Mr. Atwell immediately began serving as minister at St. Mark's Parish in Louisville, where he maintained a thriving Sunday school and operated a day school that his bishop described as "one of the best in the city."[3]

At diocesan convention in 1867, Bishop Smith reported that Atwell had presented four persons for confirmation. "This event is worthy of record," he noted, "since it is probably the first occasion in which a class, consisting wholly of colored people, and presented by their own colored minister, has ever been confirmed in a colored church, in either of the Southern or Southwestern states."[4] Smith also noted that St. Mark's had survived the discouraging years of Civil War and had begun "in a quiet way, the very work for the benefit of the colored race in our midst, required by the great change in their social condition, a work connected with their better education, and the preparation of teachers of their own race to meet the eager demand for common school instruction."[5]

Smith reported to his diocese in 1868 that a pupil of Atwell's had gone on to establish a Sunday school and a day school in Limerick, a suburb of Louisville. Another "well-educated colored person" from Barbados, a Mr. Ford, was conducting both a Sunday school and a day school in Frankfort. The diocese also learned that two other young recruits from Barbados, a D. A. Straker and a Mr. King, were "daily expected" to arrive in Kentucky.[6] Both men did arrive, and Mr. Straker became associated with the Reverend J. S. Atwell at St. Mark's. Mr. King opened a mission in Lexington, which by the time of his June 1869 report had within it a thriving day school with eighty-five pupils. King reported that he had encountered prejudice and resistance from the white population at first but that those attitudes had faded.[7]

The Reverend Mr. Atwell married Cordelia Jennings, one of the teachers at St. Mark's day school, sometime between July 1867 and February 1868.[8] The school received support from the Freedman's Commission, and Mrs. Atwell reported to the commission in early 1868 that the four schools under the aegis of St. Mark's Mission had an aggregate enrollment of 225 pupils. Two of the schools derived funding from the Pennsylvania branch of the commission.[9]

Bishop Smith reported to the diocese in 1868 that funding for work among the freed people also was coming from the Avery Fund in Pittsburgh and the American Church Missionary Society. His report also stated that teacher training was progressing and that he was anticipating expansion of the outreach to freedmen.[10] Late in the year 1868 the Reverend and Mrs. Atwell removed to Petersburg, Virginia, where they both served under Bishop Johns.[11] Bishop Smith appointed D. A. Straker lay reader at St. Mark's Church after Atwell's departure. For a time Mr. Straker not only handled that responsibility but also managed the associated day schools and taught the upper-level classes.[12] Within two years, however, both the schools and St. Mark's Church had closed.[13] The centerpiece of Bishop Smith's missionary work among the freed people had collapsed.

The fiscal troubles of the diocese and the Freedman's Commission, the ascension of Smith to the office of presiding bishop in 1868, and the tensions between Bishop Cummings and the Kentucky clergy that culminated in abandonment of the Episcopal Church by Cummings in 1873, all combined to diminish the thrust of diocesan activity among the freed people in Kentucky.

### Cicero Stephens Hawks of Missouri

At the 1866 diocesan meeting Bishop Cicero Stephens Hawks reported on the action at the 1865 General Convention that had created the Freedman's Commission: "The close of the war found all the former slaves of the country emancipated; and now the Church—which, it seems to me, was always more considerate for the slaves than other religious bodies—met this state of things for these millions of beings by establishing in her Missionary Board a new bureau in their behalf, with its consequent machinery; and now she is busily and properly at work, helping them in their temporal and spiritual necessities. She is sowing in season, and not scattering seed wildly."[14]

Hawks's mention of the creation of the Freedman's Commission under the aegis of the Board of Missions casts the board's decision in a favorable light, but his report does not outline an action plan for work among freed people within the Missouri diocese, and he did not appoint a committee or exhort the diocese to action. At that point Hawks may have been awaiting guidance or information from the new commission. A year later in 1867, however, his address also did not mention programs for freedmen.[15] By this time, however, Hawks's health had deteriorated. He died in April 1868.

In 1872 a Committee on Missions to the Colored People was appointed at diocesan convention.[16] The first point in the committee report was that "the Committee regard this [ministry to the black population] as a work of great interest, and that it is the bounden duty of the Church in the Diocese of Missouri to undertake and carry it forward at the earliest possible day."[17] The committee went on to recommend that the various parishes organize Sunday schools for the "oral and other instruction of colored persons" and that the "Missionary Board should appoint a colored missionary as itinerant for the Diocese."[18] In 1873 it was reported that there was one "excellent colored candidate for orders" and that another was "studying with that object in mind."[19] These entries in the diocesan journals for 1872–1873 are comparable to ones that appeared in the church journals for other former slave states six years earlier, indicating that the diocesan outreach effort to the freed people got off to a slow start in Missouri.

## Alfred Lee of Delaware

Bishop Alfred Lee had denounced slavery in addresses during the Civil War, and in a sermon preached on 7 December 1865, a Day of Thanksgiving appointed by President Andrew Johnson, Lee gave thanks for the demise of that institution. He referred to slavery as a "prodigious wen smothering the body" and a "malignant cancer eating the vitals of the state" and credited the "uplifted hand of God" for eradicating slavery in the United States. In the same sermon Lee noted that emancipation, to be meaningful, had to be followed by efforts that would provide education, economic assistance, and religious instruction.[20]

For decades, however, the treatment of free black people in Delaware had, in terms of the number of people affected, been a larger issue than slavery. According to the 1860 U.S. Census, there were 1,798 slaves and about 20,000 free black people in the state.[21] The ratio of free to enslaved black persons had grown steadily since the Revolution, and, instead of facilitating acceptance of black persons as citizens, that growth had spawned legislation designed to ensure that free black persons did not have equal rights with white persons. The feelings that fueled this legislation also resulted in the rejection of the Thirteenth Amendment by the state of Delaware in February 1865.[22]

The official website for the state of Delaware notes that "unfortunately, the state government put numerous restrictions on free African-Americans. Along with this sharp increase in free blacks in the late 18th century, the Delaware General Assembly imposed laws that severely limited the ability of African-Americans to rise economically, socially, and politically."[23] Free blacks did not have the right to vote, and the state did not support public education for their children. The rights of free blacks to testify in court, to own weapons, or to leave the state temporarily all were restricted by law. Employment opportunities were limited. In 1866 the Delaware legislature passed a series of resolutions protesting the passage of an act in the U.S. House of Representatives giving the right to vote to black citizens of Washington, D.C. One of the resolutions labeled the action "an insult to the free white men of this country" and another stated that "the immutable laws of God have affixed upon the brow of the white races the ineffaceable stamp of superiority."[24]

In his convention addresses during the years immediately after the war, Lee did not confront either the legal and economic repression of black citizens in Delaware or the climate of resistance against their attaining any real measure of citizenship and economic status. Nor did he vigorously issue calls to act on the educational needs of the freedmen.[25] The organization through which Bishop Lee chose to work to advance the cause of the black citizens of Delaware was the Delaware Association for the Moral Improvement and Education of the Colored People.[26] Lee chaired the executive committee of this association and for a time served as its president. The Delaware Association was a quasi-state organization that promoted the welfare of black citizens and had been given the responsibility of administering the small state appropriation for "colored" schools. The association also received private donations and supplemented the state appropriation by contributing a monthly sum to every school serving black children. Bishop Lee thus led his diocese by example; his service with the Delaware Association no doubt was controversial with some in his diocese, but Lee's participation showed his commitment to education as a vehicle for improving the lot of black citizens.[27]

### William Rollinson Whittingham of Maryland

In 1860 Maryland was listed in the U.S. Census as having 87,189 slaves and 83,942 free black persons, so that when its slaves were freed in November 1864, there were about 171,000 free black people in the state, just over half of whom had been recently emancipated.

Poor health played a major role in the life of Bishop William Rollinson Whittingham after the war, especially during the critical half decade from 1865 to 1870. In his message to the diocese in 1866 he reported on the assistance received from seven bishops in meeting Episcopal obligations in his diocese, and in 1867 he described the help received from eight colleagues in the episcopate. In both 1867 and 1870 Whittingham could barely speak, and his address was read by others. His condition precluded his undertaking firm sustained leadership of a diocese-wide outreach effort to black people in terms of religious and secular instruction. There were individual efforts by many churches, particularly in Baltimore, Annapolis, and Washington, but these were not centrally coordinated.

Two committees reported at the 1867 diocesan convention. The State of the Church report concluded that "if we would not incur the guilt of turning them away into the darkness of Romish superstition, or to the agrarian creeds of fanaticism, or to sectarian forms and preaching, we must provide churches and schools, teachers and ministers for them."[28] The Committee on Freedmen report included this statement: "Things are now tending more and more to make this people as separate and as distinct a nation as possible. If they are to be reached through the church, it can only be done by following the example on antiquity in giving to each distinct nationality churches and pastors of their own."[29]

Two points stand out in these reports. First, there was an unequivocal recommendation to do everything possible to bring freedmen into the fold of Christ but not into social union with their white brethren. There would be separate churches. The second was that no operational plan, stipulating resources and timetables or a mechanism for constructing them, was put in place; clergy were exhorted to work among black people, but how separate churches and ministers of their own were to materialize was not addressed at the diocesan level.

Bishop Whittingham supported the establishment of the Freedman's Commission, and in October 1865 discussed with Secretary Wharton the possibility of commission assistance with mission and educational work in Baltimore.[30] Diocesan journals in the next few years, however, did not reflect a formal request to the commission by the diocese.[31] At the policy level Whittingham remained strongly supportive of the commission and assisted Secretary Charles Gillette in gathering support among the bishops for funding in advance of the 1868 General Convention.[32]

In December 1864 the Baltimore Association for the Moral and Educational Improvement of Colored People, comprising leading white men in Baltimore, began an effort to establish and provide operating funds for schools to serve the black population. The association found a partner in the Freedmen's Bureau, which helped to build schoolhouses. Most schools were located in black churches or constructed on black-owned land. Financial support was received from the Baltimore City Council and from philanthropists. Beneficent organizations, including the American Missionary Association, furnished teachers, supplied transportation costs, and helped pay teachers' salaries. The association and the bureau worked closely with organizations of black citizens, involving those organizations in planning as well as responding to their requests. By November of 1866 more than six thousand students were in enrolled in some fifty schools located within rural counties in southern Maryland, the Eastern Shore, and the City of Baltimore.[33]

Bishop Whittingham was aware of the efforts of the Baltimore Association and, in fact, was invited to some of its meetings, but the degree of his involvement is not known.[34] Given this massive effort initiated by the Baltimore Association, however, and his knowledge of both the fiscal status of the Freedman's Commission and the pressing needs of freed people in the former Confederate States, Bishop Whittingham may have decided not to press for commission support in Maryland.

## Notes

1. *Diocese of Kentucky, 1867* (Cincinnati: Applegate, Poundsford, 1867), 39–40, and *Diocese of Kentucky, 1868* (Cincinnati: Applegate, Poundsford, 1868), 13.

2. George Freeman Bragg, *History of the Afro-American Group of the Episcopal Church* (Baltimore: Church Advocate Press, 1922), 267.

3. *Diocese of Kentucky, 1868*, 26–27. Marion B. Lucas, *From Slavery to Segregation, 1760–1890*. Vol. 1 of *A History of Blacks in Kentucky* (Frankfort: Kentucky Historical Society, 2003), 237–38.

4. *Diocese of Kentucky, 1867*, 23.

5. Ibid., 24.

6. *Diocese of Kentucky, 1868*, 27.

7. *Spirit of Missions* 34 (1869): 624–25.

8. *Spirit of Missions* 32 (1867): 563, and 33 (1868): 162. See also Lucas, *History of Blacks in Kentucky*, 238.

9. See reports by Mrs. Atwell and Miss Kendall in *Spirit of Missions* 33 (1868), 235–37.

10. *Diocese of Kentucky, 1868*, 27.

11. *Spirit of Missions* 34 (1869): 237.

12. *Diocese of Kentucky, 1869* (Louisville: John P. Morton, 1869), 56.

13. Lucas, *History of Blacks in Kentucky*, 237–38; *Diocese of Kentucky, 1870* (Louisville: John Morton, 1870); and *Diocese of Kentucky,1871* (New York: Hendrickson and Howard-Smith, 1871).

14. *Diocese of Missouri, 1866,* (St. Louis: George Knapp, 1866), 20. The bureau to which Hawks referred was the Freedman's Commission of the Board of Missions, established at the 1865 General Convention.

15. *Diocese of Missouri, 1867* (St. Louis: George Knapp, 1867). Exhortations for religious instruction of slaves may be found in Hawks's addresses to his diocese in 1853 and 1857, and his failure to be more aggressive with respect to the freedmen after the war is puzzling, although his health, which was failing rapidly, may have been a factor.

16. *Diocese of Missouri, 1872* (St. Louis: R. P. Studley, 1872), 17.

17. Ibid., 114.

18. Ibid.

19. *Diocese of Missouri, 1873* (St. Louis: R. P. Studley, 1873), 45.

20. Alfred Lee, *The Great National Deliverance. A Sermon Preached on the Day of Thanksgiving in St. Andrew's Church, Wilmington, Delaware; Published by Request of the Vestry* (Wilmington: Henry Eckel, 1865), 13–16.

21. Data from U.S. Census, 1860, *Historical Census Browser, Geostat Center,* University of Virginia Library, http://fisher.lib.virginia.edu/collections/stats/histcensus/ (accessed July 2008).

22. Delaware rejected the Thirteenth Amendment on 8 February 1865 and did not ratify it until 12 February 1901.

23. See the State of Delaware official website, http://www.state.de.us/sos/dpa/outreach/education/lessonr.shtml. (Accessed 7 January 2013).

24. J. Thomas Scharf, *History of Delaware, 1609–1888*, vol. 1 (Port Washington, N.Y.: Kennikat Press, 1888), 377.

25. See *Diocese of Delaware, 1866* (Wilmington: Henry Eckel, 1866), journals of the diocese published in 1867 and 1868 in Wilmington by Henry Eckel, and the diocesan journal published in 1869 in Wilmington by H. and E. F. James.

26. A mission statement for the Delaware Association was signed and released on 12 January 1867 and was published in the *Spirit of Missions* 32 (1867): 306.

27. Scharf, *History of Delaware*, 385–87. See also St. Andrews Church, Wilmington, Delaware, *Alfred Lee 1807–1887* (Philadelphia: James B. Rodgers, 1888), 25–27.

28. *Diocese of Maryland, 1867* (Baltimore: Published by the Convention, 1867), 96.

29. Ibid., 103.

30. Francis H. Wharton, Secretary, Freedman's Commission, to Bishop Whittingham, 28 November 1865, Archives, Diocese of Maryland.

31. See *Diocese of Maryland, 1868* (Baltimore: Published by the Convention, 1868), and journals of the diocese published in Baltimore by the conventions of 1869 and 1870.

32. Charles Gillette, Secretary, Freedman's Commission, to Bishop Whittingham, 17 February 1868, Archives, Diocese of Maryland. Gillette had become comission secretary following the resignation of J. Brinton Smith in October 1867.

33. Richard Paul Fuke, *Imperfect Equality: African Americans and the Confines of White Racial Attitudes on Post-Emancipation Maryland* (New York: Fordham University Press, 1999), 88–95. Fuke gives a detailed account of African American community schools in Maryland in the years just after the Civil War.

34. Two letters of invitation to Bishop Whittingham to attend Baltimore Association meetings are in the Diocese of Maryland Archives, one dated 27 January 1865 and the other 25 October 1865.

# Concluding Observations

## Theological Context: Know and Obey God's Will

Two important elements in the theology of the Episcopal bishops during the period covered by this study helped shape their responses to events and issues, to wit: (1) God was intimately involved in the day-to-day lives of individuals as well as with the affairs of nations and the workings of the universe. Their God was, in fact, the stage manager and ultimate arbiter of the affairs of each human as well as those of humanity in general. Nothing occurred unless God intended it to happen. God, on a schedule of his choosing, rewarded and punished human behavior, depending upon obedience to his will. Prayer, repentance, faith, and obedience, if strong and sincere, could stay God's wrath and gain his favor. (2) The will of God was set forth explicitly in Holy Scripture, and that will as expressed therein was to be obeyed to the letter, unless and until God revealed through events his will to be otherwise.

## Slavery: The Fundamental Issue

During the antebellum period and the Civil War the Southern bishops supported the institution of slavery. The fundamental reason for their support of this incredibly inhumane practice was not lack of the courage to buck the mores or the economics of their day or a belief that the black race was inferior, though most bishops in fact held the latter belief. These bishops were guided by their understanding of God's will as it was revealed to them through Holy Scripture. It was their literal interpretation of scriptural passages that led them to support slavery.

Until almost the end of the same period, the Northern bishops shunned slavery as a church issue. Their words and actions were also guided by their understanding of God's will, which they saw as directing them to support the United States government, the "powers that be" named by St. Paul. That government upheld slavery until the Emancipation Proclamation was issued.[1]

## Secession and War

Although three Southern bishops, Thomas Atkinson, William Meade, and James Hervey Otey, originally opposed secession, the bishops in the Confederate States all supported the South's war effort when it was clear that the North was committed to restoration of the Union by force. All Northern bishops, by contrast, saw secession as "rebellion, privy conspiracy, and sedition" and supported the Union. Bishops in both sections called down God's blessings on their armed forces and saw the Almighty as on their side. Bishops North and South reminded those in their dioceses of their Christian duty to support the "powers that be," namely their respective governments. Bishops in the Confederate States attempted to boost morale as the military outlook turned grim, assuring their flocks that the Southern cause was right.

## Civil Reunion and Church Unity

### Acceptance of War's Outcome

In accord with the view of God described above, the bishops in the former Confederate States accepted the outcome of the Civil War as God's will and exhorted their diocesan flocks to accept that outcome and to proceed to deal with postwar challenges. Dealing with the challenges at hand meant helping with the rebuilding—physical, financial, and emotional—made necessary by the disruption of war. These "accept and move on" appeals by bishops were heard throughout the Southern dioceses. The Northern bishops also saw the divine hand in the war's end. Bishop Charles Pettit McIlvaine, for example, contended that not only did God ordain and set the time for a Union victory, but the Almighty also used the war as the instrument to end slavery.

### Church Unity

When the war ended the desire among most bishops for church unity trumped all other considerations, North and South. Although bishops in both sections were disappointed at the stand taken during the war by their colleagues in the other section, there was genuine affection for one another across sectional lines. More important was the belief that Christ's apostolic church in the United States should be unified. At the 1865 national convention of the Protestant Episcopal Church in the United States, a majority of the Northern bishops endured a stinging rebuke from their fellow Northern prelates in the minority because the majority, in order to ensure that Southerners would participate in a service of thanksgiving, refused to include in the service a prayer that thanked God for the restoration of the Union and the end of slavery. Although under protest and greatly distressed, the Northern minority accepted the will of the convention. The Southern bishops, for their part, overcame their humiliation and crushed hopes and forgave the terrible wartime destruction wreaked on the church in the South. The disagreement of Bishops Atkinson, Alexander Gregg, and Henry Champlin Lay with Stephen Elliott, the senior bishop in the Confederate church, was about when and how, not about if, reunification should occur. By the middle of 1866 the church was one.

## Church and State: The Prayer Issue

From the perspective of the twenty-first century, the most bizarre issue that arose to confront the bishops was the one involving the Prayer for the President and all in Civil Authority. Episcopal churches in the South during the war and its immediate aftermath were ordered by Union military commanders in several cases to pray for the president of the United States by using this particular prayer. In Alabama this issue caused a church and state confrontation between Bishop Richard Hooker Wilmer and General George Henry Thomas, who ordered that Episcopal churches in the state be closed because the prayer was not being used. The president of the United States, upon learning of the order in Alabama, did not countermand it promptly. Most surprising, bishops in the North at the 1865 national church convention uttered an ambiguous whimper of disapproval of the order then in force in Alabama instead of a vigorous protest.

The matter was resolved when the president finally did direct that Thomas's order be rescinded. Although no rationale was formally forthcoming from the president, his action implicitly affirmed that the state had no authority in matters of church liturgy. More than thirty years later, William Stevens Perry, bishop of Iowa and church historian, wrote of Wilmer's defiance of military orders with regard to the conduct of worship services: "This action of the Bishop established for all time to come, in this land at least, the principle that in spiritualities the Church's rule is supreme."[2]

## Emancipation and Its Consequences

Two significant challenges faced after the Civil War by the Episcopal Church were (1) to reach out to the free black people, and, in the process, to bring back the "lost communicants"—the large numbers of freed people who had abandoned the Episcopal Church at the close of the war—and (2) to respond to the desperate need of the freed people for education and other assistance to help them adapt to freedom and to prepare for meaningful roles in American society.

The mindset of the bishops in most former slave states in the war's aftermath was that their obligation to the black residents of their dioceses had not changed. A diocesan bishop was still called by God to marshal the resources of his diocese to bring them the gospel. This meant providing them with religious instruction and worship opportunities. There were new barriers to fulfilling that obligation, however. The Civil War had impoverished the South, and in many states, destruction and vandalizing of church property added to the church's economic burden. Efforts to reach out to former slaves were hampered by poverty and by the fact that the social system, with its plantation chapels and plantation congregations, used by missionary clergy in the Southern Episcopal Church to bring black people into its fold had vanished. The freed people were "moving about." There was distrust of the religion that many of them had embraced as slaves, and, perhaps more important to them, they were free to encounter and explore different patterns of worship. Although there were isolated instances of success, the efforts across the South by bishops, clergy, and laity, did not stem the exodus from the church by former slave communicants or halt the general rejection of the Episcopal Church by black individuals.[3]

After the war the missionary or outreach efforts within dioceses in the former slave states were pointed toward formation of separate black congregations. An exception in the immediate postwar years was in Texas, where for a time Bishop Gregg encouraged his clergy to avoid separation of the races whenever possible and to have black and white worshippers under the same roof, but lack of success forced Gregg to change his approach. Separate congregations probably were inevitable at the time for two reasons: (1) former slaves would at best have been patronized by whites in any joint congregations, so that sharing of responsibility would have been minimal and (2) black communicants wanted to have control over their worship experiences. An unfortunate result of separate black congregations was a segregated church, which, in turn, contributed to the growth of a segregated society.

Although there were pockets of outstanding success in several dioceses, the diocesan journals and reports from the Southern dioceses to General Convention after the war are replete with accounts of frustrated efforts by the church to "reach" the black population. An excerpt from the 1877 triennial convention report of the (national) Committee on the Domestic and Foreign Missions Society revealed the nature and scope of a problem that seemed to baffle the church and its bishops:

> With respect to the mission work among the colored race, the Committee can make no favorable report. . . . There are congregations in Washington, in Richmond, Charleston, Wilmington, and some other cities in the Southern States; and there are large schools in Raleigh and a few other towns, intended to educate young men in the faith of our church, and to train candidates for the ministry. These congregations are chiefly, if not exclusively, of the better class of the colored population. They consist of those who have some education, some property, some social status. But of the four millions of blacks upon our soil, the mass is untouched by our Church. They are drifting farther away from our influence. . . . In South Carolina alone, there were 2500 colored

communicants before the Civil War. The statistics do not [now] show one-half of this number among the communicants of this Church through all the United States.

What should we do for these people more than we have done? How can we call out the zeal of the church in their behalf? The Commission for Home Missions have labored diligently to awaken the interest of the Church, but with only limited success.[4]

The decision in October 1865 to establish the Freedman's Commission reflected a recognition by the Episcopal Church of the second "Emancipation Challenge" listed above: the great need to help prepare the recently emancipated slaves for the new roles and responsibilities that came with freedom. Although a few Southern bishops at first were not supportive, the majority of bishops from North and South welcomed the establishment of the commission and endorsed its objectives. The initial programs of the commission were designed to provide both religious and secular education, but the emphasis was on helping to elevate the intellectual, social, and economic skills of the former slaves through basic secular education in reading, writing, and mathematics. After a few years the commission continued to support basic education, but the emphasis shifted to religious instruction and missionary efforts to bring freed men, women, and their children into the church.

Given the fact that slaves had not been taught to read or write, the commission's initial decision to focus on secular education for the freed people and to locate schools wherever it seemed feasible to do so was an appropriate response aimed at a serious and immediate problem. The policy change of 1870 that mandated that the educational work of the commission be based within parishes reflected a decision to incorporate Freedman's Commission activity into the ongoing work of Episcopal churches across the South and signaled that promoting the educational and religious welfare of the freed people was considered as part of the mission of the Episcopal Church.

Teachers and ministers assigned by the commission initiated and staffed a number of successful freedmen's schools, many of which had a church affiliation. These institutions had a positive impact on the lives of several thousand children and adults each year that the commission functioned, and some of the institutions continued well beyond the commission's lifetime.

### Thoughts and Speculation

None of Southern bishops in the first few decades after the Civil War attempted or even conceived of a church, either integrated or segregated, in which communicants of both races were considered equal members, especially with respect to access to leadership and governance positions. Even some tentative, small actions that could have been early steps in that direction, including efforts in South Carolina by Bishop Howe and in Virginia by Bishop Johns to admit black churches to diocesan membership, as well as Bishop Quintard's stance that white and black confirmands should be viewed as equally important in the sight of God and hence to the church at the moment when they knelt for the bishop's blessing, were blocked by convention votes or caused a storm of resistance.

These and many other unfortunate setbacks were not the fault of bishops, but these church leaders might have prevented the premature retrenchment and discontinuation of the Freedman's Commission. The great promise for the commission lay in the great need that it was created to address. Its great misfortune was that it was not funded adequately. The funding levels identified by Bishop McIlvaine were never attained.[5]

Had all bishops, North and South, intervened to seek additional support at the critical juncture in 1868 when the Freedman's Commission was attempting to broaden and strengthen its work, this expansion effort might have moved forward instead of being halted by lack of funds. As a result the impact of the commission would have been much broader, its momentum maintained for a longer period, and the shift to put more emphasis on the commission's work being parish-based could have been accomplished smoothly. Given the low membership of the Episcopal Church, the direct impact of a stronger and continuing commission still would have been that of a "candle in the darkness," but any flame would have been a welcome beacon to the freed people as the neglect and racial prejudice of the postwar decades undercut the anticipated promises of emancipation. Further, the Southern dioceses would have benefited from an increasing core of freed people educated by and instructed in the faith of the Episcopal Church.

From the late antebellum period through the first half decade after the war, the bishops of the Episcopal Church confronted first slavery and then the spectrum of issues and events that were the legacy of that institution, including the complex questions of social justice that arose after the war. These issues soon receded in importance, however, and did not engage the passion of the church prelates until more than three-quarters of a century later when the movement toward civil rights and inclusiveness demanded a place on the bishops' agenda.

### Notes

1. As indicated above, in "Bishops in the Slave States: Their Beliefs About and Responses to Slavery in the Antebellum Period," some Northern bishops, notably John Henry Hopkins, also accepted the scriptural sanction for slavery. The Southern bishops would not have disagreed with the view that slavery was an institution subject to civil governance, but the basic approaches of bishops in the two sections were on the grounds indicated.

2. William Stevens Perry, *The Episcopate in America* (New York: Christian Literature Company, 1895), 155.

3. The abandonment of the Episcopal Church by former plantation slaves is discussed above, in "Aftermath in South Carolina: Thomas Frederick Davis."

4. *Journal of the General Convention, 1877* (Boston: Printed for the Convention, 1878), 491.

5. See the essay above entitled "The Freedman's Commission" for Bishop Charles Pettit McIlvaine's recommendations early in the life of the commission.

# Bibliography

Diocesan journals are cited in the notes using the name of the diocese and the convention year, such as *Diocese of Georgia, 1865*. Single journals of the General Convention of the Protestant Episcopal Church in the United States are similarly cited, such as *Journal of the General Convention, 1871*. Both diocesan and general convention journals are available in libraries at Episcopal seminaries as well as the New York Public Library and other repositories.

## Primary Sources

*Manuscripts, Papers, and Archival Materials*

Hopkins, John Henry. Papers and Correspondence, Archives, Diocese of Vermont.
———. Collection, Special Collections, University of Vermont Library.
Lay, Henry C. "Private Journal, 1861–1863" and "Private Journal, 1864–1865," Henry C. Lay Papers, Southern Historical Collection, University of North Carolina at Chapel Hill Library.
"Letters of the Northern Bishops of the Protestant Episcopal Church on Reunion with the Bishops of the South after the Civil War," Kenyon College Archives.
McIlvaine, Charles Pettit. Personal Correspondence, Kenyon College Library.
Polk, Leonidas. Papers and Correspondence, Southern Historical Collection, University of North Carolina at Chapel Hill Library.
Potter, Alonzo. Pastoral Letters, 1861, 1863, and 1864, Keller Library Archives, General Theological Seminary.
"Proceedings of the Board of Missions, Protestant Episcopal Church, Meeting of 5 October 1865," Miscellanies 1815–1868, Protestant Episcopal Church in the United States of America. Keller Library Archives, General Theological Seminary.
Whittingham, William Rollinson. Papers, Keller Library Archives, General Theological Seminary.
———. Personal Correspondence, Archives, Diocese of Maryland.
———. "Various Pastoral Letters and Prayers, 1861–1865." Keller Library Archives, General Theological Seminary.

*Books, Journals, and Pamphlets*

Atkinson, Thomas. *Christian Duty in the Time of Present Trouble: A Sermon Preached at St. James' Church, Wilmington, N.C., on the Fifth Sunday after Easter, 1861*. Wilmington: Fulton and Price, 1861.
———. *Extract from the Annual Address of the Rt. Rev. Thomas Atkinson, D.D. to the Convention of the Diocese of North Carolina, July 10th, 1861*. Raleigh: Church Intelligencer Office, 1861.

———. *A Sermon Commemorative of the Rt. Rev. William Rollinson Whittingham, D.D., LL.D., Late Bishop of the Diocese of Maryland.* Baltimore: William Boyle, 1879.

Bowen, Nathaniel. *A Pastoral Letter on the Religious Instruction of the Slaves of Members of the Protestant Episcopal Church in the State of South Carolina Prepared at the Request of the Convention of the Churches of the Diocese.* Charleston: A. E. Miller, 1835.

Clay, Henry. *An Address delivered to the Colonization Society of Kentucky at Frankfort, Ky, February 17, 1829, by the Honorable Henry Clay.* Lexington: Thomas Smith, 1829.

*Diocesan Records of the Year A.D. 1865.* Charleston: Walker, Evans, and Cogswell, 1865.

Elliott, Stephen. *Ezra's Dilemma. A Sermon Preached in Christ Church, Savannah, on Friday, 21 August 1863.* Savannah: George H. Nichols, 1863.

———. *Funeral Services at the Burial of the Right Reverend Leonidas Polk, D.D., together with the Sermon Delivered by Bishop Elliott in St. Paul's Church , Augusta, GA, on June 29, 1864.* Columbia: Evans and Cogswell, 1864.

———. *God's Presence with Our Army at Manassas Junction. A Sermon Preached on 28 July 1861, in Christ Church, Savannah.* Savannah: W. Thorne Williams, 1861.

———. *New Wine Not to Be Put into Old Bottles. A Sermon Preached in Christ Church, Savannah, on Friday, February 28th, 1862.* Savannah: John M. Cooper, 1862.

———. *Our Cause in Harmony with the Purposes of God in Christ Jesus. A Sermon Preached in Christ Church, Savannah, on Thursday, September 18th, 1862.* Savannah: John Cooper, 1862.

———. *Pastoral Letter from the Bishops in the Confederate States of America 1862. Delivered Before the General Council, in St. Paul's Church, Augusta, Georgia, Saturday, Nov. 22d, 1862.* Augusta: Steam Power Press and Chronicle, 1862.

———. "Patience." In *Sermons by the Right Reverend Stephen Elliott, D.D., Late Bishop of Georgia, with a Memoir,* edited by Thomas Hanckel, 490–94. New York: Pott and Amery, 1867.

———. *Samson's Riddle. A Sermon Preached in Christ Church, Savannah, on Friday, March 27th, 1863.* Macon: Burke, Boykin, 1863.

———. *"So He giveth His beloved sheep": The farewell message from Bishop Nicholas Hamner Cobbs to his clergy, the address delivered by Elliott at Cobbs' funeral; and obituary notices for Bishop Cobbs.* Montgomery: Barrett, Wimbish, 1861.

———. *Vain Is the Help of Man. A Sermon Preached in Christ Church, Savannah, on Thursday, September 15, 1864.* Macon: Burke, Boykin, 1864.

*The Episcopal Recorder.* Philadelphia: Published 1831–1939.

Gillette, Charles. *A Few Historic Records of the Church in the Diocese of Texas during the Rebellion, together with a Correspondence between the Right Reverend Alexander Gregg, D. D., and the Reverend Charles Gillette.* New York: John A. Gray and Green. 1865.

Hanckel, Thomas, ed. *Sermons by the Right Reverend Stephen Elliott, D.D., Late Bishop of Georgia, with a Memoir.* New York: Pott and Amery, 1867.

Hopkins, John Henry. *The American Citizen: His Rights and Duties, According to the Spirit of the Constitution of the United States.* New York: Pudney and Russell, 1857.

———. *The Bishop of Vermont's Protest, and Draft of A Pastoral Letter.* N.p.: 1862.

———. *Episcopal Government: A Sermon Preached at the Consecration of the Rev. Alonzo Potter, D.D., as Bishop of the Diocese of Pennsylvania.* Philadelphia: King and Baird, 1845.

————. *A Letter to the Bishops and Delegates Now Assembled at Montgomery.* New York: 1861.

————. *A Scriptural, Ecclesiastical, and Historical View of Slavery, from the Days of Patriarch Abraham, to the Nineteenth Century, Addressed to the Right Reverend Alonzo Potter, D.D.* New York: W. I. Pooley, 1864. Reprinted, New York: Negro Universities Press, 1969.

————. *Slavery: Its Religious Sanction, Its Political Dangers, and the Best Mode of Doing It Away: A Lecture Delivered before the Young Men's Association of the City of Buffalo, and Lockport, on January 10 and 13, 1851.* Buffalo: Phinney, 1851.

Johns, John. *Sermon on the Occasion of the Funeral of the Rt. Rev. William Meade, March 17, 1862.* Baltimore: Entz and Bash, 1862.

*Journal of Proceedings of an Adjourned Convention of Bishops, Clergymen, and Laymen of the Protestant Episcopal Church in the Confederate States of America, held in Columbia, South Carolina, October 1861.* Montgomery: Montgomery Advertiser Job Printing Office, 1861.

*Journal of the Proceedings of the Convention of the People of Florida, 1861.* Tallahassee: Office of the *Floridian* and *Journal,* 1861.

*Journals of the General Convention of the Protestant Episcopal Church in the United States, 1785–1835,* edited by William Stevens Perry. Vol. 1, *1785–1821.* Claremont, N.H.: Claremont Manufacturing, 1874.

*Journals of the Protestant Episcopal Church in the Confederate States of America, Facsimile Edition,* edited by William A. Clebsch. Austin, Tex.: Church Historical Society, 1962.

Lay, Henry C. *The Devout Soldier: A Sermon Preached By Request to the Powhatan Troop at Emmanuel Church, March 6, 1864.* N.p., n.d.

————. *Sermon delivered 18 May 1881 in Christ Church, Raleigh, at the Diocesan Convention of North Carolina, Commemorating the Late Thomas Atkinson, D.D., LL.D., Bishop of North Carolina.* New York: James Pott, 1881.

Lee, Alfred. *The Great National Deliverance. A Sermon Preached on the Day of Thanksgiving in St. Andrew's Church, Wilmington, Delaware; Published by Request of the Vestry.* Wilmington: Henry Eckel, 1865.

————. *Thanksgiving Discourse: A Sermon Delivered in St. Andrew's Church, November 27, 1862.* Wilmington: Henry Eckel, 1862.

Marsh, Leonard. *Review of Bishop Hopkins' "Bible View of Slavery," by a Vermonter.* Burlington: Burlington Free Press, 1861.

McIlvaine, Charles Pettit. *Pastoral Letter from the Bishops of the Protestant Episcopal Church. Delivered Friday, October 17, 1862, at the PECUSA Annual Convention.* New York: Baker and Godwin, 1862.

————. *The Sermon at the Consecration of Right Reverend Leonidas Polk, D.D., as Missionary Bishop for Arkansas.* New York: T. A. Wright, 1906.

McNamara, John. *Three Years on the Kansas Border by a Clergyman of the Episcopal Church.* New York: Miller, Orton, and Mulligan, 1856.

Potter, Alonzo, and 164 clergy from the Diocese of Pennsylvania. *PROTEST of the Bishop and Clergy of the Diocese of Pennsylvania against Bishop Hopkins' Letter on African Slavery.* Philadelphia: Diocese of Pennsylvania, 1863.

*Proceedings of a Meeting of Bishops, Clergymen, and Laymen, of the Protestant Episcopal Church in the Confederates States, at Montgomery, Alabama on the 3d, 4th, 5th, and 6th of July 1861.* Montgomery: Montgomery, Barrett, Wimbish, 1861.

*Spirit of Missions.* Burlington, N.J.: Published by the Board of Missions, 1836–1939.

*The War of the Rebellion: A Compilation of the Official Records of the Union and Confederate Armies.* Series I, Vol. 22, Part 2. Washington, D.C.: Government Printing Office, 1888.

*The War of the Rebellion: A Compilation of the Official Records of the Union and Confederate Armies.* Series 1, Vol. 31, Part 3. Washington, D.C.: Government Printing Office, 1888.

*The War of the Rebellion: A Compilation of the Official Records of the Union and Confederate Armies.* Series I, Vol. 32, Part 3. Washington, D.C.: Government Printing Office, 1891.

Whipple, Henry Benjamin. *Lights and Shadows of a Long Episcopate.* New York: Macmillan, 1899.

Wilberforce, Samuel. *A History of the Protestant Episcopal Church in America.* London: James Burns, 1844.

## Secondary Sources

### Books, Dissertations, and Pamphlets

Abels, Jules. *Man on Fire: John Brown and the Cause of Liberty.* New York: Macmillan, 1971.

Adams, Ephraim Douglas. *Great Britain and the American Civil War.* 2 vols. New York: Russell and Russell, 1924.

Adams, Henry. *The Letters of Henry Adams.* Edited by J. C. Levenson et. al, 1982–1988. 6 vols. Cambridge: Belknap Press of Harvard University Press, 1982.

Addison, James Thayer. *The Episcopal Church in the United States, 1789–1931.* New York: Charles Scribner's Sons, 1951.

Armentrout, Donald S. *James Hervey Otey: First Episcopal Bishop of Tennessee.* Nashville: Episcopal Diocese in Tennessee, 1984.

———, and Robert Boak Slocum. *An Episcopal Dictionary of the Church: A User-Friendly Reference for Episcopalians.* New York: Church Publishing, 1999.

Bancroft, Frederic. *Slave Trading in the Old South.* Baltimore: J. H. Furst, 1931. Reprinted. New York: Ungar, 1959.

Barnes, Kenneth. *Journey of Hope: The Back to Africa Movement in Arkansas in the Late 1800s.* Chapel Hill: University of North Carolina Press, 2004.

Beary, Michael J. *Black Bishop: Edward Demby and the Struggle for Racial Equality in the Episcopal Church.* Urbana: University of Illinois Press, 2001.

Benjamin, Marcus. *The Consecration of Bishop Wilmer of Alabama in 1862.* Philadelphia: Church Historical Society, 1927.

Bradley, Mark L. *Last Stand in the Carolinas: The Battle of Bentonville.* Campbell, Calif.: Savas Woodbury Publishers, 1996.

Bragg, George Freeman. *History of the Afro-American Group of the Episcopal Church.* Baltimore: Church Advocate Press, 1922.

———. *Men of Maryland.* Baltimore: Church Advocate Press, 1914.

Brand, William Francis. *Life of William Rollinson Whittingham, Fourth Bishop of Maryland.* 2 vols. New York: E. and J. B. Young, 1883.

Breihan, Carl. *Quantrill and His Civil War Guerrillas.* New York: Promontory Press, 1959.

Burton, E. Milby. *The Siege of Charleston, 1861–1865.* Columbia: University of South Carolina Press, 1970.

Butts, Sarah Harriet, ed. *Mothers of Some Famous Georgians of the Last Half Century.* New York: J. J. Little, 1902.

Carley, Kenneth. *The Sioux Uprising of 1862.* St. Paul: Minnesota Historical Society, 1961.

Carus, William, ed. *Memorials of the Right Reverend Charles Pettit McIlvaine,* 2nd ed. London: E. Stock, 1882.

Cheshire, Joseph Blount. *The Church in the Confederate States.* New York: Longmans, Green, 1912.

Clayton, Sarah "Sallie" Conley. *Requiem for a Lost City: A Memoir of Civil War Atlanta and the Old South.* Edited by Robert Scott Davis, Jr. Macon: Mercer University Press, 1999.

Cleaves, Freeman. *Rock of Chickamauga.* Norman: University of Oklahoma Press, 1948.

Cohen, Saul B., ed. *The Columbia Gazeteer of the World.* New York: Columbia University Press, 1998.

Coleman, J. Winston. *Slavery Times in Kentucky.* Chapel Hill: University of North Carolina Press, 1940.

Conway, Moncure D. *Testimonies Concerning Slavery.* London: Chapman and Hall, 1865.

Coughtry, Jay. *The Notorious Triangle: Rhode Island and the African Slave Trade, 1700–1807.* Philadelphia: Temple University Press, 1981.

Cozzens, Peter. *This Terrible Sound: The Battle of Chickamauga.* Chicago: University of Illinois Press, 1992.

Department of the Interior. *Report on Statistics of Churches at the Eleventh Census 1890.* Washington, D.C.: Government Printing Office, 1894.

Du Bois, W. E. B. *The Suppression of the African Slave Trade to the United States of America, 1638–1870.* New York: Russell and Russell, 1965.

Eppes, Susan Bradford. *Through Some Eventful Years.* Macon: J. W. Burke, 1926.

Fehrenbacher, Don E. *Sectional Crisis and Southern Constitutionalism.* Baton Rouge: Louisiana State University Press, 1995.

———. *The Dred Scott case, its Significance in American Law and Politics.* New York: Oxford University Press, 1978.

Ferris, Norman B. *The Trent Affair: A Diplomatic Crisis.* Knoxville: University of Tennessee Press, 1977.

Filler, Louis. *Crusade against Slavery: Friends, Foes, and Reforms, 1820–1860.* Algonac, Mich.: Reference Publications, 1986.

Fleming, Walter L. *Civil War and Reconstruction in Alabama.* New York: Peter Smith, 1949.

Folwell, William Watts. *A History of Minnesota.* Vol. 2. 1924. Revised edition, St. Paul: Minnesota Historical Society, 1961.

Foote, Shelby. *The Civil War: A Narrative.* Vol.1, *Fort Sumter to Perryville.* New York: Random House, 1958.

Fremantle, James Arthur Lyon. *The Fremantle Diary.* Edited by Walter Lord. Boston: Little, Brown, 1954.

Fuke, Richard Paul. *Imperfect Equality: African Americans and the Confines of White Racial Attitudes on Post-Emancipation Maryland.* New York: Fordham University Press, 1999.

Goodwin, William A. R. *History of the Theological Seminary in Virginia and Its Historical Background*. 2 vols. New York: Edwin Gorham, 1923–1924.

Green, William Mercer. *Memoir of the Life of the Rt. Rev. James Hervey Otey, D.D., LL.D., First Bishop of Tennessee*. New York: J. Pott, 1885.

Gregg, Wilson. *Alexander Gregg: First Bishop of Texas*. Edited by Arthur Noll. Sewanee, Tenn.: University Press, 1912.

Groom, Winston. *Shrouds of Glory, from Atlanta to Nashville: The Last Great Campaign of the Civil War*. New York: Atlantic Monthly Press, 1995.

Hassard, John. *Life of the Most Reverend John Hughes, First Archbishop of New York*. New York: Appleton, 1866.

Haywood, Marshall. *Lives of the Bishops of North Carolina: from the Establishment of the Episcopate in that State down to the Division of the Diocese*. Raleigh: Alfred Williams, 1910.

Higgins, Kathleen J. *"Licentious Liberty" in a Brazilian Gold-Mining Region: Slavery, Gender, and Social Control in Eighteenth Century Sabara, Minas Gerais*. University Park: Penn State University Press, 1999.

Hodges, George. *Three Hundred Years of the Episcopal Church in America*. Philadelphia: Jacobs, 1906.

Hopkins, J. H., Jr. *Life of the Late Right Reverend John Henry Hopkins, First Bishop of Vermont and Seventh Presiding Bishop by One of His Sons*. New York: F. J. Huntington, 1873.

Hoskins, Charles Lwanga. *Black Episcopalians in Georgia: Strife, Struggle, and Salvation*. Savannah: Hoskins, 1980.

———. *Yet with a Steady Beat: Biographies of Early Black Savannah*. Savannah: Gullah Press, 2001.

Howe, M. A. DeWolfe. *Memoirs of the Life and Services of the Right Reverend Alonzo Potter D.D., LL.D., Bishop of the Protestant Episcopal Church in the Diocese of Pennsylvania..* Philadelphia: J. B. Lippincott, 1871.

Hughes, Nathaniel Cheairs, Jr. *The Battle of Belmont*. Chapel Hill: University of North Carolina Press, 1991.

Hunter, Augustus. *A Narrative of the Campaign of the First Rhode Island Regiment*. Providence: Sidney S. Rider, 1862.

Insko, W. Robert. *Kentucky Bishop: An Introduction to the Life and Work of Benjamin Bosworth Smith*. Frankfort: Kentucky Historical Society, 1952.

Jewett, Clayton E., and John O. Allen. *Slavery in the South: A State-by- State History*. Westport, Conn.: Greenwood Press, 2004),

Johns, John. *A Memoir of the Life of the Right Reverend William Meade, D.D., Bishop of the Protestant Episcopal Church in the Diocese of Virginia, with a Memorial Sermon by the Reverend William Sparrow, D.D.* Baltimore: Innes, 1867.

Jones, Jacqueline. *Soldiers of Light and Love: Northern Teachers and Georgia Blacks, 1865–1873*. Chapel Hill: University of North Carolina Press, 1980.

Klein, Philip S., and Ari Hoogenboom, *A History of Pennsylvania*. New York: McGraw-Hill, 1973.

Knight, Edgar W., ed. *Educational Theories and Practices*. Vol. 5 of *A Documentary History of Education in the South before 1860*. Chapel Hill: University of North Carolina Press, 1953.

Lass, William E. *Minnesota: A History.* New York: W.W. Norton, 1997.

Levy, Patricia. *Liberia.* New York: Cavendish, 1998.

Lines, Stiles B. "Slavery and Churchmen: the Work of the Episcopal Church among Southern Negroes." Ph.D. thesis, Columbia University, 1960.

Lucas, Marion B. *From Slavery to Segregation, 1760–1890.* Vol. 1 of *A History of Blacks in Kentucky.* Frankfort: Kentucky Historical Society, 2003.

Manross, William Wilson. *A History of the American Episcopal Church.* New York: Morehouse-Gorham, 1950.

McClain, Frank. *James Hervey Otey of Tennessee.* New York: National Council, 1956.

McClurken, Kara M. "Charles Pettit McIlvaine and the Civil War: The Public Crusades of an Evangelical Episcopal Bishop." Honors thesis, Kenyon College, 1999.

McDonough, James Lee. *Shiloh, in Hell Before Night.* Knoxville: University of Tennesee Press, 1977.

McDougle, Ivan E. *Slavery in Kentucky, 1792–1865.* 1918. Reprint, Westport, Conn.: Negro Universities Press, 1970.

McWhiney, Grady. *Braxton Bragg and Confederate Defeat.* Vol. 1, *Field Command.* New York: Columbia University Press, 1969.

Meade, George. *The Life and Letters of George Gordon Meade.* Vol. 2. New York: Charles Scribner's Sons, 1913.

Meisner, Marian Keefe. *History of Millburn Township.* Millburn, N.J.: Millburn/Short Hills Historical Society and Millburn Free Public Library, 2002.

Melville, Herman. *Battle-Pieces and Aspects of the War.* New York: Harperand Brothers, 1866.

Meyer, Roy W. *History of the Santee Sioux.* Lincoln: University of Nebraska Press, 1967.

Meyers, William Starr. *General George Brinton McClellan.* New York: Appleton-Century, 1934.

Monaghan, Jay. *Civil War on the Western Border, 1854–1865.* Boston: Little, Brown, 1955.

Moorman, John. *A History of the Church in England.* London: Adam and Charles Beck, 1953.

Nelson, Truman John. *The Old Man: John Brown at Harper's Ferry.* New York: Holt, Rinehart and Winston, 1973.

Osgood, Phillips Endecott. *Straight Tongue.* Minneapolis: T. S. Denison, 1958.

Owens, Herbert W. *Georgia's Planting Prelate.* Athens: University of Georgia Press, 1945.

Parks, Joseph H. *General Leonidas Polk, C.S.A.: The Fighting Bishop.* Baton Rouge: Louisiana State University Press, 1962.

Perry, William Stevens. *The Episcopate in America.* New York: Christian Literature Company, 1895.

———. *A Handbook of the General Convention, 1785–1874.* New York: Thomas Whitaker, 1874.

———. *The History of the American the Episcopal Church, 1587–1883.* 2 vols. Boston: Osgood, 1885.

Phelps, W. Chris. *The Bombardment of Charleston, 1863–1865.* Gretna, La.: Pelican Publishing, 2002.

Polk, William Mecklenburg. *Leonidas Polk, Bishop and General.* 2 vols. New York: Longmans, Green, 1893.

Prichard, Robert W. *A History of the Episcopal Church*. Harrisburg: Morehouse Publishing, 1991.

Pugh, Loren Dale. "Bishop Charles Pettit McIlvaine: The Faithful Evangel." Ph.D. diss., Duke University, 1985.

Quintard, Charles Todd. *Doctor Quintard, Chaplain C.S.A., and Second Bishop of Tennessee: Being His Story of the War*. Edited by Arthur Howard Noll. Sewanee: University Press, 1905.

———. *Doctor Quintard, Chaplain C.S.A. and Second Bishop of Tennessee: The Memoir and Civil War Diary of Charles Quintard*. Edited by Sam Davis Elliott. Baton Rouge: Louisiana State University Press, 2003.

Reaves, William M. *Strength through Struggle: The Chronological and Historical Record of the African American Community in Wilmington, North Carolina, 1865–1950*. Beverly Tetterton, editor. Wilmington: New Hanover County Public Library.

Reed, John C. *The Brothers' War*. Boston: Little, Brown, 1905.

Robins, Glenn. *The Bishop of the Old South: The Ministry and Civil War Legacy of Leonidas Polk*. Macon: Mercer University Press, 2006.

Roscoe, Theodore. *The Trent Affair, November 1861: U.S. Detainment of a British Ship Nearly Brings War with England*. New York: Franklin Watts, 1972.

Ross, Ishbel. *First Lady of the South: The Life of Mrs. Jefferson Davis*. New York: Harper, 1958.

Row, Stephen E. *Emmanuel Church—Brook Hill, 1860–1985: A Parish History*. Richmond: Emmanuel Church History Committee, 1988.

Ruffin, Edmund. *The Diary of Edmund Ruffin*. Edited with an introduction and notes by William Kauffman Scarborough. 3 Vols. Baton Rouge: Louisiana State University Press, 1972–1989.

Scharf, J. Thomas. *History of Delaware, 1609–1888*. Vol. 1. Port Washington, N.Y.: Kennikat Press, 1888.

Schneider, Dorothy, and Carl Schneider. *Slavery in America: From Colonial Times to the Civil War*. New York: Facts on File, 2000.

Schem, Alexander. *The American Ecclesiastical Year Book: The Religious History and Statistics of the Year 1859*. New York: H. Dayton, 1860.

Shattuck, Gardiner H. *Episcopalians and Race: Civil War to Civil Rights*. Lexington: University of Kentucky Press, 2000.

Sherman, William Tecumseh. *Memoirs of General William T. Sherman*. New York: Library of Classics of the United States, 1990.

Shippee, Lester B., ed. *Bishop Whipple's Southern Diary 1843–44*. Minneapolis: University of Minnesota Press, 1937.

Slaughter, Philip. *Memoir of the Life of the Right Reverend William Meade*. Cambridge: John Wilson and Son, 1885.

Smythe, George Franklin. *A History of the Diocese of Ohio until the Year 1918*. Cleveland: Diocese of Ohio, 1931.

St. Andrews Church, Wilmington, Delaware. *Alfred Lee 1807–1887*. Philadelphia: James B. Rodgers, 1888.

Staudenraus, P. J. *The African Colonization Movement, 1816–1865.* New York: Columbia University Press, 1961.

Stevens, Ann Heathcote. "The Unofficial Commission to England in 1861." M.A. thesis, Occidental College, 1937.

Sturtevant, Mary Clark. *Thomas March Clark: Fifth Bishop of Rhode Island.* Edited by Latte Griswold. Milwaukee: Morehouse, 1927.

Tadman, Michael. *Speculators and Slaves: Masters, Traders, and Slaves in the Old South.* Madison: University of Wisconsin Press, 1996.

Thomas, Albert Sidney. *A Historical Account of the Protestant Episcopal Church in South Carolina, 1820–1957.* Columbia: R. L. Bryan, 1957.

Tiffany, Charles Comfort. *A History of the Protestant Episcopal Church in the United States of America.* New York: Christian Literature Company, 1895.

Van Deusen, Glyndon G. *Thurlow Weed, Wizard of the Lobby.* Boston: Little, Brown, 1947.

Wakeman, Henry Offley. *An Introduction to the History of the Church of England: From the Earliest Times to the Present Day.* 10th ed. London: Rivingtons, 1923.

Warner, Margaret, Gary Gallagher, and Paul Finkelman, eds. *Library of Congress Civil War Desk Reference.* New York: Simon and Shuster, 2002.

Warren, Gordon H. *Fountain of Our Discontent.* Boston: Northeastern University Press, 1981.

Webb, Samuel L., and Margaret E. Armbrester. *Alabama Governors* (Tuscaloosa: University of Alabama Press, 2001.

Weddell, Elizabeth Wright. *St. Paul's Church Richmond Virginia: Its Historic Years and Memorials.* 2 vols. Richmond: William Byrd, 1931.

Weed, Harriet A. *Autobiography of Thurlow Weed.* 2 vols. Boston: Houghton, Mifflin, 1883.

Whitaker, Walter C. *History of the Protestant Episcopal Church in Alabama, 1763–1891.* Birmingham: Roberts and Son, 1898.

———. *Richard Hooker Wilmer, Second Bishop of Alabama.* Philadelphia: George W. Jacobs, 1907.

White, Greenough. *A Saint of the Southern Church: Memoir of the Right Reverend Nicholas Hamner Cobbs, with Notices of Some of His Contemporaries.* New York: James Pott, 1897.

Wilson, Alexander. *American Ornithology; or the Natural History of Birds in the United States.* Philadephia: Bradford and Inskeep, 1808–24.

Wolfe, Allis. "Women Who Dared: Northern Teachers of the Southern Freedmen, 1862–1872." Ph.D. diss., Columbia University, 1982.

Wood, Sumner. *The Virginia Bishop: A Yankee Hero of the Confederacy.* Richmond: Garrett and Massie, 1961.

Woodbury, Augustus. *The Second Rhode Island Regiment: A Narrative of Military Operations.* Providence: Valpey, Angell, 1875.

*The World Almanac 1868.* Commemorative Edition. New York: Pharos Books [Scripps Howard], 1992.

Wormeley, Katharine Prescott. *The Cruel Side of War: With the Army of the Potomac. Letters from the Headquarters of the United States Sanitary Commission during the Peninsular Campaign in Virginia in 1862.* Boston: Roberts Brothers, 1898.

*Magazine and Journal Articles*

Brewer, H. Peers. "The Protestant Episcopal Freedman's Commission, 1865–1878." *Histori-cal Magazine of the Protestant Episcopal Church* 26 (December 1957): 361–81.

Brydon, G. MacLaren. "The Diocese of Virginia in the Southern Confederacy." *Historical Magazine of the Protestant Episcopal Church* 17 (December 1948): 384–410.

———. "Memorial on Proposed Disestablishment of the Church in Virginia, 1776." *His-torical Magazine of the Protestant Episcopal Church* 2 (March 1933): 47-50.

Duncan, Richard. "Bishop Whittingham, the Maryland Diocese, and the Civil War." *Mary-land Historical Magazine* 61 (December 1966): 329–47.

Kinsolving, Arthur. "The One Hundred and Fiftieth Anniversary of the Organization of the Diocese of Maryland." *Historical Magazine of the Protestant Episcopal Church* 3 (March 1934): 2–18.

Lay, Henry C. "Grant before Appomattox." *Atlantic Monthly* 149 (March 1932): 333–40.

———. "The Return of the Southern Bishops to the General Convention of 1865: A Sketch, with Sundry Letters and Documents." *Churchman* 47 (April 1883): 422–23.

———, continued. "The Return of the Southern Bishiops to the General Convention of 1865: A Sketch, with Sundry Letters and Documents." *Churchman* 47 (May 1883): 478–79.

———. "Sherman in Georgia." *Atlantic Monthly* 149 (February 1932): 166–72.

Lefler, Hugh T. "Thomas Atkinson, Third Bishop of North Carolina," *Historical Magazine of the Protestant Episcopal Church* 17 (December 1948): 422–34.

Moore, Janie M. "Praying for the President." *Alabama Heritage,* no. 24 (Spring 1992): 32–39.

Pennington, Edgar Legare. "Bishop Stephen Elliott and the Confederate Episcopal Church," *Georgia Review* 4 (Fall 1950): 243–46.

———. "The Organization of the Protestant Episcopal Church in the Confederate States of America." *Historical Magazine of the Protestant Episcopal Church* 17 (December 1948): 308–336.

Rightmeyer, Nelson Waite. "The Church in a Border State—Maryland." *Historical Maga-zine of the Protestant Episcopal Church* 17 (December 1948): 411–21.

Schmidt, Jay H. "Mission to Europe, 1861–1862." *Michigan Alumnus Quarterly Review* 62 (August 1956): 311–16.

———. "The *Trent* Affair," *Civil War Times Illustrated* 1 (January 1963): 11.

Shanks, Henry T. "Documents Relating to the Diocese of Arkansas, 1861–1865, and Bishop Henry Lay's Papers." *Historical Magazine of the Protestant Episcopal Church* 8 (March 1939): 67–90.

Stowe, Walter Herbert. "Polk's Missionary Episcopate." *Historical Magazine of the Protes-tant Episcopal Church* 7 (September 1938): 341–59.

Walmsley, James Elliott. "Documents: The Change of Secession Sentiment in Virginia in 1861." *American Historical Review* 31 (October 1925): 82–101.

Willis, Lee L., III. "Secession Sanctified: Bishop Francis Huger Rutledge and the Coming of the Civil War in Florida." *Florida Historical Quarterly* 82 (Spring 2004): 432.

*Electronic Sources*

"About North Georgia." http://ngeorgia.com/history/polk.hrm. Accessed 7 January 2013.

"BlackPast.org." http://blackpast.org/?q=aah/delany-henry-beard-1858–1928. Accessed 7 January 2013.

"The Call for Volunteers." *Harper's Weekly,* 27 April 1861, 253. http://www.sonofthesouth .net/leefoundation/civil-war/1861/april/call-for-volunteers.htm. Accessed 22 August 2007.

"Civil War Battle Summaries by State." http://www.nps.gov/hps/abpp/battles/bystate.htm. Accessed 7 January 2013.

"The Compromise of 1850 and the Fugitive Slave Act." *Judgment Day* (PBS Online website), Part 4, *1831–1865.* http://www.pbs.org/wgbh/aia/part4/4p2951.html. Accessed 17 July 2007.

"Crittenden Compromise Text." http://sunsite.utk.edu/civil-war/critten.html. Accessed 7 January 2013.

"Digging Up the Past at a Richmond Jail." http://www.smithsonianmag.com/history -archaeology/Digs-Devils-Half-Acre.html. Accessed 7 January 2013.

"The District of Columbia Emancipation Act." http://www.archives.gov/exhibits/featured _documents/dc_emancipation_act/ .Accessed 7 January 2013.

Historical Census Browser. Geostat Center, University of Virginia Library. http://fisher.lib .virginia.edu/collections/stats/histcensus/. Accessed 1 November 2006.

Linder, Douglas O. "The Dakota Conflict Trials." http://www.law.umkc.edu/faculty/ projects/ftrials/dakota/Dak_account.html. Accessed 7 January 2013.

"List of the Bishops of the Episcopal Church in the United States of America." http://en .wikipedia.org/wiki/List_of_Episcopal_bishops_(U.S.). Accessed 7 January 2013.

"Religious Affiliation of the Senators and Representatives in the First United States Congress." http://www.adherents.com/gov/congress_001.html. Accessed 1 July 2007.

"State of Delaware Official Website." http://www.state.de.us/sos/dpa/outreach/education/ lessonr.shtml. Accessed 7 January 2013.

"Statutes of the United States Concerning Slavery." The Avalon Project, Yale School Library. http://www.yale.edu/lawweb/avalon/statutes/slavery/sl004/htm. Accessed 22 January 2013.

"Trent Affair News Stories." http://www.civilwarhome.com/washstartrent.htm. Accessed 7 January 2013.

# Index

Page references given in *italic type* indicate illustrations or material contained in their captions. Page references followed by *t* indicate tables.

Burks, Edward Calohill, 102, 167–68
Butler, C. M., 81

Caldwell, Elias B., 39
Calhoun, John C., 65
California, 18
Calvary Church (Memphis, Tenn.), 246,
 392–93
Calvary Church (New York, N.Y.), 373
Cambridge University, 128
Campbell (Va.), 41
Camp McClellan (Davenport, Iowa), 307
Cape Palmas (Liberia), 44, 73, 147
Carnes Hospital (Atlanta, Ga.), 270
Carolinas Campaign (1865), 203–5, 212, 400
Carus, William, 294
Cassville (Ga.), 259
Cavalry Church (Charleston, S.C.), 204
Central Presbyterian Church (Atlanta, Ga.),
 272
Chancellorsville, Battle of (1863), 183, 194
Charleston (S.C.): Freedman's Commission
 school in, 380, 381, 403; PECCSA General
 Council proposed at (1868), 363; Union
 bombardment of (1863-1865), 201–3
Charlotte (N.C.), 342
Chase, Carlton, 82, 352
Chase, Philander, 7, 66, 136n10, 281
Chase, Salmon P., 126, 128, 129–30, 134, 135,
 136–37n10, 155, 316
Chatham County (Ga.), 37n34
Chattanooga (Tenn.), 185, 254–55, 257, 258–59
Cheatham, Benjamin F., 249, 252
Cheraw (S.C.), 203, 204
Cherokee Indians, 67
Cheshire, Joseph Blount, 53, 54, 358n13
Chickamauga Creek, Battle of (1863), 185, 254,
 259, 275n60, 337
China, 106, 147, 321
Chippewa Indians, 298–99, 299 map
cholera epidemics, 68
Christ Church (Columbia, S.C.), 204
Christ Church (Nashville, Tenn.), 272
Christ Church (Philadelphia, Pa.), 281
Christ Church (Poughkeepsie, N.Y.), 330
Christ Church (Savannah, Ga.), 26, 30,
 175–77, 186–89
Christ Church (St. Simons Island, Ga.), 27
Christ Church (Winchester, Va.), 41

church construction, 25
*Church Intelligencer,* 358n9
*Church Journal,* 155
Church of England, 3–4, 8n5, 127–29
Church of St. James the Less (Philadelphia,
 Pa.), 350
Church of the Advent (Nashville, Tenn.),
 246, 272
Church of the Advent (Spartanburg, S.C.),
 200
Church of the Epiphany (Philadelphia, Pa.),
 353
Church of the Holy Cross (Claremont Parish,
 S.C.), 403
Church of the Holy Innocents (Henderson,
 N.C.), 210–11
Church of the Nativity (Huntsville, Ala.), 251
church/state separation, 313n20; loyalty oaths
 and, 234; military service and, 347–48;
 Northern controversy over, 324–27, 330–33;
 "Prayer for the President" controversy
 and, 221
"Churchyards" (poem; Coxe), 393n6
Civil War: beginning of (1861), 95, 102–3,
 111; church responsibility for, 345; clergy
 battlefield visits during, 236; as divine
 plan, 320–21; as divine punishment, 155–56,
 175–77, 183–85, 187–89, 316; as divine test,
 207–9; end of, 236, 241n26, 271–72, 344;
 "false oaths" made during, 221; federal
 desecration of churches during, 195–96,
 197n17, 202–3, 204–5, 217, 433–34; morale-
 building during, 223–24; Northern vs.
 Southern bishops' views of, 432; PECUSA
 Convention services honoring, 148–49;
 "praying for the president" during, 107n36;
 prisoner exchanges during, 246, 267, 329;
 slavery as root cause of, 156; Trent Affair
 (1861–1862), 129–32, 137nn26–27; Union
 "Unofficial Commission" during, 126–29,
 132–34, 138n29
Civil War battles: Antietam (1862), 135, 180,
 211, 235, 237, 310–11; Atlanta Campaign
 (1864), 186, 200, 257, 258 map, 259–60, 264–
 65, 295; Belmont (Mo.; 1861), 245; Bentonville (N.C.; 1865), 207; Carolinas Campaign
 (1865), 203–5, 212, 400; Chancellorsville
 (1863), 183, 194; Chickamauga Creek (1863),
 185, 254, 259, 275n60, 277n105, 337; Fort

T. FELDER DORN began his academic career in Sewanee, Tennessee, on the faculty of the University of the South. He retired as dean emeritus from Kean University in Union, New Jersey, where he held positions as professor of chemistry, dean, and vice president. He is the author of *The Tompkins School: 1925–1953; A Community Institution; The Guns of Meeting Street: A Southern Tragedy;* and *Death of a Policeman, Birth of a Baby: A Crime and Its Aftermath.*